1972

GEORGE CRABBE
AND HIS TIMES
1754—1832

Painted by Thoˢ Phillips, R.A.   Engraved by W. Holl.

REVᴰ GEORGE CRABBE.

From a Picture in the possession of John Murray, Esq.

GEORGE CRABBE

AND HIS TIMES

1754–1832

A CRITICAL AND BIOGRAPHICAL STUDY

BY

RENÉ HUCHON

Translated from the French by
FREDERICK CLARKE

To show virtue her own feature, scorn her
own image, and the very age and body of
the time his form and pressure.—*Hamlet* iii. 2

NEW YORK

BARNES & NOBLE, INC.

Publishers · Booksellers · Since 1873

Published by
FRANK CASS AND COMPANY LIMITED
67 Great Russell Street, London WC1
by arrangement with John Murray (Publishers) Ltd.

Published in the United States
in 1968
by Barnes & Noble, Inc.
105 Fifth Avenue, New York, N.Y. 10003

First edition   1907
New Impression   1968

Printed in Great Britain

TO

MONSIEUR EMILE LEGOUIS

PROFESSOR AT THE SORBONNE

THIS VOLUME IS INSCRIBED

IN ALL AFFECTION AND REGARD

PREFACE

THE author of this work has endeavoured, firstly, to rewrite, with the help of all the original documents still accessible, the biography of Crabbe published in 1834 by his eldest son,[1] and secondly, to analyse and to criticise in detail the talent of the poet.

The first part of my task proved by far the more interesting one. I aimed at revising, by comparison with the originals, that *Life of Crabbe* which all contemporary critics, Mr. Kebbel and Canon Ainger among others, agree in considering as definitive, and which, however, they sometimes find fault with. Its mistakes had to be corrected, its gaps filled up, its

---

[1] George. See below, p. 189, n. 3, and p. 469, n. 1. He died at Bredfield in September, 1857. Besides the *Life* of his father, he wrote two theological works, *An Outline of a System of Natural Theology*, dedicated to Lockhart, 1840, and *Short Conclusions from the Light of Nature*, 1849. He is the " Radiator " of Carlyle, referred to in the *Latter-Day Pamphlets* and in the *Letters of Edward Fitzgerald* (cf. *More Letters of Edward Fitzgerald*, ed. by Wm. A. Wright, p. 38, to T. Carlyle, from Woodbridge, Sunday, August 26th, 1855). In an article published by *The Monthly Review* (March, 1904, p. 117) I have accused him wrongly of having allowed certain manuscripts of his father to be sold in his lifetime. In reality these papers were put up to auction at the death of an employee of Murray, named Wright, and bought in by Murray at the request of the Biographer. He left five children, three daughters and two sons, the elder of whom, George, married, in 1851, his cousin, Emily Louisa, daughter of John Waldron Crabbe, became Rector of Merton (Norfolk), and died on August 9th, 1884, at the age of sixty-five. Fitzgerald, his intimate friend, expired at Merton in June, 1883 (cf. as to George Crabbe, the grandson of the poet, *The Norfolk Miscellany*, vol. iii. pp. 113-14. The younger son of the Biographer, Thomas Crabbe, studied law and practised as a solicitor at Uttoxeter.

useless matter eliminated; in a word, a psychological biography of the poet, with a view to the interpretation of his works, had to be written, and everything sacrificed to that intention. If the plan has been carried out, even imperfectly, the labour will not have been in vain.

The *Life of Crabbe* by his son cannot be denied the merit of having handed down to us information and documents which would have been lost without it, in particular the "Journals" of the poet for the years 1780 and 1817. But its composition is not always above criticism. It is the biography of a poet-parson written by a non-poetical clergyman, who appears in too many places, with his characteristic reserve. The style, although straightforward, is not decided enough; the tone, although sincere, sometimes becomes apologetic. It was necessary to restore the poet his rights and keep the minister in the background. Besides, the Biographer had parted with the control of his work. He had been commissioned to write it by John Murray,[1] but on two conditions: firstly, it was not to exceed one volume, and secondly, Lockhart, the editor of *The Quarterly Review*, and the future author of the *Life of Scott*, was to revise the manuscript, and make such corrections and excisions as he thought fit.[2] He

---

[1] A week after Crabbe's death, on February 13th, 1832, Murray wrote to George: "I hope the family have materials for communicating an interesting account of his life to the public, for he is allowed on all hands to have been one of the most eminent of British poets." For a year it was intended to publish, not only the work of the Biographer, but also the *Posthumous Tales*, preceded by a "memoir" from Miss Hoare, a friend of the poet (see below, pp. 471 *seq.*). This lady gave up her plan in May, 1833, and George remained the sole biographer.

[2] George did not submit without a struggle. But his first draft seems to have been very careless, for Rogers writes to him bluntly, on March 1st, 1833: "As to the Memoirs, they are certainly now very unfit for publication." Lockhart consequently obtained permission to do as he liked. In November, 1833, he wrote to George: "I perceive that, as the work proceeds, the alterations to be suggested by me will be lessening gradually both in number and importance." The *Life of Crabbe* appeared on February 10th, 1834, and had a considerable success.

largely used, he even abused, this power. Not only
did he cut out a great number of letters,[1] but he also
often changed the dates of those which were retained,
and ventured to correct the poet's epistolary style,
which was not elegant enough for his taste. In short,
he partly spoilt this *Life of Crabbe*, as later on his own
Life of Scott, by small inaccuracies. He seems to have
lacked the conscientiousness, the veracity, which is
indispensable to every historian.

I should not have been able, seventy years after
Crabbe's death, to write the history of his life, if I had
not been assisted in my investigations by kindly help
from numerous persons. Mr. F. J. Furnivall, Mr. Henry
Bradley, and Canon H. Thompson have supplied me
with useful information; the late Duke of Rutland
gave me access to his library at Belvoir Castle; Mr.
Dowden and Mr. Aldis Wright have, with extreme
courtesy, communicated to me, the former, some interesting unpublished poems, the latter, some singularly suggestive manuscript notes by Fitzgerald. At
Mr. H. Buxton-Forman's house I have been able to
peruse a letter which is all the more interesting
because it belongs to a period in which documents are
rare. Mr. John Murray has entrusted to me, for
months together, his Crabbe papers: sermons, letters,

---

[1] Miss Hoare, on Wordsworth's advice, refused to publish those which
Crabbe had written to her. See Wordsworth's *Poetical Works* (Dowden,
vol. v. pp. 359-60): "He [Crabbe] was upon terms of intimate friendship
with Mrs. Hoare, and still more with her daughter-in-law [*sic*], who has a
large collection of his letters addressed to herself. After the poet's decease,
application was made to her (by Rogers, at Lockhart's request) to give up
these letters to his biographer, that they, or at least part of them, might
be given to the public. She hesitated to comply, and asked my opinion
on the subject. 'By no means,' was my answer, grounded not upon any
objection there might be to publishing a selection from these letters, but
from an aversion I have always felt to meet idle curiosity by calling back
the recently departed to become the object of trivial and familiar gossip."
As if that was the point at issue! Now these letters have disappeared,
with the exception of a few in the Broadley Collection. They are, as a
rule, very interesting.

rough drafts of all sorts.[1] Mrs. Orr, of London,
Mr. and Mrs. Rivett-Carnac, of Swefling, descendants
of the poet, placed at my disposal, at a time when they
still possessed them, all the letters of Crabbe which
had been bequeathed to them. Mrs. Mackay, of Trowbridge, gave my researches a most hospitable welcome,
and I found unlooked-for treasures in her library.
Above all, I owe a heavy debt of gratitude to Mr.
Broadley, of Bridport, who has managed to get
together, in a few years, a collection of Crabbe's
autographs, which for excellence and completeness
is without a rival.

[1] Among others a tale, published by me in *The Monthly Review* for March,
1904.

CONTENTS

FIRST PART

YOUTH AND EARLY POEMS

(1754—1781)

CHAPTER I

ALDBOROUGH (1754—1768)

CHAPTER II

WICKHAM BROOK AND WOODBRIDGE (1768—1775)

xi

CONTENTS

THIRD PART

THE CLERGYMAN AND HIS PARISH REGISTER

(1786—1807)

CHAPTER I

CRABBE AS A CLERGYMAN; HIS RELIGIOUS OPINIONS

CHAPTER II

"THE PARISH REGISTER"

FOURTH PART

CRABBE'S REALISM

SINGLE CHAPTER

"THE BOROUGH"

FIFTH PART

CRABBE AS WRITER OF TALES AND MORALIST

CHAPTER I

THE " TALES IN VERSE "

CHAPTER II

PRESENTATION TO TROWBRIDGE AND JOURNEYS TO LONDON
(1813—1818)

CHAPTER III

THE " TALES OF THE HALL "

CHAPTER IV

CLOSING YEARS (1819—1832)

LIST OF ILLUSTRATIONS

FIRST PART

YOUTH AND EARLY POEMS

(1754—1781)

CHAPTER I

ALDBOROUGH (1754—1768)

I. The family: the grandfather and the father.—II. Aldborough and its surroundings.—III. Home life in childhood and early youth.—IV. A "dame-school." Early curiosity. An excursion on the Alde.—V. At school in Bungay. First literary reading. The Stowmarket school. Return to Aldborough: the sea, the river, and the common.

IT has been very justly remarked that Taine's critical theory, which finds the adequate explanation of an author and his works in his race, his age, and his environment, applies more to talent than to genius. What likelihood was there that the son of a small burgess of Stratford-on-Avon, bred amid the peaceful country scenes of Warwickshire and in the dulness of provincial life, should one day prove able to breathe a soul into the old chronicles, and to resuscitate peoples and monarchs? The explanation is that genius, the highest form of human activity, is also the most unfettered and the most baffling. On the other hand, traces of some predominant and fruitful influence can generally be discovered in the early years, in the upbringing of a writer of talent. Did not Thomson and Wordsworth feel, from their childhood, the charm of the "native regions" to which, in varying degrees, they owed their best inspirations? True, they possessed a power of intelligence and of sensibility which remains an irreducible element for the critic and is the only possible explanation of their superiority over the little peasants their playfellows. But the materials which this intelligence and sensibility turned to account were, to a great extent, supplied them by the surroundings amid which their youth was passed. The writer of talent, whether circumstances have aided or thwarted him, whether he has had but to give free scope to his energy, or has had to struggle in order to overcome the obstacles piled up by destiny, is like

3

a plant whose roots plunge deep into the soil which
has given it birth and has more or less generously
nourished it. To understand and explain it, we must
know the seed from which it has sprung, the soil
on which chance has flung it, the atmosphere in which
it has developed, the fruits which it has produced.
Then and then only can we realise the vital force
which it possessed. The analysis cannot be carried
further. It is the duty of the biographer, as Goethe
says, to "replace the individual in his age and his life,
to show how far they have helped or hindered him,
what idea of the world and of mankind he has formed
under these circumstances, and, if he is a poet, a
writer, or an artist, what outward form he has given
to this idea." And this is more than ever the biographer's duty when the subject of his research is a
poet whose gaze always remained fixed on his native
soil, on the sights and the individuals familiar to his
childhood, and who has described them with such
faithfulness as George Crabbe.

I

BORN on December 24th, 1754, at Aldborough, a
small seaport in the county of Suffolk, Crabbe belonged to a family which was too obscure to possess
a history. It does not figure in any of the voluminous
genealogical repertories in which the aristocracy and
even the middle class have carefully inscribed their
annals; and it would be lost labour to try to find a
possible ancestor for our poet among the numerous
"Crabbes" or "Crabs"[1] of whom the archives of the
Middle Ages bear traces. These researches, however,
cannot be abandoned without a feeling of regret: it
would be so tempting to identify Crabbe, "the most
Dutch of the English poets," with one of the descend-

---

[1] The two spellings were used indifferently, as in Flemish and Middle
English. In a letter written on November 7th, 1822, the sculptor Chantrey
regretted the presence of two useless letters at the end of his friend's name.
"Many a letter," he says, "you must write weekly to friends who admire and
esteem you, and the two superfluous letters at the end of your name have been
as often repeated as would have enabled you to compose a poem as long and
enduring as your *Borough*. Think, my dear Friend, what a noble work we
have lost by so many BE's." And Crabbe replies, in a letter the original of
which is in the British Museum, that he cannot in fact account for this whim
of one of his ancestors. (The text is given in a note in the son's Biography,
Murray, 1861, p. 2.)

ants of John Crabbe,[1] Flemish adventurer and pirate,
an adept in plundering the subjects of Edward II.,
high-born ladies and Gascon traders alike. Would not
the origin of his talent be better accounted for in this
way? We might indulge in the supposition that
among the numerous Flemish craftsmen who settled in
England during the Middle Ages there happened to be
a son or a nephew of the pirate; him we should prove
to be the ancestor of the William, Thomas, or John
Crabbe so often mentioned in the history of Norfolk[2]
among the burgesses of Norwich or the inhabitants of
the village of Kimberley, and we should have the satisfaction of throwing some light on the obscure origins
of the poet's family.

The facts, unfortunately, do not justify such bold
conjectures. We must confine ourselves to repeating,
after the poet's son, his standard biographer, that the
members of this family were " for many generations in
the station of farmers," that they perhaps raised themselves to the rank of yeomen, and that their advancement stopped there. The southern part of the county
of Norfolk seems to have been their favourite residence;
at the end of the seventeenth century the Crabbes
probably lived in the little parish of Seething,[3] a few
miles north of Bungay, and thence, it may be, Robert
Crabbe, the poet's grandfather, moved when he settled
at Aldborough.[4] Here he gained a modest but

---

[1] Cf. the *Close Rolls of Edward II.* (1310-21), published by the Record
Office, and the *Patent Rolls of Edward III.* (July 18th, 1332).

[2] Cf. Blomefield's *History of Norfolk, passim*, in particular vol. i. pp. 303
and 315; vol. v. pp. 223 and 326; also *The East Anglian* of 1869, vol. iv.
p. 233.

[3] In reply to a question from his nephew, Robert Crabbe, the brother of the
poet, wrote on May 10th, 1833, that "Mr. John Crabbe, farmer at Seeden
[evidently Seething], and *my* father were first cousins." Robert Crabbe, the
grandfather, had probably left a farmer brother at Seething when he moved to
Aldborough. This origin of the family is confirmed by particulars given by
the poet himself to a Suffolk antiquary, the Rev. Dr. Jermyn, in 1827. They
were published in *The East Anglian*, vol. ii. p. 259. I owe this piece of
information to the kindness of Mr. Walter Rye.

[4] Probably towards 1720. Mr. Casley, Town Clerk of Aldborough, has
shown that on January 23rd, 1720, Robert Crabbe "was given his freedom
as a favor," that on September 3rd, 1726, he was elected " inferior burgess,"
and "capital burgess" on August 25th, 1729. The parish register of Aldborough
mentions an "Elizabeth Crabbe, wife of late to Mr. Robert Crabbe, formerly
to Wm. Miller, who departed this life January the 22nd, 1721, aged 32 years."
This inscription was copied in the Aldborough churchyard by the antiquary
Davy, whose valuable manuscript collections were bought by the British
Museum. Can Elizabeth Crabbe have been Robert's first wife? The point
remains doubtful.

honourable position: on April 5th, 1732, he was appointed Collector of Customs, with a salary of £60 a year.[1] This official post brought him into notice: on September 8th, 1733,[2] his fellow-citizens elected him "Bailiff," or Mayor, of the town. Unfortunately, he did not enjoy these honours long, for in less than a year after his election death carried him off, when he was probably still young, on September 5th, 1734.[3] He left a widow, whose Christian name, Rachel,[4] alone is known, and a son George, baptised on November 15th, 1733, born no doubt a week before. We may suppose, with the Biographer,[5] that Robert Crabbe's premature death placed his family in a precarious position, and that George, the poet's father, must have experienced, from his tenderest childhood, the humiliations and privations of want. He thus acquired qualities of activity and energy which made him conspicuous in later life; forced, from his early years, to earn his own living, he gave up trade, the career for which he was originally intended, and became a schoolmaster. In the porch of Orford church, a short distance to the south of Aldborough, he assembled the "ragged lads" of the parish, sons of fishermen and of "men who heave coals or clean causeways,"[6] and tried to teach them the catechism and reading. Improvised gatherings of this kind, in fact, were the only

---

[1] Cf., in the publications of the Record Office, the *Calendar of Treasury Books and Papers* for 1732, p. 355: "April 5: Robert Crabb, collector Aldeburgh, loco John Burwood, dismissed"; and also in the *Treasury Records, Customs Quarterly Establishment,* No. 174, Midsummer Quarter, 1732, Aldeburgh: "Robert Crabbe, to act as deputy to the Customer of Yarmouth, for his ffees here, or 20*l.* per annum, and from the King 40*l.* per annum, per warrant 5 April 1732, to be paid from 29 do."

[2] According to Davy (cf. *Borough,* ii. 154) these officers were chosen annually, and he adds: "Their election takes place on the Feast of the Nativity of the Virgin Mary, and they come into office on the Feast of Saint Michael." Hence the date given in the text, and confirmed by the records of Aldborough. Robert Crabbe had been elected "Junior Bailiff" on September 18th, 1731, "Chamberlain" (or Treasurer) on September 29th, 1732 (dates extracted by Mr. Casley).

[3] Parish Register, Aldborough: "Mr. Robert Crabbe, bailiff of the Corporation, died Sept. 5th, mortuary 10 shillings (his emoluments exceeding 40*l.*), buried Sept. 8th, 1734." Besides his son George, he had a daughter, Mary, who died in infancy: "Mary Crabbe, inf^t. da. of Robert Crabbe, bailiff, buried February 2, 1733" (*i.e.* February 13th, 1734).

[4] We may note that a "Rachel Crabb" was buried at Aldborough on May 2nd, 1765. Perhaps this was Robert's widow.

[5] That is, George Crabbe, the poet's eldest son. I shall refer to him by this title throughout the book.

[6] *Borough,* xxiv. 96-8.

schools of the Church of England up to the end of the eighteenth century : no special building was set apart for them; the bishop merely empowered a master to collect his pupils in the porch or the aisles of the church. The emoluments of such a post must have been slender indeed, and George Crabbe soon left Orford to live near the cradle of his family. A few miles to the east of Seething is the little village of Norton ; he spent several years there as schoolmaster and parish clerk, and then returned to Aldborough. He was now nearly twenty years old. Wishing, no doubt, to settle in a place where his father's name was still respected, he obtained in the Customs the subordinate post of warehouse - keeper, and on February 2nd, 1754,[1] he married Mary Lodwick, the widow of a publican.[2] Of this marriage six children were born, the eldest of whom was the poet.[3] Let us pause for a moment in his native town.

II

THE traveller who visits Aldborough to-day can hardly recognise the " village " or the " borough " described by Crabbe. Since the beginning of the last century the

[1] Cf. the parish register of Aldborough : "Marriages 1754, Feb. 2nd George Crabb, single man and Mary Lodwick Wid. both of this Parish, by license . . . were married."

[2] Mary Lodwick's calling appears from the following note, added by John Crabbe, the Biographer's brother, to a letter from Miss Hoare : " In the talk with Miss Hoare . . . she says by all means mention that your great-grandfather was parish clerk ; this truly describes station in life, but why say your Grandmother was Landlady of a public house : it leaves an unpleasant impression and is not absolutely called for " (December 19th, 1832). We have seen that Miss Hoare's excessive scrupulousness, added to Wordsworth's, has deprived us of a probably considerable number of the poet's letters.

[3] Cf. Parish Register, Aldborough, for the exact dates of the baptisms (we can be almost sure that the birth precedes the baptism by a week) : George, the poet, January 1st, 1755; October 24th, 1756, Mary ; July 16th, 1758, Robert ; February 12th, 1761, William, who died in infancy, and was buried on June 11th, 1762 ; September 2nd, 1763, another William ; and lastly, March 25th, 1768, John. It may be observed that this simple inspection of the authentic documents enables us to correct some of the pretty numerous mistakes which have crept into the son's Biography : thus Mary is by no means " the youngest of the family " (B. p. 3), and William is John's elder brother. Moreover, it is amusing to note that Crabbe himself, in writing on April 16th, 1816, a poem entitled *Infancy*, the dated MS. of which belongs to Mr. Murray, speaks erroneously of the death " of a sister in infancy." It is evidently his "infant brother " William that he was referring to. The Biographer naturally follows his father (B. p. 3).

population has nearly trebled,[1] and the occupations of the inhabitants have changed. The fishing-boats moored to the shore are now few and far between ; Slaughden Quay, on which the custom-house formerly stood and where Crabbe and his father toiled as simple labourers, still exists, it is true, but bereft of that noisy animation which the arrival of numerous sailing-ships gave it in former days. The direct line of railway between London and Yarmouth has monopolised the traffic of this part of the world ; small towns like Aldborough and Orford, which in the eighteenth century served as intermediaries between London and the country districts of Suffolk, were unable to meet such a formidable competition. Little by little most of the fishermen departed,[2] and the seaport was transformed into a watering-place. Along the shore stand a few smart hotels, which are filled by visitors in the summer. The White Lion itself, although improved and enlarged, no longer possesses that supremacy over its rivals which the poet conceded to it. Instead of the modest "brick-floor'd parlour,"[3] sublet by the butcher in Crabbe's time, almost all the small houses of the little town take in lodgers at the present day.

Nature herself seems to have become more civilised. As if weary of having stormed this luckless coast for so many years, of having insensibly scooped out the slight curve of the bay of which Aldborough occupies the centre, the sea has raised against its own fury a rampart of shingle, behind which the houses on the shore extend in safety. It restores to the land what it formerly wrested from it. At low tide the receding waves lay bare a strip of close, fine sand, which imparts its elasticity to the tread of the pedestrian. When walking on it one would never suspect that the sea has swallowed up the ruins of perhaps the most

---

[1] Cf. Davy's manuscript collection under the heading "Aldborough": "Population = 1801 : 804.—1811 : 1066.—1821 : 1212.—1831 : 1341," and at the present day 2159, according to Crockford's *Clerical Directory*. Davy adds : "This population [in 1831] is distributed into 12 families employed in agriculture, 156 in trade or manufactures,—others : 162." At the same date, out of 330 houses, there were only thirty-one rated at a (no doubt letting) value of £10 and upwards; seven only exceeded £20. It is clear that even in 1830 Aldborough was still far from its present prosperity.

[2] This is noted by Fitzgerald, writing from Aldborough on August 18th, 1873 : "This place is duller even than it used to be, because of even the fishing having almost died away. But the sea and the shore remain the same" (*Letters*, ed. by Aldis Wright).

[3] *Borough*, ix. 19.

populous quarter of Aldborough three hundred years ago,[1] and that the quaint old town-hall, an advanced sentinel facing the ocean, that solitary " Moot Hall," almost tottering on foundations of less breadth than its first and only storey, more like a large cottage than a public building, with its outside wooden staircase and its two disproportionate chimneys, at that time formed the centre of the little town and the south side of the market-place, which was separated from the shore by four rows of houses. These, swept away one after the other by the successive storms which burst over them, have sunk beneath the waves. To-day man has stepped backwards, the ocean has ceased its encroachments, and its tempests, although furious, no longer work such havoc on the reassured town.

But the environs and the configuration of Aldborough [2] have changed less than the character of the inhabitants and the aspect of the houses. As in Crabbe's time, the main street extends for nearly a mile, parallel to the coast and at the foot of a low hill surmounted by the church. In the eighteenth century this massive edifice, too wide for its length, with its square tower, which seems to have been built of shingle, stood outside the village. To-day it faces the most modern part of the little town, which rises in tiers upon the hillside and to the left of the road that, ascending towards the west, penetrates inland. If from this culminating point you look northwards, you see nothing but a vast, sterile stretch of country, dotted here and there with meagre clumps of fir-trees, whose gnarled branches and scanty dark foliage bend without breaking under the attacks of the fiercest gales. What are the aridity of the soil and the withering blast of northerly storms to these hardy offshoots ? The short, fine grass which grows at their foot is of a pale, sickly green ; it looks very poor beside the broad-leaved bracken or the gorse bushes which abound in the dry places, and sometimes develop into regular shrubs, rude and twisted, like brambles on

[1] According to a plan of Aldborough preserved in the Moot Hall, and dated 1594. Another plan exists, dated 1790, in which the town appears to us in its present aspect. Only the " Parade," the row of houses facing the beach, has changed considerably. In particular, the lime-kilns (cf. *Borough*, i. 98), built at the southern end of the town, have disappeared Wilkie Collins has given some celebrity to this region by his description of it in *No Name*.

[2] This is Crabbe's familiar spelling. It is now written " Aldeburgh."

the top of knotted sticks. Such is the vegetation
of the flat and desolate heath which runs along the
coast at some distance from the shore. Near the sea
there is nothing but extensive marshes, to which the
aquatic plants, carefully noted by our poet, lend a
dark brown hue, singularly monotonous and dismal
under a too often overcast sky. This space is traversed
by embankments, and the pedestrian is obliged to
follow them, for the tide, trickling through the sand
and shingle on the beach, floods the soil and divides
it into a network of straight ditches,[1] sometimes fringed
with reeds, and always full of slime and a stagnant,
blackish water. Farther away, up to the hamlet of
Thorpe which bounds the horizon, stretches the dull
sheet of water called " The Mere," a sort of inland lake
formed by the influx of the sea.

If the spectator turns southwards, on all sides, from
the foot of Aldborough hill to the sea and the village
of Orford, the church and ruined castle of which can
be descried in the distance, nothing is visible but a
vast plain intersected by the same reedy " dykes," and
flecked here and there by groups of black cattle. Here,
it is true, the monotony of this landscape of a more
than Dutch uniformity is broken by the many windings
of the River Alde. Formed by the junction of two
small streams, one of which rises near Framlingham,[2]
and the other a few miles from Swefling, it suddenly
widens on coming within sight of Aldborough, and,
when the sun shines, expands in the midst of the plain
into a silvery sheet which is really the " landscape's
eye." But its glance is deceptive, and woe betide the
rowers that venture along its sides at high water.
They will be stranded on the mudbanks, which the
tide re-covers at regular intervals, and between which
the Alde has cut a narrow bed. Hither resort in winter
flocks of wild birds—duck, geese, and teal—driven from
the open sea by the violence of the storms, and
hastening inland to find shelter and repose.[3] Through
its meanderings the Alde flows peaceably eastwards,
about two-thirds of a mile from the south of the
town, and one would imagine that it is going to

---

[1] Or " dykes," as our poet and the inhabitants call them.
[2] Celebrated for its ruins of the old castle of the Howards, Dukes of Norfolk, and for the church, which contains the tomb of the poet Surrey.
[3] Cf. *Notes and Jottings about Aldeburgh*, by N. F. Hele, surgeon, 1870, p. 8.

mingle its waters leisurely and unregretfully with those of the German Ocean close to this spot. Nothing of the kind, however : at about two hundred yards from the shore it encounters a narrow strip of land, or shingle rather, which deflects it abruptly towards the south, and it has to flow alongside the sea for twelve miles, and below Orford to change its name of Alde into Ore, before it can find an outlet, barred, however, by a sandbank that prevents vessels of heavy tonnage from entering the river.[1] Others—fishing-boats or coasting craft—can easily ascend as high as Slaughden Quay, a sort of tongue of land, resting on stakes, which projects less than a hundred yards from the left bank of the Alde, at the very point where the river turns from the east to the south.

Slaughden is the " suburb " of Aldborough, so well known to the poet's readers, the centre of the commercial activity of the port in the eighteenth century, to this very day the most characteristic and picturesque spot in this part of the world. It is there that we must go if we want to form a correct idea of what was, on a larger scale, Crabbe's " village." Modern luxury has not crossed the two-thirds of a mile which separates Slaughden from the little town ; no smart hotel spoils the austere gloom which broods over this locality. Let the reader imagine, on a slip of land where the feet sink into the shingle, a group of houses imprisoned between the Alde and the sea : a small public-house, a timber-yard, some more or less humble dwellings, and close by, at the entrance of the "quay" described above, a cluster of ruins, gaping roofs, walls with great rents, whole pieces of them lying on the ground, bricks, scraps of old iron, and he will call to mind the havoc which the waves formerly wrought on Aldborough itself. He will reflect that a sudden shifting of the wind from south to north-west [2] is enough to let loose upon Slaughden furious storms in which the sea and the river, barely two hundred yards apart, unite, leagued together against the few human habitations cowering on their brink. Like serpents entwined around their prey,

---

[1] *Aldborough Described*, by J. Ford, Ipswich, 1819 (and not 1815, as the catalogue of the British Museum erroneously states), p. 56. The Alde does not flow into the sea at Orford, as the Biographer asserts (p. 3), but more than six miles farther south ; still less at Aldborough, as Mr. Kebbel has it, *Life of Crabbe*, pp. 12, 13.

[2] *Notes and Jottings*, p. 6.

the waves slowly but surely encompass the hapless walls, so stout in appearance, so frail before their irresistible enemy : too often they collapse before the tide recedes, and one can see, as in Crabbe's time, the wretched inhabitant of the hovel levelled by the waters " weep from door to door, and beg a poor protection from the poor." [1] The fisherman was wiser who, having dragged his tarred and probably worn-out craft up the beach, turned it upside-down, made two holes in its side, one to serve as window, the other as chimney, and settled himself very comfortably in it :

> . . . View his boat,
> With bed and barrel—'tis his house afloat ;
> Look at his house, where ropes, nets, blocks, abound,
> Tar, pitch, and oakum—'tis his boat aground. [2]

The water glides harmlessly off it, and if the storm becomes too threatening, his other refuge is close at hand. [3]

Let us cross the Alde by the ferry which plies between Slaughden and the opposite bank ; let us land with circumspection amid the plashing of a high tide and on the wet grass, let us climb the " wall " [4] which protects the neighbouring meadows from the encroaching wave, let us walk along the narrow, muddy, and slippery path which leads to Orford. Let us not be discouraged by the too numerous stiles which we have to climb, nor by the dangerous stumbles which threaten to fling us down the bank, into the river, or into the meadow dykes. Let us observe the landscape which spreads at our feet : to the left, the Alde with its dull yellowish waters, edged with banks of slime and irregular rows of stakes, swollen in places by streamlets which flow from the plain through the wall, and whose clear, silvery sound cheers the pedestrian weary with so much silence and monotony ; farther on, a desolate

---

[1] *Village*, i. 129-30.
[2] *Borough*, xviii. 270-3.
[3] Cf. as to these storms, a letter from Fitzgerald to Professor Norton, dated March 7th, 1883 (ed. Aldis Wright) : " A newspaper cutting [' ALDEBURGH. *The Storm.*—On Tuesday evening the tide ran over the Promenade, in many places the river and sea meeting. The cattle are all sent inland, and all the houses at Slaughden are evacuated '] will tell you what it was about on my very old Crabbe's shore. It [the sea] will assuredly cut off his old borough from the Slaughden river quay."
[4] The " wall " of which Crabbe speaks (*Borough*, ix. 173). This " wall " is in reality nothing but a long mud-embankment covered with grass.

stretch of swamp and shingle between the river and
the sea, studded with ships which seem to be sailing
along the low sky ; to the right, meadows of a whitish
green, dykes full of brackish water, on which sea-birds
alight for a moment and where the "bittern gives its
bellowing boom."[1] The whole beauty, the whole
picturesqueness and impressiveness of this landscape,
lie in the contemplation of the ruins piled up by the
blind forces of nature.   Here land and sky are "cruel" to
man, to quote the favourite expression of the inhabitants.
It is the "sad world" of which the poet speaks in his
old age, "where he had never seen the earth pro-
ductive or the sky serene."[2]

> But few our acres, and but short our grass ;
> In some fat pastures of the rich, indeed,
> May roll the single cow or favourite steed ;
> But these, our hilly heath and common wide,
> Yield a slight portion. . . .
> No crops luxuriant in our borders stand,
> For here we plough the ocean, not the land.[3]

Such landscapes may inspire a Crome, or even
a Constable, but not a Turner. What could
suggest to the artist the idea of the grand in nature,
the love of dazzling colours and infinite distances ?
The horizon is narrow on all sides, even towards the
sea ; grey or sombre tints predominate in the sky,
almost always overcast, and on the ocean, often
darkened by clouds or by the scouring of the sands.
Even in summer, when a resplendent sun plays on the
surface of the green and blue waters, a slight haze
seems to rise from the shore and veil the brilliance of
its rays.   The mind would feel depressed, if the sight
of the winged ships in the offing did not continually
recall it to the contemplation of human activity, if
this monotony of things did not force us to descend
into ourselves and take cognisance of the innate
strength which dwells in each one of us.   In presence
of an inhospitable nature, man feels his energy increase :
he confronts it in a challenging attitude, reproaches it
with its injustice, and asserts his superiority to it.
He observes it as if it were an enemy, he studies it in
order to criticise it.   In a moment of revolt and despair,

---

[1] *Borough*, xxii. 196-7.
[2] *Posthumous Tales*, xxii. 195-6.
[3] *Borough*, iii. 167-75.

he may flee from it; but later on, his need of activity once satisfied, his dreams partly realised, he will remember with gratitude the hard and salutary education it gave him. The desolate heaths, the marshy wastes amid which his austere and needy youth was spent, will be revisited without bitterness, and, if he is a writer, he will describe them with a minute accuracy, a scrupulous fidelity akin to sympathy.

III

THE humble cottage in which Crabbe first saw the light and in which his early years were passed was among those which the waves have swallowed up. Too near the sea, it could not resist its attacks, and seems to have disappeared even before the poet reached manhood. " The chambers," the Biographer tells us, " projected far over the ground-floor; the windows were small, with diamond panes, almost impervious to the light "[1]—a very vague description, which would have equally suited most of the old houses in the town. The home of Crabbe's parents cannot have been very different from that in which Burns, the peasant-poet, had his glorious " Vision ": on the ground-floor one room, or two at the most, in which the squalls from the open sea and the common drove the smoke down the chimney; above, under a somewhat ill-fastened thatched roof, a garret approached by a ladder or an outside staircase. Let us picture the child, as yet indifferent to the humiliations of poverty, ignorant of the trials which life has in store for him, absorbed in the naïve pleasure of pursuing the receding waves or fleeing from their advance almost up to the threshold of his dwelling. On certain autumn and winter days, when, more encroaching, they demolish the neighbouring houses and flood his own, his childish glee gives place to terror. The sea already reveals to him " its variety and vastness, the sublimity of all its forms."[2]

In a few years the family moved into another cottage, which Stanfield thought he had sketched in a drawing reproduced by Bernard Barton[3] during Crabbe's

---

life-time, and afterwards by the Biographer.[1] Long and
low, this hovel, of which the entrance is level with the
street, seems to be also composed of two rooms on
the ground-floor, with two attics overhung by the roof.
On the shed which flanks it is a boat upside-down ;
inside are fishing-lines, ropes, and other tackle. " You
would take it for the home of a poor fisherman."[2] And
yet, according to Crabbe's own showing, his parents'
real dwelling was even far more humble. " Bernard
Barton's print," he writes to one of his sons, " is of
my father's house many years after he left it ; never
very respectable, it was then a miserable building
divided into three poor dwellings. I lived in it, as
near as I recollect, on my return from school once
or twice, when my father removed into that more
southward, where we dwelled some years."[3] The
house sketched by Stanfield had disappeared in 1840 ;
the curious visitor who asked about Crabbe was shown
another not far off and rather like it,[4] probably on the
site of the house which is still called " Crabbe's house "
at Aldborough. It is in the main street, nearly in the
centre of the town, equidistant perhaps from the spot
where the poet was born and from that where his
father lived towards 1770. Let us bear in mind this
fact : from his earliest childhood Crabbe was lulled
to sleep by the monotonous and unceasing murmur
of the waves breaking on the beach ; he chased their
light flakes of foam, as other poets have chased butterflies ; the only flowers known to him were the seaweed ;
and all the poetry he saw and heard in nature was the
sparkle of the calm sea under a summer sun, and the
roar of the surf under the howling of the easterly gales
in winter.

The existence of his parents was one of dogged toil; an
ever-increasing family demanded constant care from the
mother, and forced the warehouse-keeper to put forth
all his energy, in order to augment his slender resources.
He became, at what time is not known, collector of
the salt duties, with the exceedingly modest salary of

---

[1] In the definitive edition of Crabbe's complete works, in eight volumes,
Murray, 1834. This print serves as frontispiece to the first volume.
[2] Hermann Pesta, *George Crabbe*, p. 2.
[3] Unpublished letter to John Crabbe (without date). B. Barton had sent
the vignette in a letter to Crabbe dated June 26th, 1829 (Fitzgerald notes).
[4] Cf. Wodderspoon's *Historic Sites of Suffolk*, with Introductory Verses by
Bernard Barton : Ipswich, 1841.

£10 a year.[1] He took an active part in the deliberations of the vestry, as the registers show.[2] On November 8th, 1761, for instance, he was among those who decided that an umbrella should be purchased for their Rector, the Rev. Mr. Benet, at the expense of the parish; and in 1764 he voted for an expenditure of ten shillings from the same fund, to enable the board to. have a jollification in a local public-house. This was one of the traditional perquisites of the office. In 1763 he goes to London to protect the interests of the parish, and on several occasions the vestry is indebted to him for relatively considerable sums. We are therefore not surprised to find him, five years later, raised to the dignity of churchwarden.[3] He discharged his professional duties with great zeal. " He was a man of short stature, but very robust and powerful." His " highly marked " countenance reminded his son of that of the illustrious philanthropist Howard, with less serenity.[4]

His duties at the custom-house took him every day to Slaughden Quay, and he did not hesitate to undertake, when occasion required, long rides in pursuit of the smugglers who abounded on the coast and throughout the country : " In *The Public Advertiser* of April 7th, 1767,[5] we read that on Sunday last were seized near Martlesham [6] by Mr. John Church, Mr. Geo. Crabbe, and Mr. Samuel Aldrich, of Aldeburgh, three bags containing near 1,000 yards of muslin, upwards of 600 yards of lace, 130 yards of silk gauze, some tea, and other goods from three foreigners who were set on shore from a Dutch hoy at or near Sizewell,[7] and the abovementioned Mr. Church and Mr. Crabbe, with the

---

[1] See in the Public Record Office, "An Account of the Offices and Employments existing in the Salt Duties on October 25th, 1705 (compared with January 5th, 1779), distinguishing the time when any increase in the number of such officers or their salaries was first made : Assistant Searchers and Boatsmen—Aldborough : George Crabbe—salary per annum £10."

[2] Cf. Vestry Book, Aldborough. These registers, as well as those of births, deaths, and marriages, were very kindly placed at my disposal by the Rev. H. Thompson, Rector of Aldborough in 1902.

[3] From April 17th, 1768, it would appear, and up to 1775, according to Canon Ainger (*Crabbe*, English Men of Letters, 1903, p. 11).

[4] B. p. 3.

[5] Copied by Davy (MS. collection in the British Museum) under the heading "Crabbe" in his *Pedigrees Alphabetically Arranged*, in 43 vols. (Add. 19114-19156).

[6] A mile and a half south-west of Woodbridge.

[7] On the coast, six miles north of Aldborough. It is about twenty miles, as the crow flies, from Sizewell to Martlesham.

assistance of another officer, have seized the said hoy near Harwich and carried her to Aldeburgh, where the goods are lodged in the Custom-House." We may be sure that this capture was a considerable event for the family, and that the child was never weary of hearing his father describe to him the ways of these bold adventurers, their wary manœuvres before landing, the feverish haste with which they loaded their horses, their hurried start and the perilous pursuit across the commons which extend to the south-west of Aldborough in the direction of Woodbridge. The personal interest which he took in these tales redoubled the curiosity of the future portrayer of the vices of the *Village* and the *Borough*; on his lively, imaginative mind scenes of this kind remained engraven for life.

When his business did not keep him at the custom-house or send him in pursuit of smugglers, George Crabbe turned fisherman. " He possessed a share in a fishing-boat, in which he not unfrequently went to sea."[1] In his mode of life he much resembled his neighbours, who dwelt in huts or cottages along the beach ; his activity was mainly physical ; sometimes he moved chests or rolled casks from Slaughden Quay to the customs warehouse, sometimes he stored sacks of salt in the sheds used for this purpose, and of which there is still a faint recollection at Aldborough, sometimes again he proved, like the others, "skill'd to take the finny tribe."[2] He too belonged to that amphibious race[3] which his son excelled in describing. In short, he was a man whose aptitudes made him fit for very different kinds of work, and who soon became the "factotum"[4] of the place. For he had as much intelligence as vigour, and in that respect was far above most of his fellow-citizens. When he came home in the evening, he liked to resume his early studies : he would take up the poetical works "of Milton, of Young, or of some other of our graver classics," selecting passages "with much judgment," and reading them to his family "with powerful effect"; and now and then he would try his hand at rhyming.[5] Many years

[1] B. p. 4.
[2] *Village*, i. 113.
[3] *Ibid*. i. 85.
[4] B. p. 2.
[5] Cf. in *The Correspondence of Sir Th. Hanmer . . . and Other Relicks of a Gentleman's Family*, edited by Sir H. Bunbury (1838, Moxon), pp. 384-95,

afterwards his son still remembered these readings, which had no doubt so much contributed to awaken in him the poetic vocation and impress on his ear the music of verse.[1]

But George Crabbe's favourite relaxation was the study of mathematics. Having, it appears, "an extraordinary faculty of calculation,"[2] he sent problems for solution to Benjamin Martin's *Miscellaneous Correspondence*, and answered his own questions as well as those of others.[3] So far as an outsider can judge, he had extensive acquirements in geometry, and was acquainted with the elements of astronomy and trigonometry. These were very remarkable scientific attainments for the age; and in a man who had received an elementary education only, which moreover had been very soon interrupted, they prove an uncommon intellectual activity and power of assimilation.

Robust in body and mind, George Crabbe evidently possessed a rich nature. But this wealth of vital energy, so precious when its owner remains master of it, may become a source of danger when it overpowers the will and is not subject to a firm moral guidance. This was the rock on which the existence of our poet's father was shipwrecked. He was "a man of imperious temper and violent passions."[4] He was liable, even in his best years, to fits of sombre rage which terrified his son, still quite young. The child was barely eight years old when his brother William died (in June, 1762), at the age of about eighteen months.[5] This bereavement plunged his parents into profound grief, and Crabbe, fifty-four years later, still remembered the distressing time which he had then gone through. It was not the sudden apparition of death so near him

a very interesting and quite unknown letter from Crabbe to Burke (see Appendix I). Its existence has since been pointed out by Canon Ainger (*Crabbe*, 1903, pp. 35-6). Among other things, it is said that "my Father was a rhymer himself."

[1] B. p. 4.
[2] B. p. 2.
[3] Cf. Benjamin Martin's *Miscellaneous Correspondence*, in Prose and Verse, October, 1760, pp. 521-2; December 9th, 1760, pp. 575, 576. As to this miscellany, see below, p. 29.
[4] B. p. 3.
[5] Cf. above, p. 7, n. 3, where it is proved that it was a brother and not a sister, as the Biographer wrongly states, p. 3, following the poet himself (*Infancy*, l. 58, p. 261 of the one-volume edition of 1861).

that touched him most, nor the sorrow caused by the
death of a little playfellow; it was rather "a mother's
tears and a father's terrors," the poignant anguish
of the over-strong man wrestling with grief, the dread
with which this anguish inspired his wife and his sons.
And the poet adds:

> Though greater anguish I have since endured,
> Some heal'd in part, some never to be cured,
> Yet there was something in that first-born ill,
> So new, so strange, that memory feels it still![1]

George Crabbe had not tenderness enough to try
to shake off his depression and console his family.
Worse still, he had not enough strength of will to
resist the temptations which, in that country of fishermen, carters, and smugglers, met him on all sides. He
became a more and more constant frequenter of the
public-house. In the eighteenth century drunkenness,
as is well known, was rife in every class of English
society, and perhaps it is not necessary to attribute
to the election of 1774,[2] in which George Crabbe is
supposed to have acted as agent, the bad habits in
which he now habitually indulged. True, the meetings
in public-houses, necessitated by the purchase of votes
and other electioneering operations, were bound to
develop this fatal propensity, but they were not the
cause of it. Violence of temper increased in a nature
whose moral side had been neglected. His wife, whose
health was precarious, began to dread his return home;
domestic scenes became more and more frequent. If
his food did not please him, "he would fling the dishes
about the room."[3] Robert Crabbe, writing in 1833,
relates that during the terrible inundation of January
1st, 1779, when the water flooded the ground-floor

---

[1] *Infancy*, 61-4.

[2] Cf. B. p. 9, who says that in 1774 there was a contested election at
Aldborough, and that George Crabbe was an active supporter of the Whig
candidate, Mr. Charles Long. It must be noted that this statement is borne
out only by the testimony of Robert Crabbe, the poet's brother, in answer
to one of the Biographer's queries. *The Public Advertiser* of Tuesday, October 18th, 1774, says, on the contrary, that "On Friday last, Thomas Fonnerau,
Esq., of Christ Church, and Richard Combe, Esq., of Earnshill in Somerset-
shire, were both returned for Aldborough, in Suffolk, without opposition."
According to *The Ipswich Journal*, the election of September, 1780, was as
uncontested as that of 1774. The Biographer (cf. also Kebbel, *Life of Crabbe*,
p. 23, note) has doubtless fallen here into one of the many small mistakes that
to a certain extent mar his work.

[3] B. p. 9.

room up to a height of three or four feet, his father
hastily carried a cask of gin upstairs, while his mother,
not less eagerly, put her tea-kettle in a safe place.[1]
A hard drinker, at home and abroad, George Crabbe
was bound to lose gradually the respect of all, even of
his children. "My father," the poet wrote to Burke
in 1781, "has a large family, a little income, and no
œconomy."[2] And when in later life he wished to
depict the insensible deterioration of a mind ravaged
by vice, he must sometimes have thought of the father
from whom he had inherited his energy and his
intellectual strength, but whom he had seen a prey to
the degradation of drink. He had witnessed heart-
rending, wellnigh tragic scenes, caused by drunkenness, in his own family and among his neighbours.
Thus his father remained for him the type of the
inhabitants of the "Borough," fishermen and others, of
those "men of masculine and robust frames, rude
manners, stormy passions," who spent their days in toil,
and their nights occasionally in noisy orgies.[3]
    There is no trace, in these stern natures, of the
tenderness and sensibility indispensable to a poet. His
father's influence therefore might have been fatal to the
young man, if it had not been corrected by that of his
mother. Born in 1725,[4] Mary Lodwick was twenty-nine
when she took for her second husband George Crabbe,
eight years younger than herself. This disparity of
age, added to the repeated fatigues of maternity and of
daily toil, early deprived her, I fear, of the affection
of a husband who became more and more estranged
from his home. She was not happy. Conscious of her
intellectual and physical inferiority, she often had to
suffer in silence with that meekness and resignation
which gained her the love of her eldest son. "She
was a woman of the most amiable disposition, mild,
patient, affectionate, and deeply religious."[5] She
cared little, the Biographer tells us, for the theological

---

[1] Letter quoted above (p. 5, n. 3).
[2] Letter quoted above (p. 17, n. 5, and Appendix I).
[3] B. p. 4 ; and cf. Wodderspoon's *Historic Sites of Suffolk*, 1841 : "There is
still that recklessness of conduct to be perceived inherent in the race he
[Crabbe] so justly condemns, and the same disposition to excite unruly
passions and feelings."
[4] She was fifty-five at her death in 1780 (Aldborough Parish Register; cf.
Davy MSS. under the heading, *Aldeburgh Churchyard*).
[5] B. p. 2.

doctrines of her clergyman:[1] her simple faith, of a
practical turn, was satisfied if she took her seat in
her pew regularly every Sunday, with all her children
beside her;[2] if she imparted to her life and to her
disposition something of that goodness and humility
which she heard inculcated in the sermon; above all,
if she brought up her children by her example. A little
of this tender piety early sank into the mind of her
son, and unsealed the fountain of sensibility which the
roughness of his father and his companions would
inevitably have dried up; he knew—

> How feelingly religion may be learned
> In smoky cabins, from a mother's tongue—
> Heard while the dwelling vibrates to the din
> Of the contiguous torrent, gathering strength
> At every moment—and with strength, increase
> Of fury; . . . . . . while the wind,
> A sightless labourer, whistles at its work. . . .
> And piety is sweet to infant minds.[3]

Later on, when dark hours came, Crabbe remembered
that he had been the beloved son of his mother, that
on his return from long excursions she had always
welcomed him with open arms,[4] and he rewarded her
affection by protecting her against his father. Seeing
that she was suffering from dropsy, " he became her
friend and her physician." He took pleasure in catching some small fish, which were the only food that
she could consume. He consoled and supported her
valiantly;[5] very often, no doubt, angry words were
exchanged between the indignant son and the father
inflamed by drink after a hard day's work.

Such was the home life of Crabbe as a child and youth,
an unhappy and dreary life, devoid of that comfort
which enhances the value of existence by lifting it above
petty cares, troubled by the quarrels of his parents,
exalted only by the example of laborious activity and
intelligence which his father had set him during his
first ten years, and also by the feelings of piety,
affection, and devotion with which his mother had
inspired him.

[1] B. p. 30.
[2] *Parish Register*, iii. 625.
[3] Wordsworth, *Excursion*, iv. Cf. also *Posthumous Tales*, i. 146 *seq.*
Silford Hall is partly autobiographical.
[4] *Tales of the Hall*, iv. 485.
[5] B. p. 9.

IV

In the absence of regularly installed primary schools, every English village in the eighteenth century had an "old matron," generally a "deaf, poor, patient widow," who was called the schoolmistress, and who boasted "unruly brats with birch to tame." In return for a trifling sum, she ensured the too busy house-wives freedom throughout the day by undertaking to look after the children and teach them to read. The little ones at Aldborough, about thirty in number, met every morning in her "lowly shed":

> Her room was small—they could not widely stray;
> Her threshold high—they could not run away.

The old "dame," looked upon as the mother of the street, was respected by all, especially by her little pupils. They could not see without admiring "her cap, far whiter than the driven snow," her apron as blue as the hare-bell of the fields, her "russet stole over her shoulders thrown," her "russet kirtle," woven by her own hands. And then she was so quick-sighted, so wide awake. "Spells, or tell-tale birds" always ready to whisper in her ear, enabled her to divine the slightest mischievous intention, the smallest attempt at a trick. Then woe to the culprit, who was sure to feel the mistress's dreaded sceptre—the birch-rod so relentlessly wielded—descend upon his "dainty skin, fair as the furry coat of whitest ermilin," unless she preferred keeping the rogue pinned to her gown for the rest of the day. From time to time she would stop knitting and solemnly give the order to resume work: forthwith the boys would take up their books, their little primers guarded on one side by a piece of "pellucid horn," and adorned on the other with a fine picture of the doughty deeds of St. George, the conqueror of the dragon. Thus were the first steps in the path of learning taken in that day.[1]

Crabbe "was a great favourite with the old dame who taught him,"[2] and did not fail to pay her a tribute in his poems:

[1] Cf. Shenstone's *Schoolmistress*; Crabbe's *Borough*, xxiv. 1-18; Cowper's *Tirocinium*, 119-24; and Tickell's *Hornbook*.
[2] B. pp. 4·5.

Shall I not think what pains the matron took,
When first I trembled o'er the gilded book?
How she, all patient, both at eve and morn,
Her needle pointed at the guarding horn;
And how she soothed me, when, with study sad,
I labour'd on to reach the final zad?
Shall I not grateful still the dame survey,
And ask the Muse the poet's debt to pay?[1]

In the hours when the "noisy, joyous troop" recovered
its liberty, the child took in instruction through his
eyes and his imagination. He lingered in front of
the little shops, and, if he found the door open,
hazarded a question suggested by his curiosity. He
was answered kindly; his gentleness, his boldness
mixed with timidity, inspired sympathy, and almost
enforced attention.[2] He crept into the inns, and,
drawing near the fire, listened to the talk of the
customers sitting round the chimney. No one turned
him out, for he "had patrons" who thought he was
harmless and incapable of noticing what went on.[3]
Involuntarily, his attention was already attracted to
the manners and customs of his fellow-men; sitting
around him were certain personages whom he afterwards described with minute accuracy: the portly
innkeeper, the deep drinkers, boatmen and petty
traders concerting a nocturnal venture with smugglers;
and, towards the evening, the poor "dredger," wet to
the skin, who tried to sell the fruit of his hard toil.
Or he walked along the beach, observed curiously all
the refuse and wreckage thrown up by the tide, and
now and then went into the cottage of some sailor,
whose wife welcomed him "like a son." She would
make him a confidant of her anxiety and wonderment;
she loved to tell him what storms endangered the
precious life of her husband, the marvels to be seen
in foreign parts—"lands without bounds and people
without law."[4] She would show him and obligingly
explain the prints on the walls: some historical, like
that in which Charles I., taught by misfortune, draws up
his twelve Golden Rules of conduct; others, legendary
or fanciful, representing the "kind" Lady Godiva, or

[1] *Borough*, xviii. 25-32.
[2] *Tales of the Hall*, iv. 411-16. The character of Richard is autobiographical.
[3] *Ibid.* iv. 417-26.
[4] *Ibid.* iv. 309-12. Cf. also *Tales of the Hall*, v. 11-73.

"the magic mill that grinds the gran'nams young." [1]
She would let him examine at leisure the books on the
" shelf of deal beside the cuckoo-clock," and the child
would devour marvellous stories about ghosts, witches,
and fairies, which were the favourite literature of
young folk in that day : [2]

> Ballads there were of lover's bliss or bale,
> The kitchen story, and the nursery tale.
> His hungry mind disdained not humble food,
> And read with relish keen of Robin Hood ;
> Of him, all powerful made by magic gift,
> And giants slain—of mighty Hickathrift. [3]

He was interested in the adventures of the Wandering
Jew, of Tom Thumb the Great, and especially in
Hickathrift's rival, Jack the Giant-killer, whose arm,
" by wizard-power upheld," had done wonders :

> His shoes of swiftness on his feet he placed ;
> His coat of darkness on his loins he braced ;
> His sword of sharpness in his hand he took,
> And off the heads of doughty giants stroke ;
> Their glaring eyes beheld no mortal near ;
> No sound of feet alarmed the drowsy ear ;
> No English blood their pagan sense could smell,
> But heads dropt headlong, wondering why they fell. [4]

Happy moments for a credulous imagination, always
prompt to forget the reality and to wander into
dreamland after his heroes; precious moments, too,
since these stories awakened in the child the creative
faculty, without which the choicest gifts of observation
would have remained unfruitful ! Crabbe retained,
up to the close of his life, a half-ironical gratitude
and a strong partiality for marvellous tales of this
class. [5] He liked to give them to his grandchildren, [6]
whom he wished to share the pleasure he had
taken, perhaps still took, in them. Like Wordsworth, [7]

---

[1] *Parish Register*, i. 51-60.
[2] B. p. 5.
[3] *Posthumous Tales*, i. 96-101.
[4] *Parish Register*, i. 119-26. Cf. a passage in the *Prelude*, vii. 274 *seq.*, in
which Wordsworth notes the illusion produced by the same hero on a popular
audience at the suburban theatre of Sadler's Wells.
[5] B. p. 5.
[6] B p. 86.
[7] *Prelude*, v. 341-7, and Legouis, *La Jeunesse de W. Wordsworth*, pp. 37-40.

he wanted to develop disinterested imagination, fancy even, at an early age; he preferred stories of fairies or giants to the "utilitarian" tales of Mrs. Trimmer, or even of Miss Edgeworth, long narratives written to point a moral, or object-lessons with plot and dialogue. He remembered his own childhood, and the books which he had read of winter evenings to the old blind women in his native village.[1]

However varied the spectacle of the sea and of the activity of the port might be, young Crabbe's life remained narrow and monotonous. His horizon therefore seemed all of a sudden to expand on the day when, at the request of "his fond mother," his father promised to take him to Orford in a "newly purchased" sailing - boat. A fine excursion was planned, and a large party expected. They were to sail, as usual, down the Alde, and pass near Orford and the island of Havergate, whose bare, isolated mass divides the river into two arms; farther on they would see, to the right, the green meadows, to the left, the long strip of shingle, the Beach,[2] which dams the ocean on one side and the river on the other. They were to stop for luncheon either at Orford or on the beach, where they could enjoy themselves for part of the afternoon, and towards evening they were to return to Aldborough along the right bank of the Alde. A day full of pleasing anticipations for a child who had never been so far from home! About fifty-five years afterwards the poet reproduced from the depths of his memory the impression which it had left on him, and noted it in a fragment entitled *Infancy*. If we put aside the moral lesson which Crabbe, too didactically, draws from his recollections, if we try to distinguish, beneath the old man's lament, the naïve voice of the child who relates his first disenchantment, we shall penetrate deeply into the secret of his nature:

> Sweet was the morning's breath, the inland tide,
> And our boat gliding, where alone could glide
> Small craft—and they oft touched on either side.
> It was my first-born joy. I heard them say,
> "Let the child go; he will enjoy the day."

[1] B. p. 5.
[2] Cf. Ford, *Aldborough Described*, p. 58.

For children ever feel delighted when
They take their portion, and enjoy with men.
Give him the pastime that the old partake,
And he will quickly top and taw forsake.

The linnet chirp'd upon the furze as well,
To my young sense, as sings the nightingale.
Without was paradise—because within
Was a keen relish, without taint of sin.

A town appear'd,—and where an infant went,
Could they determine, on themselves intent ?
I lost my way, and my companions me,
And all, their comforts and tranquillity.
Midday it was, and, as the sun declined,
The good, found early, I no more could find :
The men drank much, to whet the appetite ;
And, growing heavy, drank to make them light ;
Then drank to relish joy, then further to excite.
Their cheerfulness did but a moment last ;
Something fell short, or something overpast.
The lads played idly with the helm and oar,
And nervous women would be set on shore,
Till " civil dudgeon " grew, and peace would smile no more.

Now on the colder water faintly shone
The sloping light—the cheerful day was gone ;
Frown'd every cloud, and from the gather'd frown
The thunder burst, and rain came pattering down.
My torpid senses now my fears obey'd,
When the fierce lightning on the eyeballs play'd.
Now, all the freshness of the morning fled,
My spirits burdened, and my heart was dead ;
The female servants show'd a child their fear,
And men, full wearied, wanted strength to cheer ;
And when, at length, the dreaded storm went past,
And there was peace and quietness at last,
'Twas not the morning's quiet—it was not
Pleasure revived, but Misery forgot :
It was not Joy that now commenced her reign,
But mere relief from wretchedness and pain.[1]

Thus ended a day so radiant, when viewed from
afar, and so well begun. Is it not singular that the
expedition should have left in the heart of the child
a painful impression, persistent enough for the old
man to remember it ? Other children would have forgotten everything except the pleasure of having seen

[1] *Infancy*, 72-114 (p. 261 of *Life and Works*, 1861). Cf., as to this poem,
supra, p. 7, n. 3, and also B. p. 4.

something new, of having felt the breeze waft the boat along the glittering stream. They would have been overjoyed at the possibility of running about freely in the streets of Orford; even the rain and the storm at the end would not have put them out—they would have almost delighted in it. Think of young Wordsworth launching forth boldly upon his lake, climbing the rocky paths of the mountains, with the ardour of a child starting to discover unknown regions. His joyous activity is so great that at certain moments he forgets his own existence, and, lost in ecstasy, lets the outside world penetrate into him. He opens his soul to nature, receives life from it and imparts life to it.[1] Crabbe, on the contrary, coils up and retires into himself. Full of confidence, he sets out one sunny morning in quest of happiness; at midday the first clouds appear on the horizon: he grows uneasy, anticipating the storm which is about to darken the sky. He stops, and indulges in his gloomy reverie. A sort of homesickness makes him retrace his steps, for he lacks the fearless confidence that great enterprises require; too careful in calculating his strength, he ends by questioning its existence. He will never make a good sailor, as his father, annoyed at his clumsiness, has often reproached him.[2] Far from attracting him, the sea rivets him to the shore. He already prefers observation and reflection to action. The stern and sterile nature which surrounds him, the dull life which he leads, have already, it would seem, checked his aspirations and implanted in his pensive mind the germs of pessimism. However, he is an uncommon child, of a gentle disposition and lively intelligence, for whom some sacrifice should be made. The father therefore, in spite of his poverty, determined to send him to school for a time.

V

THE place chosen was Bungay, a small town on "the borders of Norfolk,"[3] about thirty miles to the north of Aldborough. It is impossible, however, to fix the date on which this change occurred, or the time spent by the child in his first absence from home. He must indeed have been very young if it is true, ·as two of

---

[1] *Prelude*, ii. 340-52. [2] B. p. 4. [3] B. p. 5.

his biographers state, that on his arrival there he was unable to put on his collar or even his shirt without help [1]—an additional reason for the abrupt change from home to school life being distasteful to him. The discipline was severe : the story goes that one day Crabbe and some of his schoolfellows were punished for playing at soldiers in forbidden hours by being thrust into a large dog-kennel called the " Black Hole," in allusion to a well-known recent event at Calcutta. Crabbe had got in first, and was farthest from the door, which was tightly shut. The poor child in vain shrieked out that he was being suffocated. At last, in despair, he bit the hand of the boy next to him, whose roars gave the alarm, and the sentinel at length decided to let out his prisoners. "A minute more, and I must have died," said the poet afterwards to his son.[2] As regards the teaching, it was very elementary—a little reading and writing and ciphering, no doubt.

On his return to Aldborough, Crabbe resumed the life described above. He once more ransacked his father's books and those of his neighbours. Tales of fairies and giants no longer satisfied him; he added to them—

> Romance in sheets,
> Soft tales of love, which never damsel read
> But tears of pity stain'd her virgin bed.

He became interested in " Jane Shore and Rosamond the Fair," and " in humbler heroines frail as these " : one of them, in particular, forsaken by her lover, had " till her death the work of vengeance stay'd." When the fatal hour arrived, the faithless man was at sea, surrounded " by a dauntless crew." Suddenly—

> . . . The angry ghost pursued.
> In a small boat, without an oar or sail,
> She came to call him, nor would force avail,
> Nor prayer ; but, conscience-stricken, down he leapt,
> And o'er his corse the closing billows slept.[3]

---

[1] Cf. B. p. 5, and the same anecdote in another form in Kebbel's, *Life of Crabbe*, p. 14.

[2] B. p. 5. It appears that the room in which Crabbe slept is still shown at the Bungay Grammar School ; at least, this is so stated by Mr. Kebbel, and the fact has been confirmed to me by a trustworthy informant. But I do not vouch for the identity of the room shown.

[3] *Posthumous Tales*, i. 79-91.

Nothing could be more moral or more sentimental than such a tale. The child's imagination had a craving for marvellous adventures and " wild fictions." " At your age," he wrote in 1830 to his granddaughter Caroline, " I read every book which I could procure." [1] *The Arabian Nights* delighted him, as afterwards they did Wordsworth; the *Persian Tales*, Quarles's *Emblems*,[2] *Æsop's Fables*, with "the coats in tatters, and the cuts in wood," pleased him as much as *Robinson Crusoe* in his " delightful isle," or Bunyan's famous *Pilgrim's Progress*.

Nothing came amiss to him ; his curiosity devoured everything, just as it fell in his way. He learned the history of England in the sixpenny numbers of " Dr. Cooke and other learned men." His father's mathematical books alone repelled him : " fluxions, sections, algebraic lore, he left for others to explore." But what joy when he became engrossed in *The Monthly Magazine*—that is, the collection in which Benjamin Martin, month by month, retailed the most varied information to his readers. In the fourteen volumes of his *General Magazine of Arts and Sciences* might be found a philosophy for young people of both sexes, the natural history of England and Wales, a complete system of all the philological sciences, a " corpus " of the mathematical sciences, and last, and not least, a miscellany containing, not " scraps from sermons, scenes removed from plays," as the ungrateful poet irreverently asserts,[3] but the most tasty morsels of the whole collection: a varied correspondence, problems solved or to be solved, a chronological narrative of the events of the month, and—supreme bliss!—the " Poet's Corner." The mathematician in Crabbe's father had a poor opinion, it would seem, of the innocent odes and innumerable prologues, epilogues, and occasional pieces which encumbered this " corner." He had the problems bound, and the verses sewn into a paper cover.[4] While the volumes were carefully placed on the shelves, the papers were "left to the chance perusal of the children,"

---

[1] B. p. 83.

[2] Francis Quarles (1592—1644). The *Emblems* appeared in 1635, with very numerous illustrations (cf. Pope's allusion in the *Dunciad*, i. 140 : " And Quarles is saved by Beauties not his own "). His works have been reprinted in three volumes by Grosart in his *Chertsey Worthies Library*.

[3] *Posthumous Tales*, i. 131.

[4] *Ibid.* i. 79, " poetry unbound."

who were at liberty to read them, " if the eye of any of them should be attracted by the view of words placed in parallel lines of about the same length." This was the very direction which young Crabbe's eyes took, "and he read, scarcely knowing what, pleased with the recurrence of similar sounds and with his ability of retaining a vast number of unmeaning verses in his memory." [1] Poor models in fact, very unsuited for giving the child an idea of great poetry, in which vigour of thought is allied to perfection of form ! Who knows if Crabbe does not owe some of his slovenliness to his premature acquaintance with the platitudes of these rhymesters ? No doubt the reading of Shakspeare, of Spenser, and of Milton [2] partly corrected the effect of such bad examples ; perhaps too these indifferent poems, being within easier reach of the child's mind than great masterpieces would have been, were more calculated to inspire him with a wish to imitate them and to become a poet himself.

He was in his twelfth year when he was sent to school again, this time to Stowmarket, a small town about five-and-twenty miles to the west of Aldborough, where the woollen industry was then in a thriving state.[3] A certain Richard Haddon kept a school there, in which Crabbe spent two years.[4] This was not the happiest time of his life, to judge by his poems, in which he evidently recalls his impressions. School seemed to him a " world " in which boys indulge in brutal passions, untamed by culture or by adversity. He saw a master whose " dull labour and laborious life " brought him but " small compensation," and whose " power was despised." [5] Like Cowper at Dr. Pitman's, he had to submit to the persecutions of a brute, " the stout, tall captain, whose superior size the minor heroes view with envious eyes." [6] He was under

---

[1] See the *Autobiographical Sketch*, given by Crabbe to *The New Monthly Magazine*, published on January 1st, 1816, and several times quoted by his son. It is in vol. iv. of the British Museum Collection, pp. 511-7, *Memoirs of Eminent Persons*.

[2] *Posthumous Tales*, i. 140.

[3] Cf. Arthur Young's *Tour to the East of England*, 1771, vol. ii. pp. 178-85.

[4] B. p. 5, and *Bunbury Letter* (Appendix I): " He [my father] kept me two years at a country boarding-school."

[5] I quote these and the following passages from *The Borough*, xxiv. 240-340, and from *Tales of the Hall*, iii. 1-22 and 55-70.

[6] Cowper's *Tirocinium*, 220-30.

the sway of a bully, a sort of "proud viceroy, ever near," more respected than the real master. In other words, he shrank beneath the blows of an older school-fellow, reproached himself with cowardice, and felt profoundly humiliated. He was one of the poor little "fags," servants of the big boys, doomed to a slavery which, before the reforms of later days, was a blot on English schools. He had to cower before the redoubt-able captain, of whom he has drawn a lifelike portrait :

> Hark ! at his word the trembling youngsters flee,
> Where he is walking none must walk but he ;
> See ! from the winter fire the weak retreat,
> His the warm corner, his the favourite seat,
> Save when he yields it for some slave to keep
> Awhile, then back, at his return, to creep ;
> At his command the poor dependants fly,
> And humbly bribe him as a proud ally ;
> Flattered by all, the notice he bestows
> Is gross abuse, and bantering and blows. . . .
> How hot the vengeance of a heart so cold !
> See how he beats whom he had just reviled
> And made rebellious—that imploring child :
> How fierce his eye, how merciless his blows !

His stupidity equals his brutality :

> Learn he could not ; he said he could not learn,
> But he profess'd it gave him no concern :
> Books were his horror, dinner his delight,
> And his amusement to shake hands and fight ;
> Argue he could not, but in case of doubt,
> Or disputation, fairly box'd it out.

One day, the master asking him how much six times five make, he was puzzled, shut his eyes and heaved a sigh :

> " Come, six times count your fingers—how he stands !
> Your fingers, idiot ! "—" What, of both my hands ? "

In school, painfully conscious of his inferiority, he asks his victims to correct the blunders in his exercises. Yet his tyranny renders the school "odious." He makes—

> The soft, ingenuous, gentle minds endure
> Ills that ease, time, and friendship fail to cure.

This abuse of brute strength increases the timidity

of a naturally shrinking boy. But young Crabbe remains an observer, and the bully is not the only type which attracts his attention. He sees another schoolfellow pass with a longing look in front of some fruit exposed for sale, then ask the price in a low voice, and finger the pennies in his pocket for a long time, unable to take his eyes off the " sweet seduction," or to make up his mind to buy. Suddenly a "spendthrift " rushes up, money in hand, and carries off the fruit. Whereupon the young satirist smiles at the satisfaction with which the little miser drops the pennies one after the other into his pocket, pleased at this enforced economy, and saying to himself that the " spendthrift," once he has satisfied his appetite, will no doubt give away the rest of his purchase. Then there are sons of farmers, whose shouts astonish the much quieter Crabbe :

> They who, like colts let loose, with vigour bound,
> And thoughtless spirit, o'er the beaten ground, . . .
> Their minds are coursing in their fathers' fields.

Work is a torture to them, dancing lessons a bore, and they have such a voracious appetite that they could not wait for their meals,

> Did they not slily to the chamber steal,
> And there the produce of the basket seize,
> The mother's gift ! still studious of their ease.

Brutality or greediness, these are the very defects which Taine, thirty years ago, found in the English schoolboy.[1] Crabbe had suffered from them, and had not forgotten them.

Like so many other poets, he held aloof. His work, of a higher order than at Bungay, filled his time. He made progress in mathematics. His father, who, it would appear, already destined him for the medical career, was highly pleased to receive occasionally from the pupil a solution of the " difficult " problems which he propounded to the master.[2] Greek was not taught at Stowmarket, and Crabbe was never very familiar with the language of the gods.[3] On the other hand, he learnt the rudiments of grammar, read no doubt some

---

[1] *Notes sur l'Angleterre*, pp. 143-9.   [2] B. p. 5.   [3] Cf. below, p. 206, n. 1.

easy pages from Latin authors, and this rapid initiation
enabled him later to pursue his classical studies and take
orders.[1] It should not be forgotten that he left school
for good in his thirteenth year, and that he never went
to a university; all the culture which he gave himself
is therefore his own, and testifies to his strength of
mind and character. Signs of this originality showed
themselves as early as the Stowmarket days. Like
the "elder brother"[2] in the *Tales of the Hall*, he was
"a still, retiring, musing, dreaming boy. He relished
neither sudden bursts of joy nor the tumultuous
pleasures of a rude, noisy, careless, fearless multitude."
He had his own pleasures, his unexpected amusements.
He tried to write down from memory the very indifferent poems published by B. Martin; if certain passages
escaped him, "he supplied the defect by his own
invention, and thus at a very early period of his life
became a versifier."[3]   Less precocious than Pope, he
was also less well trained. He remembered the fairy
tales and stories of adventure which he had read, "the
religious and moral principles" which his mother had
instilled into him, and with them he—

> Wove the wild fancies of an Infant-Muse,
> Inspiring thoughts that he could not express,
> Obscure sublime ! his secret happiness.
> Oft would he strive for words, and oft begin
> To frame in words the views he had within ;
> But ever fail'd : for how can words explain
> Th' unform'd ideas of a teeming brain ?[4]

Or he turned to real life, and practised the art of satire.
According to the Biographer, his first victim was a
little damsel who came to the school in the evening,
and was too proud of a new set of blue ribbons in her
straw bonnet. Vanity or simple coquetry deserves
correction, thought the future moralist, who expressed
his ironical disapproval in some doggerel lines.[5]   The
vices and failings of human nature struck him already,
either in his playfellows or in ridiculous outsiders like
"Neddy," "the mimic for a schoolboy's pay," and afterwards a quack doctor.[6]   Thus it may be said of Crabbe,

[1] Cf. Burke's remark, B. p. 27.
[2] George. Cf. *Tales of the Hall*, ii. 98-102.
[3] *Autobiographical Sketch*, see above, p. 30, n. 1.
[4] *Posthumous Tales*, i. 166-73.
[5] B. p. 5.
[6] *Borough*, vii. 233 *seq.*

as of Wordsworth, and no doubt of each one of us, that "the child was father of the man."

The end of 1767 and the early months of 1768 were spent at Aldborough, where Crabbe waited for a place to be found for him. His recovered liberty and his mother's affection must have seemed sweet indeed to him after the apprehensions inspired by the rule of the stronger. No more lessons of arithmetic or grammar; his life was now a long holiday, of which he took advantage to read over again his precious note-books of verses, and to venture beyond the limits hitherto set for his excursions. From his own state-ment it appears that at this time he led the same kind of life as his Richard in the *Tales of the Hall*.[1] He walked through the town:

> Where crowds assembled I was sure to run,
> Heard what was said and mused on what was done;
> Attentive listening in the moving scene,
> And often wondering what the men could mean.

The masts of the ships seen from a distance attracted him to Slaughden Quay:

> Strange sounds to hear, and business strange to me,
> Seamen and carmen, and I know not who,
> A lewd, amphibious, rude, contentious crew—
> Confused as bees appear about their hive,
> Yet all alert to keep their work alive;
> I saw their tasks, their toil, their care, their skill,
> Led by their own and by a master-will.

He helped them sometimes, when his father required his services, which he willingly gave, I believe, not being old enough to "abhor manual labour,"[2] but rather glad to be thought able to assist grown men in an important and urgent task. More gladly still he turned to the ocean and gave it "his mind and thoughts, as restless as the wave." When the ships at sea made signals of distress, he followed with curiosity the prompt man-œuvres of the sailors and of the ever-watchful pilots:

> Mix'd in their act, nor rested till he knew
> Why they were call'd, and what they were to do.

One day, when squalls and calms succeeded each other, he had climbed the hill and was gazing on the troubled waters. Suddenly a gun is heard, two

---

[1] iv. 287-485.　　　[2] B. p. 6.

sailing-boats appear, racing each other, sometimes
one and sometimes the other ahead. One of them,
seeing itself distanced, hoists a sail which had been
kept in reserve—a fatal piece of imprudence : the
wind sends the boat ahead like an arrow, but it
capsizes, and all the anxious inhabitants, massed on
the shore, see it sink before their eyes. "Then were
those piercing shrieks, that frantic flight;" . . . "all
ask, all answer, none attend, none hear."[1] Crabbe
notices a young girl who stands apart, her eyes fixed
on the waves "meeting and clashing o'er the seamen's
graves." 'Tis a poor maiden betrothed—"a few
hours more, and *he* will lie, a corpse, upon the shore."
Tears of pity rise to the child's eyes ; he returns to his
mother, who feels alarmed and distressed by such a
keen sensibility. He has so much curiosity and sympathy that even painful emotions have an attraction for
him :

> No ships were wreck'd upon that fatal beach,
> But I could give the luckless tale of each ;
> Eager I look'd till I beheld a face
> Of one disposed to paint their dismal case ;
> . . . and suffering in their fate
> I long'd the more they should its horrors state.

If sailors returned from the polar regions, he interro-
gated them and heard with terror of "boats uplifted
by enormous whales," and this perilous pursuit
appeared to him cruel, criminal almost.
On fine summer days he left the little town, and
going in a northerly direction, wandered over the
heath. There he met the shepherd, the only denizen
of these solitudes, and stopped to speak to him, for
"shepherds love to talk." The superstition of this
man astonished him : "he with tales of wonder stored
my mind, wonders that he in many a lonely eve had
seen himself, and therefore must believe." In Crabbe's
eyes he was simply an untutored peasant, in an arid
and monotonous landscape, and by no means a well-
nigh supernatural being like that which Wordsworth
sometimes descried on the Cumberland hills, "in size
a giant stalking through thick fog," and "glorified by
the deep radiance of the setting sun."[2] Regardless of

---

[1] Cf. a similar scene on the Alde, *Posthumous Tales*, xviii. 195-235.
[2] *Prelude*, viii. 262-70.

hunger, and sure of finding "crabs" or "brambles," "cress embrown'd by summer sun, in the dry bed where streams no longer run," and a "crystal spring,"[1] Crabbe, like Cowper,[2] continued his walk :

> I loved to walk where none had walked before, . . .
> Or far beyond the sight of men to stray,
> And take my pleasure when I lost my way ;
> For then 'twas mine to trace the hilly heath,
> And all the mossy moor that lies beneath :
> Here had I favourite stations, where I stood
> And heard the murmurs of the ocean-flood,
> With not a sound beside except when flew
> Aloft the lapwing and the grey curlew,
> Who with wild notes my fancied power defied,
> And mock'd the dreams of solitary pride.

The child felt the peculiar attraction of these vast expanses, which the spectator's eye seems to take in at a glance : he stepped out more quickly, for he fancied himself one of the heroes whose romantic adventures he had been reading, "an abdicated king, driv'n from his state by a rebellious race."[3] When he reached the environs of Dunwich, he turned towards the shore, which is fringed by cliffs at this point only; in one of their recesses he discovered the smugglers' refuge, the hut in which "poor, pious Martha served the lawless tribe," whose good and bad points she obligingly described to her young visitor, adding. "I talk, my child, to you, who little think of what such wretches do." And Crabbe returned to Aldborough, tired out, but ready to start the next morning in an opposite direction, to explore the banks of the Alde, to "visit every creek and bay, made by the river in its winding way," on which the seagulls float listlessly, with folded wings.

Thus, at the early age of fourteen, Crabbe already possessed some of the gifts to which he afterwards owed his fame. Impelled by the instinct of imitation, he was beginning to learn to write in verse; he had unconsciously accumulated, in the course of his childhood, a multitude of observations on his natural surroundings, his fellow-countrymen, and his companions; he had made in fairyland and dreamland the

---

[1] *Posthumous Tales*, xxii. 103-15.
[2] *The Task*, i. 107.
[3] *Posthumous Tales*, xxii. 115-18.

sojourn which is indispensable to every poet. His
character was taking definite shape : reserved, almost
timid, possessed of an energy more fitted for resistance
than initiative, keenly observant, with a turn for satire,
endowed at the same time with a sensibility which
might have easily become sentimentality. His existence and that of his parents had remained humble and
poor, but he had suffered little from this, being ignorant
of any other. He had also tasted the delights of
solitary reverie and of much unrestrained reading.
He was liked for his naïve tenderness, he was respected
for his " learning "[1] and his intelligence. The "fair
seed-time "[2] had passed for him ; he was now about to
serve the rude apprenticeship of life.

[1] B. p. 5 : " Walking one day in the street, he chanced to displease a stout
lad, who doubled his fist to beat him ; but another boy interfered to claim
benefit of clergy for the studious George. ' You must not meddle with *him*,'
he said ; ' let *him* alone, for he ha' got l'arning.' "
[2] *Prelude*, i. 301.

CHAPTER II

I

IT was with a Mr. Smith,[1] an apothecary at Wickham Brook, that Crabbe made his start in life. He thus passed from one extremity to the other of the county of Suffolk, from the shores of the German Ocean to the plateaus which extend south of Newmarket and Bury St. Edmunds. Wickham Brook is a tiny village, little more than a hamlet, nestling in a hollow, about twelve miles south-east of Newmarket. Low hills, here and there crowned by a windmill, enclose it on every side except one, by which penetrates the streamlet that gives its name to the place. A poor church at the end of a cemetery, a few scattered houses, some built by a charitable hand, others, somewhat smarter, clad with creepers and surrounded with flower-beds, a rustic bridge, a modest inn ; then, on the crest of the slope which ascends northwards in the direction of the village of Lidgate, a newly built school—such is at the present day this neat and unpretending little spot, which seems to slumber peacefully in the shade of its trees, at the foot of its hills.

To cross the whole breadth of Suffolk was not an easy or a pleasant journey in the year 1768. It was a trying experience for Crabbe, who performed the greater part of it in the company of two farmers returning from Aldborough, and the last ten miles alone. Let the reader picture him, exhausted by a long tramp, his clothes bespattered with the mud of

[1] Cf. letter quoted above, p. 5, n. 3. " I recollect my brother went as an apprentice to a Mr. Smith at Wickham Brook," writes Robert Crabbe.

the broken tracks which in those days did duty for
cross-country roads, with "a very ill-made scratch-
wig" on his head,[1] arriving in this remote village to
which the paternal will consigns him, and finding
himself suddenly confronted by his new master's
daughters, who, seeing his melancholy appearance
and shabby attire, burst into an uncontrollable fit of
laughter, and exclaim in mocking astonishment, " La!
here's our new 'prentice!" The youth, already proud
and sensitive, more ready to criticise than to be
made fun of, reddens with humiliation, and is at a loss
for an answer. The case becomes much worse when
he discovers that this master, to whom he is bound by
a seven years' contract,[2] is poor, and has little business,
that the apothecary's income is derived more from a
neighbouring farm than from the sale of drugs, and
that the apprentice is expected to share the attic and
bed, nay, even to help in the work, of a ploughboy.
When there are no blood-lettings to be done or
errands to be run in the village or the neighbourhood,
Crabbe follows the plough up and down the hills,
helps to get in the harvest and to sow the land. He
has no consciousness of discharging a noble mission.
He grows sad when he hears the wind that sweeps
over these plateaus and bends the tree-tops with a
sound like the low roar of the sea. He thinks of the
beach, of the animation at home, of his "indulgent
mother," so tender, when compared with these indifferent, unfeeling strangers. As at Stowmarket, he
takes refuge in his dreams, he has a world of his own,
a "magic circle" into which none can follow him. He
scribbles poetry, and fills a whole drawer with it in
his two years' stay.[3] He reads tales of adventures,
glad to throw off in this way the burden of his
degrading existence, and to imagine an ideal life in
which the mind is free:

> A thousand visions float around my head:
> Hark! hollow blasts through empty courts resound,
> And shadowy forms with staring eyes stalk round;
> See! moats and bridges, walls and castles rise,
> Ghosts, fairies, demons, dance before our eyes:

[1] B. p. 6.
[2] Cf. *Bunbury Letter*: "I was bound by indentures"; and B. p. 6: "Not
being bound by indentures," which is another obvious mistake.
[3] B. p. 7.

Lo ! magic verse inscribed on golden gate,
And bloody hand that beckons on to fate :—
" And who art thou, thou little page, unfold ?
Say, doth thy lord my Claribel withhold ?
Go, tell him straight, Sir Knight, thou must resign
The captive queen, for Claribel is mine."
Away he flies ; and now for bloody deeds,
Black suits of armour, masks, and foaming steeds ;
The giant falls, his recreant throat I seize,
And from his corselet take the massy keys :—
Dukes, lords, and knights in long procession move,
Released from bondage with my virgin love :—
She comes ! she comes ! in all the charms of youth,
Unequall'd love, and unsuspected truth !
Ah ! happy he, who thus in magic themes,
O'er worlds bewitch'd, in early rapture dreams,
Where wild Enchantment waves her potent wand,
And Fancy's beauties fill her fairy land ;
Where doubtful objects strange desires excite,
And Fear and Ignorance afford delight.[1]

But what cruel regrets and what bitterness he
feels when he has to awake from his dream and
relapse into the narrow groove of reality ! For his
life is a trying one, and his distractions are few and
far between. From time to time, perhaps, a longer
errand than usual takes the little messenger to the
environs of Newmarket, up to Cheveley Park, for
instance, where the Duke of Rutland then owned a
country seat. From Wickham Brook almost a whole
day is required for the journey there and back, by the
winding, hilly road that runs through Lidgate, and
climbs a plateau commanding an extensive view, and
revealing, at some distance to the left, the dark mass
of the foliage of the park. It is towards this spot that
Crabbe is walking, with a parcel of medicine which he
has to deliver at the hall. Alas ! he has not had, like
the Peter Perkin of his *Posthumous Tales*,[2] a fond
mother to dress him in his best clothes—a green coat,
cut large in view of future growth, a white waistcoat,
a frill with a black riband to show it off, a pair of
stockings "white as driven snow," and smart shoes
on the black varnish of which " shone the large buckle
of a silvery hue." He has had to do without a horse,
however long the journey ; his dress is of the simplest,

---

[1] *Library*, 545-70.   [2] i. 195 *seq.*

as becomes a pedestrian whose clothes may be dirtied by the mud of the roads. He reflects, as he walks along, that the house contains, he has been told, wonderful treasures of art, and his curiosity will not be satisfied unless he is allowed to see them. So, having done his errand, he lingers in the "small room" to which he has been admitted; hesitating and timid, he dares not express his wish, when a sympathetic housekeeper appears who understands him at once, and takes him "through rooms immense and galleries wide and tall," where he "walks entranced." He is shown sumptuous chambers, containing beds with heavy canopies, and mirrors astonishing to him, in which he can see his whole figure, "from the pale forehead to the jet-black shoe." He penetrates, holding his breath, into the dim, silent chapel, along the majestic aisle lit by "strange, partial beams" from the stained glass of the "narrow windows." It is almost a relief to him to find himself in the gallery, where he takes a rapid glance at the various pictures—historical subjects, which, to the great surprise of his guide, his reading enables him to understand, or family portraits ; a moment he lingers before the "figures of stone," the statues whose nudity astonishes him. At last they come to the library, a novel spectacle, an imposing room, where books "of every kind are disposed, the food for every mind."

> With joy perplex'd, round casts he wondering eyes,
> Still in his joy, and dumb in his surprise.

When his first wonder has passed, he "sharp for close inspection grows." He begins with the prints lying on the table, then turns his attention to the books, hastening from one volume to the other, as fancy suggests, looking curiously at the bindings and reading the titles. "Lost in delight, and with his freedom pleased," he seizes three huge folios from their shelf, one of which is illustrated with—

> . . . Prints of every race
> Of beast and bird most rare in every place,
> Serpents, the giants of their tribe, whose prey
> Are giants too—a wild ox every day.

A second volume tells—

> Of battles dire, and dreadful to behold,
> On sea or land, and fleets dispersed in storms;
> A third has all creative fancy forms,—
> Hydra and dire chimera, deserts rude,
> And ruins grand, enriching solitude.

A thrill of fear comes over him and would have changed into terror if the housekeeper, who had left him for a moment, had not returned and taken him to see the gardens and the park. In the deep shade of venerable trees, "more aged than the mansion" which they surround, hard by a brook which murmurs unseen, the child, overcome with pleasure and fatigue, falls asleep and dreams till dinner-time. He is then abruptly awakened; his kind protectress welcomes him in most amiable fashion, and places him, flattered by such an honour and blushing with modesty, at her side; on his right is "Mistress Kitty," and opposite him Lucy, a "maiden sly." Then the butler, the groom, the footman, the laundress, the coachman, and the cook all take their respective seats at the table, for "all their station and their office knew, nor sat as rustics or the rabble do." They address each other with much respect. One of the maids invites the lucky guest to hobnob with her, and all encourage him:

> Wine, fruit, and sweetmeats close repast so long,
> And Mistress Flora sings an opera song.

Now, at nightfall, he has to return to Wickham Brook and servitude. What a contrast between this luxurious abode, in which the servants themselves seem to share the wellnigh royal splendour of their masters, and the humble dwellings of the fishermen of Aldborough, between the comfortable life of some and the privations of others, between the repose of the stately trees of this park and the fury of the breakers lashed by the gale! Are certain folk then so happy on earth that dreamland has become for them a reality? What a privileged existence is that of these lords and ladies, surrounded with all the resources of wealth and with treasures of art and literature! And what a contrast to himself, poor little apprentice to an apothecary without customers, and farm-labourer against his will!

At length, this slavery became galling to him. He

felt angry at learning nothing, at being forced to do
servile work. He considered himself more unfortunate
than his bedfellow, a servant, it is true, but hired by
the year, and free from all engagement by contract.[1]
With a singular force of will, at once passionate and
contained, calm but unshakable, he rebelled against
the oppressor and went through the first of the crises
by which the youth was changed into a man. He
must have suffered much, for he was naturally affectionate and would have preferred to live at peace with
those around him. And then it requires so great an
effort for a child to assert himself and stand up against
his elders! But he was in despair, and, as he says in
language which still breathes the indignation of that
melancholy time, "he rebelled in his servitude, for it
became grievous." To make matters worse, his "father
was informed of his idleness and disobedience," and the
correction inflicted was severe. A rough hand, which
he had learned to fear, but not to hate, descended
heavily upon him and forced him to remain in this
odious house. But the boy's resolution was taken ;
instead of flinching, his courage and his obstinacy
redoubled at the thought that he had been unjustly
treated. His father had to be sent for again, and this
time he decided to take back his son, as well as two-
thirds of the small premium paid for apprenticeship
two years before. Crabbe was in his sixteenth year
when he thus returned to Aldborough. It may be
supposed that, except from his mother, he did not meet
with a very warm reception under the paternal roof.

II

His stay there was not of long duration, for a new
place offered itself almost immediately, in 1771, and on
very favourable conditions, with a Mr. Page, surgeon
and apothecary at Woodbridge.[2] This little town, of
much the same importance as Aldborough, about ten
miles west of Orford, lies on the right bank of the River
Deben, almost at the end of one of the narrow, winding,
and deep inlets which the sea has worn into the coast
of Suffolk by flowing up the small rivers. The Deben,

[1] For all this phase of Crabbe's life, see Appendix I (*Bunbury Letter*),
which is a useful complement and correction of p. 6 of the Biography.
[2] B. p. 6, and Appendix I.

like the Alde, fills regularly at high water, and, when the tide recedes, leaves an expanse of wet mud. Its " brilliant rippling " waters, obeying the daily rhythm of ebb and flow, are gay with the sails of small fishing-craft and pleasure-boats, which reach the open sea after a run of twelve miles. Its banks, where no " stately villas " rise, have " their own befitting charm " : their silent heaths, where the spring clothes the broom with a " sumptuous golden livery," their fertile farms—

> With here and there a copse to fling
> Its welcome shade where wild birds sing.[1]

But the town itself is dull and badly built. Edward Fitzgerald, who spent a great part of his life there, describes it in 1844[2] " as one of the ugliest and dullest places in England; it has not," he says, " the merit of being bleak on a grand scale—pollard trees over a flat clay, with regular hedges." Such as it is, this quiet little country place, from which the first gleams indicating the proximity of the sea can be descried on the horizon, and where the moan of the distant surf can occasionally be heard,[3] is indebted to Crabbe's short stay and to Bernard Barton's and Fitzgerald's longer residence for a very enviable literary fame.

The business of the Woodbridge apothecary prospered, and Crabbe found himself transported into surroundings more congenial to his tastes. No more humiliating work or repugnant contacts. In fact, his master, not considering him as a " regular apprentice," did not feel obliged to show him interesting cases, and thus initiate him into the practice of medicine. Crabbe therefore remained in the dispensary, and spent his time in " putting up prescriptions and compounding medicines."[4] He somewhat regretted the state of ignorance in which he was kept, but he was well treated in other respects, and several times in the week was free to meet of an evening some kindred spirits, with whom he dined and talked of literature. He showed the poems which he had just written, and

---

[1] Bernard Barton, *To the Deben*, Selections from Poems and Letters (London : Hall, Virtue & Co., 1849.) *
[2] Letter to Frederick Tennyson (ed. by Aldis Wright).
[3] Fitzgerald, letter quoted above, p. 12, n. 3.
[4] *Bunbury Letter* (Appendix I).

spoke of his hopes of seeing them appear in a newspaper or magazine. I am not sure that at this period
Crabbe may not have indulged in some youthful indis-
cretions—of a tolerably innocent nature, however—that
the sittings of the "club" may not have been unduly
prolonged amid the warmth of discussions animated
by generous libations, poetical enthusiasm, and the
sociable character of the members. Perhaps even the
religious faith of his childhood was beginning to wither
in this hostile atmosphere ; reason, awaking in a youthful mind, is apt to launch into formidable speculations,
and doctors, too engrossed in matter, were, in the
eighteenth century at least, such dangerous sceptics !
The restraint of pious scruples was being removed
just at the moment when the young man might need
it most. As he says himself, in some rather feeble
lines :

> A wanton chaos in my breast raged high,
> A wanton transport darted in mine eye ;
> False pleasure urged, and every eager care,
> That swell the soul to guilt and to despair.[1]

Let us take note of the confession contained in these
last words, and agree that it was no doubt opportune
that an influence, at once gentle and irresistible, should
come to remind the young man of his mother's lessons,
which time had somewhat obliterated.

III

AMONG the members of the club was another doctor's
apprentice, William Springal Levett, the son of an
Aldborough surgeon, and only a few months older
than Crabbe.[2] He was engaged to a young Framlingham [3] girl, Miss Brereton, who afterwards, Levett
having died in 1774 at the age of twenty, married,
it would appear, a certain Dr. Lewis, emigrated to
America, returned to England and published from

---

[1] See the poem entitled *Mira* (p. 573 of ed. 1861), and dated Aldborough,
1777, lines 1-4, and B. p. 30.
[2] Parish Register, Aldborough, and Davy MSS. : " Wm. Springal, son of
Wm. and Elizabeth Levett, baptized February 11, 1754 "; " Mr. Wm. Levett,
Surgeon, died 1st March 1762, aged 49." For the death of his son William
Springal, at Framlingham, on October 2nd, 1774, and the epitaph composed
by Crabbe on this occasion, see B. p. 6, n. 4, and Green's *History of Framlingham*, p. 163.
[3] See above, p. 10, n. 2.

1794 onwards several rather indifferent novels.[1] It is she who probably wrote the three letters signed "Alethea Lewis" which have been preserved in the family papers.[2] They reveal to us a sprightly character, much vivacity of mind not unmixed with pretension, and, above all, a great intimacy with Crabbe and his future wife, Miss Sarah Elmy. The two girls, in fact, were close friends: Miss Brereton lived barely three miles from Miss Elmy, who at that time was staying with her uncle Tovell in the village of Parham. The Biographer tells us that one day Levett, on starting for Framlingham, said to Crabbe half jokingly, "Why, George, you shall go with me to Parham; there is a young lady there that would just suit you."[3] The introduction took place, a mutual liking sprang up, and Crabbe, at the age of eighteen, found himself bound by one of those long engagements of which moralists are fond of discussing the drawbacks and the advantages.

Born on December 12th, 1751, at Beccles,[4] in the extreme north of Suffolk, Sarah Elmy belonged, through her father, to the manufacturing *bourgeoisie* of the place, and through her mother, Sarah Tovell, sister of John Tovell, of Parham, to the land-owning middle class. But fortune had not favoured James Elmy, tanner at Beccles, for he had become bankrupt in the month of November, 1759, and had gone to Guadeloupe, where he died "some time before Mr. Crabbe knew the family."[5] His widow, of a calm and cheerful temper, in spite of "the many heavy

[1] Under the pseudonym of Eugenia de Acton, according to B. p. 6; more likely, I believe, anonymously. Cf. *The British Critic*, vol. iv. (London: December, 1794), p. 674: *Vicissitudes in Genteel Life*, a novel in four volumes, and by letters, which the critic finds tedious in parts; *ibid.*, vol. xviii. p. 197 (August, 1801): *The Microcosm*, by the author of *Vicissitudes in Genteel Life*, five volumes "somewhat above mediocrity." As for the *Tale without a Title*, it appeared in three volumes before 1811 (cf. Wm. Bent's *London Catalogue*); and that is all I can say of this now quite forgotten woman of letters, whose name, it would seem, does not appear either in the *Dictionary of National Biography* or in the *Catalogue* of the British Museum.

[2] The first dates, no doubt, from the end of 1789, and was sent to Belvoir Castle; the two others are much later. On May 21st, 1825, she writes: "On the 4th of last January, I entered my 76th year."

[3] B. p. 6.

[4] Beccles Parish Register, December 12th, 1751: "Sarah, daughter of James and Sarah Elmy, was born and baptized the same day."

[5] B. p. 10, n. 2, and Davy MSS. (*Pedigrees*, under the heading "Elmy"): "James Elmy of Beccles, Tanner, Bankrupt. *Ipswich Journal*, Nov. 3rd, 1759."

afflictions " she had to endure, averse to " all violent
emotions "[1] and to the display of them, no doubt
endowed with that happy apathy which enables its
possessor to go through life without feeling its shocks
too keenly, had remained at Beccles, where, with her
three daughters—Sarah, Mary, and Eleanor[2]—she
lived modestly " on the interest of a capital of £1,500."[3]
Her brother John Tovell, who was comfortably off,
made up her yearly income to £100, defrayed the
educational expenses of her son James, the eldest of
her children,[4] then a pupil of Cosway at the Royal
Academy, and often invited Sarah, the eldest of the
daughters, to make long stays at Parham. It was
during one of these visits that she became engaged
to the poet.

One would like to picture her in imagination, to see
her as she appeared at the dawn of their young love.
Unfortunately, Crabbe and his son, both excellent psy-
chologists, were more observant of moral than physical
qualities, and the features of Sarah Elmy, of the " Mira "
of the early poems, are lost to us. We only know
that she was " remarkably pretty," of a " lively and
cheerful disposition," very capable of prudence and
of boldness in her resolutions, and that nature had
endowed her with " a great share of penetration and
acuteness, a firm, unflinching spirit, and a very warm
and feeling heart." She was a tender and devoted
mother, and her eldest son still recollected, many years
afterwards, an evening in 1788 when, by the flickering
light of the fireside, she had combed his hair and sung
to him a plaintive ditty.[5] The same impression is left
by the only two letters of hers which we possess.[6] The

---

[1] B. p. 38.
[2] Cf. Davy, *Pedigrees* (" Elmy "). Mrs. Elmy died at Beccles on August 31st,
1802, at the age of seventy-eight years (and not ninety-two, as the Biographer
states, p. 38, confounding her with his grand-aunt Tovell).
[3] Appendix I, *Bunbury Letter*.
[4] For James Elmy and his almost tragic destiny, see an interesting note to
Tales of the Hall, iii. (*Works*, p. 386, n. 4). He failed in the profession of painter
which he had chosen, and died of languor and despair on August 31st, 1788
(Davy MSS., *Beccles Churchyard*), at the age of thirty-eight. He was born
on August 18th, 1750, as is indicated by a touching family relic (a birthday
cup) in the possession of the Rev. G. Cl. Rivett-Carnac, at Swefling. Crabbe
has made him one of his humble and melancholy heroes, with some change in
the circumstances of his life (Charles, the patronised Boy, *Tales of the Hall*,
iii. 116-326).
[5] B. pp. 11, 39, 59.
[6] See below, pp. 145 and 192, n. 4.

"Lucy" of the eighth *Tale* is no doubt her portrait, somewhat idealised :

> There was such goodness, such pure nature seen
> In Lucy's looks, a manner so serene ;
> Such harmony in motion, speech, and air,
> That without fairness she was more than fair,
> Had more than beauty in each speaking grace,
> That lent their cloudless glory to the face ;
> Where mild good sense in placid looks was shown,
> And felt in every bosom but her own. . . .
> A tender spirit, freed from all pretence
> Of wit, and pleased in mild benevolence.[1]

Such seems to have been "Mira" in her early years—pleasing, affectionate, and sensible. Why was it that life, there too, had in store a painful disenchantment for the poet?

Accustomed to the feminine society of Beccles, to the genteelness, to the ceremonious and somewhat formal manners of the provincial middle class, to visits correctly paid and punctually returned, Sarah Elmy found herself out of her element at Parham. This little village at the end of a narrow inland valley, more than twelve miles west of Aldborough, was almost a solitude for her. The refinements of modern civilisation had hardly penetrated into these districts, then more isolated than can well be imagined, vegetating in the dulness of their sluggish life, devoid of regular and direct communications with the towns or large boroughs of the neighbourhood, Aldborough, Woodbridge, and Ipswich. Only the wealthy land-owners, the aristocracy of squires, such as Lord Rochford at Easton, some way to the south, the Norths of Little Glemham, not far from Parham, and, farther north, the Longs of Saxmundham, went to London from time to time, and brought back the new fashions and inventions. As for the middle class, the "yeomen," who were one step higher than the mere farmers, because they cultivated their own lands, they remained as deeply rooted to their soil as the venerable trees which shaded their rustic dwellings. John Tovell, among others, belonged to a family which had been established at Parham for more than two hundred

---

[1] *Tales*, viii. 98-109.

years, and several members of which had already
borne the title of "gentlemen."[1] When Crabbe was
introduced to him he had just succeeded his eldest
brother William,[2] and settled with his wife, Jane
Kemp, daughter of a farmer of the same village,[3] in the
paternal mansion, which was known by the picturesque name of "Ducking Hall."[4] The Biographer, who
lived in it with his parents about twenty years later,
has left a description of it which is one of the best
passages in his book and deserves to be quoted.[5]
Mr. Tovell possessed "an estate of some eight
hundred pounds per annum, a portion of which he
himself cultivated. Educated at a mercantile school,
he often said of himself, 'Jack will never make a
gentleman,' yet he had a native dignity of mind and of
manners." His house was "large," built· no doubt of

---

[1] Davy, *Pedigrees* ("Tovell"), "Wm. Tovell, gent., died 1690."
[2] *Ibid.*, " William died 1774, aged 52."
[3] *Ibid.*, Jane, sister of Henry Kemp, of Parham, farmer. She died August
17th, 1882, aged 93 (cf. p. 47, n. 2.)
[4] The vignette of the third volume of the 1834 edition of Crabbe's works is
a reduced reproduction of a picture by Wm. Clarkson Stanfield, now in the
South Kensington Museum, and entitled, " Parham Hall, Suffolk, the Moat-
house of the Poet Crabbe." It represents a two-storied house, the upper
story projecting over the lower one, with gables and old chimneys, and foundations resting in the moat. The whole resembles a peninsula running into a
small lake. In front of the house are big trees which bend over the water and
are reflected in it, inclined by the force of the winds. This house still exists; it
is on the crest of the hill of Parham, a little beyond the church, ascending from
the valley towards Little Glemham. It is called Parham Old Hall, and is so
picturesque that one would wish that the poet had inhabited it. This unfortunately is incorrect. Mitford, the future editor of *The Gentleman's Magazine*,
Vicar of Benhall from 1810, a lover of gossip and small details, asserts
positively, in his almost illegible MS. Notes preserved in the British
Museum, that "the vignette of his house at Parham is not correct. That
was not his house which lies on the top of the hill." Cf. an article,
evidently by the same author, in *The Gentleman's Magazine*, New Series,
vol. i. pp. 253-64 (March, 1834) : " The house where Mr. Crabbe resided [at
Parham] is very near the seat of Mr. Dudley North." In a note : " It is
now called Parham Lodge, and is tenanted by Colonel Windsor. It has been
much altered and modernised since the poet resided there ; the moat has been
filled up and some handsome rooms added. Its situation is extremely pleasant,
and it commands more extensive and varied views than any other mansion
in the neighbourhood." Finally, in the *Supplement to the Suffolk Traveller*,
compiled by Aug. Page, Ipswich and London, 1844, p. 189, we read : " The
old mansion, so pleasingly described by Mr. Crabbe's Biographer as the
residence of the late Mr. Tovell, has since been almost rebuilt in the modern
style, and what was formerly designated ' Ducking Hall ' is at present known
by the name of Parham Lodge." According to Mitford (MS. notes) and
Davy ("Parham") the house was again entirely rebuilt in 1851-2 by its owner,
Mr. Corrance. This gentleman still lives there, and, according to him,
"Ducking Hall was on the exact ground of the east wing of the present
Parham Lodge" (information communicated by Mr. Ch. Ganz, of Aldborough).
[5] B. pp. 40-1.

red brick, or of plaster and cross timbers.[1] "The surrounding moat, the rookery, the ancient dove-cot, and
the well-stored fish-pond, were such as might have
suited a gentleman's seat of some consequence;"
unfortunately, "one side of the house overlooked a
farmyard, full of all sorts of domestic animals, and the
scene of constant bustle and noise. On entering the
house, there was nothing at first sight to remind one
of the farm : you came into a spacious hall, paved with
black and white marble," from which the flitches of
bacon, its former ornament,[1] had perhaps disappeared.
"At one extremity was a very handsome drawing-
room," furnished with "Turk-worked" chairs, and
hung with family portraits,[2] "at the other a fine old
staircase of black oak, with a chime-clock and a barrel
organ on its landing-places. But this drawing-room, a
corresponding dining-parlour, and a handsome sleeping apartment upstairs were all *tabooed* ground," and
were used on great occasions only, in honour of Lord
Rochford, for instance, when he came to visit his
neighbour Tovell, or at Christmas, when the farmers
on the estate assembled for a rent dinner. Woe to the
servant who ventured to encroach on the privileges of
the mistress by scrubbing the floors or dusting the
chairs in this " preserve "—she was speedily packed off
to the scullery with a contemptuous scolding ! The
members of the family themselves lived in the kitchen.
" My great-uncle occupied an armchair, or, in attacks of
gout, a couch on one side of a large open chimney,
where in winter a noble block of wood, sometimes
of the circumference of a whole tree, blazed on the
hearth. Mrs. Tovell sat at a small table, on which, in
the evening, stood one small candle in an iron candle-
stick, plying her needle, and surrounded by her maids,
all busy at the same employment." It was there that
the family received the visits of intimate friends, of
a "jolly old farmer, with much of the person and
humour of Falstaff, and a face as rosy as brandy could
make it," or of a "relative of the family, a wealthy
yeoman, middle-aged, thin, and muscular," an indis-

---

[1] In the fashion noted by Grose (*Olio*, quoted by Lecky, *History of
England in the Eighteenth Century*, vol. vi. p. 170).
[2] Cf. Lecky, *ibid.* p. 171 : "The men, in the character of shepherds with
their crooks, . . . the females likewise, as shepherdesses, with the lamb and
crook." Cf. also Goldsmith, *Vicar of Wakefield*, ch. xvi.

criminate lover of the other sex, who was said to have
" peopled the village green." The house was a regular
bee-hive, thanks to the activity of the mistress, a sort
of "widow Goe,"[1] or Mrs. Poyser without her caustic
humour. " At a very early hour in the morning, the
alarum called the maids, and their mistress also;" the
slightest delay produced "a louder alarum" and a
chiding from Mrs. Tovell, whose scolding "regularly
ran on through all the day, like bells on harness,
inspiriting the work, whether it were done ill or
well . . . .After the important business of the dairy
and a hasty breakfast, the respective employments
were resumed." At twelve o'clock, or one at the
latest, everybody, masters and servants, assembled
in the kitchen: the family took their seats "at an old
table with, perchance, some travelling rat-catcher, or
tinker, or farrier, or an occasional gardener in his
shirt-sleeves"; the maids sat at a side-table a little
farther off, and the farm-hands stood in the adjoining
scullery, the door of which remained open. Then
began a meal of which "Mira" often partook and with
much the same feelings as Nancy Moss[2]:

Used to spare meals, disposed in manner pure,
Her father's kitchen she could ill endure:
Where by the steaming beef he hungry sat. . . .
The air, surcharged with moisture, flagg'd around,
And the offended damsel sigh'd and frown'd.
The swelling fat in lumps conglomerate laid,
And fancy's sickness seized the loathing maid,
And when the men beside their station took,
The maidens with them, and with these the cook;
When one huge wooden bowl before them stood,
Fill'd with huge balls of farinaceous food;
With bacon, mass saline, where never lean
Beneath the brown and bristly rind was seen;
When from a single horn the party drew
Their copious draughts of heavy ale and new;
When the coarse cloth she saw, with many a stain
Soil'd by rude hinds who cut and came again—
She could not breathe; but with a heavy sigh
Rein'd the fair neck, and shut th' offended eye;
She minc'd the sanguine flesh in frustums fine,
And wonder'd much to see the creatures dine.

[1] *Parish Register*, iii. 125 *seq.*; cf. *ibid.* ii. 408-13.
[2] *Tales*, vii. 6-30.

To digest such meals, sleep was necessary; so, when the table was cleared, " the kitchen sanded, and lightly swept over in waves," the mistress and the maids, taking off their shoes, retired to their bedrooms "for a nap of one hour to the minute." Surrounded by the dogs and cats, " Mr. Tovell dozed in his chair, and no noise was heard, except the melancholy and monotonous cooing of a turtle-dove, varied by the shrill treble of a canary." When the hour's siesta came to an end, the bustle and noise began afresh ; and while the bottles circulated between the host and his guests, the women attended to the work of the farm, stopping only in the evening, to resume their needlework.

However humble Crabbe's extraction and position may have been, his intelligence gave him a superiority over these rustics of which Sarah Elmy speedily became aware. True, he was three years younger than she, but his seriousness and force of character made up for this slight disparity of age. Perhaps his pronunciation was a trifle provincial,[1] but Sarah and all her people spoke in just the same way. And then how many good points to set against such insignificant defects ! Was he not distinguished for his " learning," that " d——d learning " for which uncle Tovell had such sovereign contempt ? Who else would have invented for her and her friend those pretty names of " Mira " and " Stella," [2] which sounded so well and lent themselves to such pointed allusions ? Who could have pleaded his cause in better-turned verses, or invoked the " gentle gales," the " winds," and the "tempests" more poetically, or better described his " sighs " and his " languishments " ? [3] Were not his manners and his language simple, straightforward, and manly, and the tone of his voice a sort of guarantee for a lifelong affection ? He was worthy to be loved; and on the hill of Parham, where the wanderer can to

---

[1] At least this is so stated by the gossipy Mitford, who speaks of the poet's Suffolk " accentuation."

[2] Cf. letter of Alethea Lewis, end of 1789 (see above, p. 46, n. 1). The name of Mira (or Myra) already figured in Sidney's *Arcadia*, in William Browne's, Lansdowne's, and Mallet's poems, that of Stella in Browne and in Swift. Mr. Saintsbury (*Essays in English Literature, 1780—1860*) points out ingeniously that " Mira " combines the last two syllables of Elmy-Sarah.

[3] Cf. *Complete Works*, p. 572, the very insignificant poem called " Ye gentle gales," dated Woodbridge, 1776 (an obvious mistake, as Crabbe left Woodbridge in 1775 ; see below, p. 62).

this day follow his trace, the poet passed the least
troubled moments of his young life:

> Oh ! days remember'd well ! remember'd all !
> The bitter-sweet, the honey, and the gall ;
> Those garden rambles in the silent night,
> Those trees so shady, and that moon so bright ;
> That thick-set alley by the arbour closed,
> That woodbine seat where we at last reposed ;
> And then the hopes that came and then were gone,
> Quick as the clouds beneath the moon pass'd on :
> " Now in this instant shall my love be shown,"
> I said. Oh ! no, the happy time is flown ! [1]

Tender doubts and fears, which were soon set at rest!
And when, his visit ended, Crabbe returned across
the heath to Woodbridge, he said to himself, with
the practical sense which characterised him, that his
betrothed was assuredly the most charming of women,
and that one day she would inherit " a share of her
mother's small fortune." [2]

IV

LOVE proved a safeguard and an education for the
young man.[3] It opened to him a world of sensations
and feelings hitherto almost unsuspected. It gave an
object and a reality to his life, it revealed in his distant
horizon, on the heights which his energy had to climb,
the bright prospect of an ardently desired happiness.
Crabbe had his heroine in his turn, like all the knights
of the marvellous tales in which his childish imagination had delighted. To deserve the hand of Sarah
Elmy, whose rank was so much higher than his own,
he would have to gain a position and make himself
worthy of " Mira " by charm of manner and purity of
life. The meetings of the " club" lost much of their
attraction : he foresaw the dangers to which they
exposed him, and felt less need of them now that a
beloved confidant, always ready to listen to his poetic
effusions, awaited him at Parham. If it is true, as
Crabbe asserts in one of his sermons, that there is

---

[1] *Tales of the Hall*, vi. 128-37.

[2] *Bunbury Letter*: " £1,500, which at her decease is to be divided betwixt
her children."

[3] Lockhart had already noted this point in an interesting article in *The
Quarterly Review*, vol. i. January, 1834, pp. 468-508 (quoted by B. p. 381, n. 6).

" with most men a time, commonly an early one, which in a great measure determines their future life, a time when they feel the force and necessity of religion, bear up against their vices, and become virtuous," [1] then the influence of Mira, as pious as the Matilda of the *Tales of the Hall*, came at its appointed hour and proved a blessing for the future clergyman. She strengthened his faith and warned him against unprincipled companions :

> The sweet enthusiast, so I deem'd her, took
> My mind, and fix'd it to her speech and look, . . .
> Her sole design that I should think aright
> And my conversion her supreme delight. . . .
> Hers was the thought correct, the hope sublime,
> She shaped my creed and did the work of time.[2]

A short poem, of much earlier date than these lines, is still more explicit :

> Then Mira came ! be ever blest the hour
> That drew my thoughts half-way from folly's power.
> She first my soul with loftier notions fired ;
> I saw their truth, and as I saw admired ;
> With greater force returning reason moved,
> And as returning reason urged, I loved ;
> Till pain, reflection, hope, and love allied
> My bliss precarious to a surer guide,
> To Him who gives pain, reason, hope, and love. . . .
> One beam of light He gave my mind to see,
> And gave that light, my heavenly fair, by thee ;
> That beam shall raise my thoughts, and mend my strain,
> Nor shall my vows, nor prayers, nor verse be vain.[3]

He had found his muse, and henceforth abandoned himself to reverie and composition. If he was left alone in the dispensary he often forgot his work, and would "lean upon the pestle and compose." [4] Or he would read the romance-writers and the poets, even the Elizabethans, whom he liked to imitate. Spenser was one of his favourite authors, and the Spenserian stanza already had an attraction for him which it never

[1] Unpublished sermon delivered at Stathern on June 27th, 1784 (in the MSS. belonging to Mr. John Murray).
[2] *Tales of the Hall*, i. 238-9 ; vi. 92-3 and 101-2.
[3] *Mira*, Aldborough, 1777 (p. 573); cf. above, p. 45, n. 1.
[4] *Newspaper*, 444.

lost. He wrote a *Judgment of Life* in this metre; he addressed the muse like Sir Walter Raleigh replying to Marlowe's Passionate Shepherd by a refusal to go and " live with him." For he asked himself at certain moments, when the flame of inspiration burnt low within him, whether all these lucubrations were not so many follies, whether " the Muses were not real enemies," whether the following course would not be best?—

> Go! to your desks and counters all return ;
> Your sonnets scatter, your acrostics burn ;
> Trade, and be rich.[1]

Did not his master from time to time foretell ruin for him, and did not his father advise him to give up all this nonsense? But what was to be done, when the former approved with a smile what he seemed to condemn, when the latter, in spite of his paternal advice, was himself an impenitent rhymester,[2] above all, when inspiration returned, at the thought of his beloved, or of some passage that he had read? Must he not proclaim to the " shepherds who haunt the vale" the wondrous beauty of Mira and the softness of her voice, like " fancy's song when poets dream"?[3] It was so amusing to make fun of himself and of all other lovers in tripping lines which sound like a long peal of laughter![4] Ah! the nimble gaiety, the enthusiasm of this budding fancy and of this requited affection, who can describe them now? And then the triumph of printing one's rhymes, even under the veil of anonymity, in the newspapers and magazines, where " Damons and Delias begin a correspondence which does not always end there," of reading one's " first-born work a thousand times," of feeling " the infection spread," of seeing couplets " grow apace, stanzas to Delia's dog or Celia's face," of " taking a name," " Philander" perhaps, of hearing oneself praised, maybe

---

[1] *Newspaper,* 459-61.
[2] See *Bunbury Letter* (Appendix I).*
[3] B. p. 7 : *The Wish.*
[4] *Ibid.* This little poem in the four-stress metre is, according to the Biographer, a parody of a poem by Shenstone beginning with the words, " My time, oh ye Muses." In reality Crabbe here imitates the " Pastoral " of John Byrom (*Colin and Phœbe*), written by the student of Trinity College in honour of Joanna, daughter of Dr. Bentley, and published in the eighth volume of *The Spectator,* No. 603, October 6th, 1714.

for an ode in the style of Cowley, of believing that
one's "dark pages please th' enlightened age"![1]

The ladies of the neighbourhood, fair readers of Mr.
Wheble's *Lady's Magazine*,[2] are well acquainted with
the signature of "G. C.," who lives at Woodbridge, in
the county of Suffolk; they know that in 1772, in
a volume now, alas! unprocurable,[3] he has published
no less than five agreeable and edifying poems, one,
impassioned, addressed to a too happy "Mira," a
second intended for "unbelievers" ready to be converted, a third, entitled *Hope*, which received a prize
from the editor of the magazine. Had not the prize-
winner extolled this cardinal virtue as the most
precious for the poet, that which impels him "to write,
and, unsuccessful, write again"?[4] His last and most
laborious effort was not in vain. "Our young candidate," writes Crabbe of himself, "had the misfortune
to win this prize, in consequence of which he felt
himself more elevated above the young men, his
companions, who made no verses, than it is to be
hoped he has done at any time since, when he has
been able to compare and judge with a more moderate
degree of self-approbation. He wrote upon every
occasion, and without occasion; and, like greater men,
and indeed like almost every young versifier, he
planned tragedies and epic poems, and began to think
of succeeding in the highest line of composition, before
he had made one good and commendable effort in the
lowest."[5]

Three years afterwards, on the eve of ending his
apprenticeship and leaving Woodbridge, Crabbe published at C. Punchard's, bookseller in the Butter

---

[1] B. p. 7, and *Newspaper*, 449-56.

[2] According to Pesta (*George Crabbe*, p. 5, note), this magazine is one to
which Goldsmith contributed in 1759 (J. Forster's *Life of Goldsmith*, Minerva
edition, p. 135). I fancy this is a mistake. Wilkie's venture seems to have
been most ephemeral, and the collection of *The Lady's Magazine* in the British
Museum begins only in 1770. On the other hand, Wheble, whose name is not to
be found in the *Dictionary of National Biography*, was perhaps the John Wheble,
printer of *The Middlesex Journal*, who in the preceding year had been vainly
summoned to the Bar of the House of Commons for having dared to publish
the real names of the speakers in Parliament (cf. Besant, *London in the
Eighteenth Century*, pp. 26-8, and Lecky, *History of England*, vol. iii.
p. 258).

[3] The third volume (1772) is missing, as Kebbel (*Life of Crabbe*, p. 17)
had already noted.

[4] B. p. 7, n. 5.

[5] *Autobiographical Sketch* (see above, p. 30, n. 1), quoted by B. p. 7.

Market at Ipswich, a poem in three parts, of about
seven hundred lines, entitled *Inebriety*, and priced at
1s. 6d.[1] In a preface as modest as it is carefully
worded, the author submitted to the judgment of his
little world "this trifle," his first independent work,
assured beforehand of the "clemency of the climate."
He apologised to the critics for the many liberties he
had taken with Pope, the "Swan of the Thames," and
declared, as a humble disciple, that the passages
modelled on the master seemed to him "the best part
of the performance."[2] Too much humility is a mistake.
Not that *Inebriety* is a remarkable work, unjustly
neglected. The style, it must be admitted, abounds
in strained inversions,[3] odd,[4] often obscure,[5] sometimes
incomprehensible,[6] or incorrect,[7] expressions, verbal
antitheses,[8] degenerating into verbal jingles,[9] personified abstractions,[10] extremely misplaced mythological
allusions,[11] and very strange incongruities: following
long passages, the framework of which is borrowed

---

[1] B. p. 8, n. 6. Canon Ainger possessed a copy (cf. *Crabbe*, English Men of
Letters, p. 11), which Dr. A. W. Ward (*Poems by George Crabbe*, Cambridge
English Classics, 1905, pp. 13-36) has reprinted in its entirety. The Biographer
had suppressed the third part, in which Crabbe, unaware that he would one
day become a clergyman, wrote a somewhat indecorous sort of parody of
Pope's "Essay on Man," and gave a regular "Essay on Woman in a State of
Inebriety."

[2] Quoted by B. p. 7.

[3] Lines 7-8: "The sparkling ill is shed, The heart which hardens." Cf.
73-4.

[4] Line 82: "leaden vengeance."

[5] Line 41: "hollow [hollow-sounding?] panes"; line 53 (speaking of the
coffee-house politicians): "Who wage no war with an avenger's rod";
line 88: (sleep's) "rooky pinions"; and lines 128-9:
  The semi-globe by hieroglyphics crown'd,
  Where canvas purse displays the brass enroll'd,
which is better as a rebus than as poetry.

[6] Line 103: "The King who nods upon his rattle throne." Should we read
"rattling"?

[7] Line 228: "in joy-feign'd gaze," instead of joy-feigning; line 257:
"And senseless titt'ring sense of mirth confound," unless "titt'rings" is
the proper reading. And even then the suppression of the article would be
incorrect.

[8] Line 166: "The canvas general [in politics], or the general doom" (Last
Judgment).

[9] Line 66: "And *madly* thunders on the *muddy* walls"—a line, however,
which produces a genuine picturesque effect.

[10] To begin with line 99: "See, Inebriety! her wand' she waves," which
recalls the line quoted by Coleridge (*Biographia Literaria*, p. 188): "In-
oculation, heavenly Maid, descend!" with this difference, that, in the first case,
the reader is reminded of Circe. Cf. also line 29: "Nature's sister, Art";
line 190: "Shame and all her blushing train," etc., etc.

[11] Line 55: "Lucina"; line 230: "Titan," for the sun and moon.

from Pope,[1] are found reminiscences,[2] almost parodies,[3] of Gray, or, worse still, medical terms in veterinary language.[4] The versification, though elaborate, is not faultless, if the rules of the "couplet," to which the poet has evidently wished to conform, are applied to it; even the rhyme is sometimes very slovenly.[5] It is therefore not surprising that the critics have generally treated this work with contempt, as a youthful indiscretion of Crabbe's which they would like to pass over in silence.[6] They have omitted to point out how original and characteristic the choice of the subject is. Crabbe here does the reverse of Gay, who in a poem in blank verse, flowing and pleasant enough, had sung the virtues of "wine," his favourite drink, had taken us into the old Devil's Tavern near Temple Bar, had shown us the "majestic dame, in semi-circular throne enclos'd," giving out orders and scribbling "mysterious characters"; and by her side the obsequious waiter, who hurries downstairs to meet the customers and usher them into the famous "Apollo room," in which the wits of Queen Anne's day continued the traditions of Ben Jonson. What can be more amiable and more "innocent" than this enthusiastic toasting of the royal family, of the celebrities or beauties of the day, than these cheerful conversations which make "the unnumbered hours flow insensibly," than the last shouts of laughter on seeing the sleepy waiter appear at midnight,

---

[1] Cf. lines 1-18 and Pope, *Dunciad*, i. 1-8; line 9 repeated in line 184, and Pope, *Windsor Forest*, 346: "The gulfy Lee his sedgy tresses rears." For the artificial connection of the "couplets" by the deliberate repetition, in the first hemistich of the second, of the last words of the first, cf. with Crabbe, lines 19-22, Pope, *Pastorals*, "Winter," 61-6. Cf. also lines 109-35 with Pope, *Essay on Man*, i. 99-118; and very many passages in the third part (ed. Ward, pp. 25-36).

[2] Cf. line 86: "And sheds her poppies on the ambient air," with Gray, *Elegy*, 14: "And waste its sweetness on the desert air."

[3] Cf. line 62: "Fire in his head and frenzy at his heels," with Gray, *The Bard*, ii. 2: "Youth on the prow and pleasure at the helm," a resemblance which provokes a smile.

[4] Lines 25-8: "The opening valves, which fill the venal road" (*i.e.* the system of the veins); "the sanguine flood"; "the labouring pulse"; "the tendons stiffen."

[5] Lines 23-4: God, flood; lines 25-6: road, flood; lines 49-50: plain, green; lines 165-6: come, doom; lines 167-8: soul, fool; and lines 230-1: scene, swain.

[6] Cf. Saintsbury (Essay quoted above, p. 52, n. 2), p. 15: "*Inebriety* and such other youthful things are not to be counted"; and Sir Leslie Stephen (*Hours in a Library*, vol. ii. ed. 1892, p. 35): "*Inebriety*, an unblushing imitation of Pope," which is true, but not the whole truth. Mr. Kebbel (*Life of Crabbe*, p. 18), Herr Pesta (*George Crabbe*, pp. 15-16), and the Biographer (p. 8) are less severe, and I agree with them.

stumbling and rubbing his eyes, or the departure of the
company with a firm tread, "of cares and coin bereft"?[1]
Are we not here in the best of company, among people of
fashion and polished men of letters? The Woodbridge
poet, on the contrary, asks us to follow him into a
country inn. He will tell us what he has seen with
his own eyes, and then draw an appropriate moral
therefrom. It is winter, and "a sable void the barren
earth appears." The blood freezes in the veins, "the
tendons stiffen and the spirit cools." To get warmth
and shelter, the "labouring peasant" enters a room
where the wind, it is true, whistles through the
cracked panes, but where the kitchen fire diffuses its
heat. He draws near the chimney, takes his seat on
"the settle's curve or humbler bench," and, asking
"no limpid punch or rosy wine," plunges into "the
muddy ecstasies of beer." He listens to a certain
"Colin, the prince of rural wits," relating for the
hundredth time tales of "spirits" and "imps," "from
sire to son retold." It is so cosy by the bright fireside
in this bitter weather that our toper lingers ; and when,
by the light of "Lucina, gleaming in the vaulted arch,"
the "jovial savage" has to ascend the hill and descend
into the valley, he staggers along and makes the silent
air resound with his "unsteady voice" :

> Fire in his head and frenzy at his heels,
> From paths direct the bending hero swerves,
> And shapes his way in ill-proportioned curves.

On arriving home he "madly thunders on the muddy
walls," and awakens his slumbering partner with loud
shouts ; but she, knowing what this clamour means, is
moved " by equal fury " :

> In vain the waken'd infant's accents shrill
> The humble regions of the cottage fill ;
> In vain the cricket chirps the mansion through,
> 'Tis war, and blood, and battle must ensue.

The two antagonists, "big with vengeance," lose, the
one "a remnant night-cap," the other "an old cut
wig"; "unmusical" epithets are exchanged,

> Till equal valour equal wounds create,
> And drowsy peace concludes the fell debate,

and at last—

> Sleep in her woollen mantle wraps the pair.[2]

---

[1] *English Poets* (*Chalmers*, 1810), vol. x. pp. 493-4.   [2] *Inebriety*, 55-85.

Let us leave these two boors snoring side by side
and return to the inn, where, in a private room, has
assembled a collection of eccentrics in whom we shall
be able to study "the various forms of Bacchic folly."
"The vicar at the table's front presides," and Crabbe,
with the audacity of a beginner, does not spare his
future colleague:

> His presence a monastic life derides,
> The reverend wig, in sideway order placed,
> The reverend band, by rubric stains disgraced,
> The leering eye, in wayward circles roll'd,
> Mark him the pastor of a jovial fold,
> Whose various texts excite a loud applause,
> Favouring the bottle and the good old cause.
> See ! the dull smile which fearfully appears,
> When gross indecency her front uprears,
> The joy conceal'd, the fiercer burns within.

He lingers even when immoral jokes and blasphemy
go round : he "takes the last loved glass, and then the
board forsakes "[1]—a portrait overflowing with life and
spirit, but perhaps more remarkable for fancy than for
observation. By the side of the jovial and rubicund
vicar sits indolence personified, "old Torpio," who
snores and nods in his armchair, and ever and anon
wakes up with a start to laugh and drink with the rest.
Then comes "honest Curio," whose "gentle skull, of
heavy, native, unwrought folly full," produces the "dull
treasures of a brain at peace " : tales of midnight ghosts
passing over terrific vaults, dancing upon graves, and
sliding along the grass. Near him is young Fabricio,
who has stolen from his "guardian's side," who sips
the stream of pleasure without daring to plunge into
it, who really "hates the bottle," but drinks out of
bravado, and "labours to grin away the horrid dose,"
while Timon, a hardened debauchee, an unscrupulous
blasphemer, a hypocrite on occasions, gives him lessons
of vice, carefully treasured up and faithfully repeated
by the stupid "Milo."[2]

We are now a long way from Gay and his friends ;
we are among boors and vicious boors ; we ought to
be quite convinced now that the "charms of wine"
are pernicious and that the "sober joys" of "social

[1] *Inebriety,* 175-85 ; 191-2.
[2] *Ibid.* 157-60, 201-12, 221-7, 232, 240-4, 266-72.

evenings" are preferable to them.[1] Let us forgive the young doctor the care which he already takes of our souls, let us eliminate from his composition the numerous faults of clumsiness which disfigure it, let us forget the weakness of the execution, let us give a little more collective life to this group in which the individuals remain too isolated, and we shall have an excellent Dutch drinking scene. We shall regret that the poet did not return to the same subject in later years, there to seek a new source of inspiration. Lastly, we shall acknowledge that the youthful satirist, a pupil of Pope and also of Young, in trying to collect into one typical picture individual traits of character drawn from the life, has already succeeded in portraying to us some of his humble contemporaries, and is not so far removed as seems to be thought from the author of *The Village* and of *The Borough*.

Such were Crabbe's first steps in the career of letters. Lost in the remoteness of Suffolk, his voice awoke no echo, and his timid appeal was followed by a long and trying period of silence.

[1] *Inebriety*, 280-1.

CHAPTER III

ALDBOROUGH (1775—1780)

I. On Slaughden Quay. The Aldborough apothecaries: Raymond,
Maskill, and Crabbe. First stay in London. Failure at
Aldborough.—II. The lover's journey. Poetry and religion.—
III. Despair, poverty, and departure for London.

I

IT was no doubt during the summer of 1775[1] that
Crabbe returned to Aldborough. His seven years of
apprenticeship had brought him neither money nor
science, and, on his return to his native town, he
found his father still struggling with poverty, and
unable to defray the expense which an educational trip
to London or a life of studious leisure at home would
have entailed. He was, therefore, obliged to resume
the dress of a common labourer, to set to work once
more at rolling barrels of salt, at unloading and piling
up butter-casks, among the carts stuck in the mud of
Slaughden Quay or sinking into the shingle on the
beach, pell-mell with a number of shouting and swearing rustics. This was certainly not the kind of
existence which the surgeon-apprentice, poet in his
unemployed moments, had dreamed of, or even had had
glimpses of, during his long talks with his companions
at Woodbridge, or in his tender *tête-à-têtes* at Parham
with Mira. It was degrading to submit to such
humiliation, caused by the improvidence of a father
who had taken to drink and was destroying the peace
of his home, instead of thinking of the happiness and
the future of those dependent on him. Crabbe had
a proper pride, natural to a man conscious of great
abilities. As in earlier days at Wickham Brook, he

[1] And not "towards the end" of it, as the Biographer states, p. 8; see
below, p. 64, the proceedings of the parish meeting of September 17th, 1775.

rebelled against the slavery which was imposed on him. The day would begin with ill-suppressed anger and often end in violent quarrels between father and son. How could the young man help feeling a thrill of indignation and bitter shame on hearing himself addressed one day by a Woodbridge friend, now a doctor, who, after looking for him all over the town, had at last found him on Slaughden Quay, working like a common labourer ? He had to follow his friend to the nearest inn,[1] and there listen in " sad silence " to a " long lecture" and an exhortation to revolt. Alas! it was not the want of will, but the want of power, that kept Crabbe in a " servitude" the remembrance of which made him shudder many years afterwards.[2]

He had a gleam of hope, however. After the death of William Levett, in 1772, there were two apothecaries at Aldborough, a certain Burham Raymond, fifteen years older than Crabbe,[3] who had the better practice in the place, and one James Maskill, who had settled there recently, an overbearing, brutal man, of scandalous conduct, whose service the poet had thought for a moment of entering.[4] Maskill's excesses brought him into complete disrepute ; he had to leave the town, and " his enemies," Crabbe tells us, " invited me to fix there immediately."[5] In England in the eighteenth century seven years' apprenticeship conferred the right to the title of apothecary or surgeon : there was no need even of a vague University degree, such as " Dr." Goldsmith paraded before or after his name. Yielding to his father's entreaties and to the flattering solicitations of his own self-love, the young man bought on credit " the shattered furniture of an apothecary's shop and the drugs that stocked it." In spite of his want of competence, he had some prospect of success : just at that moment the parish was engaged in a dispute with Raymond, who, in December 1770, had agreed to supply attendance and remedies to the poor for the

---

[1] Already no doubt called " The Three Mariners" (cf. Ford, *Aldborough Described*, pp. 79-80).

[2] B. p. 9.

[3] He died in November, 1822, at the age of eighty-three (Parish Register, Aldborough). His activity appears from B. p. 10.

[4] *Bunbury Letter :* " I meant to serve in a shop, but an unlucky opportunity offered itself at Aldboro'," from which it may be inferred, contrary to B. p. 10, that Crabbe was never Maskill's assistant.

[5] *Ibid.*

annual sum of twenty shillings,[1] and since then, finding
no doubt that he had made a bad bargain, had been
continually raising his terms, demanding first £4, and
then £20, for one year.[2] This threatened to become
ruinous ; the poor would soon absorb the whole income
of the parish in medicines ! It was necessary to put
things to rights and make Raymond feel the pressure
of competition. Here they had the very man for their
purpose in " young Crabbe," warmly recommended by
his father, and only too anxious to work. Accordingly,
on September 17th, 1775, the parish meeting decided
that " Geo. Crabbe junr. should be employed to cure
the boy Howard of the Itch, and that, whenever any
of the poor shall have occasion for a surgeon, the
overseers shall apply to him for that purpose." And
in the following January " Dr. Crabbe " was able to send
in to this same vestry an account for £4.[3] How many
" fractures " must he have reduced, or tried to reduce,
for this sum ! How many times must he have entered
the humble, unpaved cottage, open to all the winds
of heaven, which then did duty for a poor-house, and
which can still be seen, standing alone in the middle
of a field facing the railway station.[4] How many vices
must he have discovered, how many poor wretches
must he have heard groaning on the seven miserable
beds for which five pairs of sheets, four pairs of blankets,
and one pair of curtains had to suffice. And this
handful of shivering and emaciated paupers, huddled
together round the five tables and upon the ten chairs
of which the furniture was composed,[5] dressed in their
uniform, on the right sleeve of which burned the
bright red of the piece of cloth with the two large
black letters P A,[6] the cruel badge of their odious

[1] Vestry Book, Aldborough, December 12th, 1770. The text of the "contract"
is not devoid of interest : " At a parish meeting pursuant to publick notice we
. . . do agree to pay Burham Raymond twenty shillings a year to attend and
supply with all necessaries in the physical, surgery, and midwifery way
(fractures excepted) all the parish poor and all such as may become chargeable
hereafter."

[2] In 1772 and 1775.

[3] In exact figures £4 0s. 3d., paid on February 17th, 1776.

[4] The old "workhouse," well known to the inhabitants and now used for
other purposes. It stands on the right of the road which runs from the station
to the beach (see above, p. 9).

[5] Vestry Book, Aldborough : " An Inventory of Goods in the Workhouse "
(1760).

[6] That is, Parish of Aldborough. Cf. 8 & 9 William III. (quoted by
Nicholls in his *History of the English Poor-law*, ed. 1898, vol. i. p. 341) :

servitude—must not these poor creatures have shown the young doctor to what depths vice and human ingratitude may lead?

Conscious of his technical ignorance, and wishing to have some warrant for the professional air which he assumed in imitation of his Woodbridge master, Crabbe devoted himself to study. "The time had come," he writes, "when he was told, and believed, that he had more important concerns to engage him than verse ; and therefore, for some years, though he occasionally found time to write lines upon 'Mira's Birthday' or 'Silvia's Lapdog,' though he composed enigmas and solved rebuses, he had some degree of forbearance, and did not believe that the knowledge of diseases and the sciences of anatomy and physiology were to be acquired by the perusal of Pope's *Homer* and a *Treatise on the Art of Poetry*."[1] He "read a great deal," even medical books written in Latin,[2] from which he made extracts, with the twofold object of scientific and literary progress. He studied the *materia medica* ; with laudable zeal he dissected dogs which the sea generously threw up for him, and fancied himself an anatomist, because he had entirely given up " poetry, novels, and books of entertainment."[3] Like " his friend the Weaver,"[4] he walked along the shore, in search of the flies and of the tiny insects which swarm in the sand. He became strongly interested in botany, a science which developed his gifts of exact and minute observation. He analysed the characters and the properties of the flora of the neighbouring marshes, gathered poppies and "the blue bugloss," the "slimy mallow" with its "silky leaf,"[5] the charlock, and

"It is enacted that every person receiving relief of any parish shall, together with his wife and children, openly wear upon the shoulder of his right sleeve a badge or mark with a large Roman P, and the first letter of the name of the parish whereof such poor person is an inhabitant, cut thereon either in red or blue cloth." Not only the inmates of the workhouse therefore (cf. *Borough*, xiv. 204), but also those in receipt of outdoor relief were dressed in this way. The obligation ceased in 1810.

[1] *Autobiographical Sketch* (see above, p. 30, n. 1). This passage is quoted by B. p. 9.

[2] Some of these extracts, of a rather later date, are to be found in a notebook which the poet brought with him to London in 1780. It now belongs to Mr. John Murray. It contains, among other things, the summary of a pamphlet entitled *De curandis intermittentibus febribus*, the work of a Dr. Norford, and published at Bury in 1780.

[3] *Bunbury Letter*.

[4] *Borough*, viii. 69 *seq.*

[5] *Village*, i. 71-6.

the tare. He lingered on the beach at low tide, examining the " sea-wrack," organisms which science "knows not where to place," " sea-nettles of nearly oval form, varied with serrated longitudinal lines," so tender that no preparation, even in spirits of wine, can preserve them. He saw them—

> . . . Floating by or rolling on the shore,
> Those living jellies which the flesh inflame,
> Fierce as a nettle, and from that its name ;
> Some in huge masses, some that you may bring
> In the small compass of a lady's ring ;
> Soft, brilliant, tender, through the wave they glow,
> And make the moonbeam brighter where they flow [1]—

all observations which, carefully noted down during this period, were brought out again later on by the poet, put into verse, and introduced just as they were into his works.

A year passed in this way.[2] Crabbe had no doubt saved some money, for he resolved to carry out a plan of long standing—to go up to London, where a stay of a few months would, as he thought, enable him to add to his knowledge and to undertake at last, without too many misgivings, the responsibilities of his profession. He entrusted, rather imprudently, his " little business," his dispensary and his patients, to the care of a "neighbouring surgeon," and then embarked at Slaughden on one of the trading vessels sailing for the capital. According to his son, he lodged with an Aldborough family, " humble tradespeople who resided somewhere in Whitechapel." [3]   For eight or ten months, as long as his slender resources lasted, he attended the lectures on midwifery of Messrs. Orme and Lowder; he "occasionally stole round the hospitals to observe those remarkable cases, which might indeed, but which probably never would, occur to him again."[4]   He worked hard, as is proved by an anecdote related in the Biography. At that time the progress of anatomy was encouraging the practice of dissection; the doctors, though ready to buy corpses from all comers, could

---

[1] *Borough*, ix. 82-6, 89-90, and note 2.

[2] Autumn, 1775—autumn, 1776. Crabbe probably spent the end of 1776 and the first six months of 1777 in London. One sees how inaccurate the Biographer's narrative is in this place (cf. especially pp. 9 and 10).

[3] B. p. 9.

[4] *Bunbury Letter*.

not procure enough, and a strange industry, that of the
" resurrectionists," or body-snatchers, had arisen from
this new demand. Braving the watch and the indignant
population, these male and female ghouls descended
in troops by night on the churchyards of the capital,
and "in less than forty minutes" would exhume and
carry off a body, for which they obtained nine to
twelve guineas.[1] As it happened, Crabbe's landlady
had just lost one of her children ; scenting something
uncanny in her lodger's closet, she took it into her
head that "Dr. Crabbe had dug up William," asserted
his guilt, and threatened to summon him before the
Lord Mayor. Fortunately, Crabbe returned home at
the critical moment, and produced the corpse, the face
of which "had not yet been touched with the knife."
It proved not to be William, and the good lady's
apprehensions were allayed.[2]

On his return to Aldborough, Crabbe had a disagreeable surprise. He found that his substitute had con-
spired with his rival Raymond to cheat him in his
absence and deprive him of his practice. The poor
were all that remained to him, and, to make matters
worse, his diagnosis and his manual skill were sometimes at fault. He was deficient in promptness of
perception and in self-confidence. Too clear-sighted
and too sincere to indulge in illusions, he was aware
of his shortcomings, and his apprehensions increased
his incapacity. The second woman whom he attended
died in less than a month after her confinement : he
was doubtless in no way to blame for this mishap, but
he seems to have taken it to heart, and henceforth the
prospect of an operation made him almost as nervous as
his patients. People left him or did not pay him. The
old women of the place, seeing his passion for botany,
thought that they owed him nothing for medicines
picked up in the ditches.[3] He also, it appears, had a
good many poor relations who, on the strength of the
connection, would come and ask him for a cordial,
which could not well be refused. Lastly, he possessed
too many talents at once, all the more as poetry was
now throwing its old spell over him. How was it

[1] Cf. for more details Sir W. Besant, *London in the Eighteenth Century*,
1902, pp. 372-3, 549, and 551.
[2] B. p. 9.
[3] B. p. 10.

possible to have confidence in a doctor-poet, or to take an interest in the verses of a poet-doctor ? Apollo himself, if he had met him musing on the beach of Aldborough, would not have known how to address him. Was he really a " doctor," this man who paused at "midnight" before the ocean, comparing its restlessness to that of his own mind :[1]

> There wave on wave, here thought on thought succeeds,
> Their produce idle works, and idle weeds :
> Dark is the prospect o'er the rolling sea,
> But not more dark than my sad views to me ;

and then was suddenly uplifted by the sight of the moon :

> Yet from the rising moon the light beams dance
> In troubled splendour o'er the wide expanse ;
> So on my soul, whom cares and troubles fright,
> The Muse pours comfort in a flood of light ;

and finally exclaimed with rapture :

> Shine out, fair flood, until the day-star flings
> His brighter rays on all sublunar things !

Was he really a poet, this man who spoke of "landing a stranger on this world of woe," who boasted of his knowledge of midwifery, and enumerated his talents as a doctor, as a " skilful surgeon," able to perform an operation, as well as to write a prescription, and to make up his own medicines, for fear of " all the vile compounding tribe"? What are we to think of such boasting? However, the Warwickshire Regiment, one of the two battalions of militia quartered at Aldborough[2] in 1778, employed our doctor-poet, and the concluding months of that year were a period of comparative prosperity and cheerfulness for him. He became acquainted with some of the officers of the regiment, perhaps with the Colonel, Viscount Beauchamp, eldest

---

[1] *Works* (ed. 1871), p. 575: *Fragment, written at Midnight.*
[2] The Biographer (p. 10) makes a blunder here. His sole authority is a letter from his uncle Robert (see above, p. 5, n. 3), who writes : " The Norfolk Militia quartered at Aldbro' *in the summer*, the Warwickshire in the *winter.*" The Biographer states the contrary. Subsequently he asserts that his father was also surgeon to the Norfolk Militia, contradicting Robert, who says: "The Norfolk Militia were quartered at Aldboro' while my brother was surgeon there, but I believe he did not act as *their* surgeon, but *was* surgeon to the Warwickshire."

son of the Marquis of Hertford,[1] especially with the Colonel's younger brother, Captain the Honourable Henry Seymour Conway, then thirty-two years old, who had long been Member of Parliament for Coventry, and afterwards sat for Midhurst, already no doubt remarkable for the philanthropy and eccentricity which in later years made the bachelor owner of Norris Castle, near Cowes, in the Isle of Wight, an object of wonder to all his neighbours.[2] It was this Captain Conway who, during the flood of January 1st, 1779,[3] tried to save with a rake the furniture of the poor people, who had to cross the streets of Aldborough in boats; it was he too who, sharing Crabbe's taste for botany, presented him with Hudson's *Flora Anglica*,[4] a terribly dry work, from which his too naïve Biographer would have us believe that the poet learned to read Horace and to write in Latin.[5]

Unfortunately, these less sombre days were only a break in a sky which became more and more lowering. The militia left the town, and Crabbe found himself isolated. Little by little he fell into abject poverty; it was then that he knew the dire pangs of hunger, which paralyse mind and body— very often he had not even bread to give his sister Mary, who had come to live with him in his hut.

---

[1] Who at that time had a country seat at Sudbourne, near Orford. Sudbourne Hall was afterwards purchased and rebuilt by Sir Richard Wallace. The names of the officers of the Warwickshire Militia will be found in *A List of the Officers of the Militia of England and Wales for the year* 1778 *corrected to the Month of August* (London, J. Almon, Piccadilly, 1778, 1s. 6d.). There is no mention in it, as may well be supposed, of the future "Field-marshal Conway" (B. p. 10), the Conway of Horace Walpole's Letters. He had been a general since May 26th, 1772, and at this time (January, 1779) was drinking the waters at Bath. The Biographer's mistake, already suspected by Kebbel (*Life of Crabbe*, p. 20), is all the less intelligible, as Robert Crabbe had described the personage clearly enough in the following terms: "The Warwickshire Captn. Convay [*sic*] son to the Earl of Hertford, Sudbourn Hall."

[2] Lord Henry Seymour Conway, "the friend of mankind," as Crabbe (B. p. 10, n. 1) calls him, was born on December 15th, 1746. He was Member for Coventry in 1766, for Midhurst in 1774, and died on Friday, February 5th, 1830, "at his residence of Norris Castle." Cf. *Collins's Peerage*, edited by Brydges, 1812, vol. ii. pp. 564-5; *The Times* of February 8th, 1830; and the obituary notice in *The Gentleman's Magazine* (April, 1830): "He then retired to the Isle of Wight, where the greater number of his days have been spent in building Norris Castle and laying out the grounds of his estate."

[3] Letter of Robert Crabbe, quoted above.

[4] Wm. Hudson, F.R.S., *Flora Anglica*, editio altera . . . aucta, 2 vols., London, 1778. A copy of the first edition, covered with notes, was found among Gray's papers (*Life*, by Gosse, p. 200). The two poets had the same scientific tastes.

[5] B. p. 10.

And this poverty had to be concealed to spare the feelings of a father who was himself pressed by want, so that brother and sister "fasted with much fortitude."[1] There is a tear in the faint smile of this avowal.

II

WE may wonder if in the hours of gloom the thought of Mira was a solace or an added bitterness to her lover. Sure of a warm welcome, he often went to see her at Parham ; on the way he would meditate on the uncertainty of his destiny, on the troubles of the present, on the struggles of the future, on the ever-receding prospect of one day obtaining the hand of his betrothed. He would reflect that love, differing from mere friendship, which is always calm and unvarying, is like virgin gold, which has to pass through many an ordeal, and to be purified and refined in the crucible of life.[2] Would theirs resist the flame, or would it evaporate ? Sometimes Miss Elmy left Parham and returned to her mother at Beccles. Crabbe would then ride the long distance that separated him from Mira. Like the lover of one of his *Tales*,[3] he crossed the "barren heath beside the coast," admired "the neat low gorse, with golden bloom," and the "gay ling, with all its purple flowers." On arriving at the village of Thorpe, he turned to the left ; passing through lanes in which, under the fierce heat, "dust rose in clouds before the horse's feet," he came to a "common pasture, wide and wild,". where a few small black-legged sheep wandered round some hovels scattered amid square brown stacks of turf. Going uphill and downhill, and then uphill again, he passed near the ivy-clad ruins of the old abbey of Leiston, and not far from there, the landscape changing suddenly, found himself in the middle of a level fen, where the road ran between two dykes filled with brackish water, or over the single arch of a bridge beneath which "the straiten'd flood rolled through its sloping banks of slimy mud." Farther on, a "wide and sandy road," with deep ruts, sinking under the traveller's feet, mounted the slope of a desolate hill,

---

[1] *Bunbury Letter.*
[2] *Works*, p. 573 : *The Comparison*, dated Parham, 1778.
[3] *Tales*, x. : *The Lover's Journey, passim*, especially 34-9, 46-8, 63-9, 102-10, 141-4, 232-4, 264-71.

and the "lover" saw before him an undulating waste, its poor soil barely covered with yellowish grass, brown heather, and here and there a clump of fir trees. Under their shade, in a hollow, a family of gipsies had perhaps pitched their tents, and Crabbe would observe their behaviour curiously as he passed them. He quickened his pace and rode rapidly along the Blythburgh and Beccles road until he came in sight of the little town, neat, well built, paved, and prettily situated on the River Waveney.[1] If he had not been so eager to see Mira again, he would have stopped a moment before the imposing and massive tower, which stands apart from the handsome church and seems to be rather the sole remnant of an older building ; he would have lingered in front of the porch, and on the terrace with its commanding view of the "marshes,"[2] dyed a deep green by the waters of the Waveney, by the rain and the mists ; he would have walked down the narrow street, which still has tanneries in it, to the bridge, and from there, casting a general glance at the town, would have seen only roofs nestling in foliage. But who can restrain the impatience of a lover? What joy at last to grasp her outstretched hand ! what a disappointment, what a thrill of jealousy even, if he is told that Mira has accepted the pressing invitation of some friends, and asks him to join her ! And who are these friends, that she should prefer them to him ? Simply a group of "four or five spinsters," who, under the leadership of the "elegant and pleasing" Miss Blacknell[3] and the "masculine and hearty" Miss Waldron, have formed a small community in the environs of Lowestoft, about eight miles east of Beccles, at a spot called Normanston, in a park which runs along the high road, and through the trees of which can be seen the sparkling surface of Lake Lothing, a sort of natural basin worn by the sea. They have taken it into their head to "polish" Mira, in anticipation of her introduction into the world,[4] and

[1] Arthur Young's *Farmer's Tour through the East of England* (1771), vol. ii. p. 164.

[2] The local word for the meadows bordering on the river.

[3] In 1799 she was living at Ducking Hall, or Parham Lodge, and she married later Admiral Sir Thomas Graves (cf. B. p. 41 ; Davy MSS., *Parham* ; and *Works*, p. 260, n. 1).

[4] Letter from Sarah Elmy to Crabbe (about 1782) : "I am still with the dear Ladies at Normanston ; they are endeavouring to give me a polish against I see the world. It is said, you know, we learn anything better from those we love."

also to amuse her, for Miss Waldron is excellent company, and can "sing a jovial song and toss her glass" as well as a Squire Western.[1] Crabbe will soon learn to appreciate these friends of his betrothed; he will call them the "Ladies of the Lake," will later on [2] pay them one of those honeyed compliments which are always welcome,[3] will praise the elegance and ease of their life, their goodness, their taste, the charm of their manners, "the pleasant scenes that round them glow, like caskets fraught with gold . . . which owe their worth to what they hold":

> Trees may be found, and lakes, as fair,
> Fresh lawns, and gardens green :
> But where again the Sister-pair
> Who animate the scene?

For the moment he is a stranger to them; he follows, not without some ill-humour, the road which runs at some distance from the winding Waveney, with its "smooth and full" waters; he sees, at Worlingham and at North Cove, at the end of a park or on a lawn, one of those "mansions fair and tall," which are the delight of the traveller in England; he beholds "the grazing steer, the full-fed steed, and herds of bounding deer" fly at his approach; he observes children attended by a nurse, but allowed to play around the noble elms and over the "checkered shade" of their foliage; he gallops past inns and village churches, and does not stop till he arrives at Normanston, where Mira is awaiting him. And then come a few delightful hours, when the "burden of existence seems to be lightened for him," a flight into the ideal, far away from the sad reality. Does not Normanston or Beccles hold the treasure which perhaps will transform his life? Not that the reality always failed to assert itself, and that from time to time some accident did not come to remind the moralist of the fragility of human hopes. It was thus that, according to the Biographer,[4] the poet, on a warm summer day, had left Mira fishing

---

[1] B. p. 41.

[2] In 1785. See the piece entitled *The Ladies of the Lake* (*Works*, p. 260).

[3] It was religiously preserved by the two friends and returned to the Biographer by Lady Smith (cf. *Works*, p. 260, n. 1 : "A lady of rank in Norfolk . . .") in a letter dated Norwich, March 20th, 1834, now in the possession of the Rev. Cl. Rivett-Carnac.

[4] B. p. 11.

in the Waveney near Beccles, and had retired some
way off to bathe. Suddenly, he lost his footing:
unable to swim or to cling to the bank, he struggled
desperately; as the water closed over his head, " an
undefined sensation stopped his breath,"

> Disordered views and threatening signs of death
> Met in one moment, and a terror gave
> —I cannot paint it—to the moving wave ;
> My thoughts were all distressing, hurried, mix'd,
> On all things fixing, not a moment fix'd.
> 　. . . Man has not the power
> To paint the horrors of that lifelong hour ;
> Hour !—but of time I knew not—when I found
> Hope, youth, life, love, and all they promised, drown'd.[1]

" He could never," adds his son, " clearly remember
how he was saved. He at last found himself grasping
some weeds, and by their aid reached the bank."

If it be true that a blessing is all the more precious
the more fear there has been of losing it, then Crabbe's
and Mira's affection was strengthened by illness, by
their devoted care of each other, and by the terrible
anxiety which they successively experienced. " Cordi-
ally invited " by the poet's relations, Sarah Elmy had
come to Aldborough, had grown intimate with her
future sister-in-law Mary,[2] when Crabbe was seized
with a " dangerous fever," accompanied by a violent
delirium and ending in the extreme weakness of a
prolonged convalescence. " The attentions of his betrothed were unwearied," says the amiable Biographer ;
she helped him to walk when, bent by two months
of suffering, he could at last leave the house and
saunter for an hour on the beach :

> Stopping, as one unwilling to advance
> Without another and another glance, . . .
> With what a pure and simple joy he sees
> Those sheep and cattle browsing at their ease !
> Easy himself, there's nothing breathes or moves
> But he would cherish ;—all that lives he loves."[3]

---

[1] *Tales of the Hall*, iv. 209-41. The poet makes Richard experience his
own adventure, in a modified form.

[2] She calls her " our dear Polly " in the letter already quoted (see
above, p. 71, n. 4).

[3] *Borough*, xvii. 26 *seq.*

Hardly had he recovered and Mira returned to Parham, when the disease, which was probably infectious, attacked her in turn with still greater violence. Her life was supposed to be in danger ; Crabbe was invited to stay in the house, and in this cruel suspense, chafing under his own impotence, the poet, writes his son,[1] used to water the flowers which Mira herself had planted, and which he intended to keep in remembrance of her if she succumbed. Death, which spared Sarah Elmy, inflicted a heavy blow on the Tovells by taking their daughter " Jenney,"[2] who was carried off by diphtheria on January 12th, 1778. She was their only child, and the event made a "permanent alteration at Parham."[3] Her parents' grief was so great that " Mr. Tovell's health declined from that period," and her mother abated some of her bustling activity. A gloom which neither friends nor the bottle could dispel settled on the countenance of the yeoman. He fretted at the thought that his money would now go to persons less dear to him—to his two sisters, Miss Elizabeth Tovell and Mrs. Elmy, and, through the latter-named, to his niece Sarah, and so to this stranger, this poet who, when he was gone, would doubtless take his daughter's place. "Ah ! she is now out of *everybody's* way, poor girl !" he remarked one day on seeing Crabbe enter the room.[4]

Altogether, in spite of the anxieties of an uncertain future, love remained a source of consolation for the young man. This single star, which shone in his firmament amid banks of clouds, guided, encouraged him in the storm, prevented him from yielding to despair, from letting himself drift like one of the waifs and strays of life. A ray of warm sympathy emanated from his beloved and spread over the earth, kindling his imagination and his heart, and uplifting his thoughts. He had returned to his pen and his favourite books—his Horace, his English poets.[5] He was gradually turning aside from medicine and reverting to his true vocation. Perhaps he was dreaming of becoming celebrated one day, of " burst-

[1] B. p. 11.
[2] She was in her fourteenth year, having been baptised at Parham on September 13th, 1764.
[3] B. p. 11.
[4] B. p. 12.
[5] B. p. 12.

ing to light" and "exciting the admiration of the world":

> Fame shall be mine, then wealth shall I possess,
> And beauty next an ardent lover bless.[1]

In a noble piece, of truly prophetic inspiration, he exclaims:

> Give me, ye Powers that rule in gentle hearts!
> The full design, complete in all its parts,
> Th' enthusiastic glow, that swells the soul—
> When swell'd too much, the judgment to control—
> The happy ear that feels the flowing force
> Of the smooth line's uninterrupted course;
> Be it my boast to please and to improve,
> To warm the soul to virtue and to love;
> To paint the passions, and to teach mankind
> Our greatest pleasures are the most refined;
> The cheerful tale with fancy to rehearse,
> And gild the moral with the charm of verse.[2]

Few and fortunate are those whose early "wishes" have come so true!

While his mind was thus reopening to poetry, it was also becoming more and more engrossed in religious meditation, either because Mira's influence grew daily more penetrating, or because in sickness and poverty he felt the need of some support. In the great division of men's minds which began in Europe at the Renaissance, and has gone on deepening in the course of the last two centuries, Crabbe took a side distinctly and definitively from this period, at a time when no preoccupation of creed or self-interest could warp his judgment. He has not enough confidence in himself to view the destiny of mankind with calmness, to believe in the perfectibility of the race without divine aid, in the natural and necessary triumph of its good over its bad instincts. He is one of those who tremble before the mystery of existence without daring to probe it. He mistrusts his intellect and his heart, his

---

[1] *Tales*, v. 63-70, quoted by B. p. 12.

[2] *Works*, pp. 572-3, where the poem is dated Aldborough, 1778, and entitled *The Wish*. But, as we have seen (above, p. 52, n. 3), and shall see still more clearly, the dates given by the son are by no means to be depended on. The merit of *The Wish* had already been pointed out by Messrs. Abbey and Overton in their work, *The English Church in the Eighteenth Century*, vol. ii. pp. 341-2.

reason and his inclinations. He is fain to exclaim with
the Psalmist, "Lord, what is man that Thou art
mindful of him?" He likes to humble himself: the
audacity of this atom in face of the universe, of this
"proud, little creature," the sport of every error, seems
to him presumptuous folly:

> Is not the earth thou tread'st too grand for thee?
> This globe that turns thee, on her agile wheel,
> Moves by deep springs, which thou canst never feel; . . .
> A busy fly, thou sharest the march divine,
> And flattering fancy calls the motion thine,—

till some convulsion of nature "joins thy flimsy substance to the dust."[1] The "Spirit of Light" which the
poet invokes is not the conscience and the reason of
man, proud of their power and of their purity; it is
not Pallas Athene, inspirer of the "heathen arts,"[2]
but divine grace which will impart the "majestic
truths" of religion, will teach him how "vain his
powers, how poor his frame," and show him the path
to heaven. He is willing to forgo all "philosophic
researches" and "learned definitions"; he does not want
to dispute, "but to be saved."[3] He will not allow himself to be led away by the brilliant wit and specious
reasoning of unbelievers like "Hume and Voltaire";
if there is any need of "solid argument" to answer
them, it is to be found in abundance in the "tedious"
works[4] of Young and Tillotson; but what is the good
of "disputing," when it is feeling, and not reason, that
is taken for a guide, when the sorrowful, humbled soul
seeks a consoler, and finds him, or thinks it finds him,

---

[1] See the fragment, "Proud, little man, opinion's slave . . ." (*Works*,
p. 573).
[2] Cf. *Hymn, ibid.*
[3] Cf. B. p. 25 (iv.). There will be found here (B. pp. 24-5) several extracts
from a notebook already referred to above (p. 65, n. 2). The son, in publishing them, dates them from 1780. But he forgets that in the manuscript
they all come before a prayer dated December 31st, 1779 (see below, p. 79,
n. 2), to which they are probably anterior. Besides, the text given by the
Biographer is sometimes very inaccurate and arbitrarily altered. Thus, in the
original, iii. and iv. do not form two prayers, but *one* "Meditation." Of
the five prayers properly so called, the first and the fourth have not been
published; i. represents the second, ii. the third, and v. the fifth, the text of
which is correct.
[4] "It is plain, I think, that Infidelity depends more upon wit and ridicule than
upon solid argument, so that I have but little hope in refering [*sic*] these men
to Young and Tillotson, etc., as antidotes to Hume and Voltaire, since the
former in their system will never be favourites, and moreover are tedious"
(Another unpublished "Meditation" in the same notebook).

in its God and in its Redeemer? For there are moments when Crabbe, in spite of all his courage and his distant hope, finds his burden too crushing; then he looks to heaven and composes one of those pathetic prayers which breathe such a deep and' genuine affliction. He would like to lay aside all " over-care-fulness and anxiety after the affairs of this mortal body," and think only of "the care of his immortal soul." He is conscious of his shortcomings; he is "afflicted in mind, in body, in estate"; he addresses " Him from Whom all help cometh," and exclaims :

Oh ! be Thou my refuge. . . . I cast off all dependence on the world or mine own endeavours : Thou art my God, and I will trust in Thee alone ; . . . comfort me, for I go mourning. . . .

My God, my God, I put my trust in Thee ; my troubles increase, my soul is dismayed, I am heavy and in distress ; all day long I call upon Thee : O be Thou my helper in the needful time of trouble.

Why art Thou so far from me, O my Lord? Why hidest Thou Thy face? I am cast down, I am in poverty and affliction : be Thou with me, O my God ; let me not be wholly forsaken, O my Redeemer !

Behold, I trust in Thee, blessed Lord. Guide me, and govern me unto the end. O Lord, my salvation, be Thou ever with me.[1]

And this piety is strengthened by careful religious observance. Crabbe already belongs to the Church of England : it is she who best " satisfies his reason."[2] He acknowledges the two sacraments which she admits, Baptism and the Lord's Supper, as well as the twofold meaning, material and mystic, which she gives to them.[3] But his adhesion has nothing superstitious about it, and is compatible with a certain breadth of view and with much liberty of judgment. If the "sober stillness of the night, that fills the silent air,"[4] invites him to solemn meditation, he thinks with horror of the " intoxicated spirit of licentious wit, blaspheming holy doctrines," of " pleasure revelling with the libertine"; and, on the other hand, he deplores the coldness of the

---

[1] See above, p. 76, n. 3, and B. p. 25 (v).
[2] Cf. the same MS., *Reflections on the Communion* : " The Church to which I and my reason assents [*sic*]. . . . In our Church are two sacraments, Baptism and the Lord's Supper."
[3] *Works*, p. 574, the last stanza of *The Sacrament*.
[4] *Ibid.: Night.*

preachers of the holy word, of the Church of England
" divines " as well as of the dissenting " holders-forth."
Where, then, is truth ? In the pulpits of the former or
in the tabernacles of the latter ? Where are we to seek
the infallible guide for all, learned and unlearned ?
He replies : In the " blessed Gospel," independently
of all sects ; for "serious examination, deep humility,
earnest prayer will obtain a certainty." [1] Utterances
of a fervent [2] but also impartial Christian, of a man
whom long habit and a preference, reasoned rather
than enthusiastic, keep in the Church of England, in
the compromise of her dogmas and of her majestic yet
simple rites.

III

But a time was drawing near when love and religion
would be of no avail. Material existence was becoming
impossible for Crabbe at Aldborough. Hunger was
pressing him, and there seemed to be no way out of
his difficulties. The clouds which had gathered for a
moment on the horizon of his childhood, and then
dispersed, now covered the sky and blotted out every
friendly gleam. Despair confronted him at every turn ;
all further effort seemed useless. The pure joys of
the springtide of life had not been a " promise," but an
illusory " payment." Like the " jovial swain that yokes
the morning team, and all the verdure of the field
enjoys," and then languishes " when the noontide beam
plays on his brow and all his force destroys," [3] Crabbe
has no sooner reached the " summit of his hill " than
he sees " love and pleasure fled," and " the gay lights
of youth " disappearing under the ever " deepening
clouds of care." His birthday plunges him into a

---

[1] This curious passage, prudently garbled by the Biographer, is, in the
manuscript, part of the " Meditation." It immediately precedes the "profession of faith " (B. p. 25, iv.). Instead of " Amid the errors of the best . . .
will obtain certainty " should be read, " How strong is the intoxicated spirit of
licentious Wit, blaspheming Holy Doctrines ; how cold the preachers of Thy
word, *yet joining to hunt down the spirit of Enthusiasm* ! Where is truth?
In Pleasure revelling with the Libertine ? In Pulpits with the Divine or
Tabernacles with the Holder Forth ? All assert they have Reason ; which are
we to believe ? Where is unlettered Hope to cast her anchor ? Even in Thy
blessed Gospel. . . . But to whose tenets should we subscribe ? To neither as
sects. Serious examination, deep humility, earnest prayer, will obtain a
certainty."
[2] Cf. *The Resurrection* (*Works*, p. 574).
[3] *Works*, p. 574 : *Life*. See in *The Village*, i. 142-7, a similar idea.

melancholy which finds utterance in an almost dirge-like lament:

> Through a dull tract of woe, of dread,
> The toiling year has pass'd and fled:
> And lo! in sad and pensive strain,
> I sing my birth-day date again.
>
> Trembling and poor, I saw the light,
> New waking from unconscious night:
> Trembling and poor, I still remain
> To meet unconscious night again.
>
> Time in my pathway strews few flowers,
> To cheer or cheat the weary hours;
> And those few strangers, dear indeed,
> Are choked, are check'd, by many a weed.[1]

Admirable power of profound feeling! Nowhere has Crabbe come nearer to lyrism than in these few lines; never has his voice thrilled with greater eloquence than in a prayer composed a week later, on December 31st, 1779:[2]

A thousand years, most adored Creator, are in Thy sight as one day. So contract, in my sight, my calamities.

The year of sorrow and care, of poverty and disgrace, of disappointment and wrong, is now passing on to join the Eternal. Now, O Lord! let, I beseech thee, my afflictions and prayers be remembered; let my faults and follies be forgotten!

O Thou, Who art the fountain of happiness, give me better submission to Thy decrees; better disposition to correct my flattering hopes; better courage to bear up under my state of oppression.

The year past, O my God! let it not be to me again a torment—the year coming, if it is Thy will, be it never such. Nevertheless, not as I will, but as Thou wilt.

But God was far and men were hard. His poverty was known to all, and he was "dunned for the most trifling sums." His landlord, a redoubtable Justice of the Corporation, compelled him to pay the rent of his "hut" every week. His druggist, an indispensable purveyor and an unctuous Quaker, "gave him some friendly hints."[3] All those who had urged him to settle in his native place "deserted him for this reason

---

[1] *Works*, p. 574. The piece is dated Aldborough, December 24th, 1778. I think we should read "1779," the preceding year having been less sad for Crabbe (see above, pp. 68-9).

[2] B. p. 12 (cf. above, p. 65, n. 2).

[3] *Bunbury Letter*.

only, that he had not been successful by following their advice." His father was astonished at his failure, and reproached him with the expense, trifling though it was, to which he had put his family.[1] But the "struggle" had been going on for more than three years without hope of success, and had now ended in a crushing defeat.

There was no alternative but to turn his back on this thankless spot and its unfeeling inhabitants, to flee from " these shores where guilt and rapine reigned."[2] He must give up medicine, he must put aside the crude productions of those ignorant writers on whom he had " wasted" so many " tedious hours," the "first seducers of his easy heart, who promised knowledge they could not impart."[3] He must consign to " silence " and to the " dust," to the " emblematic " web of the " slow and subtle spider," the pages of these charlatans. Why should he not devote himself wholly to literature, to poetry ? Did he not share the hopes of those who " fly night's soft repose, and sleep's mild power defy," that " after ages may repeat their praise " ?—

> Delightful prospect ! when we leave behind
> A worthy offspring of the fruitful mind !
> Which, born and nursed through many an anxious day,
> Shall all our labour, all our care repay.[4]

The dangers of the career were not altogether unknown to him. True, he had heard nothing of Chatterton, of his " extraordinary abilities, his enterprising spirit, his writing· in periodical publications, his daring project, and his melancholy fate,"[5] but he had some knowledge of Goldsmith's adventurous and often miserable life. He knew what it may cost to " love the Muses," even when one is beloved by them ; he had pretended to receive a hint from the eccentric " Doctor,"[6] warning him against ambition for poetic fame, the brilliance of which is often a mask for a sad destiny. However, he thought perhaps that with much less talent, but more good sense and economy, he might achieve greater success in life. He also remembered that his father

[1] B. p. 13.
[2] *Village*, i. 123.
[3] *Library*, 407-18.
[4] *Ibid.* 83-90.
[5] *Autobiographical Sketch*, quoted by B. p. 12.
[6] *Works*, p. 573, "Goldsmith to the Author, Aldborough, 1778."

"had attended at the House of Commons on some election business" several years previously,[1] and been received by the all-powerful Chancellor of the Exchequer, Lord North, with "condescension and affability."[2] Might he not obtain, by means of this high protection, "employment in some department that he should be thought qualified for"? In any event, the attempt ought to be made, for this was his last chance.[3] On the winter day of 1779-80 when Crabbe, pausing on the hill above Aldborough, near the "Leech-pond,"[4] which has now disappeared, made up his mind to go to London, he played a bold game: he staked his future and perhaps his life on a single throw.

The preparations for his departure were quickly made. A last visit to Parham, where Mira was going to wait trustfully for him, a last poem to lament the too rapid flight of their "happiest hours,"[5] and towards the beginning of April, 1780, he embarked at Slaughden Quay on the *Unity* smack,[6] in which he had to live with the sailors during the voyage.[7] He took with him five pounds begged from Dudley Long,[8] a case of surgical instruments, a number of detached pieces of poetry, as well as a notebook containing pious effusions and the first rough draft of *The Library*. When, at the bend of the Alde, he lost sight of Aldborough and its hill, he

---

[1] Doubtless in 1768, about Fonnereau's complaint against Benet (see Hor. Walpole's *Letters*, ed. Paget Toynbee, 1904, vol. vii. p. 168 and n. 3).

[2] *Bunbury Letter.*

[3] *Autobiographical Sketch* (*loc. cit.*): "His health was not robust, his spirits were not equal; assistance he could expect none, and he was not so sanguine as to believe he could do without it."

[4] "The Leech-pond," B. p. 12. It was, I believe, on the right of the road as one goes down to the beach.

[5] B. p. 13, "The hour arrived . . ."

[6] See the letter from Fitzgerald already quoted (p. 12, n. 3). This piece of information was given to Fitzgerald by his friend Robert Hindes Groome, Archdeacon of Suffolk (cf. *Two Suffolk Friends*, by Francis Hindes Groome, 1895, pp. 67-8): "In the summer of 1859, we were staying at Aldeburgh, a favourite place with my father as the home of his grandfather. They were seafolk; and Robinson Groome, my great-grandfather, was owner of the *Unity* lugger on which the poet Crabbe went up to London."

[7] B. p. 13.

[8] In a remarkable letter, it would appear (B. p. 13), but the original of which has not been found. Dudley Long at that time lived at Saxmundham with his eldest brother, Charles Long. In 1789 he came into the property of the Dudley Norths at Little Glemham, bequeathed to him by his aunt, the Hon. Anne Herbert, and took the name of Dudley North. In 1812, on the death of his brother, he joined the two names and was called Dudley Long North. He sat in Parliament for many years, wielded a certain political influence, was a friend of Fox, and had known Johnson (cf. Boswell's *Life of Johnson*, Globe ed., p. 558).

must have felt that he was leaving poverty behind him and sailing for the unknown. He started "with the most serious apprehensions,"[1] with the inexperience of a country-bred man of twenty-six ; but his heart beat with a fervent love, and his mind was sustained by the energy of a character tempered by adversity.

[1] *Autobiographical Sketch* (B. p. 12).

CHAPTER IV

LONDON (1780—1781)

I

A UNIQUE spectacle presented itself at that time to the traveller arriving in London by the Thames. From the deck of his ship, surrounded by a crowd of vessels—Indiamen with sails set, hoys carrying excursionists, coasting craft and barges—he could see the old town of Deptford with its filthy streets full of taverns and sailors, and its shipbuilding yards for the navy. A little farther, at the bend of the river, he entered the " Pool," the port of the capital in the days when docks were as yet unknown ; through a " prodigious forest " of yards entangled like so many branches could be descried London Bridge, without the houses which covered it twenty years earlier. It seemed as if all the ships in the world had gathered together on the spacious surface of these deep and rapid waters. A picturesque animation reigned on all sides ; an incessant clamour resounded at every point. Hardly had a vessel come to anchor when it was assailed by a swarm of small craft filled with lightermen and followed by barges for transhipping cargo in the middle of the river. Three times a day these porters left the ships and landed in gangs on the muddy bank, where the stinking lanes, the stalls, and the low public-houses of the ill-famed districts of Shadwell and Wapping were huddled together. These labourers, all of them thieves, carried bags of sugar and bottles of rum hidden under their large aprons ; the surplus booty was often concealed inside their hats. They were waited for by women, slatternly, stay-less, their breasts uncovered,

83

wearing long square shoes with wide buckles, and then all repaired together to the receiver's shop, where the stolen goods were exchanged for a few coins which at once found their way into the tavern-keeper's pocket. Or perhaps the band espied a stranger landing, and flung themselves on his baggage. The traveller was lucky who in that case found an old sailor to pilot him through the labyrinth of the adjoining streets and rescue his trunks from these plunderers.[1] He had little inclination to turn round and see, beyond London Bridge, the numerous arches of Blackfriars and West-minster Bridge, both about thirty years old, and the light wherries floating with the tide or propelled by oars, and carrying, under their blue awnings,[2] busy tradesmen to the City, and merry parties of young folks to Lambeth and Chelsea, to Vauxhall and Ranelagh Gardens.

Obliged to husband his slender resources, Crabbe decided to lodge in the City and avoid the aristocratic " West End." Anxious as he was, moreover, to make a good impression on his future publishers, and to be able to give them a respectable address, wishing also to live near a family of linen-drapers who were friends of Miss Elmy, he hired a garret[3] at a Mr. Vickery's, a hairdresser of Cornhill. The rent seemed to him rather high, but the position was central and very convenient, close to the Bank and the Exchange, the façade of which, at that time looking southwards on Cornhill, afforded a glimpse of a courtyard and of spacious porticos under which merchants in wigs and three-cocked hats walked to and fro and discussed their business. In the house of Mira's friend, Mrs. Burcham, Crabbe was always sure of a kindly welcome, and also of finding " that domestic and cheerful society " the loss of which " he doubly felt in a world of strangers."[4] This " worthy woman and her husband " had asked him to look on their house as his own, and to take his

---

[1] Cf. Besant, *London in the Eighteenth Century*, 1902, pp. 352-3, 510; and a scene of this kind described by H. Brooke in *The Fool of Quality*, vol. ii. (ed. Kingsley), pp. 267-8.

[2] Besant, *op. cit.* p. 78; and Gay's *Trivia*, i. 164.

[3] B. pp. 14, 16, and 19; " my loft," says the poet in his very interesting Journal, begun on his arrival in London on April 21st. He moved into Vickery's house on Monday, the 24th.

[4] *Autobiographical Sketch*, quoted by B. p. 14. Cf. also Lockhart's letter (B. p. 79): " He hardly ever tasted butcher's meat, except on a Sunday, when he dined usually with a tradesman's family."

place at their table whenever he felt the need or the wish to do so. He did not abuse this invitation, preferring to hide his poverty and silence his hunger, rather than beg for the pity and assistance of his equals. He had too much pride and independence to stoop to the position of shamefaced parasite : it was better to take refuge in his garret and work and meditate there. Nobody came to disturb his musings. Mr. Vickery was an "honest fellow, hasty, and not over-distinguishing," an almost learned hairdresser. A lover of books himself, he had some regard for his studious lodger, whom he looked on as a "careless, easy-tempered" young man, incapable of making a disagreeable observation, as "one not quite settled in the world" and without "much knowledge of it." To Mrs. Vickery, a "clear-sighted woman," a "good wife and mother," Crabbe was a "soft-tempered gentleman," but "not quite nice enough," a little wanting in distinction. He had, however, purchased, on taking up his quarters with this ungrateful tradeswoman, a smart tie-wig, which was very expensive, though a trifle out of fashion.[1] But he was evidently too absent-minded : did he not leave the portrait of a lady lying on his pillow, and were not loose scrawls found all over his room? And whence his indifference to a certain "hawk-eyed" little maid-servant, accustomed to more attention from the lodgers?[2] There was a mystery about his work and even about his comings and goings.

How was he to live in the great city while waiting for fame or for some post in the public service? It was no use thinking of medicine; a journeyman apothecary's place would bring in only a trifling salary, out of which it would be impossible to save the amount of the debts he had left at Aldborough.[3] Crabbe therefore resolutely turned towards poetry. He gave up his philosophical and theological studies, laid aside the preparation of a "methodical examination of our moral and religious opinions," of which a brief sketch, divided into eight chapters, has been found among his manuscripts.[4] To refute atheism, to defend deism, and

---

[1] B. pp. 14 and 19. Men of fashion began to give up wigs about 1760 and wear their hair powdered (Besant, p. 252).
[2] B. p. 19.
[3] See *Bunbury Letter*.
[4] Cf. notebook already quoted, p. 65, n. 2, and B. p. 15.

complete it by the sanctions and promises which
"natural religion" does not give and revelation alone
can supply, was to run the risk of developing the
critical faculties at the expense of the sensibility so
precious to the poet. By meditating too much on
"substance, on the nature of man and on the notions
of brutes," his Muse, Crabbe tells us with a smile,
had lost her wings and the "phlogiston" which his
betrothed used to admire. Why not try to rekindle
in his own mind and in that of his future readers the
torch of poesy which had been extinguished in England
for some years ?

> When Pope is gone, and mighty Milton sleeps,
> When Gray in lofty lines has ceased to soar,
> And gentle Goldsmith charms the town no more,[1]

what rival was left for him to fear? On the approach
of winter the humblest flower looks beautiful : in
the isolation of her "widowhood" the Muse would
perhaps welcome the most modest of her "bards."
For a beginning, one must not be too ambitious,
but simply try to gain the ear of the public and of
some powerful protector. As it happened, Prince
William Henry, the youngest son of George III.,[2]
had just made his first campaign at the age of fourteen
under Admiral Rodney, the conqueror at Cape St.
Vincent and the liberator of Gibraltar. It was known
that the Prince was about to put to sea again : the
moment seemed well chosen for addressing to him a
panegyric which was also a petition. On the very
day, therefore, of his arrival at Vickery's, April 24th,
Crabbe began a poem entitled *The Hero*,[3] which he
finished on the 27th. We have only a brief fragment
of this evidently very poor composition, in which the
writer, with frigid enthusiasm, pretends to hear, "amid
the shouts of Fame, each jolly victor hail his Henry's
name," and begs this young Royal Highness not to
forget in his triumph the "numerous band" of children
of the "drooping Muse," the sad but interesting story
of Eustace Budgell, who "madly sank for ease,"[4] of

[1] B. p. 14, note : lines written in 1780.
[2] Who became William IV. in 1830, and whom Burns, in 1786, nicknamed
"Young Royal Tarry Breeks," in an ironical ode entitled *A Dream*. He
lives again with all his bluffness, his free-and-easy ways, and his familiarity, in
a passage of Fanny Burney's *Diary* (May 2nd, 1789).
[3] B. pp. 16-17.
[4] He drowned himself in the Thames in 1736.

Savage, who "sickened by degrees," of "helpless" Otway, who "shed the proud, big tear on song-extorted bread."[1] One of these "wretches," continued Crabbe in a really too abject tone :

> Slave to the Muses and to Misery son,
> Now prays the Father of all Fates to shed
> On Henry, laurels ; on his poet, bread.

As soon as it was finished, this ill-conceived and too rapidly written piece was sent to the publisher, James Dodsley, of Pall Mall, with a request that it should be read as soon as possible and "returned the next day if not approved," otherwise the author would call on the publisher. Crabbe was saved the trouble, for on April 28th he received the following letter : " Mr. Dodsley presents his compliments to the gentleman who favoured him with the enclosed poem, which he has returned, as he apprehends the sale of it would probably not enable him to give any consideration. He does not mean by this to insinuate a want of merit in the poem, but rather a want of attention in the public."

Crabbe, in no way discouraged, met this first rebuff by a second effort. "Judging it best to have two strings to his bow," and anticipating Dodsley's refusal, he had on the same day taken up a piece composed previously, with the "awkward" title of *The Foes of Mankind*, had amplified it, and given the "still more odd name of *Epistle from the Devil*"[2] to the three hundred and

---

[1] The only energetic expression in the whole of this piece.

[2] Cf. B. pp. 17, 18, and *Literary Anecdotes of the Nineteenth Century*, 1895-6, edited by W. Robertson Nicoll and Th. J. Wise, vol. ii. pp. 146-71, where the two pieces, entitled *Poetical Epistles* (1) *From the Devil, An Epistle General;* (2) *From the Author* (to Mira), have been published, as well as the *Introduction to the former of these, by the learned Martinus Scriblerus*, from the MS. in the possession of Mr. Henry Buxton Forman. They have no merit. The first is a letter of ironical congratulations addressed by the Devil to his "Beloved and Trusty" newswriters, monarchs, statesmen, Frenchmen, his most loyal subjects, and lastly deists. The second is a farewell from the poet to his philosophic studies; like the preceding one, it is written in the four-stress metre with couplet rhymes. The following is the least harsh passage :

> O blest be the Time when, my Mira, we stray'd
> Where the nightingale perch'd and the wanton winds play'd,
> Where these were the secrets of nature we knew,
> That her Roses were red, and her Vi'lets were blue,
> That soft was the gloom of the summer-swell'd shade,
> And melting the fall of the dying Cascade.

The passage quoted by B. p. 16 ("of substance . . . behind") belongs to the same Epistle (ed. Robertson Nicoll, pp. 169-70).

fifty lines which it now contained. A fair copy was about to be made and submitted to Thomas Becket, another publisher, when Crabbe fancied that this small work might appear too light. He therefore added to it about a hundred lines *From the Author* (to Mira), and styled the whole " Poetical Epistles, with a Preface by the learned Martinus Scriblerus ":[1] the longer of the two was a satire on the follies of mankind, and the author proposed, in case it should be well received, to work this vein well, as it seemed to him a most promising one. The manuscript was sent to Becket on May 3rd ; on the 10th, Crabbe, becoming impatient, called on the publisher, who gave him much the same reply as Dodsley : " 'Tis a very pretty thing, but, sir, these little pieces the town do not regard : it has merit,—perhaps some other may——" "It will be offered to no other, sir." "Well, sir," rejoined Becket, "I am obliged to you, but——" And so, remarks Crabbe mournfully in his Journal to Mira, "these little affairs end " in sad disappointments, against which one must bear up bravely by protesting that one has not lost heart. But we feel, all the same, that his confidence is beginning to give way.

Happily, there were moments when the real poet who was slumbering in Crabbe, and whom these feeble attempts certainly could not satisfy, awoke all at once in the transport of an unexpected inspiration, with its accompaniment of strong emotion and felicitous expression. Then he forgot all his disappointments ; he said to himself with a tremor of joy that a day would perhaps come in which his talents would be recognised and "win him applause." He notes in his Journal, on May 12th,[2] that " for the first time in his life he has written three or four stanzas which have so far touched him" as to make him forget "that they were things of his own fancy." And he adds that " if he ever does succeed, he will take particular notice if this passage is remarked," for if it is not, he will conclude that this fine enthusiasm was the effect of his self-love, though " in the strangest and at the same time strongest disguise she had ever put on." A very characteristic remark !

[1] The nickname of Swift in the famous "Scriblerus Club," founded by him with the help of Pope and Arbuthnot. Let us note again Crabbe's taste for satire in the manner of Pope or Young.
[2] B. p. 18.

No sooner has the poet spoken in Crabbe than the
moralist interrupts him with his distrust, and the
psychologist intervenes with his candid and penetrating analysis, aimed now at himself, as later on it
will be aimed at others. No wonder that he complains
immediately afterwards of feeling "heavy and dull, and
unable to go on with his work"! The inspiration has
died out too quickly; it has not carried him far from
earth, into an ideal world where it would have
awakened many-sounding echoes. The reality forces
itself on him; he is absorbed once more in the cares
of his life. He thinks[1] of the "slender web" of the
illusions which he has too long cherished, of the
dreams of "wealth, and peace, and love" with which
he has deluded himself in his poverty, how he has
"been fool'd by wishes, and still wish'd again." "Gain
by the Muse!" he exclaims, alas!—

> As soon grow rich by ministerial nods,
> As soon divine by dreaming of the gods,
> As soon succeed by telling ladies truth,
> Or preaching moral documents to youth. . . .
> Gain by the Muse! alas, preposterous hope!
> Whoever gained by poetry—but Pope?
> And what art thou? No St. John takes thy part;
> No potent Dean[2] commends thy head or heart.

It would be better to "deal in soft grimace," to don a
"genteel livery," to become wherryman, thrasher, or
"draw teeth"—anything rather than write and incur
the fate of Hogarth's "garret-bard,"[3] with his "unpitied
mate and children stinted in their daily meal." The
compassion which he had always felt for this poor
wretch was to him a "portentous" omen, a dim
presentiment of his own destiny. But he had not yet
come to this:

> No! thank my stars, my misery's all my own,—
> To friends—to family—to foes unknown:[4]
> Who hates my verse, and damns the mean design,
> Shall wound no peace—shall grieve no heart but mine.

---

[1] See the piece entitled *The Choice* (*Works*, Appendix, pp. 575-6), and
dated, by an obvious mistake, February, 1780. It could not have been
written "in London" before April, perhaps even it is of later date than *The
Candidate*. The fact that lines 62-3 and 76-9 of *The Choice* are already to
be found in the *Epistle to Prince William Henry* inclines me to the belief that
the first of these poems was composed immediately after the second.

[2] Swift, appointed Dean of St. Patrick's, Dublin, in 1713.

[3] The celebrated picture of "The Distrest Poet."

[4] Crabbe preserved his anonymity in his first publications.

Why not abide by the result after this attempt? Shall
he rest, or make one more endeavour?

> Rest here, if our relenting stars ordain
> A placid harbour from the stormy main :
> Or that denied, the fond remembrance weep,
> And sink, forgotten, in the mighty deep.

Ruin, in fact, seemed to be closing over him. The
publishers had refused his poems, on the proceeds
of which he had hoped to live until he was in a
position to apply to Lord North. It was in vain
that on April 25th he had endeavoured to obtain
a place by answering an advertisement in *The Daily
Advertiser* from "a gentleman not well versed in the
English language," who wanted an amanuensis "of
grammatical education" and with a gift of style.
Crabbe, "having no doubt of his capacity," had offered
himself, and two days afterwards he went, not without
some hope, from the City to the Haymarket, where his
fate was to be decided. On arriving there he was
informed that "the gentleman was provided." The
walk back seemed long to him: "Twelve long miles
walked away"—in reality it was only about four—
"loss of time, and a little disappointment," he writes
in his Journal[1]; "and now for my philosophy. I
reflected that the 'gentleman' might not have so very
much of that character as I at first supposed : he
might be a sharper, and would not, or an author
himself, and consequently could not, pay me. He
might have employed me seven hours in a day over
law or politics, and treated me at night with a Welsh
rabbit and porter!—It's all well; I can at present buy
porter myself, and am my own amanuensis." On the
following day, April 28th, nothing was left of Dudley
Long's five pounds,[2] and our poet, really "in distress,"
found himself "under the disagreeable necessity of
vending or pawning some of his more useless articles; . . . they cost about two or three guineas, and
being silver, had not greatly lessened in value." The
"conscientious pawnbroker" agreed, not without some
diplomatic hesitation, to advance him half a guinea,
which Crabbe readily accepted, being determined to

[1] B. p. 17.
[2] See above, p. 81, n. 8. The journey from Aldborough to London seems
to have cost him two pounds.

claim his property back as soon as possible, and then, if need be, take it "to some less voracious animal of the kind." On May 1st the "good broker's money was reduced to five shillings and sixpence," Crabbe's daily expenses being about three shillings, and he had to sell twenty-five shillings' worth of books to "recruit his purse." He thus reached the middle of the month. On the 10th he was driven almost to the last extremity, and yet he smiled : "I don't think," he wrote, "there's a man in London worth but fourpence-halfpenny—for I've this moment sent seven farthings for a pint of porter—who is so resigned to his poverty. Six days afterwards an affectionate letter from Miss Elmy drew from him a cry of anguish which he immediately stifled : "O! my dear Mira, how you distress me ; you inquire into my affairs, and love not to be denied,—yet you must. To what purpose should I tell you the particulars of my gloomy situation ; that I have parted with my money, sold my *wardrobe*, pawned my watch, am in debt to my landlord, and finally, at some loss how to eat a week longer? Yet you say, tell me all. Ah! my dear Sally, do not desire it ; you must not yet be told these things. Appearance is what distresses me : I *must* have dress, and therefore am horribly fearful I shall accompany fashion with fasting." On the 18th an impatient tailor duns him for twenty shillings : how is the debt to be paid with the thirteen and threepence which Crabbe possesses ? He once more has recourse to the pawnbroker, pledges his surgical instruments for eight shillings, and by cleverly redeeming and repledging his watch [1] clears a balance of ten shillings, which will keep the wolf from the door, and encourage the visits of the Muse, "who does not love empty pockets nor poor living." After counting over his treasure, he exclaims, in a burst of youthful merriment : "A rare case, and most bountiful provision of fortune!" Then he becomes pensive again, and his mirth ends in a fervent thanksgiving : "Great God! I thank Thee for these happy spirits : seldom they come, but coming, make large amends for preceding gloom."

His life, which was regularity itself, exposed him only once, it would appear, to an irresistible "temptation,"

[1] Cf. B. p. 19 : "Now, you must know, my watch was mortgaged for less than it ought ; so I redeemed and repledged it."

and it was to the poetical attractions of Dryden that he
succumbed. An " unlucky " chance had led him to one
of those bookstalls where—

> . . . Many a weary walker, resting, reads,
> And pondering o'er the short relief, proceeds,
> While others, lingering, pay the written sum,
> Half loth, but longing for delight to come,[1]

as Crabbe did on this occasion. Dryden's works in
three octavo volumes were to be had for five shillings.
The opportunity was a tempting one, but fortunately
his prudence, always on the alert, " got the better of the
devil " and suggested that he should bid a lower sum.
The precious tomes became his for three shillings and
sixpence, " a fair bargain, I believe," he remarks, " but
a very ill-judged one." All the more, as poverty
turned the slightest mishaps into painful embarrassments. " It's the vilest thing in the world," he writes
on the same day, " to have but one coat. My only one
has happened with a mischance, and how to manage
it is some difficulty. A confounded stove's modish
ornament caught its elbow, and rent it half-way.
Pinioned to the side it came home, and I ran deploring
to my loft. In the dilemma, it occurred to me to turn
tailor myself; but how to get materials to work with
puzzled me. At last I went running down in a hurry,
with three or four sheets of paper in my hand, and
begged for a needle, to sew them together. This
finished my job, and but that it is somewhat thicker,
the elbow is a good one yet. These are foolish things,
Mira, to write or speak, and we may laugh at them;
but I'll be bound to say they are much more likely to
make a man cry, though I was too much of a philosopher
for that, however not one of those who preferred a
ragged coat to a whole one." [2] Here speaks the pride
of a man who respects himself and for whom decorum
will always remain a social duty. He will " fast " perhaps, but his clothes will be neat; he will never let
himself be like his " old friend Morley," [3] who knew
the smiles of Fortune before her frowns, and who has

---

[1] *Posthumous Tales*, i. 142-5. About this time (B. p. 19) Vickery removed
from Cornhill to Bishopsgate Street, whither Crabbe followed him. To escape
from his father's solicitude, he sent his new address to Aldborough, without
adding that his landlord was still the same.
[2] B. p. 19.
[3] B. p. 18.

now grown slovenly under the influence of depression
and ill-health. It is better to fight on.

Besides, all is not yet lost. During the month of
May he has doggedly pursued the execution of his
"great design,"[1] the completion of a "volume of verses,"
with which he intends to support his petition to Lord
North.[2] Let us "make hay while the sun shines," he
says on Wednesday the 3rd; "when the spirits are
tolerable, we'll pursue our work, for it's plaguy apt to
be clouded." On the 6th he has almost finished the
plan of the book, which he hopes to write in a week;
on the 10th he has made good progress, and is debating
with himself whether an ode or a small lyric poem
should have the next place in the collection—a point
which seems to him to deserve serious consideration.
On the 20th he feels "somewhat exhausted" after
writing more than thirty pages; finally, on the evening
of Sunday the 21st, after returning from church, he
begins the all-important document, the "long and
laboured" letter in which he explains to Lord North
"the motives of his application." He is evidently very
proud of this production, for, after re-reading it, he
declares it to be the "most consequential piece he has
ever executed, whether in prose or poetry." "You
will perceive there is art in it," he says to Mira,[3]
"though art quite consistent with truth, for such is
actually the case with me. My last shilling became
eightpence yesterday. The simplicity of the style is,
I hope, not lost in endeavouring at the pathetic, and if
his Lordship is indeed a literary man, I am not without
hope that it may be a means of obtaining for me a better
fortune than hitherto has befallen us." "Success will
soon prove whether it is in the power of my talents
to obtain me favour." The next morning he finishes
his book and "consecrates" it by "begging of Him,
who alone can direct all things, to give him success in
it or patience under disappointment." In the afternoon
he goes to Lord North's residence in Westminster[4]

---

[1] "My principal work" (B. p. 16), "my principal design" (*ibid.* p. 17),
"my principal business" (*ibid.* p. 18), "my book" (*ibid.*). The third letter to
Burke (*Bunbury Letter*, Appendix I) leaves no doubt as to the nature of this
"book," contrary to what Canon Ainger says (*Life of Crabbe*, p. 21).

[2] Appendix I, "A volume of verses, etc., . . ." "a long and laboured
account of my motives for this application."

[3] B. p. 21.

[4] In Downing Street.

and delivers his letter and poems. Then follow two
long days of " dread and expectation." He has. presumed too much on his powers, he thinks, and now his
" hopes are flying " ; his three failures in one month
have robbed him of all confidence. " God help me, my
Sally, I have but a cowardly heart, yet I bear up as
well as I can ; and if I had another shilling would get
something to-night to keep these gloomy thoughts at
bay, but I must save what I have in hopes of having a
letter to pay for to-morrow.[1] How, let me suppose,
shall I be received ? The very worst I can possibly
guess will be to have my book returned by the servant,
and no message ; next to this a civil refusal. . . .
Oh," he continues in an outburst of fervent piety,
" what pains do we take, what anxiety do we feel, in
our pursuit of worldly good—how reproachful a comparison does it make to our more important business !
When was I thus solicitous for the truly valuable
riches ? O my God, forgive a creature who is frailty
itself, who is lost in his own vileness and littleness,
who would be happy, and knows not the means. My
God, direct me ! " A more heart-felt prayer than many
of those which resounded in places of worship, and
which, however, does not bring him peace of mind !
Alternately waking and sleeping, he spends a restless
night, dwelling on his " old views, his romantic expectations," his successive disappointments : " such as the
past has been," he says, " shall be the future." Then
a return of his vanity gives him a glimpse of " fairer
things," " magnifies his little talents," which he ends by
considering as worthy of notice. In the morning he is
" more composed," and engaged in copying out for his
" dearest Sally " the letter to Lord North, which is
unfortunately lost.[2]

It was no doubt in the afternoon of the following day,
Wednesday, May 24th,[3] that he had an audience of the
Prime Minister who had once received his father with
cordiality. A singular mixture of physical ugliness
and apparent amiability, of caustic wit and sleepy indolence, of good sense in the handling of administrative

---

[1] Evidently from Mira herself. In those days the addressee had to pay the
postage of the letters which he received.
[2] The leaves of the Journal on which it was copied have been torn out.
There is a gap from May 23rd to June 5th (B. p. 21).
[3] B. p. 21 : " I shall call again on Wednesday."

detail and blind obstinacy in the conduct of general policy, North was reputed a man of letters on the strength of a few Latin verses composed at Eton, and perhaps he would have assisted Crabbe if he had taken the trouble to look at the manuscript. But he was daily assailed by applications of this kind, and just then was struggling with the insurmountable difficulties of the American War. He received the young man "with attention," but with none of the "affability" that Crabbe hoped for; he asked about his affairs and his recommendations, expressed himself as satisfied with the latter, invited him to come again, and fixed a day for the audience. " Unnecessary and cruel civility," wrote the poet afterwards in his third letter to Burke; "it has greatly added to the inconveniences I now labour under, besides the anxiety of a long attendance growing daily more hopeless; for not only on the day fixed, but on all other days, I went regularly to Downing Street, but from my first to my last interview with his Lordship were three months. I had only a variation in the mode of answer as the porter was more or less inclined to be civil; the purport of all was the same. I wrote and entreated his Lordship to accept or refuse me; I related my extreme poverty and my want of employment, but without effect. I again begged him to give some message to his servant, by which I might be certain that I had nothing further to hope for: this also was ineffectual. At last I had courage to offer so small a sum as half a crown, and the difficulty vanished: his Lordship's porter was now civil and his Lordship surly; he dismissed me instantly and with some severity."[1] It was on the eve of the General Election of 1780.

But long before this [2] Crabbe, growing impatient at the dilatoriness of the head of the Government, had turned to one of the leading personages of the Opposition, Lord Shelburne, who owned the princely residence in Berkeley Square, begun and afterwards abandoned by Lord Bute. Imbued with the literary traditions of Queen Anne's time, forgetting also that

[1] Cf. Appendix I. We see how mistaken Canon Ainger is in saying, "When, after a fortnight's suspense, this request for assistance had been refused." He is misled by the letter to Shelburne (see below).

[2] From June 6th (B. p. 22).

what Harley and St. John had paid for, was services
rendered, and not the genius of the authors, Crabbe was
" not conscious of losing the dignity becoming a man "[1]
when, in his poverty, he sought assistance in every
quarter. The lines in which the " Right Honourable
Earl " is described as "blest with all that's good or
great, t' adorn a rich or save a sinking state," are feeble
indeed ; the *Epistle to a Friend*, in which a distant
echo of Spenser makes " Shelburne's fame through
laughing valleys ring," is almost unreadable ; and this
poor stuff is accompanied by a distressingly humble
letter. The poet, with diplomatic shrewdness, makes
Lord North responsible for his misfortunes : " Starving
as an apothecary in a little venal borough in Suffolk,
it was there suggested to me that Lord North, the
present minister, was a man of that liberal disposition
that I might hope success from a representation of my
particular circumstances to him. This I have done. . . .
My request had bounds the most moderate : I asked not
to feed upon the spoils of my country, but by an honest
diligence and industry to earn the bread I needed. . . .
Why I complain of his Lordship is not that he denied
this, but for his cruel and unkind delay. . . . My
repeated prayers for my sentence were put off ; and
at length a lingering [2] refusal, brought me by an
insolent domestic, determined my suit, and my opinion
of his Lordship's private virtues. My Lord, I now turn
to your Lordship, and entreat to be heard. I am
ignorant what to ask, but feel forcibly my wants—
Patronage and Bread. . . . May I not hope it will occur
to you how I may be useful ? " Let us not blame
Shelburne too much if he refused to listen to these
lamentations or to read these verses ; rather let us
pity the poet, who, unlucky as ever, exposed himself
to fresh mortification by applying to the blunt Lord
Chancellor Thurlow, the surliest man, the craftiest
and most pompous judge of his day.[3] To his first
letter enclosing a poem, Thurlow replied by " a cold,

---

[1] B. p. 20.

[2] But not definitive ; cf. the third letter to Burke, quoted above (p. 95).

[3] He is the "Niger" of Cowper in his *Valediction*, the poet's farewell to a
forgetful friend of his youth :

> Your brain well furnished and your tongue well taught
> To press with energy your ardent thought,
> Your senatorial dignity of face,
> Sound sense, intrepid spirit, manly grace.

polite note, regretting that his avocations did not leave him leisure to read verses." Crabbe rejoined with a second composition, of a satirical turn, in which he reminded the Chancellor that his predecessors had made a point of encouraging letters. Thurlow, of course, paid no attention to this remonstrance, the simplicity of which must have appeared highly entertaining to him.[1]

The poet's Journal, from which I have quoted so many passages, is a unique document in the history of English eighteenth-century literature. In it can be followed day by day, and sometimes hour by hour, the struggle with poverty of a "candidate" for fame, aspiring to "cleave his natal gloom." Nothing can be more characteristic of a time when authors, abandoned by the noblemen who had formerly encouraged them, turned towards the public, and, owing to their obscurity, were obliged to become the drudges of the publishers to get a "glass of porter" and a garret in the neighbourhood of "Grub Street." And nothing reveals the man better than these pages, written under the influence of the humble events they relate, especially if Crabbe's conduct is compared with that of some of his seniors. Where is the sturdy independence of Johnson, who, on his arrival in London, writes to Cave, the proprietor of *The Gentleman's Magazine*, to offer him Latin verses, critical articles, or even translations, and who never thinks for a moment of seeking a "protector." Crabbe comes up to the capital to beg for a place, and if he has poems to dispose of, he submits them to the most famous publisher of the day. He is by nature an official and a gentleman; what he wants is some modest but safe post, which will give him consideration and leisure. In our day his ambition would have been to scribble his verses on a desk in a Government office. He has none of the heedlessness and absent-mindedness of Goldsmith; none of the irregularity of Boyse or Savage, who, once their pockets were full, spent the money in drink and debauchery; none of their indifference to the opinion of society. He likes regularity and purity of life. Against the coarse seductions of cities he possesses an all-powerful charm in the love of her whom he "wants" so badly, of her who can "throw a beam of gladness"[2] on his deepest

gloom—his Mira, left behind at Parham. His religious
convictions, which are becoming more and more deeply
rooted, take him to church on Sunday and suggest to
him the naïve idea of sending Miss Elmy an abstract
of the sermons of his "favourite clergyman."[1] His
poverty prevents him from going to the play; the
only distraction which he allows himself is to spend
an occasional evening at a "small coffee-house near
the Exchange," where he meets a group of friends,
accomplished mathematicians with a distinguished
career before them, but young as yet, and supporting
themselves by giving lessons[2]

He associates more especially with John Bonnycastle,
the future Master of the Military Academy at Woolwich, the "good fellow" whom Leigh Hunt knew
afterwards, and whom he describes, not without some
exaggeration, as "a tall, gaunt, long-headed man, with
large features and spectacles and a deep internal voice,
with a twang of rusticity in it, and an equine laugh." Of
an impetuous temperament, Bonnycastle was capable,
in a fit of hypochondria, of throwing his insolent landlord downstairs; an active-minded man, moreover,
who not only put the discoveries of astronomy into
elegant language, but also, as early as the year 1771,
sent a poetical *Morning Soliloquy* to *The Lady's
Magazine*,[3] and professed an exclusive admiration for
Pope's well-turned couplets.[4] Crabbe liked to listen
to his interminable stories and to his quotations from
Shakspeare, to accompany him into the rural environs
of the capital of those days, and then to lose his way,
with an Ovid or a Horace in his hand, amid woods

[1] B. pp. 20, 24.
[2] B. p. 15. Besides Bonnycastle, Reuben Burrow and Isaac Dalby used to
come there.
[3] See Leigh Hunt's *Lord Byron and some of his Contemporaries*, 2nd ed.
1828, vol. ii. pp. 3 *seq.* ; reprinted in Leigh Hunt's *Autobiography*, ed. 1860,
pp. 90-1. Leigh Hunt used to meet him about 1808 at the table of Hunter,
the publisher, of St. Paul's Churchyard, the successor of Johnson. The last-
named had published Cowper's works in 1782 and 1785, and in 1786 a work
by Bonnycastle, entitled *An Introduction to Astronomy in a Series of Letters
from a Preceptor to his Pupil*. The *Morning Soliloquy* was printed in *The
Lady's Magazine* of June, 1771 (p. 520).
[4] He is evidently the man who, in 1784, ventured to correct a line in
Cowper's second volume of poems, a piece of audacity which drew down on
the publisher, Johnson, an indignant protest from the poet (see in The Golden
Treasury Series, p. 120, Cowper's letter to "Mr. Johnson, printer "). The
note of Crabbe's Biographer (B. p. 15, n. 4) proves that Bonnycastle was the
"accidental reviser" mentioned by Hayley.

and valleys, until sunset and the approach of night
forced the belated pedestrian to cease his reading or
botanising, and to sit down under a haystack, where he
once had to spend the night.[1] This predilection for
science and for the tranquil pleasures of a modest
existence will reappear in all the works of the poet.

II

AT the beginning of June an unforeseen event, a regular
revolt of the London mob against society and the
constituted authorities, interrupted Crabbe's labours,
hampered his movements, and spread terror in the
capital. In those days, perhaps even more than now,
there was a startling contrast between the luxury of
the rich and the degrading wretchedness of the poor.
At many points London was beginning to assume a
modern aspect : it was no longer the city described by
Gay, with its often narrow streets, irregularly paved,
and divided in the middle by a fetid gutter, blocked by
heaps of domestic refuse. The stakes which formerly
alone protected the muddy sidewalks from the wheels
of the heavy carts, the multifarious signs which creaked
in the wind, the poles from which the hosiers used to
hang their stockings, the picturesque pent-houses of the
shops, along the edge of which stood rows of dripping
flower-pots—all this had given place to spacious, well-
ventilated,"[2] and solidly paved thoroughfares, where
there was no longer a risk of falling at night through
gaping holes into the cellars. The famous " Fleet Ditch,"
the stream of slime and filth on the banks of which
people came to eat oysters in Gay's time, had been
filled up in 1769, and no longer offended the nasal
organs of the poor women imprisoned in Bridewell
and of the bankrupts who begged at the railings of the
" Fleet Prison " hard by. Between 1760 and 1771 the
old gates and the useless walls of the City had been
successively demolished to admit light and air. Elegant
shops, full of obsequious and neatly dressed assistants,[3]
lined the hill which descends from St. Paul's Cathedral
to Fleet Street ; along the Strand, especially at Charing
Cross, there was a constant traffic of vehicles of all

---

[1] B. p. 15.
[2] Smollett, *Humphrey Clinker*, to Dr. Lewis (May 29th).
[3] Cf. Fanny Burney's *Evelina*, pp. 18, 19 (Bohn's Library, 1892).

kinds, of coaches, driven at full speed by coachmen in scarlet coats, or entering the courtyard of an inn to the cheerful blast of the guard's horn. At night the shops were lit by the faint gleam of candles, and the streets, lighted by oil-lamps, were full of sedan-chairs, preceded by torches, and carrying people of fashion from the theatre or to the masquerade.

But this pleasing exterior barely concealed an unparalleled wretchedness and depravity. In Westminster, in Southwark, in Shoreditch, even in the centre of the town, there were whole districts into which one could not venture without danger, where every malefactor arrested by the police was at once rescued by "twenty or thirty armed comrades."[1] If the pedestrian, walking towards Charing Cross, turned to the right, and, passing through Chancery Lane, entered the large deserted space which is still known as "Lincoln's Inn Fields," he espied rows of beggars standing along the palings, who imposed upon public charity and at nightfall used their crutches as bludgeons.[2] If he wanted to reach the great thoroughfare of Holborn, he had to cross a number of filthy lanes which were called, no doubt ironically, Whetstone Park, a sort of outpost of the famous parish of " St. Giles'," which was the refuge of outcasts, thieves, and prostitutes, and the whole tribe of those who flock to great cities for a hiding-place. In the dens which swarmed there a bed could be procured for twopence in a room open to creatures of both sexes; for another penny one could sleep two in a bed or buy a quarter of a pint of gin. When the men of the watch ventured to make a raid into one of these houses, which were full from " cellar to loft," they sometimes found more than fifty persons " whose stench was so intolerable" that they had to beat a speedy retreat.[3] Brutalised by ignorance and drunkenness, living on robberies encouraged by the numerous receivers of stolen goods, this populace had no amusements but gambling, cock-fighting, or bearbaiting. Sometimes they would collect in front of the pillory and nearly stone to death some poor wretch

---

[1] Fielding's *Causes of the Increase of Robbers* (Bell, 1889), p. 785.
[2] Gay's *Trivia*, iii. 132-8.
[3] Fielding, *op. cit.* p. 784 (Report of "Mr. Welch, the high constable of Holborn"). What Fielding wrote in 1750 remained true up to 1792, when the London police was completely transformed (cf. Besant, *op. cit.* p. 522).

who happened to be in it. On the day of an execution they would cheer the condemned men as the cart or carts carrying them to the gallows of Tyburn passed slowly by. One and all were ready to descend into the streets on the first favourable opportunity, and to commit the worst excesses.

As it happened, an outburst of religious fanaticism took place in London towards the end of May, 1780. On the motion of Sir George Savile, Parliament had decided to repeal the disabling laws then in force against the Roman Catholics, and this measure had aroused the anger of a certain number of mistrustful Protestants. They had formed an " association," and chosen for their honorary president a young Scottish nobleman, Lord George Gordon, Member of the House of Commons, a man of vain character and ill-balanced mind. In order to force Parliament to retract its vote by proving clearly to it the hostility of public opinion, Lord George had got up a monster petition, and declared his intention of presenting it to the House attended by all his adherents. On Friday, June 2nd, at ten o'clock in the morning, the heat being intense, " an enormous crowd," wearing cockades and carrying blue flags, singing hymns and formed in military order, had gathered to the south of London, on the right bank of the Thames, in " St. George's Fields." At noon Lord George in person gave the signal for the start, and the demonstrators, divided into three columns, invaded the City, the Strand, and Westminster by the three bridges which then crossed the river. Two hours later they met in front of the Houses of Parliament, and at once occupied its approaches and lobbies. Every Member arriving was obliged to don the cockade and cry " Down with the Papists ! " Not a Peer was spared ; the Archbishop of York, who was hissed and hooted, managed, not without difficulty, to extricate Lord Mansfield, whose carriage was smashed and whose life was in great danger. All this violence, however, was of no avail, for the House of Commons, in spite of the tumult outside and the entreaties of Lord George, refused to take the petition into consideration, and about nine o'clock the Horse Guards at last arrived on the scene and cleared the approaches of Parliament. But before the close of the day the first acts of pillage had been committed—two Roman Catholic chapels of foreign embassies were sacked and burnt. A deceptive lull had barely reassured the population when, on Sunday evening and during the whole of Monday, incendiary fires broke out more violently than ever. The news spread that Sir George Savile's house had been gutted, that the troops were paralysed by the inaction of the civil authorities, and that the rioters, furious at the imprisonment of some of their number in Newgate, had sworn to be avenged on the magistrates who had dared to have them arrested. The mob now had a free hand, and, for the space of two days, lorded it over the terrorised city. The strangest scenes were then witnessed : boys, armed with iron bars, blackmailed the shopkeepers of Holborn with impunity ; a highwayman stopped the passers-by and refused to accept anything but gold.

Crabbe, an astonished spectator of these bloody revels, relates in his Journal some episodes of Tuesday, June 6th. About three o'clock in the afternoon, no doubt just after he had been dismissed by Lord North's porter,[1] he saw a dense mob in front of the Houses of Parliament stopping the Members who were going in. They allowed all to pass except the First Lord of the Admiralty, the unpopular and disreputable Lord Sandwich, "whom they treated roughly, breaking his coach windows, cutting his face, and turning him back."[2] A detachment of infantry and cavalry was immediately sent for, " but did no particular service, the mob increasing and defeating them." Bands of " vile-looking fellows, ragged, dirty, and insolent, and armed with clubs," made their appearance at different points in the City, evidently preparing for the exploits of the evening. Between seven and eight o'clock, in fact, Crabbe, returning from Westminster, where there remained only a few persons, "and those quiet, and decent in appearance," arrived at the Old Bailey, and " there saw the first scene of terror and riot ever presented to him." The new prison, just finished after eight years' building, "was a very large, strong, and beautiful building, having two wings, and besides these the keeper's (Mr. Akerman's) house, a strong intermediate work, and other parts." The keeper had in

---

[1] "My own business being decided" (B. p. 23), and see above, p. 95, n. 2.
[2] B. p. 23. Crabbe seems not to have noted his impressions until two days later, on June 8th.

his custody four prisoners who had been arrested in
the course of the riot, and the mob demanded their
release. Meeting with a refusal, they broke into his
house by the windows, and threw all the furniture
they could find into the street, piled it against the
prison door, and set fire to it. The fire-engines
arrived, "but were only suffered to preserve the
private houses near the prison." Worse still, a
hundred policemen, sent to the assistance of the head-
keeper, saw the ranks of the crowd open in front of
them and then close upon them, so that they found
themselves struggling with a furious multitude who
snatched away their staffs and used them as torches.
By a singular coincidence, at that very moment Lord
George Gordon, the instigator of these disturbances,
happened to pass by in a coach drawn by the mob,
and surrounded by five hundred of his adherents, on
his way to the house of a no less strong Protestant,
Mr. Bull, Alderman and Member of Parliament.
Crabbe noted the "lively" appearance of this "hero"
of the moment, who replied by bows to the cheers of
the more and more excited mob. By eight o'clock
Akerman's house was in flames, and the sight was
"dreadful." The prison was of great strength, but the
assailants, "determined to force it," had managed to
break open the gates with crowbars and other weapons.
They now "climbed the outside of the cell part, which
joined the two great wings," and Crabbe watched their
operations from a distance. "They broke the roof, .
tore away the rafters, and, having got ladders, they
descended. Not Orpheus himself had more courage
or better luck; flames all around them, and a body
of soldiers expected, they defied and laughed at all
opposition." They seized the prisoners by the hair,
the legs, the arms, by anything they could lay hold
of, dragged them upon the roof, and then set them at
liberty. Crabbe saw twelve women and eight men,
still "in their chains," pass before him; three of them
were to have been hanged on the following Friday.
All the malefactors in Newgate, to the number of three
hundred, escaped that evening. "You have no conception," writes Crabbe, "of the phrensy of the multitude." After the criminals, it was the debtors' turn to
be set free : the part of the building which contained
them was also invaded and set on fire, and ten or

twelve rioters, standing on the blazing roof, enveloped in a volume of black smoke and lighted up by a sudden outburst of flame, appeared to the poet to realise the vision of Milton's demons. Below, Akerman's house was now a mere shell, in which the incendiaries kept "a store of flame," and the walls becoming red-hot made "the doors and windows like the entrance to so many volcanoes."

Here Crabbe's Journal stops, several pages having been torn out. We do not know whether he witnessed the no less terrible scenes of the following day : the burning of the Langdale distillery at Holborn, in which men and women, stupefied by drink, were carbonised in pools of blazing alcohol, the destruction of three other prisons, the attack on the Bank of England, fortunately repulsed, the firing on the mob by the order of the King, the sanguinary repression of the riot.[1] But we may be certain that the sight of all these horrors, perpetrated by a maddened and almost barbarous populace, left on Crabbe's mind an indelible impression, which was subsequently deepened by the accounts of revolutionary excesses in France. He thus understood more clearly the necessity for an unquestioned hierarchy, for a strict social discipline, able to curb "the wild wish" and check "the strong desire."[2]

III

THE storm having passed over, and "patrons" remaining deaf to the poet's appeal, he had to set to work again and try once more to find readers. He had no lack of verses : his notebooks and drawers were full of the "idler things that soothed his hours of care";[3] tired of languishing on his "modest shelf," they longed to

---

[1] For further details of these events see Lecky, *History of England*, vol. iii. pp. 510 *seq.* (ed. 1890). It contains an excellent list of authorities, to which must be added a passage from Beavan's *James and Horace Smith*, pp. 29 *seq.*, and a letter from Ch. Burney, the father of Fanny, in Twining's *Recreations and Studies of a Country Clergyman*, pp. 80-4. Most of the particulars given in the text will be found in a small contemporary work, *A Plain and Succinct Narrative of the Late Riots and Disturbances in the Cities of London and Westminster*, 2nd ed. 1780, by William Vincent, of Gray's Inn (*i.e.* Thomas Holcroft). The reader will also call to mind Dickens's *Barnaby Rudge*.

[2] *Borough*, xiii. 83.

[3] *Works*, p. 576. "An Introductory Address of the Author to his Poems." As Crabbe knew no French at this time, there is probably no direct imitation of Boileau (épître x.) here.

fly to the publishers' shop-windows, "where princely
Popes and mighty Miltons lie." But he feared the
unknown dangers of publicity for them; he knew that,
once gone, they could no longer find a refuge in his
"tongueless mansion," and he hesitated to abandon
them all to the tender mercies of the critics. For then
"ye'll grieve," he apostrophises them—

> Ambition's plumage stript; . . .
> Your unsoil'd page each yawning wit shall flee, . . .
> Its place, where spiders silent bards enrobe,
> Squeezed between Cibber's Odes and Blackmore's Job;
> Then sent disgraced—the unpaid printer's bane—
> To mad Moorfields, or sober Chancery Lane,[1]
> On dirty stalls I see your hopes expire,
> Vex'd by the grin of your unheeded sire.

No, upon such dangerous ground one must venture
with prudence, send forward a "scout" who will
"view the strange land, and tell us of its worth"; if
he meets with "barbarian usage," this will be a warning
to retreat. This scout was *The Candidate*, an epistle
in verse to the authors of *The Monthly Review*,[2] of
which Crabbe managed, how and on what conditions
is unknown, to get two hundred and fifty copies
printed by John Nichols.[3]

Never was such naïve and clumsy humility seen
as in this anonymous poet. He is like an awkward
countryman in the middle of a drawing-room. With
downcast eyes, his hat in one hand, his manuscript in
the other, he solicits "the opinion of the candid and
judicious reader," and then turns to the authors of *The
Monthly Review*, "as critics of acknowledged merit, an
acquaintance with whose labours has afforded him a
reason for directing it to them in particular, and, he
presumes, will yield to others a just and sufficient
plea for the preference."[4] "I address you," he continues, "not because I have much to say, but because
I should like to know if, after hearing me, you think
me capable of saying something. I am not one of

---

[1] Where second-hand books were sold. Moorfields has become Finsbury.

[2] *Works*, p. 576. "The Candidate, a Poetical Epistle to the Authors of *The Monthly Review*, 4to, 1 sh. 6 p., H. Payne." Cf. *Gentleman's Magazine*, vol. l. p. 475.

[3] See *Bunbury Letter*. Nichols was chosen because he had "printed some remains of Dryden and other poets."

[4] "Preface to the Reader," *Works*, p. 577.

those, you will observe, who 'write enraptured,' who
'dream idle dreams and call them things of taste,'
who discover beauties 'in every paltry line,' who
'see, transported, every dull design,' and 'seldom
cautious, all advice detest.' Nor am I a 'supple
slave' who to 'regal pomp bows down, prostrate to
power, and cringing to a crown.' I am neither 'mad
nor mean,' neither a flatterer nor presumptuous. 'I
despise each extreme, and sail between.' I do not
long for the wings of Icarus, 'who flew too near the
sun'; I also dread the fate of him who, creeping along
the shore, is swept away by the waves and 'found no
more.' 'I hope for fame and dare avow my hope;
humbly at Learning's bar I state my case.' Above all,
I am circumspect, because misfortune has taught me
prudence, which has since then become my constant
attendant:

> Life's hopes ill-sped, the Muse's hopes grow poor,
> And though they flatter, yet they charm no more ;
> Experience points where lurking dangers lay,
> And, as I run, throws caution in my way." [1]

Yes, that is what the poet ought to tell us, and that
alone. Why does he not discard these incongruous
metaphors, these frigid antitheses, this schoolboy
rhetoric, and relate to us the dreams of his boyhood
and youth, the sufferings of his manhood? The
language of emotion would not fail him ; his strong
and simple diction would move his readers and his
critics ; his accents would be thrilling ; he would stand
upright ; he would abandon his ignominious attitude of
suppliant. But nothing is more difficult to discover
than the truth, which always lies hidden under the
artificial. The poet, imprisoned in the imitation of his
models, cannot burst his bonds unless inspiration gives
him superhuman strength. And Crabbe, at this particular juncture, is not inspired. If he wants to tell
us to what painful experience he owes his " prudence,"
he bethinks him of Addison's " visions," of Pope's
allegories in *Windsor Forest* or the *Dunciad*; and this
is what he invents : On a wintry night, when the wind
was raging, " hard by a ruin'd pile," covered with " moss,
its spreading beard," resounding with hollow echoes
and the hoots of fleeing owls, he has met " a sage," whose

---

[1] *Works*, p. 577, ll. 21-2, 31-2, 49, 57-61, 75-8, 83-8.

"threadbare coat the supple osier bound," his "breast bronzed by many an eastern blast," his head hoary, his frame bowed by "fourscore winters." He was a fisherman, it would appear, "pressing with slow feet the trodden ground," and the poet, whom white hairs always inspire with respect, accosted him deferentially. "Father," he said, "tell me the pains and pleasures of the poor. . . . There was a time "when, by Delusion led, a scene of sacred bliss around me spread," but now I resemble Moses, "who gazed upon the good he ne'er possessed":

> My Hope just spent requires a sad adieu,
> And Fear acquaints me I shall live with you.

"Son," answered the Sage—

> . . . Be this thy care suppress'd,
> The state the gods shall choose thee is the best. . . .
> But other thoughts within thy bosom reign, . . .
> Poetic wreaths thy vainer dreams excite,
> And thy sad stars have destined thee to write. . . .
> Be not too eager in the arduous chace : . . .
> Venture not all, but wisely hoard thy worth,
> And let thy labours one by one go forth ;
> Some happier scrap capricious wits may find,
> On a fair day, and be profusely kind ; . . .
> And watch the lucky Moment of Success.

Who is this fisherman endowed with such profound wisdom? No longer a man, but a god. All of a sudden the poet witnesses the transformation :

> His white locks changing to a golden hue,
> And from his shoulders hung a mantle azure blue. . . .
> Beauteous and young the smiling phantom stood,
> Then sought on airy wing his blest abode.[1]

Is all this parade necessary to express such a simple idea, and to express it so tamely? What prodigious efforts for such a poor result! And Crabbe, still timid, turns once more to the arbiters of taste. Do you think, he goes on, that "Hope may indulge her flight, and I succeed?" I do not covet "India's spoils, the splendid nabob's pride," nor all "the gold the Ganges laves or shrouds." May Virtue, "brighter than the noontide ray, my humble prayers with sacred

---

[1] *Candidate*, 89-162.

joys repay!" Let others sing the exploits of heroes,
of the "mighty Wolfe, who conquered as he fell," of
Rodney, "whose triumph comes on eagle wing": as
for me, I wish to chant the praise of divine Mercy, the
"softest attribute of Hope's and Thought's eternal
King." I would also sing, in many a fond and flowing
strain, of love, the unquestioned sovereign of my heart,
recall my schoolboy dreams, "of laughing girls in
smiling couplets tell, and paint the dark-brow'd grove,
where wood-nymphs dwell," and, lastly, describe that
radiant summer morn when first I heard the "syren-
song" of the Muse, "her magic felt, and all her charms
revered":

> May she not hope in future days to soar
> Where Fancy's sons have led the way before? [1]

Here unquestionably is a poet animated by the
best intentions. He loves piety and virtue more than
money; if the critics have no objection, he will sing
the praises of the Deity and of Mira; he who once
described, not without some vigour, the noisy gaiety
of village topers, is bent on trying some innocent
pastoral under an Arcadian sky. He will endeavour
to adorn his lines with all the elegances of Pope's
rhetoric and style, will be lavish of personified abstractions,[2] of plays on words and alliterations,[3] will
introduce the Bible in one line and mythology in the
next. If the authors of *The Monthly Review* are not
satisfied with so much modesty and readiness to
oblige, they must be hard to please.

Their reply was not long in coming; a month, probably, after the publication of the poem[4] its author was
informed that "his rhymes were not always regulated

---

[1] *Candidate*, 166-335.

[2] "Ambition's plumage" (*Introductory Address*, p. 576, 13), "Fancy's
bow" (*ibid.* 43), "Genius' wings" (*ibid.* 44), "Fame, Envy, Fate"
(*Candidate*, p. 579, 217-18), etc., etc.

[3] *Candidate*, p. 577, 36:
> But he whose soul . . .
> Nor meanly flatters power, nor madly flies.

P. 579, 219:
> Crimson'd fields, where Fate, in dire array,
> Gives to the *breathless*, the *short-breathing* clay.

[4] *The Candidate* was, I think, composed in June and July, and printed in
August, 1780 (and not "early in 1780," as the Biographer says at p. 15). The
articles in *The Monthly Review* and *The Critical Review*, which both appeared
in September (and not in August, B. p. 25), must have followed very closely
on the publication.

by the purest standard of pronunciation,[1] but that these
petty blemishes might be removed in a future edition,"
and that in that case he might also correct an essential
defect, "the want of a subject to make a proper and
forcible impression on the mind." This was some of
the "mutilated praise" which Crabbe had declined
beforehand,[2] but he found it preferable to the ironical
castigation [3] inflicted on him by the rivals of *The
Monthly Review*, the formidable judges of *The Critical
Review*, who wrote as follows: "The anonymous
author of this Poetical Epistle is, it seems, an unfortunate gentleman who, having long laboured under a
cacoethes scribendi, humbly requests the advice and
assistance of Dr. G—— [4] and his brethren of the faculty
concerned in *The Monthly Review*. The patient, it is
observable, takes no notice of us Critical Reviewers,
though we have been pretty famous for eradicating
disorders of this kind. . . . Although we have received
no fee, we shall give our advice gratis. Temperance
in this, as in almost every other case, is the grand
specific : we shall confine our prescription, therefore,
in a very few words ; viz. *Abstine a pluma et atramento*."
Then follow a number of quotations, which the writer
tries to turn into ridicule, and of objections, which are
often well-founded.[5] In conclusion, this smart critic

---

[1] For instance, shone-moon (p. 579, l. 266-7), gods-abodes (*ibid.* 304-5),
licences which, however, are less objectionable than the following : stoop-hope
(p. 576, l. 45-6, and p. 577, l. 41-2), road-good (p. 580, l. 326-7).
[2] *Works* (p. 580, l. 360).
[3] Third letter to Burke (Appendix I) : "My patrons spoke of my poem
rather favourably ; but Messrs. the Critical Reviewers trimmed me handsomely."
[4] Dr. Griffiths, Goldsmith's exacting "employer," who founded *The
Monthly Review* in 1749.
[5] For instance, awkward expressions, such as (p. 579, l. 217) :
    Heroes born . . .
    Whom Fame anoints, and Envy tends whose grave ;
or (*ibid.* l. 257) :
    Nor Flattery's silver tale, nor Sorrow's sage (tale) ;
not to mention grammatical mistakes which the critic omits to point out—p. 579,
l. 277 :
    Such is that sound, which fond designs convey (*for* conveys) ;
p. 579, l. 316 :
    Let those whose ill-used wealth their country fly (*for* flies) ;
or a painfully inappropriate expression like the following (p. 577, l. 51) :
    As busy thought her wild creation apes,
that is probably "imitates," "draws."
On the other hand, *The Critical Review* very unjustly censures one of the
best lines of the passage in which Crabbe describes the "summer morning,"
which the apparition of the Muse made so radiant for him. He is at the

expresses the opinion that if this Candidate sets up
for the borough of Parnassus, he will most probably
lose his election, as he does not seem to be possessed
of a foot of land in that county "—an ingenious witticism
which a third review, *The Gentleman's Magazine*,
reproduced a month later.[1] Can we wonder if articles
of this kind deterred the public from buying this very
mediocre poem and discouraged the author? In a
year's time the two hundred and fifty copies printed
by Nichols were probably still in Payne's (the publisher's) shop.[2] They had met with the fate which
Crabbe dreaded so much : they had joined the ranks
of " the unpaid printer's bane."

IV

THERE remained another resource : in default of a
public, the poet, who learned prudence from these
repeated humiliations, might perhaps find subscribers
to a new work, and thus obtain a little money for
himself, and some security for his future publisher.
He selected, from among all his manuscripts, a piece
composed in the preceding year at Aldborough, to
which he afterwards gave the name of *The Library*,[3]
circulated prospectuses among his acquaintance,
especially at Beccles, and easily obtained from Lord
Rochford, a neighbour of Mr. Tovell,[4] permission to

sea-side, near "a crumbling ruin, once a city's pride " (p. 579, l. 281 ; the
place is evidently Dunwich—see above, p. 36) :

> The glowing east in crimson'd splendour shone,
> What time the eye just marks the pallid moon. . . .
> The vivid dew hung trembling on the thorn,
> And mists, like creeping rocks, arose to meet the morn (p. 579, ll. 266-72).

The critic, who no doubt had never crossed the Channel and been caught in a
bank of fog, cannot understand mists being compared to rocks, and especially
to " creeping rocks."

[1] October number (vol. l. p. 475), quoted by B. p. 16.

[2] At least this is what appears from a passage in the third letter to Burke
(Appendix I) : " 250 copies . . . which I believe are now [June 26th,
1781] in the warehouse of Mr. Payne the bookseller, as I never heard of any
sale they had," which would seem to prove that Crabbe made a mistake when,
in his Autobiographical Sketch of 1816, quoted by B. p. 15, he attributed his
disappointment to a supposed bankruptcy of Payne.

[3] Appendix I : " I am desired to send my poem in whatever manner
it comes out . . . " This explains two expressions in the first letter to Burke
(B. p. 26) which have hitherto remained obscure : " . . . my little work . . .
copies of the enclosed Proposals."

[4] See above, p. 48. Lord Rochford was also the brother of R. Savage
Nassau, whom Crabbe knew and who had represented Malden in the House of
Commons.

dedicate to him a book "free from all political
allusions and personal abuse." But this ungenerous
nobleman took care to inform the poet that he must
rely not so much on the dedication as on the merit
of his work to extricate himself from his difficulties.
At Beccles the Elmy family, by means of its connections, got together about one hundred and fifty
subscribers. This was enough to start printing.
Unfortunately, little progress was made, and Crabbe
soon perceived that the expense would be too great to
leave him any profit. Nothing could be expected from
this undertaking.

All his hopes had vanished in succession. Already,
at the end of May, 1780, we have seen him reduced to
the last expedients, and we should not so much as
know how he managed to reach, even with difficulty,
the month of February, 1781, if he had not revealed the
secret in one of his letters to Burke.[1] He was relieved
by a devoted hand, by Mira herself. "From the family
at Beccles," he writes, "I have every mark of attention,
and every proof of their disinterested regard. They
have from time to time supplied me with such sums as
they could possibly spare, and that they have not done
more arose from my concealing the severity of my
situation, for I would not involve in my errors or
misfortunes a very generous and very happy family by
which I am received with unaffected sincerity, and
where I am treated as a son by a mother who can have
no prudential reason to rejoice that her daughter has
formed such a connection." But this assistance, in-
valuable as it was to him, could not support him long
in his struggle with obscurity and want : towards the
end of February the time was drawing near when,
as at Aldborough ten months previously, he would be
obliged to admit his defeat. His landlord and the
clear-sighted Mrs. Vickery, being aware of his poverty
and believing him to be friendless, cheated him, persecuted him with their insults and their threats, and had
forced him to sign a promissory note for seven pounds
on pain of being arrested for a debt of about fourteen
pounds which he owed them. When the note fell
due, he was unable to pay. It was in vain that he had
written to Beccles—Mrs. Elmy was too poor to supply
him with this sum; it was in vain that he had explained

[1] The third, or "Bunbury," Letter. See Appendix I.

his situation to Lord Rochford, requesting him to advance the amount for one month, until the money derived from the subscriptions came in. He had received no reply, and was afraid of having offended the Earl by his insistence. He had been obliged to admit his insolvency, to beg, to implore even a week's delay, which had been granted him as a special favour. He knew that at the expiration of these few days he would have to go to gaol. He could not reproach himself with anything but his imprudence and his temerity, caused, and to some extent excused, by his inexperience; he thought that if his circumstances were known, somebody would come to his assistance.[1] He resolved to apply to the man who, among all his contemporaries, appeared to him to combine the most brilliant qualities: by a happy thought, he wrote to Edmund Burke, "one of the first of Englishmen, and, in the capacity and energy of his mind, one of the greatest of human beings."[2]

This time Crabbe's petition was destined to find a hearing. His letter, the manuscript of which has come down to us,[3] is not dated; it was delivered, I believe, towards the end of February or the beginning of March, 1781, at the house which Burke then occupied in Charles Street, near St. James's Square.[4] It is straightforward and full of genuine emotion, with no presumption or excessive humility; we feel that the poet is speaking to a man of letters in whom he has confidence, and no longer to a nobleman whose title and influence had intimidated and dazzled him. In a few words he relates the trials of his youth and his disappointments in London. "I am sensible," he writes, "that I need even your talents to apologise for the freedom I now take; but I have a plea which, however simply urged, will, with a mind like yours, Sir, procure me pardon: I am one of those outcasts on the world who are without a friend, without employment, and without bread. . . . I had a partial father, who gave me a better education than his broken fortune would have allowed; and a better than was necessary, as he could give me that only. I was designed for the

---

[1] See first and third letters to Burke (B. p. 26; and Appendix I).
[2] *Autobiographical Sketch* (1816), quoted by B. p. 25.
[3] It now belongs to Mr. Broadley. A facsimile of it is given herewith.
[4] Morley's *Life of Burke* (English Men of Letters), ed. 1889, p. 87.

I am sensible that it requires your Talents to appolo
give for the Freedom I now take but I have a Plea
which however simply urged will with a Mind
like yours Sir procure me Pardon; I am one of those out
casts on the World who are without a Friend without
Imployment & without Bread. Pardon me a short Preface
I had a partial Father who gave me a better Education
than his broken Fortune would have allow'd & a better
than was necessary as he could give me that only.
I was design'd for the Profession of Physic, but not
having sufficient to compleat the requisite Studies,
the Design but served to convince me of a Parent's Affection, & the Error it occasion'd. In April last
I came to London with 5£ & flatter'd myself it was
sufficient to supply me with the common Necessaries
of Life, til such my Abilities shou'd procure me
more; of these I had the highest Opinion & a poetical Vanity contributed to my Delusion; I knew little
of the World & had read Books only; I wrote &
fancied Perfection in my Compositions, when I
wanted Bread they promised me Affluence, &
sooth'd me with Dreams of Reputation, whilst
my Appearance subjected me to Contempt.

Some Reflection, & Want, have shewn me my
Mistake; I see my Trifles in that which I think
the true Light; & whilst I deem them such, have yet
have yet the Opinion that holds them Superior
to the ordinary run of Poetical Publications
P I had some Knowledge of the late Mr. Nassau
the Brother of Lord Rochford; in consequence of
which I ask'd his Lordship's Permission to inscribe
my little Work to him. Knowing it to be free from
all Political Allusions & personal Abuse it was no very
material Point to me to whom it was dedicated; His
Lordship thought it none to him & obligingly consented
to my Request —

I was told that a [...] would be the more profitable method to [...] before endeavour'd to
circulate Copies of the enclosed Proposals. —
I am afraid Sir I disgust you with this very dull
Narrative, but believe me punish'd in the Misery
that occasions it — You will conclude that during
this Time I must be at more expence than I could
afford, indeed the most Parsimonious could not have
avoided it. The Printer deceived me & my little
Business has had every Delay. The People with whom
I live perceive my situation & tend me to be indi-
-gent & without Friends. — about ten Days since I
was compell'd to give a Note for y.e to avoid an
Arrest for about double that Sum, which I owe; I
wrote to every friend I had, but my friends are p
likewise; the time of Payment approach'd & I wrote
to represent my case to Lord Rochford; I begg'd to be
credited for this Sum til I received it of my Subs
=bers which I believe will be within a Month; to this
Letter I had no Reply & I have probably offended by my Impor
=tunity. Having used every honest means [...]
confess'd my Inability & obtain'd with much entreaty & a
the greatest favor a Week's forbearance, when I am positi
=ly told that I must pay the Money or prepare for a Pris
You will guess the Purpose of so long an Introduction; I ap
=peal to You Sir as a good & let me add a great Man
I have no other Pretensions to your favor than that I am
an unhappy One. It is not easy to support the Thought
of Confinement & I am coward enough to dread the
an End to my Suspense

    Can you Sir in any Degree aid me with Prop
will you ask any Demonstrations of my Veracity? I have
=posed upon myself but I have been guilty of no other I
=position. Let me if possible interest your Compassi
I know those of Rank & fortune are teized with freq
Petitions & are compell'd to refuse the Requests of Men w

...they know to be in [...] it is therefore with a reluctant hope I venture to solicit such favor; but you will forgive me Sir if you do not think proper to relieve [...] is impossible that Sentiments like Yours can proceed from any but an humane & generous Heart

I will call upon You Sir tomorrow & if I have not [...] Happiness to obtain credit with you, I will [...] to my tale. My Existence is Pain to me, & every one near & dear to me are distress'd in my Distresses; my Connections once the Source of Happiness now embitter the Reverse of my Fortune; & I have only to hope a speedy End to a life so unpromisingly begun: In which (tho' it ought not to be boasted of) I can reap some Consolation from looking to the End of it.

I am Sir with the greatest Respect
Your Obedient
& most humble Servant
George Crabbe

Edmond Burke Esq.r
1781

profession of physic; but not having sufficient to
complete the requisite studies, the design but served
to convince me of a parent's affection, and the error
it occasioned. In April last I came to London with
three pounds, and flattered myself it was sufficient
to supply me with the common necessaries of life
till my abilities should procure me more; of these
I had the highest opinion, and a poetical vanity contributed to my delusion. I knew little of the world,
and had read books only : I wrote, and fancied perfection in my compositions ; when I wanted bread, they
promised me affluence, and soothed me with dreams
of reputation, whilst my appearance subjected me to
contempt. Time, reflection, and want have shown me
my mistake. I see my trifles in that which I think the
true light ; and whilst I deem them such, have yet the
opinion that holds them superior to the ordinary run
of poetical publications."

Lord Rochford's silence and his landlord's demands
have reduced him to despair. " You will guess," he
continues, " the purpose of so long an introduction.
I appeal to you, Sir, as a good and, let me add, a great
man. I have no other pretensions to your favour than
that I am an unhappy one. It is not easy to support
the thoughts of confinement ; and I am coward enough
to dread such an end to my suspense. Can you, Sir,
in any degree, aid me with propriety? Will you ask
any demonstrations of my veracity? I have imposed
upon myself, but I have been guilty of no other impo-
sition. Let me, if possible, interest your compassion.
I know those of rank and fortune are teased with
frequent petitions, and are compelled to refuse the
requests of men whom they know to be in distress :
it is, therefore, with a distant hope I venture to
solicit such favour ; but you will forgive me, Sir, if
you do not think proper to relieve. It is impossible
that sentiments like yours can proceed from any but
a humane and generous heart. I will call upon you,
Sir, to-morrow, and if I have not the happiness to
obtain credit with you, I must submit to my fate.
My existence is a pain to me, and every one near and
dear to me are distressed in my distresses. My connections, once the source of happiness, now embitter
the reverse of my fortune, and I have only to hope a
speedy end to a life so unpromisingly begun : in which

(though it ought not to be boasted of) I can reap some
consolation from looking to the end of it. I am, Sir,
with the greatest respect, your obedient and most
humble servant." After having delivered this letter,
together with a copy of *The Library* and of his pro-
spectus, Crabbe, a prey to uncontrollable agitation,
spent the night in walking up and down Westminster
Bridge.[1]

His fate was wholly in the hands of the orator and
writer who for the last fifteen years had gained a constantly increasing influence over Parliament and the
public.[2] Without ever having held high office, Burke
none the less remains the most illustrious of English
statesmen in the eighteenth century. He is the only
one whose speeches retain a permanent interest, independent of the quarrels of the moment, the only one
whose pamphlets are inspired by political principles
and doctrines of a universal application. These rare
qualities of his writings are due, not only to the vigour
of his thought and the extent of his knowledge, but
also to the richness of his nature and the beauty of his
character. Few men possessed in such a high degree
the most exquisite, the most dangerous also, of all the
gifts of heart and intellect—the sympathetic imagination which enables its owner, by intuition alone, to put
himself in the place of others, to feel and to think in
unison with minds differing most widely from his own.
From 1774 to 1777 he had supported, with as much
eloquence as disinterestedness and clearsightedness,
the cause of the American colonists in their revolt
against the meddlesome impotence of George III. and
Lord North; in 1788 he was to constitute himself the
champion of the Hindus, who had been ground down,
defrauded and massacred by the pitiless proconsul
Warren Hastings; and if, later on, he condemned the
French Revolution with a passion which sometimes
amounted to fury, it was not only because that popular
upheaval seemed to him the rushing to perdition of a
society carried away by violence, but also because he

---

[1] At least this is what he declared, forty-one years later, to Sir Walter
Scott; cf. the letter from Lockhart (B. p 79): "The night after I had
delivered my letter at his door, I was in such a state of agitation that I walked
Westminster Bridge backwards and forwards until daylight."

[2] " Perhaps, if we were to point out the period of his life when he stood on
the highest ground as a public man, in the estimation of all parties, we should
name the year 1781," says Wraxall, in his *Historical Memoirs*, ed. 1904, p. 354.

had once, in the chapel at Versailles, gazed upon the future Queen Marie Antoinette, then resplendent with youth and beauty. He was at once chivalrous and realistic, an opportunist and an enthusiast. He had made his start in the career of letters before entering political life ; he had been acquainted with Goldsmith and was in the habit of meeting Johnson : he knew the trials they had gone through to win their fame. No one was better prepared to lend a kindly ear to the poet's petition and to give a sympathetic welcome to the poet himself. When Crabbe presented himself on the following day, he was received and assisted. His debts were evidently paid and funds advanced to enable him to resume his work. Burke had "saved him from sinking," and was about to guide his first steps along the shore.[1]

V

AN enlightened patron and a kind critic, Burke began by reading "a large quantity of miscellaneous compositions which the young man submitted with timidity, indeed, but with the strong and buoyant expectation of inexperience."[2] He proved an impartial judge, who soon taught the poet to appreciate his writings at their proper value, and, at the same time, a friend full of sympathy and consideration, who, " in the very act of condemnation, found something for praise." Crabbe sometimes had the satisfaction of being told that, " if his verses were bad, his thoughts deserved better, and that if he had the common faults of inexperienced writers, he had frequently the merit of thinking for himself." From among all these manuscripts Burke selected *The Library* for speedy publication, a poem which had long been promised to the Beccles subscribers.[3] He advised the author to touch it up, and on March 27th Crabbe sends him " the poem in its former state," as well as a corrected copy, to be

---

[1] Second letter to Burke, dated March 27th, 1781.
[2] *Autobiographical Sketch*, quoted by B. p. 27.
[3] B. p. 27 (*Autobiographical Sketch*) : " Among those compositions were two poems of somewhat a superior kind, *The Library* and *The Village*; these were selected by Mr. Burke." This was written by Crabbe himself in 1816, but it seems highly probable that only a few isolated lines, and not even a general sketch of *The Village*, existed in March, 1781. None of the letters of 1781 mention *The Village*.

printed as soon as Burke has read it and a publisher has been found.[1]

Two months passed, during a part of which Crabbe, leaving his garret in Bishopsgate Street, lived at Beccles with the Elmys, added about fifty names to the list of his subscribers, and put the finishing touches to his composition. On his return to London he wrote to Burke, on June 26th, that " he will wait upon him as soon as possible with a fresh copy of his poem, correct as he has power to make it."[2] Burke, on his side, using his influence in favour of his *protégé*, had himself brought the manuscript of *The Library* to the publisher Dodsley and had taken the trouble to read and comment on a good many passages. " Mr. Dodsley," says Crabbe in his *Autobiographical Sketch*,[3] " listened with all the respect due to the reader of the verses, and all the apparent desire to be pleased that could be wished by the writer. . . . ' He declined the venturing upon anything himself: there was no judging of the probability of success. The taste of the town was exceedingly capricious and uncertain. He paid the greatest respect to Mr. Burke's opinion that the verses were good, and he did in part think so himself, but he declined the hazard of publication, yet would do all he could for Mr. Crabbe and his poem.' " The meaning of which was that the prudent Dodsley did not care about buying *The Library*, but was ready to print it for the two hundred subscribers. On these terms the poem appeared on July 24th,[4] and the "worthy" publisher, mindful of his promise, pushed the sale of the little quarto so well as to insure it a certain success. Although very fond of money, he even went so far as to make over to Crabbe his profits as a publisher and vendor of the work.

The Library is one of those descriptive, didactic, and satirical poems of which the eighteenth century was so prolific in England as well as in France. No symptom

---

[1] Second letter to Burke, dated " B. Street, March 27, 1781 " (published in *The Correspondence of the Rt. Hon. Edm. Burke*, edited by Earl Fitzwilliam and Lieutenant-General Sir Richard Bourke, in 4 vols. 1844, vol. ii. pp. 413-15).

[2] *Bunbury Letter* (Appendix I).

[3] Quoted by B. p. 27.

[4] In June, according to B.; cf. *Works*, p. 101, n. 1: " *The Library* appeared anonymously in June, 1781." But on June 26th (*Bunbury Letter*) Crabbe was still engaged in correcting it, and we read in *The Public Advertiser* of July 24th: " This day is published, 4°, 2 sh., The Library, a Poem."

better reveals the decay and the perversion of poetic feeling than the choice of such subjects and this melancholy production of insipid copies or indirect imitations of the *Georgics*. It may be said that Virgil, misunderstood, had a pernicious influence on the English literature of that time. He suggested to writers that a certain number of descriptions, accompanied by a few precepts and embellished by extravagant digressions, might constitute a poem. His unfaithful imitators forgot this truth—that " all verbal description, though never so exact," cannot have the smallest effect if the writer does not use language "which marks a strong and lively feeling in himself."[1] They consequently too often chose subjects incapable of producing the faintest emotion in themselves or their readers.[2] It was thus that the facetious John Philips took it into his head that it would be original to sing the properties of "cider" and the culture of the apple in Miltonian lines. The fumes of the yellow liquor inspired him with a poetical intoxication of the most placid kind. Half a century later, poor Christopher Smart lost his way in his *Hop Garden* and left us asleep there ; the highly respectable English clergyman John Dyer, landscape-painter in his unemployed moments, offered to teach us the art of breeding and shearing sheep, and the ingenuous James Grainger, doctor of medicine, on his arrival in the Antilles, conceived and carried out the plan of "writing a poem on the culture of the sugar-cane." We need not wonder, then, if Crabbe, encouraged by these examples, resolved to describe a library. The subject had, at any rate, the merit of novelty.

Let us follow this poet-librarian who constitutes himself our guide ; let us contemplate with him "this spacious scene, this sacred dome, this noble magazine" of intellectual treasures ;[3] let us wander with a religious

---

[1] Burke, *Essay on the Sublime and Beautiful* (1756) (Cassell's National Library, 1891), p. 191.

[2] Almost the only exceptions are a few passages of Falçoner's *Shipwreck* and the greater part of Somerville's *The Chase*.

[3] I quote from the text of the first (anonymous) edition, the lines of which I have numbered. *The Library* has come down to us in three forms : the first, dating, I believe, from 1779, is that of Mr. Murray's manuscript, of which the Biographer has reproduced (sometimes inaccurately) certain fragments (cf. the notes in the *Works*, pp. 101-5, 108, 110-11) ; the second is that of the edition of 1781 (reproduced in the second edition of 1783, signed by Crabbe) ; the third, that of 1807, reprinted in the *Works* (pp. 101-13). In Appendix II will be found a comparison of the two texts of 1781 and 1807.

respect through these silent avenues peopled with the
lasting monuments of the dead :

> "The dead !" methinks a thousand tongues reply ;
> "These are the tombs of such as cannot die !
> Crown'd with eternal fame, they sit sublime,
> And laugh at all the little strife of time."

Hail then to those immortals who, each in his sphere,
shine like a Jove of letters ! hail also to the stars of the
second magnitude, the humbler crowd of nameless
deities who trod the mazes of history and science, of
philosophy and poetry ! Let us look at their works,
which " all in silence, all in order stand " before us :

> The mighty folios first, a lordly band ;
> Then quartos their well-order'd ranks maintain,
> And light octavos fill a spacious plain :
> See yonder, ranged in more frequented rows,
> A humbler band of duodecimos ;
> While undistinguish'd trifles swell the scene,
> The last new play and fritter'd magazine. . . .
> First let us view the form, the size, the dress ;
> For these the manners, nay, the mind express : [1]
> That weight of wood, with leathern coat o'erlaid ;
> Those ample clasps, of solid metal made ;
> The close-press'd leaves, unclosed for many an age ;
> The dull red edging of the well-fill'd page ;
> On the broad back the stubborn ridges roll'd,
> Where yet the title stands in tarnished gold ;
> These all a sage and labour'd work proclaim.
> A painful candidate for lasting fame ;
> No idle wit, no trifling verse can lurk
> In the deep bosom of that weighty work ;
> No playful thoughts degrade the solemn style,
> Nor one light sentence claims a transient smile,
> Hence, in these times, untouch'd the pages lie,
> And slumber out their immortality. . . .
> Ah ! needless now their weight of massy chain ;
> Safe in themselves, the once-loved works remain ; . . .
> Abstracts, abridgments, please the fickle times,
> Pamphlets and plays, and politics and rhymes.[2]

The reason of this is that we read mainly to divert
our minds. Here the poet, leaving his exact but frigid
descriptions, turns didactic, and a little emotion trembles

---

[1] *Works*, pp. 104, 143-56. The whole of this passage was added in 1807,
as well as ll. 157-78. It is perhaps the most remarkable of the whole poem.
[2] *Ibid.* p. 104, ll. 157-8, 173-4, 195-6.

in his voice. Without our having perceived it, perhaps,
he proceeds to speak of himself:

> When the sad soul, by care and grief oppress'd,
> Looks round the world, but looks in vain for rest ;
> When every object that appears in view,
> Partakes her gloom and seems dejected too ; . . .
> Alas ! we fly to silent scenes in vain ;
> Care blasts the honours of the flow'ry plain ;
> Care veils in clouds the sun's meridian beam,
> Sighs through the grove, and murmurs in the stream. . . .
> . . . in the calms of life we only see
> A steadier image of our misery,
> But lively gales and gently clouded skies
> Disperse the sad reflections as they rise ;
> And busy thoughts and little cares avail
> To ease the mind, when rest and reason fail.

In that case, where are we to find those " lenient cares "
which, with our own combined, will—

> Steal our grief away, and leave their own behind,
> A lighter grief ! which feeling hearts endure
> Without regret, nor e'en demand a cure ?

Those precious consolers, those physicians of the
soul, for ourselves as well as for the poet, " will be
books." By showing us misfortunes worse than our
own, they will reconcile us with our destiny ; better
still, they will open new prospects to us and " teach us
how to live." Sincere friends and always accessible
to all, " they fly not sullen from the suppliant crowd,"
and " show to subjects what they show to kings." [1]
After making these sage reflections, the Librarian
returns to his shelves and discusses his books once
more—not their outward form this time, but their
contents. He pauses complacently before the works
of Science and of Moral Philosophy, shows us a volume
of Botany, and, in a style which gives a foretaste of
Erasmus Darwin,[2] describes the generation of plants:

> Whose fruitful beds o'er every balmy mead
> Teem with new life ; and hills, and vales, and groves,
> Feed the still flame, and nurse the silent loves ; . . .
> There, with the husband-slaves, in royal pride,
> Queens, like the Amazons of old, reside ;
> There, like the Turk, the lordly husband lives,
> And joy to all the gay seraglio gives ;

---

[1] *Works*, p. 101, ll. 1-50.
[2] Whose *Loves of the Plants* appeared in 1789.

> There, in the secret chambers, veil'd from sight,
> A bashful tribe in hidden flames delight;
> There, in the open day and gaily deck'd,
> The bolder brides their distant lords expect;
> Who with the wings of love instinctive rise,
> And on prolific wings each ardent bridegroom flies.[1]

At the apex of creation, man arrests our gaze by the mystery of his moral nature and the spectacle of his passions. Here are books in which, " at little price," inexperience can buy " the wisdom of the wise"; here we see how some, " won by virtue, glow with sacred fire," and others, " lured by vice, indulge the low desire," while the majority, sometimes virtuous and sometimes vicious, are " ever wretched, with themselves at strife." Truly, our Librarian seems to be a singular poet: all his enthusiasm has been spent on the natural sciences, and now that he begins to speak of man and of the other branches of human knowledge, he indulges his turn for satire. Not that he tries to imitate Pope or Boileau, to attack poor books or personal enemies: his criticism, of a very general and abstract order, is aimed not at men, but at mankind. You think yourselves very wise, he seems to say to us, because you have collected a vast number of volumes under this roof; you are quite wrong—they are almost all useless. Look at these piles of books on Medicine:

> Glorious their aim—to ease the labouring heart,
> To war with death, and stop his flying dart:
> But man . . .
> Oft finds a poison where he sought a cure ;
> For grave deceivers lodge their labours here,
> And cloud the science they pretend to clear. . . .
> What thought so wild, what airy dream so light,
> That will not prompt a theorist to write ?
> What art so prevalent, what proof so strong,
> That will convince him his attempt is wrong ? . . .
> Some have their favourite ills, and each disease
> Is but a younger branch that kills from these :
> One to the gout contracts all human pain,
> He views it raging in the frantic brain,
> Finds it in fevers all his efforts mar,
> And sees it lurking in the cold catarrh.

---

[1] *Library*, 1st ed. ll. 167-82, reprinted by B. p. 106, n. 26. He himself points out a resemblance between Darwin and the lines 310-17 of the edition of 1807, without being aware that the latter are the old ones recast and of a much later date than Darwin's (*Works*, p. 106, n. 28).

All of them are "truth's destructive foes," whose "stupid prose" will mislead us as it has misled the poet. Works on Law are just as unsatisfactory, those "huge abridgments" which, as numerous as our vices, "spread their guardian terrors round the land":

> Knaves stand secure, for whom these laws were made, . . .
> And Justice vainly each expedient tries.

Theology itself will not be a safer guide for us, whether we consult the pious works of the divines who "vigils advise, and yet dispose to sleep," or whether we lose ourselves in endless controversies of doctors, "wolves in their vengeance, in their manners sheep, . . . who friend from friend and sire from son divide." Let us rejoice to see their Zeal "sleeping soundly by the foes she fought":

> Calvin grows gentle in this silent coast,
> Nor finds a single heretic to roast ;
> Here, their fierce rage subdued, and lost their pride,
> The Pope and Luther slumber side by side.

If we pass to History and examine the volumes in which "every nation its dread tale supplies," we shall see that she too "has her doubts," and that "every age with sceptic queries marks the passing page":

> Records of old nor later date are clear,
> Too distant those, and these are placed too near,

so that the real aspect of things is hidden from us, either by time, or by our passions and those of the writer. And if we could know the truth, what a melancholy spectacle is that of a state which, long "guarded by virtue," reaches the summit of its glory only to "sink to slavery again." The history of mankind resembles that of Rome—it is a continual and inevitable decay. After all this, of what avail is the support given to morality by "the profane delusions of the stage," the tears which Tragedy draws from us, the indignation which she arouses against vice, the feeble darts which Comedy in vain launches against folly ? Of what use are the "ancient worthies of

Romance,"[1] the fabulous exploits in which childhood alone can take pleasure ?

> . . . lost, for ever lost, to me these joys,
> Which Reason scatters, and which Time destroys,
> Too dearly bought : maturer judgment calls
> My busied mind from tales and madrigals ;
> My doughty giants all are slain or fled,
> And all my knights—blue, green, and yellow—dead !
> No more the midnight fairy tribe I view
> All in the merry moonshine tippling dew ;
> E'en the last lingering fiction of the brain,
> The churchyard ghost, is now at rest again.
> And all these wayward wanderings of my youth
> Fly Reason's power, and shun the Light of truth.

The Librarian now comes to the Critics, and is seized with terror at the sight of such an army of foes. He remembers all at once certain reviews which trounced him in the preceding year, when he made his first venture in poetry. For our guide is a poet, although owing to timidity, or perhaps ignorance, he tells us nothing of his art. But now he will show us his ability by constructing one of those ingenious machines which "the sons of Imagination" felt bound to invent in those days :

> Pensive I spoke, and cast my eyes around ;
> The roof, methought, return'd a solemn sound ;
> Each column seemed to shake, and clouds, like smoke,
> From dusty piles and ancient volumes broke ;
> Gathering above, like mists condensed they seem,
> Exhaled in summer from the rushy stream ;
> Like flowing robes they now appear, and twine
> Round the large members of a form divine ;
> His silver beard, that swept his aged breast,
> His piercing eye, that inward light express'd,
> Were seen,—but clouds and darkness veil'd the rest.

It is the "Genius of the place" who thus appears to us. Addressing the poet, he delivers himself of these remarkable words :

> Care lives with all ; no rules, no precepts save
> The wise from woe, no fortitude the brave ; . . .
> Partial to talents, then, shall Heav'n withdraw
> Th' afflicting rod, or break the general law ?

---

[1] The passage has been quoted above (pp. 39-40).

> Shall he who soars, inspired by loftier views,
> Life's little cares and little pains refuse?
> Shall he not rather feel a double share
> Of mortal woe, when doubly arm'd to bear?

For, in his case, "every wound the tortured bosom feels,"

> Or virtue bears, or some preserver heals;
> Some generous friend of ample power possess'd;
> Some feeling heart, that bleeds for the distress'd;
> Some breast that glows with virtues all divine;
> Some noble RUTLAND, misery's friend and thine. . . .
> Go on, then, Son of Vision! still pursue
> Thy airy dreams; the world is dreaming too.
> Ambition's lofty views, the pomp of state,
> The pride of wealth, the splendour of the great,
> Are visions far less happy than thy own;
> Go on! and, while the sons of care complain,
> Be wisely gay and innocently vain;
> Blow sportive bladders in the beamy sun,
> And call them worlds![1]

What matter if they are illusions! They will bring happiness to the poet, and give some pleasure to his readers. Crabbe could not have composed his work more harmoniously, since the conclusion brings us back to the beginning.

Such is, in its essentials, this poem of *The Library*, which cannot be denied the merit of originality in the choice of subject, of clearness of arrangement and much ingenuity in development, of real amplitude and elegance of style in a few passages, and, lastly, of a satirical power which makes certain lines as incisive as epigrams. But it was almost throwing down a challenge to poetic inspiration to ask it to feel emotion in describing shelves full of books, in depreciating almost all human knowledge, except natural science, in defining poetry itself as an illusion or an innocent pastime. It was deliberately drying up the source of enthusiasm, giving up all thought of touching the reader in an attempt to obtain the approval of his intellect and his taste only. Crabbe, not being really moved himself, remains a critic and a satirist. He had not as yet, perhaps he never had, that love of books which inspired a man of learning like Southey

[1] *Library*, 1st ed. ll. 197-611.

with the tender accents of the most delicate of his lyric poems. He could not say to us, with the recluse of Keswick :

> My days among the Dead are past,
>   Around me I behold,
> Where'er these casual eyes are cast,
>   The mighty minds of old ;
> My never-failing friends are they
> With whom I converse day by day.[1]

Crabbe was far more of an observer than a reader. If he wished, like Southey, to " leave a name that would not perish in the dust," he gave this aspiration a purely intellectual and slightly ironical form, which did not allow the idea to develop into a feeling meet for song.[2] His lines have the force and the clearness of his reason, but also its coldness. They interest us not so much in themselves as by what they tell us of their author : his struggles, at last victorious, with poverty, his study of the natural sciences, especially of botany, his contempt for the works on medicine which made him waste so many precious years, his youthful taste for romances and his sly criticism of their absurdities, his irresistible turn for satirical poetry, and his want of enthusiasm. But it is clear that this revelation of the author in his work, which is visible to us to-day, must have escaped the first readers of this anonymous poem, who gave Crabbe a *succès d'estime* and nothing more. Horace Walpole, in a letter dated September 4th, 1781, states that he has read *The Library* and found some pretty and easy lines in it, but that the whole poem seems to him too long.[3] *The Critical Review* for August said : " A vein of good sense and philosophic reflection runs through this little performance, which distinguishes it from most modern poems, though the subject is not sufficiently interesting to recommend it to general attention. The rhymes are correct, and the versification smooth and harmonious." It quotes with commendation the satire on medical works, gives suitable praise

---

[1] *Southey's Poetical Works*, ed. 1837 (Longmans), vol. ii. pp. 257-8 (*Occasional Poems*, xviii.).

[2] See *Works*, p. 103, ll. 83-90 (quoted above, p. 80).

[3] To the Countess of Ossory (*Letters*, ed. Cunningham, 9 vols., Bentley, 1858, vol. viii. p. 75) : " One thought is charming, that a dog, though a flatterer, is still a friend " (see 1st ed. l. 196 : " And in the fawning follower find the friend," suppressed in 1807). And Walpole adds : " It made me give Tonton a warm kiss, and swear it was true."

to the "description of romance, which is full of fancy
and spirit," and ends by observing that the author has
carefully abstained from "characterising or entering
into the merits of any particular writer." In the
month of October *The Gentleman's Magazine*, somewhat
offended by Crabbe's disrespectful allusion to "fritter'd
magazines,"[1] was more brief; but in December *The
Monthly Review* pronounced our Librarian "an agreeable and intelligent guide," and his poem "the production of no common pen." The critics and the public
had come up to Burke's expectation, and the anonymous
poet, without being richer for it, had acquired some
reputation.

VI

BUT he had as yet no profession. With his habitual
foresight, he had, as early as the month of March,
explained his position to Burke, and on the 27th he
once more told him of his anxieties: "I will apply
myself diligently," he wrote, "to the study of the
Greek and Latin languages; my great inclination to
the Church, and your late hints to me on this subject,
give me, perhaps, too fair a prospect of success; but I
am ignorant of the difficulty, and you will pardon me
if I hope too much. There is a family in Oxford who
would be of service to me, should my good fortune
ever lead me there. I, in the strict sense of the words,
'know not what I ask' when I hint these things, and
only do it with a firm confidence that you, sir, will feel
for my circumstances, in which I hope much and have
much to fear."[2] Crabbe, one can see, is a shrewd
enough diplomatist. He delicately intimates to Burke
that he is ready to take orders and to pursue the
necessary studies at Oxford, if some benefactor will
supply him with the means of doing so. Unfortunately, Burke's finances had long been encumbered by
the purchase and upkeep of his Beaconsfield property,
and he could not defray the considerable expense
of a University education. Crabbe had to wait.
He reduced his expenditure by leaving London for
Beccles,[3] and perhaps Aldborough, where he had the

---

[1] *Library* (1807), l. 134 (p. 104).
[2] See the letter quoted above, p. 116, n. 1.
[3] See above, p. 116.

grief not to see his mother again, her sufferings having ended on July 20th in the preceding year.[1] On June 26th, as we are aware, he had returned to Vickery's, and was reminding his 'patron of his existence in a long letter which is a living autobiography. " I am totally at a loss," he wrote, " how to act and what to undertake. I cannot think of living with my friends without a view of some employment or design, and I can form none, and I cannot continue in town without such, where the expense is (to me) much greater. My present undertaking[2] can be of no material service, I find, and the unlucky circumstance of printing so much of my miscellany makes it less so. . . . I entreat your consideration on my present state and my future propects. . . . I only wish to live and to be as little a burden as possible to my friends, but my indiscretion and my ill-fortune have so far carried me away that it requires a better judgment than my own to determine what is right for me to do."[3] Burke, somewhat embarrassed, had recommended Crabbe to the Duke of Rutland,[4] and had tried to find a bishop who would ordain him without delay. In addition to this, the Parliamentary session having come to an end on July 18th, he invited him to Beaconsfield, where the poet spent several happy weeks. In this large, square, one-storied house,[5] built on the top of a terrace, he was given a convenient apartment, supplied with books for his information and amusement, and made a member of a family " whom it was honour as well as pleasure to become in any degree associated with."[6] Mrs. Burke treated him with all the consideration which others perhaps

---

[1] See above, p. 20, n. 4, and her tomb in Aldborough churchyard. She was buried on the 23rd. As the Biographer remarks (p. 30), Crabbe probably alluded to this loss in two passages of his works : *Parish Register*, iii. 619-28, and *Infancy* (p. 261), 65-71.

[2] *The Library.*

[3] See Appendix I.

[4] Through Lord John Townshend, according to Lord Holland (*Memoirs of the Whig Party*, 1852, vol. i. p. 256). On Burke's advice Crabbe had probably made the first advances : cf. above, p. 123, the line 589 of the first edition of *The Library*: "Some noble Rutland, misery's friend and thine," and the following passage in the second letter to Burke (March 27th, 1781) : "If the line wherein the Duke of Rutland is indirectly mentioned be such as would offend his grace, or if you disapprove it, it is almost unnecessary, I hope, to say it shall be immediately altered."

[5] Called Gregory's, or Gregories.

[6] *Autobiographical Sketch*, quoted by B. p. 27.

would have reserved for personages of a higher rank.[1]
Burke himself made Crabbe his companion in his
walks through the park and over the one farm on
his property. He questioned him once more about
his misfortunes, his former studies, and his views for
the future, treated him to some of those classical
quotations which English orators delighted to make,
and was struck with the extent and the variety of
his knowledge. " Crabbe," he said about this time to
Sir Joshua Reynolds, "appears to know something of
everything."[2]

In the month of August the poet returned to
Beccles, while active steps were being taken in
two quarters simultaneously to get him ordained.
Burke had applied to two Suffolk friends: one of
them, Sir Charles Bunbury, Member of the House of
Commons, celebrated for his conjugal misfortunes,[3]
and his racing triumphs on Newmarket Heath, had
interceded with Dr. Warren,[4] Bishop of St. David's, at
the extreme end of Wales; the other, Dudley Long,
already known to us,[5] was making interest with
Dr. Yonge, Bishop of Norwich. These two recommendations were an embarrassment to Crabbe, as
appears from his letter to Burke of August 24th,[6]
of which the following are the principal passages:
" I enclose a letter I received from Sir Charles Bunbury, with a copy of my answer; in writing which I
lamented my absence from Beaconsfield, though at the
only place where that absence would not, at all times,
be lamented. I hope I need not speak my sentiments
of Sir Charles's generosity, nor of yours, on which it

---

[1] B. p. 28 : "As a trivial specimen of the conduct of the lady of the house,
I may mention that, one day, some company of rank that had been expected to
dinner did not arrive, and the servants, in consequence, reserved for next day
some costly dish that had been ordered. Mrs. Burke happened to ask for it ;
and the butler saying, ' It had been kept back, as the company did not come,'
she answered, ' What ! is not Mr. Crabbe here ? Let it be brought up immediately.' "

[2] B. p. 28.

[3] Sir Charles Bunbury (1740—1821) had married the celebrated Lady Sarah
Lennox, daughter of the Duke of Richmond and great-granddaughter of
Charles II. In 1769 she left Sir Charles, and a divorce was granted in 1776.

[4] John Warren (1730—1800), appointed Bishop of St. David's in 1779 and
of Bangor in 1783, was the second son of Richard Warren, Archdeacon of
Suffolk, which explains his relations with Sir Charles Bunbury.

[5] See above, p. 81, n. 8.

[6] See *Burke's Correspondence*, 1844 (cf. above, p. 116, n. 1), vol. ii.
pp. 429, 431.

was founded. Feeling the effect of his kindness, I must be lost to reflection as well as gratitude, not to see and be thankful to the cause of it. I lately visited the Mr. Longs at Saxmundham, and was received by both with more than civility. Mr. Dudley Long spoke to me concerning the Bishop of Norwich, and the probability of his consent to my ordination. I had not then received Sir Charles's letter, and must beg your directions on the occasion ; as Sir Charles will probably inquire of the bishop he mentions, and it is not improbable but Mr. Long may also make such inquiry, yet I can write to neither, with propriety, of the other's intention ; and should the more fear to do it, as one may not succeed. . . . I shall certainly prefer the diocese of Norwich; both for the reasons you give, and because they are your reasons."

The Bishop of St. David's seemed to hesitate, to express doubts as to Crabbe's "moral worth," and to demand a year of probation or of " quarantine," as it was called by Burke, who was surprised at so many scruples. " Dudley Long," he wrote to Sir Charles Bunbury on October 4th,[1] " says he has the best moral character possible among all those he has always lived with. He had even when I saw him some smattering of Greek, and I daresay what would do on the common examination for orders. He has been studying since I saw him. It is a disadvantage to him that he always puts the worst face on his own qualifications." The Bishop of Norwich was less exacting, and allowed Crabbe, a few months later, to become a clergyman. About the time when Parliament reassembled, on November 27th, Burke invited the poet to live, if not in his house,[2] at all events close by, introduced him to the eminent men, such as Charles Fox and Sir Joshua Reynolds, who were then his intimate friends, and recommended him to the " stern and formidable " Chancellor Thurlow. The latter apparently remembered[3] that he had, six months before, roughly dismissed Crabbe, and showed

---

[1] See this letter from Burke to Sir Charles in *The Bunbury Correspondence* (cf. above p. 17, n. 5), pp. 395-6.

[2] B. p. 28 : " It being inconvenient for them to afford him an apartment *at that time* in their town house." The Biographer evidently thought that Burke had from the first received Crabbe in his house (see p. 27 : " Mr. Burke domesticated him under his own roof and treated him like a son "), a mistake corrected by a careful perusal of letters unknown to the Biographer.

[3] B. p. 29.

himself anxious to make amends. He received Burke's *protégé* with extreme condescension, told him that " he ought to have noticed his first poem and heartily forgave him the second," invited him to breakfast, assured him of his interest and his favour, and, on parting from him, handed him a bank-note for one hundred pounds in " a sealed paper." This sum came in the nick of time and extricated Crabbe from pecuniary difficulties, which were continually recurring, and which his new life, on the skirts of the fashionable world, was bound to increase. At last, on December 21st, 1781, "at a general ordination held at Park Street Chapel, near Grosvenor Square,"[1] he was ordained deacon, with the title of curate to the Rev. James Benet, Rector of Aldborough.

Thus the first part of his life ended in a complete victory. He could now forget his protracted anxieties, his struggles, desperate at times. He had triumphed over poverty and obscurity. He was entering a profession to which he had been long called by the seriousness of his conduct and character, by his habits of religious meditation and of psychological analysis of himself and of others. He was to obtain in it not only leisure for further writing and for improving his style, but also opportunities for probing the character of his fellow-men and for fresh observation. He had just composed the most elegant poem which England had seen for ten years ; he was now to produce a really powerful work. He had found his professional vocation, and was soon to find his vocation as a writer, his true manner. His innate vigour, aided by a friendly hand, had surmounted every obstacle : reinforced by fresh contact with his native soil, it was about to burst forth in a number of original compositions.

[1] These are the terms of the official "attestation."

SECOND PART

THE CHAPLAIN AND POET OF COUNTRY LIFE

(1782—1785)

SINGLE CHAPTER

THE CHAPLAIN ; HIS " VILLAGE " AND " NEWSPAPER "

I. Curate at Aldborough.—II. Ducal chaplain. Life at Belvoir Castle.
—III. Pastoral poetry in the eighteenth century and the sources
of its inspiration : the golden age, the natural man, the man of
feeling. Attacked by Crabbe in his *Village*. Description of the
real countryman.—IV. Marriage.—V. *The Newspaper*.

I

To return with an official position and as an appreciated poet to a place from which poverty has driven
you eighteen months previously is to take, it would
seem, a fine revenge on adverse fortune. Crabbe must
have tasted a few moments of intense happiness on
the day when, comfortably reinstalled with his sister
Mary, he was able to receive in his house and at his
table his brother Robert and his father [1]—the latter
at last convinced of the injustice of the reproaches
which he had formerly levelled at his son, the author
of that *Library* which he now, in a fit of enthusiasm,
copied out with his own hand.[2] But it would argue a
slight acquaintance with the spirit of Little Pedlington
to suppose that the family joy was shared by the
inhabitants of Aldborough. The new curate was
coldly received. What right, people said, has he to
come and lecture his fellow-townsmen, this upstart
whom we have known as a fisherman in his father's
boat, as a common labourer, like all his belongings,
as a poverty-stricken and clumsy apothecary, who
killed his patients or gave them herbs gathered on the
marshes instead of drugs ? Depend upon it, he owes
his success to some low intrigue with great people,
and this poem, on which he prides himself so much,
is only half his own ! Where could he have invented

[1] Letter from Robert Crabbe to his nephew, John Crabbe, dated June 18th,
1833 : "The year following, my brother was got to his lodgings as curate of
Aldbro I was there shortly after on a visit on a Saturday evening, and
supped with him at his lodgings, my father being with us" (Broadley Collection).
[2] B. p. 29.

all this, never having been to the University? And
was it certain what kind of a clergyman he would
make? Was it not common talk that not long ago,
at Woodbridge, at Aldborough even, he had led a gay
life, like his boon companions, and ogled the pretty
girls, after a glass of wine?[1] His doctrines apparently
were not more orthodox than his conduct. Had not
a sailor from Aldborough, entering a Methodist chapel
in Moorfields, seen him standing on the steps of the
pulpit in which Wesley was preaching? Would it be
possible to tolerate the airs which he would be sure to
give himself with his betters and his equals of yesterday? So the cue was to run him down; to say, like
the daughters of a local ship-owner, while "smoothing
their black mittens," "*We* never thought much of
Mr. Crabbe"[2]; and when he preached his first sermon
he saw nothing but "unfriendly countenances" around
him. The young curate, full of indignation, did not
care what they thought of him or his discourse. But
he bore them a grudge; he remembered this reception
when, in writing *The Village* a few months afterwards,
he referred to the "bold, artful, surly, savage race"
which peopled these shores, and, for the present, he
confined himself to doing his duty on Sunday, to
preaching an occasional sermon or performing a
marriage ceremony.[3] On Monday mornings he generally betook himself to Beccles, where Mira was the
attraction; half-way he would meet his brother Robert,
at the village of Blythburgh: they would take "their
tea and a glass of punch" together, and then resume
their journey, the one to Beccles, the other to Southwold.[4] In the meanwhile Crabbe became more and
more anxious that one of his influential friends should
rescue him from this untenable position.

It was Burke who once more came to his aid.
Although the resignation of Lord North's Ministry,
on March 20th, 1782, and the advent to power of the
Whigs and their leader, Lord Rockingham, had imposed on him the twofold duty of managing his office

[1] See B. pp. 29-30, Mitford MS. notes (British Museum), and *Gentleman's
Magazine*, March, 1834, p. 256. Mitford gives this piece of gossip in another
form.

[2] *Two Suffolk Friends* (see above, p. 81, n. 6), p. 58.

[3] On February 18th, 1782, as the Rev. H. Thompson has noted in the
parish register.

[4] Letter from Robert Crabbe (p. 133, n. 1).

of Paymaster of the Forces and of defending his
plan of "administrative reform" before the House of
Commons, Burke did not forget his *protégé*. He had
ascertained, in the course of a conversation with the
Duke of Rutland, that the Rev. George Turner, rector
of the parish of Knipton and chaplain to the ducal
family, was about to give up the second of these offices
for "reasons of health," and that the Duke would
gladly appoint Crabbe to it, as soon as the latter could
find a substitute at Aldborough. Burke wrote to
Crabbe,[1] who replied on April 16th, from Beccles.
He congratulates, but not without some of his habitual
circumlocutions, the new minister on his accession to
office; he thinks perhaps, without exactly saying so,
that it is hardly worthy of Burke's talents or legitimate
expectations; and he continues with a categorical
profession of his political creed: "Most heartily do I
rejoice, being well assured that if the credit and happiness of this kingdom can be restored, the wisdom and
virtues of my most honoured friend, and of his friends,
will bring forward so desirable an event; and if not,
it will be some satisfaction to find such men lost to the
confidence of the people, who have so long demonstrated their incapacity to make a proper use of it."[2]
From this flattering eulogium of the Whigs and
severe censure of the Tories he passes to his own
affairs, states that he has "procured a successor," and
that he will shortly come to London for a few days,
probably to arrange matters with the Duke of Rutland.
He hopes to see Burke at least once on this occasion,
for he cannot bear to think that "any honours, or
business, or even the calls of his country should make
him totally forgotten."

We know nothing of this short journey to London,
which was probably followed by a stay of several
months at Beccles, where Crabbe pursued his studies
with a view to his ordination to the priesthood.
Hoping perhaps to kindle a fresh access of generosity in
the surly Chancellor, who was now Burke's colleague,
he wrote to him on May 14th in rather vague terms,
complaining of the difficulties and unpleasantness of
his position.[3] Lord Thurlow seems to have thought

---

[1] B. p. 31.
[2] *Burke's Correspondence* (above, p. 116, n. 1), vol. ii. pp. 475-6.
[3] This letter has not been found.

that a donation of £100 was enough for one year, for
his reply, dated May 29th, though encouraging for
the future, was evasive as to the present. "I have
thought," he says, "of writing to you frequently in
answer to your last letter of the 14th of May, but have
stopt for want of imagining how to shape my answer,
and this is only to tell you that when you think fit to
take full orders, as you must come to town on that
account, I shall be glad to see you and enter more
fully into the affairs you allude to. . . . I wish you
well, and if you make yourself capable of preferment, I
shall try to find an early opportunity of serving you."[1]
Crabbe, therefore, was bound to complete his theological
studies without loss of time. He could less than ever
count on assistance from his father, who married again
on June 5th,[2] severing family ties by a hasty act disapproved by all his sons. At length, on August 4th,
1782, Crabbe was ordained priest "in the Chapel
belonging to the Palace in the city of Norwich."[3]
Shortly afterwards he left for Belvoir Castle, where
the Duke of Rutland was spending the summer.

II

THE position of "domestic chaplain" to an English
nobleman had, with the progress of manners, per-
ceptibly improved in the course of the eighteenth
century. It was no longer quite that of the "young
Levite" described to us by Eachard, Oldham, and
Macaulay[4] with the exaggeration and generalisation
of satire. The chaplain had ceased to be a sort of
footman, "with a little better wages than the cook or
butler," dressed "in silken scarf and cassock," which
were but "a gayer livery," "consecrating with holy
words the meat" which he had barely time to devour,
saying grace for the masters and prayers for the servants. When, after long solicitations, he obtained the

---

[1] Letter dated May 29th, 1782 ; a part of it is published by the Biographer,
without date.

[2] A widow named Mary Revett, from the village of Monewden, in Suffolk
(cf. Davy MSS. *Pedigrees* [Crabbe], in the British Museum). See also the
allusion in B. pp. 38-9.

[3] Official attestation of Philip (Yonge), Bishop of Norwich.

[4] Eachard, *Causes of the Contempt of the Clergy and Religion* (1670),
Works, ed. 1774, vol. i. p. 84; Oldham's *Satire addressed to a Friend that
is about to leave the University*, quoted by Addison in *The Tatler*, No. 225,
November 25th, 1710 ; Macaulay's *History of England*, ch. iii.

much-coveted living, he was no longer obliged to marry,
before leaving, some elderly lady's-maid, the cast-off
mistress of his noble patron. More fortunate than
Addison's correspondent,[1] he ran no risk of being
turned out of the room if, on the arrival of dessert, he
forgot to rise from table and slink away, "picking his
teeth and sighing with his hat under his arm." He
could help himself to tarts and sweetmeats without
being reproached by the mistress of the house for a
sweet tooth. He was no longer obliged to "make great
ravages on all the dishes that stood near him and to
distinguish himself by the voracity of his appetite," for
fear of not having time to gorge himself. He could now
remain till the end of dinner without seeing glances,
impatiently fixed on him, demanding his prompt departure; he no longer heard, as soon as the door was
shut, a cry of relief proceeding from the guests, glad
to be left to themselves at last and to be able to shout,
swear, and drink without being lectured by the chaplain. The position accepted by Crabbe was no longer
humiliating, but still very delicate, as is always the case
when there is a conflict between the inherent authority
of an office and the social inferiority of its holder.

However, it was no small advantage to find oneself
transplanted from hostile and vulgar surroundings
into a princely abode and into a society conspicuous
for its rank or intelligence. This select circle, on the
fringe of which Crabbe was about to live, was to afford
him an opportunity of studying the manners and the
life of the great world and of comparing them with
those of the rustics and fishermen of Aldborough.
Nothing could be more whole-hearted than the devotion
to pleasure which reigned at Belvoir Castle in that
day. Charles Manners, fourth Duke of Rutland, had
in 1779 inherited the title from his grandfather, the
third Duke, the first who settled definitively at Belvoir,
where his hermit's existence had obtained for him
the patriarchal name of "John of the Hill."[2] At the
age of sixteen Charles Manners, who was only a
few months older than Crabbe,[3] had prematurely lost

---

[1] *Tatler, loc. cit.*; cf. *Guardian*, No. 163, September 17th, 1713.
[2] T. F. Dale, *The History of the Belvoir Hunt* (1899), pp. 22-3.
[3] According to the *Dictionary of National Biography*, he was born on
March 15th, 1754. Crabbe, therefore, makes a slight mistake when he writes
to Sir Walter Scott in 1813 (letter quoted by B. p. 57), that the Duke and he
"were of an age to a week."

his father, the illustrious Marquis of Granby, the
brilliant cavalry general whose heroic charges at
Minden and in other engagements had made him a
popular favourite, but who had somewhat lost caste
through excesses at the table and senseless extravagance
towards the close of his life. He had transmitted to
his son his love of good living and of pleasure of every
kind.[1] In 1775, at the age of twenty-one, the future
patron of Crabbe had married Lady Mary Isabella
Somerset, daughter of the Duke of Beaufort, the rival
in beauty and the political opponent of Fox's enthusiastic
admirer the Duchess of Devonshire. Educated at Cambridge, where William Pitt had just graduated, Rutland
cherished a cult for Lord Chatham's memory and for
the second Pitt's future which was alike generous and
interested. He liked to sing the praises of " that
unparalleled statesman " and to maintain that the nation
ought, out of gratitude, to pay the great minister's
debts and provide for his family, his idea being that
the officers of State should learn to be " indifferent
about the emoluments of office," in the certainty that
henceforth, if they died, the nation would, as a reward
for their services, pay their tradesmen's bills and give
pensions to their widows and their children. " Sublime
nonsense," declared the sceptical George Selwyn, on
hearing his interlocutor develop these theories.[2]
Rutland, however, had put his principles into practice.
At the General Election of 1780 he had warmly supported Pitt's candidature for the University of
Cambridge; and on his *protégé's* failure had recommended him to Sir James Lowther, afterwards Lord
Lonsdale, owner of nine seats in the North of England,
and it was thus that in February, 1781, at the age
of twenty-one, Pitt had been able to enter the House
of Commons as Member for Appleby.[3] To this signal
service the Duke of Rutland owed the successes
of his short political career. Towards the end of
1782 Pitt, then Chancellor of the Exchequer in Shelburne's ministry, got his friend appointed Lord Privy

---

[1] Dale, *op. cit.*, pp. 44-7.
[2] See *George Selwyn : his Letters and his Life*, edited by E. S. Roscoe and
Helen Clergue (1899), p. 182.   The conversation took place on January 8th,
1782, at Brooks's, between Fox, Selwyn, and Rutland.
[3] See *Pitt*, by Lord Rosebery (Macmillan, 1891), pp. 9-10. Wraxall,
Historical Memoirs of my own Time, relates the matter in great detail,
pp. 378-80 of the Askham ed. (London, 1904, Kegan Paul).

Seal,[1] and in December, 1783, having become Prime
Minister, he bestowed the same office on him, and,
a few weeks later, made him Lord-Lieutenant of
Ireland. In power, as in private life, Rutland seems
always to have preserved his good humour, his open,
affectionate,[2] and passionate disposition, his jovial
optimism, so different from the reserve and the somewhat melancholy gravity of his chaplain.

Belvoir Castle, where the young Duke used to come
with a large party to shoot and hunt in the autumn,
was not then the sumptuous abode known to us at
the present day, the alike imposing and handsome,
mediæval and modern edifice, with its massive, three-
storied flanking towers, and all the complicated details
of its irregular architecture. It did not then emerge
from waves of foliage which rise and fall with the
undulation of the hills ; no restful lawns or tasteful
gardens spread at its feet. All these splendours date
from 1816 only.[3] Situated in Leicestershire, near the
north-eastern point of a triangle formed by Nottingham,
Grantham, and Melton Mowbray, Belvoir Castle in
1782 was simply a large, square, flat building, with
a low single storey, planted heavily on the top of its
hill, a sort of terrace commanding a view, to the
south-east, of the ridge that stretches towards Stathern
and Melton Mowbray, of the spires of Lincoln Cathedral in the distant north, and, all round, of the village
churches scattered over the vast plain. A few statues,
some plantations on the hillside, and, in the " valley,"
to the east of the castle, a sheet of water fed by
the little River Devon alone broke the monotony of
the landscape.[4] Then, as now, this part of England

---

[1] In place of the Duke of Grafton (Lecky, *History of England*, vol. iv.
p. 268).

[2] See an anecdote related by B. p. 33. Some time before Crabbe's arrival
at Belvoir, the younger brother of the Duke of Rutland, Lord Robert Manners,
commander of the *Resolution*, had been mortally wounded in a naval engagement. His hat, riddled with bullets, was sent to Belvoir, and, according to
the Biographer, " The Duke first held it up with a shout of exultation and
triumph, glorying in the bravery of his beloved brother ; and then, as the
thought of his danger flashed suddenly into his mind, sank on his chair in
a burst of natural and irrepressible feeling."

[3] The rebuilding, begun in 1801, was interrupted by a fire at the end of
1816 which destroyed a great number of valuable pictures. The work was
immediately resumed (Dale, *op. cit.* p. 99).

[4] Arthur Young, who visited Belvoir in 1776, three years before the death
of " John of the Hill," criticises it very severely : " The house is now almost
entirely unfurnished and the gardens neglected, so that it looks more like the

was a favourite hunting country. The owner of
Belvoir possessed a famous pack of hounds, and every
year his own friends, the country gentlemen of the
district, the sporting clergy, and the neighbouring
farmers used to meet in the hunting-field. Crabbe
does not seem to have taken to this amusement. He
preferred, the Biographer tells us,[1] to ride with the
Duke to some secluded part of the property and talk
of literature, the drama, and poetry. What he liked
better still was to ascend the valley of the Devon
in a southerly direction to the plateau surmounted by
Croxton Park, where the Dukes of Rutland had already
built a shooting-box, and where there was complete
liberty to fish, to botanise, to catch and examine insects
and butterflies, while the rooks wheeled and cawed
in the air above. On his return, Crabbe perhaps found
some one ready to talk with him : either the Duke of
Queensberry, a fanatical devotee of pleasure, always
on the look-out for " a black eye and a low forehead,"[2]
when he was not betting with or against Fox at
Newmarket ; or Richard Watson, Regius Professor
of Divinity at Cambridge, and just made Bishop of
Llandaff[3] through the interest of Rutland, his old
pupil ; or again the eccentric Dr. Glynn, the younger
Pitt's physician, recognisable by his " three-cornered
hat and scarlet cloak " and his habit of " saying whatever came uppermost into his mind." But Crabbe could
hardly become intimate with personages of this kind,
and his only close friend at this time seems to have
been a certain Robert Thoroton, the son of a relation
and confidential agent of the ducal family,[4] a bold rider,
as impetuous in his amusements and actions as he was
generous in his disposition.[5] There is no doubt that

habitation of one in distress than the seat of one of our most opulent nobles—at
least such was its appearance in 1776 " (*Tour through Great Britain,* 8th ed.
1778, vol. iii. pp. 32-3).

[1] B. p. 32.

[2] George Selwyn, *op. cit.* p. 80.

[3] In July, 1782. For Watson, see the curious *Anecdotes of the Life of
R. Watson,* London, 1817, and a summary of his career in Legouis, *La Jeunesse
de Wordsworth,* pp. 230-1.

[4] Thomas Thoroton, of Scrieveton, Member for Newark and Bramber (Dale,
op. cit. p. 65).

[5] According to B. (p. 33), he one day spurred his horse up the steep terraces
to the castle walls ; on another occasion, to escape from Crabbe, whom he
was evidently teasing, he sprang over the boundary of the glacis. In 1784 he
accompanied the Duke to Ireland as private secretary, and Sir Jonah Barrington
(*Personal Sketches,* 1869, vol. i. p. 102) speaks of him in these terms : " He

the etiquette at Belvoir was often burdensome to the poet, and that he preferred Cheveley,[1] where the Dukes of Rutland led a simpler life, when they went to Suffolk for Newmarket races.   It was thither that Crabbe, a humble and timid youth, had once carried the medicines of his master at Wickham Brook.   He had got on since then.

But he lacked the suppleness and the ease required for those who would succeed with the great.   He had not the art of obtaining influence by insinuating himself. In his reserve, in his humility even, one could feel the jealous independence and pride of the plebeian.   His duties as chaplain were sometimes delicate : if his advice was asked, he had to reply discreetly, without appearing to claim the privileges of an intimate friend[2]; if the Duchess brought him one of her children to be scolded for swearing, it was necessary to measure out the blame so as to spare the mother's feelings and preserve the respect due to the little " lord " of four years old.[3] If some female friend or relation arrived at the castle, the chaplain was asked for a poetical effusion, and Crabbe would bring his verses with his sweetest smile and most high-flown compliments.   The reader can judge from the following note [4] addressed to the Duchess : " Madam,—I have the honour of sending you my verses to Lady Elizabeth, and am much more proud of obeying your commands than of the performance which was written in obedience to her ladyship.   I confess that my muse is one of the poorest of your Grace's servants and cannot decorate you to advantage, but you will, I hope, forgive her, because nobody so little needs the arts of decoration.   It is unfortunate for me that every one is able to judge how much I fall below the subject of my praise, but your Grace is bound to

---

had the manner of a coxcomb, but the heart of a friend and the sentiments of a gentleman.   He was clerk of the [Irish] House of Commons, and, being by no means a common man, formed a necessary part of all our societies. . . . I was aware that circumstances existed which were the cause, to him, of great anxiety ; and, finally, the death of Mr. Thoroton by his own hand deprived me of one of the sincerest and most useful friends I ever possessed."

[1] See above, pp. 40-2.

[2] *Tales* (*The Patron*, 276).

[3] See the manuscript note of Fitzgerald on B. p. 32 : " Their Graces' children . . ." Fitzgerald was told by B. himself that " *She* came in one day with one of them by the hand to be reproved by the chaplain for *swearing* something [some oath?] picked up from the then common conversation of dukes royal and other."

[4] Dated July 23rd, 1873 (Mackay Collection).

vindicate the error of which you are the cause. Had
the object been less perfect, I should have been able to
have taken a nearer likeness. I have the honour to be
with the highest respect your Grace's most obliged,
obedient and very humble servant." On other occasions
his patience was subjected to a more trying ordeal:
even in his presence certain guests would be too free
in their speech, and Crabbe, with an imprudence
which he blames in one of his tales,[1] would constitute
himself " religion's advocate," without fearing to compromise his cause by his zeal in defending it :

> With wine before thee, and with wits beside,
> Do not in strength of reasoning powers confide ;
> What seems to thee convincing, certain, plain,
> They will deny, and dare thee to maintain ; . . .
> Men gay and noisy will o'erwhelm thy sense,
> Then loudly laugh at truth's and thy expense ;
> While the kind ladies will do all they can
> To check their mirth, and cry, " *The good young man !* "

Or perhaps the conversation ran on politics, and
Crabbe, whose Liberal opinions we are acquainted
with,[2] would defend Burke, Fox, and the Whig party
against the Duke of Rutland, a fervent admirer of
Pitt, and against the Duchess herself, the most uncompromising of Tories. Did she not write to Crabbe in
1807[3] that Fox's " principles both private and public
were bad, and that his shining talents would have
rendered them more dangerous to his country had
not the superior and more transcendent abilities and
eminent virtues of Mr. Pitt happily prevented their
being so"? What reply could be made to such an
opponent? Crabbe had, it appears,[4] " more than once
to drink a glass of salt water because he refused to
join in Tory toasts "—a very coarse sort of joke for a
society that laid claim to distinction. The poet must
have felt himself humiliated, must have thought, with
the " proud disdain" of a superior man, that these high-
sounding titles often covered " common parts,"[5] and
have aspired to the day when he would " have a little

---

[1] *Tales*, v. 321-36. The autobiographical nature of the passage is all the
more certain because it forms a very long digression.

[2] See above, p. 135.

[3] Letter dated " Belvoir Castle, Thursday, December 10th, 1807 " (Broadley
Collection).

[4] B. p. 49.

[5] *Tales*, v. 228.

hut, that he might hide his head in, where never guest might dare molest, unwelcome and unbidden." [1] He seems to have always had a grudge against Belvoir for the little annoyances to which he was subjected there.

In December, 1782, Rutland was made a minister, and Crabbe accompanied the family to London. According to the Biographer,[2] there was no room for him in the town-house in Arlington Street, and he "accidentally procured" the lodgings which had just been occupied by the well-known Hackman,[3] the officer who became a clergyman and, in a fit of jealousy, killed Martha Ray,[4] Lord Sandwich's mistress, at the door of Covent Garden Theatre. Crabbe's reputation as a poet and position as chaplain to a nobleman gave him more access to the fashionable and literary society of the capital than even Burke's protection had done. He saw Sir Joshua Reynolds again, in his luxurious mansion in Leicester Fields, frequented the octagonal studio where the painter, standing at his easel near the narrow window, was working of a morning at the preliminary studies for his great picture ordered by the Empress of Russia, *The Infant Hercules strangling the Serpents*. He was invited, with the Duke of Rutland, and no doubt with Burke, to the hospitable board at which Miss Palmer, Reynolds's niece, afterwards Marchioness of Thomond, received a select company. He must have admired the indefatigable activity and the probity of the great artist, his luminous and penetrating intelligence, which conveyed into his sitters' expressions a spark from the flame of his own genius; he perhaps envied him his calmness of temper, unruffled by deafness and the approach of a premature old age, and the distinction of his manners, invariably easy, whatever the rank of his interlocutor.

It was also at Sir Joshua Reynolds's house that the young poet was introduced to the redoubtable Cerberus of the temple of Fame, the illustrious Dr. Johnson, the tyrant of English criticism at that time. Their first

[1] Lines quoted by B. p. 32.
[2] B. p. 34.
[3] According to *The Criminal Recorder*, "Hackman lodged in Duke's Court, St. Martin's Lane."
[4] On April 7th, 1779. She had several children by Lord Sandwich, among others Basil Montague. Lord Sandwich, born in 1718, is the "Jemmy Twitcher" of Gray's *Candidate*.

interview was not, it would appear, a great success.[1] Crabbe, having timidly hazarded some commonplace remark, was greeted with a "growl" from the doctor, and a visit to Bolt Court, where Johnson was living, was required to set things right. Crabbe remembered a hint which the critic had given him on this occasion: "Never fear putting the strongest and best things you can think of into the mouth of your speaker, whatever may be his condition"—a dangerous piece of advice, which seems to inculcate the neglect of all dramatic probability. But the value of the remark was of little consequence: Johnson had deigned to be amiable, and that was the main point. The Chancellor Thurlow was not less so: at Fox's suggestion[2] he asked Crabbe to breakfast again, said to him on parting, "You are as like Parson Adams as twelve to the dozen," and gave him the livings of Frome St. Quintin and Evershot,[3] small parishes in Dorsetshire, which were worth together about £200 a year.[4] At the same time, on March 22nd, 1783, Bishop Watson, at the Duke of Rutland's request, put Crabbe's name on the books of Trinity College, Cambridge, to enable him to take the degree of Bachelor of Divinity at the expiration of ten years.[5] Fortune at last was smiling on the poet, and, to crown all, he had in reserve a work which was about to win him fame.

III

THIS was *The Village*, begun perhaps in 1780,[6] continued at intervals, on occasions which cannot be specified owing to the absence of dated documents,

[1] B. p. 28.

[2] See *Lord Holland's Memoirs of the Whig Party* (1852), vol. i. p. 255: "While Lord Thurlow was in office, he [Fox] overcame his reluctance to asking favours of a political enemy, and urged that Chancellor to encourage genius by giving Mr. Crabbe some preferment."

[3] Ten miles to the north-west of Dorchester. The presentation was made in February or March; it is mentioned in *The British Magazine*, number for March, 1783, p. 244. Thurlow at that time belonged to the Shelburne ministry, which was supplanted by the coalition between Fox and Lord North on April 2nd, 1783.

[4] Letter from Crabbe to his son George, dated Trowbridge, March 7th, 1831.

[5] See the extract from the books taken by M. W. White: "1783, March 22, Admissus est—Crabbe Clericus annos natus 24." This was not Crabbe's real age, but the minimum limit of age for admission. These candidates were called "ten-year men." They had to keep three terms only in the course of the ten years, a condition no doubt not strictly enforced.

[6] See above, p. 115, n. 3.

resumed and finished at Aldborough, Beccles, and Belvoir during the year 1782. On December 26th, in fact,[1] Burke had received the manuscript of the new poem, and he wrote to Crabbe as follows: "I have got the poem, but I have not yet opened it. I don't like the unhappy language you use about these matters. You do not easily please such a judgment as your own—that is natural; but where you are difficult every one else will be charmed." Such delicate praise must have pleased the poet, and have made him forget for a moment the scruples and fears of his exaggerated modesty and distrust. He looked out for a publisher, and asked advice of Mira, whose reply[2] shows all her tenderness and her naïve admiration for her "dearest Mr. Crabbe." "I hope," she writes, "you don't deceive me as to your health; pray, my dearest Mr. Crabbe, in this as in all other things show your affection by your sincerity. And depend on my doing the same. I have considered and reconsidered your proposals[3] to my uncle, and depend upon me when I say I approve them because tho' I cannot be assured they *will* please yet I am convinced they ought. . . . I am still with the dear ladies[4] at Normanston. . . . I am obliged to you, my dearest Mr. Crabbe, for taking my opinion respecting Mr. Dodsley. If you had none of your own, the compliment would not be very great—but as you are much better calculated to instruct than to be instructed, I must be alway proud to give my opinion and pleased to see it adopted." It was thus that Dodsley, the publisher of *The Library*, was chosen to bring out *The Village*. Owing to the good offices of Sir Joshua Reynolds, Dr. Johnson had consented to read the manuscript; and on March 4th, 1783,[5] he returned it full of erasures

[1] This date, not mentioned by B. p. 33, is on the original letter (Broadley Collection). Canon Ainger (p. 44) by mistake substitutes for it the month of May, 1783, and does not see that it was the manuscript, and not a printed copy of the poem, that Crabbe sent to Burke.

[2] Not dated. On it Crabbe has noted, "Written about two years before we married," which probably should be reduced to about one year (Broadley Collection).

[3] Of marriage, evidently, made by Crabbe to Mr. Tovell. This detail fixes approximately the date of the letter, for Crabbe could not have made such proposals at any time in the year 1781.

[4] Cf. above, pp. 71-2.

[5] See B. p. 33, and Crabbe's Preface to his Poems published in 1807, *Works*, p. 98. Sir Joshua transmitted Johnson's letter to Crabbe, with the following note of the same date: "Dear Sir,—I have returned your poem with Dr.

and accompanied with a most flattering note. " Mr. Crabbe's poem," he wrote, " is original, vigorous, and elegant. The alterations which I have made I do not require him to adopt; for my lines are, perhaps, not often better than his own : but he may take mine and his own together, and perhaps, between them, produce something better than either. . . . His dedication will be least liked; it were better to contract it into a short sprightly address. I do not doubt of Mr. Crabbe's success." In May, 1783, the poem appeared without a dedication,[1] and the public at once ratified the verdict of the critic. This telling satire on pastoral poetry was read with eagerness.

From the time when Virgil, departing from the Doric and realistic rusticity of Theocritus, had uttered his famous *O fortunatos nimium*, and sung the supposed attractions of country life, " its security and quiet, its innocence, its varied resources, its spacious leisure, its caves, its fresh lakes, its cool valleys," the charm of " lowing oxen and of refreshing slumbers beneath a tree," [2] the bucolic poets had not ceased to vie with each other in blowing their Arcadian " pipes." Themselves confined within the narrow limits of cities, cloyed with the enjoyments of a refined civilisation, they let their imagination wing its flight towards the haunts of freedom which they had never visited, towards a state of innocence alike ideal and sensual. Their peasants had become " eclogue shepherds," contemporaries of the golden age. Like the first men of whom Ovid [3] speaks, their herdsmen were ignorant of " the penalties and terrors of the laws " because, of

Johnson's letter to me; if you knew how sparing Dr. Johnson deals out his praises, you would be very well content with what he says. I feel myself in some measure flattered in the success of my prognostication. Yours sincerely " (Broadley Collection).

[1] " *The Village* was published in May, 1783," says B. p. 34; on the 23rd of May, according to *The Public Advertiser* of the same day. In the first edition, the poem is a grey quarto, like *The Library*, and entitled " *The Village, a poem in two books*, by the Rev. G. Crabbe, chaplain to H. Gr. the Duke of Rutland. London. Printed for J. Dodsley, Pall Mall, 1783."

[2] *Georgics*, ii. 467-71.

[3] *Metamorphoses*, i. 89 *seq*. It is not in the plan of this work to relate the history, which is long and often tedious, of pastoral poetry. As regards England, a complete bibliography of the school will be found in an essay by Mr. Gosse, *On English Pastoral Poetry*, in the third volume of Mr. Grosart's *Spenser*. For France I have read with advantage M. Arnould's study of Racan and an article by M. Baldensperger on *Gessner en France* in the *Revue d'Histoire littéraire de la France*, 1903, pp. 437 *seq*.

themselves and without constraint, they "cultivated
honesty and virtue." Crime was not to appear in this
earthly paradise, the harmony of which it would have
disturbed, and rare were the wolves that were allowed
to molest the flocks. In these blissful regions, where
war was unknown, neither "helmets nor swords" ever
gleamed, and the pine-trees, left unharmed on the
mountain peaks, "never descended into the rivers to
visit alien shores." The earth, "unwounded by rake
or ploughshare," yielded grass to the sheep, and to
men the wild fruits, which sufficed for them. It was
"an eternal spring, whose warm and gentle breezes
caressed the flowers which no hand had sown." These
"first shepherds," real "kings of their flocks" and of
boundless domains, were supposed to have enjoyed
absolute "leisure and tranquillity," to have "lived their
own life in great opulence" and complete liberty.
They were pictured as sitting from early dawn at the
foot of some beloved Sylvia or Daphne, watching with
a careless eye their docile goats and sheep, which they
had just let out of the fold, and singing, to please their
companion or to compete with another herdsman, the
charms of their "fair" or the amorous distress of a
friend. What a pleasing lot was theirs! Ever and
anon the shepherdess would rise to "milk the ewes
and wean the lambs,"[1] her hand, "white as the lily,"
would take up the crook and drive the thriving flock
before her, while, to beguile the fatigues of the way,
the shepherd's pipe and song would make their sweetest
harmony. How delicious was love in this enchanted
land, where honour and modesty "had not yet concealed the source of bliss, where nymphs and swains
mingled caresses and murmurs with their words, and
kisses with their murmurs; and the maiden, young
and unclad, revealed her fresh roses" and, like Chloe,
sported with her lover in a lake or a fountain![2] If their
sky became overcast, it was with the lightest of clouds—
a too fortunate rival, an unfaithful shepherdess, might
throw the hapless wooer into a plaintive and melodious
languor, but were never to drive him to despair.[3]

[1] Ambrose Philips, *Pastorals*, i. (Chalmers's *English Poets*, vol. xiii. p. 110).
[2] Tasso's *Aminta*, act i. chorus—a passage which has become very celebrated, and which was translated by Samuel Daniel (*A Pastoral*, Chalmers's
English Poets, vol. iii. p. 559).
[3] Contrary to the opinion of La Motte-Houdar, in this case in revolt against
his master, Fontenelle. Cf. La Motte, *Œuvres*, ed. 1754, vol. iii. p. 295.

Stormy ambitions or violent passions would have
devastated the trim gardens of this artificial Arcadia;
the rough work of field and stable would have
reddened the arms of the shepherdesses, would have
disordered their pretty lace and their beribboned hats.
In this conventional existence, invented by the poets,
plenty, peace, and comfort were always to reign;
the "vulgarity and poverty" of real life were to be
ignored at all hazards. Work of a too laborious kind,
such as that of fishermen, was not suited to the
pastoral school, from which Fontenelle, Steele, and Sir
William Jones[1] wished to expel with ignominy the
impertinent innovator Sannazaro, author of *Ecloga
piscatoriæ*. In vain had Phineas Fletcher, taking up
the same subjects, extolled the happiness of fishermen:

> Ah, would thou knew'st how much it better were
> To bide among the simple fisher-swaines;
> No shrieking owl, no night-crow lodgeth here;
> Nor is our simple pleasure mixt with pains:
> Our sports begin with the beginning yeare;
> In calms, to pull the leaping fish to land;
> In roughs, to sing and dance along the golden sand.[2]

In vain had he tried to win the adherents of
"bucolics" by showing them a group of "merry
shepherds, clad in green, accompanied by their
charming nymphs," on a "sward" by the sea, and
fishermen, "clad in blue," engaged in competing
for the prize of poetry, a competition ever undecided.[3]
He was not listened to, and his master did not find
favour. The rules which Fontenelle laid down for
the idyll in 1688 were largely adopted by Steele; and
Marmontel, in an article in the *Encyclopédie*, gave this
decisive definition of the eclogue: "The object of
pastoral poetry has been hitherto to show to men the
happiest condition which they are allowed to enjoy
and to afford them mental enjoyment of it by the
magic of illusion." What with the golden age of some

---

[1] See Fontenelle, *Discours sur la nature de l'églogue* (*Œuvres*, ed. Belin,
1818, vol. iii. pp. 58-9); Steele, Nos. 22 and 32 of *The Guardian* (April
6th and 17th, 1713), the first almost translated from Fontenelle; Sir William
Jones, the illustrious Orientalist, *Arcadia*, published in 1772 (Chalmers's
English Poets, vol. xviii. p. 449), a reproduction in verse of Steele's article in
The Guardian (No. 32).
[2] Phineas Fletcher, *Piscatory Eclogues*, i. (1633), st. xviii. (Chalmers's
English Poets, vol. vi. p. 135).
[3] *Piscatory Eclogues*, vii. st. ii.-iv. p. 150-1.

and "the refinement and politeness" of others,[1] the
poetical shepherds of the eighteenth century were
departing more and more from the reality.

They strongly resembled, however, the near relation
whom Rousseau's imagination had found for them—
the gentle and amiable "savage" of the *Discourse
on the Origin of Inequality among Men*.[2] This "simplicity of early times," this "handsome countenance
adorned by nature's hand alone," in which the
youthful race presented a "happy mean between the
indolence of the primitive state and the petulant
activity of our self-love," were they not, in a form hardly
renewed by the philosopher of Geneva, the Arcadia of
tradition, with its country life and its manners ? Both
contemporaries of the golden age, the "eclogue
shepherd" and the "natural man" were bound to
come to terms and join forces for the conquest of the
public. Living in seclusion, the one among the fields
with his sheep and his shepherdess, the other in the
depths of the forest with his "food, his female, and his
repose," they were so far removed from our artificial,
perfidious, and tyrannical society, so independent of
any master who, "having enclosed a plot of ground,"
chose to say: "this belongs to me!" They roamed
hither and thither free and proud, in the plenitude of
their strength as yet not "enervated" by civilisation,
in the purity of their "naturally good" instincts.
Feeling an innate pity for the sufferings of others, they
practised without being aware of it the "morality of
sympathy," and would have shuddered at our cruelties.
"When they had dined, they were at peace with all
nature," with their fair partners especially, and if they
had to fight for the latter or for their repasts, "a few
blows" sufficed: the "conqueror satisfied his hunger,
the conquered departed to try his fortune elsewhere,
and all was harmony."[3] How delightful it would have
been to tear oneself from the fever and the tumult of
cities in order to cultivate the society of this ideal
peasant or "savage," and to share, for a few moments,
their careless and unsophisticated existence![4] For

[1] Fontenelle, *op. cit.* p. 64.
[2] Written in 1754 ; cf. also the *Discourse on Arts and Sciences* (1750).
[3] *Discours sur l'inégalité*, n. 9.
[4] This aspiration is that of Tasso in the chorus cited above, and that of Mme.
Deshoulières in the pretty idylls called *Les moutons* (1674), *Les oiseaux*, *Le ruisseau*,
La solitude (1688), some lines of which seem timid forerunners of Rousseau.

there is a pleasure in following, even in imagination only, the "path which leads civilised man back to the charms of primitive life."[1]

Especially when one may hope not to be too much out of one's element amidst rustic "innocence" and "simplicity," when there is a good prospect of finding there, if not the elegance and polish of civilisation, at all events the refinements of sentiment. These last were introduced into pastoral poetry by Gessner, whose first *Idylls*, published in 1756, drew their inspiration alike from Theocritus and Rousseau.[2] The "eclogue shepherd," who, in Virgil and the writers of the Renaissance, had almost always[3] been the harmonious poet of peace and love-making, who had become a wit with Fontenelle, was a "man of feeling" in Gessner. Without discarding Arcadia and the golden age, he became the contemporary of Diderot, of Greuze, and of all that generation who talked of, rather than practised, virtue. One must be hard-hearted indeed not to rise edified from the perusal of the Idylls of Gessner and of Léonard, his French imitator. These little works,[4] somewhat like fables, often try to inculcate, by an appeal to our good feelings, some moral lesson which, "nourishing our soul," will make us "respect and cherish virtue."[5] The "inborn pity" of Rousseau's savages streams from the eyes of Gessner's shepherds in a flood of rapture and tenderness. See the affectionate Mirtil pause in front of the arbour formed by the vine on the threshold of his "solitary hut": he has just espied "his old father, who has sunk back and is slumbering peacefully under the rays of the moon"; he folds his arms and casts a long look on the old man; ever and anon he glances towards the sky through the resplendent foliage, and tears of joy burst from his eyes. "O my father," he cries, "thou whom I honour almost as a god, how sweet is thy slumber! . . . Of a surety thou hast fallen asleep in

---

[1] G. Sand, *La Mare au Diable*, notice, p. 2 (ed. 1856).
[2] See the preface *An den Leser* (ed. Kürschner, pp. 63-5), esp. the lines 22-5, p. 63. and the last two paragraphs (64-5).
[3] Except when controversy or political allusions found their way into pastoral poetry. Virgil set the example in his first Eclogue ; he was followed by the Mantuan, by the Pléiade, and especially by Spenser in *The Shepherd's Calendar*.
[4] Those of Gessner in poetic prose, those of Léonard in prosaic verse.
[5] Florian, *Essai sur la pastorale*, prefixed to *Estelle*. The *Galatée* of the same author is preceded by a "Letter to M. Gessner."

praying, and in praying for me also, my father! . . .
Ah, my best friend, soon I must lose thee—what a sad
thought! Ah, then, then I will raise an altar near thy
tomb, and whenever the happy day recurs on which I
shall have succoured the afflicted, then, my father, I
shall come to pour milk and scatter flowers on thy
grave."[1]   Singular mixture of old pious customs, of
tearful filial love, and of mawkish philanthropy!
These flowers did not come from the fields; they
grew in a hot-house, and this made their perfume
all the more intoxicating to fastidious nostrils in the
eighteenth century.

Under one or the other of these influences, the portrayal of peasant life had remained idyllic and conventional. In the early days of English literature Chaucer,
giving the "Ploughman" a humble place among his
pilgrims, had made him the Parson's brother and
depicted him as a hard worker and worthy man, loving
God with all his heart, and his neighbour "right as
himselve," always ready to pay tithe, "to thresh and
dike and delve, for Christe's sake, for every poore
wight, withouten hire, if it lay in his might."[2] Thomson,
later on, pausing amid the snowstorms of his native
Scotland, had a vision of the cottager, indifferent to
the rigour of the season, bending over the cheerful
blaze of the hearth, and relating at great length one of
his innocent tales or some terrifying "goblin-story":

> . . . Rustic mirth goes round,
> The simple joke that takes the shepherd's heart,
> Easily pleased; the long, loud laugh sincere,
> The kiss snatched hasty from the sidelong maid
> On purpose guardless, or pretending sleep;
> The leap, the slap, the haul, and shook to notes
> Of native music, the respondent dance.[3]

More poetical evenings assuredly than those of
modern French peasants, in a stable overheated by
"exhalations" from the cattle, and lighted by one
wretched candle.[4] Neither the inclemency of winter

---

[1] Fifth idyll, p. 71. Cf. also the curious scene (idyll vii.) in which Amyntas,
a woodman, saves a young oak on the point of being uprooted by a torrent,
sacrifices his time and his bundle to it, and for his only recompense asks the
grateful "dryad" to cure his neighbour Palemon. Balzac's hags were not so
kind to the oaks of the forest (*Les Paysans*, 2nd part, ch. vii.).

[2] Prologue to *The Canterbury Tales*, 529-41.

[3] *The Seasons: Winter.*

[4] Zola, *La Terre*, 1st part, v.

nor the heat of summer can ruffle the good humour of
Thomson's herdsmen or labourers : if the sun burns
too fiercely, the shepherd leads his flock back to the
fold, stretches himself on the " downy moss" near his
" watchful dog," and goes to sleep, " his careless arms
thrown round his head."   When the young villagers,
" brown with meridian toil," set to work to cut the
grass, they all appear " healthful and strong"; " the
ruddy maid" is " half-naked," " her kindled graces
burning o'er her cheek "—

> . . . From dale to dale,
> Waking the breeze, resounds the blended voice
> Of happy labour, love, and social glee

At the close of day, after the shearing-feast,[1] a
shepherdess [2] sometimes slips into a " hazel copse,"
undresses, and plunges timidly into a " refreshing
stream," while her swain watches her unperceived
from a distance.

We are now back in Arcadia, in a voluptuous
region where the bathing Musidora recalls Longus
and Boucher's " Pastorales."   In a graver, but hardly
less optimistic tone, Gray sketches, in a few stanzas
of his *Elegy*,[3] the calm and happy life led by the
" rude forefathers of the hamlet": " the breezy call
of incense-breathing morn," the return to the " blazing
hearth," when " the busy housewife plies her evening
care," and " the children climb his knees the envied
kiss to share "; their joyous labour also—

> How jocund did they drive their team afield !
> How bow'd the woods beneath their sturdy stroke !

And Goldsmith, in his turn, in the first part of *The
Deserted Village*,[4] makes his " Auburn " an earthly
Paradise, describes the " village sports beneath the
spreading tree," the melodious sounds when "up
yonder hill the village murmur rose," the " splendours " of the whitewashed inn parlour,

> Where village statesmen talk'd with looks profound,
> And news much older than their ale went round,

---

[1] *The Seasons : Summer*, a passage imitated by Dyer in his poem *The
Fleece* (1757), book i. conclusion.
[2] Musidora, *ibid.*
[3] *Elegy written in a Country Churchyard* (1750).
[4] Published in 1770.

the strict but kindly schoolmaster, the "modest mansion" of the "village preacher,"

> . . . A man to all the country dear,
> And passing rich with forty pounds a year.

Such is the flattering picture which the poets drew up to 1780[1] of village life and manners, either because they were carried away by their imagination, or because, owing to the continuance of patriarchal customs and to the prosperity of agriculture, English country life really did afford a happiness unknown in later times.

There was a notion, however, that the reality very seldom resembled these ideal descriptions, and certain writers had incidentally revealed the truth. Virgil's first eclogue, for instance, leaves a feeling of melancholy, for the happiness of Tityrus only brings out more clearly the misfortune of Melibœus preparing for exile. The Mantuan himself interrupts for a moment his disquisitions on "honest friendship" and the "madness of love," on the "nature of women" and "religion," to describe, in a few precise and forcible terms, the hardships of country life. "See!" exclaims his Fortunatus, "by what toil we procure our wretched food, and what suffering the poor shepherd must undergo for his flock, his wife, and his children. He is scorched by the cruel heat of summer; he is frozen by the cold of winter; he sleeps in the rain on the ground or on a bed of rough stones; infection, in a variety of forms, threatens his cattle; he is terrified by numberless dangers; brigands, wolves, and soldiers, fiercer than wolves, lie in wait for his sheep."[2] It is the same complaint that is uttered, in a more passionate tone, by La Fontaine's[3] woodman; and La Bruyère, in a terrible passage,[4] shows us the fearful privations

---

[1] In 1776 John Scott (of Amwell), in the poem to which he owes this surname, described his village after Goldsmith (*English Poets*, vol. xvii. p. 475), and exclaimed :

> Such rural life! so calm, it little yields
> Of interesting act, to swell the page
> Of history or song ; yet much the soul
> Its sweet simplicity delights, etc., etc.

One is reminded of the "mechanick echoes of the Mantuan song" of which Johnson and Crabbe speak (*Village*, i. 18).

[2] Battista Spagnuoli, called "The Mantuan," eclogue iii. His collection, published in 1498, contains ten of them.

[3] *Fables*, book i. xvi.

[4] *Caractères*, ch. xi.

of the peasants of the old régime, of "those wild
animals, male and female, scattered over the country
districts, black, livid, and sunburnt," who "dig the
soil with dogged obstinacy," and "at night withdraw
into their holes, where they live on black bread, roots,
and water." Nearly a century later, Johnson, finding
nothing but rudeness, ignorance, and spitefulness
among the "shepherds," called them "envious
savages."[1] In 1782 Cowper, anticipating Crabbe,
wrote that "nowhere but in feigned Arcadian scenes"
do the poor "taste happiness or know what pleasure
means."[2] Long before this time, in fact, illusion had
become impossible, and the adherents of the "golden
age"—Fontenelle and Gessner among others—informed
their readers that they were going to visit an imaginary
world, to escape from the brutal reality. In 1783
pastoral poetry had quite lost touch with the truth,
on which, after all, poetry must rest, even when it
idealises life ; and Fréron's *Année littéraire* was able
to declare that the reign of bucolics "had gone, never
to return," and that "the eclogue now met with only
unfeeling and incredulous readers."[3] The countryman
ran the risk of being forgotten, after having been
misrepresented.

It was time that attention should be redirected to
him by a clear-sighted and honest observer who
ventured to describe things as he saw them. It is not
surprising that the impulse should have come from
England, where literature had always, and especially
in the eighteenth century, been swayed by the instinct
of realism. Pastoral poetry itself had felt this irresistible influence ; it had modelled itself on Theocritus,
whose rustic accent Spenser and most of his successors[4]

[1] *Rasselas*, ch. xix.
[2] *Hope*, 7-10.
[3] Vol. vii. of the year 1783, with reference to *L'Age d'or* of " M. Maréchal."
This journal does not mention Crabbe's *Village*.
[4] Mr. Gosse, in his *Essay on the English Pastoral*, asserts that it comes
straight from the Mantuan, and not from Theocritus or Virgil. This seems a
mistake. *The Shepherd's Calendar*, by Spenser, is derived in equal proportions
from the Mantuan and Theocritus. With Spenser's disciples (Drayton,
Browne, A. Philips) it is the influence of Theocritus that predominates.
Dryden (*Preface* to the translation of Virgil's Pastorals) and Steele (*Guardian*,
Nos. 28 and 30) obviously prefer Theocritus to Virgil as a bucolic poet. A.
Ramsay, in his graceful dramatic idyll, *The Gentle Shepherd* (1725), has left
us the best work extant in this intermediate style, half realistic, half idealistic.
On the other hand, in the beginning of the eighteenth century, William Walsh,
Pope's literary adviser and a Waller among English pastoral poets, aimed at

had tried to reproduce by inventing for their shepherds a harsh, archaic language, of a somewhat improbable kind, or simply by giving them familiar names, sometimes of grotesque invention. Far from launching boldly into the ideal, like its sisters of France and Germany, it had stopped halfway up the hill, not knowing whether to redescend into the plain or climb the heights. It was thus paying an involuntary homage to unadorned truth, and exposing itself to pitiless criticism from matter-of-fact and pessimistic minds. Crabbe was of this number. He did not believe in the much-vaunted "golden age," in the idle fancies with which the "young" poets beguiled their imagination. He knew that "each nation first was rude," that the first men were "cheerless sons of solitude," strangers to "the joys of social life," and that "none felt a care that was not all his own."[1] He did not share Rousseau's theoretical optimism ; far from considering human nature as originally good, and civilisation as corrupting, he felt that the duty of each man and the object of the laws is to combat the evil instincts inherent in human nature, and to ensure the triumph of good.[2] As for Gessner's shepherds and their beautiful sentiments, they would have seemed extremely odd to him, who had been received by his fellow-townsmen in the way described above.[3]

He therefore does not conceal his contempt for the classic pastoral—true perhaps in antiquity, but out-of-date in our day :

> On Mincio's banks, in Cæsar's bounteous reign,
> If Tityrus found the Golden Age again,
> Must sleepy bards the flattering dream prolong,
> Mechanick echoes of the Mantuan song ?[4]

Virgil's elegance and correctness ; he drew Pope after him, and made his pupil a disciple of Fontenelle. But the movement remained abortive, for Gay's ironical *Shepherd's Week* is one of those hybrids that mark and cause the extinction of a race. We know that the French Pastoral, sprung from the Italians and Virgil, evolved in a contrary direction and returned to Theocritus through Gessner (cf. Baldensperger, *loc. cit.*).

[1] *Library*, 1st ed., ll. 317-26. Thomson (*Spring*) had already made the same objection :
> But now those white unblemished manners, whence
> The fabling poets took their golden age,
> Are found no more.

[2] See above, pp. 75-6.

[3] See pp. 133-4.

[4] In the *Works* (p. 114, n. 4) will be found the text of Crabbe's manuscript and (*Village*, i. 15-20) Johnson's corrections, religiously adopted by the

Let us candidly admit that—

> Fled are those times, when, in harmonious strains,
> The rustic poet praised his native plains :
> No shepherds now, in smooth alternate verse,
> Their country's beauty or their nymphs' rehearse.

Let us abandon " the tender strain " in which " fond Corydons complain,"

> And shepherds' boys their amorous pains reveal,
> The only pains, alas ! they never feel.

If the Muses still talk of rustic felicity, it is because they have never experienced the wretchedness of country life, because they are unaware that " peasants now resign their pipes and plod behind the plough "; it is mainly because " no deep thought the trifling subjects ask," " to sing of shepherds " being " an easy task " :

> The happy youth assumes the common strain,
> A nymph his mistress, and himself a swain ;
> With no sad scenes he clouds his tuneful prayer,
> But all, to look like her, is painted fair.[1]

Let us discard these pleasing fictions, and, leaving the imaginary for the real world, follow the poet into the country which he knows best—the Aldborough of his childhood and his youth.   It is not an Arcadia :

> Lo ! where the heath, with withering brake grown o'er,
> Lends the light turf that warms the neighbouring poor ;
> From thence a length of burning sand appears,
> Where the thin harvest waves its wither'd ears ;
> Rank weeds, that every art and care defy,
> Reign o'er the land, and rob the blighted rye ;
> There thistles stretch their prickly arms afar,
> And to the ragged infant threaten war ;
> There poppies nodding mock the hope of toil ;
> There the blue bugloss paints the sterile soil ;

poet.   It is certain that Johnson's first four lines are better than Crabbe's, but this is not the case with the last.   Compare Crabbe's
>   Where Fancy leads, or Virgil led the way ?
with Johnson's
>   Where Virgil, not where Fancy, leads the way ?
in which the word " Fancy " is used in the very inaccurate sense of " poetic or creative imagination," and the superiority of the original line becomes evident. Canon Ainger is of the same opinion, but does not clearly state the reason for his preference (*Life of Crabbe*, pp. 49-50).

[1] *Village*, i. 7-38.

> Hardy and high, above the slender sheaf,
> The slimy mallow waves her silky leaf;
> O'er the young shoot the charlock throws a shade,
> And clasping tares cling round the sickly blade;
> With mingled tints the rocky coasts abound,
> And a sad splendour vainly shines around.[1]

In the minute and too scientific precision of these details, which in themselves are picturesque and characteristic, but which, from not being fused into a general impression, do not form a picture, we recognise the apothecary and the botanist, walking with his eyes fixed on the plants that he is studying, and indifferent to the rest of the landscape. We are also reminded of the laborious years spent by Crabbe in his native " village," of his escape from a poverty which seemed to him part and parcel of its marshy heath, in reading these touching lines:

> As on their neighbouring beach yon swallows stand,
> And wait for favouring winds to leave the land,
> While still for flight the ready wing is spread,
> So waited I the favouring hour, and fled, . . .
> And cried, Ah! hapless they who still remain;
> Who still remain to hear the ocean roar,
> Whose greedy waves devour the lessening shore.

Hapless, above all, those whom fate condemns to live among a people as wretched and thankless as their soil! They have nothing in common with the shepherds in eclogues. Even health, " labour's fair child, that languishes with wealth," is often denied them. Their strength is prematurely exhausted by unremitting labour on their unfertile land:

> Go, then! and see them rising with the sun,
> Through a long course of daily toil to run;
> See them beneath the dog-star's raging heat,
> When the knees tremble and the temples beat;
> Behold them, leaning on their scythes, look o'er
> The labour past, and toils to come explore;
> See them alternate suns and showers engage,
> And hoard up aches and anguish for their age;
> Through fens and marshy moors their steps pursue,
> When their warm pores imbibe the evening dew.

Let the rich admit that " labour may as fatal be to these their slaves" as their own excesses to them-

---

[1] *Village*, i. 63-78.

selves. Too often "a manly pride" makes the poor
"strive in strong toil the fainting heart to hide":

> There you may see the youth of slender frame
> Contend with weakness, weariness, and shame;
> Yet urged along, and proudly loth to yield,
> He strives to join his fellows of the field :
> Till long contending nature droops at last,
> Declining health rejects his poor repast,
> His cheerless spouse the coming danger sees,
> And mutual murmurs urge the slow disease.

Yes, the countryman's life is a sad one, harassed by
intolerable hardship and hopeless poverty:

> Or will you praise that homely, healthy fare,
> Plenteous and plain, that happy peasants share!
> Oh! trifle not with wants you cannot feel,
> Nor mock the misery of a stinted meal.

Addressing the well-to-do admirers of pastoral poems,
the indignant satirist exclaims :

> Ye gentle souls, who dream of rural ease,
> Whom the smooth stream and smoother sonnet please;
> Go! if the peaceful cot your praises share,
> Go, look within, and ask if peace be there;
> If peace be his—that drooping weary sire,
> Or theirs, that offspring round their feeble fire ;
> Or hers, that matron pale, whose trembling hand
> Turns on the wretched hearth th' expiring brand.[1]

Of what avail, in the midst of all this sadness, are the
"few hours of sweet repose" and the "gleams of
transient mirth" which Sunday brings? The pleasures
of the villagers are too short ! Some, perhaps, disport
themselves on the green, between "the squire's tall gate"
and the "churchway walk "; others, "a little tribe of
friends," loiter around and talk of the sermon, which
they "loudly praise," if it has been preached in a loud
voice. The "rural beaux their best attire put on, to
win their nymphs"—

> While those long wed go plain, and by degrees,
> Like other husbands, quit their care to please ;
> Some on the labours of the week look round,
> Feel their own worth, and think their toil renown'd ;
> While some, whose hopes to no renown extend,
> Are only pleased to find their labours end.

[1] *Village*, i. 146-79.

A group of farmers hard by are full of the suppressed discontent peculiar to that class :

> Much in their mind they murmur and lament,
> That one fair day should be so idly spent ;
> And think that Heaven deals hard, to tithe their store
> And tax their time for preachers and the poor,

while it affords them no protection from " nightly pilferers," who steal the fish from their ponds and the fruit from their gardens ; nor from " the meaner rivals " who interfere with their sport :

> Just rich enough to claim a doubtful right.[1]

It seems that in the country there is no security for property, no tranquillity for its inhabitants. The labourer, poverty-stricken already, completes his ruin by his vices. Sunday has not come to an end before quarrels break out on the green ; they arose in the " noisy inn " :

> What time the weekly pay was vanish'd all,
> And the slow hostess scored the threat'ning wall ;
> What time they ask'd, their friendly feast to close,
> A final cup, and that has made them foes ;
> When blows ensue that break the arm of toil,
> And rustic battle ends the boobies' broil. . . .
> See the stout churl, in drunken fury great,
> Strike the bare bosom of his teeming mate.

And now that darkness has fallen, Slander creeps out and taints the green :

> At her approach domestic peace is gone,
> Domestic broils at her approach come on ;
> She to the wife the husband's crime conveys,
> She tells the husband when his consort strays.

Immorality[2] is just as rife in the country as in the

---

[1] *Village*, ii. 1-24 and 55-62. Ll. 59-62 were not in the first edition, their place being taken by the two lines quoted by B. p. 119, n. 1. They appeared for the first time in the edition of 1807, where l. 60, almost incomprehensible in the editions of 1834 and 1861 (Just *right* enough), is correctly printed " Just *rich* enough," the allusion being that, up to 1831, no one in England had a right to shoot who had not an income of not less than £100 a year derived from land (see Sydney Smith's *Essay on Game* [*Edinburgh Review*, 1819], and Boutmy, *Le développement de la constitution anglaise*, p. 240).

[2] *Village*, ii. 50-4, where Crabbe is thinking of his medical experience and perhaps of Hogarth (*The Harlot's Progress*, 1st plate).

capital; see the "silent nymph appear" before the magistrate:

> Frail by her shape, but modest in her tears;
> And while she stands abash'd, with conscious eye,
> Some favourite female of her judge glides by,
> Who views with scornful glance the strumpet's fate,
> And thanks the stars that made her keeper great;
> Near her the swain, about to bear for life
> One certain evil, doubts 'twixt war [1] and wife;
> But, while the faltering damsel takes her oath,
> Consents to wed, and so secures them both.[2]

The distress and the failings common to all country districts are accompanied by special drawbacks in small seaports. Their population of labourers and sailors has all the violence of the ocean beside which it lives, and produces a dangerous type:

> Here joyless roam a wild amphibious race,
> With sullen woe displayed in every face;
> Who far from civil arts and social fly,
> And scowl at strangers with suspicious eye.

Enticed away by the agents of a lawless trade, "drawn from the plough" in a state of intoxication, they have become smugglers:

> . . . Beneath yon cliff they stand,
> To show the freighted pinnace where to land;
> To load the ready steed with guilty haste,
> To fly in terror o'er the pathless waste,
> Or, when detected, in their straggling course,
> To foil their foes by cunning or by force;
> Or yielding part (which equal knaves demand)
> To gain a lawless passport through the land.

Or, with a cruelty worse than any crime, they watch for a wreck:

> Wait on the shore, and, as the waves run high,
> On the tost vessel bend their eager eye,
> Which to their coast directs its vent'rous way,
> Theirs or the ocean's miserable prey.

This was done, even as late as 1811, by the "wreckers" in Cornwall; they used to tie false lights to the tails of tethered horses, and thus lure the ships which they

---

[1] *Village*, ii. 84. Bastards having to be supported by the parish, the justices of the peace had the right to imprison the culprit or force him to enlist.
[2] *Ibid.* ii. 63-70, 33-4, 39-44, 77-86.

wished to plunder on the rocks.[1] How was it possible
for the poet, who had witnessed such scenes, to believe
in the fables of the golden age and in the beautiful
"simplicity of natural life"? He had found nought,
in his long wanderings "amid these frowning fields,"
but "rapine, and wrong and fear."[2] In lamenting his
own wretchedness, he had felt all the more deeply that
of others.

Especially had he felt compassion for the old men
who, with no family or resources, had reached the
brink of the grave. The melancholy of their desolate
existence inspired him with the most eloquent passages
of his poem, those which most impressed his contemporaries and ensured its success. See, he says,
"that hoary swain, whose age can with no cares
except its own engage," who, "propt on a rude staff,"
gazes at the bare branch of a tree, on which one
"withered leaf remains behind, nipt by the frost, and
shivering in the wind"—a sad image of himself and
symbol of his decay. He thinks of his early triumphs:

> He once was chief in all the rustic trade ;
> His steady hand the straightest furrow made ;
> Full many a prize he won, and still is proud
> To find the triumphs of his youth allow'd ;
> A transient pleasure sparkles in his eyes,
> He hears and smiles, then thinks again and sighs ;
> For now he journeys to the grave in pain ;
> The rich disdain him, nay, the poor disdain,
> Alternate masters now their slave command. . . .

He has become one of those poor for whom, by order
of the overseers, the farmers reluctantly find a job, with
food and sixpence a day[3]:

> Oft may you see him, when he tends the sheep,
> His winter charge, beneath the hillock weep ;
> Oft hear him murmur to the winds that blow
> O'er his white locks and bury them in snow,

[1] Sydney, *The Early Days of the Nineteenth Century in England*, London,
1898, pp. 51-2.
[2] *Village*, i. 85-118.
[3] Plus fourpence given by the parish. These were the "roundsmen"
referred to by Sir Frederick Eden (*State of the Poor*, Account of the Parish of
Kibworth Beauchamp in 1795) : "When a man is out of work, he applies to
the overseer, who sends him from house to house to get employed. The
employer is obliged to give him victuals and sixpence a day, and the parish
adds fourpence." Wordsworth, in his *Simon Lee*, shows us the scanty labour
that these worn-out old men could still perform.

When, rous'd by rage and muttering in the morn,
He mends the broken hedge with icy thorn—
" Why do I live, when I desire to be
At once from life and life's long labour free ? "

Why live, when he is thrust on one side by the younger generation, and, unable to help others, is left without help himself? Why live, if he must end his days in " the House that holds the parish poor," the abhorred refuge, the miserable cottage[1] in which the old men, too feeble to work, are herded together? The " village," in fact, has not sufficient funds to build and maintain one of those large asylums or quasi-prisons, in which for more than half a century many large towns and rural districts had housed, sometimes all together and sometimes in separate wards, incorrigible vagabonds, unemployed workmen, and incapables. Without sharing the poet John Dyer's blissful and ridiculous enthusiasm for these " delightful mansions,"[2] without forgetting that, in spite of all precautions and improvements, life in these workhouses is still monotonous and repellent from its sordid surroundings and associations,[3] one may yet believe that the poor, even in the eighteenth century,[4] enjoyed more comfort in them than in the sordid " parish houses" which Crabbe thus describes to us:

Theirs is yon House that holds the parish poor,
Whose walls of mud scarce bear the broken door ;
There where the putrid vapours, flagging, play,
And the dull wheel hums doleful through the day ;
There children dwell who know no parents' care ;
Parents, who know no children's love, dwell there ;
Heart-broken matrons on their joyless bed,
Forsaken wives, and mothers never wed ;

[1] Cf. above, p. 64.
[2] Dyer's *Fleece* (1757), Chalmers's *English Poets*, vol. xiii. pp. 241-2.
[3] Cf. Miss Edith Sellar's *In the Day-room of a Workhouse* (*Nineteenth Century*, September, 1902).
[4] See the numerous details on the Nacton Workhouse, in Suffolk, given by Arthur Young (*Tour to the East of England*, vol. ii. pp. 178 *seq.*, 1771): " There are various apartments for men with their wives—for single men and lads—and also for single women and girls, for the sick, etc., and a surgery. . . . The poor are undoubtedly taken excellent care of, both sick and well. . . . They are clothed in a warm comfortable manner, and are in general pretty well satisfied with their situation, but the confinement disgusts them." For the opposition between the " workhouses " and the " parish poorhouses " see Nicholls, *History of the English Poor-Law*, ed. 1898, vol. ii. p. 101.

Dejected widows with unheeded tears,
And crippled age with more than childhood fears ;
The lame, the blind, and far the happiest they !
The moping idiot, and the madman gay.

How can one live or die in such surroundings, amid
the " clamours of the crowd below" and the "loud
groans" proceeding from above, from the sad room
where "the sick their final doom receive"? Let us
follow the relentless poet through this chamber of
horrors ; he is too much in love with the truth,
especially when it is painful, to spare us the slightest
detail. Let us ascend with him into the sick-room :

. . . That room which one rude beam divides,
And naked rafters form the sloping sides,
Where the vile bands that bind the thatch are seen,
And lath and mud are all that lie between,
Save one dull pane, that, coarsely patch'd, gives way
To the rude tempest, yet excludes the day ;
Here, on a matted flock, with dust o'erspread,
The drooping wretch reclines his languid head ;
For him no hand the cordial cup applies,
Or wipes the tear that stagnates in his eyes ;
No friends with soft discourse his pain beguile,
Or promise hope, till sickness wears a smile.

But suddenly " a loud and hasty summons " is heard,
which "shakes the thin roof and echoes round the walls":

Anon, a figure enters, quaintly neat,
All pride and business, bustle and conceit ;
With looks unalter'd by these scenes of woe,
With speed that, entering, speaks his haste to go,
He bids the gazing throng around him fly,
And carries fate and physic in his eye ;
A potent quack, long versed in human ills,
Who first insults the victim whom he kills ;
Whose murd'rous hand a drowsy Bench protect,
And whose most tender mercy is neglect.
Paid by the parish for attendance here,
He wears contempt upon his sapient sneer ;
In haste he seeks the bed where Misery lies,
Impatience mark'd in his averted eyes ;
And, some habitual queries hurried o'er,
Without reply, he rushes on the door :
His drooping patient, long inured to pain,
And long unheeded, knows remonstrance vain ;
He ceases now the feeble help to crave
Of man. . . .

But before dying some "pious doubts" and "simple fears" arise in his mind:

> Fain would he ask the parish priest to prove
> His title certain to the joys above;
> For this he sends the murmuring nurse, who calls
> The holy stranger to these dismal walls:
> And doth not he, the pious man, appear,
> He, "passing rich with forty pounds a year"? [1]
> Ah! no; a shepherd of a different stock,
> And far unlike him, feeds this little flock;
> A jovial youth, who thinks his Sunday's task
> As much as God or man can fairly ask;
> The rest he gives to loves and labours light,
> To fields the morning, and to feasts the night;
> None better skill'd the noisy pack to guide,
> To urge their chace, to cheer them or to chide;
> A sportsman keen, he shoots through half the day,
> And, skill'd at whist, devotes the night to play;
> Then, while such honours bloom around his head,
> Shall he sit sadly by the sick man's bed,
> To raise the hope he feels not, or with zeal
> To combat fears that e'en the pious feel?

No, he will let the poor wretch die without the consolations of religion.   Let us attend the funeral:

> Now once again the gloomy scene explore,
> Less gloomy now—the bitter hour is o'er,
> The man of many sorrows sighs no more.
> Up yonder hill, behold how sadly slow
> The bier moves winding from the vale below. . . .
> Now to the church behold the mourners come,
> Sedately torpid and devoutly dumb;
> The village children now their games suspend,
> To see the bier that bears their ancient friend:
> For he was one in all their idle sport,
> And like a monarch ruled their little court;
> The pliant bow he form'd, the flying ball,
> The bat, the wicket, were his labours all;
> Him now they follow to his grave, and stand,
> Silent and sad, and gazing hand in hand;
> While bending low, their eager eyes explore
> The mingled relics of the parish poor. . . .
> The busy priest, detain'd by weightier care,
> Defers his duty till the day of prayer;
> And, waiting long, the crowd retires, distrest
> To think a poor man's bones should lie unblest.

[1] See above, p. 153.

But what is the contempt of the world to the wretched
man ? Is he not now one of the happy ones who are
free from pain ?

> No more, O Death ! thy victim starts to hear
> Churchwarden stern, or kingly overseer ;
> No more the farmer claims his humble bow,
> Thou art his lord, the best of tyrants thou ![1]

Begun in poverty, continued in hardship, concluded
in the desolation of want, such is, affirms Crabbe,
the existence of the countryman—far removed, alas !
from the Arcadian felicity with which people liked to
invest it.

One has only to place *The Library* and *The Village*
side by side to measure the progress made by the
author in this last poem. Still satirical and descriptive, but taking his subject from real life and no longer
from an artificial literary tradition, he has contrived,
by the accuracy and force of his inward vision, by the
minute distinctness of his reproduction, to give his
work such a stamp of originality that he has added a
new province, so to speak, to the realm of poetry and
secured a place in the history of literature. None
of his later poems, though much longer, have the
vigour and significance of this. To escape from the
atmosphere of illusion which Goldsmith had thrown
over the first part of his *Deserted Village*, Crabbe sat
down in front of the reality, copied it with all the
energy and impartiality in his power, and divided it
into a series of little pictures taken from life and transported unchanged into his verses. The reader has
only to recall the various scenes which I have tried to
bring out in the foregoing analysis—the reapers sinking under a scorching sun, the sick labourer dragging
himself to his work, the groups which form of a Sunday
on the village green in front of the church, the poor
girl insulted in the magistrate's court, the repulsive
poorhouse—and he will admit that these sketches,
remarkable in themselves for the scientific precision
of the details, form collectively an ample composition,
quite a realistic epic, in fact, of country life. No one
had attempted this before Crabbe : no attention was
paid to rustics other than pastoral shepherds ; their
rough ways being known, they were considered at

[1] *Village*, i. 180-346.

the most as useful for supplying a comic scene—a
fight, for instance, in a churchyard, with fragments of
skeletons;[1] and if a respectable yokel was introduced
in a novel, care was taken to give him a little polish
before the *dénouement*.[2] Crabbe had no scruples of
this kind; as he had known the rustic, so he painted
him, and he was rewarded for his plain-speaking
by the attention of the public. *The Critical Review*
for July, 1783, strongly commended the style and the
sentiments of the poem, compared Crabbe's *Village*
with Goldsmith's *Deserted Village*, and was of opinion
that the former showed "more justice and almost
an equal warmth of colouring."   In November, *The
Monthly Review* made some objections, and wondered if
all villages were like Crabbe's, if the author had not
taken the exception for the rule, and if there were not
as much exaggeration in "representing a peasant's life
as a life of unremitting labour and merciless anxiety"
as in describing the country as wearing a perpetual
smile and its inhabitants as enjoying a round of un-
interrupted pleasures. But it added, in conclusion,
that "the poem contained many splendid lines, many
descriptions that were picturesque and original, and
such as would do credit to the ingenious author of *The
Library*."   In the following month *The Gentleman's
Magazine* recommended the public to read a work
"which was well worth the trouble"; and Horace
Walpole anticipated the verdict of posterity by declaring that Crabbe could "write lines that one can
remember."[3]

Not that *The Village* is a masterpiece, free from all
defect. Without at present entering into the question
of Crabbe's realism, of its artistic value and its drawbacks, without looking beyond the poem before us,
one cannot help admitting that the composition has
serious imperfections. The author has managed to
contradict himself at least once: when, in the description of the poorhouse, he takes us to the pauper's
bedside and shows us his forlornness, he points out
that "no hand the cordial cup" applies, and yet this
same sick man, a little further on, sends his "nurse"

[1] Fielding, *Tom Jones*, book iv. ch. viii.
[2] Cf. in very different styles the *Paysan parvenu* of Marivaux, and Pamela's
parents, "John and Elizabeth Andrews," in Richardson's novel.
[3] Letter to the Rev. William Mason. *Letters*, ed. Cunningham (1858),
vol. viii. p. 377.

to fetch the clergyman.[1] In another place [2] Crabbe
introduces a development which he suddenly interrupts and then resumes in a subsequent passage. In
the series of pictures that makes up the work there
reigns a certain disorder which is not the effect of art.
Over and over again, in order to present a methodical
analysis, I have had to depart from the author's plan—
to go from one place to another, at one time to the
middle, at another to the end, and then retrace my
steps. Especially is it difficult to understand why
Crabbe has divided his poem into two "books": why
begin a second, when the pauper, his hero, has been
buried in the first? This second book has too much
resemblance to one of those "continuations" which
are never so good as what has gone before. The
opening is unfortunate: the cheerful description of
Sunday in the village follows too closely on the
labourer's death, and is a bad introduction to the
ironical portrayal of quarrels and vices that comes
next. It is a too transient smile, an over-bright patch
on a dark ground. Lastly, can anything be more out
of place than the conclusion of the poem, than the
funeral oration on Lord Robert Manners, the brother of
the Duke of Rutland? Not that this young man, who
died a hero's death at the moment of a naval victory,[3]
was unworthy of the praises which Crabbe bestows on
him in singularly eloquent and powerful lines;[4] but,
in order to connect this accessory with the rest of the
work in some way or other, the poet has been obliged
to distort his intention, to do violence to his idea. He
wanted to show the rich, who were misled by pastoral
effusions, the real lot of the rustics, to contrast the
luxury of the former with the misery of the latter, and
thus draw the attention of the great to a class which
has no share of the good things of this life. His
pessimism was to be limited, and not to go beyond the
country districts: he knew perfectly well that a large
fortune gives some individuals chances of happiness
which they perhaps neglect, but which they none the
less have once possessed. Only, in order that Lord

---

[1] *Village*, i. 270 and 300.
[2] *Ibid.* 42-6 and 140-63.
[3] See above, p. 139, n. 2.
[4] *Village*, ii. 115-207, and the appendix of the poem (ed. 1834), where the
obituary notice written by Crabbe for *The Annual Register* of 1783 is reproduced (*Works*, pp. 121-3).

Robert Manners should be mourned even in the
"village," he had to begin by telling the poor that
they are wrong to "lament their fate" and "envy the
great,"[1] misfortune being the lot of all mankind; he
had to display a universal and commonplace pessimism,
dictated by circumstances and foreign to the original
conception of the work.   Here the chaplain has spoilt
the poet.

And it is not only in the composition, but also in the
tone that a want of unity is observable.   If some of the
pictures enumerated above are examined again—for
instance, the most important of all, the description of
the poorhouse—it will be seen that Crabbe wishes to
make us feel pity for the sufferings of the humble; on
the other hand, if one turns to such sketches as those
of the quarrels and of the smugglers, one will incline
to the belief that the author feels the most profound
contempt for his heroes.   The reader will therefore
hesitate.   He will be tempted to say to the poet, How
am I to pity the distress and the forlornness of your
poor, when you have depicted them to me as vicious
and unworthy of my sympathy?   The explanation of
this contradiction seems to be that Crabbe, a satirist
by nature, cannot resist his propensity: he must have
something to criticise.   If he can find fault with others
besides the village people, he readily does it: he attacks
successively the doctor, the clergyman, the magistrate,
and, by way of contrast, is moved with pity for the
rustic, their victim; but, if he happens to be dealing
with the poor only, he administers the lash to them
impartially.   Crabbe always had the plain-spokenness
of the realist and of the man of science.

There remains the question whether the satirical
bent of his mind has not interfered with the truth of
his descriptions, whether the objections of *The Monthly
Review* are not well-founded, and whether the
poet has not exaggerated the wretchedness of the
country districts.   Here a distinction must be made:
the countryman portrayed by Crabbe in *The Village*
is not the "peasant" with whom Balzac's and Zola's
novels have made us so familiar, the man bound to the
land by ancestral ties, the small proprietor, a slave of
routine and inured to hardship, who wears himself out
and, if need be, becomes a criminal in order to keep

[1] *Village*, ii. 101-6.

his patrimony or increase it.   This middle class had
existed among the English cultivators; the yeomen
who formed it had played a decisive part in history by
supplying Cromwell with his sturdiest recruits.   But
in the course of the eighteenth century it had lost
much of its importance: some members of it had
raised themselves to the rank of country gentlemen;
others—the majority—had become mere farmers, after
having sold their land to noblemen, squires, or wealthy
merchants.   Under the name of "dalesmen" or "statesmen" they still subsisted, but much impoverished, in
the "Lake country," where Wordsworth knew them,
admired the patriarchal dignity of their frugal, laborious manners, and described them in his portrait of
Michael.[1]   The farmers who had replaced them in
England, becoming more and more prosperous as the
century drew to a close, found that "fields and flocks
had charms"[2] for those who turned them to account.
Far from including such among the poor, Crabbe likes
to represent them as satisfied with their position and
comfortably off.   But he had remarked that the richer
they grew the more hopeless the poverty of their
labourers became, and it is with these alone that
he deals in his *Village.*   The picture which he gives of
them, in spite of its copious details, remains generic
and abstract, somewhat like the satirical portraits
drawn by Young: Crabbe's peasant is not a *particular*
peasant, with his individual character added to that of
his class; he is a typical peasant, a less artistic conception, perhaps, than the other would have been, but
all the more representative of the English labourer in
1783.   And this picture, as we have seen, is a profoundly pessimistic one: the green fields amid which
the worker toils are to him only a vale of tears, with
no prospect but destitution and death.   Is the sombre
poet right?   Was the life of these labourers all privations and vices, varied at the most by a few transient
gleams of pleasure?   Did they not taste the lasting
joys of family life, which Burns was to sing a few
years later?[3]   Were they strangers to the happiness

[1] See, on this point, a letter from Dorothy Wordsworth written from Windy
Brow in 1794 (Knight, *Life of Wordsworth*, vol i. p. 90), and a letter from
Wordsworth to Fox (Knight, *ibid.* p. 220), accompanying *The Brothers* and
Michael.   "This class of men," says the poet, "is rapidly disappearing."

[2] *Village*, i. 39-40.

[3] *The Cotter's Saturday Night*, st. iv. vi. xii.-xiii.

of seeing now and again a loved daughter, now a
"woman grown" and bashfully courted by an honest
and strapping "neebor lad"? On "Saturday nights"
did the family never gather round the paternal hearth
and listen, bareheaded, to the father reading the Bible
or chanting some ancestral hymn? Alas! I much fear
that the gloomier picture is also the truer one. Who
does not remember the failure of Burns's and his
father's hopes, in spite of their dogged struggle,
of their "hard labour and most rigid economy"?
When want wrings the heart of man, it stifles the
poetry of life. And we must not forget that, according
to the unanimous testimony of historians, the English
agricultural labourer was in 1783 passing through a
crisis which was still far from its close. The prosperity which had marked the commencement of the
century seems to have been followed about 1770 by a
trying period in which the agricultural labourers, and
not the farmers, felt the effect of bad harvests, of more
and more burdensome wars, and of repeated encroachments on common lands. In 1782 corn had been
dearer than in the preceding fifty years; the American
War raised the price of all the necessaries of life,[1]
while wages on an average were not more than nine
shillings a week.[2] Again, noblemen who wished to
round off their properties, business men or "nabobs"
in quest of the political influence attaching to the
possession of land, drove the poor out of the cottages
which they occupied on the still free lands, deprived
them of their gardens, and often even of their work.
In many places cattle-breeding was substituted for
corn-growing, and a few shepherds sufficed, instead of
a number of reapers; the commons were claimed
by the lord of the manor, wrested from the poor and
fenced in.[3]   The agricultural labourer, seeing his

[1] Cf. Toynbee, *Lectures and Industrial Revolution* (ed. 1896), p. 100; and
Lecky, *History of England*, vol. vi. pp. 201-3.

[2] Arthur Young's *Eastern Tour*, vol. ii. pp. 78 *seq.* : "Labour: in harvest,
2s. a day and beer; in haytime, 1s. 6d. and beer; in winter, 1s. 2d." In 1840
these wages had rather diminished than increased (Toynbee, p. 69). To-day
they are nearly 16s., which does not prevent intelligent labourers from leaving
the country for the towns (cf. *Life in our Villages*, Cassell, 1891, *passim*, and
an interesting article in the *Western Daily Press*, August 20th, 1903,
Farmers and Labourers).

[3] And the inhabitants would leave the village, like those of Auburn (see the
second part of Goldsmith's *Deserted Village*, and also Langhorne's allusion to
the "gilt Nabob" in *The Country Justice*, part iii., written in 1776: Chalmers's
English Poets, vol. xvi. p. 455).

resources diminish and his expenditure increase, de-
spaired of the future and sank into that apathy which
is still the great blot on his condition.

Thus *The Village* is a faithful picture, within the
limits which the author has set himself. More than
this, it is, on the whole, a sympathetic· description of a
class hitherto unknown or despised. The indignation
which Crabbe displays on the subject of pastoral
poetry is due not only to his hatred of all unreality,
but also to his conviction that in flattering the illusions
of the rich, the traditional eclogue was fatal to the very
peasants whom it wished to idealise. Hence the insistence with which the poet addresses his aristocratic and
middle-class readers, takes them to the pauper's
deathbed, and exclaims:

> Say, ye, opprest by some fantastic woes,
> Some jarring nerve that baffles your repose ;
> Who press the downy couch, while slaves advance
> With timid eye to read the distant glance ;
> Who with sad prayers the weary doctor tease,
> To name the nameless ever new disease ;
> Who with mock patience dire complaints endure,
> Which real pain and that alone can cure :
> How would ye bear in real pain to lie,
> Despised, neglected, left alone to die ?
> How would ye bear to draw your latest breath
> Where all that's wretched paves the way for death ? [1]

The hand which wrote these lines was a virile one,
and it was a noble heart that inspired them. Beneath
Crabbe's pessimism and satirical humour there lies a
profound feeling of the equality of all men before vice,
misfortune, and death. In London and at Belvoir he
was living in the midst of a fashionable and frivolous
society, engrossed in political intrigue and in pleasure,
devoting to card-playing the time which it could spare
from the pursuit of game or of honours; he could read
in the conversation and the manner of those around
him that contempt for the poor so naïvely revealed
to us in the following letter from the Duchess of
Buckingham to the pious Countess of Huntingdon:
"I thank your Ladyship for the information concerning
the Methodist preachers; their doctrines are most
repulsive and strongly tinctured with impertinence
and disrespect towards their superiors, in perpetually

---

[1] *Village*, i. 250-61.

endeavouring to level all ranks and do away with all distinctions. It is monstrous to be told you have a heart as sinful as the common wretches that crawl on the earth. This is highly offensive and insulting, and I cannot but wonder that your Ladyship should relish any sentiments so much at variance with high rank and good breeding." [1]   To such arrogance as this, Crabbe replies in *The Village*, as Wesley might have done in one of his sermons :

> Yet why, you ask, these humble crimes relate,
> Why make the Poor as guilty as the Great?
> To show the great, those mightier sons of pride,
> How near in vice the lowest are allied ;
> Such are their natures and their passions such,
> But these disguise too little, those too much ;
> So shall the man of power and pleasure see
> In his own slave as vile a wretch as he ;
> In his luxurious lord the servant find
> His own low pleasures and degenerate mind :
> And each in all the kindred vices trace
> Of a poor, blind, bewilder'd, erring race,
> Who, a short time in varied fortune past,
> Die, and are equal in the dust at last. [2]

Since rich and poor are on a level morally, the only superiority which the former can have is to help the wretched out of their distress.   Such is the lesson to be learned from *The Village* : by it Crabbe is akin to those members of the enlightened middle-class, to the Wesleys, the Raikeses, the Howards, and the Wilber-forces, who, from 1750 onwards, devoted themselves to the improvement of the moral and material condition of the outcasts of society.   He shares with Goldsmith and Langhorne the glory of having introduced philan-thropy not only into poetry, but also into literature, and of having anticipated by half a century those who, like Ebenezer Elliott and Mrs. Gaskell, drew the atten-tion of their contemporaries to the destitution of the workers in field and factory.

IV

HAVING acquired a competence and fame, Crabbe found himself at the end of the heroic period of his life.   He was now a successful man, in a position to settle and

---

[1] Quoted by Abbey and Overton, *The English Church in the Eighteenth Century*, vol. ii. p. 119 (ed. 1878).

[2] *Village*, ii. 87-100.

realise the dream of his youth. Eleven years of waiting
had not weakened the affection of Mira, still faithful,
in spite of the flight of her springtide and the evident
ill-will of her uncle, who was more exacting than
generous. The poet therefore availed himself of the
leisure afforded by the rising of Parliament, on
July 16th, 1783, to return to Beccles, after an absence
of ten months, and resume with his betrothed their
long walks and rides in the neighbourhood. The
climate that year had been most bewildering : the
summer was advancing, and yet the sun was continually hidden by dense clouds and mists. Nature
seemed to have put on mourning, and people were
puzzled to account for it.[1] On Monday, August 18th,
about nine o'clock in the evening, Crabbe and Mira
were returning on horseback from one of their ex
cursions, when there suddenly appeared in the sky
two globes of fire, each about two feet broad, and
followed by eight others, which gradually diminished
in size and dissolved into a luminous dust ; a long trail
of flame ending in a bright point completed the meteor,
whose dazzling radiance, made up of a soft yellow and
of all the other prismatic colours, lighted the earth for
about two minutes.[2] Miss Elmy, says the Biographer,[3]
thought that the end of the world had come, while
Crabbe, his hand raised, transfixed with admiration
and terror, watched the phenomenon slowly disappear
in the south-east.

Shortly afterwards the poet was recalled to
Belvoir by his duties as chaplain ; from there he
went to London about the middle of November,[4]
visited, with a pleasure which he never tried to
conceal, Drury Lane Theatre, where Kemble was then
playing Richard III. and Mrs. Siddons Constance,[5]

[1] Cf. Cowper, *The Task: The Timepiece*, ll. 57 *seq.* and the notes ; also
the letter to Newton of June 17th.
[2] See the description given in *The Gentleman's Magazine* for September,
1783, p. 744 (a letter from Greenwich).
[3] B. p. 35.
[4] Parliament met on the 11th.
[5] Cf. Genest, *History of the Stage*, 1832, vol. vi. pp. 293 *seq.* Kemble,
coming from Dublin, had made his first appearance in London in *Hamlet* on
September 30th in the same year. Mrs. Siddons played Isabella (*Measure
for Measure*) on November 3rd, the Mrs. Beverley of Moore's *Gamester* on
November 22nd for the first time, and Constance of *King John* on December 10th. The Biographer is mistaken in saying that his father admired Mrs.
Abingdon's and Mrs. Jordan's acting at this time. The latter acted Sir Harry
Wildair (in Farquhar's *Constant Couple*) on May 2nd, 1787, for the first time

and had the honour of being presented to His very
youthful Royal Highness the Prince of Wales, afterwards George IV.[1] A few days later he left for
Beccles, where, on December 15th, was celebrated his
marriage with Miss Elmy, then in her thirty-third
year.[2] The newly married couple had hardly arrived
at Belvoir, where a suite of rooms had been reserved
for them, when news came of the fall of Fox's and
Lord North's Coalition Ministry,[3] of Pitt's accession to
the dignity of Prime Minister, of the Duke of Rutland's
return to office and his approaching appointment to
the Lord-Lieutenancy of Ireland.

When Rutland went to Ireland, in February, 1784,
Crabbe did not accompany him, either because the
post of vice-regal chaplain had been given to some
more influential personage, or because the poet did
not wish to be exiled to a country where, for want of a
university degree, he could not aspire to any well-paid
canonry. He remained therefore at Belvoir until the
kindness of the Chancellor or the interest of his "noble
protector" could provide him with a more lucrative cure
than his two livings in Dorsetshire. These, adminis-
tered by a curate,[4] required the presence of their
incumbent at the beginning of 1784. Crabbe, accompanied by Mira, undertook that journey, then somewhat tedious. On March 25th he was at Evershot,
where he expounded to his parishioners " the duties
of the ministers of the Christian religion."[5] After a
stay in this part of the world, where Mr. George Baker's[6]

(cf. Genest, *ibid.* p. 480). As for Mrs. Abingdon, she was acting in March,
1784, at Covent Garden when Crabbe returned to London (see also *The
Newspaper*, l. 340.)

[1] Thoroton, Crabbe's friend, had taken him into the box of the Prince of
Wales's equerries, and His Highness happening to be there, an explanation
had to be given, and afterwards a formal presentation took place (B. p. 35).

[2] Parish Register (Beccles) : " George Crabbe, Clerk, of this parish, single-
man, and Sarah Elmy, of the same, single-woman, were married in this church
by licence from the Chancellor this fifteenth day of December 1783 by me
P. Routh, Curate."

[3] Burke also belonged to this Ministry, which lasted barely nine months
(April 2nd—December 17th, 1783). It succeeded Shelburne, and was
replaced at the King's command by Pitt and Thurlow.

[4] Cf. *Notes and Queries for Somerset and Dorset*, vol. viii. March, 1903 :
" It seems probable that the Rev. Nathaniel Bartlett acted as Crabbe's curate
during the whole time he was rector " (Note by Mr. Broadley).

[5] See a sermon in Mr. Murray's manuscripts dated " Evershot, Dorset,
1784 : Discourse for March 25th at Evershot Chapel."

[6] A local journal, the name of which cannot be ascertained, states : " Some-
time previous to 1784 Mr. Baker commenced a contest for one of the then

hospitality must have been particularly acceptable to him, he returned to London, paid a visit with Mira to Burke, "who received them with the greatest cordiality," and invited them to meet at dinner his old schoolfellow and friend Richard Shackleton,[1] whose daughter, known under the name of Mary Leadbeater, subsequently kept up an assiduous correspondence with Crabbe. Shackleton, it appears, had a great admiration for the works of our poet, and told him, not without provoking a modest disclaimer, that "Goldsmith's Village would henceforth be really the deserted Village."[2] Returning to Belvoir,[3] Crabbe spent another year there in various occupations—in taking the duty for Dr. Thomas Parke[4] at Stathern, or devoting the leisure left him by the cares of family life[5] to the composition of an epistle in verse to the Duke of Rutland[6] or of a new poem.

undivided county seats, but he does not seem to have gone to the poll. Above the classic porticos of Frome St. Quintin House one may still read the words 'Geo. Baker, A.D. 1782.'" Crabbe's host died in 1803. Cf. B. p. 37.

[1] Born in 1728, two years after the foundation—by his father, Abraham—of the school at Ballitore, to which Burke was first sent. The Shackletons, settled in Ireland but originally from Yorkshire, were Quakers.

[2] Cf. *Leadbeater Papers*, 2nd ed. 1862, vol. i. p. 135, and B. pp. 64, 65. This meeting took place on June 6th.

[3] And not to Stathern, as B. says, p. 37.

[4] Cf. Ainger, *Life of Crabbe*, p. 61. According to Mr. Taylor, Rector of Stathern in 1902, Thomas Parke was Archdeacon of Stamford, where he resided, as well as incumbent of Stathern. A sermon preached by Crabbe at Stathern on June 27th, 1784, is still in existence (Murray Collection).

[5] B. p. 36: "A child born to my parents, while still at Belvoir, survived but a few hours."

[6] See the publications of "The Historical MSS. Commission," report 12, London, 1889, vol. ii. p. 330: "*An Epistle*, 1784, August, Belvoir," where the MS. of this poem now is. It has little interest, and is full of faults. It shows especially that Crabbe was anxious not to be forgotten. The following is the most characteristic passage:

> Think you, my Lord, your Belvoir's heights infuse
> Vigor, like old Parnassus, to the Muse?
> Not so: Parnassus was a dismal scene,
> And hunger made the wretched Tenants keen:
> Still the same kinds of Inspiration last:
> A London garret and a long day's fast.
>
> I—and I thank your Grace—have ceased to strive
> For niggard rhymes that keep us just alive;
> And little care if now it pleased the State
> To tax your poets as they tax your plate;
> Exempt from both, my useless Life I'd close,
> Use humbler ware, and correspond in prose.

This is almost autobiography. The poem contains 126 lines. Contrary to what the "Commission" asserts, it was never published in the *Works*. The piece entitled *Belvoir Castle* (*Works*, p. 263) is quite different. Since this note was written, some extracts from the *Epistle* have appeared in *The Book Monthly*, May, 1906, pp. 546-7.

V

As if Crabbe had failed to see what constituted the originality of *The Village*, its human interest and its direct contact with life, he reverted in *The Newspaper*, published on March 15th, 1785,[1] to impersonal satire and frigid description, to the literary tradition from which *The Library* had sprung. By a truly singular contrast, one of the dullest of his writings was inspired by an extremely keen political struggle. In March, 1784, Pitt and his colleagues, raised to power by the abrupt intervention of the royal authority, exposed for the last three months to the furious but ineffectual attacks of Fox and his majority, had seized the propitious moment, dissolved Parliament, and appealed to the country. The two opponents personified antagonistic principles : the triumph of Pitt would be for George III. the recognition of his " prerogative," of his absolute right to choose his own ministers ; the victory of Fox would mean the humiliation of the Crown, and its subjection to the will of the House of Commons in the selection of the head of the Cabinet and its members. Fox, unfortunately, had made two consecutive mistakes which had deprived him of his great popularity : to force the hand of George III., he had, in the preceding year, contracted an impolitic alliance with his old opponent, Lord North, and availed himself of his short stay in office to bring in a Bill curtailing the privileges of the East India Company, thus alarming all vested interests.[2] After a violent campaign, the election ended in a crushing defeat for him and the Whigs.

Crabbe seems to have followed the various incidents of this contest with considerable indifference, either because, in spite of his sympathy for Burke and Liberal ideas, the coalition of Fox and Lord North was distasteful to him, or because his obligations to the Duke of Rutland,[3] a colleague of Pitt in the ministry, had made him assume a prudent attitude and an air of disillusion. He therefore does

[1] See an advertisement in *The Public Advertiser* of the same day.

[2] For the Parliamentary history of this time, see the very interesting and copious work of a contemporary, Sir Nathaniel Wraxall, *Historical Memoirs of my own Time* (ed. 1904, pp. 499 *seq.*).

[3] We may also note that Crabbe, diplomatic as usual, dedicated the poem to Thurlow, thus reminding the Chancellor of his existence.

not aim the shafts of his satire at one of the parties
before him, but at party spirit in general. He condemns its excesses, he ridicules its follies with his
habitual moderation and good sense. It is not, he says
in his Preface,[1] at the moment when I am censuring
the " temerity and ignorance " of the newspapers, that
I shall " adopt their rage." The poet would be ill-
advised who descended into the arena, carried away
by the passions of a turbulent and troublous time. He
might choose some "subject of the day" for his
effusions, and obtain a hearing for a few hours perhaps,
but the next morning some new wonder would " puff
his praise away." He would reap more ill-will than
fame in such a contest :

> . . . Should we force the peaceful Muse to wield
> Her feeble arms amid the furious field,
> Where party pens a wordy war maintain,
> Poor is her anger, and her friendship vain ;
> And oft the foes who feel the sting, combine,
> Till serious vengeance pays an idle line ;
> For party-poets are like wasps, who dart
> Death to themselves, and to their foes but smart.

Let them leave to the newswriters the sorry task of
spreading hatred, calumny, and lies throughout the
land ; animated by a generous contempt, let them
reproach the town for preferring the harshest prose
to the smoothest numbers, and let them "sing their
rivals with a rival's pride." Organs of party spirit,
newspapers take different sides :

> Some champions for the rights that prop the crown,
> Some sturdy patriots, sworn to pull them down ;
> Some neutral powers, with secret forces fraught,
> Wishing for war, but willing to be bought :
> While some to every side and party go,
> Shift every friend, and join with every foe.

Most of them, however, swim with the tide :

> Fickle and false, they veer with every gale ;
> As birds that migrate from a freezing shore
> In search of warmer climes, come skimming o'er,
> Some bold adventurers first prepare to try
> The doubtful sunshine of the distant sky ;
> But soon the growing summer's certain sun
> Wins more and more, till all at last are won ;

[1] *Works*, p. 125.

> So, on the early prospect of disgrace,
> Fly in vast troops this apprehensive race ;
> Instinctive tribes ! their failing food they dread,
> And buy, with timely change, their future bread.

And it is in guides of this kind that the public puts its
trust ! How many an "honest zealot" have they not
taken from trade ; how many pious clergymen have
been made "factious tools" by them ! They are to
be found everywhere, in—

> . . . Tavern haunts where politicians meet ;
> Where rector, doctor, and attorney pause,
> First on each parish, then each public cause :
> Indited roads, and rates that still increase ;
> The murmuring poor, who will not fast in peace ;
> Election zeal and friendship, since declined ;
> A tax commuted, or a tithe in kind ;
> The Dutch and Germans kindling into strife ;
> Dull port and poachers vile ; the serious ills of life.

Nothing resists the contagion, not even the "peaceful,
pleasant" villages, which are full of Whig farmers and
Tory labourers, not even the inn frequented by the
yokel whose forty-shilling freehold gives him a vote.
There he sits, with the newspaper before him :

> Here he delights the weekly news to con,
> And mingle comments as he blunders on ;
> To swallow all their varying authors teach,
> To spell a title, and confound a speech :
> Till with a muddled mind he quits the news,
> And claims his nation's licence to abuse ;
> Then joins the cry, "That all the courtly race
> Are venal candidates for power and place " ;
> Yet feels some joy, amid the general vice,
> That his own vote will bring its wonted price.[1]

Satisfied with having thus ridiculed party spirit in
the sheets which propagate it, and in the person of the
elector who is its victim, Crabbe now undertakes to
describe to us in detail a newspaper of his time.

In 1785, two years before the foundation of *The
Times*, the English Press, which was about a century
and a half old,[2] had already attained considerable

---

[1] *Newspaper*, ll. 5-12, 115-20, 125-40, 154-62, 183-92.
[2] " The first English publication which tried to appear at regular intervals
seems to have been *The Weekly News from Italy*. . . . (1622)," says M.
Beljame (*Le public et les hommes de lettres en Angleterre*, p. 163).

proportions. Its principal organs, *The Morning Chronicle* and *The Public Advertiser*, played an important political part. William Woodfall, the editor of *The Morning Chronicle*, had been the first to give, in 1769, a daily report of the Parliamentary debates; his elder brother, Henry Sampson Woodfall,[1] had from 1767 to 1772 opened the columns of *The Public Advertiser* to the celebrated pamphleteer who concealed his identity under the pseudonym of "Junius." Yet it is enough to cast a glance at one of the ninety sheets[2] which were published in Great Britain and Ireland at that time to form an idea of the progress that had to be accomplished, and which was gradually accomplished, from the day when the second John Walter ensured the success of *The Times*.[3] Let us open *The Public Advertiser* of January 1st, 1784, for instance, and see what its readers got for their threepence. Its four pages of yellowish paper are covered with indistinct type, of an uneven black which sometimes runs into grey patches. The advertisements of the theatres are at the top, being doubtless the best paid, then come those of the publishers, which are followed by a series of "letters to the printer," in which obliging correspondents communicate their political opinions to the public. Happy "printer"! He lives in the golden age of his art; he knows nothing of the painful obligation incumbent on his modern successors of paying handsomely for news and leading articles; he looks to his kind readers to fill his columns, and by a generous exchange, supplies them gratis with his pale ink and his rough paper. Members of the public vie with each other in rendering him aid; some bring him "their dramatic criticism"; others send him a summary of Parliamentary debates from Ireland; he receives news from the Court, from the country, and from every corner of society; the poet laureate, Mr. William Whitehead, communicates to him a "New Year's Ode to the King"; he records the price of consols, makes out a list of crimes, robberies, ships arrived in port, bankruptcies, and auction sales, leaves

---

[1] The "cruel Woodfall" referred to by Crabbe (*Newspaper*, l. 411).

[2] The list may be seen at the head of all the numbers of *The Gentleman's Magazine* for the year.

[3] Which he joined in 1803 (cf. Bourne, *History of English Newspapers*, ed. 1887, vol. i. p. 266).

the doctors and midwives the space required for giving
"advice to the fair sex," and, having at length covered
his last page with printing ink, can rest from his
labours and feel that he has done a good day's work.

But he has many competitors, whom Crabbe enumerates amusingly:

> For soon as morning dawns with roseate hue
> The *Herald* of the morn arises too ;
> *Post* after *Post* succeeds, and, all day long,
> *Gazettes* and *Ledgers* swarm, a noisy throng ;
> When evening comes, she comes with all her train
> Of *Ledgers*, *Chronicles*, and *Posts* again,
> Like bats, appearing, when the sun goes down,
> From holes obscure and corners of the town. . . .

Even Sunday is not a day of rest for the Press, for
then—

> . . . The sainted *Monitor* is born,
> Whose pious face some sacred texts adorn. . . .
> But all is carnal business in the rear,
> The fresh-coin'd lie, the secret whisper'd last,
> And all the gleanings of the six days past.[1]

By a favour of destiny, refused to laborious poets,
these sheets demand but slight efforts from their
"careless authors":

> . . . They only strive to join
> As many words as make an even line ;
> As many lines as fill a row complete ;
> As many rows as furnish up a sheet :
> From side to side, with ready types they run,
> The measure's ended, and the work is done.

In those days, as we have seen, a newspaper is made
up of odds and ends. It does not require an editor,

---

[1] This list of names is accurate, if not complete. *The Morning Herald*,
founded by a young clergyman of the name of Bate Dudley, had appeared for
the first time on November 1st, 1780, and defended the interests of the Prince
of Wales against the King; on the other hand, *The Morning Post and
Daily Advertiser*, which dated from 1772, conducted a violent campaign
against Fox, who was standing for Westminster. *The London Gazette* had
been "the organ of the Court" from 1665 ; *The Public Ledger*, started by the
publisher Newbery on January 12th, 1760, had counted Goldsmith among its
contributors. Many evening papers appeared only three times a week—for
instance, *The London Evening Post*, *The General Evening Post*, and *Lloyd's
Evening Post*. As for *The Monitor*, published every Saturday (to be read on
Sunday), it dated from 1755, and in 1784 had a rival in *The Oglio*, which
Crabbe mentions in the first edition of his poem, and to which Cowper alludes
in a letter to Newton of December 13th, 1784. (See, for more details,
Bourne, *op. cit.*, vol. i. p. 144 and pp. 194-228).

but it needs reporters of the kind described by Foote
in *The Bankrupt*[1] :

> . . . Their runners ramble day and night
> To drag each lurking deed to open light ;
> For daily bread the dirty trade they ply,
> Coin their fresh tales, and live upon the lie. . . .
> No anxious virgin flies to fair Tweed-side ;
> No injured husband mourns his faithless bride ;
> No duel dooms the fiery youth to bleed ;
> But through the town transpires each vent'rous deed.

Miscellaneous news with spicy comments—that is the
reader's favourite dish.   He also likes information
about the price of stocks, those " state-barometers that
rise or fall by causes known to few"; he likes to
know—

> Promotion's ladder who goes up and down ;
> Who's wed, or who seduced, . . .
> What new-born heir has made his father blest,
> What heir exults, his father now at rest.

With a more or less careless eye he runs over the
advertisements of the "illustrious race, whose drops
and pills have patent powers to vanquish human ills":
quacks are so numerous in England in the eighteenth
century that perhaps he will be taken in by " Katterfelto's skill, and Graham's glowing strain."[2]   Here is
the "simple barber" of former days, now transformed
into a "gay perfumer, on whose soft cheek his own
cosmetic blooms."   To "faded belles, who would their
youth renew," he offers the "wonders of Olympian
dew"; for "batter'd beaux, whose locks are turned to
grey," he has "flaxen frontlets with elastic springs."
He is followed by a "venal throng" of "degenerate"
poets :

[1] Foote's *Bankrupt*, act iii. sc. ii., in which the "printer," Mr. Margin,
appears surrounded by his Parliamentary staff, "politicians pro and con,
Messrs. Pepper and Plaister," his critics "Thomas Comma and Christopher
Caustic," and his "collectors of paragraphs, Roger Rumour and Phelim
O'Flam." Ben Jonson's *Staple of News* will also occur to the student. Crabbe
probably knew neither of these comedies.

[2] For Gustavus Katterfelto, see an advertisement in *The Morning Post* of
July 31st, 1782 : "Wonders, wonders, wonders, and wonders ! are now to be
seen at No. 22, Piccadilly, by Mr. K.'s new improved and greatly admired
solar microscope . . ." (cf. Cowper's *Task*, iv. 86-7, a passage which
much resembles Crabbe's).—For James Graham, installed at Schomberg
House, Pall Mall, about 1781, for his "Templum Æsculapio Sacrum," his
"Elixir of Life," and his "Celestial Bed," hired at "£500 a night for an
offspring of surpassing loveliness," see Sydney, *England in the Eighteenth
Century*, vol. i. pp. 316-17.

> . . . Amid this rabble rout we find
> A puffing poet to his honour blind :
> Who slily drops quotations all about
> Packet or post, and points their merits out ;
> Who advertises what reviewers say,
> With sham editions every second day.

These arts, if report speaks true, are not unknown to the poets our contemporaries. Are they then all " degenerate," and is it possible that the eighteenth century was the precursor of our own to such an extent ? Let us pursue with Crabbe this investigation which is so full of surprises : we come to the most original part of the newspapers of that time, the rich " correspondence," which they contain. Let us listen to the malicious observer :

> These are a numerous tribe, to fame unknown,
> Who for the public good forego their own ;
> Who volunteers in paper-war engage,
> With double portion of their party's rage :
> Such are the Bruti, Decii, who appear
> Wooing the printer for admission here ;
> Whose generous souls can condescend to pray
> For leave to throw their precious time away.
> Oh ! cruel Woodfall ! when a patriot draws
> His gray-goose quill in his dear country's cause,
> To vex and maul a ministerial race,
> Can thy stern soul refuse the champion place ?
> Alas ! thou know'st not with what anxious heart
> He longs his best-loved labours to impart ;
> How he has sent them to thy brethren round,
> And still the same unkind reception found :
> At length, indignant will he damn the state,
> Turn to his trade, and leave us to our fate.

And lastly, what is to be said of the " Muses' meanest race," of those " scribblers " who are given a place, out of charity, in the " Poet's Corner," and whose lines "the eye disdainful views and glances swiftly by"? Woe, replies the writer, mindful of his own trials—woe to the youth "whose mind such dreams invade," and who devotes to poetry " the talents due to trade"!

> I know your day-dreams, and I know the snare
> Hid in your flow'ry path, and cry " Beware ! "
> Go ! to your desks and counters all return ;
> Your sonnets scatter, your acrostics burn ;
> Trade, and be rich ! [1]

[1] *Newspaper,* ll. 53-60, 77-84, 219-24, 291-4, 299-302, 310-16, 323-4, 330, 361-4, 392-6, 403-20, 432-5, 445-6.

It must be confessed that Crabbe has an irresistible turn for satire, and that his gifts of exact observation, of mockery and banter, are his strong points. When he criticises, in two little genre pictures in the style of *The Village*, the excesses and the follies of party spirit in the newspapers and in country districts, nothing can be more natural or more clearly show his love of moderation and peace, his dislike of all forms of enthusiasm. If he laughs at the rough-and-ready methods with which the " printers " of that day made up their papers, if he ridicules the emptiness of these ephemeral productions, no doubt many of their readers had already done the same thing. Only this satire of his is often of a very special kind, very different, for instance, from that of Cowper, who, three months later, treated the same subject at the beginning of the fourth book of *The Task*.[1] Strange contrast! The valetudinarian of Olney, whose religious terrors are continually threatening him with fits of madness, is the poet of comfortable family life, of the delights of intimacy; the arrival of the post on a winter evening, the reading of the newspaper by the fireside, with doors closed, shutters fastened, and curtains drawn, gives him an unalloyed pleasure, all of which he makes us share. If he despairs of the future, he is an optimist in the present; he enjoys to the full, and we enjoy with him, if only for a few moments, the sweets of life. Crabbe, on the contrary, who is chaplain to a Duke, who has escaped from his poverty and is the possessor of happiness in the person of a beloved wife, is the ironical portrayer of our disillusions, the severe critic of all our little shortcomings. He will not describe to us the arrival of the coach, with the jingle of the bells and the blast of the horn; he dwells rather on the hopeless dulness of the day on which the post does not make its appearance :

> . . . The dull morn a sullen aspect wears ;
> We meet, but ah ! without our wonted smile,
> To talk of headaches, and complain of bile ;
> Sullen we ponder o'er a dull repast,
> Nor feast the body while the mind must fast.[2]

There is good-nature in Cowper's raillery and sarcasm in Crabbe's. To this satirical *Newspaper* the critics

[1] It appeared in June, 1785.   [2] *Newspaper*, ll. 274-8.

of the day gave a *succès d'estime* only. Some of them told
the author that " his talents were more conspicuous in
the pathetic and descriptive than in the satyric line ";[1]
others reproached him with having "parodied" a
couplet of Pope's[2] and declared *The Newspaper* to be
inferior to *The Library*.[3]   All, however, gave a respectful greeting to the new work of a poet who was already
famous ; the style was considered "easy and forcible,
the rhymes chaste and carefully chosen," the satire
ingenious, and copious extracts from it were reproduced. But the subject, in spite of its real novelty,
had no interest, or even justification. Why take the
trouble to describe a newspaper, especially in five
hundred lines ? Why be anxious about "transitions"[4]
for such a dry and monotonous topic ? Did Crabbe
hope to check the "harm done by the Press," and prevent it from "injuring the character of individuals "?
That is hardly likely. Did he simply wish to excite
the curiosity of the reading public ? In that case his
success was moderate, for a single edition satisfied it.[5]

Whether the coolness of the public discouraged the
poet, or whether he gradually yielded to the charms of
a life of leisure and of the comparative affluence which
he was able to enjoy, or whether the successive deaths
of his friends and patrons, first of Johnson, then of the
Duke of Rutland, of Sir Joshua Reynolds, and of Burke,
kept him away from the world of letters, Crabbe, from
the year 1785, entered on a period of silence which
lasted not less than twenty-two years. He followed
literally the advice which he gives to his "youth" at
the end of *The Newspaper*; he returned to "his desk
and his counter"—that is to say, to his pulpit and his
parish; he "burnt his sonnets and his acrostics," as
if, weary of his long union with the Muse, he had
repudiated her for good.

---

[1] *Critical Review* for April, 1785.
[2] See line 76 and line 12 of the *Epistle to Arbuthnot*.
[3] *Monthly Review* for November, 1785.
[4] See the Preface (*Works*, p. 125), in which Crabbe complains of this
difficulty.
[5] See the " Preface to Poems published in 1807 " (*Works*, p. 98): ". . . the
impression was disposed of."

THIRD PART

THE CLERGYMAN AND HIS PARISH REGISTER

(1786—1807)

CHAPTER I

CRABBE AS A CLERGYMAN AND HIS RELIGIOUS OPINIONS

I. Crabbe's life at Stathern, Muston, Parham, Great Glemham, and Rendham.—II. A clergyman's duties : sermons, visits, and tithes. Crabbe's recreations : scientific and literary study and composition.—III. Crabbe's religious opinions : reason and faith, foundations of belief, importance of "works." Crabbe ranked among the Liberals.—IV. His dislike of scepticism, of Arminian or Calvinistic Methodism, and of Huntington's Antinomianism. Conclusion. Importance of practical morality.

I

A FEW pages will suffice to relate the life of the poet during these twenty years, insignificant for the reader, all spent in various migrations, in the humble duties of a country curate and rector, in the often interrupted labours of a mind fond of science and literature, and amid those domestic joys and sorrows under the insensible influence of which the character is definitively moulded. Shortly after the publication of *The Newspaper*, Crabbe and Mira resolved in their turn to leave the vast, empty apartments of Belvoir Castle, where a gloomy silence now reigned, and the servants, in the absence of the master and mistress, paid little regard to the comfort and the authority of the chaplain.[1] They went to live in the parsonage of Stathern, a little village at the south-west end of the valley, at the foot of the well-stocked covers which extend for about three miles along the slopes leading to Belvoir. In this solitude, surrounded by woods and by roads which the winter rains, even in the present day, convert into regular swamps, Crabbe spent four years as curate of the parish.[2] It was, he afterwards told his son, the happiest time in his life. If he had neither the wealth

---

[1] B. p. 36, and *The Patron* (*Tales*, v. 464-81 ; *Works*, p. 298), a partly autobiographical passage.
[2] See above, p. 175, n. 4.

nor the brilliant society of Belvoir at his command, on the other hand he enjoyed a modest competence, excellent health, and complete liberty. He corresponded assiduously with his " noble patron," and communicated to him his apprehensions and the difficulties which he encountered from the all-powerful Chancellor Thurlow. "Your Grace having indulged me hitherto by hearing me speak of my own affairs," he wrote on September 29th, 1785, ". . . I once more have to thank Your Grace for your very kind permission for my returning to Belvoir, should we find Stathern very unhealthy. At present we are well, but are much threatened by report that in the winter we shall be troubled with agues, impassable roads, and the petty larcenies of my poor parishioners. . . . I take the liberty of informing you that Lord Thurlow keeps me yet in suspense, neither giving me the living I applied for in exchange to any other,[1] nor giving me any reason to hope for it. . . . This suspense is a real hindrance to me, and if it be to end in a disappointment, no inconsiderable one, as I believe I could at this time make an agreement, though something disadvantageous, with a clergyman within a few miles of me." [2]

Perhaps the clergyman to whom allusion is made here was Dr. Edmund Cartwright, from 1779 rector of Goadby Marwood, a village six miles south of Stathern. Crabbe had gone to preach there in the month of January, 1785,[3] and had begun a cordial intercourse with the incumbent, which lasted several years. A community of scientific and literary tastes led to an exchange of visits, and Cartwright, a poet of repute,[4] and still more famous as an inventor, often came to Stathern, where his extensive knowledge, his rare conversational power, and the dignity of his manners were much appreciated.[5] In 1785, as it happened, Cartwright, fired by the example of Arkwright, whose workshops he had visited in the preceding year, had just conceived the idea of his " power-loom," and was thinking

[1] Frome St. Quintin and Evershot, in Dorsetshire (see above, p. 144, n. 3).
[2] The original of this letter is at Belvoir Castle and has been published by the Historical MSS. Commission, report 12, vol. i. pp. 244-5, London, 1889.
[3] He repreached the sermon mentioned above, p. 175, n. 4.
[4] He was the anonymous author of a poem, *Armine and Elvira*, published in 1772 and well received by the public.
[5] B. p. 38.

of leaving Goadby in order to start a factory at Doncaster. Why should not Crabbe have acted as curate
for him, as he already did for Thomas Parke at
Stathern ? Nothing came of it, however ; but there is a
peculiar interest in seeing the poet of " rural England "
thus coming into casual contact with one of the initiators
of that " industrial revolution " which, although Crabbe
could not foresee it, was soon to transform the aspect
of the country and give the towns a preponderance
over the rural districts.

Leaving his ingenious brother-clergyman to follow
a path beset with obstacles, Crabbe remained at
Stathern, where, towards the end of October, 1787,
the unexpected news of the Duke of Rutland's
death[1] reached him. The Lord-Lieutenant, a victim
of his popularity and of his love of good living and
pleasure, had succumbed to a slight attack of fever,
which carried the poet's best hopes into the grave.
A solemn funeral service was held at Belvoir and at
Bottesford, after which Crabbe pronounced an eulogium
on his patron, extolled, without too much flattery, " his
respect for things divine," his " essential " virtues, such
as justice and mercy, and, in conclusion, invited his
dependants to follow his example, by practising, like
him, " charity at all times and towards all men." This
tribute of deserved gratitude and this not unskilful
praise must have pleased the Duchess, for the sermon
was published by her order.[2] Crabbe, more solitary
than ever, deprived of Rutland's support and of Cartwright's society, confined himself to the circle of his
increasing family.[3] Thus passed the four years of his
life at Stathern, far from any contact with the outside
world, except a journey to Suffolk in 1785,[4] and, in

[1] On October 24th.
[2] By Dodsley, with this title : " *A Discourse on II. Corinthians*, i. 9, *read
in the chapel at Belvoir Castle after the funeral of the Duke of Rutland*,
London, 1788, 4°, 1 shilling." It is dedicated to the Duchess, and dated
Belvoir, January 31st, 1788.
[3] He had three children at Stathern ; the eldest, his son George and future
Biographer, baptised on November 16th, 1785 ; the second, John, baptised on
October 17th, 1787 ; and a daughter, Sarah Susannah, baptised on January
23rd, 1789. In the meanwhile, his father had died at Aldborough on June 3rd,
1786 (and not in 1789, as the Biographer mistakenly asserts, p. 38). His
sister Mary, a milliner at Ipswich from 1782 or 1783 (cf. *Works*, p. 360, n. 1),
had married, on October 2nd, 1786, Thomas Sparkes of Aldborough (Parish
Registers of Stathern and Aldborough).
[4] Cf. the poem entitled *The Ladies of the Lake*, already quoted (p. 72),
and written " during a visit to Normanston " (*Works*, p. 260, n. 1).

1787, an excursion to Doncaster, where the noise of Cartwright's machines made such an impression on Mira that, according to her son's account, she burst into tears.[1]

The Duchess of Rutland, wishing, it would appear, to keep the late Duke's chaplain near her and to see him settle in the neighbourhood, had given him in 1788 a letter of recommendation to Thurlow, and Crabbe, returning to London, had once more faced the surly dispenser of favours. But a disagreeable reception was in store for him; he had hardly stated his request for an advantageous change of parishes, when Thurlow interrupted him with a "growl" and exclaimed, "By God, I will not do this for any man in England."[1] The Duchess herself had to intervene, to exert her power and her charm over the intractable Chancellor, in order to make him consent at last to present Crabbe to the two livings of Muston (in Leicestershire) and West Allington (in Lincolnshire), which were in the gift of the Crown. Their joint income was about £270 a year, £80 more than that of Evershot and Frome St. Quintin.[2] This presentation, dated January 9th, 1789, demanded many formalities. After the Chancellor, it was necessary to see the Archbishop of Canterbury, obtain from him a "dispensation," empowering the recipient to hold the two livings at the same time, and, with that object, pass the examination for the degree of Master of Arts or Bachelor of Laws in Lambeth Palace. At the appointed day and hour Crabbe complied with the summons of the Archbishop's chaplain, was waited on by a servant, who brought him pens, ink, and paper, as well as a dictionary, and was invited to discuss in his best Latin a subject of the following kind: *Aevum quo advenit Jesus, unde constet esse commodissimum.*[3] Two hours were allowed him for the composition of his thesis. When it was finished, the chaplain reappeared, declared himself satisfied, and on January 10th, 1789, the author of *The Village*

---

[1] B. p. 38.

[2] See above, p. 144, n. 4, and a passage from the letter to Scott, quoted by B, p. 38.

[3] See the amusing description by the conceited P. Stockdale, in the *Memoirs of his Life and Writings, written by himself,* 1809, London, vol. ii. pp. 233-6, and in Moore's *Memoirs* (ed. 1853, vol. iv. p. 60), an anecdote of the same kind, about Sydney Smith, in April, 1823.

was granted the ecclesiastical degree of Bachelor of Laws.[1]

His induction to Muston, which was delayed by the birth of a daughter, took place on February 25th. It is about nine miles from Stathern to Muston, skirting the Castle in the direction of Grantham. The place lies in the centre of the Vale of Belvoir, in a level and open plain, intersected here and there by hedges which divide fields of root and corn crops, and watered by several streams, one of which, the Devon, runs by Muston. The parsonage, situated on the right bank of the rivulet, to the east of the village and just north of the little church, in Crabbe's time stood in the middle of a garden adjoining the churchyard, which was partly concealed by large elm-trees. Between the foliage one could espy the little river gliding by the graves, and lingering on its banks before flowing under the bridge which leads to the first houses of the village. The eye, shut in on all sides by verdure, rested with pleasure on a "Gothic arch cut in the hedge," which made a sort of frame for the massive structure of Belvoir Castle in the distance.[2] Crabbe was destined to spend in this spot twelve years of his life, divided into two very unequal periods, the first of which lasted a little less than four years. Several of his children were born and died there;[3] he left it only at long intervals, to make flying journeys to Suffolk with his family.

It was thus that in September, 1790, Crabbe and Mira revisited the places where their attachment had sprung up long ago—the farm at Parham, still inhabited by Uncle Tovell, Beccles, and the retreat of the "Ladies of the Lake" at Normanston. They

[1] By abbreviation LL.B. This information has been given me by Mr. Kershaw, librarian at Lambeth Palace. The list of the "Lambeth degrees" was reproduced in *The Gentleman's Magazine* for May and June, 1864. The Biographer (p. 35) has made a mistake of six years. The "dispensation" followed closely on the degree; it was granted on January 14th.

[2] For Muston and its environs, see B. pp. 56 and 57, Kebbel (*Life of Crabbe*, pp. 57-60), and an article by Mr. W. H. Hutton, *Some Memories of Crabbe*, in *The Cornhill Magazine* for June, 1901, reprinted in *The Burford Papers*, pp. 282-302 (a passage is quoted by Ainger, *Life of Crabbe*, p. 65).

[3] Two sons were born: the one, Edmund, in January, 1790 (baptised on the 25th); the other, William, in October, 1792 (baptised on the 10th). Two daughters died: Sarah Susannah (buried September 12th, 1789), and Sarah (baptised on February 10th, 1791, and buried on the 17th). See the parish register of Muston.

even went so far as Lowestoft, on October 15th,[1] to hear Wesley preach one of his last sermons, at the age of eighty-seven. In a chapel " crowded to suffocation " the indefatigable old man ascended the pulpit that evening leaning on the arms of two young ministers ; he quoted, with a playful seriousness, the lines in which Anacreon advises his readers to " live, for death is coming," and Crabbe felt so profoundly the beauty of his character, of a career so vigorously and joyously accomplished, that he forgot Wesley's dissent for a moment and introduced himself to him after the service : he was received, the Biographer tells us, with benevolent politeness.

In June, 1792, we find the poet at Aldborough[2] again, and on October 6th in that year John Tovell died, appointing Crabbe his executor, and leaving his property in equal shares to his two sisters, Mrs. Elmy, Mira's mother, and Miss Elizabeth Tovell, a disagreeable old maid who lived at Parham.[3] In spite of the recent birth of his last child, Crabbe had to start for Suffolk again, face the hostility of the relations and friends of the deceased man, carry out the provisions of a will not very favourable to himself, since nothing was left to Mira personally, and return in haste to Muston with plans for taking up his abode at Parham.[4] Crabbe, in fact, was convinced that

---

[1] The date is fixed by a passage in Wesley's *Journal*: "Friday, Oct. 15, 1790. I went to Lowestoff, to a steady, loving, well-united society. The more strange it is that they neither increase nor decrease in number." The *Journal* comes to an end on Sunday the 24th, and Wesley died on March 2nd of the following year (cf. B. 41-2).

[2] From a manuscript sermon dated Aldborough, June 10th, 1792 (Murray Collection).

[3] Cf. Aug. Page, *Supplement to the Suffolk Traveller*, 1844, p. 189, *Davy Pedigrees* (Tovell), and B. p. 42.

[4] See an interesting letter from Mira to Crabbe, with the Grantham stamp, October 22nd, 1792, and addressed to "the Rev. Mr. Crabbe, to be left at Miss Moore's, Parham." Here are a few extracts (I omit a couple of pages of stories about the " dear boys") : " I do confess my dearest Mr. Crabbe I was disappointed this afternoon in not hearing from you. But consider says I to myself he has let you know he got safe there and was well . . . then Saturday evening. Your letter, my dearest Mr. Crabbe, is received ! And I am certainly the most obedient wife in the kingdom. You said ' expect nothing my dear Sally '—from that moment I expected nothing. ' But ultimately the will may be a good one '—I read over the particulars—it may so, says I—and really there is nothing so much left out of the family as I expected, tho tis true not all together to my liking in it. In this Reverie was I in, forgetting the children were with me, I turn'd up my Head : George was as red as scarlet, and the water started into his Eyes : 'Is my papa well?' Yes my dear Boys ! He is well and *all is well*. Such my dearest George is the force of affection,

his own interests demanded that he should leave his parishes in charge of curates and reside himself at Ducking Hall, where he hoped to feel really at home, in the neighbourhood of his native place. The Muston people, vexed at this selfish desertion, still bore him a grudge for it when he returned among them thirteen years later.

On November 28th, 1792,[1] after a three days' journey, the poet and his family arrived at Parham, where a most frigid reception awaited them. "Mrs. Tovell and her sister-in-law," writes the Biographer, who was an eye-witness of the scene, "were sitting by the fireside weeping; they did not even rise to welcome my parents, but uttered a few chilling words, and wept again." It was in vain that Mira had hired the farm and bought her uncle's furniture : she was not allowed to manage the house. Miss Elizabeth Tovell, relying on her sixty-four years, her domineering character, and her relationship to the deceased, ordered everybody about, not excepting Crabbe himself, whom the old lady boasted she could " screw up and down like a fiddle." With her long ivory-tipped cane, "a foot, at least, above her head," she personified the past, opposed to all innovation. Not a piece of furniture could be moved or a picture touched without provoking objections. Then Tovell's friends and neighbours, accustomed to hobnob with the master of the house every evening, were angry with the intruder, whom they accused of making Ducking Hall as formal and as melancholy as himself. What was he doing on other people's property, this wet blanket who wouldn't crack a joke or take his glass, this son of a custom-house officer who thought fit to reprimand smugglers ? We'll soon show him what we think of his high moral tone and his airs of self-importance !

and such may it always be with us. For you were well and I really felt as if all was right. [It is here that Crabbe wrote the note quoted by the Biographer on p. 59, col. 2, ll. 3-7 ; instead of "was denied" it should read "was not granted."] You talk my dearest Mr. Crabbe about living at Parham, but *can* we live there? For even the rent of the House is part of it my Aunt's [Miss Elizabeth Tovell, or perhaps the widow Tovell], furniture the same, and she will part with her teeth, if she had any, as soon as her Rent. Well, no matter! thank God I am well, the children are well and if you are so I am happy. . . . *Frugality* must still be *our* Motto. That I do not mind if it please God you are well . . . another Ewe is dead. . . ." (Broadley Collection).

[1] The date is given by B. p. 42, and by a manuscript note of Fitzgerald (in the possession of Mr. Aldis Wright).

And, sure enough, when the demand for parish rates was presented, Crabbe found with indignation that he had been rated at a much higher sum than had been paid by Uncle Tovell. He protested strongly, and the malcontents had to forego their little revenge. But a whole year passed in friction and worry of this kind, and it was not till July 22nd, 1794, that Crabbe, writing to the son of his friend Cartwright, was able to inform him that "peace had been established," and that "Mrs. Crabbe enjoyed that freedom and authority which were her due long before she had them."[1]

Happily the poet and his wife had found a relief from their troubles in change of scene: the first months of 1793 were spent at Aldborough,[2] with Mary Crabbe, now Mrs. Sparkes; in June of the same year Muston was visited by its incumbent;[3] and occasional invitations to Dudley North's country house at Little Glemham brought Crabbe once more into contact with the Liberal society of the day—with Fox and Grey, with Dr. Parr, the eccentric pedagogue, and Roger Wilbraham, a jovial antiquary and collector of Italian books.[4] These distractions were soon reinforced by professional duties: on October 27th, 1793, Crabbe preached at Great Glemham, a small village of which he undertook the curacy from the beginning

---

[1] Letter dated Parham, Wickham Market, and addressed to Lieutenant Edmund Cartwright, who was godfather of the poet's youngest son but one (Broadley Collection).

[2] See B. p. 43, and two manuscript sermons (Murray Collection) dated April 21st and 28th, 1793.

[3] See in Mr. Murray's collection two sermons for June 2nd and 16th. Crabbe returned there in 1794, as is proved by two other sermons of September 7th and 14th, and the following fragment of a letter to Cartwright, dated August 30th, 1794: "As I mean to leave Suffolk very early on Monday (1st of September), I write principally to request that any letter I may be favoured with from you may be directed to Muston near Grantham till the 20th of September, after which your favours will be received at Parham again." The visits to Muston, although pretty frequent, were not perhaps regularly annual.

[4] For Wilbraham, see *The Gentleman's Magazine* for June, 1829, p. 569. He died in February, 1829, at the age of eighty-six. In May, 1817, he read at the Society of Antiquaries, of which he was a member, a paper called "An Attempt at a Glossary of some Words used in Cheshire" (*Society of Antiquaries, Archæologia*, vol. xix.) His Italian and Spanish library contained all the rarest and most valuable works of ancient and modern poetry and romance. It was extremely useful to Ugo Foscolo, as is proved by the Preface to the *Discorso storico sul Testo del Decamerone* (1825), dedicated "al Signore Ruggiero Wilbraham" (Foscolo, *Opere edite e postume*, Florence, 1850-90, vol. iii. p. 5).

of 1794, while he acted in the same capacity at Swefling for the Rev. Richard Turner,[1] who was detained by more important avocations at Great Yarmouth.

Unfortunately, after the successive bereavements which had saddened his life at Muston came the loss at Parham of his two youngest sons—of William in September, 1793, and of Edmund in March, 1796.[2] Irritated for some time past by many worries, worn out by the anxiety of nursing a " promising " and tenderly loved child, Mira seems to have given way under this last ordeal, and to have lost her cheerful temper and her health in it. Her constitution was not a very robust one ; perhaps she unconsciously harboured the germs of a hereditary malady : her brother James had died in 1788 in a fit of hypochondria, and her sister Eleanor, according to Fitzgerald,[3] went out of her mind, and was for years under the charge of Mary Elmy. Mira was attacked by a nervous disorder of a somewhat similar kind, and from the year 1796 to the day of her death was never herself again. During the hotter months she sank into profound dejection and sullen silence, and on recovering from this condition alarmed her family by going into the opposite extreme.[4] The return of cooler weather brought on an access of feverish gaiety, of talking and singing, which, although less gloomy, was almost equally distressing. We can imagine the grief of the poet, obliged to humour the caprices of her whom he had formerly respected,

[1] Crabbe and Turner struck up a friendship, and his name will reappear occasionally in this work. Richard Turner, Rector of Swefling from October 29th, 1785, was the uncle of Dawson Turner, the bibliophile. A cultivated man and a judicious critic, he gave the poet advice which was followed. He was for twenty years " Perpetual Curate " of Great Yarmouth, where he died on October 13th, 1835, at the age of eighty-four. (See *The Ipswich Journal* of October 24th, 1835.)

[2] Parish register of Parham. William was buried on September 6th and Edmund on March 11th.

[3] Manuscript note in Mr. Aldis Wright's copy : " There is a beautiful face, done in chalk, of Miss Elmy's [Mira's] sister, who I think turned crazy : Eleanor Elmy was for years mad under charge of her sister Mary."

[4] B. pp. 45-6 and 59. See also the portrait of Jane in *Tales from the Hall* (Book viii. *Works*, p. 419, ll. 731-42).

> Fits of long silence she endures, then talks
> Too much, with too much ardour as she walks.

It is remarkable that Crabbe, a matter-of-fact mind if ever there was one, has described with singular vigour the hallucinations of weakened brains. His use, a very moderate one, of narcotics with opium for the principal ingredient was perhaps not the only reason of his success.

and who now, like a little child, collected the most ordinary stones,[1] insisted on being taken to London,[2] and was in a nervous dread of being left alone.[3] He had hoped for a less evanescent happiness,[4] for a more lasting interchange of feelings and ideas. He repeated to himself, in his solitary meditations, that a "long continuance of happiness cannot be looked for in this world";[5] he felt the burden of years grow heavy on him, and his natural melancholy was deepened by it.

The death of Edmund having made Parham distasteful to Mira, Crabbe gratefully accepted the advantageous offer made him by Dudley North of a large house about two miles farther east, close to the hamlet of Great Glemham. Built at the foot of a gentle declivity, between two hills, one to the north

---

[1] Bath-stones, which Ralph Allen, Fielding's Allworthy, had brought into fashion for building. When the Crabbes left Suffolk in 1805, says Mitford (*Gentleman's Magazine*, new series, vol. i. March, 1834, p. 260, note), "The collection of Bath stones, a fancy of Mrs. Crabbe's, was *prodigious.*"

[2] In 1813, B. p. 58.

[3] See in the South Kensington Museum, in the Forster Collection, a series of letters from Crabbe to Wenn, an attorney at Ipswich, which will be referred to later. Here are two passages relating to Mira: "Aldborough, 1st August, 1805. . . . Mrs. Crabbe lies at this place extremely and (as she supposes) even dangerously ill, and tho' I am in hope of a more favourable termination, yet I cannot look to a day when I can leave her . . ."; and on the 12th of the same month : ". . . Mrs. Crabbe is so ill that I am obliged to contrive this affair [a journey of a few hours to Wickham Market] with some secrecy." This painful state of things had not escaped the poet's acquaintances, and Southey had heard of it : see a letter from Neville White, dated Keswick, September 30th, 1808, quoted by Ainger, *Life of Crabbe*, p. 74, and published by John Wood Warter (*Selections from the Letters of Rob. Southey*, 4 vols. 1856, vol. ii. pp. 90-1): ". . . It was not long before his wife became deranged, and when all this was told me by one who knew him well, five years ago, he was still almost confined in his own house, anxiously waiting upon this wife in her long and hopeless malady." The very exact expressions used by Southey are, as we see, confirmed by Crabbe's own letters. Only I think the word "deranged" should be taken in its mildest sense, and that there is no ground for saying, as Ticknor does in his Journal, on Rogers's authority, that "Crabbe was nearly ruined by grief and vexation at the conduct of his wife for above seven years, at the end of which time she proved to be insane," which appears to be more brutal than true.

[4] See above, p. 192, n. 4, and B, p. 59.

[5] Letter to his brother John, dated North (*i.e.* Great) Glemham, November 21st, 1796. John, the youngest of Crabbe's brothers, had become captain of a slave-ship. Successful at starting, he had just married the owner's daughter, and Crabbe congratulates him in the following terms: "We all wish you much happiness, but indeed, my dear John, it is not a world to look for it for any long continuance. You and your wife will, I hope, have a full share, and that is the utmost which can be expected." These apprehensions were only too well grounded : in his next voyage the captain was thrown overboard by his slaves (B. p. 2).

and the other to the south, surrounded by a park with
an irregular growth of underwood and fine timber,
and here and there a few violets, skirted at the south
by a stream which runs down a lane, this new residence,[1] already called Great Glemham Hall, was,
according to the Biographer's enthusiastic account,
the most pleasant of all those that the poet inhabited.
In this part of the county, though not far from the
coast, Suffolk is not the marshy heath which we have
had occasion to describe: the slightly undulating
ground is broken up by valleys of no great depth which
rise in soft and flowing outlines, the grass is of a
deeper green, and although there is nothing picturesque
about the landscape, the well-farmed land and the
woods surrounding the country seats make a pleasing
impression. It was here that Crabbe took up his
abode on October 17th, 1796 ;[2] he remained there five
years, up to the end of 1801, when Dudley North and
his brother Charles Long decided to sell the property.
Nothing occurred to break the monotony of this
secluded life: we may note that in 1799 Crabbe
received an invitation,[3] which he declined, to the
festivities connected with the young Duke of Rutland's
majority; and that on December 31st, 1800, he sat up
till midnight in his library and " began the nineteenth
century by reading a small portion of each Latin
book."[4] Let us hope there were not too many of
them. It may also be noted that in July of the same
year Crabbe learned with regret that his bishop, Dr.
Pretyman,[5] had declared in one of his charges that
non-resident clergymen could not properly perform
the manifold duties of their office, and that he
required "from every incumbent in his diocese who
did not reside upon his benefice, the reasons of his

---

[1] See B. p. 44, and Mitford (article quoted above, p. 196, n. 1): ". . . It
[Crabbe's house at Glemham] was pulled down soon after Mr. Crabbe left ;
it stood at the bottom of the park near the village, and the house in which
Mr. Moseley's gamekeeper resides formed its stables."

[2] B. p. 44.

[3] Note by Fitzgerald (Aldis Wright copy): "1799, æt. 14. Invitation to
the Duke of Rutland's 21st birthday " (B.)

[4] Note by Fitzgerald (Aldis Wright copy).

[5] George Pretyman, better known under the name of Tomline, which he
took in 1803, had been Pitt's tutor at Cambridge, and always had the
greatest influence on the Minister's ecclesiastical appointments. He became
Bishop of Lincoln in January, 1787, and was translated to Winchester in
1820. Muston and Allington were in the Lincoln diocese.

non-residence in writing." [1] Crabbe could only allege
his personal convenience, an obviously inadequate
excuse. Dudley North therefore took the trouble to
plead his cause with Pretyman, dwelling, it would
appear, on the devotion of the curate of Swefling and
Great Glemham to the interests of his parishioners
in Suffolk. The powerful bishop, who owed everything to Pitt and nothing to the Whigs and Dudley
North, proved inflexible; his only concession was a
leave of absence for four years, which enabled Crabbe
to settle his affairs gradually, and prepare for a return
to Muston. [2] In October, 1801, as we have already
seen, the poet had to leave Great Glemham, and he
moved to Rendham, a small village a mile or two
farther north, hardly distinct from Swefling. There
he spent, in a much more unpretending house, [3] the
last years of his stay in Suffolk, absenting himself
only on occasional visits to Muston or Aldborough.
He was in his native town in the month of October,
1803, when the threat of a French invasion spread
terror [4] among the inhabitants of the eastern counties,
and the Biographer tells us [5] that one morning, alarm
signals having been fired at sea and on shore, he
burst into his father's room and awoke him with
some difficulty, saying, "Do not be alarmed, but the
French are landing, and the drum on the quay is
beating to arms"; to which Crabbe replied, "Well,
you and I can do no good, or we would be among
them; we must wait the event." Such was his indifference to these warlike rumours and his resignation

[1] See his *Charge to the Clergy of the Diocese of Lincoln, Visitation of June
and July*, 1800, p. 23, and B. p. 47.

[2] B. p. 47, and manuscript note by Fitzgerald, from which it appears that
North tried to keep Crabbe near him by offering him two livings, probably
Blaxham and Great Glemham, in exchange for Muston and Allington. But
their value was less, and the poet's family expenses were increasing.

[3] See the article by Mitford already quoted (p. 196, n. 1): "He moved to
Rendham, to a house at the bottom of the hill, just opposite the new
parsonage, which is now inhabited by a farrier, and which always went by the
name of Lady Whincup's"; and B. p. 47.

[4] The expression is not too strong, as is proved by this passage in a letter
from Thomas Twining, dated Colchester, October 13th, 1803 (ed. Murray,
1882, pp. 235-6): "I suppose you will not ask me why I leave Colchester.
I leave it because I am afraid to stay in it. Many have left, more are preparing
to leave it; though I myself think there is very little danger, yet I should be
very uneasy to stay here and run the risk. And if I stay till the moment of
alarm upon the coast, I may not be able to get away at all unless I walk
away with a knapsack on my back."

[5] B. pp. 48 and 50.

to the inevitable that he soon afterwards fell fast asleep. At the end of July, 1805,[1] having sold part of his furniture, books, and numerous herbals, he returned to Aldborough, and about September 1st[2] he once more reached the parsonage at Muston and the monotonous plain of the Vale of Belvoir.

II

IF we except Mira's illness, these trivial events and various moves were only the outward side of an existence almost entirely devoted to the routine of parish work. At Muston, as in Suffolk, the main point was that, at the end of each week, the Sunday sermon should be ready and duly written on its dozen sheets of small-sized paper. It was therefore desirable not to put off till too late the choice of the text and the period of meditation necessary for its composition. At the hour of divine worship the congregation of farmers and labourers, gathered in the little village church, would see the minister of the Gospel, clad in a white surplice, take his place at the desk, read, in a "tone of authority," though rather rapidly,[3] the service and the lessons for the day, then ascend the pulpit with a firm step, and, his precious manuscript in his hand, begin the edifying moral discourse which lasted about twenty minutes.[4] A good many people came to hear him : in a grave and sometimes affecting voice he would speak of the hardships and calamities which beset the path of life, but which should not rob the pious Christian of the holy joy imparted by the consolations of faith. Or he would inculcate true

[1] See a manuscript note on a sermon of the Murray Collection : "Last Sunday at Swefling, July 14th, 1805"; a letter to Wenn, dated Rendham, July 25th, 1805 : "My goods are advertized for auction (such as I do not take with me) within a few days, and I shall have no house that I can call my home." "The sale lasted three or four days," Mitford tells us (article quoted above), ". . . his books were also sold, and his numerous herbals are now scattered among the farmhouses of the county." On August 1st he was at Aldborough (cf. p. 196, n. 3).

[2] And not in October, as the Biographer says, p. 50. See a manuscript note on a sermon of the Murray Collection : " Muston, 22nd September, 1805, third sermon." Crabbe had consequently preached at Muston on September 1st.

[3] B. p. 45.

[4] B. p. 45. On occasion he could be familiar. One evening, when it was growing dark, he shut up his sermon, saying, "I cannot see ; I must give you the rest when we meet again." Another time he stepped upon a seat near the window and finished his sermon there.

repentance, which, like the prodigal son, breaks away from all vice, does not put its trust in the creed of a Church or a sect, but returns to virtue and to lowliness of heart, to a life of communion with God and charity towards man. Difficult subjects to treat, especially Sunday after Sunday! Our pastor therefore was glad, after some years of assiduous preaching, to find himself the possessor of an ample collection of sermons from among which he could choose when time pressed. What did it matter if they looked rather ancient, if the edges were worn and the ink faded? What harm was there in preaching them over and over again?[1] As Crabbe himself judiciously pointed out, if people remembered them, then they had produced their effect and deserved to be heard again; if they had been forgotten, then they ought to be repeated.

Free from this demand on his time, he could display more physical activity: on certain Sundays he might be seen trotting along the roads, hastening from parish to parish, and producing the same old manuscript at each place. A twelve miles' ride and three services in one day were not impossible in these conditions: in the morning at Saxmundham, for instance, in the afternoon at Swefling, and in the evening at Stratford St. Andrew.[2] Another advantage was that he obtained additional leisure for paying his flock the visits demanded by the care of their souls and sometimes of their bodies; it was known, both at Muston and at Parham, that Crabbe had formerly practised as a doctor, and not only needy parishioners but even well-to-do farmers used to ask him for gratuitous consultations, which he always granted to the former and rarely refused to the latter. How was it possible for him to decline, when on urgent occasions an appeal was made to his skill as an accoucheur?[3] Was not this the best way of know-

[1] George Eliot has humorously noted the same habit in Mr. Gilfil (*Scenes of Clerical Life*, Blackwood, 1899, p. 71).

[2] This was done by Crabbe on February 14th, 1804 (cf. a sermon in the Murray Collection). On June 2nd, 1793, he took the duty at Bottesford and at Allington; on the following Sunday the congregation at Muston heard the same sermon. Every one of the Leicestershire and Suffolk sermons was, after frequent touchings-up, preached again at Trowbridge.

[3] In the "*Memoir* of the Rev. G. Crabbe, by C. T. . . .," at the beginning of the Galignani edition of the poet's *Works*, is the following passage: "Being on a visit to a gentleman, the lady of the house was suddenly taken

ing, and winning the confidence of, his parishioners, to take them from their birth and attend to their bodily as well as spiritual health from the very beginning? Crabbe was therefore well liked in Suffolk and at Muston during the first part of his life there. Like the "Author-Rector" of his *Parish Register*, he pleased by the simplicity of his dress, by the amiability of his manners and his cordiality to all, rich and poor, by his charity, which, more generous than prudent, was extended even to "gipsies and vagabonds." [1] When he lived in the Vale of Belvoir he had so far complied with local custom as to don a sporting attire; [2] but his son tells us that he had neither the eye nor hand for a good shot, and " the cry of the first hare he saw killed struck him as so like the wail of an infant " that he gave up this form of amusement.

It must be admitted, on the other hand, that he was not exempt from the annoyances of his profession. In particular, the recovery of tithes was at that time a source of endless disputes from which none could escape. Crabbe had no sooner arrived at Muston in February, 1789, than he found out that his predecessor, the Rev. Francis Bacon, had improperly appropriated some corn, thereby causing him serious loss. Always pertinacious in the defence of his interests, he consulted Richard Burke, the son of the great orator, but was advised by him that he had no case. [3] Every

in labour; the midwife not arriving in time, Mr. Crabbe was obliged to return to the duties of his first profession, and delivered the lady of a son. The boy whose birth was attended by so singular a circumstance received the equally singular name of Lemuel. He became an officer, and was slain on the field of Waterloo." Now, on p. 163 of vol. vi. of Davy's *Original Letters* (British Museum MSS.) we read that a solicitor named Shuldham, a friend of Crabbe's and owner of Marlesford Hall, near Parham, had a second son named Lemuel, who was "in the Scots Greys and was killed at Waterloo." Illustrious in his birth and in his death, may this " Lemuel " no longer be forgotten !

[1] *Parish Register*, iii. 871-82.

[2] B. p. 36; cf. also Mr. Gilfil (p. 72). According to Sir Leslie Stephen (*English Thought in the Eighteenth Century*, vol. ii. p. 123, ed. 1902), "Paley was a keen sportsman."

[3] See a letter from Richard Burke to Crabbe dated Lincoln's Inn, March 3rd, 1789: "My dear Sir, I must trust to your goodness to pardon my almost inexcusable delay in answering your letter of 10th February. . . . I more than fear that you have no sort of title to the arrears in question. The moment the corn and other subject-matter of tithe was severed from the soil, it vested in the Rector. . . . The property was in him on the severing; he (as it were) sold it and the person taking became his debtor for so much money and not for tithe. I believe that the case admits of no doubt " (Broadley Collection).

year, about February, the rector had to call upon the
farmers to pay their dues, and the poor clergyman
then went through a terribly anxious time, which
Cowper has humorously described:

> This priest he merry is and blithe
> Three quarters of a year;
> But oh! it cuts him like a scythe
> When tithing time draws near.
>
> .   .   .   .
>
> For then the farmers come jog, jog,
> Along the miry road,
> Each heart as heavy as a log,
> To make their payment good.[1]

Crabbe's apprehensions, it would appear, were not so
lively: at the end of a sermon he would simply say, " I
must have some money, gentlemen," and then quietly
descend from the pulpit. Nevertheless, the tithe-
payers were never in a hurry, and if on the appointed
day half the amount due was forthcoming, it was
considered satisfactory. Besides this, claims and
excuses had to be listened to, and perhaps a dinner
given.[2]

Thus the life of a clergyman slipped away, divided
between meditation and the discharge of his social
duties. Standing half-way between the country folk
and the "lord of the manor," he was the centre and
the connecting-link of the rural population, all of
whom he knew intimately. Confidant and umpire of
petty jealousies and conflicts, he owed to his intellectual
superiority, sometimes to his University education or
to his literary skill, a prestige in no way impaired by
his disputes with his parishioners about tithes. Up to
the end of the eighteenth century the country districts
of Leicestershire and Suffolk remained outside the
Methodist movement, with its sectarian rivalries
and discussions on points of dogma. The Church of
England clergymen in those tranquil regions were

---

[1] *The Yearly Distress, or Tithing-time at Stock, in Essex*, st. 2 and 4.
[2] B. p. 45; cf. a letter from Crabbe to his son George, dated Trowbridge,
February 13th, 1827: ". . . I expect my Tithe people on Thursday, and
shall be glad to get that business over. There are many defaulters and many
backward who ought not to be, but we take the evil with the good." On
February 16th, 1824, Crabbe wrote from Bath: "We had a rather better day
on the Tithe business than I expected, and I received about half: five or six
and twenty came" (Broadley Collection).

strangers to the feverish activity displayed by their
successors in good works of every kind, or in associations of propaganda and philanthropy. Less criticised,
they enjoyed more complete liberty ; in those days no
one was surprised that the Rector of Muston should
leave his benefice and settle in Suffolk because he
preferred the life there. Did not Bishop Watson, the
incumbent of the see of Llandaff, reside permanently
in the Lake Country ? Irreproachable conduct, reasonable zeal for the welfare of souls, equal dislike of
indolence and "enthusiasm," such were the qualities
required of a clergyman, and Crabbe possessed them
in an eminent degree.

His sermon finished, his visits paid, he spent the rest
of his time with his family, in taking the necessary care
of Mira, and in educating his sons.[1] Or he resumed his
favourite studies, his geological, botanical, and entomo-
logical investigations. The plants gathered in the course
of his walks were transferred to his garden[2] or to his
herbal, being selected more for their rarity than their
beauty. The scientific works which were too expensive
to buy were carefully analysed and their plates copied.
In his journeys to Muston he never passed through
Cambridge without exploring the botanical garden,
the amiable curator of which, James Donn, used to
receive him with open arms.[3] A naturalist as well as
a poet, Crabbe was led by his observation and his
reading to undertake labour which at the present day
would be considered of a highly technical and dry
character. John Nichols, the editor of *The Gentleman's*

---

[1] George, after having been taught to read by an old "dame" at Aldborough
in 1793 (B. p. 43), was sent to a school kept by a Mr. King at Ipswich. He
remained there till June, 1798. From that date up to October, 1803, when
he went to Trinity College, Cambridge, his education, as well as that of his
brother John, was somewhat irregularly carried on by his father (B. p. 44).

[2] He had just made a walled botanical garden when Tovell's death recalled
him from Muston to Suffolk (B. p. 42). A letter to Edmund Cartwright
shows his ardour in collecting rare specimens : " Muston, Sept. 5, 1792.—My
dear Sir, . . . I am much in your debt for the plant you have favoured me
with. . . . I was in hope that the seed of this specimen might vegetate, but
on examination this morning I find it improbable : you will much oblige me
therefore by either procuring me a few ripe seed (for the plant, *Bupleurum
tenuissimum*, is annual, I think) or a root that will grow and produce them
this year ; . . . the *Atriplex pedunculata* I should also be glad to receive. . . .
This is really taking too much of your time, but a new inhabitant for a botanical
garden is too great a prize to be sacraficed [*sic*] : you will therefore pardon
me. . . . I find much to be pleased with in the *Systema Entomologiæ Fabricii*
and frequently recur to it."

[3] B. 48.

Magazine, having asked him for some contributions in 1791, received from him a paper on the fauna, flora, and fossils of the Vale of Belvoir, and this article, published in 1795 in *The History of the County of Leicester*, is simply an enumeration of plants—especially fungi—insects, and petrifactions, preceded by brief remarks on the monotony of the landscape, more "extensive than agreeable," on the absence of nightingales and other "little warblers," whose notes would form a pleasing contrast to those "of their more harsh and dissonant inhabitants."[1]

His arrival in Suffolk, which awakened recollections of his early days, coincided with a marked revival of scientific curiosity. He carried on an active correspondence with his friend Lieutenant Edmund Cartwright, and on July 22nd, 1794, wrote to him as follows, from Aldborough : ". . . Almost all this coast, however uninteresting in appearance, has in it stores for the Botanist. . . . A light sand constitutes the surface, and you are obliged to look minutely before you be able to discover any vegetable cloathing in many parts of it. It was to this coast I alluded in some verses I formerly wrote, wherein I spoke of the poppy, mallow, darnel, and the bugloss as the few ornaments (and those ornaments of sterility) which the soil could boast of : it is, however, my fortune in some measure to sing (at least to say) a recantation ; for this dispised [sic] place has afforded me much amusement, and not that only, but has impowered me (so far as I know at present) to introduce to the botanical world a new species of British plant, or rather a new species speaking more generally, for I can neither find it in the *Flora* of these kingdoms, nor the *Species Plantarum* of the last and enlarged editions. . . . I was observing the progress of the vegetation on the beach at Aldborough, where the sea had a few years since overflown [sic], and where the stones were nearly bare, or partially covered with a little light sand blown from the neighbouring banks. Here I found the *Pisum maritimum*, the *Chelidonium glaucum*, . . . and several other hardy and frugal plants which live on little and thrust their roots far

---

[1] *The History and Antiquities of the County of Leicester*, 4 vols. fol. by John Nichols, 1795. *The Natural History of the Vale of Belvoir* is in the first volume, pp. cxci-cciii.

in the soil in search of food, but among these I was
struck with the more than usual number of Trefoils,
and some of them the very scarcer kinds." Crabbe
then goes on to claim the discovery of this unknown
species, and begs Cartwright to ask Sir Joseph Banks,
President of the Royal Society, if his claim is well
founded. For, he adds, " if I can once more shake off
my complaints and gain a little life and spirit, I verily
believe that I shall publish an account of my plant "—
subsequently enlarged into "a short history of all
the Trifolia that he had cultivated with some care
for 3 or 4 years past." [1] The plan was promptly
carried out: the Essay on Trefoils or on Incipient
Vegetation, which the Biographer calls a " Treatise on
Botany," had been offered to Dodsley,[2] and was about
to be printed, when a friend of Crabbe's, the Vice-
Master of Trinity College,[3] objected that a savant
could not, on pain of losing caste, write in any
language but Latin. With a regrettable but quite
intelligible modesty, the author followed this piece of
advice from such an exalted quarter, and the " Essay
on Botany " was thrown into the fire.[4]

It is not impossible that this disappointment, by
diverting Crabbe from science, may have brought him
back to literature, where he could at all events write
in English. As a matter of fact, he had never altogether neglected it. In the Stathern woods or on the

[1] Letter dated Parham, August 4th, 1794. Cartwright wrote to Sir Joseph
Banks on August 11th from " Tynemouth Barracks, North Shields, where I am
quartered with the first West York Militia." On the 30th Crabbe returned
to the charge : ". . . I shall be glad to find Sir Jos. Banks sufficiently
disengaged to examine my Trefoil, but if not I shall go on with my intended
work " (Mackay Collection). But on February 3rd, 1795, in a letter dated
by mistake 1794, Crabbe, better informed, gave up his supposed discovery :
"I found my Trifolium out before Sir Joseph was so kind as to inform me.
I fear the materials at Aldbro' are very scanty ; however, I do not lay
aside my purpose, but I should be glad if you could obtain for me some information of what would be expected of him who wrote the History of incipient
vegetation " (Buxton Forman Collection).
[2] It was consequently finished before February 19th, 1797, the date of James
Dodsley's death.
[3] John Davies ; cf. B. pp. 37-8 and 46.
[4] Besides *The Natural History of the Vale of Belvoir*, Crabbe wrote two other
contributions to botanical science : first, *A Catalogue of Plants growing in and
near the Parish of Framlingham*, as an appendix to the *History of Framlingham*, by Hawes and Loder, published in 1798 ; and secondly, a number of notes
in *The Botanist's Guide through England and Wales*, compiled by Turner and
Dillwyn (1805). In this work " Crabbe contributed records of 84 species for
Suffolk, 15 for Leicestershire, 13 for Lincolnshire, 4 for Nottinghamshire, and
1 for Cambridgeshire " (communicated by Mr. James Groves).

roads around Glemham, when he drove out with Mira in a "huge old-fashioned one-horse chaise, heavier than a chariot," he was in the habit, his son tells us, of reading aloud the books of the day. In the evening he would take up a volume of travel, or an Italian or French work, unless he happened to tackle Demosthenes and the Greek tragedians with the help of a Latin translation.[1] Poetic composition had remained familiar to him : in the course of his botanical or geological excursions, he was sometimes seen to "quicken his pace and move his hand up and down," as if he was scanning a line that occurred to him. In 1799, Dodsley being dead, he proposed to the bookseller Hatchard[2] the publication of a volume containing, among other pieces, three very incongruous tales : one taken from the Bible, and relating how the prophet Elisha healed the leper Naaman, the "captain of the host of the King of Syria";[3] the second entitled *Gipsy Will*, probably the first version of *The Hall of Justice* composed in 1798[4]; the third founded on the legend of the "Pedlar of Swaffham Market," the John Chapman who dreamed of a treasure, came to London, and by the most miraculous chance heard from a merchant whom he met on a bridge the secret of its hiding-place,[5]—all subjects of an almost romantic kind which would have revealed a very different Crabbe to the man we know. But the Rev. Richard Turner, who was consulted at the last moment on the merit of this collection, made some objections with which the poet agreed, and the work was abandoned. During the winters of 1801[6] and 1802 Crabbe, incited by his reading, spent his evenings in writing three novels : the first was called *The Widow Grey*, and

---

[1] See a letter to Messrs. Lackington & Co., booksellers, Finsbury Square, in which Crabbe, writing from Rendham on July 6th, 1803, asks for "Euripides : Phœnissæ, etc., . . . Greek and Latin, or any edition of the same play with the Latin interpretation (not without); . . . Æschines and Demosthenes, . . . any edition with the Latin interpretation" (Mackay Collection).

[2] John Hatchard, bookseller in Piccadilly, born in 1768, died in 1849.

[3] 2 Kings v.

[4] See Crabbe's preface to the poems of 1807 (*Works*, p. 100) : "When first I had written *Aaron, or the Gipsy*, I had no unfavourable opinion of it ; and had I been collecting my verses at that time for publication, I should certainly have included this tale. Nine years have since elapsed."

[5] For further details cf. Blomefield's *History of Norfolk*, London, 1807, vol. vi. pp. 211-14.

[6] According to a manuscript note by Fitzgerald.

portrayed a certain Dr. Allison, a "benevolent humourist," whose name suggests the Dr. Harrison in Fielding's *Amelia*; the second, *Reginald Glanshaw, or the Man who commanded Success*, was a story of an overbearing ambitious man who had some good points, but eventually fell into an imbecile state; the third, the title of which is unknown to us, "opened with the description of a wretched room." It appears that Mira, on hearing this passage read, thought it very inferior to the well-known picture of the poorhouse in *The Village*, and Crabbe, agreeing with her, resolved to burn the three novels in one of those "grand incremations" which afforded such sport to his sons. Taught at last by so many fruitless efforts, he returned to the line struck out in *The Village*, and in 1802 began *The Parish Register* and in 1804 *The Borough*.[1]

III

THIS dignified and tranquil existence, this harmonious alternation of labour and repose, was matched by opinions of equal moderation. Mysticism and scepticism—these are the two foes of the true belief, according to Crabbe and all the Anglican divines of the eighteenth century. The "truths" of dogma, like those of science, are dependent on Reason, which judges before it submits. Far from being thrust on man by an infallible authority or by a sudden intuition of the illumined soul, religion, declares Tillotson, is susceptible of proof; the moral law and miracles are its best vouchers. If the Spirit of God is sent to enlighten the human mind, our reason is the faculty which becomes imbued with it, whose powers of investigation and attention are heightened, whose authority over our conduct is reinforced.[2] Crabbe agrees with the illustrious Archbishop, whose sermons he had imitated at the age of twenty. "The Believer," he wrote later on, "who being possessed of learning and an understanding and judgment fitted to the inquiry enters with solemn purpose and a soul devoted to the truth,

[1] See B. p. 47, and a manuscript note by Fitzgerald : "1804. . . . Second vacation passed at Rendham [the Biographer is speaking]. My father begins to write *The Borough*. *Sir Eustace Grey* written or begun."

[2] Cf. Abbey and Overton, *The English Church in the Eighteenth Century* (1878), vol. i. pp. 292-8.

on the search of that which is verily and indeed true,
. . . implores the God of all to guide him in the way
he is desirous of going, . . . weighs all arguments and
objections, . . . and when he has done all, says with
all his heart and mind : I believe. . . . When he concluded that the Christian religion was true, he became
a member of Christ's Church with the full consent of
his mind, as his judgment directed him, and when his
heart consented, it was because his reason had prepared the way for his affections."[1] Nevertheless, this
confidence in Reason, so naïve and so unshaken in
Tillotson, is already less implicit in Crabbe, after a
century of metaphysical and historical controversy.
He admits that certain " difficulties " appear to him
" invincible," and that, without being " a coward and
afraid of truth," one must be " prudent and afraid of
those who think the inquiry dangerous."[2] What is to
be said also of certain mysterious and consequently
"inexplicable and incomprehensible dogmas : the divine
nature of the Redeemer, for instance, His voluntary
sacrifice for our sins, the Incarnation, and the unity of
the person of Jesus Christ"? These are all subjects
which "the pride and subtlety of human wisdom seek
in vain to elucidate."[3] The fact is that Reason,
" insulted when all was gospel that a monk could
dream," has since asserted herself too strongly :

> But now, when Reason has assumed her throne,
> She, in her turn, demands to reign alone ;
> Rejecting all that lies beyond her view,
> And, being judge, will be a witness too.[4]

She forgets that the co-operation of Faith is indispensable, and that, having ascertained the essential
" truths," she ought not to let herself be shaken by
objections on points of detail, even if she cannot
confute them.

Now, these " essential truths," the foundations of
belief, were almost exclusively historical. Since
Hume's fearless criticism had challenged Descartes's

---

[1] Manuscript sermon in the Murray Collection, preached at Trowbridge on
October 22nd, 1826.

[2] Letter to his son George, dated Trowbridge, April 20th, 1831 (Broadley
Collection).

[3] *Posthumous Sermons*, edited by J. Hastings, 1850, p. 141.

[4] *Library*, ll. 267-80, a passage written in 1807. It is clear that Crabbe's
religious opinions underwent very little change, if any.

" ontological" argument and Clarke's "cosmological" proof, theologians asserted less confidently that " God exists because He can be thought," and because the creation implies a creator.   They preferred to abide by the argument of "final causes," to exhaust, like Paley, the catalogue of the harmonies of nature : from the presence of the watch and the contrivance of its machinery a providential watchmaker was inferred.[1] This demonstration completed, the domain of meta- physics was speedily quitted, and, by a return to the controversies of the beginning of the century, an attempt was made, in opposition to Paine and reviving deism,[2] to establish the inadequacy of "natural religion," the necessity and the reality of Revelation, of its promises and its sanctions.   Philosophical investigations were superseded by a minute study of the New Testament and by a criticism of the evidences.   It was no longer a question of ideas pure and simple, but of facts.   And this method, so well adapted to the bent of his mind, is that which Crabbe always adopts.   " My confidence," he writes to his son, "is in the relations themselves and in the absolute proofs we have that the Epistles which go under the name of St. Paul were *bonâ fide* written by him"[3] . . . "I certainly agree with you respecting the strong and powerful evidence which arises from the fair, candid perusal of the Gospels.   I see no reason to doubt the authenticity of them, and if authentic, if Matthew and John, the disciples of Christ, wrote the Gospels which go under their name, they *were* witnesses of the miracles and auditors of the dis- courses.   Nay, Mark must, as the son of a woman so early an attendant on Christ and hostess, if I may so call her, of His disciples, must, I should think, have been a witness also.   Luke was not.   He gathered from those who were, all he could, and fairly gave the story to his converts.   At any rate, the three first Gospels were written before the siege of Jerusalem : that, I think, Lardner has satisfactorily made out.[4]   I think also St. John.   That the Acts of the Apostles were, and St. Paul's letters to his converts, there can

[1] Paley, *Natural Theology* (1801), ch. i.
[2] *The Age of Reason*, by Thomas Paine, was published at Paris in 1794.
[3] October 23rd, 1822.
[4] The five volumes of Lardner's work, entitled *The Credibility of the Gospel History* (1727-43), are one of the sources from which Paley took his *Evidences of Christianity* (1794).

be no doubt : the *Horæ Paulinæ*[1] of Paley proves
that beyond question. Let us think of this, and then
go back to the three chapters of St. Matthew which
contain the morality of the Gospels, and then we have
the evidence that is of all most convincing. Doctrinal
points I must leave, but facts are very powerful and, I
think, cannot be resisted. . . . Jesus Christ is a character
that commands love, admiration, respect, obedience : of
whatever we may doubt, of Him we cannot."[2] His
divine mission is attested not only by His miracles and
His sacrifice, by His prophecy of the fall of Jerusalem
so many years before the event,[3] but above all by His
resurrection, the "very strength and pillar of Revelation"[4] and of the Christian belief in a future life.
"However delayed His coming, yet our Lord will
come, and *all* will stand before His judgment-seat,"[5] to
be judged according to their works. With minds ever
fixed on this dread prospect, it behoves us to curb our
"natural propensity to evil," to "accept mercy and
pardon for our sins," to consider this earthly existence
as a "preparation for eternity," and to bear with confidence the crushing burdens which divine love sends
to mankind, the temptations of youth, and the sadness
of declining years.[6] There is so much to be gained,
if this belief and this rule of conduct are true ; there is
so little to lose if they are not so. "He must make a
most miserable choice who would not be religious even
if there was no more than a chance, and that a very
slight chance, of living again ; and how much greater
his folly and how much deeper his sin, who, with our
evidence of the truth of Christianity, continues in
neglect of its duties and is become careless of its
rewards ! As the comforts of a pious mind greatly
overbalance the restraints our duties lay upon us, and
the disappointments and stings of our evil passions
are more than a balance also for their enjoyments, it
follows that even in this world the more prudent and
they who would enjoy most of the good and avoid most

---

[1] Published in 1790.
[2] Letter to George, the Biographer, dated Trowbridge, January 20th, 1831
(Broadley Collection).
[3] Crabbe's *Posthumous Sermons*, p. 111.
[4] Manuscript sermon of June 2nd, 1816 (Murray Collection).
[5] *Posthumous Sermons*, p. 111.
[6] *Ibid.* p. 112, a manuscript sermon of May 1st, 1825, and *Parish Register*,
iii. 217-20.

of the evil must take the side of religion and virtue."[1]
We can recognise here the "wager" argument,
familiar to English pulpit oratory in the eighteenth
century. Utilitarian, rational, and matter-of-fact,
Crabbe's theology is only a colourless reproduction
of that of his contemporary Paley.[2]

Faithful to its principle, it gives a preponderant
importance to "works." True, it admits that human
actions, however virtuous they may be, cannot ensure
salvation without the aid of faith, and that the justice
of the Redeemer, imputed to believers, is alone capable
of rendering their conduct meritorious and acceptable
to God. But "we must endeavour to co-operate with
the assisting grace. God worketh *in* us and *with* us,
not without us." Faith must be "fruitful" and be
known by certain signs, as "a tree is known by its
fruits." "Let it be the Faith," exclaims Crabbe, "which
turns us from our sins, and I am sure it will have one
great sign of being the true Faith." As the physician
ascertains bodily health by external symptoms, so
Crabbe, the physician of souls, finds out the spiritual
condition by the general course of life. An ironical
and distrustful observer, he demands, before giving
his opinion, convincing evidence, acts and not mere
intentions. He is realistic even in the discharge of his
holy office. He ridicules those "ardent and sudden
conversions," those pious outbursts which come after
a career of vice or indifference. The awakening of
faith seems to him sincere and lasting only if it is preceded by a heartfelt repentance, caused by "the fear
of God's justice, the conscience bearing witness against
the sinner." When summoned to a penitent, Crabbe
first "dwells on his actual sins"; rather than dilate on
the "general depravity" of mankind, he tries to "excite
a horror" of vice and its consequences. "We ask no
questions respecting the Feelings, but, as well as we
can, speak to the understanding. We read the service

---

[1] Last sermon preached at Swefling, July 14th, 1805.

[2] Cf. with the passage just quoted a curious parallel between "virtue" and
"prudence" instituted by Paley in his *Moral and Political Philosophy* (1785)
and quoted by Sir Leslie Stephen (*English Thought in the Eighteenth Century*,
vol. ii. p. 123): "The difference, and the only difference, between prudence
and virtue is that, in the one case, we consider what we shall gain or lose in
the present world; in the other case, we consider also what we shall gain or
lose in the world to come." Compared with this coldly systematic egoism,
Bentham's altruistic utilitarianism is generous and disinterested.

in the Prayer-book, and we judge it right to speak of
conditions of acceptance which a Calvinist will not
admit; we tell men that repentance is necessary and
a virtuous and religious life for the future, and for this
we inform them that grace will be given if faithfully
asked and the life regulated by the rules and precepts
of the Gospel."[1] It is not the heart, which is always
unstable, that has to be converted, but the reason,
which produces solid convictions and deliberate actions.
Such is the method of this frigid religion of the
philosopher and moralist, for which faith rests on a
syllogism and is valued by its practical results only.
Devoid of all warmth and enthusiasm, it remains powerless to stir the masses, the "ignorant and the poor,"
whose minds can be reached only through their feelings.

Do Crabbe's religious opinions thus defined enable
us to assign him a place in one of the three parties
which had arisen within the Church of England at the
beginning of the nineteenth century? I think so. He
certainly ought not to be classed among the "orthodox," with whose narrowness and exalted conception
of sacerdotal functions he had no sympathy. To him
the Church was not merely "a flock whom bishops
govern and whom priests advise."[2] The illuminism
which the "Evangelicals" had borrowed from Methodism, their exclusive doctrine of justification by faith
without works, made him hold aloof from the second
party, one of the leaders of which, Charles Simeon,[3]
he had heard preach at Cambridge. There remain
the "Liberals," among whom it seems, on the whole,
that Crabbe should be ranked, on the same grounds as
his contemporary Sydney Smith. Like them, he holds
by "essentials," and does not insist upon "inferior
points." "Are you," he writes, "of this or that Church
is a matter of no very great importance. Are you a
Christian is one of the most important."[4] His definition
of the Church is the widest possible:

---

[1] Letter to Miss Hoare, dated Beccles, December 3rd, 1825 (Broadley
Collection).

[2] *Borough*, ii. 6 and 1-4. Cf. a fragment of a letter quoted by B. (*Works*,
p. 380, n. 2).

[3] B. p. 54. For his influence at Cambridge at the beginning of the nineteenth century, see Overton, *The English Church in the Nineteenth Century*
(1800-33), London, 1899, p. 54.

[4] Letter to the Biographer, dated Trowbridge, August 15th, 1831 (Broadley
Collection).

> "What is a Church?"   Let Truth and Reason speak,
> They would reply, "The faithful, pure, and meek,
> From Christian folds the one selected race,
> Of all professions, and in every place."[1]

He has an indulgent tolerance for the Roman Catholics, then deprived of their political rights, and a reverence for the ruins which their time-honoured religion has left on English soil.   In an eloquent passage he evokes—

> . . . The seats where priests mid tapers dim
> Breathed the warm prayer, or tuned the midnight hymn;
> Where trembling penitents their guilt confess'd,
> Where want had succour, and contrition rest;
> Where weary men from trouble found relief.[2]

And this poetic enthusiasm for mediæval monasticism is compatible in his case with an equal tolerance for his Nonconformist colleagues, strong Puritans and determined opponents of Catholicism. "Our dissenting brethren," he said at Trowbridge on June 5th, 1814, "differ from us in many things, in no one, I trust, essential [and] indispensable. . . . There is difference in the opinions men form of the very dignity, nature, and office of the Redeemer; there is difference in the interpretation of texts and doctrines, and in the lesser matters of Church government and discipline, nor can it be otherwise, so long as freedom of discussion and communication takes place among us: no evil would come of this, if mutual charity attended the discussion, and if men would allow the same indulgence which they assuredly need. In points where the best and most deeply read have held various opinions, it becomes all to be diffident, all to admit the possibility of error . . ."[3] These characteristic words do not come from an "Evangelical,"[4] nor from one of the "orthodox" school, but from one of those "Liberals" who, later on, were to rally round Arnold and Stanley and form the "Broad Church."

[1] *Borough*, ii. 1-4.
[2] *Ibid.* iv. 134-43.
[3] Manuscript sermon in the Murray Collection.
[4] Contrary to what the Biographer asserts (p. 31), no sermon, manuscript or printed, and no letter indicates that Crabbe drew nearer to the Evangelicals towards the end of his life. If he discusses questions of dogma and apologetics rather frequently in his correspondence between 1825 and 1831, the reason is that his son, who was himself interested in theology, consulted him on knotty points.

IV

THERE are, however, two forms of opinion which Crabbe combats energetically—Methodism and unbelief. On the one hand, Hume's uncompromising scepticism and Voltaire's deism appear to him reprehensible. He read very attentively the famous Essay[1] in which the Scottish logician argues that no human testimony can be sufficient to prove a miracle, and that the resurrection of Christ is as improbable as would be that of Queen Elizabeth, even if attested by her contemporaries. Crabbe rejects all analogy of this kind : " Nobody has written thus of Queen Elizabeth, but it has been written that Jesus Christ was crucified and rose from the Sepulchre and was seen of those who related the event and staked their lives on its truth . . . There is nothing but perplexity in such arguments."[2] And this is what we ought, above all, to avoid. " If we wait till all doubts be cleared away, we shall die doubting." This world will "be lost in thinking of the next." Like the deists, we shall be refusing to accept " a religion which has satisfied the wisest, converted the most wicked, and consoled the most afflicted of our fellow-creatures,"[3] on pretence of examining it before we declare it to be true. The "Glad Tidings" will be read with unconcern, " searched without awe," perhaps with contempt, " refused without fear,"[4] and in this way vice will be encouraged. Scepticism, according to Crabbe, is the best auxiliary of corrupters and the best excuse for the corrupted. Look at Abel Keene, one of the outcasts in *The Borough* :[5] his young office-companions, who wanted to lead him astray, have overcome his scruples by destroying his faith. With the aid of the tales of "the admir'd Voltaire " and all the amusing and scandalous stories they could quote about the clergy, they have convinced their victim that religion is a farce, a piece of humbug cleverly got up by priests. Then why should he refrain from pleasure ? If his

---

[1] Hume, *Of Miracles* (1748). A summary of Hume's argument will be found on p. 526 of the *Essays* (World's Classics, 1903).

[2] Note perhaps written in 1814 (Murray Collection).

[3] Letter of December 24th, 1828, quoted by B. p. 83, and *Tales of the Hall*, xvi. 510.

[4] *Borough*, iv. 28-37.

[5] *Ibid.* xxi. 28 and 234-7.

conscience happens to sting him in the midst of his excesses, the infidel stills his "pangs" by reading appropriate books; like Crabbe's Blaney, he opens his Mandeville, who teaches him the utility of vice; Blount and Chubb confirm him in his contempt for revealed religion, and he learns—

> How Hume had dwelt on Miracles so well,
> That none would now believe a miracle.[1]

Since the last judgment and a future life are so many "monkish stories and nursery lies," man can safely indulge his passions. An irresponsible being, he obeys the determinism of his instincts,[2] and not the divine law. This is where unbelief leads, concludes Crabbe. According to him, if we wish to act and to act well, we must believe. For the moral conscience, like reason, is powerless without the aid of faith.[3]

On the other hand, mysticism, the opposite excess, is not less dangerous than impiety. On his return to Muston in 1805, Crabbe had been disagreeably surprised to find that, owing to his long absence and the frequent changes of his substitutes,[4] Methodism had taken root in his parish, and was making converts among his flock. This rivalry, all the more annoying because he considered himself personally responsible for it, intensified his dislike of Wesley's doctrines and gave him a taste for controversy. Mistrust enthusiasm, he cries in his sermons and sometimes in his poems; resist the impulses of your imagination: the Spirit of Christ is a spirit of truth and of moderation. Do not believe Whitefield and Wesley when they assert that "conversion," independent of works and conduct, consists in a sudden illumination of the soul torn by remorse, in a "new birth," in an intimate and intuitive union of the believer with his Redeemer. If these apostles of regeneration and of justification by faith wield a despotic influence over the crowds that hang upon their lips, this is because they dramatise religion for the needs of their cause and "imagine" a constant struggle between themselves and the demons; because

---

[1] *Borough*, xiv. 75-7 and 91-5.

[2] It may be noted that some of Crabbe's characters plead fatality, supernatural or otherwise, as an excuse for their faults : *e.g.* Edward Shore, *Tales*, xi. 355, and Fanny, in William Bailey, *Tales of the Hall*, xix. 480.

[3] This is the gist of Edward Shore (cf. ll. 77-8).

[4] B. p. 51. Between 1793 and 1803 no less than eight names of curates and "officiating ministers" are found on the Muston registers.

they consider every nervous crisis brought on by their eloquence as a defeat of Satan, expelled to make room for the triumphant Christ. But what is the value and the duration of these epileptic conversions, the effect of a "spiritual influenza"?[1] Just as great as that of the feelings which gave them birth. Reason alone can "find" the foundations of belief and make them immovable.[2]

The instability of faith is not the least of the evils engendered by Methodism. The reader is aware that at a very early stage[3] Wesley and Whitefield disagreed on essential points, the first maintaining, as a true disciple of Arminius,[4] that the divine grace is within the reach of all, the second asserting, in the name of the narrowest Calvinism, that the prescience of the Almighty implies the predestination of a certain number of elect and the reprobation of the rest, damned without pity. Now, Whitefield insisted as strongly as his colleague on the necessity of regeneration, of the "new birth" of the soul suddenly illumined by a ray of grace. This was to him the infallible sign of pardon and of election. It followed that those who were not visited by this revelation considered themselves as lost from the very beginning and destined to eternal torment. They consequently fell into a profound despair.[5] Against this cruel and pernicious doctrine Crabbe protests repeatedly. His Abel Keene, arrested in his vicious courses by poverty and ripe for repentance, consults a famous "doctor" of "souls diseased," one of those Calvinistic Methodists or Church of England Evangelicals who, like Whitefield and Toplady, had "wrought cures past belief." He confesses his sins to him, asks him for a "cordial" that will give rest to his soul, for he "trembles" at his state:

>   ... "Tremble more,"
> Said the good man, "and then rejoice therefore !
> 'Tis good to tremble; prospects then are fair,
> When the lost soul is plunged in deep despair:

[1] *Borough*, iv. Introduction, p. 186, and p. 192, ll. 334-43.

[2] *Tales*, xix. 85-102 : " The Faith that Reason finds, confirms, avows. . . ."

[3] Southey's *Life of Wesley*, Chandos Classics, 1893, p. 114, and the whole of ch. xi.

[4] Hence the name of Arminian Methodists given by Crabbe to the Wesleyans (*Borough*, iv. 387).

[5] This was the case with Cowper (cf. *The Castaway*).

> Once thou wert simply honest, just, and pure,
> Whole, as thou thought'st, and never wish'd a cure :
> Now thou hast plunged in folly, shame, disgrace,
> Now thou'rt an object meet for healing grace ;
> No merit thine, no virtue, hope, belief,
> Nothing hast thou, but misery, sin, and grief;
> The best, the only titles to relief."

What must I do, rejoins Keene, to "free my soul"?

> "Do nothing, man; it will be done for thee."
> "But must I not, my reverend guide, believe?"—
> "If thou art call'd, thou wilt the faith receive.
> Attend on us, and if 'tis Heaven's decree,
> The call will come—if not, ah ! woe for thee ! "

And the disconsolate Keene devoutly attends public worship, where the preacher's denunciations draw "tears and sighs" from the congregation—all in vain: the pains and the joy of the "new birth" are withheld from him. Eternal reprobation then must be his lot! Would it not be better, he thinks, to make an end at once of such a miserable life? He disappears, and at last is found "hanging in a pedlar's shed," a wretched victim of his own vices and of the fanaticism of others.[1]

Another and still more mischievous consequence was that the logic of the Calvinistic doctrines led their adepts to that contempt for works and the "divine law" which characterises Antinomianism. While, in Wesley's view, the illumination of the soul assures it of its present justification, but in no way of its final perseverance in Christian perfection, to the extreme Calvinists, on the contrary, the "new birth" is at once a promise and a realisation.[2] The elect are absolved in the present and perfect in the future. According to Wesley's ironical expression, they "shall be saved, do what they will."[3] In Crabbe's time no one maintained this opinion with more energy than the curious "prophet of the Lord" known by the name of "William Huntington, S.S."[4] Successively

---

[1] *Borough*, xxi. 257-8, 263-89, and 211-12.
[2] See on this point Southey's *Life of Wesley*, pp. 138 and 433.
[3] *Ibid.* p. 198.
[4] That is to say, W. H., Sinner Saved. See a good article on this personage by Southey in *The Quarterly Review*, vol. xxiv. January, 1821, pp. 462-510 (quoted in Crabbe's *Works*, pp. 186-7, note 2, p. 192, n. 20), his works pub-

cobbler, stevedore, and leader of a sect, endowed with
a pleasant voice, an extraordinary memory, and superhuman assurance, Huntington had managed to obtain,
by dint of prayers and of drafts on the " Bank of
Faith,"[1] a modest competence, money enough to build
a meeting-house in London,[2] and finally the hand of
the widow of a lord mayor.[3] Although he was of a
rather sedentary habit himself, his disciples travelled far
afield, and one of them, in the course of a tour in the
neighbourhood of Muston, succeeded in converting a
maid and a gardener in Crabbe's service.[4] This was
enough to provoke the pastor's wrath against the new
sect, against this Huntington who went about repeating that unless the Most High was to be called "a liar,"
it was inadmissible that people could " be children of
God to-day and be cast away as children of the devil
to-morrow."[5] How, he exclaims in a sermon in verse
which Crabbe put into his mouth—

> Can Grace be gradual, can Conversion grow ?
> The work is done by instantaneous call ;
> Converts at once are made, or not at all ;
> Nothing is left to grow, reform, amend,
> The first emotion is the Movement's end :
> If once forgiven, Debt can be no more ;
> If once adopted, will the heir be poor ?
> The man who gains the twenty-thousand prize,
> Does he by little and by little rise? . . .
> We're pardoned neither for belief, nor deed,
> For faith nor practice, principle nor creed ;
> Nor for our sorrow for our former sin,
> Nor for our fears when better thoughts begin ;

lished in twenty volumes (1811), and the *Memoirs of the Rev. Wm. Huntington,
S.S., the Coalheaver,* 2nd edition, revised and improved by one of his congregation, London, Bailey, 1813. He was buried at Lewes, and his epitaph
is as follows : " Here lies the Coal-Heaver, who departed this life July 1st,
1813, in the 60th year of his age, beloved of God, but abhorred of men. The
Omniscient Judge, at the grand Assize, shall ratify and confirm this, to the
confusion of many thousands ; for England and its metropolis shall know that
there hath been a prophet among them ! W. H. S.S."

[1] Divine grace according to him, contributions from simpletons in reality.
See his *Bank of Faith*, published in 1784 ; the passage quoted in Crabbe's
Works (pp. 186-7, n. 2) is an extract from it (pp. 87-90).

[2] Providence Chapel in Tichfield Street, burned down on July 13th, 1810,
and New Providence Chapel in Gray's Inn Lane, inaugurated on June 23rd,
1811 (*Memoirs*, p. 12).

[3] Lady Saunderson.

[4] B. p. 51.

[5] *Huntington's Autobiography* (1811, in the first volume of the *Works*,
pp. 183-4).

> It is the *Call!* till that proclaims us free,
> In darkness, doubt, and bondage we must be;
> Till that *assures* us, we've in vain endured,
> And all is over when we're once assured.[1]

The elect, being united to God, are above human morality. Thus Methodism, pushed to its final consequences, destroys reason if it is Arminian, and both reason and morality if it is Calvinistic.

For doctrines so extreme and subversive Crabbe could have nothing but aversion. He was neither a thinker nor a mystic. The philosophic intrepidity of a Hume, shrinking from none of the conclusions of his system, the enthusiasm, the prophetic frenzy of a Wesley and a Whitefield, illuminating this life with the glory of Paradise or shrouding it in the darkness of infernal night, remained equally foreign and perhaps incomprehensible to him. The real and the supernatural were never blended to his eyes, save in death, where they were reunited. A prudent and matter-of-fact mind, he had accepted a compromise between these two hostile principles, reason and faith, looking to the first to legitimate, as far as possible, the exigencies of the second. The "facts" of revelation once admitted to be true, the Resurrection clearly established, he was reassured about the meaning of life and the necessity of practical morality, to which he attached paramount importance: lead a peaceable, virtuous, and pious existence, he never wearied of repeating to his parishioners, and you will obtain happiness in this world and salvation in the next; indulge your evil propensities, from ignorance or from want of energy, and punishment will overtake you on earth. The picture of human life, even in a humble village, was, he thought, the best of all moral lessons.

[1] *Borough*, iv. 309-32. All this part of the fourth "Letter" of *The Borough* gave great offence to the Methodists (cf. below, p. 306, n. 2).

CHAPTER II

"THE PARISH REGISTER"

I. The immediate causes and the circumstances of the publication.—II. The moral thesis of the work.—III. Rural society in England at the end of the eighteenth century : the aristocracy, the middle class, the clergy.—IV. The agricultural classes : farmers and labourers.—V. The small shopkeepers.—VI. The oddities and failures. Crabbe and the "rustic novel."—VII. Verdict of contemporaries, and conclusion.

I

To draw a minute and accurate picture of village life from personal observation, to extract from the humblest misfortunes the lessons they suggest, to combine realistic description with moral comment—this was Crabbe's object in writing his new poem. *The Parish Register* was composed in about four years. For a long time influential friends had been urging him to break silence. Charles Fox, meeting him in the autumn of 1794 or 1795 [1] on a visit to Dudley North at Little Glemham Hall, had complained of his prolonged inactivity, and had offered to help him with advice and criticism, in case he decided to publish. Towards the end of June, 1806, the manuscript of *The Parish Register* was finished, and Fox, then Foreign Secretary in the Ministry of "All the Talents," was gradually sinking under an incurable malady. Remembering his promise, however, he "repeated an offer which the poet had not presumed to expect, but was happy to receive." Lord Holland, the nephew of the illustrious statesman, used to come to his uncle's bedside every evening and read to him for an hour or two. "The books we chose," he says, "were chiefly novels. . . . I also read the whole of Crabbe's *Parish Register* over to him in MS. Some parts he made me read twice ; he remarked several passages as exquisitely beautiful, and objected to some few, which I mentioned to the author, and

[1] B. p. 43.

which he, in almost every instance, altered before publishing. Mr. Fox repeated once or twice that it was a very pretty poem, that Crabbe's condition in the world had improved since he wrote *The Village*, and his view of life and of mankind had improved likewise. *The Parish Register*," he added, " bore marks of some little more indulgence to our species, though not so many as he could have wished, especially as the few touches of that nature are beautiful in the extreme. He was particularly struck with the description of the substantial happiness of a farmer's wife." [1] The pathetic history of Phœbe Dawson had equally interested him in his last moments. The good opinion of a man of such " capacious and candid mind " [2] and such fine taste seemed a guarantee of success to the poet.

Material considerations, even more than the encouragements of his friends, were pressing Crabbe to turn his talents to account. His domestic expenses had been continually increasing since his eldest son, George, had gone to Cambridge. On August 8th, 1804, he informed Wenn, his Ipswich attorney, that he would require a considerable sum, about £80, to pay the yearly bills at Trinity College, where the course of study lasted no less than eight years, four for the degree of B.A. and four for that of M.A. From 1807 onwards the expenses of the younger son, John Waldron, who was at Gonville and Caius College, were added to those of George, so that in January, 1808, the poet's accounts for the past year showed a formidable deficit. The publication of *The Parish Register* had not yielded its first profits; the death of Mrs. Elmy in 1802, and of Miss Elizabeth Tovell in 1803, had brought Mira and her children an inheritance which promised well for the future, but was burdened with encumbrances and difficulties in the present. " Circumstances by me wholly unavoidable," wrote Crabbe at this time, " have within the last three years drawn from me about £1,300 exclusive of the common expenses of my family, but including the college bills of my elder

---

[1] *Parish Register*, ii. 390-430: Lord Holland's *Memoirs of the Whig Party* (1852, vol. i. pp. 254-6); cf. Crabbe's Preface to the 1807 Poems (*Works*, pp. 98-9).

[2] Crabbe's Preface, *Works*. On July 26th Fox's condition was desperate. He died on September 13th; Thurlow had passed away the day before.

son till he took his degree,[1] and the first term of his brother, and the continuance of this charge I cannot any longer maintain. Some help from Mrs. Elmy's will enabled me to bear it hitherto, but, sir, the keeping two young men at an University in these times is, I find, beyond my ability, and at the same time I am under an engagement to treat my sons in like manner, nor could I with a quiet mind make a distinction, if I had not pledged my word that I would not. The young men being one in his 23rd, and the other in his 21st year, and their mother earnestly and anxiously joining in our request, I am disposed to think that we shall not meet with difficulty in our wishes to dispose of so much of the funded property left to Mrs. Crabbe and her children by her aunt as will reach £200."[2] The request thus made was refused by the executors, as vigilant guardians of the interests of George and John Waldron Crabbe. Their father had, against their wish, to look to the sale of his works for the sum required. Very fortunately, the moment happened to be propitious for his poetic resurrection, after twenty-two years of silence. His former contemporaries, Burns and Cowper, had not been succeeded in public favour either by Rogers or Campbell, still less by the authors of the *Lyrical Ballads*,[3] which were coolly or ironically received. Scott and his *Last Minstrel* had alone excited enthusiasm in recent years. But there was still room, by the side of romantic

---

[1] George Crabbe took his degree of B.A. in 1807, of M.A. in 1811; John Waldron became B.A. in 1811, M.A. in 1814 (cf. *Graduati Cantabrigienses*).

[2] Letter to Wenn, one of the trustees, dated Muston, January 20th, 1808 (Forster Collection). Wenn's unfavourable reply was a great disappointment to Crabbe, who could not forgive the attorney for it. The following is his answer, written on August 12th of the next year, to the bill of costs and the threatening letter which accompanied it: ". . . Sir,—That I have had such difficulties as you allude to is certain, for you were applied to when they became oppressive, and, whenever you have two young men to support at so expensive a place as a University, you may possibly feel those difficulties which now happily escape your commiseration, and I find by your letter that, were they ever so grievous, they would not prevent the increase your demand would in that case have made. Fortunately, sir, they are removed by means more pleasant and honourable than by an application to gentlemen in your profession, nor was your bill refused. All I claimed was the common right of every man, examination into the nature of the demand made upon him. . . . Why this should draw from you a threatening letter is to me extraordinary, but I allow much for habit" (same Collection). The "attorneys" were not forgotten in *The Borough*.

[3] *The Pleasures of Memory* by Rogers (1792), *The Pleasures of Hope* by Campbell (1799), *Lyrical Ballads* by Coleridge and Wordsworth (1798), reprinted with numerous additions in 1800, 1802, and 1805.

mediæval and border legends, for a realistic picture of
the manners of rural England, and this is what the
reading public appreciated in *The Parish Register*,
published on October 29th, 1807.[1]

II

LET us enter the vestry of a village church, and ask
the clergyman who accompanies us to take, from the
chest where they are kept under lock and key, the
precious registers, bound in yellow parchment or
grey cloth, which contain the already ancient history
of the families of the place. Here is a list of all the
" forefathers of the hamlet " who from the time of Queen
Elizabeth, perhaps, down to about 1830, have seen the
light, married, and passed away in this parish. Their
names, at all events, have not crumbled into dust;
their memory survives in that past which the sympathetic imagination evokes without difficulty in surroundings so tranquil and so little changed. Stepping
back a century, we become for a moment the contemporaries of Fox and of Crabbe; leaning our elbows on
the chest at the poet's side, the register open before
us, we seem to " explore " with him " the simple annals
of his parish-poor " :

> What Infant-members in his flock appear,
> What pairs he bless'd in the departed year;
> And who, of Old or Young, or Nymphs or Swains,
> Are lost to Life, its pleasures and its pains.[2]

We listen attentively to the remarks which each name
suggests to him, and, our curiosity aroused by his
penetrating sympathy, we beg him to conduct us
through his village.

We go out together; after a few steps he bids us
stop in front of a cottage, his clerk's, no doubt, so neat
and even smart is it :

> Screen'd from the winter's wind, the sun's last ray
> Smiles on the window and prolongs the day;
> Projecting thatch the woodbine's branches stop,
> And turn their blossoms to the casement's top.

---

[1] See the advertisement in *The Times* of the same day : "*Poems* by the Rev.
George Crabbe, 8*sh*. 6*d*." The book, which was dedicated to Lord Holland,
also contained a reprint of *The Library*, *The Village*, and *The Newspaper*, as
well as three new poems, *Sir Eustace Grey*, *The Hall of Justice*, and *Woman*,
which will be referred to later on.
[2] *Parish Register*, i. 3-6.

A garden, graciously assigned by the lord of the manor, surrounds the dwelling:

> Here—till return of morn dismiss'd the farm—
> The careful peasant plies the sinewy arm,
> Warm'd as he works, and casts his look around
> On every foot of that improving ground. . . .
> Here grow the humble cives, and, hard by them,
> The leek with crown globose and reedy stem ;
> High climb his pulse in many an even row,
> Deep strike the ponderous roots in soil below ;
> And herbs of potent smell and pungent taste
> Give a warm relish to the night's repast.

The agreeable is mingled with the useful, for close to the cottage can be seen through a reed-fence brilliant hues of carnations, of " proud hyacinths, tall-stemm'd tulips and pounced auriculas." Look at this " fair scene of peace," says the poet to us :

> Here on a Sunday-eve, when service ends,
> Meet and rejoice a family of friends ;
> All speak aloud, all happy are and free, . . .
> And the same stories are for ever told. . . .
> Yet theirs is joy that, bursting from the heart,
> Prompts the glad tongue these nothings to impart,

and finds vent in cries of delight that we, perhaps wrongly, despise. At nightfall the members of the family come home and admire, for the hundredth time, the pictures on the walls : Louis XVI. on his throne, Louis XVI. in prison with Marie Antoinette, Nelson conquering at Aboukir Bay, Nelson dying in the moment of his triumph. Devoutly they open a " newly bound Bible," bought by " sixpence weekly saved " ; its " choice prints, by famous hands engraved," its notes by celebrated commentators form the subject of conversation and discussions, which sometimes lead the " rustic readers " to " doubt."[1]

Without lingering further over this smiling picture of honest rural felicity, we resume our walk, and, passing rapidly through the village, arrive at its opposite end. What a contrast ! The feet sink into the muddy road, lined with shanties inhabited by vicious and miserable creatures, the outcasts from society. We advance with difficulty and not without repugnance ; but our guide, whose curiosity grows

[1] *Parish Register*, i. 33-6, 132-4, 139-55, 43-4, 66-7, 82-6.

visibly stronger, encourages us with his advice and example. Come, he says—

> Come ! search within, nor sight nor smell regard ;
> The true physician walks the foulest ward.

Let us follow him, then, into every corner :

> Between the roadway and the walls, offence
> Invades all eyes and strikes on every sense ;
> There lie, obscene, at every open door,
> Heaps from the hearth and sweepings from the floor,
> And day by day the mingled masses grow,
> As sinks are disembogued and kennels flow.
> There hungry dogs from hungry children steal ;
> There pigs and chickens quarrel for a meal.

Farther on, a group of " sots, cheats, and shrews " are quarrelling: we hear the oaths of a man and the screams of a woman whose insolence increases under his blows; the children shriek and try to separate their parents, begging alternately for the life of their mother and for a morsel of bread. In a corner are poachers and smugglers dividing their booty. Let us pluck up courage, and enter another hovel which is open to all comers, for its mistress spends her time in gossiping with her neighbours :

> See ! on the floor what frousy patches rest !
> What nauseous fragments on yon fractured chest !
> What downy dust beneath yon window seat !
> And round these posts that serve this bed for feet ;
> This bed where all those tattered garments lie. . . .
> Beds but ill parted by a paltry screen
> Of paper'd lath, or curtain dropt between ;
> Daughters and sons to yon compartments creep,
> And parents here beside their children sleep.
> Ye that have power, these thoughtless people part,
> Nor let the ear be first to taint the heart.[1]

Let us leave this sordid spot at last, not without casting a final glance at the dilapidated garden palings, and at the pothouse whose "walls of clay hide sots and striplings at their drink or play," as well as the cruel sport of cock-fighting.[2] What was the pastor's intention in showing us that pretty cottage and those horrid dens immediately afterwards ? We

---

[1] *Parish Register*, i. 188-95, 170-5, 204-19,
[2] *Ibid*. 243-68. The reader will remember Hogarth's *Cockpit*.

put the question to him. The village, the two ends of which you have just seen, he replies, is much the same as that which I formerly described in rough outline and without definite ideas. In the name of truth, I protested then and I still protest against the pastoral fictions which persist in turning our country districts into a land of love, of freedom, and of prosperity, where labour does not exhaust, where no care interrupts the even tenour of a perpetual happiness. I wished, by raising the veil and dispelling illusion, to bring the shepherds and shepherdesses of Eden back to our poor earth and to show that they are human beings like the rest of us, liable to all our vices and to all our calamities. But I did not go farther. It was enough for me to see and copy the reality: I did not attempt to explain it. Since then I have spent many years among our village folk; I know their character from having visited them day by day and from having stood by them on the happiest and saddest occasions of their lives. Experience has taught me that vice and misery, virtue and happiness, are indissolubly connected. Toil, care, and patience bring reward to the few, while fear, shame, and want pursue the thoughtless majority.[1] Hence the startling contrast between the wretchedness of the latter, led astray by their evil propensities, and the success of the former, due to frugality, hard work, and good conduct. For most of us, our fate is in our hands and depends on our behaviour. One can be happy, even in the country, if one knows how to control oneself. My universal pessimism of former days must be blended with a small—a very small—admixture of optimism to arrive at the truth. The sky is seldom so overcast that not a break in the clouds can be seen.

III

LISTENING all the while to the poet, we return towards the church, and skirt a wall overhung with trees which leads to a half-closed gate. This is the entrance to the park, which, from the moss on the roads and the encroaching undergrowths, would appear to be abandoned, if it were not for the irregular felling practised by a wasteful management. At the farther

[1] *Parish Register*, i. 29-30.

end is seen a "forsaken" mansion: the lady who owns this domain, the clergyman explains, always lives in town, and the house is tenantless:

> Worms eat the floors, the tap'stry flees the wall:
> No fire the kitchen's cheerless grate displays;
> No cheerful light the long-closed sash conveys:
> The crawling worm, that turns a summer fly,
> Here spins his shroud and lays him up to die
> The winter-death: upon the bed of state,
> The bat shrill shrieking woos his flickering mate;
> To empty rooms the curious come no more;
> From empty cellars turn the angry poor,
> And surly beggars curse the ever-bolted door.
> To one small room the steward finds his way,
> Where tenants follow to complain and pay;
> Yet no complaint before the lady came,
> The feeling servant spares the feeble dame,
> Who sees her farms with his observing eyes,
> And answers all requests with his replies.[1]

In the absence of the noble lady who neglects the duties enjoined by her rank, the most important personage in the place is "Sir Edward Archer," an "amorous knight," whose sight is shunned by "maidens chaste and lovely." He is supposed to have paid marked attention and to have addressed impassioned language to the fair "Fanny Price":

> Hope of my life, dear sovereign of my breast,
> Which since I knew thee, knows not joy nor rest;
> Know thou art all that my delighted eyes,
> My fondest thoughts, my proudest wishes prize;
> And is that bosom—(what on earth so fair!)
> To cradle some coarse peasant's sprawling heir? . . .
> Now turn with me, and all the young desire
> That taste can form, that fancy can require,
> All that excites enjoyment, or procures,
> Wealth, health, respect, delight, and love, are yours;
> Sparkling, in cups of gold, your wines shall flow,
> Grace that fair hand, in that dear bosom glow;
> Fruits of each clime, and flowers, through all the year,
> Shall on your walls and in your walks appear:
> Where all beholding, shall your praise repeat,
> No fruit so tempting, and no flower so sweet:
> The softest carpets in your rooms shall lie,
> Pictures of happiest love shall meet your eye,

[1] *Parish Register*, iii. 236-51. For the convenience of the analysis the present tense has been used in this passage.

> And tallest mirrors, reaching to the floor,
> Shall shew you all the object I adore. . . .
> Come, then, my mistress, and my wife ; for she
> Who trusts my honour is the wife for me ;
> Your slave, your husband, and your friend employ
> In search of pleasures we may both enjoy.

But Fanny, as good and not so clever as Pamela, merely replied with meekness and firmness :

> My mother loved, was married, toil'd, and died ;
> With joys she'd griefs, had troubles in her course,
> But not one grief was pointed by remorse :
> My mind is fix'd, to Heaven I resign,
> And be her love, her life, her comforts mine.

And Sir Edward, as generous as he is passionate, helped to marry Fanny to a youth by whom she was loved.[1]

Near his mansion rises the tame modern residence of Sir Richard Monday, who has attained honours and wealth after a life devoid of dignity. He was a foundling whom the parish had had to adopt, to the great annoyance of the vestry. The choice of a name for this "unwelcome guest" had long been a very troublesome question, for to give one's own to a child of unknown parentage might set ill-natured tongues wagging. A consultation was acccordingly held :

> They looked about, they gravely spoke to all,
> And not one *Richard* answer'd to the call.

Next they inquired on what day of the week the little stranger's cry had been first heard, and when this had been ascertained, "Richard Monday," duly labelled and registered, was sent to the workhouse. He was not petted there :

> Patient in all control, in all abuse,
> He found contempt and kicking have their use :
> Sad, silent, supple ; bending to the blow,
> A slave of slaves, the lowest of the low ;
> His pliant soul gave way to all things base,
> He knew no shame, he dreaded no disgrace ;
> It seem'd, so well his passions he suppress'd,
> No feeling stirred his ever-torpid breast.

[1] *Parish Register*, ii. 502-13, 532-45, 553-63.

This was all hypocrisy, however, for one day he absconded, being anxious to see the world. He had aptitudes for success : "no small cunning," and "some little wit "; he—

> Had that calm look which seem'd to all assent,
> And that complacent speech which nothing meant.

With a keen eye to the main chance, he amassed a fortune. And now he lives ostentatiously at " Monday Place." When he dies, he will leave all his grandsons "as rich as Jews," make bequests to charities, and buy " the blessings of the blind and dumb." But, to his native place, severely just, he will leave—

> . . . A pittance bound in rigid trust—
> Two paltry pounds, on every quarter's day
> (At church produced) for forty loaves shall pay ;
> A stinted gift, that to the parish shows
> He kept in mind their bounty and their blows.[1]

Such is the aristocracy of our little village, situated in the peaceful interior of Suffolk, and unaffected by the movement of industrial progress and social re-adjustment accelerated elsewhere by the mechanical discoveries of the preceding generation. Here the eighteenth century seems to survive itself; manners and characters remain what they were fifty years since. For a long time complaint had been made of the absen-teeism of the large landowners who, spending most of their time in London, visited their country seats only in the shooting-season, and left their parks and their estates under the charge of not over-scrupulous agents. Our "noble lady" belonged to this category. What was the darling vice of the squires who lived on their properties, from Richardson's " Mr. B—— " down to George Eliot's "Captain Donnithorne," but too great a devotion to female beauty, caused by their want of employment and their exclusively physical existence ? Sir Edward Archer's warmth is equal to theirs. And had not Addison, with sympathising insight, already noted the love of successful business men like Sir Andrew Freeport for the " *latifundia* " which brought them political prestige and influence ? Sir Richard Monday, the foundling, now a rich man and proud of a title due to lucky speculation, returns to

---

[1] *Parish Register*, i. 698-717 ; 741-59.

his native village and builds "Monday Place." Evidently, Crabbe does not invent : he groups, he summarises, he personifies the aspects of contemporary society in a certain number of types, "representative" for those who can recognise them.

Let us proceed to the middle class, which is more tamely described, no doubt because it is less interesting. As we are in the "church-way walk," we see hard by, "where the brook winds round the chancel like a shepherd's crook," a small house surrounded by a green paling with jessamine growing on each side of the door, and dark shrubs—

> . . . Clipp'd in form and tantalised with skill ;
> Where cockles blanch'd and pebbles neatly spread,
> Form shining borders for the larkspurs' bed.

This is the abode of "Catherine Lloyd," a lady "wise, austere, and nice, who shows her virtue by her scorn of vice." Her erect and stately gait, her tall, thin figure, her long, tight stays, call to mind the pious lady in one of Hogarth's pictures or Miss Bridget Allworthy.[1] No one knows her income, but it is no secret that a supposed cousin lived with her for some time, to the detriment of her good name, and bequeathed to her various treasures collected in the Indies :

> If aught like joy awhile appear'd to stay
> In that stern face, and chase those frowns away,
> 'Twas when her treasures she disposed for view
> And heard the praises to their splendour due ;
> Silks beyond price, so rich, they'd stand alone,
> And diamonds blazing on the buckled zone ;
> Rows of rare pearls by curious workmen set,
> And bracelets fair in box of glossy jet—

or when with her "clipp'd French puppy" on her knees, her stuffed parrot near her, and her old grey cat licking his whiskers, she would lord it over her companion, a "widow'd aunt, compelled by need the nymph to flatter and her tribe to feed." It was of no use to apply to her for a subscription to any charity.[2]

As we are close to the church, how can we forget the clergymen who repose beneath these tombstones ? Our guide has heard something of his predecessors ;

---

[1] See the central figure of "Morning" in Hogarth's series called *The Four Times of the Day*, and Fielding's *Tom Jones*, book i. ch. xi.
[2] *Parish Register*, iii. 312-21 ; 330-41.

in fact, he knows all about them : we guess as much
from his arch smile.   First of all comes "good Master
Addle," a man of fine presence.   How dignified and
imposing he looked when he appeared "adorned with
college gown and parish hood"![1]   And when he
"paced the hallow'd aisles," how well he filled his
"seven-fold surplice"!   But hardly had he reached
his pulpit when, wearied, no doubt, with prayer—

> He sat and seem'd as in his study's chair,
> For while the anthem swell'd, and when it ceased,
> Th' expecting people view'd their slumbering priest.

Perhaps he had tired himself out in his fields, like his
contemporary, Parson Trulliber.[2]   Without lingering
over "Parson Peele," skilful at shearing his flock, or
"Doctor Grandspear," always open-handed and with
a "world of hat," we come to times nearer the poet,
to his immediate predecessor, who is guilty of having
introduced Methodist excitement into this peaceful
parish.   This youth, fresh from Cambridge, a disciple
of the Evangelical Charles Simeon,[3] made a good
impression at first by his sober and comely appearance.   He blushed with modesty and seemed as meek
as a lamb.   But once in the pulpit he became a lion :

> Loud grew his voice, to threat'ning swell'd his look ;
> Above, below, on either side he gazed. . . .
> No more he read his preachments pure and plain,
> But launch'd outright, and rose and sank again :
> At times he smiled in scorn, at times he wept. . . .
> "Conviction comes like lightning," he would cry ;
> "In vain you seek it, and in vain you fly ;
> 'Tis like the rushing of the mighty wind,
> Unseen its progress, but its power you find ;
> The proud learn'd man, and him who loves to know
> How and from whence these gusts of grace will blow,
> It shuns,—but sinners in their way impedes,
> And sots and harlots visits in their deeds :
> Of faith and penance it supplies the place ;
> Assures the vilest that they live by grace,
> And, without running, makes them win the race."

Consumed by his fiery zeal, the young pastor even
tually fell into a decline.   A hectic flush appeared in

---

[1] *Parish Register*, iii. 824.
[2] In Fielding's *Joseph Andrews*, book ii. ch. xiv.
[3] Cf. above, p. 212.

his thin cheek; worn out, he sank upon his death-bed,
regretting his charitable actions :

> The good I've wrought still rankles in my mind;
> My alms-deeds all, and every deed I've done ;
> My moral-rags defile me every one—

so great was his abhorrence of "works" and their
merits, so exclusive his belief in justification by faith.[1]

Thus speaks the satirist whom we are continually
finding in Crabbe: he contrasts the ponderous dulness
of Addle with the feverish enthusiasm of a beginner.
To these two extremes, between which the Anglican
clergy of the eighteenth century oscillated, he prefers
the golden mean, the reasonable zeal by which he
himself was guided.

IV

IN our rural community an important place is naturally due to the agricultural class, and first of all to the
farmers, nay, even to the farmers' wives. The "widow
Goe," an able woman if ever there was one, not content
with ruling her own household, reigned supreme over
the country-side. We may recognise in her an idealised
Mrs. Tovell [2] :

> Famed ten miles round, and worthy all her fame,
> She lost her husband when their loves were young,
> But kept her farm, her credit, and her tongue:
> Full thirty years she ruled, with matchless skill,
> With guiding judgment and resistless will ;
> Advice she scorn'd, rebellion she suppress'd,
> And sons and servants bowed at her behest.
> " Come," if she said, they came ; if " Go," were gone ;
> And if " Do this," that instant it was done ;
> Her maidens told she was all eye and ear,
> In darkness saw, and could at distance hear ;
> No parish business in the place could stir
> Without direction or assent from her ;
> In turn she took each office as it fell,
> Knew all their duties and discharged them well ;
> The lazy vagrants in her presence shook,
> And pregnant damsels feared her stern rebuke.

Indefatigable, always alert and full of life, she was
found sometimes in her farmyard, followed by troops
of chickens, and sometimes in her parlour conversing

---

[1] *Parish Register*, iii. 896-946.   [2] See above, p. 51.

with the neighbouring farmers, who paid her great attention. But when they made "their amorous vows, she talked of market-steeds and patent-ploughs." With her the serious business of life came first. The days, beginning with the dawn, must be spent in work; the evening was the time for amusement:

> Then to her toilet's brief concern she ran,
> And conversation with her friends began,
> Who all were welcome, what they saw, to share;
> And joyous neighbours praised her Christmas fare,
> That none around might, in their scorn, complain
> Of Gossip Goe as greedy in her gain.[1]

Without being a landowner, she enjoyed to the full the prestige given by wealth and success.

With far less means, "Robert," a small farmer, and his wife "Susan," were equally happy. They had just christened a boy, who came after three girls, but, in spite of this, "future births were neither hoped nor feared." They had health, quiet, and comfort, and this was all that they asked:

> Few were their acres, but, with these content,
> They were, each pay-day, ready with their rent;
> And few their wishes—what their farm denied,
> The neighbouring town, at trifling cost, supplied.
> If at the draper's window Susan cast
> A longing look, as with her goods she pass'd,
> And, with the produce of the wheel and churn,
> Bought her a Sunday-robe on her return;
> True to her maxim, she would take no rest,
> Till care repaid that portion to the chest:
> Or if, when loitering at the Whitsun-fair,
> Her Robert spent some idle shillings there,
> Up at the barn, before the break of day,
> He made his labour for th' indulgence pay.

Theirs was a wise frugality, "that did not give a life to saving, but that saved to live." The anniversary of their marriage, the christening of their children, were joyful occasions on which the wealthier farmers were warmly welcomed and hospitably entertained:

> For Susan served the great, and had some pride
> Among our topmost people to preside.[2]

This was a reward for her patient efforts, a luxury in her monotonous existence.

[1] *Parish Register*, iii. 155-62.   [2] *Ibid.* i. 405-37.

On the whole, our farmers were not badly off. They were even passing through an era of exceptional prosperity. The war with France, by restricting foreign trade, had fostered an excessive protectionism and driven up provisions, corn especially, to unprecedented prices.[1] A constantly increasing population required bread at any cost. All available land was turned to account, the commons were enclosed, and a higher return was sought by improved methods of cultivation, by letting to wealthy farmers or "widow Goes" large holdings which were formerly divided. The cultivator needed capital and labour if he wished to succeed. For rents had more than trebled in twenty years,[2] so eager were the squires to get rich, so strong was the competition for the farms, owing to the profit which, in spite of all drawbacks, was yielded by them. The farmers now constituted, below the landowners whose estates they turned to account, a regular rural middle class, quite distinct from the labourers. They received by courtesy the name of "yeomen,"[3] to which their predecessors could only lay claim if they cultivated their own patrimony. Along with wealth, they had won consideration. Woe to the man whose poverty seemed to exclude him from the new caste; he became the butt of all the others. See the humble "Barnaby," who sits apart in church, and listen to the remarks of the mocking circle that forms around him:

> They praise his dairy, they extol his team,
> They ask the price of each unrivall'd steed,
> And whence his sheep, that admirable breed;
> His thriving arts they beg he would explain,
> And where he puts the money he must gain.
> They have their daughters, but they fear their friend
> Would think his sons too much would condescend;
> They have their sons who would their fortunes try,
> But fear his daughters will their suit deny.
> So runs the joke, while James, with sigh profound,
> And face of care, looks moveless on the ground;
> His cares, his sighs, provoke the insult more,
> And point the jest—for Barnaby is poor—[4]

---

[1] Wheat was more than 112 shillings a quarter in 1800 and 1801 (Toynbee, *Industrial Revolution*, p. 101).

[2] In 1793 land let at 10 shillings an acre (in Essex); in 1812, at 50 shillings an acre (*Ibid.* p. 92).

[3] See the "Mr. Martin" of Abbey Mill Farm in Miss Austen's *Emma*.

[4] *Parish Register*, i. 770-86.

and that was a crime. These rough, full-blooded natures were "coarsely kind and comfortably gay"; tables laden with dishes in honour of some festive occasion, bumpers of wine in the evening to warm their hearts and loosen their tongues—these were their pleasures. For men, work and good living; for women, the refinements which gradually transformed their farmhouses into middle-class dwellings. The times had gone by when the farmer's wife, a slave to "gain," denied herself sleep, and "in her meanest room from morn till night a noisy drudge was seen." Now she must have "a decent room, adorned with carpet formed in Wilton's loom," with "fair prints" spread along the "paper'd wall." She liked to invite the "neighbourging dames" on festal days, and practise the art of conversation in which "English wives" are so skilled:

> An art it is where each at once attends
> To all, and claims attention from her friends,
> When they engage the tongue, the eye, the ear,
> Reply when list'ning, and when speaking hear.[1]

Really, the Suffolk farmers, as described by Crabbe, seem to have been fortunate people, and we might suspect the poet of an excess of optimism in this instance if Cobbett's testimony, given twenty years later and in a much less prosperous period,[2] did not agree with his: "The land," exclaims the celebrated agitator, after visiting the environs of Ipswich and Stowmarket, "is in such a beautiful state, the farm-houses all white, and all so much alike; the barns and everything about the homesteads so snug; the sheep and cattle in such fine order; the ploughmen so expert; the furrows of a quarter of a mile long, as straight as a line, and laid as truly as if with a.level: in short, here is everything to delight the eye, and to make the people proud of their country; and this is the case throughout the whole of this county. I have always found Suffolk farmers great boasters of their superiority over others, and I must say that it is not without reason." [3]

[1] *Parish Register*, ii. 394-5, 408-30; and in Miss Austen's *Emma* Mrs. Martin has "two parlours, two very good parlours indeed, one of them quite as large as Mrs. Goddard's [the schoolmistress] drawing-room, . . . and a very handsome summerhouse in their garden."

[2] From 1818, after the war, land, in Essex, was not worth more than 35 shillings an acre (Toynbee, p. 92).

[3] Written in 1830 (Cobbett's *Rural Rides*, vol. ii. p. 297, London, 1893).

Unfortunately, their prosperity was not shared by their labourers, whose condition had not improved since 1783. Growing prouder with their increase of wealth, the masters held more and more aloof from the men, and the picture which the Biographer has drawn of Tovell and his farm-hands taking their meals together [1] corresponded less and less with the reality. The high prices of provisions, so profitable to the farmers, combined with the stationary condition of wages, had reduced the labourer to abject poverty. How could he and his family live on eight shillings a week, with wheat at 112 shillings a quarter? Since he could not earn a livelihood by his work, he must needs have been dependent on public charity, and he received a regular allowance from the parish, sanctioned by the justices of the peace, and calculated according to the number of his children [2]—an excellent means of increasing the population and the scarcity along with it! [3] Marriages were made as early as possible, and families multiplied in want. "Gerard Ablett," for instance, has had an olive-branch every year, and now he is bringing a twin boy and girl to be christened. [4] Rare are the "Reubens" and "Rachels," who can combine prudence with love and wait "year after year, with savings long laid by," until they can buy "the future dwelling's full supply":

> Her frugal fancy cull'd the smaller ware,
> The weightier purchase asked her Reuben's care;
> Together then their last year's gain they threw,
> And lo! an auction'd bed, with curtains neat and new. [5]

Yet what is the use of all this forethought, since the result must be the same in the end, and the most

---

[1] See above, p. 51.

[2] This "allowance system, . . . or reducing the price of labour and eking it out of the rate," was instituted by the Berkshire magistrates at a meeting held in 1795 at Speenhamland, near Newbury. It lasted down to 1834, when the Poor Law was amended and made much more severe. (Cf. Toynbee, p. 102; De Gibbins, *Industrial History of England*, 8th ed. 1902, pp. 187-8, and an article in *The Quarterly Review*, vol. l. pp. 347 *seq.*, January, 1834). Lecky (*History of England*, vol. vi. p. 206) writes: "With the warm approbation of Pitt (speech of 1796), parochial relief was made proportionate to the number of children in a family, and a direct premium thus offered to improvident marriages. As early as 1803, it appears that out of 8,870,000 in England and Wales, not less than 1,234,000 (one-seventh) were partakers of parochial relief."

[3] Malthus's famous theories were partly due to this state of things.

[4] *Parish Register*, i. 471-2.

[5] *Ibid.* ii. 443-6.

persevering efforts cannot ensure a competence in old age or keep the most deserving out of the odious workhouse! Consider the case of "Isaac Ashford," the "noble peasant":

> Noble he was, contemning all things mean,
> His truth unquestion'd and his soul serene:
> Of no man's presence Isaac felt afraid;
> At no man's question Isaac look'd dismay'd:
> Truth, simple truth, was written in his face.

He combined cheerfulness and gentleness with a serious character:

> To bliss domestic he his heart resign'd,
> And with the firmest had the fondest mind;
> Were others joyful, he look'd smiling on,
> And gave allowance where he needed none. . . .
> I mark'd his action when his infant died,
> And his old neighbour for offence was tried:
> The still tears, stealing down that furrow'd cheek,
> Spoke pity, plainer than the tongue can speak.
> If pride were his, 'twas not their vulgar pride,
> Who, in their base contempt, the great deride;
> Nor pride in learning—though my Clerk agreed,
> If fate should call him, Ashford might succeed;
> Nor pride in rustic skill, although we knew
> None his superior, and his equals few :—
> But if that spirit in his soul had place,
> It was the jealous pride that shuns disgrace;
> A pride in honest fame, by virtue gain'd,
> In sturdy boys to virtuous labour train'd;
> Pride in the power that guards his country's coast
> And all that Englishmen enjoy and boast;
> Pride in a life that slander's tongue defied—
> In fact a noble passion, misnamed Pride.

And what a fervent piety was his:

> True to his church he came: no Sunday-shower
> Kept him at home in that important hour;
> Nor his firm feet could one persuading sect
> By the strong glare of their new light direct. . .
> I view his seat, and sigh for Isaac there;
> I see no more those white locks thinly spread
> Round the bald polish of that honour'd head;
> No more that awful glance on playful wight,
> Compell'd to kneel and tremble at the sight,
> To fold his fingers, all in dread the while
> Till Mister Ashford soften'd to a smile.[1]

[1] *Parish Register*, iii. 413-502.

What would have been the fate of this "noble" old
man if a sudden death had not providentially cut him
off! At seventy years of age, "his strength departed
and his labour done," his wife gone before him and his
children dispersed, he would have had to end his days
in that refuge for vice and poverty where a contractor
feeds the paupers at so much a head and "gauges
stomachs with an anxious look." Do we not feel that
Crabbe, now as formerly, protests against the harshness of a society which is ungrateful to its best
servants, and all the more ungrateful because the
services have been so manifest and so meritorious ?

V

BUT we have returned to the centre of the village, and
are about to make the acquaintance of the more
important tradesfolk, some of whom examine us
curiously from their doorstep. Let us begin with the
inn, the "Old Crown," and we shall find, seated in his
"huge chair" beside the fire, the blind old landlord,
"Andrew Collett" :

> Big as his butt, and for the self-same use,
> To take in stores of strong fermenting juice.

An enthusiastic admirer of the past, he despises the
present. Those were the good old days, he exclaims :

> When ale was cheap and bachelors were bold. . . .
> One, in three draughts, three mugs of ale took down,
> As mugs were then—the champion of the *Crown* ;
> For thrice three days another lived on ale,
> And knew no change but that of mild and stale ;
> Two thirsty soakers watch'd a vessel's side,
> When he the tap with dex'trous hand applied ;
> Nor from their seats departed, till they found
> That butt was out and heard the mournful sound.[1]

Or perhaps some angry wife would come to rescue "a
third-day drunkard from his ale," which was an opportunity for Collett to show how great his skill—

> That won the vex'd virago to his will,
> Who raving came—then talked in milder strain—
> Then wept, then drank, and pledged her spouse again.

---

[1] *Parish Register*, iii. 75-112. There is no exaggeration here, as is proved
by the following passage from Garnier's *Annals of the British Peasantry*,
p. 308 : "We read of four well-seasoned yeomen of Gloucestershire who,
having raised their courage with the juice of the apple, resolved to have a
fresh hogshead tapped, and sitting foot to foot emptied it at one sitting."

He also abounded in stories of sundry breakers of the
law, of a poacher, a "precious child of fun, who shot a
keeper with his own spring-gun,"[1] and of a smuggler
who tied an exciseman to a birch-tree and left him
hanging there! We are now far from Goldsmith's
inn, with its innocent "village statesmen,"[2] but we
are nearer the reality. Andrew Collett and his
customers are arrant rogues; his house is a resort
for all the scamps of the country-side: take away the
smugglers, and you might find its equivalent in the
present day not far from Parham. We leave it without regret, and, a few paces farther on, we are received
with a sweet smile by the obsequious "Peter Pratt,"
a gardener as notable as he is pedantic. He has the
amiable weakness of giving his children learned horti-
cultural names: the last was called Lonicera, and the
next will be christened Hyacinthus if it is a boy, and
Belladonna if a girl. At his suggestion we follow him
into his garden, and, as we walk along, he reveals to
us the mysteries of his science :

> Would you advance the nuptial hour and bring
> The fruit of autumn with the flowers of spring :
> View that light frame where Cucumis lies spread,
> And trace the husbands in their golden bed,
> Three powder'd Anthers ; then no more delay,
> But to the Stigma's tip their dust convey ;
> Then by thyself, from prying glance secure,
> Twirl the full tip and make your purpose sure ;
> A long-abiding race the deed shall pay.

We suspect our parson of having often talked botany
with this singular gardener, and even of having lent
him Darwin's poems; we therefore retire with all
speed. We pass, without stopping, before the door
of "Dawkins" the grocer, an ex-pedlar who has made
money by a contraband trade in lace and tea, and who,
having married late in life, is bemoaning his childless-
ness.[3] We hear from a distance old "Leah Cousins,"
the midwife of the place, who, her pipe in her hand
and a glass of ale by her side, is abusing her formidable rival "Dr. Glibb": we hasten to escape from her
intolerable chatter.[4] A more pleasing object of contemplation is the venerable schoolmistress, seated in

---

[1] *Parish Register*, iii. 95.   [3] *Parish Register*, i. 520-7.
[2] See above, p. 152.   [4] *Ibid.* iii. 635-730.

front of her house, an open Bible on her knees. She
is knitting and reading by the rays of the setting sun :

> Her idle neighbours, who approach to tell
> Some trifling tale, her serious looks compel
> To hear reluctant,—while the lads who pass,
> In pure respect, walk silent on the grass.[1]

And our stroll coming to an end at nightfall, we return
to the parsonage.

VI

Not, however, to take leave of our guide, for he still
detains us and describes, sometimes in a satirical and
sometimes in a pathetic tone, the character and career
of a few oddities or failures, the study of whom has an
irresistible attraction for him.   He tells us of an infidel
poacher, a fierce advocate of the " rights of man," who
flatly refused to have his children baptised, and whom
the drunkards of the neighbourhood dubbed their
" bishop."[2] He remembers poor " Robin Dingley,"
who one fine day was thus accosted by a crafty
attorney :

> I give thee joy, good fellow ! on thy name ;
> The rich old Dingley's dead ; no child has he,
> Nor wife, nor will ; his ALL is left for thee :
> To be his fortune's heir thy claim is good ;
> Thou hast the name, and we will prove the blood.

Thereupon Dingley, a " poor swain " and a " man of
simple heart," knowing nothing of the world but his
own parish, began to discount his expectations, sent
his daughters to school, bought books, and " hired
harpsichords " for them. Alas ! he had been misled
by a wretched cheat ; he lost the case, and with it his
reason :

> He tried in vain to labour or to rest,
> Then cast his bundle on his back and went
> He knew not whither, nor for what intent.

He reappeared long afterwards, in a " sailor's jacket,"
with " haggard cheeks " and " hollow eyes " ; he described the " battles, prisons, and storms " which he
fancied he had undergone ; he was admitted into the
workhouse, clothed and fed. But no sooner had he

---

[1] *Parish Register*, i. 600-8.   [2] *Ibid.* i. 786-823.

begun to regain his health and strength than he
resumed his vagabond life, from which eventually
he was brought back dying, on a heap of straw in a
jolting cart which wrung groans from him—a hapless
victim of one of those "vile attorneys" whom the poet
held in such detestation.[1]

Less tragic is the story of " Roger Cuff," the
Timon of our village. Shipwrecked in his youth,
he had returned home, but received no welcome
from his three brothers. "Ah!" he exclaimed, "is
this a landsman's love? Be certain, then, we part
for ever!" And so it happened: forty years elapsed,
during which he made money, and when he decided to
come back, his brothers were dead, leaving three sons
and a daughter; besides these he had a distant kinsman, much less well off, who worked in the woods,
"apart from all his kind," and was called "Surly
John." Before landing, Roger, who had experience of
mankind, said to himself:

> "Yet hold! I'm rich;—with one consent they'll say,
> You're welcome, Uncle, as the flowers in May;
> No; I'll disguise me, be in tatters dress'd,
> And best befriend the lads who treat me best. . . ."
> In piteous plight he knocked at George's gate,
> And begg'd for aid, as he described his state :—
> But stern was George ;—" Let them who had thee strong,
> Help thee to drag thy weaken'd frame along ;
> To us a stranger, while your limbs would move,
> From us depart, and try a stranger's love :—
> Ha! dost thou murmur? "—for in Roger's throat,
> Was " Rascal!" rising with disdainful note.

Next he addressed himself to James, who was a pious
gentleman:

> "Good lack," quoth James, "thy sorrows pierce my breast,
> And, had I wealth, as have my brethren twain,
> One board should feed us, and one roof contain:
> But plead I will thy cause, and I will pray:
> And so farewell! Heaven help thee on thy way!"
> "Scoundrel!" said Roger (but apart) ;—and told
> His case to Peter ;—Peter too was cold ;—
> "The rates are high; we have a-many poor;
> But I will think," he said, and shut the door.
> Then the gay niece the seeming pauper press'd ;—
> "Turn, Nancy, turn, and view this form distress'd :

[1] *Parish Register*, iii. 503-80.

> Akin to thine is this declining frame,
> And this poor beggar claims an Uncle's name."
> " Avaunt ! begone ! " the courteous maiden said,
> " Thou vile impostor !   Uncle Roger's dead :
> I hate thee, beast ; thy look my spirit shocks ;
> Oh ! that I saw thee starving in the stocks ! "

" My gentle niece ! " murmurs Roger, and hies him to
the wood where he finds Surly John :

> " I hunger, fellow ; prithee give me food ! "
> " Give ! am I rich ?   This hatchet take, and try
> Thy proper strength, nor give those limbs the lie ;
> Work, feed thyself, to thine own powers appeal,
> Nor whine out woes thine own right hand can heal ;
> And while that hand is thine, and thine a leg,
> Scorn of the proud and of the base to beg."
> " Come, Surly John, thy wealthy kinsman view,"
> Old Roger said ;—"thy words are brave and true ;
> Come live with me : we'll vex those scoundrel boys,
> And that prim shrew shall, envying, hear our joys.
> Tobacco's glorious fume all day we'll share,
> With beef and brandy kill all kinds of care ;
> We'll beer and biscuit on our table heap,
> And rail at rascals, till we fall asleep." [1]

This is quite the downrightness of an old sailor : the
whole scene, although a trifle crude, is cleverly and
vigorously drawn.   In a few lines the author gives a
distinctive touch to each of his personages, and his
story, ingenious in itself, assumes, like a fable, a
dramatic character which is rather rare in Crabbe.
Above all it helps, along with certain other passages,[2]
to enliven a composition in which the sombre note, as
always, predominates.

The poet admits this himself :

> When these my Records I reflecting read,
> And find what ills these numerous births succeed ;
> What powerful griefs these nuptial ties attend,
> With what regret these painful journeys end ;
> When from the cradle to the grave I look,
> Mine I conceive a melancholy book.[3]

---

[1] *Parish Register*, iii. 731-800. It is noticeable that Crabbe, taught by his
experience, always contrives to give his sailors characteristic bluntness, vigour,
and impulsiveness (cf. " William " in *The Parish Register*, i. 321-8 ; and
" Rupert," in *Procrastination* : *Tales*, iv. 263 *seq.*).

[2] For instance, the story of Kirk and his maidservant (ii. 19-82).

[3] *Parish Register*, iii. 17-22.

Our follies have such irreparable consequences that
an error of conduct, a mere weakness is often enough
to spoil a whole life! Crabbe had read Mrs. Inchbald's
novel *Nature and Art* on its publication in 1796, and
the sad lot of Agnes, the humble heroine, had brought
to his mind the harrowing recollection[1] of a similar
case. Perhaps in the present day we are not so keenly
alive to the charms of the winning maiden of Anfield,
endowed with a beauty unrivalled in her village and
with the tenderest disposition, destined " to inspire
and to experience real love." Perhaps we are less
touched by her intrigue with William Norwynne, an
unfeeling and ambitious man, the son of a high dignitary
of the Church; by her sufferings when, a prey to
remorse and shame, she tries to strangle her new-born
babe with her trembling hands; by her anguish when,
sinking from one degradation to another, successively
farm-help, servant in a house of ill-fame, an accomplice
of thieves and convicted of forgery, she hears herself
sentenced to death by the same William who was
formerly her seducer and is now her judge.[2] A certain
amount of melodrama and a good deal of inexperience
and simplicity enter into this tale and spoil it in our
eyes. But at the end of the eighteenth century the
work was an original one. No writer had hitherto
ventured to treat a refined public to a realistic description of the misfortunes of a young village beauty, of a
guilty Pamela.[3] A new heroine of a new school, Agnes
founded the " rustic novel." *Nature and Art* at last
depicted a pair of genuine rustics, not ridiculous nor
too superior to their neighbours, and a real country
girl, whose beauty had brought her to crime and not
to an improbable good fortune. The lovers of accurate
observation, of the unadorned fact, commonplace to the
indifferent but fascinating to students of the human
mind,[4] could not help being interested in this innova-

[1] B. p. 44: "One evening, I believe some such association almost broke
our hearts."

[2] *Nature and Art* (Cassell's National Library, 1886), pp. 68-160. On
another side, in the character of Henry Norwynne, a young "savage" more
civilised than his cousin William, this novel proceeds from Rousseau.

[3] Mrs. Inchbald herself had some misgivings, see pp. 71-2: "Reader of
superior rank, if the passions which rage in the bosom of the inferior class of
human kind are beneath your sympathy, throw aside this little history, for
Rebecca Rymer (the daughter of the curate of Anfield) and Agnes Primrose
are its heroines."

[4] Domestic drama alone had made use of it before Mrs. Inchbald.

tion, Crabbe more than any one, he whose *Village* had thrown so much light on country life. He found traces of himself in Mrs. Inchbald, a native of the same county;[1] above all, in Agnes he recognised a likeness, somewhat idealised, to one of his parishioners. She inspired him at once, and we find three portraits drawn from this model in *The Parish Register*. First of all comes " Lucy," the young miller's daughter, too ardently courted by the bold sailor William, and banished by her father to a lonely cottage, where she languishes with her child ; then " Lucy Collins," betrothed to the honest farmer Stephen Hill, but seduced and ill-treated by the elegant Daniel, a footman in an aristocratic family ; and, last but not least, " Phœbe Dawson," well known as the favourite heroine of Charles Fox :

> Two summers since, I saw at Lammas Fair
> The sweetest flower that ever blossom'd there,
> When Phœbe Dawson gaily crossed the Green,
> In haste to see and happy to be seen :
> Her air, her manners, all who saw admired,
> Courteous though coy, and gentle though retired ;
> The joy of youth and health her eyes display'd,
> And ease of heart her every look convey'd ;
> A native skill her simple robes express'd,
> As with untutor'd elegance she dress'd ;
> The lads around admired so fair a sight,
> And Phœbe felt, and felt she gave, delight. . . .
> Correct in thought, she judged a servant's place,
> Preserved a rustic beauty from disgrace ;
> But yet on Sunday-eve, in freedom's hour,
> With secret joy she felt that beauty's power,
> When some proud bliss upon the heart would steal,
> That, poor or rich, a beauty still must feel.

Unfortunately, Phœbe selected the least desirable from among her admirers, one who "pleased by manners most unlike her own":

> Loud though in love, and confident though young ;
> Fierce in his air, and voluble of tongue ;
> By trade a tailor, though, in scorn of trade,
> He served the Squire, and brushed the coat he made ;
> Yet now, would Phœbe her consent afford,
> Her slave alone, again he'd mount the board;
> With her should years of growing love be spent,
> And growing wealth ;—she sigh'd and look'd consent.

[1] She was born at Standingfield, near Bury St. Edmunds.

Then ensued a period of fallacious happiness:

> Now, through the lane, uphill, and 'cross the green,
> Seen but by few, and blushing to be seen,
> Led by the lover, walk'd the silent maid. . . .
> Slow through the meadows roved they, many a mile,
> Toyed by each bank, and trifled at each stile. . . .
> Thus pass'd th' allotted hours, till lingering late
> The lover loiter'd at the master's gate;
> There he pronounced adieu! and yet would stay,
> Till chidden—soothed—entreated—forced away,

but not without obtaining a proof of her kindness, which she " resented first and then forgave." Imprudent Phœbe!—

> Too late her loss the marriage-rite repair'd;
> The faithless flatterer then his vows forgot,
> A captious tyrant or a noisy sot;
> If present, railing, till he saw her pain'd;
> If absent, spending what their labours gain'd. . . .

Poverty and sickness followed, and now Phœbe, left alone, is no longer, alas! the beauty of former days:

> Lo! now with red rent cloak and bonnet black,
> And torn green gown loose hanging at her back,
> One who an infant in her arms sustains,
> And seems in patience striving with her pains;
> Pinch'd are her looks, as one who pines for bread,
> Whose cares are growing and whose hopes are fled;
> Pale her parch'd lips, her heavy eyes sunk low,
> And tears unnoticed from their channels flow;
> Serene her manner, till some sudden pain
> Frets the meek soul, and then she's calm again;—
> Her broken pitcher to the pool she takes,
> And every step with cautious terror makes;
> For not alone that infant in her arms,
> But nearer cause, her anxious soul alarms.
> With water burthen'd, then she picks her way,
> Slowly and cautious, in the clinging clay;
> Till, in mid-green, she trusts a placé unsound,
> And deeply plunges in th' adhesive ground;
> Thence, but with pain, her slender foot she takes,
> While hope the mind as strength the frame forsakes:
> For when so full the cup of sorrow grows,
> Add but a drop, it instantly o'erflows.
> And now her path, but not her peace, she gains,
> Safe from her task, but shivering with her pains;
> Her home she reaches, open leaves the door,
> And placing first her infant on the floor,

She bares her bosom to the wind, and sits,
And sobbing struggles with the rising fits :
In vain they come, she feels the inflating grief,
That shuts the swelling bosom from relief ;
That speaks in feeble cries a soul distress'd,
Or the sad laugh that cannot be repress'd.
The neighbour-matron leaves her wheel and flies
With all the aid her poverty supplies ;
Unfee'd the calls of Nature she obeys,
Not led by profit, not allur'd by praise ;
And waiting long, till these contentions cease,
She speaks of comfort, and departs in peace.[1]

It is thus that Crabbe, a more scrupulous realist
than Mrs. Inchbald, leaves out the romantic element
which still remained in the story of Agnes. His
unfortunate heroines are not exalted and made, as it
were, poetical by the brilliance of their conquests ;
they do not succumb to the prestige of wealth or of
rank ; they do not fall in love with the son of a squire[2]
or of a high dignitary of the Church, but with a tailor,
a footman, or a sailor. Their attachments are of a
more ordinary and more prosaic kind. But this was
the only kind that the clergyman had observed in his
village, and no poet was ever more truthful than Crabbe.

VII

THE publication of *The Parish Register* was an opportunity for the author to communicate once more with
his friends. The book had not yet appeared when
copies, accompanied by letters, were sent to Mrs. Burke,
to Richard Turner, of Great Yarmouth, to Bonnycastle,
now head of the military college at Woolwich, to
Dr. Mansel, President of Trinity College, and afterwards Bishop of Bristol, to Roger Wilbraham, to the
young Duke of Rutland, to politicians like Canning,
Grey, Lord Holland, Dudley North, and Sir Charles
Bunbury. Writing to the last named, Crabbe explained
his long silence by the isolation in which the loss of
his patrons had left him, by the " small cares " of a
clergyman with a family, and by " greater cares " which
he did not specify. "At length," he added, " the
obliging attention of Mr. Dudley North, the kindness

[1] *Parish Register*, ii. 131-245.
[2] Like George Eliot's Hetty Sorrel, the third of that line.

of Mr. Fox, and the unexpected favour of Lord Holland
have excited me to exertion and occasioned the appearance of the volume before you." [1] This delicate attention
on the part of the poet was bound to elicit eulogistic
replies, the least commonplace of which is Richard
Turner's. " Your *Parish Register*," he wrote to his old
curate, " is a gallery of exact likenesses and highly and
accurately finished portraits, and you afford in your
descriptions complete subjects for many an artist.
Better authorities than I am I conceive will tell you
that in harmony of numbers, in personification of
character, and in justness of appropriation you follow
your former course with more than *passibus æquis.*" [2]

The new work, in fact, was favourably received. *The
Monthly Review* regarded it as a continuation and an
amplification of *The Village*, as a sort of parish biography
abounding in varied characters, vigorously drawn and
skilfully shaded, as a series of anecdotes judiciously
selected on the whole, and related sometimes with
genuine emotion, sometimes with singular satirical
power. It quoted the whole of Richard Monday, and
also of the infidel poacher, considered the story of
Phœbe Dawson a touching one, although consisting
too much of description and not enough of narrative,
and was inclined to prefer that of the miller's daughter. [3]
The British Critic, in taking leave of Mr. Crabbe,
expressed a strong wish to meet him again. [4] Lastly,
in April, 1808, Francis Jeffrey, the all-powerful critic
of *The Edinburgh Review*, hailed Crabbe as an old
acquaintance whose reappearance gave him extreme
pleasure. For the opponent of " Mr. Wordsworth and
Company," *The Parish Register*, composed in classic
metre and " in the good old style of Pope or Dryden,"
was a regular windfall. " Its characteristic," he

---

[1] Letter dated Muston, October 8th, 1807 (*Correspondence of Sir Th.
Hanmer*, edited by Sir H. Bunbury, pp. 450-1).

[2] Letter dated Yarmouth, October 24th, 1807 (Broadley Collection). For
Turner, see above, p. 195. Crabbe had mentioned him in his preface to the
poems of 1807 (*Works*, p. 99, col. 2), and Turner shows himself much gratified
by it in this letter : " You make my little bark sail proudly in the company of
rank and science and save me from forgetfulness when my children's children
will only know of me that I filled up a niche in the succession of Yarmouth
ministers."

[3] *Monthly Review*, new series, vol. lvi. pp. 170-80 (1808).

[4] Vol. xxxi. pp. 590-3 (1808). Strange to say, this review selected for an
extract the story of Nathan and his servant, which was much revised by the
author for the second edition. The first text will be found in Appendix III.

declared, "certainly is force and truth of description, joined for the most part to great selection and condensation of expression. . . . A frail damsel is a character common enough in all poems. . . . Mr. Wordsworth has written more than three hundred lines on that subject, . . . but he has contrived to tell us nothing of the unfortunate fair one, but that her name is Martha Ray, and that she goes up to the top of a hill in a red cloak and cries, 'Oh, misery!' All the rest of the poem is filled with a description of an old thorn and a pond, and of the silly stories which the neighbouring old women told about them." On the other hand, "nothing can be more touching than the quiet suffering" of Phœbe Dawson, though many persons might find fault with the accumulation of "tedious and unnecessary details," which spoil the general effect and the dignity of the narrative.[1] But these objections, far from detracting from the praise, enhanced the value of it, and, two days after the publication of the article, the first edition of the work, which had been lying in Hatchard's shop for six months, was bought out by the docile readers of *The Edinburgh Review*.[2] In September of the same year Crabbe hoped to get £100 from the sale:[3] it was therefore a real and lucrative success.

How much of all this eulogy and this criticism is worth remembering at the present day, and what is the value of *The Parish Register* to us? The composition, it must be admitted, is deficient in methodical arrangement and unity. The plan of the work, which is very different from that of the foregoing analysis, is more apparent than coherent. Our parson, on opening his "annals," sees the births on one side, the deaths on the other, and the marriages between them. Without further ado he divides his poem into three parts, on the model of his register. In each of these administrative compartments he notes in detail on a separate slip the character or the adventures of the persons whose names figure in the official lists of recent births, marriages, and deaths. He posts up,

---

[1] *Edinburgh Review*, vol. xii. pp. 131-51 (April, 1808).

[2] According to B. p. 52.

[3] See a letter to Wenn of September 23rd, 1808: "By some exertions I have a fair prospect of adding £100 or perhaps more to the year's receipts; this, however, my bookseller will not expect to pay before the end of the year" (Forster Collection).

with scrupulous accuracy, but without much method, the record of his parishioners. The rudimentary arrangement of his poem does not demand a high degree of invention. A writer preoccupied with the cohesion of his work would take care to provide a connecting-link, to contrive skilful transitions between these isolated notices; Crabbe does this sometimes, but more often he passes from one portrait to another with the mere words, " Then came a new couple," or " Next So-and-so died," according as a baptism, a marriage, or a death is in question. More than this, he does not always stick to his own categories: it is not easy to see why the story of the miller's daughter is placed among the baptisms, and not among the marriages with those of Phœbe Dawson and Lucy Collins ; the lamentations of the grocer Dawkins have nothing to do with the births, since it is of the absence of them that he personally complains ; and the characters of Richard Monday and the infidel poacher would be much more in their place among the deaths.[1] These irregularities, which, by the way, are explained by the impossibility of speaking of new-born children without referring to their parents, and the lack of cohesion in this systematically fragmentary work, prevent the reader from discerning any logical connection between the different parts, so that *The Parish Register* eludes his grasp and resembles an indiscriminate collection of portraits. It may be alleged that the unity of the poem is maintained by the thesis which it tries to establish. This, no doubt, was the opinion of Crabbe himself, who in his Preface described the inhabitants of his village as " a body of

[1] For the sake of greater clearness, I give the order in which the portraits follow each other :

I. BAPTISMS : Lucy, the miller's daughter, and William—Robert and Susan—a woman of irregular life—Gerard Ablett—Dawkins and Ditchem—the schoolmistress—Peter Pratt—Richard Monday—Barnaby—the infidel poacher.

II. MARRIAGES : Nathan Kirk and his servant—Donald and Mrs. Dobson—a seduced bride—Phœbe Dawson—a fashionable young bridegroom—Lucy Collins—the Lodges, a pair of old turtle-doves—domestic happiness of farmers' wives—Reuben and Rachel—Sir Edward Archer and Fanny Price.

III. BURIALS : Andrew Collett—the widow Goe—one of the sons of Gerard Ablett—the lady of the hall—Catherine Lloyd—Isaac Ashford—Robin Dingley—Mrs. Frankford—Leah Cousins—Roger Cuff—the old sexton, who had known the former rectors of the parish : Addle, Peele, Grandspear, the Author-Rector, and the young Evangelical from Cambridge. The reader will see that I have described as living some personages whom Crabbe had represented as dead and buried.

persons, sober or profligate, and hence, in a great
measure, contented or miserable." [1] But, in the first
place, it must be pointed out that this rule suffers
exceptions, that if it is perhaps true of the shopkeepers
and farmers, it does not apply—Crabbe expressly
admits this—to the agricultural labourers like Isaac
Ashford, who have the prospect of a wretched old
age, however well spent their life may have been.
And then, even admitting that this maxim of practical
morality serves as a support and a connecting-link
for all these independent stories, will any one believe
that it can enhance the value of a work which is a
demonstration of it ? What ! you take the trouble to
write a whole volume, and a volume of poetry, to prove
that good conduct is likely to lead to happiness and
vice to misery ! Is not this the most hackneyed
proposition imaginable ? And if it be sometimes
useful to enforce this lesson, is a poet required for the
task ?

No, what constitutes the value of *The Parish Register*
is not the plan nor the leading idea, but the isolated
characters which it contains. On reading it attentively
we seem to be inspecting a gallery of pictures of
different sizes—some of them half-length or full-length
portraits, others a combination of figures, and all hung
in a haphazard way. Near us is the old schoolmistress, seated and piously reading the open Bible on
her knees ; farther off is farmer Barnaby, surrounded
by a circle of mocking neighbours ; here, old Kirk is
snug in bed, and his servant gives him a knowing
look as she tucks him up ; there, the widow Goe is
stretched on her death-bed, " Heaven in her eye and
in her hand her keys " ; or Isaac Ashford appears, his
white head bowed in the silent meditation of prayer.
These figures strike us by their picturesque attitudes,
and in contemplating them we remember, with Hazlitt,[2]
that Crabbe wrote for a public which was beginning
to take an interest in the fine arts, especially in
painting. But an attentive, repeated, and sympathetic
consideration is necessary to extract this impression
from the work. We have to follow each touch
patiently, to reconstitute, by an effort of the imagination, the general outline of each picture. For,

---

[1] Preface to the poems of 1807 (*Works*, p. 100, col. 1).
[2] *Spirit of the Age*, Bohn's Libraries, 1886, pp. 300-1.

although picturesque traits are to be found in Crabbe, they are none too numerous. More frequently the characters are left in a sort of haze, through which the poet seems to obtain but a glimpse of them. They do not stand out, they do not light each other up by those happy effects of movement and contrast of which the Prologue of *The Canterbury Tales* presents a unique example. Most of them have an inanimate appearance, and seem to have been touched by the hand of death. The reason of this is that Crabbe lacks the supreme gift, the power of communicating a spark of his own soul to his personages. Essentially descriptive, he paints from the outside, enumerates abstract qualities, piles up exact details, but it seldom happens that this inorganic matter becomes instinct with spirit and life. We are told that Phœbe Dawson, for instance, was " courteous though coy, gentle though retired," elegant in her dress and figure ; but the decisive word is not uttered, and we do not see her. We are also told that in her distress she wears a black bonnet, a red cloak, and a green gown, but a painter alone has a sufficiently lively and prompt imagination to call up such a costume instantaneously before his eyes. We who are less practised hesitate ; our perception remains partial and indistinct. And then, is it not a waste of time, even for the most gifted, to try to paint with words ? Poets know how to sing their emotions; objectively, they can describe only by superficial and consecutive traits. Painting demands simultaneousness and fixity. A series of engravings would therefore be required to illustrate *The Parish Register* and bring out all its artistic value. In that case what a delight it would be to see the chivalrous Sir Edward Archer and Fanny Price advancing along a well-kept gravel walk, he bending amorously over her, while an honest villager jealously watches the behaviour of his powerful rival from behind the park railings ! And how many other personages would thus assume a distinctness which poetry is powerless to produce !

The Parish Register presents important points of difference from *The Village*. It lacks the boldness and the aggressive force of the earlier work. It does not contribute any new idea to literature : the vigorous satire on pastoral poetry is replaced by a pulpit platitude. But what it loses in energy it gains in amplitude. The general portrayal of the typical rustic is succeeded by clearly drawn characters of individual .rustics, such as Isaac Ashford, Gerard Ablett, Reuben and Rachel ; around them hovers a crowd of squires, farmers, tradesfolk, and nondescripts, so truthfully depicted that we have been able, by combining the poet's statements and the evidence of history, to reconstitute part of the society of that day. Crabbe, guided by his experience and his reading, has at last got into touch with concrete reality ; he grasps it under the manifold aspects of its endless details. In his effort to transfer it to his pages, he is about to become, with the aid of his pathos and his humour, the greatest realistic poet that has appeared in England.

FOURTH PART
CRABBE'S REALISM

/

SINGLE CHAPTER

"THE BOROUGH"

I. Crabbe's realism, in harmony with the tradition of the eighteenth
century in England, is opposed to the dawning Romanticism.—
II. Its origin and its elements: firstly, description—flora, heath,
sea, human dwellings.—III. Its origin and its elements: secondly,
satire and poetry of disillusion.—IV. Its distinctive character:
the psychology of outcasts.—V. Verdict of contemporaries.
Realism and reality.

I

IF realism is defined as a " tendency to represent
mankind and nature as they are," we find that this
force, always active in English literature, dominated it
in the eighteenth century. In philosophy, Locke was
led by the negation of innate ideas to make experience
the sole source of our knowledge; in theology, the
deists wished to bring religion down from heaven to
earth, and to justify it, not by a supernatural revelation,
but by a rational interpretation of the creation and of
the conscience. Poetry itself, discarding lyric and
song, revelled with Thomson and Cowper in the
description of nature in her grand or familiar aspects,
became satiric, plunged boldly into party conflicts with
Dryden, lent itself to the personal spite of Pope, and
laboriously castigated the failings of contemporary
society in the antithetical couplets of Young. The
novel in Defoe's hands had all the audacity and
curiosity of youth; taking his heroines, Moll Flanders
or Roxana, into the most disreputable quarters and
into the prisons of London, he presented them to the
public in the most unstudied attitudes. Richardson
based the plot of his *Pamela* on an authentic anecdote,
selected from among the reminiscences of his youth;
it was in order to accentuate the realism of his
illustrious predecessor that Fielding wrote his *Joseph
Andrews*, and subsequently carved Tom Jones and his

companions out of "human nature."[1] The stage, declining rapidly at the beginning of the century, recovered a few moments of life only to depict, in the domestic drama of Lillo and Moore, the dangers to which profligacy and gambling expose weak characters, and to ridicule, in the comedies of Goldsmith and Sheridan, the innocent eccentricities of country folk or the graver shortcomings of people of fashion. Finally art, in the pictures and engravings of Hogarth, became an unrivalled portrayer of the vices, the foibles, and the manners of a society whose defects it exaggerated for their better correction. In every department is displayed the same anxiety to paint the real and extract a moral lesson from it.

But this realism was blended with many foreign elements. Satire, which aims at wounding or, at all events, at criticising an opponent, exaggerated the bad, left the good in the shade, and calumniated rather than described. The novel, which had sprung from mediæval romance, retained traces of its origin, and sought to astonish the reader as much as to depict things actually seen. Whatever the originality and the merits of Richardson and Fielding, it must be borne in mind that, with the exception of *Amelia*, none of their novels forego the attraction of the unexpected and the improbable. The story of Pamela pleases by its singularity more than by its truth; the birth of Joseph Andrews and of Tom Jones remains a puzzle from chapter to chapter, and finds its solution only at the catastrophe. These authors, not content with the naked unadorned reality, delight in complicated plots, in alarums and excursions, in endless quarrels and digressions. Such romantic embellishments of works which have been rightly called "anti-romantic" ended by swallowing up the more solid elements when, about the year 1770,[2] the influence of the dawning romanticism extended to every description of literature. Thereupon imagination and the love of mystery, which had long been repressed, made up for it by wild excess,

---

[1] Cf. *Tom Jones*, book i. ch. i.

[2] *Evelina*, Miss Burney's best work, which marked the end of the semi-realistic novel in the eighteenth century, dates from 1778. The romantic novel was inaugurated by Walpole's *Castle of Otranto* in December, 1764, and its most notorious imitators were Clara Reeve (*The Old English Baron*, 1777), Mrs. Radcliffe (*The Mysteries of Udolpho*, 1794, etc., etc.), and Lewis (*The Monk*, 1795).

and soared far above the real world in the most extravagant flights. Marvellous helmets, knights with gigantic swords, spectre-haunted turrets from which inexplicable moans issued, were rife in books of fiction. This fit of frenzy, which lasted not less than twenty-five years, was succeeded towards 1801 by a revival of chastened and simplified realism, of the kind which Miss Edgeworth, Crabbe himself, and Jane Austen practised.

Crabbe has a healthy and profound contempt for the inventions of the Lewises and the Radcliffes. Miss Austen had already ridiculed them in the witty pages of *Northanger Abbey*, written in 1798 and kept for twenty years in manuscript. Crabbe in his turn riddles them with his keenest satire in a passage of *The Borough*:

> I've often marvell'd, when, by night, by day,
> I've marked the manners moving in my way,
> And heard the language and beheld the lives
> Of lass and lover, goddesses and wives,
> That books, which promise much of life to give,
> Should show so little how we truly live.
> To me, it seems, their females and their men
> Are but the creatures of the author's pen;
> Nay, creatures borrow'd and again convey'd
> From book to book—the shadows of a shade:
> Life, if they'd search, would show them many a change;
> The ruin sudden, and the misery strange!

If they did this, there would be no need to imagine fairy scenes and "ideal forms" such as those of "vengeful monks, who mix with nymphs and swains, and play unpriestly tricks." No "sixpences or tears" would be wasted over the "flow'ry pages of sublime distress" which is never fatal to persecuted virtue. The mysterious episodes of Mrs. Radcliffe's novels would be read with less rapture:

> Lo! that château, the western tower decay'd,
> The peasants shun it—they are all afraid;
> For there was done a deed! could walls reveal,
> Or timbers tell it, how the heart would feel!
> Most horrid was it:—for, behold, the floor
> Has stain of blood, and will be clean no more:
> Hark to the winds, which through the wide saloon
> And the long passage send a dismal tune,—
> Music that ghosts delight in; and now heed
> Yon beauteous nymph, who must unmask the deed.

See! with majestic sweep she swims alone,
Through rooms, all dreary, guided by a groan ;
Though windows rattle and though tap'stries shake,
And the feet falter every step they take,
'Mid moans and gibing sprights she silent goes,
To find a something, which will soon expose
The villanies and wiles of her determined foes :
And having thus adventured, thus endured,
Fame, wealth, and lover, are for life secured.[1]

In fact, what does it matter if a weeping damsel is borne
away at full gallop by remorseless villains ?

Still means of freedom will some power devise,
And from the baffled ruffians snatch their prize.

Let us take Mrs. Radcliffe's *Mysteries of Udolpho*, for
instance : are we to pity Emily because, imprisoned in
" Signor Montoni's " eyrie on the top of the Apennines,
she is forced to sleep in a chamber one door of which
cannot be locked and leads to a dark staircase ? Will
our blood run cold, like hers, when she lifts the veil
which shrouds the dread picture ? and shall we give
her up for lost when she is handed over to two bandits,
fit minions of their master, to be taken to a lonely
dwelling in Tuscany ?[2] No, our minds will be as easy
as Crabbe's : we foresee that Emily will leave Udolpho
as stainless as she entered it, and that a passionately
desired union with her beloved Valancourt will put an
end to her manifold adventures.

Crabbe has no need of such heroines. Aspiring to
paint life with the minutest accuracy, he chooses his
characters among the middle class for some of the
reasons which decided Wordsworth[3] to take his from
country folk : " It is in this class of mankind," Crabbe
writes, "that more originality of character, more variety
of fortune, will be met with ; because, on the one hand,
they do not live in the eye of the world, and therefore
are not kept in awe by the dread of observation and
indecorum ; neither, on the other, are they debarred by
their want of means from the cultivation of mind and
the pursuits of wealth and ambition." The varied
situations filled by the middle class offer many oppor-

[1] *Borough*, xx. 11-22, 49-50, 59-77.
[2] *The Mysteries of Udolpho* (London, William Strange, 1844), pp. 114, 121,
196 *seq.* A comparison of these passages with Crabbe's text shows that it must
have been the castle of Udolpho that he wished to ridicule.
[3] Preface to *Lyrical Ballads*, 3rd ed. (1802).

tunities for the study of what is common to all men, of genuine humanity.[1]   Thus *The Borough* offers itself as a continuation of *The Parish Register*, on a wider plan. Begun at Rendham in 1804,[2] it was finished at Muston in December, 1809,[3] after a trip to Aldborough [4] had enabled the author to compare his poem with the reality and to consult his friend Richard Turner, who was very favourable to the new work.   It was preceded by a laboured dedication to the young Duke of Rutland, and published by Hatchard on April 13th, 1810.[5]

II

To say of a realistic writer that he tries to depict " things as they are " is to remain on the threshold of a definition.   The world is so vast and mankind so varied that no one can hope to see and reproduce every-thing.   To write, one must limit the field of observation, and the artist, ensconced in a corner of real life, reveals to us the secret affinities of his talent by the choice of his subjects.   Besides, there are but few minds which, confronted by the same spectacle, whether landscape or animated scene, would feel the same impressions, conceive the same ideas, and produce identical copies of the object of their contemplation.   The inspiration and the form of a work of art are therefore the best characteristics of the artist.   To define the realism of a writer, we must study him in his subject-matter and in his methods.

Crabbe, as we have seen, is first and foremost a descriptive poet.   Bred in the robust school of Johnson, he is imbued with that " love of truth and accuracy " which the sturdy critic enforced on his disciples.[6]   He is less preoccupied with the choice of his subjects and

---

[1] Quoted by B. p. 55.

[2] See above, p. 207, n. 1.

[3] The date is given by the dedication.

[4] Cf. B. p. 55.   The letter to Wenn of August 12th, 1809, quoted above (p. 222, n. 2), bears the Aldborough postmark.

[5] See the advertisement in *The Courier* of the same day.   B. (*Works*, p. 171, n. 1) says the month of February, which I believe is a mistake.

[6] Cf. Beechey, *Sir Joshua Reynolds*, vol. i. p. 204: "Reynolds once observed that all who were of Johnson's school were distinguished for a love of truth and accuracy which they might not have possessed in the same degree if they had not been acquainted with him " ; and Boswell, *Life of Dr. Johnson* (Globe ed., p. 334): " The value of every story depends on its being true." Hence, no doubt, Johnson's sympathy for *The Village*.

the general plan of the composition than with the
precision of the details. He takes the first object that
comes, a library, a newspaper, or his village, and sets
himself to copy it with scrupulous fidelity. If he is
staying at Aldborough and goes out for a walk over
the common, the monotony and the melancholy of the
landscape do not discourage him : he lingers by the
brink of a muddy "dyke"[1] or near an old hovel, stoops
down and gathers one of those humble flowers which
his botanist's eye examines attentively. It seems to
him so interesting in its smallness and its ugliness, so
unduly contemned by passers-by indifferent to science,
so well suited to its habitat, that he cannot resist the
pleasure of describing it :

> There, fed by food they love, to rankest size,
> Around the dwellings docks and wormwood rise ;
> Here the strong mallow strikes her slimy root,
> Here the dull nightshade hangs her deadly fruit,
> On hills of dust the henbane's faded green
> And pencill'd flower of sickly scent is seen ;
> At the wall's base the fiery nettle springs,
> With fruit globose and fierce with poison'd stings ;
> Above (the growth of many a year) is spread
> The yellow level of the stone-crop's bed ;
> In every chink delights the fern to grow,
> With glossy leaf and tawny bloom below ;
> These, with our sea-weeds, rolling up and down,
> Form the contracted Flora of the town.[2]

The tinier they are, the more they excite the admiration of the poet, who, leaving to others the sublime
aspects of forests or mountains, finds, like a man of
science with a microscope, the grand in the infinitely
little. If he seeks for a proof of the inexhaustible
fecundity of nature, he discovers it in the "living
stains" with which the church-tower is dotted :

> . . . Where the common eye
> Can but the bare and rocky bed descry,
> There Science loves to trace her tribes minute,
> The juiceless foliage, and the tasteless fruit. . . .
> Seeds, to our eyes invisible, will find
> On the rude rock the bed that fits their kind ;
> There, in the rugged soil, they safely dwell,
> Till showers and snows the subtle atoms swell,

[1] Cf. the description already quoted above, p. 157, n. 1.
[2] *Borough*, xviii. 295-308.

And spread th' enduring foliage ;—then we trace
The freckled flower upon the flinty base ;
These all increase, till in unnoticed years
The stony tower as grey with age appears ;
With coats of vegetation, thinly spread
Coat above coat, the living on the dead.[1]

Just as Crabbe prefers to study the poor outcasts
among men, so he likes to pause before the humblest
species of the vegetable world—the mosses, the lichens,
the noxious or despised herbs.   He does not, like
Thomson,[2] make up a bouquet of the fairest flowers
brought by spring in various districts; he does not care
for beauty, but for truth.   He summarily describes the
plants which he has met with on the beach and on
the marshes at Aldborough, and takes care not to
introduce any others.   His descriptions of nature are
rigorously scientific and local.

Their material accuracy is almost always reinforced
by a human interest.   Crabbe paints the outside world
as a psychologist even more than as a man of science.
As he once said to a friend at Trowbridge, " he preferred walking in the streets, and observing the faces
of the passers-by, to the finest natural scene."[3]   For
him, man is essential and nature accessory.   Nature
serves as a picturesque and significant setting for our
actions and our life.   If he dwells so complacently on
the unattractive flora of the alleys and the common, it
is because he sees in it a symbol of the hard lot of the
inhabitants : the ocean, the river, the solitary expanse
of the marshes, interesting in themselves, become far
more so through their relations with us.

Let us leave *The Borough* for a moment and return to
a tale already quoted—*The Lover's Journey*.[4]   There we
shall see how our feelings communicate themselves to
external objects, which in their turn reflect our sadness
or our joy.   Riding gaily along under the bright rays
of dawn, Orlando follows his "favourite way," that
which leads him to his beloved.   What to him is the
barrenness of the "heath beside the coast"?   Does not
happiness shed a smile over all that surrounds him ?

" This neat low gorse," said he, " with golden bloom
Delights each sense, is beauty, is perfume ;

[1] *Borough*, ii. 45-8, 69-78.   [3] B. p. 80 (letter from Norris Clark).
[2] *The Seasons : Spring*.   [4] See above, p. 70.

And this gay ling, with all its purple flowers,
A man at leisure might admire for hours;
This green-fringed cup-moss has a scarlet tip,
That yields to nothing but my Laura's lip;
And then how fine this herbage! men may say
A heath is barren; nothing is so gay:
Barren or bare to call such charming scene
Argues a mind possess'd by care and spleen."

A little farther, under the heat of the sun, the dust
rises in clouds; Orlando is still full of admiration—

" How lovely this! . . .
With what delight is labouring man repaid!
The very lane has sweets that all admire:
The rambling suckling, and the vigorous brier;
See! wholesome wormwood grows beside the way,
Where dew-press'd yet the dog-rose bends the spray;
Fresh herbs the fields, fair shrubs the banks adorn,
And snow-white bloom falls flaky from the thorn."

If he rides over a "level fen," intersected by straight
"dykes" and crossed by a narrow dam, he still
admires. The vegetation is poor and "scarcely deigns
to bloom"; the "salt lavender" rises on its "wiry
stem," the "dwarf sallows" creep by the side of the
"harsh sept-foil." Orlando discovers hidden graces in
them, and thinks with rapture of the blissful day when
he will be able to show them to his Laura. But let the
beloved fail to appear at the trysting-place, and all the
charm has flown! In vain does he skirt the imposing
reaches of a broad and tranquil river; in vain are the
banks gay with flowers, the meadows verdant and
fertile: everything fills him with disgust; the farmers
look too proud; the grazing oxen are fattening only
for the slaughter-house; and then the monotonous
colour of the landscape:

" I hate these long green lanes; there's nothing seen
In this vile country but eternal green! "

Laura alone can restore their beauty to the objects
around him. And if the beloved were there, the lover
would have eyes for her only; the spectacle of the rich
pasture with its browsing cattle, of the green valley
with its winding river, would pass unobserved. So

true is it that "in our life alone does nature live,"[1]
that man clothes it with his own pleasure or pain,
or neglects it if more absorbing cares preoccupy the
mind.[2]

Between the languishment of the declining year and
the melancholy of a disappointed spirit there exists a
harmony which Crabbe is fond of bringing out. The
autumn, with its presentiment of death, is the season
most in keeping with the sadness of his heroes. See
the inconstant Harry,[3] who, in a moment of idleness and pique, has forgotten the proud but genuine
attachment of his Cecilia, and has succumbed to the
insinuating gentleness of the insignificant Fanny—how
he laments his imprudence, how bitterly he regrets
having to marry this doll! Nature seems to groan
with him :

> Early he rose, and look'd with many a sigh
> On the red light that fill'd the eastern sky ;
> Oft had he stood before, alert and gay,
> To hail the glories of the new-born day ;
> But now dejected, languid, listless, low,
> He saw the wind upon the water blow,
> And the cold stream curl'd onward as the gale
> From the pine-hill blew harshly down the dale ;[4]
> On the right side the youth a wood survey'd
> With all its dark intensity of shade ;
> Where the rough wind alone was heard to move,
> In this, the pause of nature and of love,
> When now the young are rear'd, and when the old,
> Lost to the tie, grow negligent and cold :
> Far to the left he saw the huts of men,
> Half hid in mist that hung upon the fen ;
> Before him swallows gathering for the sea
> Took their short flights, and twitter'd on the lea ;
> And near the bean-sheaf stood, the harvest done,
> And slowly blacken'd in the sickly sun ;
> All these were sad in nature, or they took
> Sadness from him, the likeness of his look.

Accurate in detail, this description of an October
morning near Aldborough is also a symbol of the
death of hope. Its picturesque value is enhanced by
its psychological significance. And it is thus that

---

[1] Coleridge, *Dejection*, an Ode, st. iv.
[2] *Tales in Verse*, x. 1-8, 36-61, 117-22, 232-8, 338-9.
[3] *Tales of the Hall*, xiii. 701-22 (*Works*, p. 457).
[4] The north wind blowing down the Alde (see above, p. 9).

Crabbe, in his best moments,[1] interprets nature. He
does not always paint it as a mere observer, curious
about plants or fossils. On the other hand, he does
not try to penetrate the mystery of its essence with
the intense vision of a Wordsworth. He finds in it a
reflection of our feelings and a background to our life.

Born in the seaport which he proposed to describe,
Crabbe could not help assigning an important place
to the "terrible and magnificent element" which
had fascinated him from a child.[2] An irresistible
instinct impelled him from time to time to revisit the
sea-shore, and his Biographer tells us that in 1787, not
having seen the ocean for more than three years, he
rode from Stathern right across Lincolnshire to bathe
in its waves.[3] We know what pleasure he derived, in
July, 1794,[4] from his botanical excursions on the shore
of his native town. Of all the spectacles of nature, the
sea arrests his gaze longest. He admires it in all its
moods :

> . . . Sublime in all its forms,
> When lull'd by zephyrs, or when roused by storms ;
> Its colours changing, when from clouds and sun
> Shades after shades upon its surface run.[5]

He admires it as a man of science, fascinated by and
absorbed in the contemplation of its marvels. On a
fine summer's evening, "when all is calm at sea, all
still at land," he likes to linger on the broad expanse
laid bare by the ebbing tide, to step on its "firm fair
sand," and examine the "ocean's produce":

> The living jellies which the flesh inflame,
> Fierce as a nettle, and from that its name. . . .
> See, as they float along, th' entangled weeds
> Slowly approach, upborne on bladdery beads ;
> Wait till they land, and you shall then behold
> The fiery sparks those tangled fronds infold,
> Myriads of living points ; th' unaided eye
> Can but the fire and not the form descry.

[1] Cf. *The Patron* (*Tales*, v. 426-33), *Tales of the Hall*, iv. 46-64, xi.
790-800, three passages which clearly show Crabbe's preference for autumn
and its depressing or calming influences. See also in *Edward Shore* (*Tales*,
xi. 230-5) the effect of a fine night on the awakening of the passions.

[2] Cf. the remark of Renan (*Lettres du séminaire*): "I have found that
people born on the brink of this terrible and magnificent element feel a need
to revisit it."

[3] B. p. 38.

[4] See above, p. 204.

[5] *Borough*, i. 165-8.

> And now your view upon the ocean turn,
> And there the splendour of the waves discern;
> Cast but a stone, or strike them with an oar,
> And you shall flames within the deep explore;
> Or scoop the stream phosphoric as you stand,
> And the cold flames shall flash along your hand;
> When, lost in wonder, you shall walk and gaze
> On weeds that sparkle, and on waves that blaze.[1]

Crabbe admires this not only as a naturalist, but as a poet fond of minute and picturesque detail. Here is a picture of a calm, in which, by a happy coincidence, the precision of the realist combines with the unity of the general impression to convey the heaving of the tranquil ocean :

> Be it the summer-noon : a sandy space
> The ebbing tide has left upon its place;
> Then just the hot and stony beach above,
> Light twinkling streams in bright confusion move;[2]
> Then the broad bosom of the ocean keeps
> An equal motion; swelling as it sleeps,
> Then slowly sinking; curling to the strand
> Faint, lazy waves o'ercreep the ridgy[3] sand,
> Or tap the tarry boat with gentle blow,
> And back return in silence, smooth and slow.
> Ships in the calm seem anchor'd; for they glide
> On the still sea, urged solely by the tide.

In winter the observer may suddenly find himself wrapped in a dense fog :

> When you can hear the fishers near at hand
> Distinctly speak, yet not see where they stand;
> Or sometimes them and not their boat discern,
> Or half-conceal'd some figure at the stern;
> The view's all bounded, and from side to side
> Your utmost prospect but a few ells wide;
> Boys who on shore to sea the pebble cast,
> Will hear it strike against the viewless mast;
> While the stern boatman growls his fierce disdain,
> At whom he knows not, whom he threats in vain.[4]

---

[1] *Borough*, ix. 77-110.

[2] In characteristic fashion Crabbe feels bound to explain the phenomenon scientifically, and this piece of conscientiousness results in two intolerably prosy lines which spoil the whole passage:

> For heated thus the warmer air ascends,
> And with the cooler in its fall contends.
>
> (*Borough*, i. 177-8.)

[3] The correct reading is " ridgy," and not " rigid " (l. 182, *Works*, ed. 1861, p. 177). This misprint does not occur in the first edition nor in that of 1834.

[4] *Borough*, ix. 113-22.

What nicety of touch in this delicate sea-piece, with the
outlines of its almost comic figures looming in the fog!

Man, in fact, does not remain long absent from
Crabbe's landscapes. Does the poet wish to describe
a winter storm? With his habitual accuracy he
notes the forerunners of it, the "unwieldy porpoise"
that has rolled in view of the shore on the preceding
day, the clouds which have gradually gathered and
now " o'ershroud the sky." He takes us to the beach,
and, inspired by this grand spectacle, forcibly describes
the fury of the waves :

> The breaking billows cast the flying foam
> Upon the billows rising—all the deep
> Is restless change ; the waves so swell'd and steep,
> Breaking and sinking, and the sunken swells,
> Nor one, one moment, in its station dwells.
> But nearer land you may the billows trace,
> As if contending in their watery chase ;
> May watch the mightiest till the shoal they reach,
> Then break and hurry to their utmost stretch ;
> Curl'd as they come, they strike with furious force,
> And then reflowing, take their grating course,
> Raking the rounded flints.

But actors must be introduced to animate the scene
and give it all its horror. Suddenly signals of distress
are heard in the offing :

> Yes, 'tis a driven vessel : I discern
> Lights, signs of terror, gleaming from the stern,
> Others behold them too, and from the town
> In various parties seamen hurry down ;
> Their wives pursue, and damsels urged by dread,
> Lest men so dear be into danger led ;
> Their head the gown has hooded, and their call
> In this sad night is piercing like the squall.

Idle cries, for the "stoutest boat" could not live in
such a sea :

> From parted clouds the moon her radiance throws
> On the wild waves, and all the danger shows,
> But shows them beaming in her shining vest,
> Terrific splendour ! gloom in glory dress'd ! . . .
> But hear we not those sounds ? Do lights appear ?
> I see them not ! the storm alone I hear :
> And lo ! the sailors homeward take their way ;
> Man must endure—let us submit and pray.[1]

[1] *Borough*, i. 194-270.

Thus speaks the poet who had often witnessed a similar tragedy from his native shore. He makes no display of his feelings : he simply indicates, as dramatically as possible, his compassion for the unfortunate sailors. The sublime picture of the moon sailing majestic and cold over the destructive element and its victims is drawn by him with a classic sobriety, without any of the lyrical outbursts which the indifference of the universe to human woes would have suggested to a romantic poet. Still less does he sympathise, like Byron, with the fury of the ocean in revolt.[1] Such thoughts would have seemed to him cruel or impious. Chained to the shore by his impotence, he watches, with mingled curiosity and terror, the havoc wrought by the storm and the emotion of the spectators. He does not withdraw from his fellow-creatures into the solitary reverie of an enthusiastic poet. He associates himself with them, sees them struggling with the waves or praying on the beach. Man interests him more than nature. But of all English writers prior to 1815 he none the less remains the poet who has shown the most intimate knowledge of the sea and has best described it in its varied moods. Falconer, whose *Shipwreck*[2] reveals here and there a singular force of inspiration, but no gift of expression, had repelled the public by an abuse of technical terms. Thomson had taken shelter from storms, which would have disturbed his indolent meditations, and had prudently relegated them to the Baltic or the Equator.[3] Crabbe, on the contrary, paints the sea as he observed it, the German Ocean from the beach of Aldborough. We may be sure of the local correctness of his descriptions; copied from reality, they owe nothing to his imagination. The calm of summer days, the fogs and the gales of winter, the special aspect of this "amphibious"[4] region are represented to us in the pages of *The Borough* with the minute fidelity of a man of science, the picturesqueness of an essentially descriptive poet, and the human interest which a psychologist discovers in the dullest of landscapes.

[1] *Childe Harold*, iv. st. 179-84.

[2] *The Shipwreck*, in three cantos, was published in 1762.

[3] Cf. *The Seasons : Winter* and *Summer*. Thomson, says Mr. Morel (*James Thomson*, p. 269), sees the sea "only under its terrible aspect."

[4] See below, p. 294.

The dwellings of the inhabitants, no less than their natural surroundings, reveal to us their mode of life. Let us observe these modest abodes along the beach, and, at the farther end, the "half-buried buildings, where hang at open doors the net and cork."[1] There is no trace of wealth or even of comfort here, unless perhaps in the "mansion of our last year's Mayor," and in the inns which overtop the roofs of the humbler houses. Shall we derive as much pleasure from visiting these hostelries as Crabbe does from describing them ? It is more than doubtful whether their signs, so curious in his eyes, can arrest our attention long. What is it to us if on one of them—

> The rampant *Lion* shows his kingly face ;
> His ample jaws extend from side to side,
> His eyes are glaring, and his nostrils wide ;
> A mane horrific sweeps his ample chest ?

Shall we, a little farther on, join the poet in making fun of that "incongruous pair, the Bear and Crown," where a diadem adorned with "gems and ribands" is seen suspended over the unfortunate chained animal ? Shall we, because it happens to exist in our "borough" and we ought to know it, care to enter the "Queen Caroline" and note its decay ? Everything about it is dilapidated :

> . . . You call,
> But none replies, they're inattentive all ;
> At length a ruined stable holds your steed,
> While you through large and dirty rooms proceed,
> Spacious and cold ; a proof they once had been
> In honour,—now magnificently mean ;
> Till in some small half-furnish'd room you rest,
> Whose dying fire denotes it had a guest. . . .
> You saw the carpets torn, the paper stain'd ;
> Squares of discordant glass in windows fix'd,
> And paper oil'd in many a space betwixt ;
> A soiled and broken sconce, a mirror crack'd,
> With table underprop'd, and chairs new back'd ;
> A marble side-slab with ten thousand stains,
> And all an ancient Tavern's poor remains.

And the "Queen Caroline" passes in the "borough" for a third-class hotel ! What are we to expect of the "inferior houses" ? Give a wide berth to some of

---

[1] *Borough*, i. 15-20.

them, says our parson—especially to the " Boar,"
where you are received by a kind old lady, surrounded
by young and pretty nieces, between whom, it would
appear, there is not much family likeness. It is even
asserted that a worthy burgess of the town, a pious
friend of the landlady, was caught one evening with
Sylvia on his knees.[1] Let us prudently avoid this
dubious establishment, and follow the poet, who, by an
unerring instinct, leads us to the most sordid quarter
and into the most repulsive dens :

> See that long boarded building !— By these stairs
> Each humble tenant to that home repairs,—
> By one large window lighted. . . .
> In this vast room, each place by habit fix'd,
> Are sexes, families, and ages mix'd—
> To union forced by crime, by fear, by need,
> And all in morals and in modes agreed ;
> Some ruin'd men, who from mankind remove ;
> Some ruin'd females, who yet talk of love ;
> And some grown old in idleness—the prey
> To vicious spleen, still railing through the day ;
> And need and misery, vice and danger bind,
> In sad alliance, each degraded mind.
>
> That window view !—oil'd paper and old glass
> Stain the strong rays, which, though impeded, pass,
> And give a dusty warmth to that huge room,
> The conquer'd sunshine's melancholy gloom ;
> When all those western rays, without so bright,
> Within become a ghastly glimmering light,
> As pale and faint upon the floor they fall,
> Or feebly gleam on the opposing wall :
> That floor, once oak, now pieced with fir unplaned,
> Or, where not pieced, in places bored and stain'd ;
> That wall once whiten'd, now an odious sight,
> Stain'd with all hues, except its ancient white ;
> The only door is fasten'd by a pin,
> Or stubborn bar, that none may hurry in ;
> For this poor room, like rooms of greater pride,
> At times contains what prudent men would hide.
>
> Where'er the floor allows an even space,
> Chalking and marks of various games have place ;
> Boys, without foresight, pleased in halters swing,
> On a fix'd hook men cast a flying ring,
> While gin and snuff their female neighbours share,
> And the black beverage in the fractured ware.

[1] *Borough*, xi. 19-24, 54-7, 86-102, 165 *seq.*

On swinging shelf are things incongruous stored,—
Scraps of their food, the cards and cribbage-board,—
With pipes and pouches ; while on peg below
Hang a lost member's fiddle and its bow ;
That still reminds them how he'd dance and play,
Ere sent untimely to the Convicts' Bay.[1]

Here by a curtain, by a blanket there,
Are various beds conceal'd, but none with care ;
Where some by day and some by night, as best
Suit their employments, seek uncertain rest ;
The drowsy children at their pleasure creep
To the known crib, and there securely sleep.

Each end contains a grate, and these beside
Are hung utensils for their boiled and fried—
All used at any hour, by night, by day,
As suit the purse, the person, or the prey.

Above the fire, the mantel-shelf contains
Of china-ware some poor unmatch'd remains ;
There many a teacup's gaudy fragment stands,
All placed by vanity's unwearied hands ;
For here she lives, e'en here she looks about,
To find some small consoling objects out ;
Nor heed these Spartan dames their house, nor sit
'Mid cares domestic,—they nor sew nor knit ;
But of their fate discourse, their ways, their wars
With arm'd authorities, their 'scapes and scars :
These lead to present evils, and a cup,
If fortune grant it, winds description up.

High hung at either end, and next the wall,
Two ancient mirrors show the forms of all,
In all their force ;—these aid them in their dress,
But with the good, the evils too express,
Doubling each look of care, each token of distress.[2]

This passage, one of the most original that Crabbe
has written, offers us an excellent example of his
descriptive style. One is struck by his indifference in
the choice of his subjects, or rather by his preference
for the meanest objects, by the patient curiosity which
lingers over the grotesque figures on the sign-boards,

[1] Botany Bay. Up to the War of Independence the convicts had been sold
to the planters of America. From 1788 onwards they were sent to New South
Wales. Botany Bay was selected as the site for the penal settlement, but found
unsuitable and never used for that purpose. The name, however, caught the
popular fancy, and continued to be applied to any convict establishment in
Australia.
[2] *Borough*, xviii. 332-413.

or which carefully accumulates the commonest and, apparently, the most insignificant details. Shall we add, with Hazlitt,[1] that Crabbe describes with the sole object of telling us what he finds, and that if he had wished to depict the death of Buckingham in an inn, on a flock-bed "repaired with straw," he would not have thought of the contrast which Pope[2] brings out between the wretchedness of the surroundings and the former greatness of the illustrious deceased, but would have confined himself to making an inventory of the furniture in the room? Certainly Crabbe, in his description of the "boarded building," does not look out for contrast, he even avoids it. For he does not aim at reproducing the epigrammatic turn which this contrast imparts to Pope's couplets. Wishing to emphasise, not the opposition, but the agreement which he discovers between these "degraded minds" and their filthy abode, he proceeds, not by antithesis, but by piling up *characteristic* and concordant details. An impartial critic cannot require from him more than what he wished to give. He seldom describes objects without presenting them as symbols : is not the likeness of the "rampant lion" admirably suited to the "lordly host" of the principal inn in the place, and does not the faded portrait of "Queen Caroline" serve as an introduction to the "servile couple" who manage that decaying hostelry? Whether it be the flora, the common, the ocean, or a human dwelling, Crabbe always sees and describes them as a psychologist ; the observation of inanimate things invariably brings him back to his favourite study, that of man.

III

But the descriptive poet, when he turns his attention to his fellow-creatures, reproduces their looks and their ways in a series of pictures which, by an almost irresistible tendency, will be of a satirical kind. The most experienced observers, in fact, affirm that perfect characters are extremely rare in this world, and that, even if there was an abundant supply of them, their repre-

---

[1] *Spirit of the Age,* ed. Bohn's Libraries, pp. 311-12.
[2] *Moral Essays,* iii. 299-314. The comparison had been alluded to by Crabbe himself (Preface to the *Tales, Works,* p. 274, col. 2).

sentation would have but little interest.[1] Moral perfection, so far as we can conceive it, always suggests to us the monotony of a vast plain or a dead calm. We resent its uniformity; we should like to see it dotted by rough prominences on which the mind, in its headlong flight, could alight for a moment and take breath. In the human character these salient points are its defects and its passions, which constitute an inexhaustible resource for writers of the observant type.

Formed from his youth up in the school of the English satirists of the classic epoch[2]—of Dryden, whose vigorous arm had dealt his political antagonists so many staggering blows, of Pope, who made his *Dunciad* a collection of caricatures, the victims of his personal or literary grudges, of Young also, who declaimed against the society of his time—Crabbe, either from natural predisposition or inveterate habit, obeyed an obvious tendency towards sarcasm and irony. In the course of his already long and sometimes unhappy life he had met few men who could compare with his own " Eusebius," [3] the " pious moralist," the " reasoning saint," who " preached, spoke, and wrote with manly sense," and visited the wards of a hospital to carry aid and consolation to its inmates. And, no doubt, he knew but few imitators of that " frugal merchant " [4] who, his fortune once made, embraced a life of ascetic poverty, of miserly economy, scraping and saving in order to give everything to the poor and build them an almshouse, his crowning benefaction. Most men, Crabbe was aware, are not so generous and good ; many of their actions, though apparently noble, are really interested. He was therefore most careful in awarding his praise or in vouchsafing his enthusiasm. He liked to "peep behind the scenes of human nature," [5] to probe the heart of man and find out its secret

---

[1] Æsthetically, what fascinates us in the history of great saints is their repentance for past errors, their singularities, or their activity, which implies a struggle, a perfection in process of realisation.

[2] See above, pp. 17, 33, 57 *seq.*

[3] *Borough*, xvii. 74-113. According to the Biographer (*Works*, p. 230, n. 2), this portrait was a tribute to Burke, an evidently mistaken idea, as Eusebius is a clergyman. Fitzgerald (MS. notes) makes the following very appropriate remark on this : " I doubt it. The character is too general." " Eusebius " figures as the type of the worthy young nobleman in Young's *The Centaur not Fabulous.* (Cf. Thomas, *Edw. Young*, p. 455.)

[4] *Borough*, xiii. 3-61.

[5] Letter from " Mr. Duncan of Bath " to the Biographer (p. 85, col. 2).

motives and its ulterior objects. He could be "endlessly
merciful" to foibles which were generally condemned,
but which seemed to him susceptible of explanation ;
on the other hand, excessive praise led him to ascribe
the noblest conduct to motives "more mingled and
more worldly" than simple devotion to duty.   In
that case he would be heard making his remarks " in a
low voice," as if to himself.[1] He resembled " Archer," [2]
the honest attorney, who, having been long in business,
combined a certain roughness with his honesty and
some suspicion with his sincerity, and who had seen
so much baseness in the human mind that, while
remaining a friend to man, he had a poor opinion of
mankind.   Having found too often that " the strong
are led by slight temptation," he doubted of everybody, of himself as well as of others, and " trembled
for his own conscience" through excess of moral
pessimism.

   Thus Crabbe's satire is inspired by his clear-sightedness and his profound sense of human frailty.   The
style excepted, it has nothing in common with that of
Dryden and Pope, so fiercely personal and bitter.
More reserved even than that of Young, it scrupulously
avoids all offensive allusion to personages who can be
easily recognised.   The poet expressly declares his
aversion to this :

> I love not the satiric Muse,
> No man on earth would I abuse ;
> Nor with empoison'd verses grieve
> The most offending son of Eve ;
> Leave him to law, if he have done
> What injures any other son.[3]

And again :

> Man's Vice and Crime I combat as I can,
> But to his God and conscience leave the Man ;
> I search (a Quixote !) all the land about,
> To find its Giants and Enchanters out,—
> (The Giant-Folly, the Enchanter-Vice,
> Whom doubtless I shall vanquish in a trice ;)

[1] According to Joanna Baillie, quoted by B. p. 85, col. 1.
[2] *Borough*, vi. 174-195 ; cf. *ibid.* 29-30 :
> Beside, a Muse like mine, to satire prone,
> Would fail in themes where there is praise alone.

[3] *Occasional Pieces* (*Works*, pp. 262-3) : *Satire*. This little poem was written
in August, 1818 (Broadley Collection).

But is there man whom I would injure ?—No !
I am to him a fellow, not a foe,—
A fellow-sinner, who must rather dread
The bolt, than hurl it at another's head.[1]

From a remnant of sympathy for the human species,
Crabbe, like Hogarth, ridicules it in order to cure it of
its follies and its failings. His satire is social, and not
personal, aiming at moral improvement and not at the
gratification of spite.

His characters, while retaining an individuality
ensured them by the profusion of details, have a typical
value. Here is " Sir Denys Brand," the all-powerful
squire and county magistrate. Proud of his ancestors,
who are supposed to have come over with the Conqueror, he assumes a haughty demeanour when, tired
of his village, he comes into our borough to meet his
friends at the club.[2] As soon as he enters, he casts a
glance at those present, draws near the fire, orders
something to drink, and interrupting the conversation,
exclaims :

Well, what's the subject ?—what are you about ?
The news, I take it—come, I'll help you out.

And without waiting for an answer, he generously
tells everybody what he has seen and heard, gives his
opinion, explains his votes—for he is member for the
county—repeats his speeches with comments, and in
an imperious voice concludes with a " 'Tis thus," which
admits of no reply. His liberalities, far from hiding in
hovels like those of the "frugal merchant," are displayed
in broad daylight. His are no "vulgar charities": he
leaves to "meaner minds the simple deed, by which
the houseless rest, the hungry feed"; his bounties are
of the "vast and grand" order which are lauded in
public—the assembly-room which commands a view of
the street, the first life-boat, the revival of the races,
the building of a jail in which no prisoner "sits at his
ease, but he must feel the debt." Evidently Sir Denys
Brand, the village potentate, is the incarnation of pride.
An ordinary satirist—Young, for instance—would have
stopped here. The character would have seemed to
him complete as soon as the "ruling passion" had been

---

[1] *Borough*, xxiv. 450-9.
[2] I combine here two identical personages—Sir Thomas (*Borough*, x. 199-219), and Sir Denys Brand (*ibid.* xiii. 100-226).

indicated and described in some of its manifestations. Far more penetrating is Crabbe's psychological analysis. This passion must have another side to it which, by an effect of contrast, will throw it into relief and serve as a foil. This will be humility; Sir Denys Brand will become the type of hypocritical pride. Let us enter his study : we shall find him seated on a "paltry chair," at a plain deal table, a "wretched floor-cloth" beneath his feet. Let us follow him into the dining-room : half an hour suffices him for dinner, and he dines off one poor dish and takes three sips of wine. Let us go out with him : he will put on an old overcoat to hide his better clothes, and ride an "old brown pony" not worth more than £5. But his servants live on the fat of the land. True, he reproaches them for their "sumptuous feasts" :

> " . . . My friends, you make yourselves like beasts ;
> One dish suffices any man to dine,
> But you are greedy as a herd of swine ;
> Learn to be temperate."—Had they dared t' obey,
> He would have praised and turn'd them all away.

In his rides he is accompanied by a farmer's son, mounted on a splendid hunter, which has won two plates, and if any one admires the animal, he replies carelessly :

> " . . . Yes ! I think a groom
> Bought me the beast ; I cannot say the sum :
> I ride him not ; it is a foolish pride
> Men have in cattle—but my people ride."

Is not this affected simplicity, this ostentatious con-descension, an exaggerated pride ? The all-powerful Sir Denys is the laughing-stock of flatterers who know his weakness. An "idle boy" in the place managed to turn it to account : he would keep at a respectful distance, snatch a look at the great man, and then run away to hide himself in a corner, saying to the squire's attendant :

> " . . . Oh ! I dare not fix my sight
> On him, his grandeur puts me in a fright ;
> Oh ! Mister Jacob, when you wait on him,
> Do you not quake and tremble every limb ? "

The astute young rascal soon had his reward, in the shape of a livery and a place in Sir Denys's household.

With this imperious country gentleman let us contrast a cringing clergyman, very different from his
brethren of *The Parish Register*, and we shall find a
type of what Jeffrey well described as " a man without
character " :

> Few now remember when the mild young man,
> Ruddy and fair, his Sunday-task began.

When he stood up in the pulpit he would bestow on
his congregation a " soft soothing look " and a smile
which seemed at once to implore and expect the general
approbation. This unctuous amiability never failed
him. A stranger to the " haughty virtues " which
disturb the beatitude of the soul, to apostolic zeal and
detestation of vice, his object was to offend nobody
and live in peace. A faint semblance of love had once
just touched his heart. Irresolute and shy, he had
conceived a languid attachment for a " maid " whose
mother, a widow, was present at all their interviews :

> Smiling he came, he smiled when he withdrew,
> And paid the same attention to the two ;
> Meeting and parting without joy or pain,
> He seemed to come that he might go again.

The girl ended by preferring a more enterprising
rival to this bashful lover, and our gentle Vicar,
astonished perhaps, but in no way grieved, turned his
attentions to " ancient females." With them he kept
up an intercourse marked by innocent assiduities. Of
exemplary piety, they never failed to attend the
morning service, and he, touched by such meritorious
perseverance, would offer them, with a grace that was
all his own, flowers gathered in his small garden. In
presenting his bouquet to his " fair friends," he would
generally add some " moral compliment "—as, for
instance, how they " like flowers were sweet, and must
like flowers decay." The recipients of his favours
therefore made much of him : he had his seat at their
table, at that hour when conversation goes round with
the teacups and turns on town gossip, on prospective
scandals, " kitchen cabals," and " nursery mishaps."
By way of amusement he would sometimes bring his
fiddle, or perhaps propound a charade in verse. He
would never cease to dwell on the blessings of calmness, and of that unity which he considered so all-
important for the Church of England ; especially did

he dread the bold innovations of his younger brethren, who, in their contempt for the most venerable traditions, discarded the insignia of the priesthood, did the duty in a simple surplice, " lacking hood and band," and preferred the " New Version " of the Psalms to the old translation by Sternhold and Hopkins.[1] What was to become of the Church if its most cherished observances were neglected in this way ? When our worthy pastor was oppressed by thoughts of this kind, the calming influence of a day's fishing was necessary to restore his equanimity. Alas! he is no more, and his last sleep is a prolongation of the tranquillity of his days.

Our seaport being a " borough "—that is to say, a municipality with a charter—public business is often transacted in it. Under a constitution granted by Henry VIII. and often modified,[2] the government of the town is carried on by two bailiffs, elected annually by the ten "capital" and twenty-four "inferior" burgesses, sitting in full council.[3] Besides this, Aldborough has the privilege[4] of sending two representatives to Parliament, and about every six years recurs a general election in which the burgesses and the "freemen" of the place are entitled to take part,

[1] *Borough*, iii. " The Vicar." For the introduction of the " New Version " and, more recently, of the hymns, cf. at the beginning of George Eliot's *Amos Barton*, the description of a Church of England service about 1820.

[2] Cf. Davy MSS. (*Aldeburgh Corporation*): " The earliest charter known to the existing corporate body (about 1834) was granted in 1529 by Henry VIII."; and Ford, *Aldborough Described*, p. 13, speaks of the " 2nd Edward VI. (1549), confirmed by Philip and Mary, as well as by Elizabeth. James I. in the 4th year of his reign (1607), granted the borough greater indulgences and gave it a new constitution. This was confirmed by Charles I., and entrusts the government of the town to two bailiffs, ten capital and twenty-four inferior burgesses. By these, not receiving alms, two members are returned to the Imperial Parliament."

[3] Cf. Davy MSS. (*ibid.*) : " The officers composing the council, which is the governing body of the borough, are the bailiffs and capital burgesses. The bailiffs are annually elected from the capital burgesses by the bailiffs in office, the capital burgesses, and the twenty-four inferior burgesses, and they are removable by a majority of the council. . . . The capital burgesses are elected for life by the common council from the twenty-four inferior burgesses. . . . As an electoral body, they choose the capital burgesses, the inferior burgesses, the recorder and town clerk, and jointly with the inferior burgesses they choose the bailiffs and chamberlain (treasurer). They also create freemen without restriction." In 1833, the ten capital burgesses included the Marquis of Hertford, two members of his family, J. W. Croker, who was under an obligation to him, and four dependants of the Marquis.

[4] At least in Crabbe's time. Ford (*op. cit.* p. 13) tells us that " Aldborough did not send representatives until the 13th of Elizabeth " (*i.e.* 1571), and of course it sent none after 1832.

and which is the signal for a fine uproar. " Yes, our election's past," writes the poet—

> And we've been free,
> Somewhat as madmen without keepers be ;
> And such desire of Freedom has been shown,
> That both the parties wish'd her all their own :
> All our free smiths and cobblers in the town
> Were loth to lay such pleasant freedom down ;
> To put the bludgeons and cockade aside,
> And let us pass unhurt and undefied.[1]

In the eighteenth century, in fact, elections were regular saturnalia for the mob, gathered round the hustings from which the candidates addressed it, and where the electors, for several days together, came to record their votes in public and receive the cheers of one side and the hoots of the other. The highest personages condescended on these occasions to mingle with the people, to entertain them, to supply them with drink, to bribe them.[2] Each vote had its price, and a shower of gold descended on the least important of the electors :

> Among these worthies, some at first declare
> For whom they vote : he then has most to spare ;
> Others hang off—when coming to the post
> Is spurring time, and then he'll spare the most. . . .
> Some too are pious—one desired the Lord
> To teach him where " to drop his little word." [3]

The result announced, each man receives his wages,[4] and the tumult subsides. But ill-feeling remains, in spite of the efforts of the winning side, in spite of the cordiality of our Mayor, the worthy "Daniel," who longs for calm like all constituted authorities, and preaches forgetfulness of injuries and reconciliation of friends who have been in opposite camps. " Where is the profit ? what will anger gain ?" he asks with much good

---

[1] *Borough*, v. 1-8.

[2] For this curious aspect of social life, cf. Hogarth, *The Election* (four pictures in the Soane Museum) ; Grego, *A History of Parliamentary Elections and Electioneering in the Old Days*, London, 1886 ; Sydney, *Eighteenth Century*, vol. ii. p. 157 *seq.* ; and last, not least, Cowper's famous letters of March 29th and April 26th, 1784, on Grenville's election at Olney.

[3] *Borough*, v. 91-100.

[4] Cf. a passage from Wilberforce's Biography quoted by Sydney, ii. 175 : " The letter of the law was not broken, because the money was not paid until the last day on which election petitions could be presented."

sense. And optimism becomes him as a prosperous
man :

> His short stout person he is wont to brace
> In good brown broadcloth, edged with two-inch lace
> When in his seat.

He beams with pride when he thinks how he has
got on since his early days. For he began by being
a simple fisherman, "placing his nets within the
borough's bay," living on the skates, herrings, and
soles which he caught, and never dreaming of "corporation doles." [1] By dint of unremitting toil he
managed to save "twelve-score pounds," which he
carefully concealed in a trunk, not knowing what to do
with it. As the fear of thieves prevented him from
sleeping, he consulted a friend. Invest it, said the
latter. "What, give my money up ? why then I could
not live," was the ingenuous reply of Daniel, who had
never heard of capital or interest. His objections,
however, disappeared one by one, and his eyes
sparkled when he at last grasped the fact that money,
like other things, can "breed," and that for every
hundred pounds lent he would receive—

> . . . From all deductions clear,
> Five pounds for every hundred, every year,
> And then the hundred. . . .

"Now," he exclaimed, "I begin to live." With the aid
of good luck he was elected a burgess, soon rose above
his colleagues, and, "stepping from post to post he
reached the Chair," in which he now takes his ease as
Mayor of the town.[2] He has the restful aspect of the
satisfied parvenu.

The protection of municipal interests sometimes
raises knotty points :

> There is a doubtful pauper, and we think
> 'Tis not with us to give him meat and drink ;
> There is a child ; and 'tis not mighty clear
> Whether the mother lived with us a year : [3]
> A road's indicted, and our seniors doubt
> If in our proper boundary or without.

---

[1] The various sums of money which the members of the municipality
divided amongst themselves (cf. Crabbe's note, *Works*, pp. 195-6, n. 1).

[2] *Borough*, v. 133-80.

[3] According to the Settlement Act of 1662 forty days' residence in a parish
was necessary to claim relief. Hence the period of a year required for
bastards.

Shall we tamely submit to such charges ?

> What ! to a neighbouring parish yield your cause,
> While you have money, and the nation laws ?
> What ! lose without a trial that which, tried,
> May—nay it must—be given on our side ? [1]

No, we must resist manfully; we must go to law and employ the best lawyer in the town. His name is Swallow. The son of a small attorney with no business, he has risen above the humble position in which his father was vegetating, and has built himself a splendid house out of the ruin of his victims :

> . . . See that mansion tall,
> That lofty door, the far-resounding hall ;
> Well-furnish'd rooms, plate shining on the board,
> Gay liveried lads, and cellar proudly stored. [2]

It is there that the attorney prepares his baits and receives his dupes. A good dinner serves as a prelude to serious business, for "his way to starve them is to make them eat." He keeps open house : at every hour of the day choice wines and made dishes await the guest. His best auxiliary is an excellent cook; in a cheerful mood, ripe for the necessary confidences, the clients will then be ready to go into the office. Although a small room, it supports the whole edifice :

> There in his web, th' observant spider lies,
> And peers about for fat intruding flies ;
> Doubtful at first, he hears the distant hum,
> And feels them fluttering as they nearer come ;
> They buzz and blink, and doubtfully they tread
> On the strong bird-lime of the utmost thread ;
> And when they're once entangled by the gin,
> With what an eager clasp he draws them in ! [3]

Equally rapacious, Swallow sucks his clients dry after having tricked them :

> "Well, if 'tis so, the house to you belongs ;
> But have you money to redress these wrongs ?
> Nay, look not sad, my friend ; if you're correct
> You'll find the friendship that you'd not expect."
> If right the man, the house was Swallow's own ;
> If wrong, his kindness and goodwill were shown.

---

[1] *Borough*, vi. 93-105.   [2] *Ibid.* 63-6.   [3] *Ibid.* 71-8.

But his favourite clients are young spendthrifts whose
parents persist in remaining alive and in refusing
them the money for their pleasures. Swallow is
ready to become their confidant and to advance them
funds. "See," he exclaims, pointing out one of these
youths familiarly to his guests—

> "There's our friend Rupert—we shall soon redress
> His present evil—drink to our success—
> I flatter not, but did you ever see
> Limbs better turn'd, a prettier boy than he?
> His senses all acute, his passions such
> As nature gave—she never does too much. . . .
> Now view his father as he dozing lies. . . .
> And shall this dotard from our hero hold
> His lands and lordships? . . .
> Shall not our generous heir receive supply? . . .
> The means are simple, let him only wish,
> Then say he's willing, and I'll fill his dish?"[1]

On the death of the parents the son's acres will become
the property of Swallow, who hides his cunning
and unscrupulousness under a hypocritical mask of
affability and even of piety.

Passing over the doctors, who, it appears, are all
quacks in this unfortunate region, and the tradesfolk, who, like the poet, are more prudent than enterprising, and shrink from bold speculation, let us dwell
for a moment on the schools, the different categories
of which are felicitously described by Crabbe. Left
to its scanty resources, elementary education, represented by "poor Reuben Dixon," has taken refuge in
a sort of sty in "a close lane behind the Northgate-
street."[2] Thither comes a crowd of "ragged lads,"
sons of street-sweepers and coal-heavers, the "noisiest
school that ever bow'd to rule," and for a wretched
pittance Reuben undertakes to maintain a semblance
of order and teach them the rudiments of knowledge:

> T' observe his vain attempts to keep the peace . . .
> Calls for our praise; his labour praise deserves,
> But not our pity; Reuben has no nerves:
> 'Mid noise and dirt, and stench, and play, and prate,
> He calmly cuts the pen or views the slate.[3]

[1] *Borough*, vi. 242-53, 284-9, 310-11.

[2] As Aldborough never had a "gate," the street is imaginary, but this only
brings out Crabbe's precision more clearly. He must have minute details,
observed or invented.

[3] *Borough*, xxiv. 103-8.

He is a type of the resigned teacher. "Leonard," [1]
on the contrary, the keeper of a boarding-school for
boys, "loathes the station which he dares not leave."
With a soaring mind which loves to "move from pole
to pole, and view the wonders of the worlds above,"
able to "think and reason strongly," to read Dryden,
Milton, and Pope "with delight," he is humiliated
when some dunce comes up, slate in hand, with a
badly done sum which he has to correct. He feels
the disgust of the humble servants of knowledge,
"dependent helpers always at the wheel," who may
catch glimpses of, but never explore, the fascinating
region that lies beyond :

> Day after day he to his task attends,—
> Unvaried toil, and care that never ends :
> Boys in their works proceed, while his employ
> Admits no change, or changes but the boy.

And this never-ending monotony, these thwarted
aspirations, engender discouragement and bitterness.
Leonard has already become a type of the soured
teacher. We must not suppose, however, that life
is a round of happiness even for the young man
fortunate enough to leave the "borough" and go to
the university :

> . . . There is serious strife
> In the contentions of a scholar's life :
> Not all the mind's attention, care, distress,
> Nor diligence itself, ensure success :
> His jealous heart a rival's powers may dread,
> Till its strong feelings have confused his head,
> And, after days and months, nay, years of pain,
> He finds just lost the object he would gain.

Take even the "Fellow" who, foregoing marriage
and a country living, settles down in college rooms.
He may have cloistered silence and old-world gardens,
may enjoy all the honours incident to the position,
"the freshman's terror and the tradesman's bow":

> Let his apartments with his taste agree,
> And all his views be those he loves to see ;
> Let him each day behold the savoury treat,
> For which he pays not, but is paid to eat—

---

[1] *Borough*, xxiv. 109-35 and 228-47. I combine the two passages into a
single portrait.

yet his life will be dull and solitary. His honours,
"unlike the prophet's," will be confined to his own
country, Oxford or Cambridge:

> And there such honours are familiar things ;
> What is a monarch in a crowd of kings ? [1]

Especially will his solitude be irksome to him when
he leaves the "common room" after dinner and retires
to his own apartments for the night. He will almost
envy his servant, who, when his work is done, whistles
cheerfully to the college porter, passes through the
gate, and regains his liberty.[2] Without the charm of
family affections, books themselves soon cease to be
attractive.

With the clear-sightedness of a suspicious mind,
Crabbe uses satire to unmask and point out the
disappointments which lie in wait for us on every
side in life. He is the poet of disillusion, he who
in early childhood[3] had dimly felt how the reality
gives the lie to our fond imaginings. How often has
he not repeated this to us since ! You believe, he says
to us in *The Village* and *The Parish Register*, in the
patriarchal felicity of the golden age ? Undeceive
yourselves : the real country-folk are generally miserable and often vicious, and happiness, in villages and
towns, falls only to the prudent and the rich. You
think perhaps, he says to us in *The Borough*, that a
squire is an enlightened protector of his inferiors,
and a clergyman a wise mentor to his flock ? You
are mistaken : the former, eaten up with pride, is the
dupe of a cunning young rogue; and the latter, a
sort of "eunuch" or "male lily," is a pious old lady
in breeches. Hope is a deceitful flower with disenchantment hidden beneath it. You think you are
going on a pleasure excursion, and you return from
it after having been within an ace of death. Remember
that joyous party of friends who were rowed out to
an islet of sand formed by the ebbing and covered
by the rising tide. Encircled by the ocean, they
hoped to enjoy a close view of "the watery waste,"
to walk, to run, to play, to sing, to dance with nimble

---

[1] This evident allusion to the interview at Erfurt shows that the passage
(*Borough*, xxiv. 391) was not written before the end of September, 1808.
[2] *Borough*, xxiv. 347-401.
[3] See above, pp. 25-7.

feet on the "bright shelly sand that made the summer-seat":

> The urns were boiling, and the cups went round,
> And not a grave or thoughtful face was found. . . .
> The wondering mews flew fluttering o'er the head,
> And waves ran softly up their shining bed.

All was merry as a marriage-bell, when suddenly a cry of terror resounded through the air!

> For lo! a lady sage, who paced the sand
> With her fair children, one in either hand,
> Intent on home, had turn'd, and saw the boat
> Slipp'd from her moorings, and now far afloat.

What a ghastly prison the island will become as soon as the tide rises! The boatman and his mate had drunk copiously, and "slept regardless of their state":

> "Awake!" they cried aloud. "Alarm the shore!
> Shout all, or never shall we reach it more!"
> Alas! no shout the distant land can reach,
> Nor eye behold them from the foggy beach:
> Again they join in one loud powerful cry,
> Then cease, and eager listen for reply;
> None came—the rising wind blew sadly by. . . .
> Foot after foot on the contracted ground
> The billows fall, and dreadful is the sound;
> Less and yet less the sinking isle became. . . .
> Now rose the water through the lessening sand,
> And they seem'd sinking while they yet could stand.
> The sun went down, they look'd from side to side,
> Nor aught except the gathering sea descried;
> Dark and more dark, more wet, more cold it grew,
> And the most lively bade to hope adieu;
> Children by love then lifted from the seas
> Felt not the waters at the parents' knees,
> But wept aloud; the wind increased the sound,
> And the cold billows as they broke around.

But hark! the splash of oars is heard. At last they have been seen: the crew of a ship have noticed their drifting boat, and, guessing what has happened, are coming to the rescue:

> . . . "Haste!" they cry,
> "Oh! hurry, seamen; in delay we die":
> And now the keel just cuts the covered sand,
> Now to the gunwale stretches every hand:

> With trembling pleasure all confused embark,
> And kiss the tackling of their welcome ark ;
> While the most giddy, as they reach the shore,
> Think of their danger, and their GOD adore.[1]

To what is the powerful effect of this pathetic scene due? Is it not to the ruthless insistence with which Crabbe describes the progress of the devouring element and the protracted torture of the actors? Does it not almost seem as if he wished to punish them for having dared to expect a day's happiness?

This poetry of disillusion is typically represented in one of the finest passages with which it inspired Crabbe —the description of the dream of the "Condemned Felon."[2] One day in 1780 or 1781, during the period of his early struggles, he was wandering about the streets of London in search of a patron or a publisher, when a similarity of names made him apprehend that the brother of an "intimate friend" had been convicted of robbery and was imprisoned in Newgate. When shown into the prisoners' cells, he found himself confronted by an unknown individual with haggard mien and glazed eyes, and the recollection of this agonising sight still haunted him thirty years afterwards. The wretched man, fettered in body and soul—

> . . . Paced his narrow bounds some ease to find,
> But found it not, no comfort reached his mind :
> Each sense was palsied. . . .
> Since his dread sentence, nothing seem'd to be
> As once it was—he seeing could not see,
> Nor hearing, hear aright ; when first I came
> Within his view, I fancied there was shame,
> I judged resentment; I mistook the air,—
> These fainter passions live not with despair,

with that "fixed dread" which, at "every waking hour," took possession of him :

> Still I behold him, every thought employ'd
> On one dire view !—all others are destroy'd.

---

[1] *Borough*, ix. 204-96. As there is no "islet" in Aldborough Bay, I am inclined to think that the poet had in mind the island of Havergate and the excursion narrated in the poem entitled *Infancy*. In that case the tragic incident would be due to his imagination. A scene of this kind has been related by Scott (*The Antiquary*, ch. vii.) with considerable differences, which recall a passage in one of Cowper's letters (July 17th, 1799).

[2] B. p. 55. "I know," adds the Biographer, "that my father was himself much affected when he drew that picture."

This makes his features ghastly, gives the tone
Of his few words resemblance to a groan ;
He takes his tasteless food, and when 'tis done,
Counts up his meals, now lessen'd by that one.

Here the actual observation stops : Crabbe had not
seen anything more. But he has recourse to his
imagination, or rather to his psychological intuition,
and, the prisoner falling asleep before him, he divines
the dreams of a condemned man. First of all, "the
Felon" hears the sentence and the clank of fetters ;
he sees the judge and the jury ; he trembles, and
exclaims, "Not Guilty !" Then, immediately afterwards, comes the drive to the place of execution, the
crowd which accompanies, precedes, and follows him
on the road to Tyburn,[1] the heartless shouts of some,
the pity of others, the reprobation of all, for he had
killed a fellow-creature in cold blood ; then the vision
of the gallows :

He seems the place for that sad act to see,
And dreams the very thirst which then will be,[2]

and the last words of the chaplain, in whom he
recognises a friend of his better days, the guide of his
infancy. By a rapid association of ideas his youth is
conjured up before him : he is in his " native village,"
in his father's house, in the room "where he knelt and
pray'd." His "hours of innocence" return, and with
them "the timid look of his loved maid, when first her
hand he took, and told his hope." They wander
together o'er the heath, and the sweetest moments
of his life come back to him, with a " softer bloom" and
all the charm of memory. Here are the green lane
and the meadow where they linger, the purple heather
which they tread, the blossom which they pluck where
the wild bees hum, the hedge of broom which they
lightly step over, and the "lamb browsing by the

---

[1] See above, p. 101. It is curious to note how closely Crabbe adheres to his
recollections of 1780-1. The ride to Tyburn had, in fact, been abolished from
1783 (cf. the following passage of Croker's *Correspondence* quoted by Sydney,
Eighteenth Century, vol. ii. p. 297) : " It [the drop, which took the place of
the cart] was not adopted as the general mode of execution till 1783, when ten
felons were executed on November 9th in that year, for the first time in
front of Newgate, on a new drop or scaffold hung in black."

[2] Victor Hugo, in the *Dernier jour d'un condamné*, has nothing more
powerful than this line. We may also remark that the two authors agree in
evoking the early recollections of their heroes (V. Hugo, *op. cit.* par. xxxiii.).

linnet's bed." They cross a brook by a rustic bridge,
and the bay lies before them :

> The ocean smiling to the fervid sun—
> The waves that faintly fall and slowly run—
> Ships softly sinking in the sleepy sea, . . .
> The glittering waters on the shingles roll'd, . . .
> With all those bright red pebbles, that the sun
> Through the small waves so softly shines upon, . . .
> . . . The crimson weeds which spreading flow
> Or lie like pictures on the sand below, . . .
> Pearl-shells and rubied star-fish they admire,
> And will arrange above the parlour-fire,—
> Tokens of bliss !—" Oh ! horrible ! a wave
> Roars as it rises—save me, Edward ! save ! "
> She cries :—Alas ! the watchman on his way
> Calls, and lets in—truth, terror, and the day ! [1]

Perhaps it will be thought that these details are too
numerous and too precise for a dream, and that the
poet, forgetting probability, puts himself in the place
of the condemned man. But one cannot question the
insight with which Crabbe marshals the fevered recollections of his sleeper, connecting and disconnecting
the various pictures with all the skill of a practised
psychologist. And what force there is in the poignant
contrast between such intense happiness and such
profound despair, in the idea, grand and so true, of the
wave rising to swallow up the past of the wretched
man ! [2] Was there ever a more cruel disillusion, or
more suggestive poetry ? For *we* too wake daily to
that reality which is conducting us to death.

IV

DESCRIPTIVE, satirical, pessimistic—these epithets give
us the elements of Crabbe's realism. But it is not
enough to have brought them out by analysis ; we must
also recombine them by synthesis, for it is their union
which constitutes the real originality of the poet. It
has perhaps been noticed that certain portraits—those

---

[1] *Borough* xxiii. 226-332.
[2] Canon Ainger (*Life of Crabbe*, p. 112) has called this "a certain melodramatic climax," laboriously prepared. Is it not rather a stroke of genius,
showing, in a singularly natural and skilfully introduced image, the inevitable
return of terror, stupefied by sleep but always present, after the ephemeral vision
of past felicity ? Psychologically, nothing is more probable than the close
fusion of these two currents in the semi-consciousness of a dream.

of the vicar, the mayor, and the attorney—contain, in
addition to satire and moral teaching, a considerable
amount of description, and that consequently these
personages are not only portrayed as types and in
their actual state, but are also studied in their evolution.   It follows that these " characters " are changed
into " lives," into satirical monographs.   Now, among
the humble heroes whom the " borough " offers to
Crabbe's observation, which will be his favourites ?
Evidently the most unhappy ones, since, with his
sombre turn of mind, he likes to trace the gradual
decline and the death of all hope ; the most vicious ones
also, since their lamentable end will be an example and
a lesson to us.   Progressive corruption, the anatomy
of degenerate minds, the psychology of those who have
failed in life—that is Crabbe's favourite subject and
the distinguishing mark of his realism.

Among the engravings executed by Hogarth for the
edification of his contemporaries there is one which
represents the " last stage of cruelty." [1]   On a table in
the great Hall of the London College of Surgeons is
stretched, stiff and naked, the corpse of a criminal, the
rope round his neck, his features still convulsed with
horror.   The hangman, having discharged his office,
has handed over the remains of " Tom Nero " to
the scalpel of science.   This monster, a native of
St. Giles's, has breathed his last amid the execrations
of the crowd, for, after a series of tortures inflicted
on animals, he crowned his misdeeds by pitilessly
murdering a poor servant, pregnant by him and an
accomplice in his robberies.   In their turn, his limbs
are being mercilessly cut up : an assistant is taking an
eye out of its socket, another makes an incision in his
foot, a third, with an eager gaze, brandishes a knife,
and drags out, through a wide slit in the abdomen, the
intestines, which are hanging to the ground, and the
heart, which a starving dog has just fastened on.   And
the President of the College of Surgeons, impassible
and unbending in his academical chair and under his
doctor's cap, is showing those present, with the end of
his wand of office, the organs that are being dissected.
At this moment he is pointing out the place where the
heart had been.

---

[1] *The Four Stages of Cruelty*, plate iv.

Similar is the method followed by Crabbe, a surgeon of the soul after having been one of the body. He takes a culprit, sometimes a murderer, cuts him open, tears out his heart, and, with a turn of the scalpel, lays bare the defect, the hidden vice which ruined this existence or drove it into crime. The disease once known, we are better able to cure it, if it should attack us. The works of this poet are a course of moral medicine. Just as Hogarth wished to circulate cheap reproductions of his *Stages of Cruelty* among the London populace and reform it by fear, so Crabbe, by showing us the secret havoc wrought in us by vice and the fatal consequences it entails, tries to make us wiser and better.

Let us select one or two examples. Let us study the pernicious effects of pride in one of the personages offered by *The Borough*, that of " Jachin," the parish clerk. Tall and slender, he might have been taken for gravity itself when he chanted the psalms and the responses at his desk, or listened with a solemn air, which almost implied disapproval, to the vicar's jokes. He was known to be " sober, chaste, devout, and just," and this enviable reputation had won him the confidence of all, even of the young girls, who were sure of the purity of his intentions. Indeed, Jachin, although a Churchman, was in mind a descendant of the Puritans. To him the machinations of the devil were present everywhere:

> He held that Satan, since the world began,
> In every act, had strife with every man ;
> That never evil deed on earth was done,
> But of the acting parties he was one ;
> The ever-tempting, soothing, softening power,
> Ready to cheat, seduce, deceive, devour.
> " Me has the sly Seducer oft withstood,"
> Said pious Jachin,—" but he gets no good ;
> I pass the house where swings the tempting sign,
> And, pointing, tell him, Satan, that is thine :
> I pass the damsels pacing down the street,
> And look more grave and solemn when we meet ;
> Nor doth it irk me to rebuke their smiles,
> Their wanton ambling and their watchful wiles :
> Nay, like the good John Bunyan, when I view
> Those forms, I'm angry at the ills they do,
> That I could pinch and spoil, in sin's despite,
> Beauties, which frail and evil thoughts excite."

Here was a self-righteous and tiresome apostle of virtue! Not only did he lecture the too amiable girls of the place, but he even tried to convert his friends:

> "Nay, nay, my friends, from inns and taverns fly,
> You may suppress your thirst, but not supply. . . .
> Think not of beauty;—when a maid you meet,
> Turn from her view and step across the street;
> E'en I myself, with all my watchful care,
> Have for an instant felt the insidious snare,
> Till I was forced to smite my bounding breast,
> With forceful blow, and bid the bold one rest."

A valuable admission, thought his friends, who were irritated by so much arrogance and zeal. If Jachin is impressionable, he may be tempted: how delightful if he should succumb! The attempt was made: first of all they invited him to an inn to discuss points of doctrine; Jachin cleared up every difficulty, and left his glass almost untouched. Then they sent him an "artful lass," who was to consult him on supposed conscientious scruples and at the same time try to vanquish him by a skilful display of her charms:

> She came, she spake: he calmly heard her case,
> And plainly told her 'twas a want of grace;
> Bade her such fancies and affections check,
> And wear a thicker muslin on her neck.

He therefore remained unshaken.

He did not know that his real enemy was not without but within him, and that one day his pride, the only prop of his virtue, would turn against him and be his ruin. Not content, in fact, with his good reputation, he wanted to shine like richer men; he was torn with envy whenever the vulgar herd paid respect to some inferior "burgess" and appeared to despise him, Jachin, for his shabby doublet and his old shoes. The spiritual has ever been ready to ally itself with the temporal, and the possessor of moral prestige likes to derive some material advantage from it. Jachin therefore was annoyed at not being appreciated; people did not care to listen to him, and nobody touched their hats to him but the poor boys of the charity school. He suffered all the more because his poverty was increasing:

> The year was bad, the christening fees were small,
> The weddings few, the parties paupers all :
> Desire of gain with fear of want combined,
> Raised sad commotion in his wounded mind.

Once a month the clerk, having placed the con-
secrated bread and wine on the communion table, went
round the church to make a collection while the clergyman was reading the service. The wealthier members
of the congregation sat in high pews[1] which almost
concealed them from view, and deposited their offerings
on a plate handed them by Jachin. No one knew how
much his neighbour had given, and all the contributions
were mixed up together. One day, when the needy
clerk was taking his usual round and watching the
coins fall with a chink upon the plate, he said to himself—at first it was nothing more than a thought :

> . . . "These have cash and give it to the poor."
> A second thought from this to work began—
> "And can they give it to a poorer man?"
> Proceeding thus,—"My merit could they know,
> And knew my need, how freely they'd bestow ;
> But though they know not, these remain the same,
> And are a strong, although a secret claim :
> To me, alas ! the want and worth are known ;
> Why then in fact 'tis but to take my own."
> Thought upon thought pour'd in, a tempting train :
> "Suppose it done, who is it could complain?
> How could the poor, for they such trifles share,
> As add no comfort, as suppress no care. . . .
> Nought then forbids, the danger could we shun,
> And sure the business may be safely done."

The difficulty was that he had no time to put the pieces
of money in his purse, and that they might make a
noise when falling into his pocket. But if they were to
drop on some bran?

> "Why then 'tis safe, and (all consider'd) just,
> The poor receive it, 'tis no breach of trust :
> The old and widows may their trifles miss,
> There must be evil in a good like this :
> But I'll be kind—the sick I'll visit twice,
> When now but once, and freely give advice."

---

[1] "Tall spacious seats," the pews which George Eliot describes at the
beginning of *Amos Barton.*

Having made up his mind, he put his plan into execution in the following month. At the close of the ordinary service the doors were shut, and the "solemn rite" of the communion began: then the clerk might have been seen advancing with a trembling step between the high partitions, handing the plate over them, listening, with mingled joy and terror, to the chink of the precious metal, hiding behind one of the pillars as he turned into the aisle, swiftly seizing one of the coins, holding it for an instant in his hand, and then slipping it into his pocket. A few seconds later a piece of gold was put in the plate; he "took it trembling," stopped for a moment, and then let it fall with a noise which made him start, for in his confusion and fright he had forgotten the bran. But the congregation remained silent: absorbed in their solemn thoughts, they paid no heed to the sound. Jachin, made doubly cautious, managed to obtain the coveted sum and "one piece more." The operation was regularly repeated, and practice made him perfect. True, his conscience stung him for a long time. When he advanced to take the sacrament after the other communicants, he felt an "electric shock," and often he had to repeat his "reasons" to himself before he could "kneel in quiet":

> But custom soothed him—ere a single year
> All this was done without restraint or fear:
> Cool and collected, easy and composed,
> He was correct till all the service closed;
> Then to his home, without a groan or sigh,
> Gravely he went, and laid his treasure by.

Complaints were made, which boded no good for the offender. The source of charity seemed to be drying up in the parish: widows had come to ask "if they were favour'd like the rest," and all agreed with regret that their share had dwindled. The rich gave as freely as before; the poor received much less: some thief, therefore, must have pocketed the balance. The overseer of the poor that year happened to be "a stern, stout churl," a loud-voiced and angry tyrant. He resolved to clear up the mystery. He came to the next communion, and put three marked shillings in the plate. When the money was brought up after the collection, two of these coins had disappeared, and the

overseer's prying eyes detected a sprinkling of bran on
Jachin's coat. There could no longer be any doubt:
the clerk was the culprit! He was seized, his pockets
were emptied, and his guilt made patent to all. He
fainted under his disgrace, and, when he recovered
consciousness, implored permission to withdraw. No
one objected, all considered his punishment sufficient:

> For what has death in any form to give,
> Equal to that man's terrors, if he live?

He did live, to drag out a lingering and ignominious
existence:

> He saw another in his office reign,
> And his mild master treat him with disdain:
> He saw that all men shunn'd him, some reviled,
> The harsh pass'd frowning, and the simple smiled;
> The town maintain'd him, but with some reproof.

He became one of those poor wounded creatures who
retire into a corner to die:

> In each lone place, dejected and dismay'd,
> Shrinking from view, his wasting form he laid;
> Or to the restless sea and roaring wind
> Gave the strong yearnings of a ruin'd mind:[1]
> On the broad beach, the silent summer-day,
> Stretched on some wreck, he wore his life away;
> Or where the river mingles with the sea,
> Or on the mud-bank by the elder tree,
> Or by the bounding marsh-dyke, there was he:
> And when unable to forsake the town,
> In the blind courts he sate desponding down—
> Always alone; then feebly would he crawl
> The church-way walk, and lean upon the wall;
> Too ill for this, he lay beside the door,
> Compell'd to hear the reasoning of the poor:
> He looked so pale, so weak, the pitying crowd
> Their firm belief of his repentance vow'd.

Death at last released him from his sufferings:

> To a lone loft he went, his dying place,
> And, as the vicar of his state inquired,
> Turn'd to the wall and silently expired.[2]

[1] Two impressive lines—a personal experience in 1779.
[2] *Borough*, xix.

Inspired by recollections of the terrible year [1] in which he had reason to fear that he too might succumb, Crabbe likes to place his degraded characters in presence of that formidable or sordid aspect of nature which harmonises so well with their sombre mood and intensifies it.[2] Consider the fisherman known by the name of " Peter Grimes," and universally abhorred for his cruelty : he lets his boat float with the tide, either towards the mouth of the Alde or back to Slaughden Quay. His gaze fixed aimlessly on the flowing stream, he seems to bend beneath the weight of solitude and hatred. As no one will serve him, he works alone :

> Thus by himself compell'd to live each day,
> To wait for certain hours the tide's delay ;
> At the same time the same dull views to see,
> The bounding marsh-bank and the blighted tree ;
> The water only, when the tides were high,
> When low, the mud half cover'd and half dry ;
> The sun-burnt tar that blisters on the planks,
> And bank-side stakes in their uneven ranks ;
> Heaps of entangled weeds that slowly float
> As the tide rolls by the impeded boat.
> When tides were neap, and, in the sultry day,
> Through the tall bounding mud-banks made their way,
> Which on each side rose swelling, and below
> The dark warm flood ran silently and slow ;
> There anchoring, Peter chose from man to hide,
> There hang his head, and view the lazy tide
> In its hot, slimy channel slowly glide ;
> Where the small eels that left the deeper way
> For the warm shore, within the shallows play ;
> Wnere gaping mussels, left upon the mud,
> Slope their slow passage to the fallen flood.
> Here dull and hopeless he'd lie down and trace
> How sidelong crabs had scrawl'd their crooked race,
> Or sadly listen to the tuneless cry
> Of fishing gull or clanging golden-eye ;
> What time the sea-birds to the marsh would come,
> And the loud bittern, from the bull-rush home,
> Gave from the salt ditch side the bellowing boom :
> He nursed the feelings these dull scenes produce,
> And loved to stop beside the opening sluice,

---

[1] See above, p 69 and pp. 90 *seq.*

[2] This is also the case with Abel Keene (*Borough*, xxi. 191-206), where the reader will find another example of that psychological interpretation of nature already noted above (p. 264, n. 1).

> Where the dull stream, confined in narrow bound,
> Ran with a dull, unvaried, sadd'ning sound ;
> Where all, presented to the eye or ear,
> Oppress'd the soul with misery, grief, and fear.[1]

Peter had good reason for trembling before his fellow-men ; he read in their looks suspicion of his misdeeds.   The son of an honest fisherman who would have liked to bring him up in the fear of God, he left the hut "with anger and contempt" whenever he saw his father open the Bible on Sunday and begin to read aloud a chapter of "the word of life." "This is the life itself," exclaimed the young scoundrel, seizing a bottle of brandy, which set his blood on fire. When his "impious rage" burst forth in oaths and abuse, and old Grimes tried to check him, Peter would curse "the tyranny of age" : on one occasion even he had dealt a "sacrilegious blow" on the bare head of his father, who, falling to the ground with a groan, had said, "If thou art old, and hast a son—thou wilt remember me."   The man grew up like the boy—a drunkard and a thief ; he would leave his boat at night-time and, creeping along the hedges, carry off in a sack, sometimes fruit from orchards, sometimes corn or hay, "tugged fiercely from the stack" :

> And as these wrongs to greater numbers rose,
> The more he look'd on all men as his foes.

His instinct of an exasperated brute demanded a victim on whom he could wreak his vengeance.   He knew that apprentices could be procured in London, and that even a premium[2] could be obtained by applying to "workhouse-clearing men," who undertook to rid the parish authorities of pauper orphans.   One of these little slaves, in a "blue jacket and woollen cap," was made over to him without difficulty.   For the space of three years Peter's neighbours heard screams of pain issuing from the hut :

> But none inquired how Peter used the rope,
> Or what the bruise that made the stripling stoop ;
> None could the ridges on his back behold,
> None sought him shiv'ring in the winter's cold.

---

[1] *Borough*, xxii. 171-204.

[2] " Fifty shillings, to provide the boy with sea-clothing and bedding," according to the law of 1703.

They would merely remark, " Grimes is at his exercise." After long days of torture the wretched boy's sufferings came to an end. His death caused some surprise, but Peter replied with a growl to all questions, " I found him lifeless in his bed"; and, in the absence of proof, public suspicion died away, leaving Peter " untroubled and unmoved." Another premium and a new apprentice were obtained with equal ease. The latter, by a strange chance, fell from the mast into the well where live fish were kept, and was drowned there. " Yes," declared Peter, " in his play he climbed the mainmast and then fell below." The " slave-shop " was ready to provide another victim :

> Then came a boy, of manners soft and mild,—
> Our seamen's wives with grief beheld the child ;
> All thought (the poor themselves) that he was one
> Of gentle blood, some noble sinner's son,
> Who had, belike, deceived some humble maid,
> Whom he at first seduced, and then betray'd :—
> However this, he seemed a gracious lad,
> In grief submissive, and with patience sad.
>
> One day such draughts the cruel fisher made,
> He could not vend them in his borough-trade,
> But sail'd for London-mart : the boy was ill,
> But ever humbled to his master's will ;
> And on the river, where they smoothly sail'd,
> He strove with terror and awhile prevail'd ;
> But new to danger on the angry sea,
> He clung affrighten'd to his master's knee :
> The boat grew leaky and the wind was strong,
> Rough was the passage and the time was long ;
> His liquor fail'd, and Peter's wrath arose,—
> No more is known—the rest we must suppose,
> Or learn of Peter :—Peter says, he " spied
> The stripling's danger and for harbour tried ;
> Meantime the fish, and then th' apprentice died."

A cry of pity arose in the little town. The women burst into tears and exclaimed, " Thou hast thy 'prentice drown'd." Peter had to appear before the Mayor, who said to him in a threatening tone :

> " Henceforth with thee shall never boy abide ;
> Hire thee a freeman, whom thou durst not beat,
> But who, in thy despite, will sleep and eat :

> Free art thou now !—again shouldst thou appear,
> Thou'lt find thy sentence, like thy soul, severe." [1]

From that time Peter was an outcast from society.

Nothing now went right with him : a vague terror paralysed all his efforts.   The fish escaped from his nets and became the prey of the gulls, which he cursed for catching them better than he could :

> Cold nervous tremblings shook his sturdy frame,
> And strange disease—he couldn't say the name ;
> Wild were his dreams, and oft he rose in fright,
> Waked by his view of horrors in the night,—
> Horrors that would the sternest minds amaze,
> Horrors that demons might be proud to raise :
> And though he felt forsaken, grieved at heart,
> To think he lived from all mankind apart,
> Yet, if a man approached, in terrors he would start.

Even when he floated down the river in his boat he was seized with terror, especially at three spots, which he regularly avoided, as if he dreaded a hidden enemy there.   For he trembled at the idea of seeing his victims rise up before him and denounce him.   These apprehensions [2] gave rise to hallucinations, which haunted him and drove him mad.   In the end he was removed out of pity to the workhouse, where he related his visions :

> "'Twas one hot noon, all silent, still, serene,
> No living being had I lately seen ;
> I paddled up and down and dipp'd my net,
> But (such his pleasure) I could nothing get,—
> A father's pleasure, when his toil was done,
> To plague and torture thus an only son !
> And so I sat and look'd upon the stream,
> How it ran on, and felt as in a dream :
> But dream it was not : No !—I fix'd my eyes
> On the mid stream and saw the spirits rise :
> I saw my father on the water stand,
> And hold a thin pale boy in either hand ;
> And there they glided ghastly on the top
> Of the salt flood, and never touch'd a drop :
> I would have struck them, but they knew th' intent,
> And smiled upon the oar and down they went.

---

[1] *Borough*, xxii. 12 *seq.*, 120-64.

[2] And not remorse, to which he will always remain inaccessible (cf. Crabbe's own note, *Works*, ed. 1861, p. 250, n. 4).

" Now from that day, whenever I began
To dip my net, there stood the hard old man—
He and those boys : I humbled me and pray'd
They would be gone ; they heeded not, but stay'd :
Nor could I turn, nor would the boat go by,
But, gazing on the spirits, there was I :
They bade me leap to death, but I was loth to die :
And every day, as sure as day arose,
Would these three spirits meet me ere the close ;
To hear and mark them daily was my doom,
And 'Come,' they said, with weak, sad voices, 'Come.'
To row away, with all my strength I tried,
But there were they, hard by me in the tide,
The three unbodied forms—and ' Come,' still ' Come,'
          they cried.

" Fathers should pity—but this old man shook
His hoary locks, and froze me by a look :
Thrice, when I struck them, through the water came
A hollow groan, that weakened all my frame :
' Father,' said I, ' have mercy ' :—He replied,
I know not what—the angry spirit lied,—
' Didst thou not draw thy knife ? ' said he :—'Twas true,
But I had pity and my arm withdrew :
He cried for mercy, which I kindly gave,
But he has no compassion in his grave.

" There were three places, where they ever rose,—
The whole long river has not such as those—
Places accursed, where, if a man remain,
He'll see the things which strike him to the brain ;
And there they made me on my paddle lean,
And look at them for hours ;—accursèd scene !
When they would glide to that smooth eddy-space,
Then bid me leap and join them in the place ;
And at my groans each little villain sprite
Enjoy'd my pains and vanish'd in delight.

" In one fierce summer-day, when my poor brain
Was burning hot, and cruel was my pain,
Then came this father-foe, and there he stood
With his two boys again upon the flood :
There was more mischief in their eyes, more glee
In their pale faces, when they glared at me :
Still they did force me on the oar to rest,
And when they saw me fainting and oppress'd,
He with his hand, the old man, scoop'd the flood,
And there came flame about him mix'd with blood ;

He bade me stoop and look upon the place,
Then flung the hot-red liquor in my face ;
Burning it blazed, and then I roar'd for pain,
I thought the demons would have turn'd my brain." [1]

For hell itself was beginning to open for this miscreant, whose madness revived the superstitious terrors of his youth.

Pitiless for the wicked, Crabbe makes them pay dearly for their evil deeds. But, preferring psychological analysis to the violent incidents of melodrama, he makes the punishment of his culprits come from themselves : he immures them in their own unhappy minds, the most formidable of all prisons. The despair which preys upon the dishonest clerk, the impotent rage, the misery, the terror which madden the imagination of Grimes, are executioners who inflict a slow, cruel death. And never a sign of pardon, never the faintest gleam of hope ! From the day when man enters on the path of vice, he goes straight to an inevitable and irremediable ruin. Very different from Wordsworth, Crabbe is the author of *Peter Grimes*, and not of *Peter Bell*.[2] Conversions are unknown to him. He conceives the character of a fisherman cruel enough to torture three innocent boys to death, but he takes good care not to give him remorse and to make him, " after ten months' melancholy, a good and honest man." He knows that a monster who gloats over suffering is accessible only to the fear of suffering. The means employed by Wordsworth to soften his pedlar—the faithfulness of a donkey watching for four days over the corpse of his drowned master, the gentleness of the poor beast under the redoubled blows of Peter Bell, the tears of the orphan, the occurrence of mysterious sounds, the exhortations of a Methodist preacher, the sight of a weeping family—all these influences, ingeniously accumulated, would have seemed to Crabbe of doubtful efficacy. An observer and not a dreamer, he knows the tyranny of vicious instincts. He discerned, before Balzac, the logic of the passions and their inevitable consequences. In " Jachin " he shows us a man successively a precisian and a thief through pride. " Grimes " is the type of cruelty and cowardliness,

---

[1] *Borough*, xxii. 220-31 and 298-361.
[2] Written at Alfoxden in 1798, published in 1819.

inseparable from one another.   " Blaney,"¹ the spendthrift, who runs through three fortunes ; " Clelia,"² a

¹ *Borough*, xiv. It may be noted that in all these characters the analysis is
much less penetrating and the incidents much more numerous than in those of
Jachin and Grimes.   Hence my selection of these last two.   But the history
of the others may be summarised in a few words.

Blaney, having squandered his own fortune in gambling and extravagance,
at the age of twenty-five obtained the hand and the property of a " kind
widow."   Emboldened by experience and by the violence of his passions, he
embarked on a career of vice and prodigality, aspired to " singing harlots of
enormous price," and bought a racing-stud, leaving his wife, however, " to her
own pursuits."   This life lasted for ten years.   Having spent his last guinea,
Blaney went to India to retrieve his fortunes.   He had been there for a long
time when an unknown relation left him a fortune, and Blaney, with hair
growing grey and still accompanied by the " kind widow," returned to
England.

He was almost an old man.   His jaded senses now required the refinements
of vice.   Mere enjoyment was not enough for him : he wanted to corrupt and
seduce.   He must have " beauty trembling with alarms," " frail countesses
playing for his gold."   To kindle his " dormant flame," he read immoral books ;
to allay his scruples, he had recourse to Voltaire's novels (see above, p. 214) ;
to amuse himself, he built a fine country-house and bought a gallery of pictures.

When ruin came upon him once more, his wife having died, he was admitted
into an almshouse.   Ready to do anything for a dinner or a crown, he fell
into the last stage of degradation.   He told young men stories that raised
a smile, he carried notes for women of easy virtue ; a go-between and a
flatterer, he procured friends for the latter and pleasures for the former.
He is now clad in the parish uniform, and ekes out a morose and monotonous
existence among the paupers.

² *Borough*, xv.   At twenty-five Clelia, the daughter of an ex-mayor, was
very popular with the best society of the little town.   She had the art of
pleasing without endangering her reputation.   Sprightly and mischievous in
conversation—

If some soft stripling had her keenness felt,
She knew the way to make his anger melt.

She could talk about everything, without going below the surface.   " A
fortnight's visit in Whitechapel Street" enabled her to air her opinions of actors
and the stage.   A favourite with the rich, whom she flattered, and looked up to
by the poor, whom she patronised, fond of pleasure and by no means prudish
in the infectious warmth of social entertainments, Clelia was ripe for an
adventurous career.

She was dying to get married, in fact ; and the moment had come for her
to " bait each hook."   A seductive Lovelace appeared, who owed his success
with the fair sex not to his boldness but to his feigned timidity.   He affected
a " mute despair" at the slightest coldness ; he would bend forward to seize
the coveted hand, stop suddenly, as if frightened at his own daring, and content
himself with a long look.   He intended to await the advances of his inamorata
and then profit by a momentary weakness.   Clelia fell a victim to this strategy.

Ten years later we find her presiding, but not as lawful wife, " at an
attorney's board," where she liked to dwell on her grand friends of former
days.   A quarrel with her protector threw her into the arms of the landlord of
the " Griffin," whose bankruptcy and death left her penniless.   She tried to
teach a school, to write a novel, to keep a boarding-house for consolable
widowers, but failed in everything.   She was then seen to shed bitter tears
in her poverty and despair, and yet to run after pleasure, to the cheapest seats
in the theatre, or to a peep at a ball with the servants.   She would relate with
pride to her poor friends the triumphs of her youth and her past splendours.
At last, out of pity, Sir Denys Brand admitted her into the almshouse, where
she and Blaney made a pair of friends.

lively damsel who succumbs in the game of husband-
hunting and, after a series of adventures, ends in the
almshouse ; "Abel Keene,"[1] a simple and vain character, led astray by dissolute companions ; " Frederick
Thompson,"[2] incapable of steady work, by turns
student, sailor, strolling player, and "harlots' drudge";
" Benbow,"[3] a fiery-faced drunkard,—all these failures
are victims of their irresistible love of dissipation.
" Ellen Orford "[4] alone is an exception : she owes her
sad lot to a passing weakness.   But, whether it is a
case of transient error or of vicious temperament,
Crabbe's personages always remain consistent with
themselves ; they never change, they never can escape
the fatality which pursues them and which they themselves have let loose.   They remain incorrigible—for
our better correction.   As has already been pointed
out, moral intention governs all Crabbe's psychology,
and sometimes warps it by exaggerating it.   This
intention becomes its weakness after having been its
principal, if not sole, object.   As he himself observes
in one of his sermons, " It would be as foolish and even
malevolent to talk of human miseries as to describe

---

[1] See above, pp. 216-17.

[2] *Borough*, xii. 201-370.

[3] *Borough*, xvi.   Benbow was suggested by Shakspeare's Bardolph.   Like
the sexton Dibble of *The Parish Register* (iii. 855-955), he relates not his own
history, but that of various people he has known—the old " Squire Asgill,"
" Dowling," a captain in the merchant navy, the jovial gambler " Dolly
Murray"—all as fond of a glass as himself.

[4] *Borough*, xx.   Ellen Orford reminds us both of Phœbe Dawson and Agnes
Primrose.   Her unhappy youth was a foreboding of her sad life.   Her mother
had married again and had a large family, which Ellen took charge of.   Then
poverty and affliction made their appearance as formerly in Crabbe's home :
the father, " vex'd by troubles," would make a scene when he came back
from his work ; the children cried ; the mother, regretting the past, accused
herself of having wronged Ellen.   The young girl, therefore, at the age of
twenty, sought consolation in the love of a man much her superior in rank :
they met in secret, as he dared not marry ; she became incautious, and
he betrayed her trust.

It was a terrible shock to her one day to see her seducer lead to the altar
"a blooming bride," while she was languishing with her child in shame and
poverty.   Gradually, however, she regained strength and some courage : she
even married an honest tradesman, by whom she had five sons.   Unfortunately,
fate was still unkind to her : her husband's business not prospering, he became
gloomy, took to attending meetings of Calvinist Methodists, and, feeling no
sign of grace or of a " new birth," ended by hanging himself like Abel Keene.

Poor Ellen's misfortunes were not yet ended : she saw one of her sons, who
had been corrupted by the worst company, led to the gallows.   Death deprived
her of three others ; she suspected the fifth, a pale, sickly boy, of having committed an odious crime on his idiot sister, Ellen's first child.   Both are dead,
and Ellen, for a long time schoolmistress, but now blind, lives on the indoor
relief granted her by the parish.   Her old age is tranquil and resigned.

wounds and bruises and putrefying sores, but these
are described that they may be healed, and our afflictions that just inferences may be deduced from them,
and proper applications be made for their dispersion."[1]
It would be cruel to take pleasure in portraying the
progressive corruption and final ruin of so many
unfortunates, if their example were not to serve us
as a warning, if their end were not to promote our
own improvement. And the more grievous their fall,
the more impressive the lesson will be. Realism is
justified by its practical utility, and the more sombre
it is, the greater its efficacy. Jachin, Grimes, Blaney
will deter us from evil courses, from pride, from
cruelty, from profligacy; like so many bugbears, they
will curb the appetites of those who hanker after
forbidden fruit.

Compared with the realists of our time, Crabbe is
what in painting would be termed a "primitive."
Unable to produce one of those large, ample compositions from the background of which a central
figure stands out in bold relief, he lacks the creative
imagination which, subjecting a character to the ordeal
of the most varied situations, exhibits it to us under all
its aspects and in its smallest details. His analysis,
although profound, is one-sided. He excels in minia-
ture. He resembles those mediæval artists who
illuminated their manuscripts with pictures inspired
by the text. His personages emerge little by little
from the descriptive and didactic fabric of his poetry.
They are very slow to take cognisance of their independent existence. But once animated, they have a
singular energy and originality. They throw open
new vistas to fiction. They democratise it and teach
it the pathos of tragic endings. Crabbe, sprung from
the people and saddened by his early trials, does not
share the aristocratic and optimistic tendencies of the
novelists of preceding generations or of his own—
Richardson,[2] Fielding, Miss Burney, Miss Edgeworth,
and Jane Austen. His favourite heroes are not noblemen, squires, burlesqued or travestied peasants, but
poor waifs and strays; life for him is not a bed of

---

[1] Manuscript sermon preached at Great Glemham on March 4th, 1804
(Murray Collection).

[2] With the exception of "Clarissa Harlowe," an almost unique example of
an unfortunate heroine in the eighteenth century, in England at least.

roses where two lovers, long separated and at last
reunited, fondly embrace in the last act of the play : it
is an unremitting struggle with our own nature, with
those evil propensities which land us in certain ruin if
we give way to them. And the vanquished are many.
However humble they be, however inferior their surroundings, they must be described as a lesson. A
writer cannot " remain an inert spectator of good and
evil, enjoying the one and avoiding the other." He
aspires " to a higher office : he investigates the causes,
tries to explain them and influence them ; in short, he
wishes to control good and evil, to bring about and
promote the one, to contend with the other in order
to extirpate and destroy it."[1] These utilitarian and
philosophical aspirations, this marked preference for
the fallen,[2] for the meanest surroundings, for the
tragedy of life, make Crabbe a forerunner of the
boldest realists. When he dared to say that the poet,
like " the true physician, walks the foulest ward,"[3] he
stated, without foreseeing it, the formula of naturalism.
Time alone could bring out its full significance.

For Crabbe's psychological realism has obvious
limits. His province is the individual; his subject-
matter is passion isolated, considered in its essence
and in its consequences rather than in its causes.
Jachin represents pride, and we see very clearly
how this vice changes its aspect and what misery it
entails. But what is its origin ? Was Jachin born
proud, or did he become so ? In consequence of what
natural bias or what untoward companionships did
Grimes, who had been brought up in a respectable
family, come to such a bad end ? We are not told.
Crabbe's analysis, although so penetrating, lacks the
methods which science, with its superior information,
was soon to discover. To study man and his passions,
not only in themselves but in their antecedents, to
ascertain the laws of heredity and the relations

---

[1] Claude Bernard, the famous French physiologist, speaking of " modern
morality " in a passage quoted by Zola (*Lettre à la jeunesse*, at the end of
the *Roman expérimental*, ed. Bibliothèque-Charpentier, 1902, p. 84). It is
interesting to compare this passage with the extract from Crabbe's sermon
given above, pp. 301-2. Claude Bernard's and Crabbe's expressions are almost
identical.

[2] " In reality, every decomposition interests me," said Zola (*Le naturalisme
au théâtre*, p. 65, quoted by David-Sauvageot, *Le réalisme et le naturalisme*,
1890, p. 381). It is mostly " decompositions " that Crabbe studies.

[3] *Parish Register*, i. 213.

between the physical and the moral nature, to detect
the germ of the malady, instead of waiting for it to
develop and destroy in order to observe it—that was
the first step to be taken. The fatalities of the body
and of birth having been thus established, to replace
the individual in his social environment, to follow him
in his movements, in his avocations, to trace his companions—that was the second stage. It was reserved
for the French realistic or naturalistic[1] writers of
fiction, for Flaubert, the Goncourts, and Zola, to apply
this method as rigorously as possible. Without having
anticipated or influenced them, Crabbe heralds their
advent.

V

WHAT was to be the verdict of the contemporary
critics, who had received *The Parish Register* so well,
on the new work, which was at once more unequal
and more powerful? Would they forgive its weak
points out of consideration for its good ones? Would
they be impressed with the force and the originality of
the characters, whose importance was becoming more
and more marked, with the boldness of the poetry, so
resolutely close to the humble realities of life? One
could have wished it for their own sakes, but their
attitude was quite different, and the periodicals were
full of objections.[2] *The Monthly Review*,[3] for instance,

[1] If it were absolutely necessary to draw a distinction between " Realism "
and " Naturalism," we should not find it, like M. David-Sauvageot (*op. cit.*
p. 12), in the moral intention which, added to naturalism (disinterested
imitation of nature or " realism of art for art's sake "), is supposed to constitute " realism " properly so called. At that rate, Zola would be a realist
and Flaubert a naturalist. M. David-Sauvageot himself feels that his distinction does not correspond with the reality. There is sound reason for
ranking both Zola and Flaubert among the naturalists. Perhaps the real
difference is that which I have indicated above : Crabbe and Balzac are
" realists," firstly because they are opposed to romanticism, and secondly
because they isolate and exaggerate passion or vice in order to study them
in themselves ; Flaubert in the first place, and still more the Goncourts and
Zola, are " naturalists," because with true scientific intent they try to " explain "
their personage, to exhibit him as a product of heredity and the social
environment. It was the progress of biology which, about 1864, definitively
transformed " realism " into " naturalism." By a significant coincidence,
Taine's famous article on the influence of environments in literature ("Introduction to the History of English Literature ") was published in the old *Revue
germanique* in 1863 (Taine, *Vie et correspondance*, vol. ii. p. 189), and
Germinie Lacerteux appeared in 1864. These two parallel effects have the
same causes.

[2] The public, on the other hand, remained faithful to the author. A second
edition was published in 1810.

[3] New series, vol. lxvi. 1810, pp. 396-409.

considers *The Borough*, as Crabbe's "*Village*, extended
beyond all reasonable limits." Jeffrey,[1] comparing *The
Borough* with the preceding works, declares that "a
severe critic" might find "its faults greater and its
beauties less." Finally, Gifford, in the new-born
Quarterly Review,[2] thinks the volume has "all the
characteristic qualities of its author: a genius of no
common order, but misapplied and impaired by system
—a contempt for the *bienséances* of life, and a rage
for its realities." True, no critic denies the minute
accuracy of the descriptions, the abounding satirical
power, the precision and the vigour of touch possessed
by this painter of the passions, the intensity of his
pathos in certain passages. But, these merits conceded, the objections begin over again and are
continued to the end. The weakness of the composition is unanimously censured, and with good
reason. "There is no unity or method in the poem,"
exclaims Jeffrey; "it consists of a succession of
unconnected descriptions; . . . it does not admit of
analysis." The want of arrangement and connection,
declares another critic,[3] is unparalleled: "we see no
reason why any considerable passage should occupy
its particular place; and if we began at the last book
and read the books regularly backwards, or in any
other order whatever, it would be impossible to
increase the confusion." To whom are the twenty-
four "Letters,"[4] of which the work is composed,
addressed? Who is this fictitious correspondent
whom Crabbe imagines in order to have the pleasure

---

[1] *The Edinburgh Review*, April, 1810, an article written, I suppose, on a
copy supplied in advance.
[2] *The Quarterly Review*, November, 1810, vol. iv. pp. 281-312. The first
number appeared in February, 1809.
[3] *The Monthly Review*, article mentioned above.
[4] The following is a list of them : 1, General Description of the Borough ;
2, Description of the Church and its Epitaphs, with the Story of Sally and her
Sailor ; 3, Portraits of the Vicar and the Poor Curate ; 4, The Sects ; 5, The
Election and the Mayor Daniel ; 6, The Lawyers (Archer and Swallow) ;
7, Physic ; 8, Trades : Story of the Tyrannical Walter and the Kind William ;
9, Amusements ; 10, Clubs ; 11, Inns ; 12, Strolling Players (Frederick
Thompson) ; 13, The Almshouse and its Trustees (the Frugal Merchant,
Founder of the Almshouse) ; Sir Denys Brand ; Laughton, the Wealthy
Upstart, Greedy of Flattery) ; 14, Blaney ; 15, Clelia ; 16, Benbow: all three
Inmates of the Almshouse ; 17, The Hospital and its Governors (Eusebius,
etc.) ; 18, The Poor and their Dwellings (Attack on Workhouses, the Boarded
Building) ; 19, Jachin, the Parish Clerk ; 20, Ellen Orford ; 21, Abel Keene ;
22, Peter Grimes ; 23, The Prisons (Imprisonment for Debt ; Dream of the
Condemned Felon) ; 24, The Schools.

of "describing the borough" to him? Not a word is said of his identity: all we are told is that he lives somewhere near Muston,[1] and that, being desirous of knowing Aldborough without undertaking a journey, he is prepared to read more than seven thousand lines to satisfy his curiosity! It is as clear as day that this "correspondence" is a conversation between the poet and his shadow. We may add, with Jeffrey, that it often becomes intolerably prolix, that the "Letters" on the doctors, on the tradesfolk, the innkeepers, and the trustees of the almshouse, might send the most attentive reader to sleep. We may also admit that Crabbe has not the gift of selection, that he lets his pen run on, as if his object was to cover as much paper as possible; and that, in spite of the wise injunctions of Gifford and Jeffrey, he remains diffuse and confused. "Prune, prune!" the critics of the day repeat incessantly. Their words fell on deaf ears.

But here are some complainants of another kind; one of them,[2] speaking in a grave and almost heart-broken tone, appears on behalf of the Arminian Methodists, and charges Mr. Crabbe with having, in the fourth Letter of his poem,[3] "been witty at the expense of truth," and with attributing purely imaginary doctrines to the truest followers of the Gospel. He has fallen into "the error of investing fools, knaves, and madmen with the name of Methodist, and then assailing Methodism itself with all the abuse which these fools, knaves, and madmen so richly deserve." The other,[4] a venomous Calvinist under his bland smile, expresses regret that Mr. Crabbe has not received "better preferment," for then he "would have been under no temptation to lampoon the religion taught by the Calvinists." Commenting on the offensive letter, this Reviewer pronounces it "the grossest and most abominable caricature," and among other passages that he fears "have not the best tendency is the story of Jachin." Without listening any further to their pious recriminations, we may acquit Crabbe on these

---

[1] Cf. *Borough*, i. 25-35, where the "bordering brook" is the Devon of Muston (see above, p. 191).

[2] *The Christian Observer*, 1811, vol. x. pp. 502-11 (especially p. 506)[1]

[3] See above, pp. 216-17.

[4] *The Eclectic Review*, vol. vi. June, 1810, pp. 546-61 (especially p. 547, pp. 550-5).

counts of the indictment, since, as we know, he has
told the strict truth.

If it is admitted that a book is good when it suggests
ideas, one cannot refuse this enviable epithet to a poem
which made even its critics reflect. Feeling some
misgivings about this baffling *Borough*, they found
it necessary to re-examine their æsthetic conscience
and to furbish up their principles before deciding
the point. Poetry, says Jeffrey in a laborious style,
derives its greatest charm, not from the ideas and the
feelings which it presents to us, but from those which
it suggests. The most delicious music is that which
awakens the most echoes within us. Let the poet
touch a chord which makes our hearts respond to his
verse, and we shall give him the meed of praise. To
evoke as many associations of ideas as possible, let
him select familiar subjects and passions common to
all mankind. Now, is not the life of the humble the
most familiar of all subjects ? " If the poet can contrive to create a sufficient interest in subjects like
these, they will infallibly sink deeper into the mind
than subjects of greater dignity," such as princes and
rich and distinguished people.[1] Crabbe's poetry, which
is familiar enough in all conscience, is therefore very
likely to please us. Besides, it aims at pathos, and we
are partial to this. We like to be stirred, and Crabbe
does his best to gratify us in that respect. Unfortunately, he is seldom successful. Through having
forgotten that the supreme tragic emotions are " pity
and horror," pity caused by the spectacle of virtue in
distress, horror springing from the fear inspired by a
monster, he is too often apt to produce only "disgust."
His characters are at once wretched and guilty, criminal
and contemptible. They are poor girls, ashamed of
their fault, or helpless thieves. They deserve neither
sympathy nor indignation, and leave us indifferent.
Jeffrey's mind, therefore, is made up : on the strength
of his " doctrine," he condemns Thompson, Blaney,
Ellen Orford, Peter Grimes, Abel Keene, Benbow, and
Jachin in a lump. He also condemns the abuse of
descriptions. In that case, it may be asked, what is
left of *The Borough* ? Nothing but the abundance of
satirical power. The profound psychological analysis,
which constitutes the real originality of the work,

---

[1] Jeffrey shows himself a genuinely " Whig " critic here.

escaped this theory-ridden critic. Gifford, writing six months afterwards, was resolved not to lag behind his rival. He, too, felt bound to go back to first principles, and to begin his article by a definition of poetry. According to him, poetry has nothing in common with the "real world": its mission is to provide us with a retreat far removed therefrom, in the flowery plains of pastoral verse or among the heroes of epic and romance.[1] Its province is the "paradise of the fancy," and not that brutal reality in which Crabbe would like to imprison us, "in defiance of imagination and taste." Will it be maintained that every truth is suitable for description or repetition? exclaims Gifford in alarm.

To this objection, which embarrasses him, Crabbe replies, in the Preface to his *Tales*,[2] that he was not conscious of forfeiting his title to the name of poet by describing men, manners, and things as faithfully as possible; that such strictness would exclude from genuine poetry all satirical compositions which aim at the delineation of character; and that if it were observed, Chaucer, Dryden, and Pope would, whatever their superiority in other respects, be liable to the condemnation passed on himself. Poetry is incompatible with the reality, asserts Gifford; it may very properly not travel outside it, rejoins Crabbe. The truth is its province, as well as fancy. We shall return later to this interesting question. For the moment let us confine ourselves to inquiring whether Crabbe's "characters" are as "true" as he makes out, and to what extent his realism is modelled on the reality. Has he copied his personages straight from nature, or has he altered them? Is it a simple photograph, or does he touch up the picture as a painter would? His friend Mrs. Leadbeater put this question to him one day,[3] and he replied in the following terms: "I will tell you readily about my 'creatures.' . . . There is not one of whom I had not in my mind the original; but I was obliged, in some cases, to take them from their real situations, in one or two instances to change even the sex, and, in many, the circumstances.

---

[1] Gifford is a type of the "Tory" critic. He likes to consort with the great.

[2] *Works*, p. 273, col. 2, and p. 274.

[3] In her first letter of November 7th, 1816 (B. p. 64); Crabbe's reply is dated December 1st (B. p. 65, col. 1).

The nearest to real life was the proud, ostentatious man [1] in *The Borough*, who disguises an ordinary mind by doing great things; but the others approach to reality at greater or less distances. Indeed, I do not know that I could paint merely from my own fancy; and there is no cause why we should. Is there not diversity sufficient in society? And who can go, even but a little, into the assemblies of our fellow-wanderers from the way of perfect rectitude, and not find characters so varied and so pointed, that he need not call upon his imagination." In other words, the poet does not consider himself the slave of nature, and, while accepting the data furnished by experience, he takes the liberty of recasting them, if his plan requires it. Observation supplies the first idea of a personage: Mrs. Tovell lives again in the "widow Goe," and John Jasper, the clerk of Great Glemham, in "Isaac Ashford"; "Andrew Collett" is the portrait of an old innkeeper at Hacheston, a village near Parham; "Robin Dingley" reminds the Biographer of a certain Richard Wilkinson, of Muston; and "Leonard's" disgust with his life is that of Jack Haddon, a son of the schoolmaster at Stowmarket.[2] But if Crabbe sees the possibility of a telling situation or of an ingenious stroke of satire, he does not hesitate to sacrifice the truth to his inspiration. The original of Sir Denys Brand, for instance, is "Challoner Arcedekne, who built Glevering Hall," not far from Parham. The poet had taken into his service one of the squire's maids, who confessed to him that whenever she met her old master "she felt more afraid of him than of God Almighty." The reader will perhaps remember how the satirist managed to turn this naïve remark to account: for the maid he substituted a rascally boy, who was clever enough to humbug Sir Denys and obtain a place in his household. Does not this triumph of cunning over pretentious omnipotence make the potentate still more ridiculous? Or again, the moral intention needs emphasising, and Crabbe in that case exaggerates the reality with a view to edification. He makes the colours darker than nature: the sceptical blacksmith of Leiston,[3] who, when his

---

[1] Sir Denys Brand (see above, pp. 274-5).
[2] See above, p. 282.
[3] Village to the north of Aldborough (cf. above, p. 70).

hand was cut off, ironically asked " Dr. Crabbe " if
" he would not find it at the day of judgment," becomes
the drunkards' " bishop," the infidel poacher who is
drowned in a ditch. The " Blaney" of real life never
ended his existence in an almshouse after the most
degrading experiences : he was a retired military
officer, a Major Dade, of Dennington, who was
noticed one evening at the Ipswich theatre " in the
box assigned to the nameless ladies," and, offering
them a pinch of snuff, was hissed by the public.
" Clelia," the flirt, was a Miss Rebecca Carter, who
lived at Beccles ; the sister of a naval officer, she
never went through the adventures attributed to her
by the poet. As for " Peter Grimes," his name was
plain Tom Brown, and if he did lose his apprentices in
a very suspicious manner, he never saw the spectres
of his victims rise from the water. The perusal of
Richard III. and the quest of pathos alone procured
us those horrors.[1] In order that the history of these
unfortunates may serve as a lesson, the punishment of
their misdeeds must terrify us, even at the expense of
the truth. Thus is verified in anticipation the profound
remark of Zola : "A literary work can never be anything
but a corner of nature seen through a temperament."[2]

[1] The following is a list of references in support of the foregoing statements:
Isaac Ashford (*Parish Register*, iii. 413-502). Cf. *Works*, p. 151, n. 15.
Andrew Collett (*Parish Register*, iii. 75-124). Cf. the following note by
the Biographer in the copy of Crabbe which belonged to Fitzgerald, and is
now in the possession of Mr. Aldis Wright : " I think the original of Collett
was a fat old landlord of a small public-house at Hacheston, near Parham."
Robin Dingley (*Parish Register*, iii. 503, 580). Cf. *Works*, p. 151, n. 16.
Leonard (*Borough*, xxiv. 109-35). Manuscript note of B. (Fitzgerald) :
" Jack Haddon, son of the Author's schoolmaster. The Father was a much
respected man."
Sir Denys Brand (*Borough*, xiii. 88-226). Cf. Fitzgerald MS. n. : " The
late Challoner Arcedeckne, Esq., who built Glevering Hall."
The infidel poacher (*Parish Register*, i. 787-823). Cf. *Works*, p. 140, n. 43.
Blaney (*Borough*, xiv.). Fitzgerald MS. n. : " Major Dade, of Dennington.
The poor old major was hissed in the theatre at Ipswich, when, in the box
assigned to the nameless ladies, he was seen offering his snuff-box to one of
them." Cf. also *Works*, p. 223, n. 1.
Clelia (*Borough*, xv.). Fitzgerald MS. n. : " Miss Rebecca Carter, of
Beccles, sister to a naval surgeon of that name ; both have been long dead.
The incidents are imaginary." Cf. *Works*, p. 223, n. 1.
Peter Grimes (*Borough*, xxii.). Fitzgerald MS. n. : " Tom Brown. The
death of the apprentices was most suspicious. The terrors, etc., imaginary."
Cf. *Works*, pp. 246-7, n. 1.
[2] *Le naturalisme au théâtre* (at the end of the *Roman expérimental*,
p. 111). In a remarkable passage of the same volume (pp. 207-8), Zola
explains the genesis of a " naturalistic " novel. The first thing the author
does is to collect as many notes and documents as possible ; from their

That of Crabbe, utilitarian and aiming at moral improvement, bends the truth to its exigencies, just as that of Zola, rectilinear and logical, imprisons its heroes in his inflexible determinism. What they thus obtain is no longer the true, but only the probable.

unconscious elaboration springs the general idea which gives the plan, the dramatic outline indispensable to the work. And the novel "grows of itself: the novelist has only to distribute the facts logically." The general idea is, however, taken from the documents by a brain which imparts its own special tendencies to it, and a number of secondary characters may be really *invented* to fill the canvas. Whence it follows that a writer of fiction can only—Zola admits it himself—"set up living creatures, acting the world's comedy before the readers *with as much naturalness as possible*" (*ibid.* p. 206). This "naturalness" is what we call the "probable." There is more of it in the "naturalistic" than in the "idealistic" novel, and therein perhaps lies their most notable difference.

FIFTH PART

CRABBE AS WRITER OF TALES AND MORALIST

CHAPTER I

THE "TALES IN VERSE"

I. Pathos.—II. Humour.—III. Resignation and idyllic life.—IV. Verdict of contemporaries. General features of the work.

CONSIDERED from the point of view of evolution, the works hitherto analysed—*The Village, The Parish Register*, and *The Borough*—tend by a slow but steady growth to produce the "tale in verse." As if Chaucer had never composed his *Canterbury Tales*, as if Dryden and Pope had not imitated or translated them, Crabbe seems to create, little by little and out of his own resources, that literary form to which his persistent realism imparts an undeniable originality. The germ of it, not disengaged from its satirical and didactic integument, may be found in *The Village*, where the description of the labourer still remains, as we have seen, of an abstract kind; five-and-twenty years later *The Parish Register* exhibits portraits drawn from the life and distinctly individualised; finally, in *The Borough*, these characters, assuming more and more ample proportions, become regular "lives." The poet has only, by an effort of construction, to make two of these personages act and react on each other, and the "tale" will come into existence. The story of Abel Keene had already brought together the dissolute brother and the resolutely virtuous and pious sister, who grieves at the excesses of her unworthy relative and dies broken-hearted.[1] But this, in *The Borough*, was only an isolated case, a sort of stepping-stone to a future development. The new vein, which a fortunate coincidence had brought to light, had to be worked, and Crabbe, somewhat slow at making a start, was impelled in that direction by Jeffrey, who was well inspired on this occasion. "We own we have a very strong desire,"

[1] *Borough*, xxi. 138-48 and 181.

the critic had written, " to see Mr Crabbe apply his great powers to the construction of some interesting and connected story. He has great talent for narration; and that unrivalled gift in the delineation of character, which is now used only for the creation of detached portraits, might be turned to admirable account in maintaining the interests and enhancing the probability of an extended train of adventures."[1] Crabbe did not feel equal to carrying out this ambitious programme : he knew he had no turn for devising a complicated plot, and doubtless remembered his fruitless attempts at novel-writing ten years earlier.[2] With the unerring instinct of an artist conscious of his strong and weak points, he refused to court failure again, but admitted that "the characters at his disposal" might be grouped in "small societies,"[3] each of which would form a tale. Such was the origin of these *Tales in Verse*, which were published by Hatchard on September 14th, 1812.[4] Let us examine them with sympathy, let us find out what new elements they contribute to the poet's work ; perhaps on our way we shall extract from them a modest philosophy of life.

I

In fact, certain " Letters " of *The Borough* and almost all the *Tales* are variations on a single theme—the question of happiness. Not that Crabbe, as a rule, troubles his head about the means of obtaining it or about the obstacles which, in our pursuit of it, intervene between us and the object of our hopes : ambition or love, enamoured of an idle fancy and starting on some wild adventure, leaves our realist far behind. Faithful to his favourite method, which is the study of progressive corruption, he at once places his per-

---

[1] *Edinburgh Review*, vol. xvi. April, 1810, p. 55 (quoted in *Works*, p. 272, n. 1).
[2] See above, pp. 206-7.
[3] Preface to the *Tales* (*Works*, pp. 272-3).
[4] See the advertisement in *The Times* of the same day. B. (p. 56) is wrong in speaking of "the early part of the year," and on p. 271, n. 1, of the month of August. The work was dedicated to the Dowager Duchess of Rutland by a letter dated " Muston, 31st July, 1812." It is quite impossible to believe that the following note of Fitzgerald's, copied in the poet's Journal, " Nov. 7, 1810. Finish *Tales*. Not happy hour," alludes to the completion of the entire collection.

sonages in a condition of comparative but unstable felicity, whence a combination of causes, coolly and minutely analysed, will plunge them into hopeless misery. These causes are our evil passions, which the poet knows so well in all the "shapes they take," in the "strange waste of life and joy they make."[1] They are, not the impulses, but the maladies of the mind, those corroding ailments which, attacking the heart, dry up the source of generous feeling and blight the flower of life.

Here is a pair of lovers,[2] belonging to the middle class: his name is Rupert, and he works all day in his father's office; she is called Dinah, and acts as companion to a wealthy aunt, who has promised to leave the niece her money. Their occupations are monotonous, and they have grown weary with long waiting: Rupert has repeatedly begged the "widow" to consent to their union, but always in vain:

> . . . She groan'd, and cough'd, and cried,
> Talk'd of departing, and again her breath
> Drew hard, and cough'd, and talk'd again of death:
> "Here you may live, my Dinah! here the boy
> And you together my estate enjoy."

They had to yield to her objections, to give up talking of marriage, to content themselves with a short evening walk which made up for their troubles, and thus they reached "their thirtieth year," with the uneasy hope of a still distant happiness.

Impatience is often a bad counsellor: in his thirst for wealth Rupert has accepted an apparently advantageous opening in the colonies. The lovers have parted, "with a gloomy view," and no consolation but their tried fidelity. Letters have been exchanged, from which it appears that after a crisis of despair Rupert has found kind and probably true friends in his new home. And the years glide by, without bringing to either the longed-for opportunity: Rupert has no idea of returning; the aunt persists in remaining alive, and is astonished to hear Dinah continually sighing, when she ought to be "so happy" in the contemplation of her future treasures:

---

[1] *Borough*, xxiv. 433; an excellent formula, in which Crabbe sums up his manner.

[2] *Tales*, iv.: *Procrastination.*

> To vary pleasures, from the lady's chest
> Were drawn the pearly string and tabby vest ;
> Beads, jewels, laces, all their value shown,
> With the kind notice—" They will be your own."

At length Dinah was led to covet what she so often saw and handled ; insensibly cupidity crept into her heart and dislodged the passion of love :

> Now the grave niece partook the widow's cares,
> Look'd to the great, and ruled the small affairs ;
> Saw clean'd the plate, arranged the china-show,
> And felt her passion for a shilling grow.

Her letters to Rupert became much shorter and less affectionate ; she signed them " Your friend, Dinah," and often alleged " the widow's cough " as an excuse for writing only a few lines. When at last her aunt died, the joy of her youth was all forgotten. Without devoting a thought to Rupert, she took possession of her long-expected fortune : " her stocks, her bonds, and her buildings " were all cares which she had no intention of sharing :

> Month after month was passed, and all were spent
> In quiet comfort, and in rich content ;
> Miseries there were, and woes the world around,
> But these had not her pleasant dwelling found ;
> She knew that mothers grieved, and widows wept,
> And she was sorry, said her prayers, and slept :
> Thus passed the seasons, and to Dinah's board
> Gave what the seasons to the rich afford. . . .
> A love of splendour now with avarice strove,
> And oft appeared to be the stronger love. . . .
> In small but splendid room she loved to see
> That all was placed in view and harmony. . . .
> Around the room an Indian paper blazed,
> With lively tint and figures boldly raised ;
> Silky and soft upon the floor below,
> Th' elastic carpet rose with crimson glow. . . .
> Within a costly case of varnish'd wood,
> In level rows, her polish'd volumes stood.

On her table was a silver lamp, " from Grecian pattern wrought " :

> Above her head, all gorgeous to behold,
> A timepiece stood on feet of burnish'd gold ;
> A stag's-head crest adorn'd the pictured case,
> Through the pure crystal shone the enamel'd face.

In the society of two intimate friends, admitted into this elegant boudoir, Dinah delights in discussing her neighbours, and bewails the misdeeds of the rising generation:

> How tender damsels sail'd in tilted boats,
> And laugh'd with wicked men in scarlet coats.

Evidently Dinah, at her age, would not indulge in such imprudent conduct: she is wedded to piety and selfishness. Her love has died out and her heart grown hard.

When, years afterwards, Rupert returns, as poor as he started, when, with " tawny cheek and pitted face," he encounters the disdain of the " tall starch" maid-servant, and appears unexpectedly before his old sweetheart, he is received with a calculated coolness, a hypocritical austerity which contrasts strangely with his ingenuous hope and his sailor-like bluffness. What does his poverty matter? he says; " 'tis mine to share thy comforts and the glory thine." But a cruel disappointment is in store for him:

> . . . " Heavens," returned the maid,
> " This talk to one so wither'd and decay'd ?
> No ! all my care is now to fit my mind
> For other spousal, and to die resigned."

" What spousal mean'st thou ? " rejoins the lover, half angry and half in doubt:

> " . . . Thou art Rupert's spouse ;
> That chance is mine to take, and thine to give :
> But trifling this, if we together live :
> Can I believe, that after all the past,
> Our vows, our loves, thou wilt be false at last ? . . .
> Nay, speak at once ; and Dinah, let me know,
> Mean'st thou to take me, now I'm wrecked, in tow ?
> Be fair ; nor longer keep me in the dark ;
> Am I forsaken for a trimmer spark ?
> Heaven's spouse thou art not ; nor can I believe
> That God accepts her who will man deceive :
> True, I am shatter'd, I have service seen,
> And service done, and have in trouble been ;
> My cheek (it shames me not) has lost its red,
> And the brown buff is o'er my features spread :
> Perchance my speech is rude, for I among
> Th' untamed have been, in temper and in tongue ;

> Have been trepanned, have lived in toil and care,
> And wrought for wealth I was not doom'd to share;
> It touched me deeply, for I felt a pride
> In gaining riches for my destin'd bride.
> Speak then my fate; for these my sorrows past,
> Time lost, youth fled, hope wearied, and at last
> This doubt of thee—a childish thing to tell,
> But certain truth—my very throat they swell:
> They stop the breath, and but for shame could I
> Give way to weakness, and with passion cry;
> These are unmanly struggles, but I feel
> This hour must end them, and perhaps will heal."

A contrite sigh, an assurance that she loved his soul, and "hoped he had the grace to fix his thoughts upon a better place," was the only reply that this eloquent appeal extracted from Dinah. Then, looking steadily at her, "as if to see the very root of this hypocrisy"—

> He her small fingers moulded in his hard
> And bronzed broad hand; then told her his regard,
> His best respect were gone, but love had still
> Hold in his heart, and govern'd yet the will—
> Or he would curse her:—saying this, he threw
> The hand in scorn away, and bade adieu
> To every lingering hope, with every care in view.

Rupert is now in receipt of parish relief and wears the pauper's blue livery. In church he sees "the pious Dinah dropped upon her knees"; sometimes he meets her in the street, and, while she is giving orders to some tradesman, he will sit down on a bench a few paces off. He fixes his eyes intently on her, as if to find—

> What are the movements of that subtle mind. . . .
> His thoughts are wandering through his earlier years;
> Through years of fruitless labour, to the day
> When all his earthly prospects died away:
> "Had I," he thinks, "been wealthier of the two,
> Would she have found me so unkind, untrue?
> Or knows not man when poor, what man when rich will do?
> Yes, yes! I feel that I had faithful proved,
> And should have soothed and raised her, bless'd and loved."

Dinah now advances towards him, moved by "a touch of ancient tenderness" for the broken old man; but pride restrains her:

> . . . To return would prove
> She felt the shame of his neglected love ;
> Nor wrapp'd in silence could she pass, afraid
> Each eye should see her, and each heart upbraid ;
> One way remain'd—the way the Levite took,
> Who without mercy could on misery look ;
> (A way perceived by craft, approved by pride,)
> She cross'd and pass'd him on the other side.

Varying the circumstances slightly, let us take, instead of lovers, two brothers; let us unite them by the ties of gratitude; then, having implanted avarice in the heart of the indebted man, let us study the progressive transformation of fraternal affection into black ingratitude, and we shall have the case of George and Isaac Fletcher.[1] The sons of an old sea-dog, a kindly, simple soul, they have little resemblance to each other : George, the elder, has the intrepid, careless vigour of a sailor ; the feeble Isaac, on the contrary, " shrinks from the cold and shudders at the storm." Unsuited to the rough life of a fisherman, he has served his apprenticeship with a maker of blocks and ropes, has proved steady and industrious, and, having learned his trade, carries it on in a house hired for him by his brother. His business flourishes. George, on re-turning from long expeditions, is glad to see him again, and entrusts his savings to Isaac, who, besides, has made valuable friends in his native town : his obsequiousness has commended itself to " Burgess Steel," who, in exchange for his vote, has promised him " a humble place " when the first vacancy occurs. A suitable marriage too is in prospect : " an ancient friend, a maiden spare and grave," pleased with his sedate and serious ways, encourages his " gentle flame " for a favourite servant. And George rejoices in his brother's happiness, amid the perils which menace his own life ; for he has gone into the Navy, on the declaration of war, and without waiting to be dragged off by the press-gang. Twice his ship has captured a prize, twice he has returned on short furlough and, his pockets full, has brought happiness and enjoyment into Isaac's household.

Unfortunately, he loses a leg in action shortly after-

---

[1] *Tales*, xx. : *The Brothers*. The first sketch of this tale is to be found in *The Borough*, xvii. 114-57, the story of Tom, " master of a hoy," and of Isaac, " the landman."

wards : the "worthy George" would now be an "idle log," with no refuge but Greenwich Hospital, had he not a brother on whose devotion he thinks he can rely.   He arrives soon after the receipt of the bad news, shakes hands "with love and resignation in his look," is glad to "find his anchor safely cast," asks for his nephews and his grog, and begins the story of his last engagement.   Alas! he has no idea that his brother would have preferred to see him at Greenwich, that his sister-in-law is full of contempt for the "loud, rough sailor with a timber limb," that his stories, once attentively listened to and even asked for, are now thought a bore, and that objection is taken to his habits :

> The vulgar pipe was to the wife offence,
> The frequent grog to Isaac an expense ;
> "Would friends like hers," she question'd, "choose to come,
> Where clouds of poison'd fume defiled a room ?"

Let George sit in the kitchen, or, better still, let him go up to the garret, where his presence cannot annoy the relations and friends of the mistress of the house. If he complains to Isaac of these insults, the latter, alleging his love of peace and his wife's stubborn temper, replies :

> "My spouse had money—she must have her will—
> Ah ! brother, marriage is a bitter pill."

If he apologises to his sister-in-law for troubling her, she says :

> "Oh no ! you may depend
> On my regard—but watch your brother's way,
> Whom I, like you, must study and obey."

Placed between the hammer and the anvil, the poor sailor takes refuge in the garret, "where not a being saw the tears he shed," except his nephew, little George, who loves to hear of his battles and voyages. And even the child has to visit him by stealth, for his mother has forbidden him to come, and his father, surprising him one day with his uncle, had abused the latter for "disturbing his brain with his cursed stories." One night Isaac, who is on the watch, catches the boy in the act of knocking at the old sailor's door, and exclaiming, "You serpent, is it thus you act?" sends him with a "hasty blow," indignant and in tears, back

to his mother. Then, venting his rage on his brother,
he bursts into a torrent of abuse, accuses him of
" seducing his child and making his house a scene of
vile dispute," and insists on an answer. Irritated by
the dogged silence of the sailor, he draws near the bed,
where George has at last.found rest in the sleep of
death,[1] and his conscience, which had never ceased to
protest in secret against his severity, suddenly awakes,
reproaches him with his " crime," and overwhelms him
with a remorse which makes the rest of his life a
burden to him.

For cupidity[2] let us substitute resentment, and see
with Crabbe how this new germ of strife can ruin
an existence.[3] The hero is an energetic ship-owner
and merchant, who is called Paul and has become a
widower at the age of forty. His exterior inspires
entire confidence :

> Composed his features were, his stature low,
> His air important, and his motion slow :
> His dress became him, it was neat and plain,
> The colour purple [4] and without a stain ;

[1] *Tales*, xx. 342-55. This long speech of Isaac to George, who, without
his brother being aware of it, has just breathed his last, is not a happy effort.
It is rather painful to see Crabbe struggling hard to produce a melodramatic
effect, which falls flat, in spite of all his exertions.

[2] Which is also the subject of two other somewhat uninteresting tales. The
first (*Tales*, xiv. : *The Struggles of Conscience*) relates the ever-increasing
liberties which a " toyman " takes with his conscience, his close adviser and
soon his enemy. He gets up a lottery which would ruin him if he had to pay
the prizes which he has promised, but which fortunately are not drawn ; he
charges outrageous prices for his goods ; he protests against the abuses of the
vestry, and allows himself to be bought off ; although a Nonconformist, he
attends the Church of England communion in order to become a member of
the vestry ; finally, he marries a young feeble-witted woman for her money,
and then entraps her into misconduct in order to get rid of her.—The second
(*Tales*, xix. : *The Convert*) is inspired by the autobiography of the bookseller Lackington (see above, p. 206, n. 1), whom Crabbe represents, with many
points of difference, in the person of John Dighton, a convert to Methodism
during a fever, set up in a bookseller's business by his co-religionists to sell their
tracts, then emboldened by success and by his enterprising mind to throw off
the patronage of the sect and to marry an unbeliever, the sister of a doctor.
From fanaticism to scepticism there is only one step, according to our clergyman (see above, p. 216, n. 1).

[3] *Tales*, xvii. : *Resentment*.

[4] Cf. Scott's *Antiquary*, ch. vi.: "Mr. Lovel, a gentleman who, during
the scarlet-fever which is epidemic at present [1790-1800] in this our island,
has the virtue and decency to appear in a coat of a civil complexion."
Cf. B. p. 40: "My first suit of boy's clothes (and that scarlet)" ; and Abel
Keene's attire (*Borough*, xxi. 76) : "The crimson waistcoat and the silken
hose." For these showy colours of male costume the influence of the French
Revolution gradually substituted the levelling black.

His words were few, and special was his care
In simplest terms his purpose to declare. . . .
Though frugal he, yet sumptuous was his board,
As if to prove how much he could afford ;
Among his friends he sat in solemn style,
And rarely soften'd to a sober smile.

He has so much to think of, said his friends, by way of
explanation, such "vast concerns" to conduct!   His
ships are "freighted with abundant stores," his floors
"groan" under the weight of his treasures, and on a
public occasion he can display " a little army of clerks
and servants."   Really, a man so engrossed in business
must have a companion to supervise the expenses of
his household.   Paul's choice has fallen on "a gentle
lady, with a mind discreet, neither in life's decline,
nor bloom of youth."   Her modest reserve and her
sincerity are commended : "by nature cool, in pious
habits bred," she had felt a virgin's dread at the mere
hint of love, and if a youthful admirer ventured to
speak of " her all-conquering charms," she used to
become "motionless and cold" as a statue.   But she
would not repel the advances of a staid and well-to-do
suitor ; she therefore married our merchant and left
the management of her affairs in his hands.

Under a plausible exterior Paul was really a knave ;
his speculative ventures had been increasing his lia-
bilities for years past, and the resources procured by
his two marriages had delayed, but could not avert, his
ruin.   The fêtes given on the launching of his ships,
the luxury in which his wife lived, the invitations to
the neighbours, were all intended to serve as a blind.
Pressed by his creditors, he resolved to abuse his
wife's confidence in order to obtain possession of her
money.   One day when she was going, in a handsome
dress, to preside at one of his banquets, he called her
into his study, told her that her consent was required as
a legal formality, and placed before her a paper, which
she signed without looking at it, and without a suspicion
of her husband's integrity.   Not long afterwards came
bankruptcy, involving destitution for both of them.

She never forgave him.   She bore her poverty alone,
and knew the humiliation of living under " a low
thatch'd roof with walls of clay," amid "mirth that
disgusts and quarrels that degrade."   Her husband
followed her there, but she would not relent : he

begged to be allowed to share her life, said " he would turn servant for her sake, would keep the poorest school, the very streets would sweep, to show his love." He had shown it sufficiently, she replied, and " her affliction should be all her own." Even after an uncle had given her a home and then left her his property, even when she was able to return as mistress to the house which she had once quitted in disgrace, she refused to see or help her husband or have anything in common with him, including even her name. Aided by Susan, her maid, whose tender heart presents a touching contrast to the rigid, unfeeling justice of the wife, she dispenses " a plain and homely charity " to the surrounding poor :

> With her own hands she dress'd the savoury meat,
> With her own fingers wrote the choice receipt.

But if the offender ventures to join the " cheerful groups " who wait upon her bounty, and to beg a crust for himself, he receives an answer which extorts from him a groan. He applies to the parish for relief, but the authorities tell him that his wife is rich, and show him the door. He tries various means of livelihood, but " nothing prospers in his luckless hand": he becomes an usher in a school, where the uproar soon " makes him less able than the weaker boys "; he goes on errands, but forgets the names and the words in the messages entrusted to him. Lastly, he is to be seen in a mason's yard, where stone-cutters are at work, buying the waste material for a few pence, loading it on an ass's back and reselling it for a wretched pittance :

> A dreadful winter came, each day severe,
> Misty when mild, and icy cold when clear ;
> And still the humble dealer took his load,
> Returning slow, and shivering on the road :
> The lady, still relentless, saw him come,
> And said—" I wonder, has the wretch a home ? "—
> " A hut ! a hovel ! " " Then his fate appears
> To suit his crime."—" Yes, lady, not his years ;—
> No ! nor his sufferings—nor that form decay'd."
> " Well ! let the parish give its paupers aid :
> You must the vileness of his acts allow."—
> " And you, dear lady, that he feels it now."
> " When such dissemblers on their deeds reflect,
> Can they the pity they refused expect ?

He that doth evil, evil shall he dread."
"The snow," quoth Susan, "falls upon his bed—
It blows beside the thatch—it melts upon his head."
"'Tis weakness, child, for grieving guilt to feel."—
"Yes, but he never sees a wholesome meal;
Through his bare dress appears his shrivell'd skin,
And ill he fares without, and worse within:
With that weak body, lame, diseased, and slow,
What cold, pain, peril, must the sufferer know!"
"Think on his crime." "Yes, sure 'twas very wrong;
But look (God bless him!) how he gropes along."—
"Brought me to shame."—"Oh! yes, I know it all—
What cutting blast! and he can scarcely crawl;
He freezes as he moves—he dies! if he should fall.
   . . . In pity do behold
The man affrighten'd, weeping, trembling, cold:
Oh! how those flakes of snow their entrance win
Through the poor rags, and keep the frost within.
His very heart seems frozen as he goes,
Leading that starved companion of his woes:
He tried to pray—his lips, I saw them move,
And he so turn'd his piteous looks above;
But the fierce wind the willing heart opposed,
And ere he spoke, the lips in misery closed:
Poor suffering object! yes, for ease you pray'd,
And God will hear—He only, I'm afraid."
"Peace! Susan, peace! pain ever follows sin."—
"Ah! then," thought Susan, "when will ours begin?
When reach'd his home, to what a cheerless fire
And chilling bed will those cold limbs retire!
Yet ragged, wretched as it is, that bed
Takes half the space of his contracted shed;
I saw the thorns beside the narrow grate
With straw collected in a putrid state:
There will he, kneeling, strive the fire to raise,
And that will warm him, rather than the blaze:
That sullen, smoky blaze, that cannot last
One moment after his attempt is past:
And I so warmly and so purely laid,
To sink to rest—indeed, I am afraid."
"Know you his conduct?"—"Yes indeed I know,
And how he wanders in the wind and snow;
Safe in our rooms the threatening storm we hear,
But he feels strongly what we faintly fear."
"Wilful was rich, and he the storm defied;
Wilful is poor, and must the storm abide,"
Said the stern lady; "'tis in vain to feel;
Go and prepare the chicken for our meal."

Yet Susan's words had made an impression on her. Of course she could never receive him again, but she would support him, she would send her maid to relieve his wants. Alas! it was too late! Susan found only a corpse, lying on the threshold of the hovel and watched over by the ass, " half dead himself, to see his master die."

Avarice and spite, failings of common minds, offer fewer subjects to our moralist than pride, which is often fatal to noble natures. The vanity of a young poet, who, on the strength of some ephemeral successes, thinks himself intended for a brilliant destiny, and succumbs in despair—such is the subject of *The Patron*,[1] a tale partly autobiographical. In the person of " John," the son of a bailiff, Crabbe describes to us the awakening of his own talent :

> In childhood feeble, he, for country air,
> Had long resided with a rustic pair ;
> All round whose room were doleful ballads, songs,
> Of lovers' sufferings and of ladies' wrongs ;
> Of peevish ghosts who came at dark midnight,
> For breach of promise guilty men to fright ;
> Love, marriage, murder, were the themes, with these,
> All that on idle, ardent spirits seize ;
> Robbers at land and pirates on the main ;
> Enchanters foiled, spells broken, giants slain.
> Legends of love, with tales of halls and bowers,
> Choice of rare songs, and garlands of choice flowers,
> And all the hungry mind without a choice devours.[2]

Too proud to join in the games of the village boys, John had taken up his pen by way of amusement, and was imitating his precious models :

> With the like fancy he could make his knight
> Slay half a host, and put the rest to flight ;
> With the like knowledge he could make him ride
> From isle to isle at Parthenissa's[3] side. . . .
> Such were the fruits of John's poetic toil—
> Weeds, but still proofs of vigour in the soil :
> He nothing purposed, but with vast delight,
> Let Fancy loose, and wonder'd at her flight :
> His notions of poetic worth were high,
> And of his own still-hoarded poetry ;—

---

[1] *Tales*, v.
[2] See above, p. 28.
[3] A novel by Roger Boyle (1664-5), the admirer of Mrs. Katherine Philips.

These to his father's house[1] he bore with pride,
A miser's treasure, in his room to hide;
Till spurr'd by glory, to a reading friend
He kindly show'd the sonnets he had penned:
With erring judgment, though with heart sincere,
That Friend exclaim'd, "These beauties must appear."
In magazines they claim'd their share of fame,
Though undistinguished by their author's name;
And with delight the young enthusiast found
The muse of Marcus[2] with applauses crown'd.

More alarmed than charmed at this, the bailiff sent his son to the University, "where," as he thought, "verse is honour'd, and where poets live." John studied with a view to ordination, took his degree, and returned home more desirous than ever of poetic fame:

A little time, and he should burst to light,
And admiration of the world excite;
And every friend, now cool and apt to blame
His fond pursuit, would wonder at his fame. . . .
Fame shall be mine; . . .
For me the maid shall leave her nobler state,
Happy to raise and share her poet's fate.

In the meanwhile he tried his hand at satire, took advantage of an election contested by a young sprig of nobility, Lord Frederick Damer, and an old squire, Sir Godfrey Ball, to support the former and riddle the latter with epigrams, and thus win not only extravagant praise and promises from "the noble lord," but even an invitation to "Brandon Hall," the successful candidate's country seat.

Anxious not to let himself be dazzled, John had, a few days before starting, practised alone in his room "an air composed, serene, and satisfied," and an easy tone in his replies. Many a time he had said to himself:

. . . Whatever the degree
A man obtains, what more than man is he?

And on his arrival he took care to repeat:

. . . This room is but a room;
Can aught we see the steady soul o'ercome?
Let me in all a manly firmness show,
Upheld by talents, and their value know.

[1] See above, p. 30, and p. 39, n. 3.
[2] See above, p. 55.

But on the approach of his host and hostess his courage
oozed out of him ; he felt abashed and confused ; and
in spite of the praise accorded to his verses,

> The poet found he was the bailiff's son.

In the same way, at Belvoir, Crabbe, the author of *The
Library* and a duke's chaplain, had been only a sort of
upper servant.[1] Like his hero, he had on the first day
ventured to break the ice by one or two remarks, and
in the evening, on thinking over his words, had come
to the conclusion that a little practice would enable
him to " converse with lords." But, while Crabbe had
observed the most discreet reserve, John indulges in
rash hopes. He has seen Lady Emma, the sister of his
noble friend—" a lovely creature, with majestic mien."
With a soft smile on her fair countenance, she has
praised the young poet in such a friendly way, she
has expressed such a winning frankness in her glance
and paid so much attention to her brother's guest,

> That so much beauty, join'd with speech so kind,
> Raised strong emotions in the poet's mind,

and Reason was unable to defend him against the
" sweet power " of this enchantress :

> Rash boy ! what hope thy frantic mind invades ?
> What love confuses, and what pride persuades ?
> Awake to truth ! shouldst thou deluded feed
> On hopes so groundless, thou art mad indeed.
> What say'st thou, wise one ? " that all-powerful Love
> Can fortune's strong impediments remove ;
> Nor is it strange that worth should wed to worth,
> The pride of genius with the pride of birth."
> While thou art dreaming thus, the Beauty spies
> Love in thy tremour, passion in thine eyes ;
> And with th' amusement pleased, of conquest vain,
> She seeks her pleasure, careless of thy pain ;
> She gives thee praise to humble and confound,
> Smiles to ensnare, and flatters thee to wound.
> Why has she said that in the lowest state
> The noble mind ensures a noble fate ?
> And why thy daring mind to glory call ?—
> That thou may'st dare and suffer, soar and fall.

[1] See above, p. 141.

But John no longer reasons, and each succeeding week enhances the charm of his illusion. The winter arrives, bringing with it the return of the family to town for the opening of Parliament. The date of their departure is fixed; the decisive moment approaches when the young poet is to know whether the "ladies" will invite him to accompany them or leave him to the cruel disappointment which, in spite of everything, he dreads:

> Cold grew the foggy morn, the day was brief,
> Loose on the cherry hung the crimson leaf;
> The dew dwelt ever on the herb; the woods
> Roar'd with strong blasts, with mighty showers the floods:
> All green was vanish'd, save of pine and yew,
> That still displayed their melancholy hue;
> Save the green holly with its berries red,
> And the green moss that o'er the gravel spread.[1]

One by one the carriages, with "mounted lackeys," draw up on the lawn in front of the house; the ladies make their appearance; John, trembling with apprehension, casts a despairing look at them, and then withdraws his eyes:

> Not with such speed, but he in other eyes
> With anguish read, "I pity, but despise—
> Unhappy boy! presumptuous scribbler!—you,
> To dream such dreams! be sober, and adieu!"

Next comes his noble patron, who deigns to address him as follows:

> "My good young friend,
> You know my views; upon my care depend;
> My hearty thanks to your good father pay,
> And be a student."

Then everything vanishes like a dream, leaving the poet to his despair, to the gloomy silence of empty apartments, to the offensive familiarity of underlings.[2] There was nothing for it but to return home that evening.

Ah! the distastefulness of a humdrum existence, of middle-class parsimony, of the homely fare of roast and boiled with hash between, washed down, on grand occasions, by a glass of port, to a man who has known the refinements of aristocratic life! Ah! the bitterness

---

[1] On this harmony between nature and the mind, cf. above, pp. 263-4.
[2] See above, p. 187, n. 1.

of having to forego the prospect of an ardently desired
happiness :

> The youth became abstracted, pensive, dull ;
> He utter'd nothing, though his heart was full. . . .
> Questions now vex'd his spirit, most from those
> Who are called friends, because they are not foes :
> " John ? " they would say ; he, starting, turn'd around ;
> " John ! " there was something shocking in the sound :
> Ill brooked he then the pert familiar phrase,
> The untaught freedom, and th' inquiring gaze ;
> Much was his temper touch'd, his spleen provoked,
> When ask'd how ladies talk'd, or walk'd, or look'd—
> " What said my lord of politics ? how spent
> He there his time ? and was he glad he went ? "

He was sickening with deferred hope. At last, after
an interval of three months, he was summoned to
London : perhaps his patron, remembering his promises, meant to give him a good living :

> Arrived in town, he early sought to know
> The fate such dubious friendship would bestow ;
> At a tall building trembling he appear'd,
> And his low rap was indistinctly heard ;
> A well-known servant came—" Awhile," said he,
> " Be pleased to wait ; my lord has company."
> Alone our hero sat, the news in hand ;
> Which though he read, he could not understand :
> Cold was the day ; in days so cold as these
> There needs a fire, where minds and bodies freeze ;
> The vast and echoing room, the polish'd grate,
> The crimson chairs, the sideboard with its plate ;
> The splendid sofa, which, though made for rest,
> He then had thought it freedom to have press'd ;
> The shining tables, curiously inlaid,
> Were all in comfortless proud style display'd ;
> And to the troubled feelings terror gave,
> That made the once-dear friend the sick'ning slave.

A long time elapsed :

> Was he forgotten ?   Thrice upon his ear
> Struck the loud clock, yet no relief was near :
> Each rattling carriage, and each thundering stroke
> On the loud door, the dream of fancy broke ;
> Oft as a servant chanced the way to come,
> " Brings he a message ? "   No ! he pass'd the room.
> At length 'tis certain : " Sir, you will attend
> At twelve on Thursday ! "   Thus the day had end.

Irritated by this long and fruitless suspense, John left the house in disgust. The coldness and silence of his reception seemed to him to "portend disgrace"; however, he kept the appointment:

> Punctual again the modest rap declared
> The youth attended; then was all prepared:
> For the same servant, by his lord's command,
> A paper offer'd to his trembling hand:
> "No more!" he cried: "disdains he to afford
> One kind expression, one consoling word?"[1]

The contents of the letter justified his forebodings. Lord Frederick wrote that there was no prospect of advancement for him in the Church, and that he would do well to accept an appointment in the custom-house, "on the London quays." Farewell then to "honour and ease"! In his humiliation the poet felt "how vain were his dreams"; accepting the monotonous work of a copying-clerk, he spent "heavy hours" amid "busy men," tried to learn his duties and to pass the required examination. All in vain: his wounded mind had become incapable of grasping anything, and when the questions were put to him, "silent he stood, but suffering without shame." Flying from the indulgence of his superiors and his odious occupation, he wandered aimlessly about for a time, was brought home again, and passed away, consoled by his faith and by the affection of his family.

But the vanity of a poet is an isolated case. Let us venture to generalise. Pride is a failing to which we are all liable. Its final overthrow can be compassed only if our reason, after rejecting all external assistance and claiming to be sole arbiter of conduct, issues vanquished from the struggle with the passions. Enlightened by our defeat, we shall recognise the frailty of our nature and no longer decline, in critical circumstances, the aid of religion. We shall agree with Crabbe that the moral conscience, if left to its own resources, is apt to fail ignominiously. And we shall understand the lesson of humility taught us by two of his tales, the most characteristic and the most profound of the whole series. In the first,[2] a well-to-

---

[1] In this passage (ll. 520-53) Crabbe forcibly describes his reception by Lord North in 1780 (see above, pp. 94-5).

[2] *Tales*, iii. : *The Gentleman Farmer*.

do individual named Gwyn has, at the age of forty-five, retired from business and taken to farming. A bachelor, able to do what he likes with his time and his money, he devotes himself to his three favourite pursuits—the care of his landed property, the adornment of his country seat, and the cultivation of his mind. He is a breeder of stock and judge at agricultural shows, and he introduces the latest mechanical improvements on his farms—the drill, the horse-hoe, and the thrashing machine. Proud of his wealth, he likes to display his luxury to his neighbours—his crimson curtains falling in "full festoons," his sofas rising in "bold elastic swell," his mirrors in gilded frames, his "glowing carpets and his coloured prints." Evidently, Gwyn is a personage. His individuality asserts itself vigorously. His independence has been drawn from the best sources—a treatise or two on metaphysics and logic, the "splendid book" composed by "my good lord of Bolingbroke," the writings of "the sage Tom Paine," the "florid page" of Gibbon, in short, all the sceptical literature: this is the food he provides for his mind. An enthusiastic disciple of the author of *The Rights of Man*, he becomes an uncompromising advocate of untrammelled liberty. He anticipates the speculative anarchists. He is a prose Shelley of country life. Listen to him holding forth to a circle of astonished and somewhat scandalised friends:

> ". . . It grieves me to the soul
> To see how man submits to man's control ;
> The coward never on himself relies,
> But to an equal for assistance flies ;
> Man yields to custom, as he bows to fate,
> In all things ruled—mind, body, and estate ;
> In pain, in sickness, we for cure apply
> To them we know not, and we know not why ;
> But that the creature has some jargon read,
> And got some Scotchman's system in his head ;
> Some grave impostor, who will health ensure,
> Long as your patience or your wealth endure. . . .
> Next, our affairs are govern'd ; buy or sell,
> Upon the deed, the law must fix its spell ;
> Whether we hire or let, we must have still
> The dubious aid of an attorney's skill. . . .
> But most it grieves me (friends alone are round),
> To see a man in priestly fetters bound ;

Guides to the soul, these friends of Heaven contrive,
Long as man lives, to keep his fears alive ;
Soon as an infant breathes, their rites begin ;
Who knows not sinning, must be freed from sin ;
Who needs no bond, must yet engage in vows ;
Who has no judgment, must a creed espouse :
Advanced in life, our boys are bound by rules,
Are catechised in churches, cloisters, schools,
And train'd in thraldom to be fit for tools :
The youth grown up, he now a partner needs,
And lo ! a priest, as soon as he succeeds.
What man of sense can marriage rites approve ?
What man of spirit can be bound to love ?
Forced to be kind ! compell'd to be sincere !
Do chains and fetters make companions dear ?
The ring, the vow, the witness, licence, prayers,
All parties known ! made public all affairs !
Such forms men suffer, and from these they date
A deed of love begun with all they hate :
Absurd ! that none the beaten road should shun,
But love to do what other dupes have done.
Well, now your priest has made you one of twain,
Look you for rest ?   Alas ! you look in vain ;
If sick, he comes ; you cannot die in peace,
Till he attends to witness your release ;
To vex your soul, and urge you to confess
The sins you feel, remember, or can guess ;
Nay, when departed, to your grave he goes —
But there indeed he hurts not your repose."

Doctors, attorneys, priests therefore are superfluous.
Gwyn will submit to no master : he will be "lord of
himself," with his own reason for sole mentor.

He has presumed too much on his strength. A year
after his arrival, a fair damsel named Rebecca has come
to "grace his pleasant mansion." "Sly, observant,
and still," she "watches his eye and waits upon his
will." Elegantly but simply dressed, gentle in manner,
"her smiles speak for her," as she is not a talker. She
and Gwyn lead a "sweet harmonious life" together ;
they are man and wife, except in point of form. True,
the lawfully married dames of the neighbourhood
turn up their noses and show their disapproval by
refusing to notice Gwyn's mistress. But he despises
such rudeness, and Rebecca goes to church every
Sunday, reads the Bible and pious books, condemns
her friend's free-thinking, which she styles "devils'

dreams," defends the priests, "of sin's destructive
power the foes," against him, and maintains that "they
are not such blockheads as he might suppose." In
order to humour this "kind fool," Gwyn gradually
gives up more and more of his "daring freedom."
Without abdicating, the "king" parts with a little
of his authority to the "queen." But, whether it is
the effect of the constraint which he puts upon himself or of his irregular position, he gets anxious and
out of sorts :

> She must perceive, of late he could not eat,
> And when he walk'd he trembled on his feet :
> He had forebodings, and he seem'd as one
> Stopp'd on the road, or threaten'd by a dun.

"Yes," answers Rebecca :

> "A case like yours must be no more delay'd ;
> You hate these doctors ; well ! but were a friend
> And doctor one, your fears would have an end ;
> My cousin Mollet—Scotland holds him now —
> Is above all men skilful, all allow ;
> Should he attend you, with his skill profound,
> You must be safe, and shortly would be sound."

The doctor is quite ready to stay in Gwyn's house and
to attend on him ; he even consents to remain for good
when the patient, unstrung by the "east wind," is
reluctant to let him depart. In concert with his fair
cousin, he puts our swaggerer about independence
under the strictest of régimes. "Doctor," asks Gwyn,
"may I ride to-day ?" Rebecca deigns to convey
her assent by a look. "I think you may," replies
Mollet ; "but wrap up well, and do not be out more
than forty minutes." Impossible to display a more
vigilant solicitude. Yet it is not enough. Gwyn's
soul is sick as well as his body. He lives in troublous times : the newspapers are full of invasions, of
epidemics, of famines, of "perils old and new"; neither
philosophy nor lighter literature is able to dispel the
melancholy of a mind preyed upon by an undefinable
distress. Perhaps, after all, he has taken a wrong
course. A spiritual guide is evidently necessary, but
this cannot be the clergyman of the parish. No!
Gwyn has "defied, insulted, slighted him," and
cannot accept his ministrations. He prefers a fanatical

Baptist, a certain Wisp, once an ostler, and now a
Nonconformist preacher, whose first care is to win
the favour of the lady of the house by making her a
lawful wife. "You must be married," he says to
Gwyn. "Name the day," he says to Rebecca :

> Lo ! now the change complete : the convert Gwyn
> Has sold his books, and has renounced his sin ;
> Mollet his body orders, Wisp his soul,
> And o'er his purse the lady takes control.

All the fine speeches of our "free-thinker" were so
much empty verbiage.[1]

In the pride of his intellect, man conceives an ideal
and rushes forth to realise it. Through weakness of
character, he stumbles at the start, and, falling from
one point to another, plunges into the abyss. This
is the case with "Edward Shore," the hero of the
second of these tales.[2] He is twenty years old, and
his success at the University seems to promise a
brilliant career. A "pure love of virtue" and of fame
is to direct his actions. He dreams of a perfectly
disinterested morality, dictated solely by the voice
of conscience. Those who are virtuous only through
fear of the policeman and of punishment in another
world seem to him contemptible :

> "Who needs a law that binds him not to steal,"
> Asked the young teacher, "can he rightly feel ?
> To curb the will, or arm in honour's cause,
> Or aid the weak, are these enforced by laws ?
> Should we a foul, ungenerous action dread,
> Because a law condemns th' adulterous bed ? "

---

[1] The fifteenth Tale, called *Advice ; or, The Squire and the Priest*,
presents some resemblance to this. A nobleman too much addicted to the
pleasures of this life is annoyed by the rebukes of the old rector of the
parish, and has made up his mind to present James, one of his nephews, and
still at the University, to the living as soon as it falls vacant. He hopes in
this way to secure a "compliant and easy " pastor. Unfortunately for him,
things turn out quite differently. Before leaving the University (of Cambridge,
no doubt), James has been converted to the evangelical ideas of a " preacher "
who recalls Charles Simeon. He takes possession of his benefice, astonishes
his parishioners by the fervour of his prayers and his extempore eloquence,
delivers in his uncle's presence a long sermon on "the power of grace," and
thus joins the ranks of the most dangerous "fanatics." Hence a violent
hostility between the squire and his nephew, divisions in the parish, and
misgivings in the mind of the young clergyman who reminds us faintly of
George Eliot's " Mr. Tryan," *Janet's Repentance*, ch. ii., in *Scenes of Clerical
Life* (cf. also *The Parish Register*, above, p. 231).

[2] *Tales*, xi. : *Edward Shore*.

"Reason" is to be his defence against all temptations:

> "While reason guides me, I shall walk aright,
> Nor need a steadier hand, or stronger light;
> Nor this in dread of awful threats, design'd
> For the weak spirit and the grov'ling mind;
> But that, engaged by thoughts and views sublime,
> I wage free war with grossness and with crime."

A rationalist in morality, he inclines to intellectual scepticism: not that he is wholly an infidel, but he applies to "his sovereign mistress," Reason, for the key to the great enigma, and doubts assail his "ardent mind" on all sides. Questions are raised which are beyond his powers and which remain insoluble. His friends, who are in doubt themselves, unsettle him more than they reassure him, and his mode of life tends to prolong this dangerous uncertainty. He would like to enter a profession, but cannot choose one: to be a lawyer, you must plead every cause, whether you approve it or not; physicians are "a doubting, dismal tribe"; divines are always pondering over "texts and disputations"; war leads to glory, "but there again he must the cause approve." There remains literature, and Shore has tried to write: he has planned "a serious drama," but finds its "gloom" tedious; has begun a "deep and solemn story," but is ashamed of his "ghosts" and has given it up; political controversy has attracted him for a moment, but here too he would have had to take a side, and his "vacillating mind" is averse to any decision.

In this hesitating mood, he has continued to stand aloof. He constantly visits a friend whose universal scepticism, in morals as well as metaphysics, turns everything into "a query or a jest," and considers the search for truth as wasted labour. When, with an eloquence born of his ardent zeal, Shore expatiates on "the soul's prowess and the subject-will, on virtue's beauty and on honour's force," his interlocutor replies, with a sarcastic smile:

> "My dear enthusiast! thou wilt change thy style,
> When man's delusions, errors, crimes, deceit,
> No more distress thee, and no longer cheat."

Now this friend, at the age of fifty, has just married "a young beauty," fresh from the schoolroom, to whom marriage means a prospect of "dainty food and costly dress," of pleasant walks in the country and of visits "when the roads are clean." She has "the vapours" occasionally, and is ill able to bear their long philosophical discussions, which make her head go round. To relieve her impatience, her husband stops talking, instals himself in his armchair, lets the young people play cards beside him, or even bids them take a walk while he goes on with his book:

> "Do, my kind Edward—I must take mine ease—
> Name my dear girl the planets and the trees:
> Tell her what warblers pour their evening song,
> What insects flutter, as you walk along;
> Teach her to fix her roving thoughts, to bind
> The wandering sense, and methodise the mind."

Edward willingly complies, and when the lesson is finished, they gaze on the setting sun:

> In silence saw the glowing landscape fade,
> Or, sitting, sang beneath the arbour's shade:
> Till rose the moon, and on each youthful face
> Shed a soft beauty and a dangerous grace.

On her return she finds her husband asleep, and, involuntarily comparing the two friends, finds—

> In one combined
> The nobler person and the richer mind:
> He wore no wig, no grisly beard was seen,
> And none beheld him careless or unclean,
> Or watched him sleeping.

Dangerous reflections at the age of twenty, especially when the husband is fifty and is obliged to absent himself on a visit to a sick friend. Left alone by this too trustful sceptic, the "youthful pair" feel a sudden constraint. Edward cannot look at his companion without embarrassment, but his rash daring forbids him to retreat:

> While she, with tuneless hand the jarring keys
> Touching, was not one moment at her ease:
> Now would she walk, and call her friendly guide,
> Now speak of rain, and cast her cloak aside;

Seize on a book, unconscious what she read,
And restless still to new resources fled;
Then laugh'd aloud, then tried to look serene;
And ever changed, and every change was seen. . . .

*   *   *   *   *

Painful it is to dwell on deeds of shame—
The trying day was past, another came;
The third was all remorse, confusion, dread,
And (all too late!) the fallen hero fled.

But there is no escape from the punishment which
his conscience has in store for him. To have had
such noble ambitions, such lofty thoughts, and to fall
so low! His degradation is all the deeper that he
has aimed so high. He does not repent, for remorse
would abate nothing of his shame; he cannot pray,
his faith being dead; he does not implore the aid
which the contrite sinner finds in the divine mercy;
his tears do not flow in a "penitential flood" towards
an offended God. In the tumult of his fierce passions
and his pride, he seeks only to deaden his feelings:
he has recourse to wine, "the opiate which grief
applies to guilt"; his own words intoxicate him as,
surrounded by his boon companions, he holds forth
on predestination, and, a fatalist for the needs of his
cause, declares that man, when he thinks himself the
arbiter of his own conduct and plans, is really the
victim of an illusion, the sport of "superior natures."
"It is idle," he exclaims, "to lament our actions, which
are fore-ordained." His "ardent mind" throws off all
restraint, and he plunges into debauchery. Misery lies
in wait for him:

Struck by new terrors, from his friends he fled,
And wept his woes upon a restless bed;
Retiring late, at early hour to rise,
With shrunken features, and with bloodshot eyes:
If sleep one moment closed the dismal view,
Fancy her terrors built upon the true:
And night and day had their alternate woes,
That baffled pleasure, and that mock'd repose;
Till to despair and anguish was consign'd
The wreck and ruin of a noble mind.

His extravagance brings him into a debtors' prison,
which he would never have left but for assistance from

a person, at first unknown, but afterwards ascertained
to be the friend whom he had so deeply wronged:

> This was too much; both aided and advised
> By one who shunn'd him, pitied, and despised:
> He bore it not; 'twas a deciding stroke,
> And on his reason like a torrent broke:
> In dreadful stillness he appear'd a while,
> With vacant horror and a ghastly smile;
> Then rose at once into the frantic rage
> That force controll'd not, nor could love assuage.

Like Hogarth's gambler,[1] he has to be chained on a
heap of straw, which he "spurns in disdain, while
laughing loudly at the clinking chain." By degrees,
however, this frenzy subsides and gives place to a
sort of childishness, "to playful folly and to causeless
joy." His words have no sense and his actions no
object:

> He drew fantastic figures on the wall,
> And gave some wild relation of them all;
> With brutal shape he join'd the human face,
> And idiot smiles approved the motley race.

As he is now harmless, he is restored to his home,
where he is taken care of by a young girl whom he
had formerly loved, and who, out of a "mild religious
pity," remains faithful to him:

> Kindly she chides his boyish flights, while he
> Will for a moment fix'd and pensive be;
> And as she trembling speaks, his lively eyes
> Explore her looks, he listens to her sighs;
> Charm'd by her voice, th' harmonious sounds invade
> His clouded mind, and for a time persuade:
> Like a pleased infant, who has newly caught
> From the maternal glance a gleam of thought,
> He stands enrapt, the half-known voice to hear,
> And starts, half-conscious, at the falling tear.
>
> Rarely from town, nor then unwatch'd, he goes,
> In darker mood, as if to hide his woes;
> Returning soon, he with impatience seeks
> His youthful friends, and shouts, and sings, and speaks;
> Speaks a wild speech with action all as wild—
> The children's leader, and himself a child;

---

[1] *The Rake's Progress*, plate viii.

He spins a top, or, at their bidding, bends
His back, while o'er it leap his laughing friends ;
Simple and weak, he acts the boy once more,
And heedless children call him " Silly Shore." [1]

In varying degrees, a common element is to be found in the foregoing tales : the pathos of disenchantment. There is not one of their suffering heroes but has his mind shattered by the failure of his hopes. The poet of disillusion, Crabbe makes it the mainspring of his tragic stories. Sometimes his characters carry the cause of their fall within them : this is the case with all his proud subjects, with John, the bailiff's son, with Gwyn, with Edward Shore. Between the perfection of which they dreamed and their degradation such a terrible contrast breaks forth that they are over-whelmed by it. Others succumb not so much to their own vices as to the selfishness of friends or relations who might have helped or comforted them. This is the case with Rupert, counting on Dinah's affection after his return from the colonies, of George, the disabled sailor, looking forward to a home under his brother's roof, of Paul, the merchant, begging alms

[1] In the eighth tale, under the title of *The Mother*, will be found a study of feminine pride. Dorothea, a rich heiress and spoilt child, is married and has two daughters, one whom the poet calls "The Beauty," petted by her mother, the other named "Lucy," and almost despised for her unassumingness. She is therefore glad to be a companion to an aunt who sends for her. A clergyman, the younger brother of a neighbouring squire, is attracted by the gentleness and the virtues of the affectionate Lucy, who returns his love. Dorothea has just given her consent to the proposed alliance when "The Beauty" dies on the eve of making a brilliant match. Lucy, recalled to her mother, has more ambitious views thrust upon her : the young clergyman, twice repulsed by the arrogant Dorothea, forgets the affection of Lucy, who dies of grief on hearing that she is forsaken. And Dorothea continues to reign in the splendour of her somewhat faded beauty.

The twenty-first tale, *The Learned Boy*, is an uninteresting story of a certain Stephen Jones, the son of a farmer, who gets a clerkship in London, is led astray by his companions, like Abel Keene, and is ordered home by his anxious father. As soon as he arrives at the farm, Stephen begins to air his infidel views, and receives a sound whipping from the vigorous arm of the old man, who makes him abjure his heresies and burn his favourite authors, a pack of "scoundrelly" atheists. It is curious that this tale, one of the least happy, is, like *The Convert*, taken from literature and not from real life. The original of it is No. 108 of *The Tatler*, an article by Addison, in which a "gentleman" administers to his son the treatment undergone by Stephen Jones ("I remember a young gentleman," etc.). The curious reader may be referred to a discussion which Crabbe's story started in the pages of *Notes and Queries* on the legitimacy of corporal punishment (*Notes and Queries*, 7th series, vol. vii. pp. 214 and 273 ; vol. viii. pp. 116 and 298 ; vol. ix. p. 71). The controversy, a very fragmentary one, lasted from March 16th, 1889, to January 25th, 1890.

from an unrelenting wife—all of them ruined by the
unkindness of those whom they have loved best.
And as if the description of their unhappiness and
despair was not enough to touch us, Crabbe has
recourse to a second device ; he introduces alongside
his heroes, who are always more or less blameworthy,
an accessory but highly attractive figure, a weak child
or a compassionate woman, who, sharing and reflecting
the emotion of the reader, enhances it by giving utterance to it. We need only recall the part played by
Susan in *Resentment*, by little George in *The Brothers*,
and, in *Edward Shore*, by his once beloved Anna.[1]
The pathos of grief is thus reinforced by that of pity.

II

LET us suppose that, instead of being a fatal passion,
pride takes the form of mere boasting, and leads only
to amusing mishaps, then tragedy will be succeeded by
comedy, and we shall have the two humorous tales which
Crabbe has called *The Wager* and *The Frank Courtship*.

There are men who in marrying look out for a
partner to whom they can confide their cares and
a portion of their authority. Clubb,[2] an easy-going
and successful tradesman, belongs to this category.
There are others who wish to reign supreme in their
own household and make their wife a humble slave :
this is the view of Counter, Clubb's friend and partner.
He would never have chosen, as Clubb has done, a
wife who " has no meekness and is seldom mute,"
who is " quick to anger," more disposed to command
than to obey, who, if she has her way, acquits herself
very well, but is quite ready to take it if it is refused her.
No, he has preferred a wife of a very different type :

> . . . A young complying maid,
> A tender creature, full of fears as charms,
> A beauteous nursling from its mother's arms ;
> A soft sweet blossom, such as men must love,
> But to preserve must keep it in a stove.

[1] A similar effect had already been produced by Crabbe in the story of the
consumptive sailor and his sweetheart " Sally," who nurses him tenderly on
his deathbed. This passage of letter ii. of *The Borough* was much admired.

[2] *Tales*, xviii. : *The Wager*. As the quotations at the head of this tale
indicate, the first idea of it was borrowed from scene 2 of act v. of *The
Taming of the Shrew*, in which Petruchio makes himself obeyed at once by
Katharina, while the other wives are not nearly so docile.

He is proud of his choice. What husband could be happier?

> Raise but the voice, and this fair creature shook, . . .
> Chide, and she melted into floods of tears . . .
> Say but his will, no question would she ask ;
> She sought no reasons, no affairs she knew,
> Of business spoke not, and had nought to do.

At the club, where the two partners meet their neighbours of an evening, Counter is never weary of vaunting his happiness and his independence ; sometimes even, after a glass of wine, he turns towards his friend, and in a "triumphant" tone banters him for having parted so easily with his liberty.

This boastfulness at last exhausts Clubb's patience. He has long been puzzled by his partner's "teasing" mood, and half suspects its cause :

> This plainly proves him not at perfect ease,
> For felt he pleasure, he would wish to please.
> These triumphs here for some regrets atone—
> Men who are bless'd let other men alone.

Was it not strange that Counter should leave his friends so early every evening, alleging his Juliet's "tender nerves and the attention such a wife deserves"? Clubb resolved to penetrate this mystery. One day, when Counter's swagger had exasperated him more than usual, he broke out :

> " By Heaven ! " said Clubb, " excuse me if I swear,
> I'll bet a hundred guineas, if he dare,
> That uncontroll'd I will such freedoms take
> That he will fear to equal—there's my stake.

A visit to Newmarket Races is agreed on, whichever comes back first or refuses to start to lose the bet.

To make this fine plan was easy enough, but its execution did not prove so simple. What would the two wives think of it?

> " 'Twas wrong," thought Counter, " and will grieve my
>   love ; "
> " 'Twas wrong," thought Clubb, " my wife will not
>   approve :
> But friends were present ; I must try the thing,
> Or with my folly half the town will ring."

His wife, far from wishing to keep him at home, urges him to prolong his absence if necessary :

> " The husband's honour is the woman's pride :
> If I in trifles be the wilful wife,
> Still for your credit I would lose my life. . . .
> . . . Let the blockheads learn
> That though a wife may sometimes wish to rule,
> She would not make th' indulgent man a fool ;
> I would at times advise—but idle they
> Who think th' assenting husband *must* obey."

Very different was the behaviour of the gentle Juliet. In vain did Counter use the tenderest, the most caressing language to prepare her for his departure; in vain did he assert that " business " and not the races took him to Newmarket :

> Awhile the tender creature look'd dismay'd,
> Then floods of tears the call of grief obey'd :—
> " She an objection ! No !" she sobb'd, "not one ;
> Her work was finish'd and her race was run ;
> For die she must, indeed she would not live
> A week alone, for all the world could give ;
> He too must die in that same wicked place ;
> It always happen'd—was a common case ;
> Among those horrid horses, jockeys, crowds,
> 'Twas certain death—they might bespeak their shrouds ;
> He would attempt a race, be sure to fall,—
> And she expire with terror—that was all :
> With love like hers she was indeed unfit
> To bear such horrors, but she must submit."

" And the thousand pounds," rejoined Counter, inventing a new fib, " must I stay here and lose them ? "

> " Go then, my love ! it is a monstrous sum,
> Worth twenty wives—go, love ! and I am dumb ;
> Nor be displeased—had I the power to live,
> You might be angry, now you must forgive :
> Alas ! I faint—ah ! cruel—there's no need
> Of wounds or fevers—this has done the deed."

And Counter had to give way, to humiliate himself before Clubb, to write to him, on the very day fixed for the start, a letter in which he declined the journey, and added that he had been wrong in speaking of " submission and control," and that such "follies" should not " vex their future peace." He had found

out that the tearful weakness of a child may be more
tyrannical than the firmness of a serious and sensible
woman, and that the most autocratic man cannot
always do as he likes.

The next tale introduces us to a personage "six
feet high," who "looked six inches higher," a man
"erect, morose, determined, solemn, slow." His name
is "Jonas Kindred."[1] A vendor of hops and malt,
of coals and corn, he belongs to the sect of the
Independents, the rigid Puritans who in those days,
it would appear, refused to intermarry with members
of the Church of England. He rules his family with a
rod of iron:

> His faithful spouse, when Jonas was not by,
> Had a firm presence and a steady eye ;
> But with her husband dropp'd her look and tone,
> And Jonas ruled unquestion'd and alone.
> He read, and oft would quote the sacred words,
> How pious husbands of their wives were lords ;
> Himself he view'd with undisguised respect,
> And never pardon'd freedom or neglect.

Their life is precision itself : they rise early, pray and
sing hymns for an hour, and then enjoy a "plain but
plenteous " meal :

> Neat was their house ; each table, chair, and stool,
> Stood in its place, or moving moved by rule ;
> No lively print or picture graced the room ;
> A plain brown paper lent its decent gloom.

The only contrast to this monotony is a china service
standing in a corner and a portrait of the hero revered
by the Independents, of "the bold Protector of a
conquer'd land," of the stern and strong-featured
Cromwell,

> Drawn in that look with which he wept and swore,
> Turn'd out the Members, and made fast the door.

Remembering his deeds, the friends of the house,
when they meet in that austere parlour, lament the
nation's guilt,

> That would not long endure
> The reign of men so modest and so pure. . . .
> The times were bad ; the Saints had ceased to reign !
> A few yet lived, to languish and to mourn
> For good old manners never to return.

[1] *Tales*, vi. : *The Frank Courtship*.

Jonas and his co-religionists have the pessimism of beaten parties.

The family which is growing up under this roof is composed of several boys and a girl, Jonas's favourite child, baptised "Sybil" in not very Christian fashion. Vivacious and winning, she has managed from her earliest years to dispel her father's gloom and to obtain all she wishes by smiles or tears. Since then she has been entrusted to the care of a widowed aunt. Of a lively turn already, in spite of her family circle, Sybil has been transplanted into surroundings which are favourable to gaiety. The aunt, in fact, by no means shares Jonas's gloomy temper. She is "rich and frugal," two qualities which ensure her the obliging attentions of her brother and future heir. But, devoid of all Puritan stiffness, she "resides in a lively place," is very fond of playing whist, and has no prejudice against the Church or Churchmen. She takes Sybil into society, and the latter, enraptured with her new liberty, "feels the pure pleasure of the opening mind." The aunt and the niece understand each other perfectly: on three occasions they have paid Jonas a visit, and have feigned a concerted gravity in his house. When she appeared again before her father,

> In all the bloom and beauty of sixteen,
> He gazed admiring ;—she with visage prim,
> Glanced an arch look of gravity on him ;
> For she was gay at heart, but wore disguise,
> And stood a vestal in her father's eyes,
> Pure, pensive, simple, sad ; the damsel's heart,
> When Jonas praised, reproved her for the part ;
> For Sybil, fond of pleasure, gay and light,
> Had still a secret bias to the right ;
> Vain as she was—and flattery made her vain—
> Her simulation gave her bosom pain.

What will happen when Puritan despotism tries to quell this fascinating coquette ? It is bound to fail, unless the rebel falls in with its views.

Three years have elapsed, and a husband has been found for Sybil, a young Puritan, a good match in point of fortune and character. Jonas has written a rather mysterious letter, sending for his daughter, and the aunt has reluctantly had to part

from her niece. Sybil has left her chaperon without
overmuch regret, for—

> . . . In the young there lives a love of change,
> And to the easy they prefer the strange !
> Then, too, the joys she once pursued with zeal,
> From whist and visits sprung, she ceased to feel :
> When with the matrons Sybil first sat down,
> To cut for partners and to stake her crown,
> This to the youthful maid preferment seem'd,
> Who thought what woman she was then esteem'd ;
> But in few years, when she perceived, indeed,
> The real woman to the girl succeed,
> No longer tricks and honours fill'd her mind,
> But other feelings, not so well defined ;
> She then reluctant grew, and thought it hard
> To sit and ponder o'er an ugly card ;
> Rather the nut-tree shade the nymph preferred,
> Pleased with the pensive gloom and evening bird ;
> Thither, from company retired, she took
> The silent walk, or read the fav'rite book.

On her return home she proves a source of delight
and of anxiety to her parents. Her father is charmed
with her beauty and her talents, but alarmed by her
high spirits and her freedom of language, so out of
keeping with maidenly reserve. Jonas fears that
his " sinful wretch " of a sister has corrupted the
impressionable mind of his " darling child ": she seems
to know far too much, and all her knowledge is used
for display :

> Too gay her dress, like theirs who idly dote
> On a young coxcomb, or a coxcomb's coat ;
> In foolish spirits when our friends appear,
> And vainly grave when not a man is near !

" The maid is virtuous," says her mother :

> . . . Quoth he,
> " Let her give proof, by acting virtuously :
> Is it in gaping when the Elders pray ?
> In reading nonsense half a summer's day ?
> In these mock forms that she delights to trace,
> Or her loud laughs in Hezekiah's face ?
> She—O Susannah !—to the world belongs ;
> She loves the follies of its idle throngs,
> And reads soft tales of love, and sings love's softening songs."

These tendencies must be counteracted without delay, by threats in the first instance. One day therefore the grave Jonas takes his daughter aside,

> Demanding sternly, "Wilt thou be a bride?"
> She answer'd, calling up an air sedate,
> "I have not vow'd against the holy state."
> "No folly, Sybil," said the parent; "know
> What to their parents virtuous maidens owe:
> A worthy, wealthy youth whom I approve,
> Must thou prepare to honour and to love.
> Formal to thee his air and dress may seem,
> But the good youth is worthy of esteem:
> Shouldst thou with rudeness treat him, of disdain
> Should he with justice or of slight complain,
> Or of one taunting speech give certain proof,
> Girl! I reject thee from my sober roof."

> "My aunt," said Sybil, "will with pride protect
> One whom a father can for this reject;
> Nor shall a formal, rigid, soul-less boy
> My manners alter, or my views destroy."

Thereupon Jonas raises his arms to heaven, utters "something 'twixt a groan and sigh," and hands Sybil over to her mother, who has recourse to persuasion, threats being of no avail:

> "Hear me," she said; "incline thy heart, my child,
> And fix thy fancy on a man so mild:
> Thy father, Sybil, never could be moved
> By one who loved him, or by one he loved.
> Union like ours is but a bargain made
> By slave and tyrant—he will be obey'd;
> Then calls the quiet, comfort—but thy youth,
> Is mild by nature, and as frank as truth."

> "But will he love?" said Sybil.   "I am told
> That these mild creatures are by nature cold;
> "I must be loved," she added, "I must see
> The man in terrors who aspires to me;
> At my forbidding frown his heart must ache,
> His tongue must falter, and his frame must shake:
> And if I grant him at my feet to kneel,
> What trembling, fearful pleasure must he feel,
> Nay, such the raptures that my smiles inspire,
> That reason's self must for a time retire."

"Alas! for good Josiah," said the dame,
"These wicked thoughts would fill his soul with shame;
He kneel and tremble at a thing of dust!
He cannot, child":—the child replied, "He must."

Josiah and Sybil are at last introduced to each other
by her father, who leads him in and then retires:

The couple gazed—were silent; and the maid
Look'd in his face, to make the man afraid;
The man, unmoved, upon the maiden cast
A steady view—so salutation pass'd:
But in this instant Sybil's eye had seen
The tall fair person, and the still staid mien;
The glow that temp'rance o'er the cheek had spread,
Where the soft down half veil'd the purest red;
And the serene deportment that proclaim'd
A heart unspotted and a life unblamed:
But then with these she saw attire too plain,
The pale brown coat, though worn without a stain
The formal air, and something of the pride
That indicates the wealth it seems to hide;
And looks that were not, she conceived, exempt
From a proud pity, or a sly contempt.

Josiah's eyes had their employment too,
Engaged and soften'd by so bright a view;
A fair and meaning face, an eye of fire,
That check'd the bold, and made the free retire:
But then with these he mark'd the studied dress
And lofty air, that scorn or pride express;
With that insidious look, that seem'd to hide
In an affected smile the scorn and pride;
And if his mind the virgin's meaning caught,
He saw a foe with treacherous purpose fraught—
Captive the heart to take, and to reject it, caught.

Silent they sat—thought Sybil, that he seeks
Something no doubt; I wonder if he speaks:
Scarcely she wonder'd, when these accents fell
Slow in her ear—"Fair maiden, art thou well?"
"Art thou physician?" she replied; "my hand,
My pulse, at least shall be at thy command."

She said—and saw, surprised, Josiah kneel,
And give his lips the offer'd pulse to feel;
The rosy colour rising in her cheek,
Seem'd that surprise unmix'd with wrath to speak;
Then sternness she assumed, and—"Doctor, tell;
Thy words cannot alarm me—am I well?"

"Thou art," said he, "and yet thy dress so light,
I do conceive, some danger must excite ;"
"In whom?" said Sybil, with a look demure:
"In more," said he, "than I expect to cure ;—
I, in thy light luxuriant robe, behold
Want and excess, abounding and yet cold ;
Here needed, there display'd, in many a wanton fold :
Both health and beauty, learned authors show,
From a just medium in our clothing flow."

"Proceed, good doctor ; if so great my need,
What is thy fee? Good doctor! pray proceed."

"Large is my fee, fair lady, but I take
None till some progress in my cure I make :
Thou hast disease, fair maiden ; thou art vain ;
Within that face sit insult and disdain ;
Thou art enamour'd of thyself ; my art
Can see the naughty malice of thy heart :
With a strong pleasure would thy bosom move,
Were I to own thy power, and ask thy love ;
And such thy beauty, damsel, that I might
But for thy pride, feel danger in thy sight,
And lose my present peace in dreams of vain delight."

"And can thy patients," said the nymph, "endure
Physic like this, and will it work a cure?"

"Such is my hope, fair damsel ; thou, I find,
Hast the true tokens of a noble mind ;
But the world wins thee, Sybil, and thy joys
Are placed in trifles, fashions, follies, toys ;
Thou hast sought pleasure in the world around,
That in thine own pure bosom should be found ;
Did all that world admire thee, praise and love,
Could it the least of nature's pains remove?
Could it for errors, follies, sins, atone,
Or give thee comfort, thoughtful and alone?
It has, believe me, maid, no power to charm
Thy soul from sorrow, or thy flesh from harm :
Turn then, fair creature, from a world of sin,
And seek the jewel happiness within."

"Speak'st thou at meeting?" said the nymph, "thy speech
Is that of mortal very prone to teach ;
But would'st thou, doctor, from the patient learn
Thine own disease?—The cure is thy concern."

"Yea, with good will."—"Then know 'tis thy complaint,
That for a sinner thou'rt too much a saint;
Hast too much show of the sedate and pure,
And without cause art formal and demure:
This makes a man unsocial, unpolite;
Odious when wrong, and insolent if right.
Thou may'st be good, but why should goodness be
Wrapt in a garb of such formality?
Thy person well might please a damsel's eye,
In decent habit with a scarlet dye;[1]
But, jest apart—what virtue can'st thou trace
In that broad brim that hides thy sober face?
Does that long-skirted drab, that over-nice
And formal clothing, prove a scorn of vice?
Then for thine accent—what in sound can be
So void of grace as dull monotony?
Love has a thousand varied notes to move
The human heart:—thou may'st not speak of love
Till thou hast cast thy formal ways aside,
And those becoming youth and nature tried:
Not till exterior freedom, spirit, ease,
Prove it thy study and delight to please;
Not till these follies meet thy just disdain,
While yet thy virtues and thy worth remain."

"This is severe!—Oh maiden, wilt not thou
Something for habits, manners, modes allow?"
"Yes, but allowing much, I much require,
In my behalf, for manners, modes, attire!"

"True, lovely Sybil; and, this point agreed,
Let me to those of greater weight proceed:
Thy father!"—"Nay," she quickly interposed,
"Good doctor, here our conference is closed!"

Josiah, however, has won the day: he has found favour in the eyes of Sybil, who is ready to surrender at the first summons. Her father comes to upbraid her for the reception which she has given to her suitor:

"Unhappy child! what labour will it cost
To win him back!"—"I do not think him lost."
"Courts he then (trifler!) insult and disdain?"
"No; but from these he courts me to refrain."
"Then, hear me, Sybil: should Josiah leave
Thy father's house?"—"My father's child would grieve."

[1] See above, p. 323, n. 4.

" That is of grace, and if he come again
To speak of love ? "—" I might from grief refrain."
"Then wilt thou, daughter, our design embrace ? "
" Can I resist it, if it be of grace ? "
" Dear child ! in three plain words thy mind express :
Wilt thou have this good youth ? "—" Dear father ! yes."

At once realistic and satirical, Crabbe was bound
to attain to humour, if only now and again.   Whether
he was dealing with the external world or with the
workings of the mind, he knew how to describe the
concrete, and to describe it ironically.[1]   His humour
is, like his pathos, one of the aspects of the poetry of
disillusion.   The heroes of the two foregoing tales are
baffled autocrats : Counter, who aspires to complete
independence and to omnipotence in married life, is
forced to comply with his wife's caprices ; Jonas, the
Puritan, lord and master of his spouse, is foiled and
defied by his daughter.   Is it not entertaining to watch
the stupefaction of this godly man, when Sybil, who
has been brought up in the right principles, returns
transformed into a wide-awake and argumentative
woman of the world ?   He has cherished a little
serpent then in his bosom ?   And the clever dialogue
where, in a form as amusing as it is paradoxical,
Josiah and Sybil pick each other to pieces with
perfect frankness and clear-sightedness, does it not
owe its humorous effect to the struggle between
these two characters which try to get the mastery
of each other, without succeeding ?   Neither the
wilful young girl, who wants to make her suitor
"tremble," nor the opinionated suitor, convinced of
his moral superiority and too eager to prove it, wins
the victory : their conversation ends in an amicable
compromise.   "You see," Crabbe appears to say to
them, "that your illusions were a long way from
the reality.   You had too good an opinion of yourselves, and you have had to lower it.   You thought
you could control events, and events have controlled
you.   In comparing your fanciful aspirations and
your laughable failure, in confronting your idealism
with my realism, I obtain a contrast which gives

[1] I adopt here the very useful definition of humour given by M. Angellier,
in his work on Burns (vol. ii. p. 116) : " Ridicule in the observation or the
direct and concrete representation of life, or by means of them."

birth to irony."[1]   And that is the essential element
of Crabbe's satirical humour.   He teaches his presumptuous characters the severe lesson of the reality,
and he smiles at their confusion.

III

HAPPINESS is obtainable, concludes our moralist,
only by dint of prudence and moderation.   It cannot
be perfect, and whoever hopes to realise all his
ambitions and all his wishes courts a cruel disappointment.   We must know how to limit our aspirations
and to resign ourselves to the inevitable imperfection
of this world.   We must also know how to steer our
course.   Life is a hurly-burly of passions rising on all
sides, from ourselves and from others.   If we plunge
heedlessly into the fray, we run the risk of succumbing
to unforeseen attacks.   The enemy is within us and
outside us ; he lies in wait for us, and assails us at
every step : how are we to reach the goal safe and
sound, if we do not observe the utmost wariness ?
Let us try to keep cool, like the experienced player
who controls his impulses and regulates the force
of each stroke.   Let us curb our evil instincts and
protect ourselves against those of others, and we shall
have some chance of obtaining a relative felicity.   Let
us not ask for more.   Happiness comes to the wise
man who is content with a little.

Instead of autocrats like Counter and Jonas, let us
take an indulgent man, the yeoman Stafford.[2]   After

---

[1] As it would seem that irony always springs from a contrast, clearly perceived or merely implied, the definition of the particular humour of an author
will result not only from the distinctive features of his realism, but also from
the nature of the terms of the contrast from which the irony proceeds.
Cervantes, for instance, with unrivalled inventiveness and exuberance, opposes
the visionary idealism of his knight to the realism personified in Sancho Panza ;
to the physical or moral greatness of man (Gulliver at Lilliput—the
Houyhnhnms) Swift opposes his infinite physical or moral littleness (Gulliver
at Brobdingnag—the Yahoos), without being able to reconcile these two
contraries—whence the bitterness which characterises his humour.   An unstable
compound of two hostile natures, man to him is only a negative quantity.   In
certain writers, on the other hand, the reconciliation has been effected, and
their humour is of a satisfied and cheerful kind.   They like to indulge in
sentiment ; in a character which is fundamentally amiable and good, they let
us see a few failings or foibles, and their irony is kindly and playful (Addison,
Goldsmith, Lamb, and Jean Paul).   Carlyle ardently desired this equilibrium,
but never permanently achieved it.

[2] *Tales,* xvi. : *The Confidant.*

thirty years of hard toil, he has inherited, late in life, a nice fortune, and has married the "young and lovely" Anna, the companion to the lady of the hall. A slender shape and small features, bright eyes and rosy cheeks, graceful, easy, and unaffected manners— these are the charms which he admires in his wife. She, on her side, has found under his roof an independent and happy existence which she could never have hoped for. The daughter of a small official who died in debt, she had been obliged, on two occasions, to fly from the compromising attentions of the husband or the son of her successive protectresses, and to take refuge with her third and last mistress, who had given her a quiet life, but not liberty. Her almost slavish duties of secretary, of pianist, of reader, of constant loser at whist, "harassed" sometimes her body and sometimes her mind, and Stafford, seeing her thus humiliated and overworked, had at first pitied her and then loved her for her modesty, her beauty, her talents, and her unblemished reputation. He and her employer were, in fact, ignorant of a regrettable episode in Anna's past. When she was about fifteen, in her father's lifetime, she had made the acquaintance of an "Irish captain" twice her own age, and had listened too confidingly to his deceptive promises. Accompanied by an intimate friend, her "dear Eliza," she had gone to London to "hide her disgrace," had given birth to a child, which died soon afterwards, and this solitary fault had left no traces behind it, except a feeling of remorse in the mind of Anna and a valued reminiscence in that of her "confidant."

Years have passed, bringing to one the happiness of wedded life, to the other misfortunes. Eliza has also married, but has been left a widow and penniless, with a child to bring up. To a selfish and "vulgar" woman of her type, the temptation is irresistible : she will make use of the dread secret and extort money from her friend. One day, then, Anna receives a letter which she reads with terror. It is from Eliza, who complains of her poverty, of the indifference of her relations, and in a threatening tone demands assistance from the friend who had once been under an obligation to her. This strangely worded request astonishes Stafford, to whom Anna feels bound to show the letter :

" Anna, your friend has not a friendly style :
Say, where could you with this fair lady dwell,
Who boasts of secrets that she scorns to tell ? "
" At school," she answer'd ; he " At school ! " replied ;
" Nay, then I know the secrets you would hide ;
Some early longings these, without dispute,
Some youthful gaspings for forbidden fruit :
Why so disorder'd, love ?—are such the crimes
That give us sorrow in our graver times ?
Come, take a present for your friend, and rest
In perfect peace—you find you are confess'd."

Of course, Eliza does not value her silence so cheaply.
One, two, three begging letters follow one another,
each more imperious than the last. And, death having
rid her of her child, she makes her appearance one
evening, determined to thrust herself upon Stafford
and his wife.

Anna received her with an anxious mind,
And meeting whisper'd, " Is Eliza kind ? "
Reserved and cool the husband sought to prove
The depth and force of this mysterious love.
To nought that pass'd between this stranger-friend
And his meek partner seem'd he to attend ;
But, anxious, listen'd to the lightest word
That might some knowledge of his guest afford ;
And learn the reason one to him so dear
Should feel such fondness, yet betray such fear.

Soon he perceived this uninvited guest,
Unwelcome too, a sovereign power possess'd ;
Lofty she was and careless, while the meek
And humbled Anna was afraid to speak :
As mute she listen'd with a painful smile,
Her friend sat laughing, and at ease the while,
Telling her idle tales with all the glee
Of careless and unfeeling levity.
With calm good sense he knew his wife endued,
And now with wounded pride her conduct view'd ;
Her speech was low, her every look convey'd—
" I am a slave, subservient and afraid."
All trace of comfort vanish'd ; if she spoke,
The noisy friend upon her purpose broke,
To her remarks with insolence replied,
And her assertions doubted or denied :
While the meek Anna like an infant shook,
Woe-struck and trembling at the serpent's look.

> " There is," said Stafford, " yes, there is a cause—
> This creature frights her, overpowers, and awes."
> Six weeks had pass'd—" In truth, my love, this friend
> Has liberal notions ; what does she intend ?
> Without a hint she came, and will she stay
> Till she receives a hint to go away ?"
>
> Confused the wife replied, in spite of truth,
> " I love the dear companion of my youth."
> " 'Tis well," said Stafford ; " then your loves renew :
> Trust me, your rivals, Anna, will be few."

This was said playfully, but Anna, in her anxiety, can derive no comfort from a jest. She sleeps badly, sighs in her dreams, "murmurs forth her anguish," and calls for death; her sunken eyes, slow gait, and pallid cheeks betray her distress; she hardly ventures to speak.

Stafford is determined to know the truth. Near the handsome room occupied by Eliza is a small study to which he sometimes retires. An attentive ear can catch through the partition what is said on the other side. One day the yeoman overhears an animated conversation between Anna and her friend. " There was a time," says the latter,

> " When I, a tender maid,
> Flew at a call, and your desires obey'd ;
> A very mother to the child became,
> Consoled your sorrow, and conceal'd your shame ;
> But now, grown rich and happy, from the door
> You thrust a bosom-friend, despised and poor ;
> That child alive, its mother might have known
> The hard, ungrateful spirit she has shown."
>
> Here paused the guest, and Anna cried at length—
> " You try me, cruel friend ! beyond my strength,
> Would I had been beside my infant laid,
> Where none would vex me, threaten or upbraid !"

Stafford understands everything : irritated at first, he is gradually moved by pity for his wife, more sinned against than sinning. He remembers " his own failings," which " teach him to be kind," and his affection for Anna inclines him to pardon her. He determines that peace shall be restored to his household, and that the intruder shall receive a merited lesson this very day. In the evening, at the time when he generally reads aloud, he invents an apologue imitated from the

Arabian Nights: The caliph Haroun Alraschid, he says, had entrusted the custody of a valuable orchard to two of his pages: woe betide all those who should be found poaching there! Now, one of these two boys, named Osmyn, succumbed to the temptation himself:

> The tempting beauty sparkling in the sun
> Charm'd his young sense—he ate, and was undone.

No one had seen him but his companion, who promised to keep the secret if he were paid for it, and by repeated threats extorted all the offender's money. But one day the caliph, who was visiting his garden, happened to be within earshot of the two pages, and discovered their secret. At first he felt indignant, then his wrath gave place to compassion, for he pictured the agony which Osmyn had suffered, and the "bitter sorrow" with which the culprit had expiated his fault. He generously pardoned him, restored him to favour, and as for "the traitor-friend, whom pains nor prayers could move," he dismissed him from his service and banished him. The allusion was obvious and was grasped at once. Eliza fled before daybreak on the following morning. Stafford, by subduing his pride, had succeeded in preserving Anna's happiness and his own.[1]

[1] If *The Parting Hour* is excepted (see next page), *The Confidant* appears to be the only one of Crabbe's *Tales* which has left a posterity. In a letter from Charles Lamb to Bernard Barton (August 10th, 1827) we read the following words: "I am trying my hand at a drama, in two acts, founded on Crabbe's *Confidant (mutatis mutandis)*" (*Lamb's Letters*, ed. by Talfourd and Hazlitt, Bohn's Libraries). This drama, or rather this serious comedy, compressed into one act with seven scenes, and written in blank verse on the Elizabethan model, was offered to Charles Kemble, of Covent Garden, on September 27th, 1827, and refused by him. It appeared in *Blackwood's Magazine* in December 1828, under the title of *The Wife's Trial*. Stafford is called "Mr. Selby, a Wiltshire gentleman," Anna figures as "Katherine," and Eliza as "Mrs. Frampton, a widow." But as Anna's "fault" has always seemed "unpleasing" to English critics (see Jeffrey, and again in modern days Canon Ainger, *Life of Crabbe*, p. 145), Lamb conceived the singular idea of transforming this "fault" into a premature marriage, contracted by the young girl with a certain "Robert Halford" and never consummated, for Robert Halford, on leaving the church, sailed for Africa, where he died "at the age of twenty-two." Katherine Selby's anxiety becomes almost inexplicable, for her "fault" is not one at all. Crabbe had more respect for probability. His *Confidant* had not only a daughter, but also a granddaughter. Lamb's *Wife's Trial* was the foundation for Miss Edgeworth's last novel, *Helen*, begun in 1830 and finished during the summer of 1833 (cf. *Life and Letters*, ed. by Hare, vol. ii. p. 198). In this work Anna's "fault" is still more toned down. With Miss Edgeworth, we are moving in high life. A certain Lady Cecilia Davenant has married

Let us accept our destiny without a murmur, even if it does not come up to all our aspirations. Perhaps a serene old age will console us for our past misfortunes. Let us bear in mind the story of Allen Booth and Judith Flemming.[1] At the infant-school together, they were fond of each other from earliest childhood : the little Allen was her companion "in every sport" and her champion "in every fray." As years went on, this instinctive affection had changed into a deliberate attachment : "they walked together, they together danced." If occasionally some misunderstanding or friction arose between them, it was—

> A causeless quarrel, followed by a peace,
> That gave to love growth, vigour, and increase.

Everything united them, even the opposition of their families and the uncertainty of their future. For they were poor, like Rupert and Dinah in one of the foregoing tales. And Allen's career reminds us of that of Rupert : a rich and childless kinsman in the West Indies has sent for him, promising him a legacy if he will help him in his business. Tearing himself from the weeping and anxious Judith, the young man has embarked, bent on securing a competence for himself and his beloved. He little knows the misfortunes which await him. War has broken out between England and Spain : the ship falls into the hands of the enemy, and the passengers are sold as slaves into the mines of a tropical country. Despairing of escape, Allen gradually achieves a tolerable existence in those distant regions : "a good priest," who speaks "his native language," protects him, recommends him to the favour of his master, and enables him to marry "a Spanish maiden." Twenty years after his arrival, Allen, with-

---

"General Clarendon," a personage who is so jealous that he cannot bear the idea of his wife having ever loved, let alone married, any one but himself. Now, the frolicsome Lady Cecilia has in her youth kept up a rather compromising correspondence with a Colonel d'Aubigny, who, like Halford, is dead. A whole bagful of their letters has been found. If the ferocious General sees them and knows whose they are, Cecilia is lost. Very fortunately, her "confidant," Helen, is as high-minded and charming as Eliza was the reverse : she comes to the rescue and takes advantage of the resemblance of her handwriting to that of Cecilia to mislead the General. In so doing she runs the risk of sacrificing her love for Beauclerc to her friendship for Cecilia; but everything comes right in the end, for we are moving in the best society. Alas ! what has become of Crabbe's straightforward and sturdy realism in all this?

[1] Tales, ii. : The Parting Hour.

out having forgotten the attachment of his youth, is surrounded by a family with which his "fond Isabel" has presented him. He has even become rich, and this prosperity brings him fresh misfortunes. His enemies accuse him of heresy, and he is obliged to fly from his belongings and take refuge in the forests of Campeachy Bay. There he meets some English sailors, with whom he returns home. They are within sight of land, when, as bad luck would have it, he is arrested by the press-gang which infests the coasts, and forced to serve his country for years in the war that is raging. He loses a limb in the "Indian seas," but recovers and obtains employment in an office, where he gains "a fair subsistence 'mid rich aspiring men." But advancing years undermine his health, and he is seized with an intense longing to revisit England and the scenes of his childhood. In his dreams he sees his parents, sees "his fav'rite maid, no feature wrinkled, not a charm decay'd." So he embarks and returns to his native land, forty years after he had quitted it.

He reaches the port on an autumn evening, and lands alone:

> No one was present; of its crew bereft,
> A single boat was in the billows left;
> Sent from some anchor'd vessel in the bay,
> At the returning tide to sail away.
> O'er the black stern the moonlight softly play'd,
> The loosen'd foresail flapping in the shade;
> All silent else on shore; but from the town
> A drowsy peal of distant bells came down:
> From the tall houses here and there, a light
> Served some confused remembrance to excite:
> "There," he observed, and new emotions felt,
> "Was my first home—and Judith yonder dwelt;
> Dead! dead are all! I long—I fear to know,"
> He said, and walk'd impatient, and yet slow.

> Sudden there broke upon his grief a noise
> Of merry tumult and of vulgar joys:
> Seamen, returning to their ship, were come,
> With idle numbers straying from their home;
> Allen among them mix'd, and in the old
> Strove some familiar features to behold;
> While fancy aided memory:—"Man! what cheer?"
> A sailor cried: "Art thou at anchor here?"
> Faintly he answer'd, and then tried to trace
> Some youthful features in some aged face:

A swarthy matron he beheld, and thought
She might unfold the very truths he sought :
Confused and trembling, he the dame address'd :
"The Booths ! yet live they ?" pausing and oppress'd ;
Then spake again :—"Is there no ancient man,
David his name ? assist me, if you can—
Flemmings there were—and Judith, doth she live ? "
The woman gazed, nor could an answer give ;
Yet wond'ring stood, and all were silent by,
Feeling a strange and solemn sympathy.
The woman musing said—"She knew full well
Where the old people came at last to dwell ;
They had a married daughter, and a son,
But they were dead, and now remain'd not one."

   " Yes," said an elder, who had paused intent
On days long past, " there was a sad event ;—
One of these Booths—it was my mother's tale—
Here left his lass, I know not where to sail :
She saw their parting, and observed the pain ;
But never came th' unhappy man again."
" The ship was captured "—Allen meekly said,
" And what became of the forsaken maid ? "
The woman answer'd : " I remember now,
She used to tell the lasses of her vow,
And of her lover's loss, and I have seen
The gayest hearts grow sad where she has been ;
Yet in her grief she married, and was made
Slave to a wretch, whom meekly she obey'd,
And early buried—but I know no more :
And hark ! our friends are hast'ning to the shore."

In his uncertainty Allen has taken a lodging in the
town and has continued his inquiries, but in vain.
He is unaware that Judith, a widow whose children are
out in the world, has moved to a neighbouring village,
that she has just heard of the "poor wanderer," and
that all her old affection for him has revived. They
meet at last :

                    . . . Not grief nor age,
Sickness nor pain, their hearts could disengage :
Each had immediate confidence ; a friend
Both now beheld, on whom they might depend :
" Now is there one to whom I can express
My nature's weakness, and my soul's distress."
Allen look'd up, and with impatient heart—
" Let me not lose thee—never let us part :
So Heaven this comfort to my sufferings give,
It is not all distress to think and live."

Judith shares these tender feelings. Very different from Dinah, she devotes herself to her old friend and watches over him. While he slumbers under a shady tree, she protects him from the fierce rays of the sun, and sits musing at his feet :

> And where is he ? Ah ! doubtless in those scenes
> Of his best days, amid the vivid greens,
> Fresh with unnumber'd rills, where ev'ry gale
> Breathes the rich fragrance of the neighb'ring vale.
> Smiles not his wife, and listens as there comes
> The night-bird's music from the thick'ning glooms ?
> And as he sits with all these treasures nigh,
> Blaze not with fairy-light the phosphor-fly,
> When like a sparkling gem it wheels illumined by ?
> This is the joy that now so plainly speaks
> In the warm transient flushing of his cheeks ;
> For he is list'ning to the fancied noise
> Of his own children, eager in their joys :
> All this he feels, a dream's delusive bliss
> Gives the expression and the glow like this.
> And now his Judith lays her knitting by,
> These strong emotions in her friend to spy,
> For she can fully of their nature deem—
> But see ! he breaks the long-protracted theme,
> And wakes, and cries—" My God ! 'twas but a dream."

The Parting Hour probably suggested Tennyson's *Enoch Arden.*[1] But the differences between the two poets are profound and instructive. Without dwelling on the form, tame or even incorrect in Crabbe, scrupulously ornate and finished in his successor, let us examine the plan of the two works. To the simple description of the characters with which Crabbe's tale opens, Tennyson, more intent on an elaborate composition, has added a dramatic plot from the beginning : he has placed his heroine, Annie Lee, between two children, who soon grow into young men, both equally in love with her; and the repressed but intense jealousy felt by Philip Ray,[2] the miller's son, towards Enoch

---

[1] This cannot be absolutely asserted, as there is no evidence on the point. But Tennyson knew and appreciated Crabbe's works.

[2] We may note that Crabbe refers to a rivalry of this kind in Allen's parting injunctions to Judith :

> " When every lad would on my lass attend,
> Choose not a smooth designer for a friend :
> That fawning Philip !—nay, be not severe,
> A rival's hope must cause a lover's fear."
> —*The Parting Hour*, 163-6.

Arden, the son of the fisherman, at once arrests the
attention of the reader, whom Crabbe's somewhat
colourless narrative fails to touch.   On the other hand,
Tennyson has simplified the centre of the story : discarding the various adventures which Crabbe enumerates too rapidly to excite interest, he places his Enoch,
like a new Robinson Crusoe, alone on a desert island,
and magnifies him with all the immensity of this
solitude.   Like a true romantic poet, he imparts to his
characters the qualities of his own nature : his gentle
melancholy, which throws a kind of soft haze around
Enoch and Philip, his lofty aspirations, which transform
plain country-folk into real heroes, as chivalrous as
Arthur's knights. It is his heart which has implanted in
Philip's the still strong love, "the lifelong hunger"; it
is his generosity which inspires Enoch at the supreme
moment when the forgotten old man sees his wife and
children adopted by his old rival and smothers the
despairing cry which " would shatter all the happiness
of the hearth." Observation, the attentive study of
mankind, is not required to conceive and paint such
pictures : imagination and sensibility are sufficient.
Crabbe, on the contrary, is all the better inspired for
keeping closer to the reality. His description of the
tropics,[1] admired in his day, pales before the magnificent passage in which Tennyson evokes the landscapes
of the equatorial regions ; but as soon as he finds himself amid familiar scenes, on the beach at Aldborough,
near the boats moored to the shore or among groups
of noisy sailors—in a word, as soon as he describes
what he has seen—his poetry acquires an animation,
a homely truthfulness, and occasionally a humour
unknown to Tennyson.

Modest in his tastes, timid in his ambitions, our
moralist sums up his precepts and our poet defines his
ideal in an idyll entitled *Jesse and Colin.*[2] The daughter
of a vicar, from whom she has inherited two hundred
guineas, Jesse, after her father's death, has the choice
between two proposals. She can either marry the
honest and worthy Colin, by whom she is tenderly
loved and who has just urged his suit, or she can
accept the invitation of an elderly and well-to-do lady,
an old friend of her father, who, out of gratitude for

[1] See above, the end of the tale and the last twenty lines in the text.
[2] *Tales*, xiii.

past kindness, offers her a home in her well-appointed
dwelling. Jesse weighs the pros and cons :

> " Colin is mild and civil, kind and just,
> I know his love, his temper I can trust ;
> But small his farm, it asks perpetual care,
> And we must toil as well as trouble share :
> True, he was taught in all the gentle arts
> That raise the soul, and soften human hearts ;
> And boasts a parent, who deserves to shine
> In higher class, and I could wish her mine. . . .
> Still he is poor, and here my father's friend
> Deigns for his daughter, as her own, to send."

It would be imprudent to refuse.   Jesse therefore
decides to accept the lady's offer.

She takes up her abode in the " vast mansion " which
the " dame " occupies in a busy town, and soon understands that certain services are expected from her.
The mistress of the house has three attendants—a
maidservant named Jane, a housekeeper called the
" widow Issop," and a poor relation, a young and
merry girl, whom Crabbe has left anonymous. This
trio is indispensable to the lady, and yet she distrusts
them all : her vigilance may be so easily eluded ! Let
Jesse come and act as spy on them for her !—

> " Hearken, my Jesse, never can I trust
> Beings ungrateful, selfish, and unjust ;
> But you are present, and my load of care
> Your love will serve to lighten and to share ;
> Come near me, Jesse—let not those below
> Of my reliance on your friendship know ;
> Look as they look, be in their freedoms free—
> But all they say do you convey to me."

The underlings criticise their mistress with equal
animosity, and spy on one another :

> Jane was a servant fitted for her place,
> Experienced, cunning, fraudful, selfish, base ;
> Skill'd in those mean humiliating arts
> That make their way to proud and selfish hearts :
> By instinct taught, she felt an awe, a fear,
> For Jesse's upright, simple character ;
> Whom with gross flattery she a while assail'd,
> And then beheld with hatred when it fail'd ;

> Yet, trying still upon her mind for hold,
> She all the secrets of the mansion told. . . .
> But on the widow'd friend with deep disdain
> And rancorous envy, dwelt the treacherous Jane.

Issop pays her back in her own coin. One morning she engages Jesse in a conversation, and says :

> "Observe that artful maid,
> A lying, prying, jilting, thievish jade ;
> I think, my love, you would not condescend
> To call a low, illiterate girl your friend. . . .
> But she has flexile features, acting eyes,
> And seems with every look to sympathise."

By her "fawning, her vulgar flattery, and her vile reports," continues the widow, she courts the favour of her mistress, who now comes in for a share of abuse :

> "Good Heav'n ! that one so jealous, envious, base,
> Should be the mistress of so sweet a place : . . .
> She loves to see us abject, loves to deal
> Her insult round, and then pretends to feel :
> Prepare to cast all dignity aside,
> For know, your talents will be quickly tried ;
> Nor think, from favours past, a friend to gain, —
> 'Tis but by duties we our posts maintain :
> I read her novels, gossip through the town,
> And daily go, for idle stories, down ;
> I cheapen all she buys, and bear the curse
> Of honest tradesmen for my niggard purse ; . . .
> Nay, I have heard her, when she chanced to come
> Where I contended for a petty sum,
> Affirm ''twas painful to behold such care,
> But Issop's nature is to pinch and spare ' :
> Thus all the meanness of the house is mine,
> And my reward—to scorn her, and to dine."

After the housekeeper comes the niece :

> "My sweetest friend has been with us a week,
> And does she love us ? be sincere and speak ;
> My aunt you cannot—Lord ! how I should hate
> To be like her, all misery and state ;
> Proud, and yet envious, she disgusted sees
> All who are happy, and who look at ease.
> Let friendship bind us, I will quickly show
> Some favourites near us you'll be bless'd to know ;
> My aunt forbids it—but, can she expect,
> To soothe her spleen, we shall ourselves neglect ?

> Jane and the Widow were to watch and stay
> My free-born feet; I watch'd as well as they:
> Lo! what is this?—this simple key explores
> The dark recess that holds the Spinster's stores:
> And, led by her ill star, I chanced to see
> Where Issop keeps her stock of ratafie. . . .
> Thus bless'd with secrets both would choose to hide,
> Their fears now grant me what their scorn denied."

Strange creatures! thinks Jesse, who begins to regret Colin's cottage, and cannot reconcile herself to these surroundings. Besides this, her lukewarmness displeases her protectress: she cannot "lie or jest," she brings no news and cannot contribute any scandal; if she takes a walk, it is for her health or to go to church. This is not enough for the lady, who soon intimates her dissatisfaction:

> "Let me be frank—I am not satisfied;
> You know my wishes, I your judgment trust;
> You can be useful, Jesse, and you must."

To which Jesse replies, with long-suppressed indignation, that such duties are repugnant to her, and that she refuses to discharge them. On the following day she takes her departure, deaf to the entreaties and the violent reproaches of her former friend:

> . . . "Speak—yet I can forgive,
> Still live with me."—"With you," said Jesse, "live?
> No! I would first endure what you describe,
> Rather than breathe with your detested tribe,
> Who long have feigned, till now their very hearts
> Are firmly fix'd in their accursed parts;
> Who all profess esteem, and feel disdain,
> And all, with justice, of deceit complain;
> Whom I could pity, but that, while I stay,
> My terror drives all kinder thoughts away;
> Grateful for this, that, when I think of you,
> I little fear what poverty can do."

She returns to her native village. One evening when Colin, according to his custom, is waiting for the arrival of the coach at his garden gate, and his mother, in touching accents, is begging him not to be distressed at his repeated disappointments, he sees the vehicle stop and Jesse descend from it:

> She came—he saw her bending from the door,
> Her face, her smile, and he beheld no more,

> Lost in his joy—the mother lent her aid
> T' assist and to detain the willing maid. . . .
> No wishes to depart she felt, or feign'd ;
> Yet long in doubt she stood, and then perforce remain'd.

Her presence has brought contentment and joy into the household :

> In the mild evening, in the scene around,
> The maid, now free, peculiar beauties found ;
> Blended with village-tones the evening gale
> Gave the sweet night-bird's warblings to the vale :
> The youth, embolden'd, yet abash'd, now told
> His fondest wish, nor found the maiden cold ;
> The mother smiling whisper'd, " Let him go
> And seek the license ! " Jesse answer'd, " No " :
> But Colin went.—I know not if they live
> With all the comforts wealth and plenty give ;
> But with pure joy to envious souls denied,
> To suppliant meanness and suspicious pride ;
> And village maids of happy couples say,
> " They live like Jesse Bourn and Colin Grey."

We shall do the same, if we are wise, the poet seems to conclude. Dreading for our frail bark the storms [1] which threaten it on the ocean of an ambitious and worldly life, we shall return to the country-side and till the soil. Equidistant from poverty, which drags down the mere labourer, and from luxury, the parent of avarice and pride, far from the sterile agitations in which the baleful passions consume their energy, we shall find, in regular work, the peace of mind that constitutes happiness. The middle rank [2] is the most

---

[1] It will be noticed that Crabbe's ideas are in perfect harmony with his character (see above, p. 27, n. 2).

[2] In all things Crabbe loves the golden mean : this is proved by a comparison of the fourth tale (*Procrastination*) with the twelfth (*The Precipitate Choice*). Rupert was unhappy because he hesitated too long about marrying, "Squire Thomas" because he was in too great a hurry to marry. For ten years the latter has patiently borne the abuse and ill-humour of an aged aunt, whose fortune he hoped to inherit. At last he has obtained it by ousting a female cousin. A well-to-do man, he thinks of marrying, but cannot make up his mind to court any girl of equal rank to his own. The attentions which he formerly paid to his aunt he now demands for himself. He has engaged as secretary a young man named George, the son of a neighbouring farmer, and apparently full of zeal.

One day when George and the squire are returning together from a race-meeting, they lose their way, no doubt by chance. After wandering about for some hours they reach a farm, which happens, by a surprising coincidence, to be that of George's father. Thomas is received there with open arms, is waited on attentively, and is fascinated by the beauty of " Harriot," the daughter of

enviable and the safest of all: in rural England, a the house. He remains there two days, in a state of rapture, regretting only that the fair one is not rich.

But, by a second chance, George drops a letter which is forthwith picked up by the squire. It is from the farmer's wife, deploring the ill-health of Harriot, who seems to be pining away. The desired effect is produced: with a precipitation caused by his reviving passion, Thomas returns to the farm and marries his dulcinea. He is not long in repenting it. Harriot proves intractable and aggressive, proposes a separation if he will share his property with her, and tells the poor squire plainly that their marriage was a premeditated piece of revenge on the part of herself and her family, her mother being the cousin who had been supplanted by Thomas. The squire being too avaricious to consent to the sacrifice demanded by Harriot, the pair spend their lives in tormenting each other.

The two following tales give us new lessons in moderation and wisdom. The heroine of the first (*The Widow's Tale: Tales*, vii.) is a schoolgirl, Nancy Moss, the daughter of a farmer. When she returns home from school, the roughness of the farm life and the coarseness of the food are so offensive to her that she begs her father to let her take her meals alone, and not to ask her "if she has fed the pigs." Moss refuses point-blank, and bids her take the place of her deceased mother, get up early to superintend the maids, and devote her spare time to spinning or to bleaching the linen.

In a flood of tears, Nancy consults a refined "widow," whose modest but neat house, clad with jessamine, has attracted her attention. She tells the lady her troubles, the horror she has of marrying a farmer, even if it were young Henry Carr. Contrary to her expectation, the widow condemns her distaste for farm work, and discourages her ambitions. She tells Nancy the story of her own life, as a lesson of resignation. Like Dinah and Rupert, the widow and her sweetheart, who was a clerk in her father's office, waited a long time for each other: he went to the colonies, but was wounded on the way, and returned to die in her arms. At the age of forty she had to marry an affectionate and devoted man, whom she could never love, and who on his death left her the cottage which she now inhabits. Marry young Henry Carr, she concludes. Do not despise the farmer: he will give you happiness.

Nancy follows her friend's advice. Her father, to his astonishment, soon sees a complete change in her. She rises betimes, supervises the household, and pays great attention to the dairy. Henry Carr, finding her thus transformed, is not long in asking her hand and marrying her.

Arabella (*Tales*, ix.) is the story of the daughter of a clergyman named Dr. Rack. In the pride of her youth, of her beauty, of her extensive reading, she shows herself very exacting in the choice of a husband. She studies Berkeley, Bacon, Hobbes, Locke, history, Latin, Italian even; she has an unblemished reputation, and expects to find all these qualities in her future husband. She therefore rejects successively a Scotch doctor, who is an infidel and a hypocrite, a clergyman who is too old for her, and a spendthrift captain. Young Edward Huntley alone seems to have some chance of success. But on the eve of the marriage a country lass appears with a child in her arms, and tells Arabella that Huntley is its father. Great indignation of the young lady, who dismisses this vicious individual with scorn.

Twelve years later, under the influence of time, she has lowered her pretensions considerably. A merchant is paying his addresses to her, and although a confirmed old maid accuses this new suitor of having a mulatto mistress and a number of coloured children in London, Arabella refuses to make any inquiry. She accepts Beswell in full confidence, for, as she remarks:

> " If false the charge, I then shall show regard
> For a good man, and be his just reward:
> And what for virtue can I better do
> Than to reclaim him, if the charge be true ? "

Age, observes Crabbe, is apt to temper the ardour of youth.

modest, intelligent, and generous farmer is best able to order his life aright and control his inclinations. And if his beloved listens to his suit, he may even enjoy that idyllic felicity which the poets formerly attributed to all dwellers in the country indiscriminately. A destroyer of artificial and false pastoral poetry, Crabbe, in this last tale, has given a model of the realistic and true type of it.

IV

THE critics proved more favourable to the *Tales in Verse* than to *The Borough*. *The Eclectic Review*[1] alone, unable to forgive the poet his hostility to the Calvinists, received the work coldly. "We are very far from thinking," it said, "that these tales will add to the reputation of the author of *The Village* and *The Borough*. Lovers as we are of poetry, it was with no little difficulty that we toiled through this heavy mass of verse. We seemed jogging on a broken-winded Pegasus through all the flats and bogs of Parnassus. We do hope that when Mr. Crabbe has it in contemplation to appear again before the public he will employ a little more judgment in the selection of his subjects, a little more fancy in their decoration, and withal a little more time in preparing 10,000 verses for the press." Jeffrey,[2] on the other hand, thanked Crabbe in his most gracious manner for the new work. He analysed it tale by tale, considered it a series of "chapters supplementary to *The Parish Register* and *The Borough*," discovered in it the same characteristics, "the same tone, the same subjects, the same finished and minute delineation of things quite ordinary and common, the same sympathy for the innocent pleasures of the poor, contrasted with a strong sense of their frequent depravity." He also noted certain special qualities in it: a purer kind of pathos, less often blended with "disgust," a "more amiable and consoling view of human nature," a marked tendency to dwell on the strong passions and the generous sentiments of the lower and middle classes, finally a

[1] Vol. viii. December, 1812, pp. 1240-53.
[2] *Edinburgh Review*, vol. xx. November, 1812, pp. 277 *seq.* (quoted partly in *Works*, p. 276, and *passim*).

more constant and more immediate moral usefulness than in former works. *The Critical Review*,[1] in an article remarkable for the appropriateness and the clearness of some of its comments, observed that these *Tales* were rather portraits than narratives properly so called, divided them into three categories according to their merit, included in the first *The Parting Hour*, *The Patron*, *The Lover's Journey*,[2] *Edward Shore*, perhaps *The Confidant* and *Resentment*; in the second, *The Dumb Orators*,[3] *The Gentleman Farmer*, *Procrastination*, *The Frank Courtship*, *The Widow's Tale*, *The Mother*, *Arabella*, *Jesse and Colin*, *The Wager*, *The Convert*, *The Brothers*; and lumped the rest[4] together in a third group condemned as "decidedly bad." It also blamed the author for his love of useless and tedious detail, and for the slovenliness of his style, and added, with much perspicacity, that his manifest defects would weaken the effect of his real but more hidden beauties, less obvious to ordinary readers. As for *The Monthly Review*,[5] it congratulated Crabbe on his steady improvement "in grace and spirit, in copiousness, vigour, and sensibility." Comparing the *Tales* with the preceding works, it concluded that they sometimes attained a higher degree of poetical merit, while at the same time "exhibiting a larger portion of what might have been advantageously spared." Apart from these few objections, the *Tales in Verse*, which gave rise to less difference of opinion than *The Borough*, found favour with their critics. And the public read them eagerly.[6]

Let us try to characterise them in our turn. We find, in the first place, that they do not form a whole, that no link unites them, and that, like La Fontaine's *Fables*, they follow each other but are not connected. They may be studied separately without any prejudice to the entire work. We then see that each of them is easily divisible into three parts—the opening statement, the plot, the catastrophe—and thus assumes the form of a small drama with two or three actors. With

---

[1] Vol. ii. of 1812, pp. 561-79.
[2] See above, pp. 70-2 and 261-2.
[3] Cf. below, p. 453.
[4] *The Struggles of Conscience, Squire Thomas, Advice or the Squire and the Priest*, and *The Learned Boy*.
[5] Vol. lxix. 1812, pp. 352-64.
[6] Five editions were published in two years.

a loquacity which often wearies our patience, Crabbe introduces his personages to us before putting them on the scene, relates their past existence in detail, enumerates their strong and their weak points—in a word, draws their portraits by way of introduction to the story.   Then comes an unforeseen incident, a new fact which, disturbing the equilibrium of their relations, sets them at variance sometimes with one another and sometimes with themselves : for instance, Rupert's departure, which makes Dinah's heart accessible to avarice ; the arrival of Eliza at Stafford's, which brings trouble into the honest yeoman's household ; or again, the absence of the too-confiding friend, which exposes Edward Shore to the irresistible temptation.   From this turn of events, from this crisis, flows, as a logical consequence, the catastrophe brought about by the actions of the personages.   It depends entirely upon them ; chance never intervenes in these tales.   Happiness and unhappiness are strictly meted out, according to the good behaviour of some and the imprudence of others.   In their construction the *Tales in Verse* resemble sermons with three heads, embellished with descriptions, anecdotes, and even animated dialogues.[1]

Their heroes are less humble than those of *The Village* and *The Borough*. Among them are squires, literary aspirants, clerks, successful tradesmen, well-to-do farmers. The fulness of the observation, the general tone of the work, less gloomy than *The Borough*, bring us back to *The Parish Register*. And the character of the poetry, its realism with a moral aim, has not changed.   It should be noted, in fact, that, although Crabbe gives each of his personages a particular calling, he describes man as a moral being and of all ages rather than man in a social state and of a particular epoch.   But, unlike the French classics, he does not look for the universal in the abstract.   He keeps as close as possible to the reality, and if he alters it, this is not in order to simplify it, but to make it more striking and more intense.

We do not know the sources of all the tales in the collection.   Three of them are of purely literary origin,[2]

---

[1] Cf. in particular tales iv. (between Dinah and Rupert), vi. (between Sybil and Josiah), and xvii. (between the Wife and Susan).

[2] The eighteenth (in part : see above, p. 342, n. 2), the nineteenth (*ibid.* p. 323, n. 2), and the twenty-first (the last of the series : *ibid.* p. 341, n. 1).

some were no doubt invented from beginning to end,[1] others were suggested to the author by facts of his own experience which cannot now be ascertained,[2] and several recall to us certain events in his life or in that of his near relatives. In this last case we are able to follow his process of poetic elaboration. We know that *The Patron* contains a good many autobiographical details— that " John " at Brandon Hall is Crabbe at Belvoir Castle, that the timid applicant in the nobleman's sumptuous ante-room is also Crabbe waiting on Lord North. But what a contrast between the fortunate destiny of our clergyman and the misfortunes of the bailiff's son! It was necessary to touch the reader, even at the expense of the truth. A similar transformation is observable in the tale entitled *Procrastination*. Dinah, gradually fascinated by her aunt's treasures, is Mira living with Mrs. Tovell,[3] and perhaps urged to forget her luckless poet ; Rupert represents William, one of Crabbe's brothers, who died in a remote part of Central America,[4] after adventures

---

[1] In particular those which introduce the Puritans—the fourteenth (see above, p. 323, n. 2) and the sixth (*ibid.* p. 345 *seq.*) ; perhaps also the first, the ninth (*ibid.* p. 366, n. 2), the eleventh (pp. 336 *seq.*), the sixteenth (pp. 353 *seq.*), in which " the moral thesis " accounts for the incidents.

[2] Those whose heroes are squires : the third (pp. 332 *seq.*), the fifteenth (p. 336, n. 1), the twelfth (p. 366, n. 2).

[3] See above, p. 51, and *Works*, p. 290, n. 1. The aunt " motif " reappears in tales vi., viii., xii. (at the beginning), xiii. (with a variation).

[4] See above, p. 7, n. 3, and B. p. 2. William, the third of the four brothers, a sailor like John, had been made prisoner by the Spaniards and taken to Mexico, where he married and practised the calling of a tinsmith. Having acquired wealth, he was accused of heresy, and had to flee to the coast of Honduras, where, in 1803, he met a sailor who was a native of Aldborough (cf. Allen Booth, in the second tale). But William Crabbe never returned to England. The *Athenæum* of March 21st, 1840, p. 235, contains the following curious notice : " We now learn from the following paragraph in *The Belize Advertiser* of the 25th January that the poor outcast wanderer [*i.e.* William Crabbe] contrived to make for himself another home and to surround himself with other ' happy infants' : ' We [*i.e.* the Belize paper] failed to notice a week or two back the demise of the last surviving son (a coloured man) of Crabbe, the brother of the late Rev. George Crabbe, one of the first poets of his time. . . . The late deceased's parent was well known to some of our oldest settlers as following the calling of a whitesmith, and frequently journeyed to and fro between this settlement and the Mexican territory, where he had once acquired some property. One or both of the sons have left progeny behind them.' " We may take this opportunity to note that Robert, the second brother, born in 1758, died at Southwold on November 30th, 1835. He married twice, but left only one son, an idiot. For John, see above, p. 196, n. 5. As for Mary Sparkes, who was born in 1756, she died on November 17th, 1827, and her husband Thomas Sparkes, a builder and carpenter at Aldborough, died on May 19th, 1826. They had nine children, three of whom (Emma, born in June, 1792 ; Cecilia, born

identical with those of Allen Booth.[1]   Whence it
follows that his return to England, his visit to Dinah,
his frequent meetings with her when coming out of
church—all these pathetic scenes are due to the narrator's imagination.   Similarly, the story of Paul the
merchant and his unrelenting spouse is founded on
an episode in the life of Mrs. Elmy, whose husband
went to Guadeloupe after having become bankrupt,[2]
and, perhaps, behaved in a dishonourable way to his
wife.[3] With no pity for his defunct father-in-law,
Crabbe represents him in beggar's rags and living in
a wretched hovel, on the threshold of which he is
found dead of cold and hunger.   Clearly, our tale-
writer, in spite of his realism, still remains too much
of a "poet" to tell us the truth and nothing but the
truth.

in October, 1798 ; and John, born in December, 1800) appear occasionally
in Crabbe's correspondence.   We read in Fitzgerald's manuscript notes :
"Sparkes' Lodgings, afterwards Beach House, one of the roomiest in the
Aldbro' of thirty years ago, and lodged in by us about 1822."
   [1] *Tales*, ii.   The journey "motif" reappears in tales iv. and vii. (in part).
   [2] See above, p. 46, n. 5.
   [3] Cf. *Works*, p. 347, n. 1.

CHAPTER II

PRESENTATION TO TROWBRIDGE AND JOURNEYS TO LONDON
(1813—1818)

I. An exchange of livings.—II. The Indian summer.—III. Crabbe
in society

I

WHILE the reviews were re-echoing his name
throughout England and Scotland, what was Crabbe
doing himself? In the solitary Vale of Belvoir, under
the shadow of his little church and of the elms in his
garden, he continued to live a calm, almost dull life
in the bosom of his family. His money troubles had
disappeared. He could now drink wine "without
absolutely repining at the enormity of the cost": his
livings brought him in about £400 a year, Mira's
income, and perhaps that of his children, together
amounted to one-half of that sum, and every year his
publisher added something to his "privy purse." His
sons had left the University and returned to Muston,
which considerably reduced his expenses.[1] George,
the eldest, having been ordained,[2] could act as curate
for his father at West Allington. The family, now
reunited, had resumed their Great Glemham habits:
their reading in common, whenever the Colburn
circulating library sent them some new novel; their
reproductions of insects copied from plates of entomo-
logical works; the care of the botanical garden, in
which the poet still cultivated his "choice weeds."
And Crabbe was not without society in the neighbourhood: the owners of Belvoir Castle, where the
dowager-duchess received him with favour, Sir Robert
Heron, Sir William Welby, of Denton Manor, and

---

[1] See the letter to Scott, quoted by B. p. 58, and *ibid.* p. 56.
[2] Cf. Fitzgerald, MS. notes: "1808. Æt. 23. I take Deacon's orders
at Buckden and license to the curacy of Allington. December 18. G. C.
jun^r." *Ibid.*: "1809. I take Priest's orders in December."

especially the Very Rev. Dr. Gordon, Dean of Lincoln and a pluralist, who occasionally deigned to honour the village and parsonage of Sedgebrook[1] with his presence.

But a precarious state of health often disturbed the tranquillity of this family existence. Crabbe's delicate constitution, which was liable to gastric and nervous derangements, demanded constant care. During one of his trips to Suffolk, about 1790, he had suddenly been attacked with giddiness and fallen down in a street of Ipswich, and a doctor had advised him to take "opiates," which he apparently continued to do for the rest of his life.[2] Perhaps the remedy increased the excitement instead of calming it. At Muston Crabbe suffered from fits of low fever and indigestion, which produced great depression of spirits. "Life is as tedious as a twice-told tale," he was wont to say.[3] The mere thought of a journey to London[4] brought on "tremors and terrors." He was troubled with strange dreams: in one of them he thought he was followed and hooted by a set of boys, whom he tried to beat off with a stick, but to no purpose, because they were made of leather! He would sometimes reply, when he was asked whether he had slept well, "The leather-lads have been at me again."[5] Occasionally he was attacked with deafness. On September 10th, 1812, four days before the publication of the *Tales in Verse*, he wrote to Dr. Gordon after a visit

[1] About a mile and a half east of Muston, close to the road from Grantham to Nottingham.

[2] B. p. 45.

[3] *Ibid.* p. 61.

[4] Letter to Dr. Gordon: "MUSTON, 15 *April*, 1813. DEAR SIR,—You did mention that it was your purpose to visit Sedgbrook at Easter. . . . To the determined and the diligent, I find all things are possible that man can effect, and I am happy to find that your good health permits you to undertake such things as my poor nerves shrink from with tremors and terrors. . . . What you desire is done, and notice of a sacrament at Sedgbrook given for Sunday next. . . . I.render you my best thanks for your obliging offers ; I have at least half a dozen kinds of small businesses in London, but not a single one of size and interest enough to engage the time of a Dean of Lincoln. . . . And now do not dismiss the thought without giving it a moment's consideration :—Will you dine with me on Sunday? I know among other good and happy properties you can take the fare of the day as it happens, and we can give you the Sunday's joint and applepye, in short you shall have a country rector's dinner, and now on this condition, will you dine with me on Sunday? Mrs. Crabbe and her sons desire their respectful remembrances : we are in our usual state, rather I think improving than declining. . . ." (Mackay Collection.)

[5] MS. notes by Fitzgerald on the poem entitled *The World of Dreams : Works*, pp. 268 *seq.*

to Sedgebrook: "I know not in what manner to
express my sense of the good humour and polite
condescension of your friends. I am, as much as it is
right and becoming, in love with Lady J. Thynne, and
am greatly indebted for her obliging attention to a
half-deaf Village Priest who several times gave her
Ladyship the trouble of repeating what she was kindly
observing to him : were I always so fortunate, I should
feel none of that reluctance which now in a great
measure confines me to my own house, with an
exception of the visits I make to Sedgbrook." [1]

His physical inactivity, combined with his protracted
intellectual labours and his comparative isolation at
Muston, had a depressing influence on him. He could
hardly receive his friends in this old " patched and
pieced" house, which he considered neither "comfortable nor perfectly secure." [2]   Besides this, Mira
was daily growing worse, which obliged him to spend
long hours in her room and nurse her with unwearied
patience.   In July, 1813, he took her up to London for
a treat ; they spent two or three months in a hotel
near the Strand, and Crabbe availed himself of this
opportunity to see his old friends Dudley North and
Bonnycastle again, to frequent the botanical gardens
and, occasionally, the theatres. [3]   Twenty-nine years had
elapsed since his last visit to the capital in June, 1784,
when, on his return from Evershot, six months after
his marriage, he had introduced his wife to Burke.
And now Burke was dead, and Mira dying—for she
passed away on September 21st, [4] 1813, immediately
after her return to Muston.   Exhausted no doubt by
sleepless nights and anxiety, Crabbe had an acute
attack of the malady which was preying on him.   His
life was thought to be in danger : he himself desired
that Mira's grave should not be closed until his recovery was assured.   At last a judicious use of emetics
saved him, [5] after a month's illness.   On November 1st

---

[1] Broadley Collection.

[2] Letter to Dr. Gordon of December 9th, 1813.

[3] B. p. 58. The farce of *Sharp and Flat*, which is referred to in this
passage, and in which Crabbe admired Liston's acting, was played for the
first time on August 4th, 1813, at the "Theatre Royal, Lyceum." Liston's
"Solomon Wiseacre" must have been the cousin of an old astrologer whose
daughter elopes with a captain (cf. *The Times* of August 5th). The captain
was probably "Sharp" and the fool of a cousin "Flat."

[4] And not October, as B. says, p. 59 (see the tablet in Muston church).

[5] B. p. 59.

he informed Dr. Gordon that his health was sufficiently improved to enable him to offer his services at Sedge-brook.[1] He had no idea that a new chapter of his life was about to begin.

For a long time, in fact, Crabbe had given up hope of obtaining any living from the Rutland family. The son evidently took little interest in his father's *protégé*. In a humorous passage of a letter to Sir Walter Scott, Crabbe explains to us most clearly the nature of his relations with Belvoir: "Thirty years since, I was taken to Belvoir by its late possessor, as a domestic chaplain. I read the service on a Sunday, and fared sumptuously every day. At that time the Chancellor, Lord Thurlow, gave me a rectory in Dorsetshire, small, but a living; this the duke taught me to disregard as a provision, and promised better things. While I lived with him on this pleasant footing I observed many persons in the neighbourhood who came occasionally to dine, and were civilly received: 'How do you do, Dr. Smith? How is Mrs. Smith?'—'I thank your Grace, well': and so they took their venison and claret. 'Who are these?' said I to a young friend of the duke's.[2] 'Men of the *old race*, sir; people whom the *old duke* was in the habit of seeing—for some of them he had done something, and had he yet lived all had their chance. They now make way for us, but keep up a sort of connection.'" Crabbe, in his turn, belonged to the "old race"; his patron's death had been followed by a long minority. "New connections," he continues, "were formed; and when, some few years since, I came back into this country, and expressed a desire of inscribing my verses[3] to the duke, I obtained leave, indeed, but I almost repented the attempt, from the coldness of the reply. Yet recollecting that great men are beset with

[1] Letter in the Mackay Collection. In spite of the insignificance of the subjects, the reflections in it are very characteristic : "DEAR SIR,—I am almost ashamed to send so small a basket of those yellow apples which appeared to me upon the tree as a much larger quantity, nor will I undertake to prove, as I was not the operator, that all which were gathered were deposited in my receptacle. . . . I proposed this fine morning to have been at Sedgbrook, . . . but my sons persuade me that the balloon to be launched from Nottingham this day will with the present wind come near the Vale of Belvoir : I think not much of a thing which twenty other things may prevent, but yet I wait."

[2] Robert Thoroton, no doubt (see above, p. 140).

[3] *The Borough.*

applicants of all kinds, I acquitted the duke of injustice, and determined to withdraw myself, as one of the *old race*, and give way to stronger candidates for notice. To this resolution I kept strictly, and left it entirely to the family whether or no I should consider myself as a stranger, who having been disappointed in his expectation, by unforeseen events, must take his chance, and ought to take it patiently.[1] For reasons I have no inclination to canvass, his Grace has obligingly invited me, and I occasionally meet his friends at the castle, without knowing whether I am to consider that notice as the promise of favour, or as a favour in itself."[2] We can easily guess to which interpretation Crabbe leaned.

But it happened that at the beginning of December, 1813, the Duke of Rutland wanted the living of Muston for the Rev. Henry Byron, a cousin of the author of *Childe Harold* and vicar of Granby, a tiny village.[3] He offered the poet to exchange Muston for Trowbridge, a small town in Wiltshire, not far from Bath and Bristol. As for West Allington, George, the eldest of Crabbe's sons, who was already acting as curate there, would become its incumbent. Hardly was this " affair in agitation, when it gave rise to other projects than our own," wrote Crabbe to Dr. Gordon, on December 9th. " The Welbys," he added, " appear to think that if I quit West Allington, they have most claim to the presentation." Sir William Welby, in fact, wished his son John to have the living. " This would have disconcerted me more," continues Crabbe, " had not the duke been kind enough to speak of Croxton[4] as an equivalent, and indeed on inquiry I find it is equal in value to West Allington at this time or rather better."[5] The negotiations thus begun made no progress during the months of December, 1813, and January, 1814. The inmates of Belvoir had other preoccupations at that moment: the Archbishop of Canterbury, Dr. Manners Sutton, was about to baptise the young heir of the ducal house, Lord George John Frederick,

---

[1] Cf. with this sentiment *supra*, p. 366.
[2] Quoted by B. pp. 57-8.
[3] About six miles west of Belvoir. The incumbent complained of losing money by it. It is said at Muston that this clergyman went mad in the middle of the church service.
[4] About six miles south of Belvoir, on the plateau (cf. above, p. 140).
[5] Mackay Collection.

Marquis of Granby, and preparations were being made to receive the august sponsors—the Prince Regent in person, and his brother the Duke of York. Crabbe himself got out his best pen and paper to celebrate the " happy infant."[1] The ceremony was fixed for January 4th ; on the 2nd, George, Prince Regent and "first gentleman of Europe," arrived at Belvoir, where Crabbe had the signal honour of dining in his company. On the 7th the poet once more returned to the castle, and witnessed the " magnificent fêtes " which followed the christening.

A month afterwards the last echoes of the solemnity had died away, and Muston was again spoken of. On February 15th Crabbe received an unlooked-for proposal, which seemed to him almost humiliating. In a letter of that date the Duke informed him that he had "written to the Chancellor and at last obtained his consent to the measure." Then he added very unexpectedly : " Let me ask you whether the Vicarage of Granby will suit the ideas of your son. Unless it will, I fear that I shall be drawn into some difficulties in the arrangements consequent upon your translation." On the following day Crabbe told Dr. Gordon of the disappointment which the Duke's new offer had caused him : " Now, my dear Sir, if my *translation* depend upon my son's taking Granby or my taking it, it will never be accomplished, and this I can but conceive his Grace must, if he deigned to think, have thought of himself; he must surely know of a village so very near to him, that it is the poorest benefice in his gift ; that it long stood at £80, but may be now at £100, that the house is an Hovel no decent labourer would live in, and in short that if my son resided he must live in misery for this wretched sub-

---

[1] Here is stanza x. of this manuscript compliment. We do not know if it was presented :

> Heir to thy noble House, this day to thee
> Shall be, when memory wakes, a joyful date :
> Thou shalt look backward to the time, and see
> The first, the greatest in the Church and State
> All take an interest in their Granby's fate :
> What happy infant in the world is found,
> Whom so much grace and dignity surround ?
> What favoured being in his life shall say :
> I had like honours and as great a day ?

(Murray Collection.)

The young marquis was born on August 20th, 1813. Vanity of human greatness ! he died on June 15th, 1814.

sistence, and if he did not (and to that, nothing would tempt him I believe) the curacy would, and justly, take all the income."· Crabbe therefore had replied that he "considered his present livings as preferable to Trowbridge and Granby," that he felt bound to refuse this offer, but that he would, "as the very utmost he could yield in his views," accept Trowbridge and Croxton for himself, if there was any objection to giving the second of these livings to his son.[1] The bargain was concluded on these terms. On February 21st the Duke wrote as follows: "I had offered Croxton[2] to Sir W. Welby for his son John, but both Sir William and his son have in the handsomest manner possible waived all right to that living in your favour, and I can assure you there is no longer any objection to your receiving Trowbridge and Croxton upon resigning Muston and Allington. If this arrangement should be satisfactory to you, be so good as to write a letter to the Chancellor resigning the preferment which you hold under the Crown, and send me a presentation to Trowbridge and to Croxton which I shall be ready at the earliest opportunity to sign." [3]

The formalities involved in this change of residence were carried out in March. On Tuesday, the 15th, at six in the evening, Crabbe left Muston; on the 16th he arrived at Buckden, where the Bishop of Lincoln instituted him Vicar of Croxton Kerrial. On the 17th he had an interview in London with the Bishop of Salisbury,[4] in whose diocese Trowbridge was situated,

---

[1] Letter to Dr. Gordon, dated Muston, February 16th, 1814 (Mackay Collection).

[2] West Allington in that case would have fallen to Byron.

[3] Broadley Collection. Crabbe saw clearly that all this was more of a bargain than a favour. On March 7th, 1831, he wrote to his son George : "Of the Duke of Rutland's patronage I could form an opinion, but it was not such as gave me hope of succeeding according to my wishes. His livings are many, but with few exceptions they are of small value . . . and in the situations no man would choose to reside in, . . . to whom the few more acceptable benefices must be assigned : that is to one of the family connected with the Castle or to some who had interest of a kind that they could pay in another way for what they received. . . . In fact I should have been fearful even of a compliance with my request had I made one. This living was made mine, because I had almost an equivalent to resign, and what was mine, both Muston and Allington were wanted, one by the Duke and the other by Sir W. Welby. I would not be ungrateful, but I am well assured that Trowbridge had never been allotted to me—nor could it have been expected—but under these peculiar circumstances."

[4] John Fisher, from 1807 to 1825. The Bishop had been advised of his coming by Dr. Gordon. Cf. a letter from Crabbe to the latter : "MUSTON,

and his institution to this second living was signed on the 18th. That very evening, with a freedom of manners which is rather attractive in this clergyman-poet, he went to see Kean play Shylock at Drury Lane, and on the 20th he returned to the same theatre to see him act in *Hamlet*. On the 22nd he travelled by coach to Trowbridge, and on the following day met " Mr. Fletcher," the substitute of the Rev. Gilbert Beresford, who had been absent for some time. Returning to London on the 25th, he went back to Muston, where he inducted his successor on April 18th.

A short trip to Suffolk preceded his final departure. On May 2nd he was at Beccles, where the two Misses Elmy were living, on the 5th at Aldborough, where he remained up to the 10th with his sister Mary Sparkes. One of these days, his Biographer tells us, was devoted to a ramble in the environs of Parham and Glemham. In a few stanzas the poet has recorded the melancholy thoughts suggested by this excursion :

Yes, I behold again the place,
　The seat of joy, the source of pain ;
It brings in view the form and face
　That I must never see again.

The night-bird's song that sweetly floats
　On this soft gloom—this balmy air,
Brings to the mind her sweeter notes
　When those dear eyes can shine no more.

Lo ! yonder shines that window's light,
　My guide, my token, heretofore ;
And now again it shines as bright,
　When those dear eyes can shine no more.

Then hurry from this place away !
　It gives not now the bliss it gave ;
For Death has made its charm his prey,
　And joy is buried in her grave.[1]

Leaving all his past behind him, Crabbe returned to Muston on May 14th, and on Tuesday, the 19th, quitted his parish for good. Some of his parishioners, Nonconformists or others, were, his son asserts, so hostile to him that they had the bells rung for his successor

12 *March*, 1814. . . . On Thursday I mean to reach Buckden and then think of proceeding to London, where I hope to find the Bishop of Salisbury whom you have with so much kindness prepared to see me " (Mackay Collection).
　[1] Quoted by B. p. 60.

before his departure.[1] An angry sarcasm or two must have risen to his lips on the solitary road that leads from Muston to Grantham.[2]

II

TROWBRIDGE and its environs had produced a most favourable impression on him.[3] Then as now, this small town, with about twelve thousand inhabitants,[4] supported itself by the manufacture of cloth, and its population was composed "chiefly of the working class, with a sprinkling of shopkeepers and wealthy manufacturers."[5] Built along a slope, the foot of which is watered by the Biss, an affluent of the Avon, and which ascends in a north-westerly direction towards Hilperton and Devizes, it doubtless already possessed its three main, sickle-shaped streets, connected by a

[1] B. p. 59. But I suspect the Rev. Henry Byron of having started the peal. He probably rang his predecessor out by ringing himself in. We read, in fact, in a letter to Dr. Gordon, dated Grantham (and no longer Muston) on May 21st, 1814: "Mr. Byron has reproved me (I had almost said reproached) for my delay, and as he cannot judge of the motives for my late journey into Suffolk, he may think with justice, tho' he acts with precipitancy. He complains of money lost by being kept out of his house, but as I am only seven days beyond his own time, I hope the sum is not large, and if that will satisfy him, I will gladly pay it." Crabbe left his sons at Grantham (cf. B. p. 60, and this same letter to Dr. Gordon): "As we can obtain no aid at Croxton till the first Sunday in August, it is agreed among us to give up our plan, and George will remain (with his brother perhaps) at Grantham in lodging till that time."

[2] The foregoing dates are supplied by Crabbe's "Accompt-Book for 1814." The following is the text : "Wednesday Jan. 5 = Duke's invitation.—7 at Belvoir.—Monday 21 Feb. 1814: Trowbridge and Croxton from Duke of Rutland.—Call at Croxton.—24-7-8 Lincoln [at Dr. Gordon's].—3-5 March Belvoir.—Tuesday 15 March Leave Muston at night 6.—16 on to London. Institution first at Palace to Croxton.—17 London. Mrs. Osborne's hotel [cf. B. p. 58]. See the Bishop.—18 Instituted to Trowbridge. At night to see Kean in Shylock.—20 This evening at Drury Lane. Kean in *Hamlet*. First fruits office.—21 [?] Mr. Vickery.—Tuesday 22 March. Journey to Trowbridge.—23 Dine with Mr. Fletcher. He has three guineas a week.— Friday 25 in London from Trowbridge. Monday 18 April. Mr. Byron inducted to Muston.—2 May. Grantham, Beccles.—5-10 Aldbro'.—12 London.—13-4 Grantham and Muston.—Friday 27 May 1814. Kemble in *Macbeth*.—Wednesday 1 June. Arrived at Trowbridge " (Broadley Collection).

[3] Letter to Dr. Gordon, dated Muston, April 5th, 1814: "I like the country about Trowbridge extremely and Trowbridge itself very well" (Mackay Collection).

[4] These at least are the figures given by Howitt (see below, next note). In a letter to John Murray of January 28th, 1819, Crabbe speaks of a "population of more than 8,000 inhabitants."

[5] Wm. Howitt, *Homes and Haunts of the most Eminent British Poets*, 3rd ed. 1857, "Crabbe," pp. 350-69 ; for Trowbridge in particular, pp. 366-7, where there is a curious description of the Woolpack Inn.

number of short alleys. The church, half-way up the hill, just behind the central point, occupies, with its churchyard, a sort of terrace between two of these thoroughfares. At that time it was a very "old building," almost in a ruinous state. The tall and slender spire which now adorns it dates from 1847 only. About a hundred yards from its door, going away from the town, stands the parsonage, concealed by lofty trees and long greyish walls. The house, a commodious one for those days, remains the same as when Crabbe inhabited it. It consists of a one-storied central block with three windows, crowned by two gables and flanked by two wings, that on the right containing the very low but tolerably well-lighted ground-floor room which the poet made his study. How confined and dull life would seem to us in these dark and narrow apartments! How we should long to escape from them into the pure air of the spacious garden surrounded by meadows! Crabbe, who was not so exacting, would have been perfectly satisfied if the repairs undertaken by his predecessor had been finished and the floors laid down. Unfortunately, a considerable sum was still required to put the building in good order, and the Rev. Gilbert Beresford for a long time had trouble with Crabbe on this subject.[1] Never-

[1] Crabbe arrived at Trowbridge on June 1st, 1814. It is probable that Beresford had left as early as June, 1813, for on July 21st, 1814, Crabbe, who no doubt was obliged to defray the expenses of the living for the current year, wrote as follows to the banker Timbrell of Trowbridge: "As I purpose to summon the occupiers of land in this parish before the proper judges if I be not allowed what I consider as my due, it is necessary that I should give you this information, not that I have any claim upon Mr. Beresford, but because I believe that he is mistaken in his claim, and if he has taken for three quarters of the year [viz. from Michaelmas, 1812, to Midsummer, 1813] he will I apprehend be obliged to repay a part of it. I am very ready to enter into an agreement, but I thought it was a fact known to every person conversant in these matters that the tithe which falls from Midsummer to Michaelmas is of much more value than it is in any other part of the year, and certainly equal to all the rest if taken strictly."—Timbrell, sending this letter to Beresford, who was then at Aylstone, near Leicester, added: "You will observe by the note on the other side that Mr. Crabbe, altho' he does not directly charge you with the quarter due 24th June 1813, yet in fact it will eventually fall on you, as you promised to refund to me in case Mr. Crabbe had a right to it—how far he is correct in the demand he has made, not being then presented to the living, I leave to your superior judgement, not being much acquainted in the Ecclesiastical Law. He has told the Churchwardens he shall expect an answer by the 29th inst.; otherwise he will proceed" (Mackay Collection).

To the inevitable wrangle about tithes (see above, pp. 201-2), was added a claim for dilapidations, an incumbent being bound to hand over the parsonage in good and tenantable condition to his successor. Hence the

theless, Trowbridge was better than Muston. No
doubt, after heavy rain, the Biss, rising suddenly,
would flood the low-lying quarters, and the town
would be covered with mud,[1] no doubt also the
clicking of the weaving-looms might become monotonous, but the busy scene was attractive to our
realist, and the rich pastures bounded on the south
by the Westbury hills, the winding valleys of the
Frome and Avon, which led the pedestrian by easy
and shady paths to the brilliant city of Bath—all these
surroundings had an air of abundant prosperity well
calculated to gladden the heart.

Crabbe seemed to grow young again. Since his
last illness his health had much improved, the crisis
of October, 1813, having apparently purged his system
of the mischief that was undermining it. He became
stouter. "Although he began to stoop, his limbs and
motions were strong and active." His looks improved
with advancing age : " his temples getting more bare,
the height of his well-developed forehead appeared
greater." He had met with a cordial welcome from
the principal families of the place : on the evening
of his arrival, June 1st, Mr. Waldron, his future
colleague on the Bench, had received him with open
arms.[2] There was some secret opposition, it is true,
in two quarters : a certain number of the inhabitants,
enamoured of the extempore eloquence and apostolic
zeal of the Rev. Mr. Fletcher,[3] had petitioned the Duke

frequent demands made by Crabbe, which, however, were always fruitless.
On February 11th, 1815, he wrote to Dr. Gordon : " I have obtained
nothing of my predecessor in this Rectory, except an honest confession of
embarrassments, and it is evident that I must live in unfinished and even
unfloored rooms or be at the expense myself. . . . And this is not the sole
misfortune : I have indeed, by many efforts and some threatening, obtained a
promise from the late sequestrators that a part of the sums so inconsiderately
paid to Mr. Beresford and his solicitor [*i.e.* the three quarters of the income
from Michaelmas, 1812, to Michaelmas, 1813 : Crabbe claimed "the greater
part of the tithe of 1813," probably because Beresford having left in June at
the latest, had no right to the quarter from Midsummer to Michaelmas, 1813,
which brought in a good half of the year's income] shall be accounted for to
me, but I must wait long and lose a considerable part of my dues even then,
for though the law might give me a title, it cannot procure my opponents a
fund " (Mackay Collection).

[1] Cf. a letter of December 11th, 1827, in which Crabbe speaks of the
"streets of Trowbridge, where I see a man continually shovelling the mire
away."

[2] B. pp. 60-1.

[3] An excellent man, however—cf. the following passage in a letter from
Crabbe to Dr. Gordon (above, p. 381, n. 1) : " I must hasten to Trowbridge,
where, while this hurrying, yet not ill-natured successor of mine [Byron] is

of Rutland to give him the living. According to these parishioners, the more or less faded sheets which the Rev. Mr. Crabbe, "the poet," read to them every Sunday, lacked animation ; his voice was too weak to stir up their consciences as they would have wished.[1] He moralised very wisely, but did not "awaken" souls, and the Trowbridge "Evangelicals" regretted his predecessor. Besides, this manufacturing town contained many Nonconformists, for whom the fourth Letter of *The Borough* remained an abomination. In a very short time, however, Crabbe, by a combination of firmness and gentleness, contrived to command the respect and win the esteem of all. A lover of conciliation, he had discerned that this uneasiness wanted to be allayed : his first sermon, delivered on June 5th, 1814,[2] dwelt on the mutual tolerance which Christian sects should practise towards one another, in the interest of their common task.[3] The author of a *History of Trowbridge*, published in the same year, declares that "Mr. Crabb seems to be a very moderate and very peaceable clergyman."[4] Avoiding henceforth all religious controversy, he soon had no more opponents in the parish. And the upper middle class, flattered at having one of the most famous writers of the time for their pastor, sent him frequent invitations to their houses. "I was surprised as well as delighted," says his son,[5] "to observe the tempered exuberance to which his spirits, lately so sombre and desponding, were raised, how lively and cheerful he appeared in every company, pleased with all about him, and evidently imparting pleasure wherever he went."

urging me to be speedy in my exit, the patient and good-natured minister of that place, who is engaged and much wanted in a new situation, kindly and patiently waits for me, and even presses me to do all my business before I release him. It is a happiness when we find one man thus compensating by his virtues for the inconsideration of another."

[1] See a singular anonymous letter, dated Trowbridge, June 13th, 1816, of which it is enough, I think, to quote the last sentence : "You wood do Well Anofe for to Read fables and plays and poeitry : but the bible you are Quite Ignorant of you are aⁿ Ass and a fool and A Laughin Stock for decenters" (Broadley Collection). The Rev. Erskine Neale (*The Living and the Dead*, 2nd series, London, 1829, pp. 44-5) seems to have heard of some of these complaints.

[2] Fletcher had inducted him on the 3rd.

[3] See above, p. 213.

[4] James Bodman, *A Concise History of Trowbridge*, Bristol, 1814, p. 18, note.

[5] B. pp. 60-1.

Crabbe was extremely susceptible to the charm of the feminine friendships that came in his way. At Trowbridge or in the neighbourhood he had " six female friends, unknown to each other, but all dear, very dear to him." "With men I do not much associate," he wrote to Mrs. Leadbeater in December, 1816, "not as deserting, and much less disliking, the male part of society, but as being unfit for it; not hardy, nor grave, not knowing enough, nor sufficiently acquainted with the every-day concerns of men. But my beloved creatures have minds with which I can better assimilate."[1] His cheerful politeness, his affectionate cordiality, his ceremonious and well-turned compliments,[2] seemed a delicate homage, coming from such a poet. His pointed remarks on the passions common to mankind, his tranquil humour, his satirical touches gave his conversation a piquancy and an unexpectedness which women appreciated more than men, too absorbed as these are in ephemeral interests. Under the softness of his manners there lay a discreet irony, which his friends liked to draw out perhaps, for it never wounded. How pleasant life must be in his company!—some of his young female parishioners at Muston had said to themselves after Mira's death. And in the eagerness of their devotion, they had begun a tender correspondence with him. His age, which he urged by way of objection, was of little consequence. " No, Mr. Crabbe," declared one of these amiable enthusiasts, " I honor and revere age, most especially as you are entirely free from all the disagreeable qualities mostly attendant upon it, such as ill-humour, etc., etc., etc.—and give me leave to say without flattery that I never saw a young man of more amiable or pleasing manners than yourself—it would be rather dangerous for me if I should." To these protestations of his " dear Fanny " Crabbe had replied by evasive thanks.[3]

[1] Letter quoted by B. p. 65 (cf. *Leadbeater Papers*, 2nd ed. 1862, vol. ii. p. 340).

[2] Cf. Moore's *Memoirs*, under date July 5th, 1819 (vol. ii. ed. 1853, p. 335) : " In talking of Crabbe with Hallam at dinner, he quoted what Miss . . . had said of him as a companion, that the cake was no doubt very good, but there was too much sugar to cut through in getting at it."

[3] The rough draft of Crabbe's letter is written on Fanny's: " Your note affects me. I do not think that I rightly understood you. You kindly overlook my age, but I cannot. If the regard and kind wishes as well as remembrances of such a man can be in any degree gratifying to you, this

But in September, 1814, he was staying at Sidmouth, where he again met Miss Charlotte Ridout, another of his attached friends. She was " really a very pleasant, sensible and good young lady," elegant even,[1] " one of those who had for some two years past honoured him with their letters " and offered to share the solitude of the large house at Trowbridge. Should he accept the hand thus held out? He was astonished at this young girl's readiness to sacrifice herself to a man old enough to be her father; he knew that she had just rejected the addresses of a suitor of the same age as herself, an excellent match in every respect, except a certain weakness of intellect. So Charlotte had a real affection for him! This time he encouraged her, not without much imprudence. He walked with her morning and evening on "Sidmouth terrace" and breathed its " balmy air"; in her company no doubt he gazed on "the full orb'd moon" from the cliffs of Dawlish, "explored the far bay at Exmouth beacon," or rested on "Teignmouth's pebbly shore."[2] On September 22nd he made his declaration, and was accepted. On his departure he composed some lines which are a second promise :

> Yes! I must go—it is a part
> That cruel Fortune has assign'd me,—
> Must go, and leave, with aching heart,
> What most that heart adores behind me.
>
> Still I shall see thee on the sand
> Till o'er the space the water rises,
> Still shall in thought behind thee stand,
> And watch the look affection prizes.
>
> But ah ! what youth attends thy side
> With eyes that speak his soul's devotion—
> To thee as constant as the tide
> That gives the restless wave its motion?

I can promise. You flatter me by the opinion you express. I certainly do not think that age makes itself respectable by ill nature, and I believe neither man nor woman is the worse for being agreeable, but still, my dear Fanny, there must be many defects in the aged which no lightness of spirits can make up. Of this we will not dispute. I once more thank you, and assure you of my kindest regard and am affectionately yours, G. C.

"I know not whether you have any connections at Bath, where I frequently am. If at any time I can be of use, direct to Rev^d. G. C., Trowbridge, Wilts" (Broadley Collection).

[1] According to Fitzgerald, MS. notes: "Miss Ridout I remember, an elegant spinster, friend of my mother's about 1825: she had been at Sidmouth and knew Crabbe." This passage is wrongly punctuated in Canon Ainger's *Life of Crabbe*, p. 152.

[2] *Works*, p. 436, l. 567, and n. 3.

Still in thy train must he appear,
For ever gazing, smiling, talking ?
Ah ! would that he were sighing here,
And I were there beside thee walking !

Wilt thou to him that arm resign,
Who is to that dear heart a stranger,
And with those matchless looks of thine
The peace of this poor youth endanger ?

Away this fear that fancy makes
When night and death's dull image hide thee ;
In sleep, to thee my mind awakes ;
Awake, it sleeps to all beside thee.

Who could in absence bear the pain
Of all this fierce and jealous feeling,
But for the hope to meet again
And see those smiles all sorrow healing ?

Then shall we meet, and, heart to heart,
Lament that fate such friends should sever,
And I shall say—" We must not part ";
And thou wilt answer—" Never, never ! "[1]

How could she doubt the sincerity of a love expressed
with such fervour ? Alas ! a few months of separation were enough to extinguish this bright flame. On
October 5th Crabbe received a visit from Mr. Ridout,
who was doubtless anxious to obtain a formal engagement, and on December 12th "Charlotte's picture was
returned."[2] What had taken place in the interval ?
Had the lady's family offered any opposition ? I fancy
not. It seems pretty clear that Crabbe, in one of those
returns of cool reason which were apt to paralyse his
impulses,[3] reflected on the plan, that he weighed all
its drawbacks—the difference of age, the possible
dissatisfaction of his sons,[4] that he remembered his own

---

[1] *Works*, p. 266: *To a Lady on leaving her at Sidmouth.* The lines
quoted by B. p. 63 are not autobiographical.

[2] See in Fitzgerald's MS. notes the following extract from the *Poet's
Journal*: "(1814) Sept. 22, Sidmouth. Miss Ridout. Declaration. Acceptance. Oct. 5. Mr. Ridout. Dec. 12. Charlotte's picture returned."

[3] See above, p. 89.

[4] B. writes, p. 63: "On one occasion at least [evidently that of Miss
Ridout] my brother and myself looked with sincere pleasure to the prospect
of seeing our father's happiness increased by a new alliance." But the manuscript notes of the same Biographer are still more "sincere": "1814 *circiter*
July he is *transferred* to Miss Ridout and goes to Sidmouth in Septr. 1815
not broken off in [Jan. 10], but soon after."

satires,[1] and that, in the conflict between " prudence and inclination," he sacrificed his passion to his misgivings and preserved his freedom. But this decision was not arrived at without a severe pang. Solitude was irksome, and family life indispensable to him. " I am alone now," he wrote to Mrs. Leadbeater, " and since my removing into a busy town among the multitude, the loneliness is but more apparent and more melancholy."[2] " Never," he said to Dr. Gordon in a letter about Charlotte, " have I had such a call for self-denial, and even yet almost doubt my victory."[3] What he needed was not the society of a young woman, but that of his children. In the spring of 1815 his sons had undertaken a walking tour through England. They remained absent for nearly two years. He spent a few days only with them at Beccles in October, 1816.[4] But when, in December of the same year, his

[1] Cf. *Parish Register*, ii. 359: "Twice had old Lodge been tied"; and the story of Nathan Kirk, "at thy years trepanned!"

[2] Letter quoted above, p. 385, n. 1.

[3] The following is the text of this very interesting letter, which is dated February 11th, 1815 (cf. above, p. 382, n. 1): ". . . I know not whether in one of my letters I did not give some intimation of a design I had entertained of making my too large house less solitary, and there was a Lady somewhat too young indeed who had the courage to offer her assistance. She is really a very pleasant, sensible and good young Lady, and one of those who has [*sic*] honoured me by her letters for some two years past. I was astonished by her readyness to give up so much to a man as old as her father, and the more because I made out upon fair, honest enquiry that she rejected the proposal of a youth [cf. the poem quoted above, pp. 386-7] eligible in every respect except a certain degree of weakness in his Intellects. I have never had such call for self-denial, and even yet almost doubt my victory: yet I am afraid prudence and inclination are not on one side, and in this fear I remain solitary but free . . ." (Mackay Collection).
See, as to this solitude, another letter from Trowbridge, dated August 5th, 1816, and addressed to Colonel Houlton of Farleigh Castle (cf. below, p. 390, n. 2), then at Brussels : " Your most welcome letter first met my view on my return from a short excursion and entirely took off that heavy and spiritless effect which a man is disposed to feel in returning to a solitary room which he must occupy in silence. Even the plants which once grew there, though I will not part with them, create in me something very much akin to melancholy, and yet I preserve them with more than common care : such are the contradictory feelings of our nature, I mean the nature of such of us as do feel : the gloominess of the season has in some measure had its effect upon the mind." Then he thanks his correspondent for his " repeated and unwearied attention to a man situated as I am and almost standing alone in society, at least at the Time when I had first the happiness of seeing that dear seat of hospitality and cheerfulness " (Broadley Collection).

[4] In his letter to Colonel Houlton, begun August 5th, 1816, he says: "HAWLEY HOUSE, *Sunday* 11 *August*. . . . Hither, in consequence of a letter from Mrs. Norris, I came on Thursday, and with the utmost expedition because the time is limited and we part on the 14th when they proceed on a projected tour in and through Wales and I to the coast of Suffolk." Cf. also B. p. 62.

son John married Anna Maria Crowfoot, the daughter of a Beccles doctor,[1] and came to live at the Rectory of Trowbridge as curate, he no longer thought the house too large or his life too lonely. He felt that he really possessed what he had sought for,[2] and would perhaps not have found in an alliance with Miss Ridout—the happiness of a united family circle. I am afraid that in his mistake, which was due to his need of affection, he may have bruised a loving heart.[3] But he had ardently and sincerely re-experienced the best moments of his youthful love, and his poetry bears traces of this rejuvenescence.[4]

III

WITH John to help and, in case of need, to take his place in the discharge of his professional duties, Crabbe was able to entertain the idea of re-entering the "great world," which he had not frequented since 1783. One acquaintanceship after another gradually led him back towards the aristocracy of intellect and rank. On

[1] The marriage took place on Monday, December 2nd (see *The Ipswich Journal* of the 7th).

[2] See a letter to a lady (Mrs. Houlton) published in *The Sphere* of May 31st, 1902, and dated "BATH, 3 *March* 1819. . . . I am writing at the house of Mr. Hoare with whom I became acquainted since you left us. . . . I have not seen Mrs. Norris for many a day, but when I last saw her, I well remember our conversation took its way to Brussels and dwelt a while with you. . . . The Lady Longs are at Sidmouth. . . . Mr. Long and his sons are at Rood Ashton [near Trowbridge]. . . . Miss Long tells me that a certain young Lady whom I once saw at Sidmouth, and had some idea that I might see at Trowbridge is still with her aunt Floyd, and I hope as happy as an aunt can make her. I am now contented to be old and quiet and will not catch a romantic fit any more."

[3] Cf. the following passage in a letter from Miss Hoare (see above, n. 2) to the Biographer, dated Hampstead Heath, February 18th (1832): "How barbarously do the biographers of our day expose incidents which injure the characters of those who can no longer reproach them, and cut their surviving friends to the heart. . . . I know a literary friend of your Father who amused a whole company with a story at his expence, and would probably amuse the public with more such tales, were he to write his life—he might gratify malignity by detailing the story of poor Charlotte Rideout in exaggerated colours ; not many weeks since, *just before her death*, her aunt spoke of Mr. Crabbe in bitter terms and this aunt no doubt has her own coterie, and the story may get abroad." The present "Biographer" might therefore have hesitated to "detail this story" had not the late Canon Ainger already let out the secret (*Life of Crabbe*, p. 152). Perhaps "aunt Floyd" would have liked her niece to marry the young man "with a certain degree of weakness in his Intellects."

[4] Cf. *Tales of the Hall*, vi. : *Adventures of Richard* (above, p. 53, n. 1).

Thursday, February 9th, 1815,[1] he was dining with Colonel Houlton at Farleigh Castle,[2] which Moore thus described nine years afterwards : " A pretty house, beautiful girls, hospitable host and hostess, excellent cook, good champagne and moselle, charming music; what more could a man want?"[3] In the midst of these attractions Crabbe had met his "brother versifier," the Rev. William Lisle Bowles, Vicar of Bremhill. He was a valuable man to know, from the number and the nature of his acquaintances. His vicarage, about three miles north-west of the market town of Calne, was close to Bowood, the ancestral seat of the Marquis of Lansdowne. Few notabilities came to the Park without Bowles being invited to meet them, or without their paying him a visit at Bremhill. For he had a great celebrity. He was said to have been crossed in love when an undergraduate at Oxford, and this disappointment had found vent in a series of sonnets as melodious and melancholy as they are feeble in point of thought. They awakened a lyric echo in Coleridge and Southey —almost their only merit in the eyes of posterity. But in 1789 their plaintive accents had achieved the distinction of novelty. Besides this, Bowles was a character. Proud of his hill, the summit of which is still crowned by his ancient church, and of his village, whose history he took the trouble to write, he had transformed his garden into a museum of curiosities : in one corner was a grotto, in another a " hermitage " adorned with a crucifix, a missal, and inscriptions imitated from Shenstone ; farther on a fountain only awaited the arrival of a visitor to begin playing, while sheep roamed hither and thither with bells "tuned in thirds and fifths." Bowles reminded all his contemporaries of Fielding's clergymen, especially of " Parson Adams." Of an absent-mindedness and simplicity which had become a byword, he felt, he said, out of his element in London, " like a daisy in a hothouse." An amusing anecdote portrays him in all his ingenuousness. On

---

[1] Letter already quoted (p. 388, n. 3), of February 11th, 1815 (a Saturday): "I dined on Thursday with Colonel Holton of Farley—whom I think you know : there I met Mr. Bowles my brother versifier." Their acquaintance might, however, have been an older one, for according to Bowles (letter to B. of January 31st, 1834): " I rode over to Trowbridge to call on him with Lord Lansdowne when he came into the county."

[2] Four miles west of Trowbridge.

[3] Moore's *Memoirs*, vol. iv. p. 179 (April 14th, 1824).

Madame de Staël's visit to Bowood in 1813, Bowles was naturally asked to meet her. In his eagerness, or perhaps heedlessness, he fell from his horse and sprained his shoulder, but rode on notwithstanding. Lord Lansdowne having mentioned this accident and praised his guest's courage, Madame de Staël made Bowles a speech full of compliments, which he suddenly interrupted with these words: "O ma'am, say no more, for I would have done a great deal more to see so great a curiosity"; and on Lord Lansdowne explaining afterwards to Madame de Staël what Bowles was, she remarked, "I see he is only a plain country clergyman without any tact, although a great poet."[1] An excellent man, however, in spite of his foibles, and, according to Moore,[2] "the most delightful of all existing parsons or poets."

Thanks to him, Crabbe made the acquaintance of the noble inmates of Bowood. Lord and Lady Lansdowne, favoured by fortune, were winning the good opinion of society. Lord Henry Petty, third Marquis of Lansdowne from 1809, was the son of that Earl of Shelburne to whom Crabbe in his distress had formerly appealed, but in vain.[3] Chancellor of the Exchequer at the age of twenty-four,[4] liberally inclined and broad-minded, he already enjoyed that enviable reputation for disinterestedness, probity, and refined courtesy which Sydney Smith was fond of acknowledging.[5] He was accounted, along with Rogers and Sir George Beaumont, one of the most enlightened and generous patrons of English art. Taking advantage of the extent and the fortunate configuration of his park, which is divided by wooded dells converging on a large open space filled by a lake, he had made Bowood the rendezvous of all the celebrities of Europe. And Lady Lansdowne enhanced the charm of this hospitality. There is a concurrence of genuine testimony to her graciousness, to the unaffectedness of her manners and the liveliness of

---

[1] Miss Edgeworth's *Letters*, ed. by Hare, vol. i. p. 250.

[2] *Memoirs*, vol. ii. p. 181 ; cf. *ibid.* p. 153 and vol. vii. p. 204. See also a letter from Southey (*Life and Correspondence*, ed. by Cuthbert Southey, 1850, vol. vi. pp. 314-15), dated Wells, November 16th, 1836. Cf. also below, p. 462.

[3] See above, pp. 95-6.

[4] In 1806, with Fox.

[5] In an interview with Moore (Moore's *Memoirs*, vol. vii. pp. 204-5).

her conversation. "She is so amiable," Miss Edge-worth wrote, "and so desirous to make others happy, that it is impossible not to love her; and the most envious of mortals, I think, would have the heart opened to sympathy with her."[1] Among the common friends of the Lansdownes and of Bowles was the wealthy collector and poet, Samuel Rogers. Being on a visit to Bowood, he went all the way to Trowbridge, with the object of making Crabbe's acquaintance. The poet happened to be out, but he was touched with Rogers's attention, and sent him a copy of *The Borough* or perhaps of the *Tales*, with a note the highly ceremonious and involved style of which ill expressed all the pleasure given him by the proposed meeting.[2] This took place either at Bowood or at Bremhill. The result of it was that Crabbe came to London on Rogers's invitation in June, 1817.

He arrived there on Thursday, the 19th, in the com-pany of his friend Waldron, and, in a letter of the 22nd, placed himself at Rogers's disposal: "Do not how-ever permit me to intrude too much on your time, for I well know how you are consulted and engaged, but, speaking for myself alone, I would say, dear Sir, dispose of me as it seems best to you. I will dine with you when you can take me into your company, and I will wait on Lord Holland when it shall appear to you that his Lordship will be disposed to receive me. . . . My few engagements and my small business in town I reckon as nothing—the society to which you introduce me is all!"[3] A couple of days after-wards, Crabbe was breakfasting at St. James's Place, in the sumptuous abode which Rogers, banker by profession and poet by inclination, had built for him-self. Two days later Lady Holland, with character-istic impetuosity, "came and took him to Holland

---

[1] *Letters*, vol. i. p. 207 and pp. 249-52.

[2] "Mr. Crabbe feels himself much gratified by the obliging attentions of Mr. Rogers. He has great pleasure in the prospect of meeting a gentleman to whom Mr. Bowles had given him hope that he should be introduced. In the morning, Wednesday, he promises himself this satisfaction, which is abated solely by the fear that (from want of foresight) he has occasioned trouble to Mr. Rogers, when he so obligingly sought to communicate the pleasure he intended that Mr. Crabbe should receive. Tuesday morning." Quoted by Clayden (*Rogers and his Contemporaries*, pp. 242-3), who wrongly assigns to it the date of 1810 or 1812.

[3] Letter quoted by Clayden (*op. cit.*, date June 23rd, 1817, which, I believe, should be the 22nd).

House." [1] The reader may remember the praise which Macaulay, in one of his *Essays*,[2] lavishes on this aristocratic residence, the most celebrated and the most frequented of all London for about twenty years. Built on rising ground in the old village of Kensington, the house, which dated from the beginning of the seventeenth century, was rich in historic memories. Not only had Cromwell and Fairfax deliberated there, but the apartment was also shown in which Addison, Secretary of State and husband of the Countess of Warwick, used to work. The extensive park, on which modern streets and buildings have now encroached, was then attractive and intersected by long avenues. In the rooms Crabbe lingered with pleasure over the busts, the statues, and the portraits, those of Bacon and Fox among others. He was bound by close ties to this house. He could not forget that Fox and his nephew Lord Holland had encouraged him to publish *The Parish Register*[3] ten years previously, and that Lord Holland himself had accepted the dedication of it. Besides, the curiosity of so shrewd an observer could not fail to be stimulated by his host and hostess and their friends. A worthy representative of a hitherto illustrious family, Lord Holland was distinguished for the intelligence which played over his massive features, for the cordiality of his manners, for his strong good sense, and the causticity of his wit. Without being in any way an orator, he excelled in reply, and he possessed a gift of scornful mimicry, with which he defended in the House of Lords his uncle's liberal ideas on the abolition of slavery and on electoral reform. Yet he was inferior to his wife in originality of character. Lady Holland was beyond question a unique figure, morally and physically. Unfaithful to her first husband, whom she left to follow Lord Holland, she had from her youth displayed independence of conduct and imperiousness of temper. She interfered with and domineered over everybody around her. John Allen, the physician, Lord Holland's secretary and librarian,

---

[1] Cf. Crabbe's *Journal*, reproduced by B. pp. 67-71. I confine myself to a connected account of the salient events, many remarks being of too summary a kind to find a place here.

[2] Entitled *Lord Holland*. Cf. on the same subject a very full account by S. J. Reid, *The Life and Times of Sydney Smith*, ed. 1901, pp. 106-13.

[3] See above, pp. 220-1.

a distinguished biologist and historian, "equally intelligent and affable, must have had a difficult part" to play with her, and "executed it well," in Crabbe's opinion. He knew how to preserve his independence with this despotic woman, who despised all reticence and would tolerate no contradiction. "*Elle est toute assertion*," said Talleyrand, "*mais quand on demande la preuve, c'est là son secret.*" And Moore added, "Poets inclined to a plethora of vanity would find a dose of Lady Holland now and then very good for their complaint."[1] But she had the art, it would appear, of leading a conversation; her ambition was to have the first *salon* in London, and, in spite of her exacting ways, which entertained people,[2] in spite of her caprices, which they made fun of, she had succeeded.[3]

Crabbe's visit to Holland House must have been very pleasant to him: he met there two poets, much younger than himself, Moore and Campbell, and the latter has left us an account of their interview in a letter addressed to Crabbe's son: "He and Tom Moore and myself lounged the better part of a morning[4] about the park and library. Our conversation, I remember, was about novelists. Your father was a strong Fieldingite, and I as sturdy a Smollettite. His mildness in literary argument struck me with surprise in so stern a poet of nature, and I could not but contrast the unassumingness of his manners with the originality of his powers. In what may be called the ready-money small-talk of conversation, his facility might not perhaps seem equal to the known calibre of his talents; but in the progress of conversation I recollect remarking that there was a vigilant shrewdness that almost eluded you by keeping its watch so quietly. Though an oldish man when I saw him, he was not a *laudator temporis acti*, but a decided lover

---

[1] Moore's *Memoirs*, vol. ii. p. 328.

[2] She was called familiarly "The Princess of Madagascar," or simply "Madagascar," a nickname which had been given her by Lady Caroline Lamb in *Glenarvon* (cf. *The Creevey Papers*, ed. 1904, vol. ii. p. 15).

[3] Cf. Greville, *Memoirs*, vol. ii. ed. 1897, pp. 340-1: "Though everybody who goes there finds something to abuse or to ridicule in the mistress of the house, or its ways, all continue to go [in 1832]; all like it more or less, and whenever, by the death of either, it shall come to an end, a vacuum will be made in society, which nothing will supply. It is the house of all Europe; the world will suffer by the loss; and it may with truth be said that it will 'eclipse the gaiety of nations.'"

[4] On Thursday, the 26th; cf. B. p. 67 and Campbell's letter, *ibid.* p. 68.

of later times. . . . He was very frank, and even confidential, in speaking of his own feelings. Though in
a serene tone of spirits, he confessed to me that since
the death of his wife he had scarcely known positive
happiness. . . . When Moore left us we were joined by
Foscolo[1]; and I remember as distinctly as if it had
been yesterday the contrasted light in which Crabbe
and Foscolo struck me. It is not an invidious contrast—at least my feelings towards Ugo's memory
intend it not to be so—yet it was to me morally
instructive, and, I need hardly say, greatly in favour
of your father. They were both men of genius, and
both simple. But what a different sort of simplicity!
I felt myself between them as if I had been standing
between a roaring cataract and a placid stream. Ugo
raged and foamed in argument, to my amusement, but
not at all to your father's liking. He could not abide
him. What we talked about I do not recollect; but
only that Ugo's impetuosity was a foil to the amenity of
the elder bard." In the evening among the guests
at dinner Crabbe saw Lord Brougham, the future
defender of Queen Caroline. He appreciated his facile
eloquence, always ready to expatiate on all subjects,
and found in him some resemblance to Burke. He
also made the acquaintance of the Countess of Bess-
borough, mother of the celebrated Lady Caroline
Lamb, and admired her "frank and affectionate
character." He was introduced to the widow and
to the sister of Ch. J. Fox. "I remember," he wrote
in the *Journal*, "meeting Miss Fox thirty years since,
but did not tell her so, and yet could not help
appearing to know her; and she questions me much
on the subject. Parry it pretty well." For it would
not have done to hurt poor Miss Fox's feelings by
reminding her of her age.

On the following day, Friday, June 27th, there
took place a ceremony to which Crabbe was invited
by order of Lady Holland. The illustrious actor,
J. P. Kemble, brother of Mrs. Siddons, was retiring
from the stage: four days previously he had played
Coriolanus at Covent Garden for the last time, and a
committee had been formed, with Lord Holland as
chairman, for the purpose of offering him a banquet

[1] Ugo Foscolo, Italian patriot and author of *Ultime Lettere di Jacopo Ortis*
(1802).

and a memento of his long career. Crabbe and Rogers therefore repaired to this entertainment, which was given in the "Freemasons' Tavern."[1] They found the room full, and took their places "about half-way down the common seats." But Campbell, having perceived them, came up to them and invited them "into the committee-room." Dinner was announced at seven o'clock. Kemble and the chairman, Lord Holland, preceded by the members of the committee, entered the hall to the sound of music. Being thus promoted to the table "above the steps," Crabbe sat down by Lord Erskine, and was able to hear the recitation of the ode[2] written by Campbell in honour of the tragedian who had impersonated so many of Shakspeare's characters. He listened with curiosity to the toast which Talma proposed of his fellow-actor in a few "not ill-turned" English sentences. Then, remembering his engagements, he left the company before the speeches were finished, and went to Vauxhall with Rogers, whose sister was awaiting them there with a large party.[3]

A long series of invitations—this is a summary description of the month which Crabbe spent in London.[4] On June 30th he was taken for the first time to the drawing-room in which his future publisher, John Murray, received the popular authors of the day and hung their portraits. Crabbe's not being among them, the painter Phillips was commissioned to execute it. The poet consequently had to sit for some time in the morning several days running. On July 2nd, at the invitation of Campbell, who professed a respectful affection for him,[5] he dined at Sydenham; and the party, consisting of Moore, Rogers, Crabbe, and Campbell, planned the foundation of a "Poets' Club," of which our clergyman was to be the president. For want of presidential zeal, no doubt, the

---

[1] In Great Queen Street. For further details cf. J. Boaden, *Memoirs of Kemble*, vol. ii. pp. 558 and 561-4.

[2] *Valedictory Stanzas.*

[3] It will be noted that after this date there is no further mention of the Hollands in the poet's *Journal*. The reason is that they had gone to Belgium. (Cf. in the *Works* of Foscolo, Florence, 1850-90, vol. viii. p. 427, a letter from Lord Holland, in Italian, dated "Brusselle, 9 Luglio, 1817.")

[4] On June 28th he moved to a lodging at 37, Bury Street.

[5] "Something of a filial upward-looking affection for your matured genius and patriarchal reputation" (letter from Campbell to Crabbe, from Sydenham, June 25th (in reality the 27th), 1817, quoted by B. p. 67, n. 5).

project was abandoned. In a letter to his sister, Campbell is full of praise for the man whom he looked on as a venerable representative of a bygone generation, as a contemporary of "the giants before the flood," as a friend of Johnson and of Reynolds. "Crabbe is absolutely delightful," he writes; "simple as a child, but shrewd, and often good-naturedly reminding you of the best parts of his poetry. He took his wine cheerfully—far from excess; but his heart really seemed to expand, and he was full of anecdote and social feeling." [1] The fact is that Crabbe, always reserved, silent, "extinguished," as he said himself,[2] with strangers or in too large a company, felt at his ease with a small party of people whom he liked; in that case his courtesy and his liveliness made him an agreeable companion.

Hardly had he returned from Sydenham when he was invited to Wimbledon, where Lord Spencer had a magnificent property, which had already aroused Hannah More's enthusiasm.[3] "The grounds," observes Crabbe in his turn, "more beautiful than any I have yet seen; more extensive, various, rich. The profusion of roses extraordinary," not to mention the violets and the birds. On the following day, which was a Friday, Crabbe returned to London in Rogers's carriage to dine with Lord Lansdowne and revisit the "porter's lodge" where, thirty-seven years previously, he had left his timid petition. Then came an excursion to Twickenham, where his old friend Wilbraham awaited him. "I hear," wrote the latter, "that you are received by every one as you ought to be, which I always told you would be the case, and you now clearly perceive that the author of *The Library*, *Borough*, etc., is far distinguished from all the ephemeral Rimers of the last thirty years." [4] How

---

[1] *Life and Letters of Th. Campbell*, ed. by Wm. Beattie, 1849, vol. ii. pp. 333-4. Moore has alluded to this dinner in his *Verses to the Poet's* [*i.e.* Crabbe's] *Inkstand*, Crabbe's inkstand (perhaps that of Ariosto) having been offered to him by George and John Crabbe after the death of their father. This piece, written in May, 1832, appeared in *The Metropolitan* two or three months later.

[2] Letter to John Murray, of October 18th, 1819, where he speaks of "a Lady [Mrs. Murray] who has repeatedly shown me that attention which people of my turn of mind, who are extinguished in general society, find so peculiarly pleasant" (Murray Collection).

[3] *The Life and Correspondence of Mrs. Hannah More*, ed. by Wm. Roberts, 2nd ed. 1834, vol. i. p. 174.

[4] Letter dated Twickenham, July 8th, 1817 (Broadley Collection).

could he resist such a cordial and "classical" appeal? So Crabbe went to Twickenham, inspected "Pope's house," and, in the course of a three hours' drive through this pleasing country, recognised Sir Joshua Reynolds's villa at Richmond Hill, and visited Hampton Court, whence he returned to London through Richmond Park and Brentford.

On July 11th he was breakfasting again with Rogers,[1] where William Spencer called for him. "This gentleman," says Crabbe, "is grandson to the Duke of Marlborough. He married, at nineteen, a very beautiful and most accomplished woman, in the court of the Duke of Weimar. She was sixteen.[2] His manner is fascinating, and his temper all complacency and kindness. His poetry far beyond that implied in the character of *Vers de Société*." Spencer, in fact, who had been successively member for Woodstock and Commissioner of Stamps, was also a poet. In 1796, about seven years after his marriage, he had published a translation of Bürger's celebrated ballad *Lenore*, and had thus acquired a celebrity which was enhanced by his conversational powers and by his occasional poems. Like Moore, but in a higher sphere, he flitted about society, living alternately in Curzon Street and at Petersham, where he occupied a house, just outside Richmond Park, belonging to his friend Sir Henry Englefield. The last-named, a fervent Catholic, a scholar, mathematician, and antiquary, became one of Crabbe's favourites.[3] On July 20th the poet notes the pleasure given him by an evening spent in Sir Harry's London house, which overlooked Hyde Park and the Serpentine River. "Disappointed of Mr. Spencer," he writes; "but Mrs. Spencer and Miss Churchill dine with us. Mr. Murray and Mr. Standish. Nothing particularly worthy of remark at dinner; but after dinner one of the best conversations since I came to town. Mr. Spencer and Miss Churchill chiefly; on the effect of high polish on minds; chiefly female; Sir Harry sometimes joining, and

---

[1] On the 15th Rogers and Moore left for Paris. Crabbe's stay in London might thus be divided into three successive periods, each having its leading personage : Lord Holland first, then Rogers, and lastly Sir Harry Englefield.

[2] She was the daughter of "Count Jenison Walworth" (cf. Hon. Wm. Spencer, *Poems with Biographical Memoir*, 1835).

[3] Cf. *Journal* (B. p. 70), July 19th : "Go and call on Mrs. Spencer; find Sir Harry Englefield. These are two favourite characters."

Miss Spencer. A very delightful evening. Sir
Harry's present of Ariosto's inkstand. Of a double
value, as a gift, and from the giver. Part painfully
at one o'clock. Miss Churchill a very superior and
interesting woman." No wonder that Crabbe had
dreams after all this!

The charm of these visits was occasionally enhanced
by little surprises. One day, for instance, he met
Canning, who, on July 17th, sent him an invitation to
dine at Gloucester Lodge on the following Monday.
And Crabbe duly noted the beauty of the gardens and
of the house, as well as the excellence of the " minis-
terial claret." Or again, at eleven o'clock in the
evening, Lady Caroline Lamb[1] appeared at John
Murray's and offered to take him to Melbourne House
to join her party at twelve. After some hesitation,
due to " curiosity," he declined. But Lady Caroline,
struck by his amiability, sent him a letter[2] which
must have drawn a smile from him : " Will you I
say forgive me for putting you to the pain of
wasting with me a moment and first how came you
who appear so calm, so *gentle*, benevolent towards
others and really almost too kind for this world—
to think and utter such daring strong vivid thoughts
as you have done—this puzzles me a good deal—one
thing more—your words are rather too flattering
to human weakness—your lines—severe bold—
satiric—are you false—next I would say—thank
you for your two kind notes which I received one
after the other late last night and early this morning
and thank you for receiving my little offering prettily
. . . now as to the tooth-ache try the Leech it is a
French remedy no pain and the only cure, for all the
opiates inflame the gum the Leech takes the blood
away gently and the pain will subside immediately
after—you cannot think what impression you have
made on me—seeing you—soothes me—I am violent
and eager and you are gentle . . . now that all is
smooth and prosperous I feel my errors more than I
can say—and upon my honour the having given pain

---

[1] Born in 1785. She was desperately in love with Byron, who broke off
the connection in 1813. She gave vent to her rage in *Glenarvon*.

[2] Broadley Collection. Perhaps it is to this undated letter that Crabbe
alludes in his *Journal* (B. p. 70, July 19th): " Return to Bury Street, and
find a note ! ! What an unaccountable ! it is so ridiculous."

to others and mocked at the grey hairs of Samuel Rogers is like a corkscrew in my heart . . . pray forgive all this do not write an answer I need none and burn this letter." In a second note Lady Caroline, evidently in search of a confessor, begged Crabbe to "drink tea alone with her that evening, or the next day at nine, or on Sunday : only let me know," she added. But our poet, remembering the adventurous existence and the "daring thoughts" of the authoress of *Glenarvon*,[1] had some misgivings, I fancy, and maintained a prudent reserve.

In the midst of his pleasures he did not neglect his self-imposed task—the writing of thirty lines of poetry on an average every day. If now and then he got into arrears, he always tried to make up the number afterwards. With favourable inspiration he could manage as many as eighty in a few hours.[2] And his Muse was easily wooed, even in the neighbourhood of the Strand. On July 15th, for instance, we find him composing after morning church "in the solitude of Somerset House, not fifty yards from the Thames," amid surroundings "as quiet as the sands of Arabia." But he also had fits of depression,[3] and sometimes, as at Muston, unpleasant dreams. On returning from the "delightful" party given by Sir Harry Englefield,[4] "my reflections," he says, "were as cheerful as such company could make them, and not, I am afraid, of the most humiliating kind ; yet, for the first time these many nights, I was incommoded by dreams such as would cure vanity for a time in any mind where they could gain admission. None, indeed, that actually did happen in the very worst of times, but still with a formidable resemblance. . . . Why I cannot account. So it was. Awake I had been with

---

[1] A novel which Crabbe had read on its publication : cf. the following passage in a letter to Colonel Houlton (August 5th, 1816, above, p. 388, n. 3) : "You Ladies when you be good are very good and when naughty— may I not say very naughty ? I have now read the remainder nearly of *Glenarvon*, and should not give the writer as an example of the good Ladies : the woman absolutely holds forth the doctrine of irresistible passion and that if Lady Avondale falls desperately in love with Lord Glenarvon, after marrying the man of her own choice, there is no help for it : if he spare her, well and good, if not, she must fall ! Charming morality and such as my dear Miss Houltons will never be taught."

[2] On the 16th, for instance (B. p. 70).

[3] Especially on the 9th and the 15th.

[4] See above, p. 398, from n. 3 onwards.

the high, the apparently happy : we were very plea-
santly engaged, and my last thoughts were cheerful.
Asleep, all was misery and degradation, not my own
only, but of those who had been. That horrible image
of servility and baseness—that mercenary and commercial manner ! It is the work of imagination, I
suppose ; but it is very strange." He had doubtless
seen one of the visions which he relates in his *World
of Dreams*[1] with a superabundance of detail not incompatible with a certain vigour. A " poor-house"
suddenly rises before the sleeper :

> Where ? where ?—am I reduced to this—
>   Thus sunk in poverty extreme ?
> Can I not these vile things dismiss ?
>   No ! they are things that more than seem :
> This room with that cross-parting beam
>   Holds yonder squalid tribe and me—
> But they were ever thus, nor dream
>   Of being wealthy, favour'd, free !
>
> Shall I a coat and badge [2] receive
>   And sit among these crippled men,
> And not go forth without the leave
>   Of him—and ask it humbly then—
> Who reigns in this infernal den—
>   Where all beside in woe repine ?
> Yes, yes, I must ; nor tongue nor pen
>   Can paint such misery as mine !
>
> Wretches ! if ye were only poor,
>   You would my sympathy engage ;
> Or were ye vicious, and no more,
>   I might be filled with manly rage ;
> Or had ye patience, wise and sage,
>   We might such worthy sufferers call ;
> But ye are birds that suit your cage—
>   Poor, vile, impatient, worthless all ! [3]

Was it the influence of opium that gave this dream
the intensity of reality and produced this mental
anguish ?
  It was soon dispelled, however, for our poet re-

---

[1] Published in 1834 in the *Posthumous Works* (cf. *Works,* pp. 268-70).
[2] See above, p. 64, n. 6.
[3] *The World of Dreams,* stanzas xxxiii.-xxxv.

turned to Trowbridge[1] enchanted with his trip.
Rogers had "introduced him to almost every man[2]
he was acquainted with, and in this number were
comprehended all" Crabbe was anxious to know.
His visit to London, which was followed by another
in 1818,[3] had been fruitful. His sensibility, his faculties of observation, which might have lain dormant at
Muston for want of practice, had revived in all the
freshness of their last spring. He was hard at work
on a new poem.

[1] After an excursion into Suffolk, it would appear. Cf. a letter from Trowbridge, May 13th, 1817, to a Mr. Richard Sainthill (published by *The Gentleman's Magazine*, new series, vol. xlii. November, 1854, pp. 453·5): "I dare
not fix any period for my movements in this year; but, having a call into
Suffolk, I shall try and get for myself a few days in town." Thus, a month
before his departure, Crabbe anticipated only a short stay in London. He
had therefore not yet seen Rogers, and the note quoted above (p. 392, n. 2)
is probably of the end of May or the beginning of June, 1817.
[2] Letter to Mary Leadbeater of October 30th, 1819 (*Leadbeater Papers*,
vol. ii. p. 350, passage quoted by B. p. 71, but with a wrong date).
[3] Cf. Fitzgerald MS. notes: "1818. In London from May 17 to July 17
in the thick of society; sits to the two painters Phillips (the portrait wanted
touching up) and Pickersgill; always with Rogers to whom [he] read the
Introduction [to *Tales of the Hall*] and W. Bailey [*ibid*. book xix.]; has
the Game Laws and lottery suggested by Romilly." "Lines as I returned to
Sir F. Burdett's under the 'lamps'" (see also a letter from Rogers to Moore
of July 12th, 1818, *Memoirs of Thomas Moore*, vol. viii. p. 245): "Crabbe
has been here for a fortnight, and being a lover of peace and quiet, took
a lodging at the Hummums (in Covent Garden) when the Westminster
uproar was at its height." On July 26th he was back at Trowbridge (cf. a
manuscript sermon in the Murray Collection); in September he went to
Cromer, probably with the Hoare family; on October 10th he was at
Aldborough (Fitzgerald), and on the 18th he preached at Beccles, after which
he doubtless returned to Trowbridge.

CHAPTER III

THE "TALES OF THE HALL"

I. Circumstances of the publication.—II. The plan of the work.
Family life.—III. The pathos of misfortune.—IV. Verdict of
contemporaries and critical estimates.

I

BEGUN soon after his arrival at Trowbridge, the *Tales
of the Hall* occupied Crabbe for four years.[1] On
October 30th, 1817, he hoped that " his verses might
appear in some three or four months,"[2] but the delays
incidental to literary composition and also the ex-
pansion of the work itself made him write on September 7th, 1818, that " his new *Tales* were not yet
entirely ready."[3] He added, however, that " they do
not want much," and the finishing touches were given
to the manuscript in the course of a journey to Cromer,
Beccles, and Aldborough in October of the same year.

In November the poet returned to London and
opened negotiations with various publishers. His
recent visits to the capital, his conversations with men
of letters like Rogers and Moore, had inspired him
with ambitions which Hatchard could no longer
satisfy. Our relations, Crabbe wrote to him some
time afterwards, have always been " correct and fair :
we part not in complaint, in resentment, in suspicion.
Duty to my family, an increasing family, and that
common and natural desire of gain, led me to accept
a liberal offer "[4]—that of John Murray, who had been

---

[1] See letter to Murray of November 23rd, 1818, below, p. 405, n. 3.
[2] Letter to Mary Leadbeater (*Leadbeater Papers*, vol. ii. p. 349).
[3] *Ibid.*, letter quoted by B. p. 72, col. 2.
[4] Letter dated Trowbridge, November 11th, 1819 (Mackay Collection).
In this connection a mistake may be pointed out in the following book : *A
Publisher and his Friends: Memoir and Correspondence of the late John
Murray, with an Account of the Origin and Progress of the House* (1768—1843),
by Samuel Smiles, LL.D., 2 vols., London, J. Murray, 1891, in which it is
said (vol. ii. p. 72) : " Crabbe had some difficulty in getting his old poems

in relations with Crabbe since June 30th, 1817.[1] He seemed quite ready to publish the new work, as well as a complete collection of the poems that had already appeared. On November 23rd, 1818, he received the following letter from Crabbe : " My not waiting upon you for some time past makes an apology necessary, if I would not appear unmindful of your obliging attentions. The truth is that I have been considerably indisposed and even painfully so for some days. I was likewise in some degree restrained by not feeling myself perfectly disengaged from all those expectations which Mr. H—— might have in consequence of our former engagements : these are now entirely done away, and he is satisfied that I mean no more to proceed in the manner we have done. Mr. H—— in our conversation urged the integrity of his dealings by me and the success of our publications, neither of which I disputed, but argued that the integrity wanted knowledge and the success was much less than by a judicious mode of conducting our business it would have been. Being now freed from any claims or any expectations of this nature, I am at liberty to address you freely on the subject. . . . But," continues the poet, " I well know that I am placed in a situation which I could wish to avoid, for I feel the awkwardness of placing a value on my own labours and it would please me much if I knew the estimation that would be made by a person perfectly competent to judge."[2] It would seem that Murray and his advisers had a high opinion of Crabbe's poetry and of its popularity,

out of the hands of his former publisher, who wrote to him in a strain of the wildest indignation, and even threatened him with legal proceedings, but eventually the unsold stock, consisting of 2,426 copies, was handed over by Hatchard and Colburn to Mr. Murray, and nothing more was heard of this controversy between them and the poet." Hatchard and Colburn must remain quite distinct. The first complied without a murmur ; the claim of the second, which was entirely unexpected, had no foundation, as is proved by the first sentence of the following letter from Crabbe to Murray : " TROW-BRIDGE, *Jan.* 10, 1819. DEAR SIR,—I was much surprised by the enclosed letter which I received this morning. I have known Mr. Colburn some years and have been a subscriber to his public library and I was accustomed when in town to go to his shop and talk with him and I am sorry our conversation led to such expectations and such disappointment. I remember that I did speak of my dissatisfaction and wished to change at least the mode of publishing, but I entered into no contract . . . " (Murray Collection). As for Hatchard, it is probable that Crabbe shared profits with him, retaining, however, the copyright of his works.

[1] See above, p. 396.
[2] Murray Collection.

for, about December 6th, they offered £3,000 for the
copyright of the *Tales of the Hall* and of the previous
volumes. Their author had never expected to get so
much, and he considered the offer a good bargain
which should be concluded at once. But Rogers, who
was really too partial, thought that the *Tales* alone
were worth this sum, that the preceding works should
be held back, and that perhaps Longmans might accept
these unconscionable terms. On receipt of a letter
from Lord Holland, Rees, one of Longmans' partners,
called on Rogers about five o'clock. He declared that
his firm could not possibly afford to pay as much for
Crabbe's poetry as for Moore's,[1] and that, judging by
the sale of the previous works, the utmost they could
give for the whole was £1,000. This was only a third
of Murray's offer! What was to be done to prevent a
disaster, which was inevitable if any rumour of this
clandestine negotiation reached Albemarle Street?
Immediately after Rees's departure Crabbe, in consternation, had written to Murray that he accepted his
offer; but no reply had arrived by the morning of the
8th, and there was every fear of a rupture. Thereupon
Moore and Rogers, being anxious to put an end to the
suspense of poor Crabbe, who was " sitting alone in
his room, expecting the worst," resolved to call on
Murray. Rogers diplomatically first spoke of his own
poem on *Human Life*, which he was printing himself,
but of which Murray was to undertake the sale, and
then added in an indifferent tone, " I am glad to
find, Mr. Murray, that you have settled with Mr.
Crabbe for his new work." Murray replied quite
cheerfully that this was the case. Crabbe was
saved; he could pocket his £3,000,[2] and his *Tales of
the Hall*,[3] "after four years' labour, and of late

---

[1] Moore himself relates all this in his *Journal* (vol. ii. pp. 235-7). He had
received £3,000 for *Lalla Rookh*.

[2] Cf. Moore, *ibid.* p. 259 : " Crabbe's delight at having £3,000 in his
pocket. Rogers offered to take care of the bills for him, but no, he must take
them down to show them to his son John."—" Would not copies do ? "—" No,
must show son John the actual notes."

[3] The collection was to be called *Remembrances* (cf. *Leadbeater Papers*,
vol. ii. p. 350, letter of October 30th, 1817) ; then Crabbe had some
misgivings which he communicated to Murray : "TROWBRIDGE, *Dec.* 28,
1818. I have my corrections and additions for our first sheet nearly ready and
would send them, . . . but that I wished to consult you previously respecting
the title. . . . *Remembrances* I do not like, though I am not able to assign any
very good reason for disapproving it ; *Tales of the Hall* would I think be more

almost incessant," at last appeared in the beginning
of July, 1819.[1]

II

IN a sense, they mark an advance on the *Tales in Verse*.
While the latter resemble scattered fragments not
forming a whole, the new tales, on the contrary, show
a tendency to coalesce. They come before us encircled by an outline which serves to give them unity.
After having grouped his characters in isolated
narratives, Crabbe, by an effort of composition to which
he had not accustomed us, brings these narratives
together and subordinates them to a more comprehen-
sive scheme, to a sort of framework which supports
and consolidates the collection.

As far back as 1812 Crabbe had tried to find a connecting-link of this kind for his *Tales in Verse*. Well
read in the history of literature, including that of old
English poetry, he was aware of the precedents set
him by Chaucer and Boccaccio. But he did not think
it advisable to follow in their footsteps. Probability
did not appear to him to have been sufficiently observed
even by Chaucer in the Prologue to the *Canterbury
Tales*. " It is difficult to conceive," he writes, "that on

inviting, but a title has occurred to me which I prefer to either, though I
would not adopt it without your approbation. . . . What will you think of
Forty Days or a *Series of Tales told at Bunning Hall*? . . . I have—partly in
consequence of this idea—introduced my elder Brother to his hall. . . ."
Murray chose *Tales of the Hall* (cf. a letter from Crabbe, dated Trowbridge,
January 22nd, 1819).

In consequence of their length, the first idea was to publish them in
numbers, tale by tale (cf. the letter quoted above, p. 403, n. 1) : " Sir H.
Englefield, having been informed of the number of lines in my present undertaking [then about twelve thousand], judges it too long for the fastidiousness
of modern readers and suggests the idea of dividing it into parts . . . After
four years' labour and of late almost incessant, I confess that I should love to
have my books presented to the public in an advantageous and respectable
manner, but this is a secondary consideration ; what they may profit me, I own,
is the first. . . . " The idea was abandoned in March : " Such of my friends
as I have consulted highly approve the change of your purpose," writes Crabbe
on the 12th.

The seventh tale was added while the work was in the press : "TROW-
BRIDGE, 22 *Jan.*, 1819. . . . I send the three next books and they will be
followed by one more which you will either include or not at your pleasure.
It is the story of the Elder Brother and contains thirty-five of my pages. After
this the *Tales* might follow in almost any succession we preferred. . . ."
(Murray Collection).

[1] The only work of Crabbe entered at the Stationers' Register (July 3rd,
1819). It was dedicated to the Duchess of Rutland (Lady Elizabeth Howard),

any occasion the devout and delicate Prioress, the courtly and valiant Knight, and 'the poure good Man the persone of a Towne,' would be the voluntary companions of the drunken Miller, the licentious Sumpnour, and 'the Wanton Wife of Bath,' and enter into that colloquial and travelling intimacy, which, if a common pilgrimage to the shrine of St. Thomas may be said to excuse, I know nothing beside (and certainly nothing in these times) that would produce such effect. Boccace, it is true, avoids all difficulty of this kind by not assigning the ten relators of his hundred Tales any marked or peculiar characters ; nor, though there are male and female in company, can the sex of the narrator be distinguished in the narration. To have followed the method of Chaucer might have been of use, but could scarcely be adopted, from its difficulty; and to have taken that of the Italian writer would have been perfectly easy, but could be of no service." [1] Since Chaucer's joyous cavalcade was an anachronism in an age of coaches, and " Madonna Pampinea" and her young friends seemed as unreal as phantoms, it was necessary to find an idea better suited to contemporary life and more in keeping with the realism in which the poet sought inspiration.

This is what he hit upon. Two brothers, or rather two half-brothers, have remained strangers to each other since the days of their youth. George, the elder, who is more than sixty years old, has retired from business after a long and laborious career which has brought him wealth and enabled him to buy a property in his native village :

> . . . The hill
> He climb'd a boy had its attraction still ;
> With that small brook beneath, where he would stand
> And stooping fill the hollow of his hand,
> To quench th' impatient thirst.

Near the " church with lofty tower " stands " an ancient venerable hall," formerly surrounded by a moat and walls which a " squire of taste " has filled up and demolished in order to add a wing to the mansion and modernise its aspect. It is there, on the summit of this hill, which is that of Aldborough, and in this

---

[1] Preface to *Tales in Verse* ; *Works*, p. 273, col. i.

old manor-house, which reminds us of Ducking Hall,[1]
that George has settled:

> The Hall at Bihning! how he loves the gloom
> That sun-excluding window gives the room;
> Those broad brown stairs on which he loves to tread;
> Those beams within; without, that length of lead
> On which the names of wanton boys appear,
> Who died old men, and left memorials here.

Happy in at last possessing this old place, which he
formerly admired from a distance, George cherishes
an almost sentimental fondness for the past: the
ancient walls, the stately avenue of elms which have
been sacrificed to so-called improvements, he would
like to have them all back again.   He is a strong Conservative.   In politics he reproves the intolerance of—

> Those who believe they never can be free,
> Except when fighting for their liberty;
> Who by their very clamour and complaint
> Invite coercion or enforce restraint.

To ensure the stability of public liberties, let us know
how to forego some of their advantages.   Let us
acknowledge an authority which limits our rights:

> The public good must be a private care,
> None all they would may have, but all a share:
> So we must freedom with restraint enjoy;
> What crowds possess they will, uncheck'd, destroy.

The constitution is to George an "ark" which must
be defended with pious zeal, without tampering with
the Royal prerogative or with the privileges of
Parliament.   In religion, likewise, he applied his
mind "firmly yet meekly" to this great subject, and
was satisfied with the truth of Christianity; then,
accepting the doctrines of Anglicanism, with the
breadth of view of those who dislike Puritan narrowness, he has found his place and fixed his principles
in the Established Church.   Moderate in his opinions,
contented from resignation rather than optimism,
George is the wisest and most warm-hearted of
squires and old bachelors.   He likes good living,
but without excess, and to cheer his solitude he

[1] See above, pp 49-50.

receives a few friends in an informal way or listens
to " the female accent sweet."

Richard, about fifteen years younger, is the son of an
"Irish soldier," the second husband of George's mother.
Having inherited more bravery than money, he has
entered first the navy, then the army, and has served
under Wellington in Spain, where he has gathered
laurels. On his return to England he has married
and settled down. To his birth and military life he
owes an adventurous and expansive nature, a frank
aversion to all hypocrisy, a boldness of ideas in politics,
and an eclecticism in religion very different from the
reserve and moderation of his elder brother. He is a
true Liberal, no Radical :

> He loved, like George, our liberty and laws,
> But had more youthful ardour to be free,
> And stronger fears for injured liberty :
> With him, on various questions that arose,
> The monarch's servants were the people's foes ;
> And though he fought with all a Briton's zeal,
> He felt for France as Freedom's children feel ;
> Went far with her in what she thought reform,
> And hail'd the revolutionary storm ;
> Yet would not here, where there was least to win,
> And most to lose, the doubtful work begin.

And this independence of mind is accompanied by a
certain pride. He knows that his brother is rich and
that his own children will be poor. But he will not
solicit favours which might be refused him. He lets
George take the initiative. A need of affection,
imperious in a lonely man, impels the owner of
Binning Hall to make friends with Richard, who
has been too long neglected. Through the instru-
mentality of common acquaintances, the captain is
told that his brother "loves him well, and will be
rejoiced to see him when he has no better thing in
view." So they meet, with an emotion intense at first
and gradually changing into a profound attachment.
They feel that they understand and complete each
other, and, day after day, in long confidences, they
unbosom themselves of their own secrets and of those
of their neighbours.[1]

They begin by relating their life to each other. At

---

[1] *Tales of the Hall*, book i.

the age of twenty, George, escaping from the authority of his stepfather, the "Irish captain," lived with a clergyman to whom his uncle and guardian, a rich man of business, had entrusted his education. He describes himself as follows :

> " And who was I ? a slender youth and tall,
> In manner awkward, and with fortune small ;
> With visage pale, my motions quick and slow
> That fall and rising in the spirits show. . . .
> Yet awkward as I was, without the grace
> That gives new beauty to a form or face,
> Still I expected friends most true to prove,
> And grateful, tender, warm, assiduous love."

He dreamed, as youth has rarely dreamed, even at the age of twenty :

> " This was my dream.—In some auspicious hour,
> In some sweet solitude, in some green bower
> Whither my fate should lead me, there, unseen,
> I should behold my fancy's gracious queen,
> Singing sweet song ! that I should hear a while,
> Then catch the transient glory of a smile ;
> Then at her feet with trembling hope should kneel,
> Such as rapt saints and raptured lovers feel ;
> To watch the chaste unfoldings of her heart,
> In joy to meet, in agony to part,
> And then in tender song to soothe my grief,
> And hail, in glorious rhyme, my *Lady of the Leaf*." [1]

A remote corner of Binning Park served as a retreat for these passionate meditations. At that already distant period the lofty elms and hoary oaks flung their branches over the sward :

> And where the soil forbade the nobler race,
> Dwarf trees and humbler shrubs had found their place,
> Forbidding man in their close hold to go,
> Haw, gatter, holm, the service and the sloe.

Penetrating into this thicket by a gap in the hedge, George could, unobserved, indulge in his reveries and contemplate, with "respect and timid awe," the turrets of that manor, "where never yet his feet had stray'd."

One evening in June he was walking in this "green enclosure" and singing what seemed to him

---

[1] Probably an allusion to the poem entitled *The Flower and the Leaf*, long attributed to Chaucer.

a "heavenly tune," when he saw two ladies appear
arm in arm on the steps of the mansion. They
walked slowly down and crossed the park as if
coming in his direction. The beauty of one of them
dazzled him with a lightning flash :

> " One matchless face I saw
> And, though at distance, felt delight and awe :
> Fancy and truth adorned her ; fancy gave
> Much, but not all ; truth help'd to make their slave !
> For she was lovely, all was not the vain
> Or sickly homage of a fever'd brain !
> No ! she had beauty, such as they admire
> Whose hope is earthly, and whose love desire. . . .
> Their dress was such as well became the place,
> But one superior ; hers the air, the grace,
> The condescending looks, that spoke the nobler race.
> Slender she was and tall : her fairy-feet
> Bore her right onward to my shady seat. . . .
> Thus was I musing :—Is this maid, divine
> As she appears, to be this queen of mine ?
> Have I from henceforth beauty in my view,
> Not airy all, but tangible and true ?
> Here then I fix, here bound my vagrant views,
> And here devote my heart, my time, my Muse."

The two ladies continue to advance, but suddenly a
cry of alarm is heard, quickly followed by another :

> " Are my princess and her attendant maid
> In so much danger and so much afraid !
> But whence the terror ? "

Simply from a herd of badly guarded cattle, which
stand across their path with lowered horns :

> " As feeling prompted, to the place I ran,
> Resolv'd to save the maids and show the man :
> Was each a cow like that which challenged Guy,[1]
> I had resolved to attack it, and defy
> In mortal combat ! to repel or die.
> That was no time to parley—or to say
> I will protect you—fly in peace away !
> Lo ! yonder stile—but with an air of grace,
> As I supposed, I pointed to the place."

[1] Guy of Warwick, whose legend has been related by Crabbe (see *Lines
written at Warwick : Works*, pp. 264-5) in a poem the subject of which was
probably taken from Percy's collection of Ballads (series iij. book ii. 1 : *The
Legend of Sir Guy*).

The ladies understood the signal, and retreated to the other side of the stile, while their champion confronted the still menacing herd. Fortunately the opportune intervention of a milkmaid put an end to this somewhat ridiculous scene, and George was rewarded for his valour by a " gracious smile." He fancied himself loved ; and in his solitude his imagination was fired :

> " Oh ! my dear Richard, what a waste of time
> Gave I not thus to lunacy sublime ;
> What days, months, years (to useful purpose lost)
> Has not this dire infatuation cost !
> To this fair vision I, a bounden slave,
> Time, duty, credit, honour, comfort gave ;
> Gave all—and waited for the glorious things
> That hope expects, but fortune never brings."

He saw the angelic creature no more, and sought her everywhere : at the manor, where he could only ascertain that her name was Rosabella, on the Continent, in places frequented by travellers, until "youth and health and all but love were gone," leaving him a prey to "mental suffering," to a "nameless ill" which, though not exactly madness, weakened his faculties and impaired his reason.

At last the earnest requests of his uncle, who had returned from abroad, induced George to shake off his torpor. Wishing to recover, if not happiness, at least peace of mind, he went to work, learned the rudiments of business, and began to take an interest in commerce. In this he was warmly encouraged by the old merchant, who showed him his ledger "with supreme delight," and exclaimed :

> " That's poetry, my boy !
> These are your golden numbers—them repeat ;
> The more you have, the more you'll find them sweet,
> Their numbers move all hearts—no matter for their feet.
> Sir, when a man composes in this style,
> What is to him a critic's frown or smile ? . . .
> What is the puppy's censure or applause
> To the good man who on his banker draws,
> Buys an estate, and writes upon the grounds
> Pay to A. B. a hundred thousand pounds ? "

After all, reflected George, this realistic ideal is better than an illusion ! He therefore tried to win his uncle's confidence.

But what had become of the mysterious Rosabella? An unforeseen circumstance was destined to bring the pair together again, many years after their first meeting; the prosaic nature of the incident is reflected in the following remarkable lines:

> " Something one day occurred about a bill
> That was not drawn with true mercantile skill,
> And I was ask'd and authorised to go
> To seek the firm of Clutterbuck and Co."

The office being closed, he was told to go to a country house where the merchant in question spent his leisure time.   On entering he was astonished at the untidiness of the servant and of the apartment:

> " The shutters half unclosed, the curtains fell
> Half down, and rested on the window-sill.
> Late as it was, the little parlour bore
> Some tell-tale tokens of the night before:
> There were strange sights and scents about the room
> Of food high-season'd, and of strong perfume ;
> Two unmatch'd sofas ample rents display'd,
> Carpet and curtains were alike decay'd ;
> A large old mirror, with once-gilded frame,
> Reflected prints that I forbear to name;
> The cinders yet were sleeping in the grate
> Warm from the fire, continued large and late ;
> The chairs in haste seem'd whirled about the room."

In short, every sign of the recent orgy.   The master of the house was out, but a woman's voice attracts the visitor's attention and then rivets it.   She enters: it is Rosabella!   She in this place, pale and thin, with painted cheeks and haggard features, "laughing in languor," in a dirty tawdry dress!

> " But is it she?   O ! yes; the rose is dead,
> All beauty, fragrance, freshness, glory fled !
> But yet 'tis she—the same and not the same—
> Who to my bower a heavenly being came ;
> Who waked my soul's first thought of real bliss,
> Whom long I sought, and now I find her—this ! "

To hear her speak of love with voluptuous intonations which, aided by anacreontic verse, seek to rekindle passions now well-nigh extinct !   To see her weep in narrating her history of a seduced and deserted orphan who yields to vice in order to avoid starvation !   For

a moment George feels such grief and pity that with
singular imprudence he offers her his heart and hand
if she will repent and give up her mode of life. She
promises, but to no purpose :

> ". . . Alas ! she did not know
> How deeply rooted evil habits grow :
> She felt the truth upon her spirits press,
> But wanted ease, indulgence, show, excess,
> Voluptuous banquets, pleasures—not refined,
> But such as soothe to sleep th' opposing mind."

Incapable of grasping the hand held out to her, she
sank into the lowest stage of degradation, and ended
her days in a poor-house, still assisted by George, who
remains faithful to the memories of his youth amid
the melancholy disappointments of middle age.[1]

Richard, who is less of a poet and more of a man of
action, has had, on the whole, a happier though a
harder life. His youth, identical with that of Crabbe,[2]
was passed in a small cottage near the sea, the river,
and the common. As enterprising and decided as his
brother was timid, he ventured on the waves early,
" in a relation's ship." A characteristic accident marked
this excursion. It was a pleasure trip, and the youthful crew, in high spirits, had driven away care and
fear. With a craving for excitement, they courted
danger :

> " When, as the gale at evening died away,—
> And die it will at the retiring day,—
> Impatient then, and sick of very ease,
> We loudly whistled for the slumbering breeze.
> One eve it came ; and, frantic in my joy,
> I rose and danced, as idle as a boy :
> The cabin-lights were down, that we might learn
> A trifling something from the ship astern ;
> The stiffening gale bore up the growing wave,
> And wilder motion to my madness gave : . . .
> . . . In an instant, as the stern sank low,
> Chance that direction to my motion gave,
> And plunged me headlong in the roaring wave :
> Swift flew the parting ship,—the fainter light
> Withdrew,—or horror took them from my sight. . . .

---

[1] *Tales of the Hall*, book vii. : *The Elder Brother* (cf. above, p. 405,
n. 3).

[2] *Ibid.* iv. 287-485, and above, p. 23, notes 2-4, and p. 34.

> Weaker I grew, and grew the more dismay'd,
> Of aid all hopeless, yet in search of aid ;
> Struggling awhile upon the wave to keep,
> Then, languid, sinking in the yawning deep."

His friends had fortunately seen him fall overboard and had thrown him all the spars on which they could lay hands. His "heaven-directed arm" seized one of these, and plucking up courage, he at last reached the ship.[1]

Passing over his adventures in Spain, Richard describes his return to England. Worn out with toil and fever, he found a home with a "village priest," a friend of his mother, and believed that he would end his days there:

> "The man was kind, intelligent, and mild,
> Careless and shrewd, yet simple as a child. . . .
> He lost his wife when they together pass'd
> Years of calm love, that triumphed to the last."

Like the poet, who here describes himself, he devoted his leisure time to the study of natural science:

> " He knew the plants in mountain, wood or mead ;
> He knew the worms that on the foliage feed,
> And the small creatures who on bark or bough
> Enjoy their changes, changed we know not how."

Mankind were not so familiar to him, although his remarks were often shrewd and penetrating. But there was no ill-nature in him. He had three daughters, as beautiful as they were poor, and he received an officer who was still young into his house—an obvious piece of imprudence! Richard, in the course of his long convalescence, soon showed a preference for the amiable Matilda. Her remarks "made a strong impression" on him. She asked about the captain's religion, and his conversion became "her supreme delight."[2] This good work accomplished, their conversation ran on the "friendship" that can bind kindred spirits, on their "refined esteem," on—

---

[1] *Tales of the Hall,* iv. 185-264. The reader will perhaps remember that an accident of a similar kind had happened to Crabbe (see above, p. 73) : for exaggeration of the reality in order to make it more striking, cf. the remarks already made on pp. 371-2.

[2] Matilda is Mira herself (cf. above, p. 54).

> "Scenes where this is real found,
> And love subsists without a dart or wound. . . .
> This sacred friendship thus in secret grew
> An intellectual love, most tender, chaste, and true—
> Unstain'd, we said, nor knew we how it chanced
> To gain some earthly soil as it advanced—
> . . . no doubt, at length,
> We could perceive the weakness of our strength."

For, as our moralist remarks in another passage, "friendship with woman is a dangerous thing,"[1] a pretext for love.

A moment of jealousy is enough to make this suppressed passion burst forth irresistibly. One day Richard fancied himself menaced by a rival. Like Orlando in *The Lover's Journey*,[2] he had gone to see Matilda while she was visiting friends at Brandon Hall. With a joyous heart he had skirted the common and the cliff, admiring the "spacious bay" and a large fleet steering full sail towards the north, then he had descended to the sands,

> Where the small pebbles, wetted by the wave,
> To the new day reflected lustre gave.

Everything seemed to him to forebode happiness. But, on entering the "pernicious room" in which Matilda is seated, he sees beside her a "soldier," a new aspirant, no doubt, whose haughty look betrays a confidence that seems justified. Matilda receives the stranger's attentions with complacence; she returns his smile. This is too much, Richard says to himself indignantly:

> "I must approach, and find,
> Or make, a quarrel, to relieve my mind."

His attempts are in vain:

> Politeness, as a shield
> The angry strokes of his contempt repell'd.

Matilda alone is embarrassed, and casts beseeching glances at him. Suddenly every one rises and walks to a lake on which an excursion has been planned. The two culprits whisper to each other:

> "Good Heaven! they whisper! is it come to this
> Already?—then may I my doubt dismiss;
> There, forth they go! He leads her to the shore—
> Nay, I must follow."

[1] *Tales of the Hall*, xii. 587.   [2] Cf. above, p. 71.

When taking their seats in the boat, they make room
for the jealous lover, who is astonished at so much
attention; evidently, he reflects, this is the device of
a flirt:

> ". . . It tells him he must mind,
> Must not be careless :—I can serve to draw
> The soldier on, and keep the man in awe."

They land on the opposite bank:

> ". . . And will he yet support
> This part?   What favour has he now to court?"

None whatever: the "soldier" prepares to take leave
of "the fair." "My love to Julia," she says. What, is
this supposed rival only the husband of Julia, of that
schoolfellow to whom Matilda writes so frequently?
What a mistake Richard has made! How can he
obtain forgiveness for such suspicion and such ill-
tempered speeches? By redoubled tenderness:

> The boat had landed in a shady scene ;
> The grove was in its glory, fresh and green ;
> The showers of late had swelled the branch and bough,
> And the sun's fervour made them pleasant now.
> Hard by arose an oak in all its pride,
> And threw its arms along the water's side—
> Its leafy limbs, that on the glassy lake
> Stretch far, and all those dancing shadows make.

The tender charm of the scene invites apologies which
would be forthwith accepted, avowals on which depends the happiness of a lifetime. Will Richard dare
to confess that his friendship has ripened into love?
He is about to speak, when suddenly a ridiculous
shout is heard:

> "A hat! the idiot's—fallen in the lake!
> I almost wish the head had fallen too!"

mutters the poor captain, exasperated at this inter-
ruption. Suspense has never appeared so painful to
him; he longs to put the decisive question to Matilda.
They enter the boat again together, and once more
cross the lake, under the moonlight shining through
the clouds upon the water:

> "This was such bliss! even then it seem'd relief
> To veil the gladness in a show of grief:
> We sigh'd as we conversed, and said, how deep
> The lake on which those broad dark shadows sleep ;

> There is between us and a watery grave
> But a thin plank, and yet our fate we brave.
> What if it burst?—'Matilda, then my care
> Would be for thee: all danger I would dare,
> And, should my efforts fail, thy fortune would I share.'—
> 'The love of life,' she said, 'would powerful prove!'—
> 'O! not so powerful as the strength of love!'"

This was almost a declaration. In a few moments they have landed; they return in the twilight to Brandon Hall, and lose their way in a maze of lanes. The words which have so long been trembling on Richard's lips at last escape him:

> "I love thee, dear Matilda!—to confess
> The fact is dangerous, fatal to suppress;
> And now in terror I approach the home
> Where I may wretched but not doubtful come,
> Where I must be all ecstasy, or all—
> O! what will you a wretch rejected call?
> Not man, for I shall lose myself, and be
> A creature lost to reason, losing thee!
> Speak, my Matilda! on the rack of fear
> Suspend me not—I would my sentence hear,
> Would learn my fate.—Good Heaven, and what portend
> These tears?—and fall they for thy wretched friend?
> Or"—but I cease; I cannot paint the bliss
> From a confession soft and kind as this.[1]

A reciprocal attachment had united them. It has never known a break: the birth of their children, the pleasures enjoyed and the trials endured in common have rather increased it. "Do you still love this woman?" George asks his brother, to which the latter replies:

> ". . . O! beyond
> What I can tell thee of the true and fond:
> Hath she not soothed me, sick—enriched me, poor—
> And banish'd death and misery from my door?
> Has she not cherish'd every moment's bliss,
> And made an Eden of a world like this?
> When Care would strive with us his watch to keep,
> Has she not sung the snarling fiend to sleep?
> And when Distress has look'd us in the face,
> Has she not told him, 'Thou are not Disgrace'?"

---

[1] *Tales of the Hall*, vi. 25 *seq.*

When letters therefore arrive twice a week from
Matilda—

> Letters of love, all full and running o'er,
> The paper fill'd till it could hold no more ;
> Cross'd with discolour'd ink, the doublings full—

Richard beams with delight. George sees clearly that
such a couple cannot remain separated for long, and
that, when his brother is gone, his solitude will
become doubly burdensome to him. " Tell me," he
cries :

> " . . . How am I to live
> Without the comforts thou art wont to give ?
> How will the heavy hours my mind afflict,—
> No one t' agree, no one to contradict,
> None to awake, excite me, or prevent,
> To hear a tale, or hold an argument,
> To help my worship in a case of doubt
> And bring me in my blunders fairly out ! . . .
> . . . No ! I cannot part ;
> Is it in human nature to consent
> To give up all the good that Heaven has lent,
> All social ease and comfort to forego,
> And live again the solitary ? No ! " [1]

What is to be done then, since Richard has too much
independence and pride to accept the position of
hanger-on ?

In the environs of Binning Hall there is a property
which George hastens to acquire. Without making
known his intentions, he asks his brother's opinion
on his new " purchase," and tells him the way to it :

> "Southward at first, dear Richard, make your way,
> Cross Hilton Bridge, move on through Breken Clay ;
> At Dunham Wood turn duly to the East,
> And there your eyes upon the ocean feast,
> Then ride above the cliff, or ride below,
> You'll be enraptured, for your taste I know ;
> It is a prospect that a man might stay
> To his bride hastening on his wedding-day ;
> At Tilburn Sluice [2] once more ascend and view
> A decent house ; an ample garden too. . . .
> Mark well the rooms, and their proportions learn,
> In each some use, some elegance discern ;

[1] *Tales of the Hall*, vii. 23-32, xiv. 47-51, xxii. 237-44.
[2] These names, although imaginary, recall Aldborough and its bay.

> Observe the garden, its productive wall,
> And find a something to commend in all.
> Then, should you praise them in a knowing way,
> I'll take it kindly."

The rector of Binning, a friend from boyhood of the squire, has undertaken to explain George's plans to Matilda.   His negotiations have met with complete success.   While Richard is complaining of the increasing brevity of his wife's letters, the latter is preparing to move into the residence which her brother-in-law has just purchased for her and her family.   When the last day of the visit at Binning arrives, and Richard, in a somewhat gloomy mood, is about to take leave of his host, he is imperceptibly led by George to the recently acquired property, and there, to his great surprise, is addressed as follows by the kind squire :

> " It is thy wife's, and will thy children's be,
> Earth, wood, and water !—all for thine and thee ;
> Bought in thy name.—Alight, my friend, and come,
> I do beseech thee, to thy proper home ;
> There wilt thou soon thy own Matilda view. . . .
> Here, on this lawn, thy boys and girls shall run,
> And play their gambols when their tasks are done ;
> There, from that window, shall their mother view
> The happy tribe, and smile at all they do ;
> While thou, more gravely, hiding thy delight,
> Shalt cry, ' O ! childish !' and enjoy the sight." [1]

Thus George has given happiness to others and ensured his own.

An autobiographical interest attaches to the characters of the two brothers, who present more or less striking resemblances to the author.   If we bear in mind Crabbe's solitary life during the first years of his residence at Trowbridge,[2] when the conversation of a few female friends formed his sole distraction, there can be little doubt that the squire of Binning, surrounded by his old bachelors and his old maids,[3] is a poetic reproduction of our clergyman.   Richard's childhood is Crabbe's, at the age when he roamed over the common and along the banks of the Alde

---

[1] *Tales of the Hall*, xviii. 19-29, xxii. 439 *seq.* and 489-502.
[2] See above, p. 388.
[3] See *Tales of the Hall*, viii., x., and xi.

or by the sea-shore. Richard, returning from his campaigns and conceiving such a tender and constant attachment for Matilda, is Crabbe at Parham in love with Mira. Lastly, does not George, surrounded by the family circle made for him by his brother and Matilda, remind us again of Crabbe, sharing with his younger son John, Anna Crowfoot, and their children, the parsonage at Trowbridge, too large for himself alone ?

Hence the really pleasing and restful impression which the "framework" of this collection of tales leaves with the reader, and which made Edward Fitzgerald prefer the *Tales of the Hall* to Crabbe's other works.[1] After so many satires and gloomy pictures, the poet sets before us a bright ideal. He believes in happiness because he has enjoyed it in the bosom of his family. That is his concluding view on practical ethics. As he told us in his *Tales in Verse*,[2] and again by the mouth of George, we must not expect too much from life, for our dreams are often mere illusions. But, if we have the wisdom and moderation of George, the tenderness of Colin and of Richard, we shall find in love, in the devotion of a serious and sensible woman, in the joys of home life, the only durable felicity possible on earth. Crabbe, even more than Cowper, is the poet of the family : the rather selfish happiness of the recluse of Olney is not enough for him ; he must have not only the affection of a female friend, but also the fruitful love of a wife ; he wants to hear the ringing laugh of his children.

[1] A preference which Fitzgerald wished to make the public share by bringing out an abbreviated edition of the work under the title of *Readings in Crabbe*, firstly in 1879, for some friends, and then in 1882 (forty copies published by Quaritch). In his introduction he writes : "... Of all the Poet's works this one alone does not leave a more or less melancholy impression upon me. ... [It] is on this account, I do not say the best, but certainly that which best I like, of all his numerous offspring." The *Letters of Edward Fitzgerald* and *More Letters of Edward Fitzgerald* (1901), edited by W. A. Wright, contain many references to Crabbe and to the Biographer. Two will suffice : "To Donne, Aug. 27, 1865. ... Don't forget to sound Murray at some good opportunity about a selection from Crabbe. Of course he won't let me do it." Murray naturally refused (cf. letter to Norton, February 1st, 1877). In another letter to Norton just before, Fitzgerald says : "... I wish some American publisher would publish my edition of *Tales of the Hall*, edited by means of scissors and paste, with a few words of plain prose to bridge over whole tracts of bad verse, not meaning to improve the original, but to seduce hasty readers to study it...."

[2] See above, pp. 366-8.

III

It would be tedious to give in this place, as in a preceding chapter, a detailed analysis of the *Tales of the Hall.*[1] Passing over what they have in common with the *Tales in Verse*, let us try to bring out the new elements which they contain. There are two of these. The first and the most important, the plan of the composition, the link connecting the different parts, has been examined. There remains for consideration the special nature of the pathos in certain tales.

Imprudent or guilty, Crabbe's heroes are, as we have seen, all responsible for their ruin.[2] Either through misconduct or from error of judgment,[3] they have invariably gone astray. Consider these unhappy people, the poet seems to say to us, to what a depth of misery have they sunk! Their fall has been gradual, and they themselves were the instruments of it. To which the reader may reply: True, their downfall is distressing; but since they have deserved it, we only half pity them. Our sympathy, and consequently our emotion, would be more intense if you were to portray in them victims really unfortunate, overwhelmed, in spite of their innocence, or, at all events, through no fault of their own, by a relentless destiny. Not having to blame them, we should bestow on them our undivided commiseration. The more unjust the suffering, the more touching it is. Abstaining from pointing a moral, and aiming at deeper emotion, Crabbe found this kind of disinterested, irresistible pathos in the tales of Ruth, of Rachel, and of the two sisters, Jane and Lucy.[4]

A single example will suffice. In the days when Richard, still quite a young child, lived with his mother on "Barford Downs," he often spent his time in talking or reading with the wife of a fisherman,[5] whose cottage was situated "south in the port, and eastward in the street." Of a jovial temperament,

---

[1] An outline of one is given in Appendix IV.
[2] See above, pp. 341-2.
[3] Rupert and George, the sailor (pp. 317-323), are in this position.
[4] *Tales of the Hall:* v. *Ruth*; xxi. *Smugglers and Poachers* (Rachel); viii. *The Sisters.*
[5] This again is Crabbe himself (cf. above, p. 23).

equally fond of a "coarse jest" and a "pious psalm,"
old Hannah nevertheless cherished a great sorrow,
caused by the death of her daughter. One day, at
Richard's request, she confided the sad story to him:

> " Ruth—I may tell, too oft had she been told—
> Was tall and fair and comely to behold,
> Gentle and simple, in her native place
> Not one compared with her in form or face ;
> She was not merry, but she gave our hearth
> A cheerful spirit that was more than mirth.
>
> " There was a sailor boy, and people said
> He was, as man, a likeness of the maid ;
> But not in this—for he was ever glad,
> While Ruth was apprehensive, mild, and sad ;
> A quiet spirit hers, and peace would seek
> In meditation : tender, mild, and meek !
> Her loved the lad most truly ; and, in truth,
> She took an early liking to the youth :
> To her alone were his attentions paid,
> And they became the bachelor and maid.
> He wish'd to marry, but so prudent we
> And worldly wise, we said it could not be :
> They took the counsel,—maybe, they approved,—
> But still they grieved and waited, hoped and loved."

Like Phœbe Dawson, Lucy Collins, and Ellen Orford,
Ruth listened too eagerly to his tender speeches :

> " Now, my young friend, when of such state I speak
> As one of danger, you will be to seek ;
> You know not, Richard, where the danger lies
> In loving hearts, kind words, and speaking eyes ;
> For lovers speak their wishes with their looks
> As plainly, love, as you can read your books.
> Then, too, the meetings and the partings, all
> The playful quarrels in which lovers fall,
> Serve to one end—each lover is a child,
> Quick to resent and to be reconciled ;
> And then their peace brings kindness that remains,
> And so the lover from the quarrel gains. . . .
> They were as children, and they fell at length ;
> The trial, doubtless, is beyond their strength
> Whom grace supports not ; and will grace support
> The too confiding, who their danger court?
> Then they would marry, but were now too late ;
> All could their fault in sport or malice state ;
> And though the day was fix'd and now drew on,
> I could perceive my daughter's peace was gone ;

> She could not bear the bold and laughing eye
> That gazed on her,—reproach she could not fly ;
> Her grief she would not show, her shame could not deny :
> For some with many virtues come to shame,
> And some that lose them all preserve their name."

To crown their misfortunes, a few days before the ceremony a "frightful rumour" spread through the place :

> "War, who had slept awhile, awaked once more,
> And gangs came pressing till they swept the shore ;
> Our youth was seized and quickly sent away,
> Nor would the wretches for his marriage stay,
> But bore him off, in barbarous triumph bore,
> And left us all our miseries to deplore, . . .
> Not one last look allow'd—not one adieu ! "

Soon afterwards news was received of the young man's death. Ruth was left inconsolable with an orphan son.

Her beauty still attracted all beholders, especially a Methodist preacher, a weaver by trade, an apostle and spiritual adviser by vocation. He began by taking an interest in Ruth's soul, was lavish of visits, counsel, and arguments, thanks to which the young woman's grief seemed gradually to heal. At the expiration of three years she was seen to smile again, and, grateful for so much attention, would reply amiably to the observations of her improvised pastor. But the Methodist's affection was not only spiritual : it was carnal as well. Of all "the widows and maidens who flock'd to hear his voice," none had pleased him so much as Ruth. She did not encourage his preference ; she even entreated him to desist, declaring that she could never love him :

> "'Love me !' he replied,
> 'The love you mean is love unsanctified,
> An earthly, wicked, sensual, sinful kind,
> A creature-love, the passion of the blind ;
> He did not court her, he would have her know,
> For that poor love that will on beauty grow ;
> No ! he would take her as the Prophet took
> One of the harlots in the holy book ;'
> And then he look'd so ugly and severe !
> And yet so fond—she could not hide her fear.

Beset by the importunities of this imperious hypocrite, who wanted to make her his slave, Ruth on the other hand ran counter to the will of her father, who, dreading poverty for himself and for her, was in favour of this odious marriage.   If she refused, he said, she should no longer live under his roof; she must either marry the preacher or go to the work-house:

> " ' Three days I give you : see that all be right
> On Monday morning—this is Thursday night—
> Fulfil my wishes, girl ! or else forsake my sight ! ' "

Ruth's decision was soon taken.   She would not resign herself to this hateful alliance or to the humiliating and sordid existence of a pauper.   Rather would she die !

> " She left her infant on the Sunday morn,
> A creature doom'd to shame ! in sorrow born ;
> A thing that languish'd, nor arrived at age
> When the man's thoughts with sin and pain engage—
> She came not home to share our humble meal,
> Her father thinking what his child would feel
> From his hard sentence—still she came not home.
> The night grew dark, and yet she was not come ;
> The east wind roar'd, the sea return'd the sound,
> And the rain fell as if the world were drown'd :
> There were no lights without, and my good man,
> To kindness frighten'd, with a groan began
> To talk of Ruth and pray : and then he took
> The Bible down, and read the holy book ;
> For he had learning : and when that was done
> We sat in silence—Whither could we run ?
> We said ; and then rush'd frighten'd from the door,
> For we could bear our own conceit no more :
> We call'd on neighbours—there she had not been ;
> We met some wanderers—ours they had not seen ;
> We hurried o'er the beach, both north and south,
> Then join'd, and wander'd to our haven's mouth :
> Where rush'd the falling waters wildly out,
> I scarcely heard the good man's fearful shout,
> Who saw a something on the billow ride,
> And—' Heaven have mercy on our sins ! ' he cried,
> ' It is my child ! '—and to this present hour
> So he believes—and spirits have the power.[1]

---

[1] According to the popular superstition, the spectre of children who had died at sea appeared to their parents at the very moment of their death (cf. *Tales of the Hall*, iv. 431-40).

And she was gone ! the waters wide and deep
Roll'd o'er her body as she lay asleep.
She heard no more the angry waves and wind,
She heard no more the threat'ning of mankind ;
Wrapp'd in dark weeds, the refuse of the storm,
To the hard rock was borne her comely form !

" But oh ! what storm was in that mind ! what strife !
That could compel her to lay down her life !
For she was seen within the sea to wade,
By one at distance, when she first had pray'd ;
Then to a rock within the hither shoal
Softly and with a fearful step she stole ;
Then, when she gain'd it, on the top she stood
A moment still—and dropp'd into the flood !
The man cried loudly, but he cried in vain,—
She heard not then—she never heard again !
She had—pray Heav'n !—she had that world in sight,
Where frailty mercy finds, and wrong has right ;
But, sure, in this her portion such has been,
Well had it still remain'd a world unseen ! "

This passage, unsurpassed by Crabbe, is of a high
order of poetry. The author seems at last carried
away by a dramatic inspiration : he forgets to moralise,
and completely identifies himself with his characters.
Impelled by the same apprehensions, he leaves the
house with them, follows them step by step along the
beach, and shares their despair when the irreparable
is accomplished. It is old Hannah herself who speaks
through him : we recognise her by certain familiar
locutions which betray the country-woman,[1] but the
rhythm, the precision, and the force of expression
belong to the poet, who interprets, while idealising
them,[2] the feelings of his humble heroine. A penetrating melody, like that of a long lament in the minor
key, arises from these lines, more separated, more
broken up than usual, but all borne along by the
torrent of "a wild and rapid eloquence."[2] Suggested

---

[1] " My good man," she calls her husband, and—

" Then he took
The Bible down, and read the holy book,
For he had learning."

[2] Sometimes to excess, as, for instance, when he puts a comparison with
Mandane into the mouth of this fisherman's wife (v. 371-7). Nothing of the
kind, however, occurs in the passage which we are considering.

[3] The expression of Crabbe himself, who felt he was well inspired (lines
464-5).

by inspiration, felicitous expressions abound, whether the poet seeks to render in a few words the howling of the tempest, or has to portray the anguish of Ruth advancing through the waves, or that of her parents questioning the strangers whom they meet.

The Muse is a jealous mistress who brooks no rival. She claims undivided homage from the poet whom she favours. If other preoccupations beset him, if, instead of singing for her alone, he tries to amuse or to instruct, she turns away from him. She flees from all sermons, arguments, or rules. She lives on pure feeling. Her heart opens to our indignation, to our rapture, to our distress; she has tears for imaginary misfortunes, depicted with disinterestedness and sincerity. But the slightest jar disenchants her. Beneath the narrative of Phœbe Dawson's woes she detects a moral lesson and relapses into indifference. She prefers poor Ruth succumbing, not to her venial fault, but to the persecution of an odious suitor and an avaricious father. She loves this frail creature who, forsaken by all, rebels against destiny and acquiesces in death rather than degradation. And her sympathy, kindling the poet, inspires him with the most touching lines he ever wrote.

IV

No work of Crabbe's met with a better reception from the critics than the *Tales of the Hall.* Southey wrote to one of his friends[1]: "I was not disappointed with Crabbe's *Tales.* He is a decided mannerist, but so are all original writers in all ages; nor is it possible for a poet to avoid it if he writes much in the same key and upon the same class of subjects. Crabbe's poems will have a great and lasting value as pictures of domestic life, elucidating the moral history of these times. . . . He knows his own powers, and never aims above his reach." John Wilson Croker, Secretary to the Admiralty, beguiled the monotony of a cruise by reading the new work. "I had Crabbe's *Tales* with me on shipboard, and they were a treasure," he wrote to John Murray.[2] "The tales are in general so well conducted that, in prose, they would be interesting as

[1] C. W. W. Wynn, letter of July 22nd, 1819 (*Life and Correspondence*, ed. by Cuthbert Southey, 1850, vol. iv. p. 355).

[2] *The Croker Papers*, vol. i. p. 146; letter dated "Ryde, July 18th, 1819."

mere stories; but to this are added such an admirable *ease* and *force* of diction, such good pleasantry, such high principles, such a strain of poetry, such a profundity of observation, and such a gaiety of illustration as I never before, I think, saw collected.   He imagines his stories with the humour and truth of Chaucer, tells them with the copious terseness of Dryden, and the tender and thoughtful simplicity of Cowper.   This high commendation does not apply to the whole of the tales, nor, perhaps, to the whole of any one.   There are sad exceptions, here and there, which might easily be removed, but on the whole it is a delightful book." In more measured terms, Jeffrey,[1] as usual, praised Crabbe's "unrivalled and almost magical power of observation, resulting in descriptions so true to nature as to strike us rather as transcripts than imitations— an anatomy of character and feeling not less exquisite and searching—an occasional touch of matchless tenderness, and a deep and dreadful pathos strangely interwoven with the most minute and humble of his details.   Add to all this," the critic went on, "the sure and profound sagacity of the remarks with which he every now and then startles us in the midst of very unambitious discussions, and the weight and terseness of the maxims which he drops, like oracular responses, on occasions that give no promise of such a revelation."   But Jeffrey dwelt no less strongly on Crabbe's indifference in the choice of his characters and his subjects, on the homeliness of his prosaic style and the tameness of his versification.   He concluded, nevertheless, that this combination of merits and defects made up some of "the most powerful and original poetry" that the world had ever seen.   Wilson, in *Blackwood's Magazine*,[2] founded in 1817, declared that Crabbe's latest work seemed to him the best, that the plan of it was extremely happy, and that the series of tales could be read, not only without tedium, but with sustained interest.   *The Monthly Review* measured out praise and blame in the proportion indicated by Jeffrey.   As for the religious reviews, *The Christian Observer* and *The Eclectic Review*, they noted the preponderance of love stories in the present collection, the inveterate pessimism of most of the tales, which

[1] *Edinburgh Review*, vol. xxxii. July 1819, pp. 118, 119, and 125.
[2] Vol. v. July, 1819, p. 473.

thus became "triumphs of vice" rather than lessons of virtue,[1] the bitterness with which the Rev. Mr. Crabbe continued to attack the Methodists, especially in the "deeply tragical and at the same time revolting story of Ruth," and lastly, the absolute impossibility of imitating the "cool, dry manner" of this indefatigable observer and critic of mankind.[2]

Admired by most of the reviews, the new work was neglected by the public. A single edition sufficed, and even this was not entirely disposed of by John Murray, who had paid a high price for the poem.[3] It is not difficult to account for this failure. The framework of the composition was certainly not wanting in charm : the conjugal felicity of Richard and Matilda, the generosity of George, the domestic idyll which forms the general conclusion, imparted to some of the tales, and especially to the last, an optimistic and cheerful tone calculated to please people of feeling. But was it permissible to compare, as Croker did, the limited circle of this family and its acquaintances to the manifold personages, all instinct with life, all picturesque and sharply drawn, with which Chaucer has filled his canvas ? And must it not be admitted that, in spite of the abundance of biographical detail, in spite of the contrast between their respective temperaments and lives, Richard and George remain indistinct and unreal for us ? They never take shape, they never become alive. The author describes them, but he does not see them and does not make us see them. His creative imagination has little force and grasp. Besides, this framework, however ingenious it may be, does not hold the composition closely enough together. As Crabbe himself observes, the two brothers once presented to the reader, the tales might follow in any order.[4] They are not always skilfully introduced : we may allow at a pinch that George, in order to inform Richard, should tell him after dinner the story of all the neighbours met or noticed in their

---

[1] *Christian Observer*, vol. xviii. October, 1819, pp. 662 and 665.

[2] *Eclectic Review*, vol. xiii. February, 1820, pp. 122 and 132.

[3] "He [Murray] had given £3,000 for the copyright, and spent a considerable sum on the illustrations, but in the end his total loss had been about £2,500. He sold the greater part of the remainder to Mr. Tegg [1776—1845, bookseller in Cheapside] for one-third of what the poems and illustrations had cost him" (*A Publisher and his Friends*, by Samuel Smiles, vol. ii. p. 385).

[4] See above, p. 405, n. 3 ; letter from Trowbridge, January 22nd, 1819.

walks; the same privilege may be willingly conceded to "Jacques," the excellent rector; and the
"old bachelor's" confidences can be listened to with
pleasure. But how are we to believe that the "old
maid" has written her autobiography in verse and
handed it to George, in order that he may read it to
us?[1] More finished than that of the *Tales in Verse*,
the composition of this collection is still defective.

Considered separately, these tales are remarkable
for a steadily increasing prolixity. That a long
analysis of the characters should serve as preface to
the plot need not surprise us, for such is the favourite
method of our poet, who defies monotony.[2] But when
the narrator, wishing to provide a transition between
a good dinner and an often prosy story, introduces
each tale with interminable remarks, the result is pure
loquacity. The opening of *Ruth* consists of a catalogue
of the volumes in old Hannah's possession. Had
Crabbe forgotten that a similar description already
occurs at the beginning of *The Parish Register*?
George, being desirous to hear his brother's adventures, would naturally want to let him speak. He
prefers to inflict on us beforehand a ridiculous digression on the travels of the explorer Bruce[3] and the
loves of the Indian heroine Yarico.[4] It looks as if
Crabbe, from excess of realism, had persuaded himself
that every conversation is fit to be put into verse.

Lastly, the uniformity of all these stories, *Tales in
Verse* or *Tales of the Hall*, could not but repel the
public. Repetition cannot be practised with impunity,
especially in poetry. Readers grow weary and turn
to other objects of admiration. As it happened, Byron
had appeared between 1812 and 1818: the stanzas of
Childe Harold revealed to England the landscapes of
eastern Europe, and glowed with a burning enthusiasm
for the cause of liberty; *Lara*, *Manfred*, and *The
Corsair*, desperate heroes or mysterious brigands,
were captivating the public imagination, henceforth
indifferent to the humble misfortunes which Crabbe
had described in such abundance. His vein was exhausted, and his popularity at an end.

[1] *Tales of the Hall*, xi. 11, 12.
[2] See above, pp. 369-70.
[3] Who, in 1770, thought he had discovered the source of the Nile.
[4] Cf. her history, by Steele, in No. 11 of *The Spectator*, Tuesday, March 13th,
1710-11.

CHAPTER IV

CLOSING YEARS (1819—1832)

I. Relations with Sir Walter Scott. Journey to Edinburgh.—II. The *Posthumous Tales.*—III. Political opinions and social ideas.—IV. Decline and death.

I

FOR some time to come, Crabbe's state of health allowed him, not only to return to London every summer, but also to enjoy the honours and the pleasures which his fame procured him. At the end of April, 1819,[1] he once more left Trowbridge for the capital, took up his abode provisionally at the " Hummums," the well-known hotel in Covent Garden, and resumed his fashionable life. A tradition of fifty years' standing demanded that the opening of the Royal Academy exhibition should be preceded by a dinner given by the President and Members to the most distinguished representatives of rank or intellect. Crabbe was invited to it, and a letter of his, written on May 7th to a female friend at Trowbridge, acquaints us with his impressions. " It was," he writes, " singular and grand. We dined in the great room,[2] where the principal pictures were placed, which covered every part of it. Our number I judge about 180 or 200 : we had one royal duke, Sussex ; the Duke of Wellington ; we had four ambassadors (at whose table I was placed, with two English gentlemen luckily) ; and many of our nobility. The dinner itself was like all very large dinners : but the toasts, music, and speeches after we had dined,

---

[1] Cf. Fitzgerald notes : " 1819.—April 29. London.—30. Hummums.—May 5. Lodgings. Brewer Street.—June 11. Mr. Rogers. Stothard, verbose and determined. Rob Roy. Good day.—July 3. Arrive at home.—September 22. At Cromer this week.—Oct. 9. To London. 14. Trowbridge."

[2] Of Somerset House, no doubt, where the exhibition was held until the National Gallery was built, in 1838. The Royal Academy took up its abode at New Burlington House in 1869.

were in a high style. I was not a little surprised to see my picture by Phillips,[1] for, if any, I expected the other;[2] and they all said that not only the likeness was strong, but the picture good: and I believe it is so, because Lord Holland is to have it copied, and placed with those in his library. I slept two nights at Holland House, and dined three times before Lady H. was weary of me, and even at last I was treated with marvellous kindness. . . . I am going to-day to dine at the Thatched House, being elected a member of the Literary Society. When I have seen my brethren, and paid my subscription, I shall better judge whether the honour makes amends for the costs."[3] On May 17th, the philanthropic " Wiltshire Society in London,"[4] founded under the auspices of the Marquis of Lansdowne, was banqueting at the Albion Hotel. After dinner the " noble President " drank the health of the three Wiltshire poets, Crabbe, Bowles, and Moore, who

[1] Which has always belonged to the Murrays, and an excellent engraving of which is the frontispiece of all the editions published by them. It is also the frontispiece to this volume. The following is a good description of it : " The poet is represented sitting, with his hands clasped before him, in nearly a front view. He is dressed in black, with a dark porch behind him to the left and verdant vine-leaves, a bit of light sky and a view of a distant village to the right. The forehead is high and bald, excepting a single lock. The complexion clear ; the eye, if the height of the picture did not deceive us, of a mild blue ; the expression open and lively with a fine character of frank intelligence. The head is in a broad mellow style. The carnations much less toned, the transitions in the shadows more sudden, and the dark touches in the features less decided than usual with this artist. The hands are well coloured, and the general effect is bright and agreeable " (*Exhibition of the Royal Academy: New Monthly Magazine*, August 1819, p. 96).

[2] By Pickersgill. The original belongs to the Rev. Cl. G. Rivett-Carnac. The forehead is not so high as in Phillips's portrait. Cf. Fitzgerald's opinion on these two pictures : *More Letters of Edward Fitzgerald*, ed. by W. A. Wright (Macmillan, 1901, p. 153), to E. B. Cowell, from Woodbridge, October, 1873: ". . . I think I shall have Lawrence copy me the portrait that used to be at Bradford " (on Avon, with the Biographer's daughters) ; and p. 158 to W. F. Pollock (1874). ". . . If you did not observe my Laureate Crabbe's portrait at the Portrait Gallery, go and see it at Lawrence's, who is copying it for me. Phillips's portrait is the man in company, a little ' doucereux ' as Moore defined him : but Pickersgill's is The Man, I fancy : and his son, my old friend at Bredfield, so thought of it, I believe." To these portraits must be added two others, one by Millington, of Trowbridge, the other attributed to John Waldron Crabbe (Mackay Collection). There are also two sketches taken by the sculptor Chantrey with a view to a bust, the first in 1821 (National Portrait Gallery ; see the plate facing this page) the second in 1826.

[3] B. p. 74.

[4] The purport of the meeting was to promote "the ' Wiltshire Society in London' to apprentice the sons of poor Wiltshire parents settled in the metropolis" (*The Autobiography* of John Briton (1850): The Rev. Geo. Crabbe, vol. i. pp. 381-7).

Geo'ge Crabbe 1821 —

Berger-Levrault & Sc.

GEORGE CRABBE IN 1821.

From a Sketch by Sir Francis L. Chantrey, R.A.

each responded in a few words. With his usual brilliance, Moore, turning towards Crabbe, told him that " the *Musa severior* which he worshipped had had no influence whatever on the kindly dispositions of his heart," and that "while with the eye of a sage and a poet, he looked penetratingly into the darker region of human nature, he stood surrounded by its most genial light himself."[1] This toast, which, according to the author of it, was a "marvellous success," emphasised happily the contrast patent to all between the generally satirical tone of Crabbe's works and his affable manners. Sincerely modest and simple, Crabbe was quite ready to be patronised, provided it was done with good taste, and Moore, a butterfly poet and warbling bird, liked to play the part of patron, which flattered his vanity. On June 5th a banquet, presided over by the Duke of Sussex, being given to celebrate the glory of Burns, Crabbe was again invited and made to sit beside Moore at the table of honour.[2] At the beginning of July he returned to Trowbridge, which he left in September for Cromer and Suffolk.[3]

In this comparatively sedentary life, the year 1822 is marked by an event of some importance—a journey to Edinburgh. A correspondence had arisen in 1812 between Crabbe and Sir Walter Scott. The latter, hearing that the *Tales in Verse* were about to be published, had bespoken a copy at Hatchard's, and had afterwards intimated his entire satisfaction with the work in a highly eulogistic letter addressed to the publisher. Hatchard hastened to send it to Crabbe, who at once expressed his deep gratitude to the writer. " I have," he says,[4] "long entertained a hearty wish to be made known to a poet whose works are so greatly and so universally admired. I continued to

[1] Moore's *Memoirs*, vol. ii. p. 308, and B. p. 75.

[2] Moore's *Memoirs*, vol. ii. p. 332.

[3] Nothing is known of the years 1820 and 1821, except that in August and September, 1820, he was at Beccles and Cromer (MS. sermons, Murray Collection), and in 1821 in London from September 5th and at Weymouth on October 8th.

[4] In a letter dated Muston, Grantham, October 13th, 1812, and published by Lockhart, *Life of Scott*, new popular ed., Black, 1893, p. 228. It begins as follows: " SIR,—Mr. Hatchard, judging rightly of the satisfaction it would afford me, has been so obliging as to communicate your two letters, in one of which you desire my *Tales* to be sent ; in the other you acknowledge the receipt of them, and in both you mention my verses in such terms, that it would be affected in me were I to deny, and I think unjust if I were to conceal, the pleasure you give me. I am indeed highly gratified. . . ."

hope that I might at some time find a common friend,
by whose intervention I might obtain that honour;
but I am confined by duties near my home and by
sickness in it. . . . Excuse me then, Sir, if I gladly seize
this opportunity which now occurs to express my thanks
for the politeness of your expressions, as well as my
desire of being known to a gentleman who has delighted and affected me, and moved all the passions and
feelings in turn, I believe—envy surely excepted. . . . I
truly rejoice in your success, and while I am entertaining, in my way, a certain set of readers, for the most
part probably of peculiar turn and habit, I can with
pleasure see the effect you produce on all." Scott replied
by return of post with marked cordiality. He fully
shared Crabbe's wish. "It is more than twenty years
ago," he added, "that I was, for great part of a very
snowy winter, the inhabitant of an old house in the
country, in a course of poetical study, so very like
that of your admirably painted 'Young Lad,' that I
could hardly help saying, 'That's me!'"[1]   And
Scott, being unable to procure the poems themselves,
had learnt by heart all the extracts from them given
by *The Annual Register*—the conclusion of the first
book of *The Village*, and the satire on the romantic
novels in *The Library*: "You may therefore guess
my sincere delight when I saw your poems at a later
period[2] assume the rank in the public consideration
which they so well deserve. It was a triumph to my
own immature taste to find I had anticipated the
applause of the learned and the critical."[3]   The correspondence thus begun was not allowed to languish:
in 1813 Crabbe asked Scott for information about a

[1] The "Youth" whom Crabbe makes fun of at the end of *The Newspaper*
(lines 441 *seq*., cf. above, p. 182).

[2] In 1807. Scott pushed his admiration for *The Parish Register* to the point
of imitating it in a long piece called *The Poacher*, and written in 1811. Cf.
Lockhart, pp. 207-8: "This piece . . . when first forwarded to Ballantyne
was accompanied with a little note, in which he says, 'Understand I have no
idea of parody, but serious imitation, if I can accomplish it. The subject of
my "Crabbe" is a character in his line which he never touched.'" This *Poacher*,
which is almost unreadable, is very like a parody, at least in the beginning,
and is simply an amplification of the infidel poacher in *The Parish Register*,
i. 787-823. Never has the impossibility of imitating Crabbe been more
effectively demonstrated than by this failure of Sir Walter Scott.

[3] B. p. 53, with the wrong date of October 21st, 1809. It should be
October 21st, 1812, as the chain of facts demands (cf. the letter from Crabbe
to Scott of October 13th, 1812, above, p. 433, n. 4, which is evidently the
first of this correspondence).

certain "Mr. Brunton," who wanted our clergyman to contribute to a collection of Scotch hymns.[1] An allusion by Scott to his duties as "clerk" of the Supreme Court[2] led to other letters in which the two poets gave each other information about their respective modes of life.[3] Lastly, on July 16th, 1822, Scott wrote to Crabbe that he would be very glad to see him in Scotland, especially at Abbotsford. "If the King comes to Edinburgh," he continued, "I must be there for a day or two, but I fancy you will avoid that period of tumult and bustle, though, if your health permitted, it would be a curious sight to see." Scott concluded by telling his friend that to get to Edinburgh he had the choice of two routes, either by sea in sixty hours or by the great western road, through Carlisle and Selkirk.[4] Crabbe, accompanied by a servant, arrived at Edinburgh in the second week of August. He wished no doubt to see the reception which Scotland was preparing for George IV.

In his *Life of Scott*, Lockhart,[5] who did not hesitate to distort the truth in order to make it more picturesque, gives a humorous account of the supposed meeting of the two poets. On Wednesday, August 14th, about midday, a break in the weather had revealed the royal yacht, attended by its men-of-war, anchoring in the roadstead of Leith. Impelled by a feeling of loyalty, all Edinburgh had sallied forth to meet their sovereign. "But the climate is capricious in that country," observes a contemporary chronicler:[6] the sun was too soon hidden by clouds which dissolved in drizzling rain. Besides this, a distressing piece of intelligence

---

[1] Lockhart, *Life of Scott*, p. 228 (undated, but probably 1813).

[2] B. pp. 58-9, and Lockhart, pp. 228-9: "He [Mr. Brunton] is at this very moment sitting on the outside of the bar of our Supreme Court, within which I am fagging as a clerk."

[3] Crabbe to Scott (Lockhart, p. 229): "MY DEAR SIR,—Law, then, is your profession—but how fag as a *clerk*? . . ." A complete collection of the poems in three volumes no doubt accompanied this letter, which would account for Scott's reply (B. pp. 56-7, and Lockhart, pp. 229-30), sent from Abbotsford on June 1st, 1813 (and not 1812, as printed in B.): "I have too long delayed." To Scott's confidences Crabbe replies by his own (undated letter, B. pp. 57-8, often quoted): "Accept my very sincere congratulations on your clerkship."

[4] Sir W. Scott to Crabbe, dated Abbotsford, Melrose, July 16th, 1822 (Broadley Collection).

[5] P. 482.

[6] See *Blackwood's Edinburgh Magazine*, September, 1822, vol. xii. pp. 268 seq.

reached the King at that very moment : his beloved Minister for Foreign Affairs, the famous Lord Castlereagh, then Marquis of Londonderry, had committed suicide ; so that George IV., yielding to his grief and to the bad weather, decided to remain on board and disappoint his loyal subjects, whose enthusiasm defied the rain. But Sir Walter Scott, who had on this occasion constituted himself organiser of the fêtes and director of ceremonies, was unwilling to defer the homage due to his royal master. Taking with him a St. Andrew's cross in silver, a gift of the ladies of Edinburgh to His Majesty, he rowed out in a boat to the *Royal George.* "What!" exclaimed His Majesty, when the visitor was announced, "Sir Walter Scott! the man in Scotland I most wish to see. Let him come up!" With affectionate condescension the King most graciously asked for a bottle of Highland whisky, which he appreciated as much as that of Ireland,[1] and proposed the health of the poet, who acknowledged it. Scott, a great collector and fervent Tory, begged his sovereign to let him have the glass in which his health had been royally drunk. He obtained it, wrapped it up, and placed it carefully in one of his pockets. Affected by this kind reception, and wet through, Scott, says Lockhart, was returning to his house in Castle Street, when he espied "the poet Crabbe," who had just arrived. "With fraternal affection, he embraced the venerable old man," forgetting, in his surprise and delight, the precious relic which he was carrying. A moment afterwards he sat down on the glass and broke it into fragments.

This ingenious anecdote would deserve to be true in every detail. Unfortunately, on the date which Lockhart assigns to it Crabbe had been at Castle Street for a week,[2] and his presence could no longer have

---

[1] Which he had copiously partaken of the year before, in the course of his journey to Dublin.

[2] The following passages from two unpublished letters prove it. Crabbe to his son John :

"*August* 9, 1822, SIR WALTER SCOTT, CASTLE STREET, EDINBOROUGH. —MY DEAR JOHN,—Do pray consider my distance and let me hear from you once at least before I leave Edinborough. There is a letter for me on the road, I will conclude and hope for it every day till it arrives.

"I am very happy and very well—a pain now and then excepted—at Sir Walter's, who is more engaged than any man in England at this time, but who does all he can to make me comfortable and in this is joined by his whole family.

"Nor that only, for here are friends. . . . Here is Mr. Mackenzie—with

surprised his host. He had had time to explore Edinburgh, to visit, in Holyrood Palace, the "little room"
in which Rizzio was "cut down" by his murderers
under the eyes of Mary Queen of Scots. "They show
certain stains on the floor," remarks Crabbe, "and I

surprise I heard it—the author of the Man of Feeling—and indeed he is so
called. Here is Mr. Jeffery to whom I always count myself obliged, here is
Mr. Lockhart, Sir Walter's son-in-law and his pleasant wife—here is a Mr.
Murry [*i.e.* John Archibald Murray, a Whig and afterwards a "Judge"] with
whom I dined to-day,—and lastly, no, not lastly, for there are many more—
but here is Mr. Blackwood, the Editor of the Magazine which goes under his
name and who this morning—*in modo* Mr. Murry of London—very kindly
pressed me to accept a volume, and a very pleasing volume, of Miscellanies
which I will take with me if I live to reach Trowbridge again.

"All is, you may suppose, bustle and a continual accession of strangers.
The Highland Chieftain and his officers and followers make a respectable
but singular appearance. We had quite a day of it yesterday, and wine and
music, and more than I can or perhaps ought to tell you in a letter, but we
shall meet, I hope, and you will hear my stories if I do not forget or lose all
before I see you. . . . I find time in all this confusion to walk and even to
rhyme, and have a few verses on the occasion, which are not much amiss. I
dare say Mr. Blackwood would give me thanks for them, and I do not know
but I may give them to him, if I can do it with perfect concealment, but I will
consult Sir Walter.

"Hollis [his servant] is quite a gentleman. He has found a friend in Sir
Walter's attendant after his own heart: both good quiet fellows, both bachelors
of a certain age, both curious, inquisitive, obedient, orderly men ; there is quite
a friendship. I did not know that he was in the house till to-day. Lady Scott,
who by the way is a favourite with me, gave her orders secretly, and Hollis has
a good berth of it. No wonder the man is pleased.

"It is late, but I shall be engaged in the morning. . . . We expect the King
on or about Tuesday. . . . No quarries here, but many mountains ; no pits
nor fossils, but granite in abundance, and the views of the city very fine indeed.
Nothing near London equals it. . . .

" . . . I should like to earn a little money during this excursion, and will if
possible make a little volume like a thin one of the *Tales of the Hall*. I wonder
what Murray would say. I know that Constable here would like to hear of it,
but I will not do unhandsomely by my friend in Albemarle Street" (Mackay
Collection).

Crabbe to his sons :

"CASTLE STREET, 39. *August* 15*th* [a mistake for the 14th].—I was favoured
with your letter as I returned home from a dinner visit to a gentleman whom I
thought long since in his grave, Mr. Mackenzie [cf. B. p. 77, col. 2]. . . . We
are in daily and now almost hourly expectation of the King, but he is not yet
in sight. The City is a little intoxicated, but that is no wonder. . . . I am in
the very centre of preparation : the Highland chiefs come hither, and some of
their followers who speak no language except Galic exhibited yesterday specimens of the costume and manners of the Highlands . . . . I am rather at a loss
respecting my stay, but, I think, not for another letter.—I will however write
as soon as I know myself. I just learn from Hollis that the King is seen, the boat
at least [consequently written on the 14th], and of course he will be here to-day.
I am almost ashamed to say I shall be glad when it be over, and yet I have done
something for I have written five and forty congratulatory lines for him, tho'
I will not undertake to say they will be presented or that he will read them,
but somebody will. . . . Sir Walter is gone or going to meet him and do the
honours appertaining to his office. Indeed he is the guiding figure in the
exhibition " (Mackay Collection).

see no reason why you should not believe them made
by his blood, if you can." After having ascended the
historic street which leads up to the "Hill" crowned
by the "Castle," Crabbe had been shown by Lockhart, who was escorting him, the country-house of
Allan Ramsay, a bookseller and poet whose name
even was unknown to him. That very evening he
read *The Gentle Shepherd*, and was pleased with this
agreeable pastoral drama, but added, "There is a
long step between Ramsay and Burns." On another
occasion he had climbed the "Salisbury Craigs," which
rise to the south of Holyrood, and had taken as much
interest in their stratification as in the extensive landscape to be seen from their summit. "Edinburgh," he
writes, "is really a very interesting place,—to me very
singular. How can I describe the view from the hill
that overlooks the palace—the fine group of buildings
which form the castle; the bridges, uniting the two
towns;[1] and the beautiful view of the Firth and its
islands? On Sunday the streets were forsaken; and
silence reigned over the whole city. London has
a diminished population on that day in her streets;
but in Edinburgh it is a total stagnation—a quiet that
is in itself devout." With a characteristic predilection,
he had often rambled, even at nightfall, in the
"wynds" and "closes" which then branched off
from Canongate and the High Street, like so many
"fibres projected from an enormous spine." "A lane
of cobblers," he writes, "struck me particularly; I
could not but remark the civility and urbanity of
the Scotch poor; they certainly exceed ours in politeness, arising, probably, from minds more generally
cultivated." Sir Walter Scott, being uneasy about
these nocturnal peregrinations in questionable
localities, had discreetly ordered an errand-boy, a
"caddie," to follow his friend and see that he came
to no harm.

At Scott's table Crabbe had witnessed the feverish
agitation caused by the preparations for the royal
reception and by the disputes of the Gaelic clans
contending for precedence in the processions to be
formed. Invited by the feudal enthusiasm of Sir
Walter, the Highland chieftains and their retainers
seemed to be the masters of Edinburgh. Their

[1] "The Old" and "the New."

stature and their costume of kilt and tartan made them the observed of all observers. They flocked into Castle Street, attracted by the princely hospitality of their great poet. On the day after his arrival[1] Crabbe had found some of them in the dining-room. They were talking Gaelic, a language of which our clergyman could not understand a word. Good breeding, however, demanded that he should greet them. Latin would no doubt have embarrassed him. According to Lockhart, he chose French, which he had learnt at Muston and Trowbridge. The clansmen were at a loss in their turn. Fortunately Sir Walter Scott came in at that moment and addressed his guests in the only language which Crabbe had not thought of using and which all were able to understand—English. The dinner was a most cheerful one. There was plenty of "wine and music. . . . We had Sir Walter Scott's national songs and ballads, exhibiting all the feelings of clanship. I thought it an honour that Glengarry even took notice of me, for there were those, and gentlemen too, who considered themselves honoured by following in his train. There were, also, Lord Errol, and The Macleod, and The Frazer, and The Gordon, and The Ferguson ; and I conversed at dinner with Lady Glengarry, and did almost believe myself a harper, or bard, rather—for harp I cannot strike—and Sir Walter was the life and soul of the whole. It was a splendid festivity, and I felt I know not how much younger."[2]

When, therefore, on August 15th the King landed and, preceded by a group of dignitaries and Highlanders, drove along Leith Walk and by the foot of Calton Hill to Holyrood Palace, Crabbe was quite prepared to sympathise with Scott and the inhabitants of Edinburgh, who were enraptured with the fine day. On Saturday, the 17th, he attended the levée, at which George IV. appeared in a " Stewart tartan " and despatched fifteen hundred of his subjects in one hundred and twenty minutes. He perhaps waited for the grand day, Tuesday, the 22nd, on which the King, amid deafening cheers and in pouring rain, proceeded from Holyrood through the Old Town

---

[1] The 8th, and not the 15th, as Lockhart says (*Life of Scott*, p. 482, and letter quoted by B. p. 78, col. 1).

[2] B. p. 77.

to the Castle, slowly ascended the hill, stopped on the esplanade, at the top of "the highest battery," and there, alone, enveloped at intervals by the smoke of the guns, under the folds of the royal standard flapping in the wind, saluted his Scotch subjects massed at his feet. "It was a sublime sight," exclaims the chronicler. Let us hope that Crabbe was able to enjoy it, and that this singular spectacle repaid him for his long journey and for the lines which, like Scott, he had composed in honour of his King.[1]

II

ENCOURAGED by the considerable sum which he had obtained for the *Tales of the Hall*, Crabbe tried, between the years 1822 and 1824, to write a new collection of tales. "If my health will allow me," he wrote to Mrs. Leadbeater, "I will endeavour to make a few things I have by me more fit for the press. I have some friends whom I consult, and having their sanction I should proceed in my *last* trial—for so I must consider it—with some alacrity. But so much of the day is taken from me by my disorder[2] that little remains in which I can engage in any employment that requires thought, and this makes me quite uncertain of the time, or even of the publication itself."[3] Interrupted for a long time, the "correction" of them was pushed on in October, 1829[4]; two years afterwards, Crabbe, writing to his sons of the *Tales of*

[1] Scott wrote *Carle, now the King's Come*, published in his works, and Crabbe a *Vision* (see Appendix V).

[2] The "tic douloureux" (cf. below, pp. 464-5).

[3] *Leadbeater Papers*, vol. ii. pp. 385-6, letter from Trowbridge, March 26th, 1824. We may note the following sentence: "My longest attempt I have called *The Deserted Wife* (or *Family*), and I do not recollect that the principal incident has been taken before." This tale, which remained unpublished, does not figure in the *Posthumous Tales*. An analysis of it and an extract from it will be found in Appendix VI.

[4] Fitzgerald notes: "1829, October. Correcting his MSS. in good earnest." The following passage in a letter from Miss Hoare to B. (February 22nd, 1832) explains this delay: "Mr. Crabbe never spoke of the poems to me as completely prepared for publication, but said, 'My sons will know what I wish.' ... Mr. Crabbe spoke of them to Mr. Murray when last in town, for we were several times at Mr. Murray's door. . . . I heard through a friend of Mr. M. that he was not likely to give the sum for these poems which he gave for the *Tales of the Hall*, and Mr. Campbell decidedly recommended that they should not be published during your Father's life. I did not mention my conversation with Mr. Campbell to him, but I never urged him from this time to publish again." Hence the long intervals between these revisions, which were always incomplete.

the Hall, informed them that they would find in his "recess at home another series of such stories, in number and quantity sufficient for an octavo volume." "As I suppose," he added, that "they are much like the former in execution, and sufficiently different in events and characters, they may hereafter, in peaceable times, be worth something to you; and the more, because I shall, whatever is mortal of me, be at rest in the chancel of Trowbridge Church; for the works of authors departed are generally received with some favour, partly as they are old acquaintances, and in part because there can be no more of them."[1] Revised by Lockhart, and no doubt also by Rogers, the *Posthumous Tales* appeared in September, 1834, two years after the death of their author, in the eighth volume of the complete edition. A contemporary of Johnson by his first efforts, Crabbe ended his career at the moment when Tennyson was beginning his. Three generations of poets had succeeded each other since 1781, and the fourth made its appearance while the sole survivor of the first was passing away.

The *Posthumous Tales* are divided into two quite distinct parts. The first includes five stories, composed at the time of the *Tales of the Hall*[2] and rejected then as superfluous: *Silford Hall, or the Happy Day*, an autobiographical reminiscence of Wickham Brook and Cheveley Park;[3] *The Family of Love*, an amplification, in more than a thousand lines, of the story of Roger Cuff and Surly John;[4] *The Equal Marriage*, a description of domestic scenes already twice portrayed, in *The Natural Death of Love* and in *Squire Thomas*[5]; *Rachel*, in which Crabbe develops a sketch of Cowper's[6]; and lastly, *Villars*, which perhaps deserves a brief consideration.

Matilda, an elegant and imperious coquette of high

---

[1] Letter from Clifton, October 24th, 1831, B. p. 88, col. 1.

[2] Cf. especially *Rachel* and *Villars*, evidently related by one of the brothers in the *Tales of the Hall*.

[3] See above, pp. 40-2.

[4] *Parish Register*, iii. 731–800; cf. above, pp. 241-2.

[5] *Tales of the Hall*, xiv., and *Tales*, xii.; cf. below, p. 510, and above, p. 366, n. 2.

[6] Cf. *The Task*, i., towards the end, "Kate is crazed." The imitation is certain, for in the manuscript of the *Posthumous Tales* belonging to the Dyce Collection (South Kensington Museum) we read after line 66:

Rachel is crazed, but she is not like Kate:
The cause the same, yet hers the harder fate.

birth, is courted by Villars, a timid lover, and by a
very enterprising nobleman. She treats the first as
a humble slave; she receives with an air of triumph
the homage and the feigned deference of the second.
Pursued by the jealous entreaties of Villars, who
implores her to bid him "die or live," she replies with
cruel irony:

> "Or die or live"—the gentle Lady cried—
> "As suits thee best; that point thyself decide.
> But if to death thou hast thyself decreed,
> Then like a man perform the manly deed;
> The well-charged pistol to the ear apply,
> Make loud report, and like a hero die:
> Let rogues and rats on ropes and poison seize—
> Shame not thy friends by petty death like these;
> Sure we must grieve at what thou think'st to do;
> But spare us blushes for the manner too!"

Then, tempering her sarcasms with a smile, she
manages to "allay the anger" and "console the pride"
of the sentimental Villars. Less pressing, the young
nobleman confines himself to complimenting his "fair"
in flattering verses; he never asks the hand which
she would so gladly bestow on him; he seems to be
watching for the moment when Matilda's tenderness
will get the better of her reason. The moment came,
as he thought:

> He dropp'd his mask; and both were undeceived.
> She saw the vice that would no longer feign,
> And he an angry beauty's pure disdain.

Resentment throws her into the arms of Villars,
who, wild with delight, obtains the consent of her
whose reproaches he dreaded!

> Proud as a prince, and restless as a boy,
> He sought to speak, but could not aptly find
> Words for his use, they enter'd not his mind. . . .
> So full of bliss, that wonder and delight
> Seem'd in those happy moments to unite.
> He was like one who gains, but dreads to lose
> A prize that seems to vanish as he views;
> And in his look was wildness and alarm—
> Like a sad conjuror who forgets his charm,
> And when the demon at the call appears,
> Cannot command the spirit for his fears.

On the wedding day he proudly shows his lovely
bride,
> Demurely pacing, pondering, at his side.

To please her, he transforms his property, cuts down
oaks to let in the light of day, builds a new house,
gives sumptuous fêtes to which the neighbours flock
to greet their queen. On two occasions Matilda meets
the young nobleman and treats him with cool disdain.
Villars, less unrelenting in his happiness, intercedes
for the culprit:

> "Smile, my Matilda! virtue should inflict
> No needless pain, nor be so sternly strict."

The husband is destined to repent of his kindness.
Business summons him to Ireland and keeps him
there for many weeks. Matilda has remained alone
at the hall, not far from her old admirer. Who knows
if her attachment will not revive, if she will always
retain the same horror of vice and will not yield to
the ardent entreaties of the man whom she formerly
preferred? Has not Villars advised her to smile?
Has he not drawn upon himself the calamity of which
he has a kind of presentiment? On his return to
England he stops, seized by a sudden apprehension, a
few miles from his home:

> . . . The night was wet and dim;
> Thick, heavy dews descended on the ground,
> And all was sad and melancholy round.

Espying the gleaming fire of an inn, he enters to
ascertain if all is well. In the chimney corner is
seated a poacher whom he had once sentenced to a
fine, a whipping, and imprisonment for having caught
a hare. The man is already enjoying his revenge:

> ". . . Will your Honour know
> How does my Lady? that myself can show.
> On Monday morning I was early up,
> And forth without a morsel or a sup;
> There was my Lady's carriage—Whew! it drove
> As if the horses had been spurred by Love."

What, thinks Villars, still incredulous, has Matilda
gone off with her old adorer? And his anxiety

deepens. He arrives at the park gates, and finds
them wide open:

> . . . Who would dare
> Do this, if her presiding glance were there!

As he approaches the house, he sees a woman weeping
at a window lighted by a lamp. It is his own sister,
and not Matilda. A servant comes up and makes a
stammering explanation. . . . All doubt is at an end:
the guilty couple have fled.

Revenge is now his sole thought. On the sea-coast,
between rocks which forbid access to the shore and
a " stubborn heath" that resists the plough, stands a
deserted house, surrounded by "dark elms," the breed-
ing-place of herons. Villars buys it. He selects a
room, " square, small, and lofty," with a sloping sky-
light. If he can recover possession of Matilda, this
shall be the faithless woman's dungeon. He has her
watched. Fifteen months afterwards he succeeds in
capturing her and carrying her off in his carriage to
the prison which he has prepared. But how is it
possible to punish a woman whom he loves so
much?

> Features so dear had still maintain'd their sway,
> And looks so loved had taught him to obey:
> Rage and Revenge had yielded to the sight
> Of charms that waken wonder and delight;
> The harsher passions from the heart had flown,
> And LOVE regain'd his subject and his throne.

Bald in execution and prosy in style, this tale nevertheless contains one of the most original plots that
Crabbe invented. It raises a psychological problem
which is sometimes treated on the modern stage—the
revival, in the heart of a woman married in spite of
herself or out of resentment, of a youthful passion
which causes her fall.[1] Singularly bold for the time
and for a clergyman's pen, this subject was entirely
new. Unfortunately, Crabbe has indicated rather than
developed it. Preoccupied with Villars and neglecting
Matilda, he has omitted to describe the crisis which
leads to her surrender to her lover. And the abrupt
dénouement spoils the general effect. But the sketch,

---

[1] Not to mention the question of "pardon," already treated by Crabbe in
the *Tales in Verse* (xvi., *The Confidant*; cf. above, pp. 354-7) and in the *Tales
of the Hall* (xii., *Sir Owen Dale*, and xix., *William Bailey*; cf. below,
pp. 506-7 and 511-2).

such as it is, appears sufficiently interesting to deserve notice.

The second part of the *Posthumous Tales*, entitled *The Farewell and Return*, forms a series of seventeen tales, the unity of which is ensured by the person of the narrator himself. Let us suppose that a young man, quitting his native place to make his way in the world, bids farewell to his friends and acquaintances; that, twenty years later, he revisits his borough, inquires about those whom he left behind him there, and proceeds to relate their history in verse—the poet will find in this very simple idea an opportunity of placing the characters and incidents which he can best describe.[1] He will depict the youth and the old age of his heroes, the ups and downs of their existence; he will explain, as is his wont, the causes of the failure of most of them, the reasons of the success, which is always incomplete, of a few. He will identify himself thoroughly with his wanderer. For he too has felt himself a stranger in the town which gave him birth. "Beccles," he writes,[2] "is the home of past years, and I could not walk through the streets as a stranger. It is not so at Aldborough: there a sadness mixes with all I see or hear; not a man is living whom I knew in my early portion of life; my contemporaries are gone, and their successors are unknown to me and I to them." Thus disenchantment still pervades this last work of Crabbe.

Almost all the personages in it are unfortunate. A schoolfellow seemed a boy of great promise: he dies prematurely, and is barely remembered. He is described as a "decent lad," with "a long, pale face, who dressed in drab and walked as in a race," and played on the flute, his only accomplishment. A shopman, named "Barnaby," was conspicuous for his politeness, his love of work, and his cleanliness. Every morning he used to open the shop himself, sweep the doorstep, and arrange his wares. On Sunday he would put on his best clothes to go to church or to visit a rich widow whom he was timidly courting. He engaged in smuggling, and was ruined by a custom-house prosecution. A merchant dazzled his fellow-citizens by his

---

[1] Letter to Mrs. Leadbeater of March 26th, 1824 (*Leadbeater Papers*, vol. ii. p. 386), quoted by B., *Works*, p. 534, n. 1.

[2] On January 19th, 1831: cf. B. p. 87.

fleet of ships moored to the quay and by the luxury of his wife, who strutted from "stall to stall" and received the humble obeisances of the tradesmen. He ends his days in the poorhouse, and, like Blaney, curses the pauper's dress. The gentle and amiable "Jane," full of good sense, charity, and piety, fancied she had found the husband of her dreams in a stranger, of the same age as herself, of grave and manly appearance. A woman, the mistress of this hypocrite, appears to undeceive her and shatter her happiness. The pretentious "Miranda," a provincial blue-stocking, in the lifetime of her husband, the Dean, was the queen of a circle in which philosophy was talked; to-day a widow and in reduced circumstances, she has lost all her former glory. The heedless "Belinda Waters," who, a laughing, frivolous girl, thought that she would always have as much money as her soul could desire, has ended by marrying a half-pay navy surgeon, and wonders why "the rude butcher" brings his bill every week. In the ardour of youth "Richard Danvers" had fallen in love with his pretty neighbour, "Phœbe Rayner"; but, while his family inherited a country house and a handsome fortune, the Rayners sank lower and lower in the world. Phœbe, inconstant and unrefined amid vulgar surroundings, was surprised by the amorous Richard on the arm of a sailor.[1] Always

---

[1] See in succession, *Posthumous Tales*, vii. (*The Schoolfellow*), viii. (*Barnaby, the Shopman*), xi. (*The Merchant*), ix. (*Jane*), xiii. (*The Dean's Lady*), xv. (*Belinda Waters*), xvii. (*Danvers and Rayner*). To them should be added the tenth, in which an old man deplores the cutting down of the trees on an *Ancient Manor*; the eighteenth (*The Boat-race*), in which the young boatman, Charles, falls in love with the "good and graceful" Elizabeth, the daughter of another boatman, a political opponent of Charles's father. To obtain the hand of his beloved, Charles gives up his vote, and the couple are about to be united, when the young man perishes in a boat-race in which his future father-in-law had urged him to take part. The nineteenth (*Master William*) shows us the love of a youth for his mother's maid, the "charming nymph Fanny," who soon undeceives him by introducing him to her real sweetheart, a "burly swain" called John. The twentieth (*The Will*) is a somewhat strange story of a certain George, a dissipated spendthrift, who, knowing that his father is on the point of death and about to disinherit him, pretends to be a reformed character, and regains the paternal favour. Now, the father has made two wills: the first, entrusted to a friend, David Wright, cuts off George; the second, revoking the first, reinstates the son, subject to payment of £3,500 to Wright and some cousins. Not wishing to part with such a heavy sum, George burns the will. A few days afterwards Wright appears with his will and claims all the property. Overwhelmed, George is obliged to become Wright's tenant, contracts economical and even avaricious habits, and, on Wright's death, succeeds to a considerable fortune, which does not give him happiness.

"the same sort of teasing, helpless, mechanical, unimaginative distress," as Hazlitt says.

It looks as if old age had robbed the poet of his smile. Even his rare cheering tales are tinged with sadness. He describes to us two brothers—"James," a Whig, and "Charles," a Tory—whom politics have separated, and who are reconciled in the long run. But James must be threatened with bankruptcy to make Charles come to his rescue, from motives of pride, and forget his resentment. "Sophia," a prudent and serious woman, has married a captain whom she has followed to the wars and nursed in the camp, where he succumbs to his wounds. She has then married, out of devotion rather than affection, a friend of the captain, with a large family. Full of solicitude for these children who are not her own, she has not hesitated to travel alone to Barbadoes to claim her husband's share of an estate. On her return she has found her rheumatic spouse very assiduously tended by a young nurse, with whose services she has to dispense. A widow a second time, she has died respected. It may be doubted whether much happiness has fallen to her lot.[1]

This persistent pessimism would not have spoilt the effect of the tales if the execution had been equal, as Crabbe maintained, to that of the *Tales of the Hall*, and especially of the *Tales in Verse*. But this is by no means the case. Their all-pervading monotony soon disheartens the reader. Not only do the narratives lack incidents likely to awaken curiosity and are little better than mere sketches of characters, but the tameness of a slovenly style is too rarely relieved by happier passages.[2] Even these last are no longer what

---

[1] *Tales*, xii. (*The Brother Burgesses*) and xiv. (*The Wife and Widow*). The twenty-first (*The Cousins*) is at once sad and idyllic. A "frugal merchant" has retired on a fortune. His niece "Patty" keeps house for him, and cherishes a secret passion for her cousin James, a nephew of the merchant and a dissipated youth. Like "George" in the preceding tale, James feigns repentance. He ingratiates himself with his uncle, on whose death he succeeds to almost all the property, leaving Patty alone and in comparative poverty. But he has reckoned without the merchant's natural son, a sailor, long forgotten, who now claims under a clause of the will. The parties go to law. James obtains the largest share, and the rest is equally divided between Jack and the niece. But Jack has taken a liking to Patty; he marries her. James goes into the excise, and is eaten up with jealousy. The twenty-second tale is the insignificant story of the friend who has given information to the traveller, whose adventures are not related.

[2] See below, p. 448, n. 1, and *Posthumous Tales*, xiv. 150-69 (*Works*, p. 548).

they would have been in earlier days. One quotation
may serve as a proof. An arrant scoundrel named
Bonner, usurer, adulterer, and suspected murderer,
has a watch-dog to which he is attached, and by the
side of which he is found lifeless one morning. The
following is a description of this brute :

> There watch'd a cur before the Miser's gate—
> A very cur, whom all men seem'd to hate ;
> Gaunt, savage, shaggy, with an eye that shone
> Like a live coal, and he possess'd but one ;
> His bark was wild and eager, and became
> That meagre body and that eye of flame ;
> His master prized him much, and *Fang* his name.
> His master fed him largely ; but not that,
> Nor aught of kindness, made the snarler fat.
> Flesh he devour'd, but not a bit would stay ;
> He bark'd, and snarl'd, and growl'd it all away.
> His ribs were seen extended like a rack,
> And coarse red hair hung roughly o'er his back.
> Lamed in one leg, and bruised in wars of yore,
> Now his sore body made his temper sore.
> Such was the friend of him who could not find
> Nor make him one 'mong creatures of his kind.
> Brave deeds of Fang his master often told,
> The son of Fury, famed in deeds of old,
> From Snatch and Rabid sprung ; and noted they
> In earlier times—each dog will have his day.[1]

This passage may be allowed the merit of a certain
energy and of a picturesqueness which suggested to
the critic of *The Edinburgh Review*[2] the idea of pro-
posing it as a subject for Landseer's brush. But,
on the other hand, what frequent repetitions, what
absence of all co-ordination between the touches of
the picture, drawn, alas ! by an already trembling
hand ! When we reflect that these lines are among the
best in the work, we cannot but agree with all his
judges that the *Posthumous Tales* have added nothing
to Crabbe's fame, and may, without any scruple, be
left out of consideration in the study of his poetry.
They have been mentioned here only for the sake of
completeness.

---

[1] *Tales*, xvi. (*The Dealer and the Clerk*) 171-91 (*Works*, p. 551).
[2] Vol. lx. January, 1835, p. 292.

III

BEFORE this long career enters upon its closing stage, a few pages may be devoted to the examination of Crabbe's political opinions and social ideas. In 1781 Burke's protection had put an end to his hesitation[1] and made him a Whig. The reader will recollect with what ardour sharpened by resentment he condemned, in April, 1782,[2] the ill-omened ministry of Lord North, with what joy he hailed the advent to power of his illustrious friend. When, several years afterwards, in the full maturity of his intellect, the news of the French Revolution surprised him in his solitude at Muston, he could not ignore Burke's violent hostility to the Constituent Assembly, and the pathetic rupture of the old friendship which united the two great orators and leaders of the Whig party:[3] Burke, more conservative than Pitt, summoning the Tories to a European coalition against France, Fox, on the other hand, opposing with all his might such a hazardous enterprise. According to his Biographer, Crabbe took the latter view. "He was one of the good men who hailed the beginning of the French Revolution,"[4] who trembled with joy on learning that the wish expressed by Cowper as early as 1785 was at last realised, that the Bastille had fallen, and—

> That even our enemies, so oft employ'd
> In forging chains for us, themselves were free.[5]

True, he lamented the excesses which followed. In common with all his fellow-countrymen, too distant from Paris to understand its anguish, he was indignant at the execution of Louis XVI.,[6] he deplored the tragedies that were being enacted on the world's stage.[7]

[1] He had applied first to Lord North ; see above, p. 93.
[2] See above, p. 135.
[3] In the famous sitting of May 6th, 1791, in the House of Commons.
[4] B. p. 49.
[5] The Task, book v. 389-90.
[6] See for this feeling Lord Holland's Memoirs of the Whig Party, vol. i. p. 28, and a letter from Charles Grey (the Prime Minister of 1830) to Mrs. Orde, of January 24th, 1793 : " An account is come that the King of France was executed on Monday morning. . . . Bad as I am thought, I cannot express the horror I feel at this atrocity. . . . War is certain, and—God grant we may not all lament the consequences of it " (The Creevey Papers, ed. Maxwell : John Murray, 1904, vol. i. p. 1).
[7] In a manuscript sermon dated Glemham, May 4th, 1794, he speaks of " a changeful world and woeful times " (Mackay Collection).

But, like Fox and the "new Whigs," he considered the war which his country began against France in 1793 as inopportune. By no means warlike, he did not share the passions of the English people and their Government: the wish to avenge the defeats sustained during the struggle with the American colonies, the fear of seeing republican armies permanently quartered in Belgium and threatening England,[1] the royalist enthusiasm of Burke and Windham. He did not side with the landlords and the farmers, who were in favour of a war which made rents and the price of corn go up, but which starved the poor in the country districts and the towns. When he was living in Suffolk, from 1792 to 1805, he was often invited to Dudley North's house at Little Glemham, where he met Fox, an opponent of the war and an advanced Liberal. These visits made him suspected in the neighbourhood, and even at Muston.[2] A report was circulated that our clergyman was a "Jacobin," a friend of France and of the Revolution, an enemy of the King. His old parishioners took alarm, it would appear. They were wrong. No one could be more loyal than Crabbe, more faithful to his Church and his sovereign. But at that time the epithet of "Jacobin" was bestowed in England on every one who was not an unqualified supporter of Pitt, the Tories, and their policy of repression.[3]

In 1802 the Peace of Amiens, like a salutary "amnesty,"[4] reconciled the English who were most

---

[1] Cf. Emile Bourgeois, *Manuel historique de politique étrangère*, ed. 1898, vol. ii. pp. 90 and 107.

[2] B. p. 48.

[3] Cf. Edward Smith's *Story of the English Jacobins*, pp. 31-2, and Lord Cockburn's *Memorials of his Time*, ed. 1874, p. 70.

[4] The expression is Southey's, and occurs in an interesting note of his memoirs (ed. by Cuthbert Southey, 1850, vol. iv. p. 125): "He himself [Southey] says of the Peace of Amiens: 'No act of amnesty ever produced such conciliatory consequences as that peace. It restored in me the English feeling which had long been deadened, and placed me in sympathy with my country; bringing me thus into that natural and healthy state of mind, upon which time, and knowledge, and reflection were sure to produce their proper and salutary effects.' From an MS. preface to the Peninsular War." See also a poem on Robert Emmet, dated September, 1803 (Southey's *Poetical Works*, 1853, Longmans, vol. ii. p. 246), which shows the last stage of this evolution: Why didst thou not live longer, says Southey to the Irish hero, for then—

"How had that heart, . . . that noble heart of thine,
Which even now had snapt one spell, which beat
With such brave indignation at the shame
And guilt of France, and of her miscreant Lord,

favourable to France with their own country. The nation, henceforth unanimous, in the following year made a stand against the "aggression" of the First Consul. Had he not occupied Switzerland, northern Italy, and the island of Elba? Did he not claim to interfere in the government of the kingdom? Did he not demand the immediate evacuation of Malta?[1] Evidently he wanted to invade Egypt and India,[2] to despoil England after having subjugated the Continent. Against the tyranny which this Corsican, master of France, sought to impose on the world, all the lovers of freedom and justice revolted, and they sympathised with Great Britain in its struggle for existence.[3] Crabbe, it is needless to say, applauded the victories of the English fleets, and was proud of "the unsubdued spirit of his countrymen in their glorious resistance of those enemies who would have no peace throughout the world, except that which is dictated by the triumphant insolence of military success."[4] He expresses his admiration for the "defenders of our soil"—

> Who from destruction save us; who from spoil
> Protect the sons of peace, who traffic, or who toil.[5]

When, in April, 1814, he heard of Napoleon's abdication, he had a moment of enthusiasm. In a letter

> How had it clung to England! With what love,
> What pure and perfect love, return'd to her,
> Now worthy of thy love, *the champion now*
> *For freedom* . . . yea, the only champion now,
> And soon to be the avenger."

It is highly probable that Wordsworth's definitive "conversion" took place at the same time, between March 27th, 1802 (Peace of Amiens) and May 18th, 1803 (resumption of hostilities): cf. Knight's *Life of Wordsworth*, vol. i. p. 350, quoted by Legouis, *La Jeunesse de Wordsworth*, p. 389, n. 2, and *The Prelude*, book xi. 359-69). Coleridge of course had recanted much earlier, in February, 1797 (*France, an Ode*).

[1] Such is the English point of view, summarised in *Social England* (ed. by Traill and Mann, Illustrated Edition, Cassell, vol. v. pp. 703-4).

[2] Cf. Emile Bourgeois, *op. cit.* vol. ii. pp. 236-8.

[3] They would have liked to apply to Bonaparte the following lines, which the prophetic Cowper, by a curious anticipation, had written as early as 1782 in *Table Talk* (29-32):

> But let eternal infamy pursue
> The wretch to nought but his ambition true
> Who, for the sake of filling with one blast
> The posthorns of all Europe, lays her waste.

[4] Preface to poems published in 1807, *Works*, p. 99, col. 2.

[5] *Borough* (1810), vi. 20-7.

to Dr. Gordon,[1] he refers with pride to "this glorious
country, . . . a country which never from the time
when Cæsar first tried its virtue stood so high as
at the present period." And later, on seeing in an
album a sketch of the elm under which Wellington
had halted several times at Waterloo, he wrote this
prosaic but sincere stanza :

> Is there one heart that beats on English ground,
> One grateful spirit in the kingdoms round ;
> One who had traced the progress of the foe,
> And does not hail the field of Waterloo ?
> Who o'er that field, if but in thought, has gone,
> Without a grateful wish for Wellington ?[2]

Had he not ensured the safety of England and put an
end to the sanguinary excesses of the Empire ?

When the storm had blown over, public attention
turned to domestic affairs. For thirty years, with the
exception of fourteen months in 1806-1807, power
had been in the hands of the Tories, supported by
George III. What did Crabbe think of this supremacy ? Had his old Liberalism survived his youth, the
split of the Whigs into Burke's and Fox's followers, the
conservative policy imposed by a defensive attitude ?
Or had it changed into an uncompromising Toryism,
such as that of Coleridge, of Southey, of Wordsworth,
all repentant republicans ? Like a wise and sober-
minded man, Crabbe now observed a happy mean.
Rejecting the exaggerations of the two parties, he
adopted with impartiality all their sound ideas. "I
can but think," he wrote, "that two dispassionate,
sensible men, who have seen, read, and observed, will
approximate in their sentiments more and more ; and if
they confer together, and argue—not to convince each
other, but for pure information, and with a simple
desire for the truth—the ultimate difference will be
small indeed. The Tory, for instance, would allow
that, but for the Revolution in this country, and the
noble stand against the arbitrary steps of the house
of Stuart, the kingdom would have been in danger
of becoming what France once was; and the Whig
must also grant, that there is at least an equal danger
in an unsettled, undefined democracy. . . . Every state

[1] Dated May 21st, 1814 (cf. above, p. 381, n. 1).
[2] *Works*, p. 265, col. 2.

is at times on the inclination to change : either the
monarchical or the popular interest will predominate ;
and in the former case, I conceive, the well-meaning
Tory will incline to Whiggism—in the latter, the
honest Whig will take the part of declining mon-
archy."[1] In this game of see-saw, the slightest shock
may disturb the equilibrium. The restless spirits are
especially to be feared. In politics as in religion,
Crabbe dreads the hot-headed, and holds them up
to reprobation. He describes, in the first of his
Tales in Verse, an ultra Tory, "Justice Bolt," whose
bold, imperious, and inexhaustible eloquence extols the
blessings of the "glorious" English constitution :

> We have the force of monarchies ; are free
> As the most proud republicans can be ;
> And have those prudent counsels that arise
> In grave and cautious aristocracies. . . .
> Ours is a Church reform'd, and now no more
> Is ought for man to mend or to restore ;
> 'Tis pure in doctrines, 'tis correct in creeds,
> Has nought redundant, and it nothing needs.

To this inveterate Conservative Crabbe opposes a
Jacobin, an anarchist almost, the "orator" Hammond :

> "Bishops and deans, and prebendaries all,"
> He said, "were cattle fatt'ning in the stall. . . ."
> Then from religion *Hammond* turned his view
> To give our rulers the correction due ;
> Not one wise action had these triflers plann'd, . . .
> Thus with licentious words the man went on
> Proving that liberty of speech was gone ;
> That all were slaves—nor had we better chance
> For better times, than as allies to France.

The country would be safe—

> Might patriots rule her, and could reasoners guide ;
> When all to vote, to speak, to teach, are free,
> Whate'er their creeds or their opinions be ;
> When books of statutes are consumed in flames,
> And courts and copyholds are empty names :
> Then will be times of joy—but ere they come,
> Havock, and war, and blood must be our doom.

This is social renovation by fire and sword with a
vengeance ! Hammond is a disciple of Rousseau, and

---

[1] B. p. 50.

a revolutionary. If a choice had to be made, Crabbe would evidently prefer Bolt, the Tory magistrate. But he likes neither and humiliates both.[1]

Faithful to his principle, Crabbe, who had three votes,[2] gave them sometimes to one party and sometimes to the other. At the General Election of June and July, 1818, a keen struggle took place between Lord Liverpool's Ministry and the Whig Opposition. Although half the seats were, as the saying went, in the "pocket" of the Government or of its wealthy adherents, more than one hundred elections were contested. At Westminster, the Liberal, Sir Samuel Romilly, and the Radical, Sir Francis Burdett, entered the lists against the Conservative candidate, Sir Murray Maxwell, who, in his patriotic pride and enthusiasm for the Navy, had an enormous boat, drawn by six horses, driven through Covent Garden, on which the Whigs made a victorious rush.[3] In Wiltshire, the two Tories, Paul Methuen and W. P. T. L. Wellesley, were attacked by an intruder, John Benett, of Pyt House.[4] Crabbe made no secret of his sympathy for the latter. But the majority of his parishioners held different views. A Protectionist as well as a Whig, Benett was against any reduction of the duty on corn, a policy little to the taste of the trading and working-class population of Trowbridge. They showed their dissatisfaction with their clergyman. On two occasions he was assailed by a mob which hissed and hooted him. Crabbe replied by "rating them soundly" and by continuing to support Benett. "He always walked in the streets alone, and just as frequently as before." His opponents returned to the charge. On the day when he started for Devizes, where the poll took place,[5] "a riotous, tumultuous, and most appalling mob besieged his house," threatening to destroy his chaise and tear him to pieces, if he attempted to start. "In the face of the furious assemblage," writes the Rev.

---

[1] He shows us Bolt chafing with impatience in the club where Hammond holds forth, and the latter stammering before Bolt in an assembly of "priests and deacons"—an illustration of the fact that a speaker's success depends a good deal on the sympathy of his audience.

[2] For Trowbridge, Aldborough, and the University of Cambridge.

[3] On June 29th; cf. *The Greville Memoirs*, ed. 1899, vol. i. p. 4.

[4] Born on May 20th, 1773; died on October 1st, 1852. Cf. *Gentleman's Magazine* for December, 1852, pp. 636-7. He sat in the House of Commons for thirty-three years.

[5] Between June 27th and July 2nd, the poll having lasted a week.

W. L. Bowles, "he came out calmly, told them they might kill him if they chose, but, whilst alive, nothing should prevent his giving a vote at the election, according to his promise and principles, and set off, undisturbed and unhurt, to vote for Mr. Benett."[1] On the other hand, happening to be at Aldborough in 1826 during a General Election, he seconded the nomination of his excellent friend, the Tory John Wilson Croker, Secretary to the Admiralty.[2] More than this, in 1827, at a time when the unbending Conservatives, of the type of Wellington and Peel, refused to join the "moderates" and deserted Canning,[3] Crabbe declared that he "felt considerable respect" for both sides, adding that he should be glad that time and good feeling might soften "the spirit of animosity that now reigns among them."[4] It is impossible to be more conciliatory.

But his moderation did not exclude a marked preference for the Whigs. This was clearly revealed when, in November, 1830, Lord Grey had formed his Liberal Ministry and introduced, five months later, the famous Reform Bill. Every one knows how bold this salutary measure appeared, with what indignant consternation it filled the ultras of Toryism, with what delight it was hailed by the nation, bent on seeing it become law. History records also what obstruction

---

[1] B. pp. 61-2. Benett, however, was beaten in 1818 by Wellesley, the less popular of his two opponents, who received 2,009 votes to his 1,572 (cf. *The Times* of July 2nd). But in the following year, Methuen having retired, a by-election took place in July, and Benett was elected by 2,436 votes to 2,270 recorded for the Tory, J. D. Astley, after a poll which lasted a fortnight (cf. Smith's *Parliaments*, p. 106). In a letter to John Murray, dated Trowbridge, July 20th, 1819, Crabbe alludes to this contest: "I write in the midst of confusion, noise, and contention, as the place I reside in seems in this present contest to be determined that no other shall exceed it in these efforts of their public spirit. Our election will, I fear, have all the virulence and enmity of the last" (Murray Collection).

[2] Letter to the Biographer, dated Hampstead, June 28th, 1826: "Elections are now pretty well over. I was at Aldbro' during the time, and, sitting down among the freemen, which is my place, was invited *up higher* by Mr. Croker and requested to second his nomination, which I did in very few words, but quite enough, for there was not a shadow of opposition. Some witty gentleman posted up a paper, 'The Election, a Farce, by Lord Hertford, etc.' [cf. above, p. 277, n. 3], but the sailors did not understand and nobody seemed to give it notice. It is not the place for squibs" (Broadley Collection). Cf. also B. p. 49, col. 2.

[3] Who, in consequence, leaned on the Whigs (cf. Sir Spencer Walpole, *History of England*, ed. 1903, vol. ii. p. 353).

[4] Letter to the Biographer, dated Trowbridge, May 7th, 1827 (Broadley Collection).

it encountered in the House of Commons in the Committee stage, and especially in the House of Lords. It was brought in three times by the Minister in charge, Lord John Russell, on two occasions in a modified form. Crabbe followed the debates with interest: "With some it is ruin; with others it is renovation; neither my hopes or fears are very strong; the lower class of our brethren can be but little affected by the bill,[1] whatever they may be by the effects of it, and of those effects who has foresight enough to determine?"[2] Singularly wise and characteristic words! But he was in favour of this reform all the same. When the second Bill was rejected by the Lords, on October 8th, 1831, and the House of Commons, irritated by this opposition, passed a formal vote of confidence in the Whig Ministry, Crabbe wrote: "I believe there is a fund of good sense as well as moral feeling in the people of this country; and if ministers proceed steadily, give up some points, and be firm in essentials, there will be a union of sentiment on this great subject of reform by and by; at least, the good and well-meaning will drop their minor differences and be united."[3] A Liberal up to his last moments, Crabbe therefore approved of Grey's and Russell's efforts. He was dead when the Reform Bill became law, on June 7th, 1832.

Social questions had preoccupied him even more than politics. For the poet of rural England, there was no problem more urgent than that of the improvement of the agricultural labourer's condition. A wage of a few shillings a week, even when supplemented by an allowance from the parish,[4] did not enable the "peasants" of *The Village* to make a provision for sickness or old age. The parish had to take charge of their declining years. As early as the reign of Elizabeth, when England, deprived of Catholic charity by the spoliations of Henry VIII., became alarmed at the growth of mendicancy and vagabondage, Parliament had instituted a system of lay poor relief, socialistic in its principle. Under the Poor Law of

---

[1] The elective franchise was to be extended in boroughs to householders paying £10 annual rent.
[2] Letter to B. (Broadley Collection).
[3] Letter of October 24th, quoted by B. pp. 87-8.
[4] Cf. above, p. 236, n. 2.

1601, every pauper, whatever the cause of his poverty, had a right to subsistence at the expense of the rate-payers. Before long in many places "parish houses" were built, in which unemployed workmen were temporarily received and permanent shelter was given to the "lame, impotent, old, blind, and such other." From 1697 onwards, Parliament had authorised the parishes of one and the same district to combine in a single union, with a central establishment, the "work-house," in which all the poor of the neighbourhood were lodged. This "giant-building" presented some advantages:

> Be it agreed—the Poor who hither come
> Partake of plenty, seldom found at home;
> That airy rooms and decent beds are meant
> To give the poor, by day, by night, content:
> That none are frighten'd, once admitted here,
> By the stern looks of lordly Overseer:
> Grant that the Guardians [1] of the place attend,
> And ready ear to each petition lend—[2]

Yet discontent reigned within these walls, which were odious to respectable labourers like Isaac Ashford. Their inmates felt imprisoned and solitary. "Grand-sires are there," exclaims Crabbe—

> who now no more must see,
> No more must nurse upon the trembling knee,
> The lost loved daughter's infant progeny. . . .
> Is not the matron there, to whom the son
> Was wont at each declining day to run?
> He (when his toil was over) gave delight
> By lifting up the latch, and one "Good night."
> Yes, she is here; but nightly to her door
> The son, still lab'ring, can return no more.
> Widows are here, who in their huts were left,
> Of husbands, children, plenty, ease bereft;

---

[1] The "Guardians of the Poor" formed a board on which sat delegates from the respective parishes. The "overseer," instituted by the Act of 1572, on the other hand, was an inspector appointed by the Justices of the Peace, locally and annually.

[2] *Borough*, xviii. 119 *seq.* Contrary to the quotation in B. (*Works*, p. 234, n. 3), these "Houses of Industry" were not confined to Suffolk. Bristol in 1697, Worcester in 1703, Plymouth in 1707, Norwich in 1711, had set the example. In 1725 there existed more than a hundred establishments of this kind" (cf. Nicholls, *History of the English Poor Law*). For the Nacton Workhouse cf. above, p. 162, n. 4.

Yet all that grief within the humble shed
Was soften'd, softened in the humble bed :
But here, in all its force, remains the grief,
And not one soft'ning object for relief.

Society really owes more gratitude and kindness to its
old servants. "Then too, I own," continues the poet—

it grieves me to behold them sent
From their old home ; 'tis pain, 'tis punishment,
To leave each scene familiar, every face,
For a new people and a stranger race,

among whom, from indifference and torpor, "the day
itself is, like the night, asleep." Let us be more compassionate to old age worn out with toil :

Drooping and burthen'd with a weight of years,
What venerable ruin man appears !
How worthy pity, love, respect and grief—
He claims protection—he compels relief ;—
And shall we send him from our view, to brave
The storms abroad, whom we at home might save,
And let a stranger dig our ancient brother's grave ?
No ! we will shield him from the storm he fears,
And when he falls, embalm him with our tears.

Let us therefore do away with these refuges : let the
infirm and aged workers of each parish be relieved in
their own homes ; let us spare them the gloom and the
humiliation inseparable from the " workhouses," which
are no better than prisons.[1]

Imbued with these sentiments of social charity,
Crabbe approved the patient and for a long time fruitless efforts of the philanthropists who tried to introduce some humanity into the manners and the laws of
England. He admired the generous initiative of Mrs.
Fry, the " tender and delicate " Quakeress who, in 1813,
undertook to visit Newgate prison and reclaim its female
inmates.[2] Some lines composed on the news of Sir
Samuel Romilly's suicide show in what high esteem he
held this statesman, the grandson of a French refugee

---

[1] It is easy to conjecture how hostile Crabbe would have been to the reform
of 1834 which, in order to correct an abuse (that of doles in relief of wages),
fell into the opposite extreme—that of making presence in the workhouse
"proof of poverty," with one exception, seldom observed, in favour of the
"old and infirm."

[2] *Tales of the Hall*, xi. 653-64.

and a strong supporter of the reform of the criminal law :

> Whom as the first of counsellors I prized,
> The best of guides to my assuming pen,
> The best of fathers, husbands,[1] judges, men. . . .
> Yes ! I was proud to speak of thee, as one
> Who had approved the little I had done,
> And taught me what I should do !—Thou would'st raise
> My doubting spirit by a smile of praise,
> And words of comfort ! great was thy delight
> Fear to expel, and ardour to excite,
> To wrest th' oppressor's arm, and do the injured right.
> Thou hadst the tear for pity, and thy breast
> Felt for the sad, the weary, the oppress'd !
> And now, afflicting change ! all join with me,
> And feel, lamented Romilly, for thee.[2]

It was he who, in September, 1818, had suggested to the poet the story of the two rival brothers, the poacher and the keeper, set at enmity by the brutal severity of the Game Laws.[3]   And even before he knew Romilly, Crabbe had not remained indifferent to social injustice : in *The Borough* he had condemned the debtors' prisons where tradesmen, often more unfortunate than blameworthy, were confined, sometimes for life [4]; he had eloquently shown, by the example of Peter Grimes, what abuses might arise from the apprenticing of young orphans to cruel and ill-supervised masters.[5]   He had already drawn attention, in the *Tales of the Hall*, to the " Yorkshire schools," which kept their pupils for " seven gloomy winters," and sent back the survivors

---

[1] The cause of Romilly's suicide seems to have been the death of his wife.

[2] Lines dated Hampstead, November 6th, 1818 ; Romilly died on October 30th (cf. *Works*, p. 502, n. 1).

[3] They prohibited the killing of game by any one who had not an income of not less than £100 a year derived from land.   Thus a tenant could not shoot over his farm, even with the consent of his landlord : cf. an article by Sydney Smith on the Game Laws (1818): "In Northumberland, and on the borders of Scotland, there are large capitalists who farm to the amount of two or three thousand per annum, who have the permission of their distant non-resident landlords to do what they please with the game, and yet who dare not fire off a gun upon their own land."   In 1822 the Duke of Buckingham himself convicted a farmer in identical circumstances (cf. Sir Spencer Walpole, *History of England*, vol. i. pp. 138-9).

[4] Imprisonment for debt became less frequent after 1813.

[5] They were also consigned to factories in Yorkshire and Lancashire : " The children, who are sent off by wagon-loads at a time, are as much lost for ever to their parents as if they were shipped off to the West Indies," wrote Romilly in 1811 (Walpole, *ibid.* p. 163).   The children of paupers were treated as orphans by the parishes.

pale, lean, and freckled, but adepts in " the northern virtues," astuteness, dissimulation, thrift, and greed, which were taught so well in those establishments.[1] With his habitual modesty, Crabbe, we see, was a discreet champion of the weak in a country then for the most part hostile to reform.

No doubt he remained a firm defender of the principle of authority.[2] He had never varied on this point, whatever his son and certain critics may have said.[3] Even when he published *The Village*, in 1783, he had nothing of a " Radical " or a rebel in him. To make Crabbe a sort of early Cobbett is to take a strangely mistaken view of his character and his ideas. If he was indignant with the rich in this poem, it was not on account of their luxury or their social superiority, but because they shut their eyes to the reality and deluded themselves with the fictions of the conventional idyll. The love of truth, and not the hatred of a privileged class, inspired his eloquent protest. The levelling ideal of the French Revolution seemed to him a chimera, and the advocacy of the " rights of man " a dangerous agitation. " 'Tis meet and right," he says—

> That robes and titles our respect excite ;
> Order requires it ; 'tis by vulgar pride
> That such regard is censured and denied.[4]

Every society implies a hierarchy. Let a few govern and the masses obey.[5] But the rulers should not be tyrants. Let them show indulgence on occasion, even to evil-doers; for are there not—

> Thousands who must all be fed,
> Yet ne'er were taught to earn their daily bread ;
> Whom crimes, misfortunes, errors only teach
> To seek their food where'er within their reach,
> Who for their parents' sins, or for their own,
> Are now as vagrants, wanderers, beggars known,
> Hunted and hunting through the world, to share
> Alms and contempt, and shame and scorn to bear ;

[1] *Tales of the Hall*, ii. 172-81, and *Posthumous Tales*, ii. 514-23. Every one knows Dickens's Mr. Squeers and Dotheboys Hall in *Nicholas Nickleby*.
[2] Cf. above, p. 104, n. 2.
[3] B. p. 49, col. 1, and Kebbel, *Life of Crabbe*, p. 79.
[4] *Borough*, iv. 94-8.
[5] Cf. above, p. 408, and *Tales of the Hall*, i. 157 and 160.

Whom Law condemns, and Justice, with a sigh,
Pursuing, shakes her sword and passes by,—
If to the prison we should these commit,
They for the gallows will be rendered fit.[1]

Much in advance of his age, in which many minor offences were punishable with death, Crabbe had ventured to represent, in a poem written in 1798,[2] a gipsy-woman charged with robbery who appears before a " kind magistrate," and, with her granddaughter in her arms, pleads her cause in these terms :

My crime !—This sick'ning child to feed,
  I seized the food your witness saw ;
I knew your laws forbade the deed,
  But yielded to a stronger law.

Know'st thou, to Nature's great command
  All human laws are frail and weak ?
Nay ! frown not—stay his eager hand [3]
  And hear me, or my heart will break.

In this, th' adopted babe I hold
  With anxious fondness to my breast,
My heart's sole comfort I behold,
  More dear than life, when life was blest
I saw her pining, fainting, cold,
  I begg'd—but vain was my request.

I saw the tempting food, and seized—
  My infant-sufferer found relief ;
And, in the pilfer'd treasure pleased,
  Smiled on my guilt, and hush'd my grief.[4]

Touched by such distress, the magistrate discharges her.

When therefore Crabbe was appointed Justice of the Peace, in July, 1825,[5] he showed all the kindness

[1] *Posthumous Tales*, ii. 172-85.

[2] *The Hall of Justice*, published in 1807, vigorous in point of style and versification, but based on a highly melodramatic idea. The "vagrant," an illegitimate daughter of unknown parents, has followed a band of gipsies. She loves young Aaron, the son of their leader. The father also has conceived a passion for her; he drives away Aaron by persecution and forces the young girl to surrender to him. On his return, Aaron kills his father and marries the "vagrant," who is about to give birth to a daughter. The child is sold to strangers by Aaron. Many years afterwards, Aaron being dead, the gipsy is arrested for some offence and in prison finds her daughter, who is transported and leaves a child behind her. The "vagrant" adopts this new-born granddaughter, and it is to feed her that she has committed theft.

[3] Of the constable who had seen the offence committed.

[4] Lines 9-26.

[5] On the 9th, according to Fitzgerald's MS. notes.

and forbearance which his poetry demanded for the humble. Whether at the Woolpack Inn, in which the Trowbridge petty sessions [1] were held, or at Devizes, where the quarter sessions took place, he always leaned towards clemency. He backed up his brother-clergyman and friend, the Rev. W. L. Bowles, in the case of the unfortunate Catherine Cook. This woman, after fifteen years of excellent service, had had the misfortune to steal some cups and saucers, valued at four shillings and sixpence, from her master, Ernle Warriner. Being brought up before the magistrates, she was sentenced, by a bench of harsh and ignorant squires, to six months' imprisonment and a fine of £40. " It might have been £400," observes Crabbe, " for she was utterly unable to raise the sum." Moreover, the judges were informed, after sentence had been pronounced, that they " had no power to fine a criminal." But this trifle was easily got over : they recalled the wretched woman, and commuted the fine into six months of solitary confinement, over and above the term of imprisonment. Bowles, who does not seem to have taken part in the decision, was " shocked by this severity." He went to the prosecutor and all the magistrates in turn, begging for mercy. He met with a unanimous refusal. He then addressed a petition to the King, and his prayer was granted. But his brother-magistrates, annoyed at his success, took action against him. On Tuesday, January 15th, 1828, they held a largely attended meeting : Paul Methuen made a violent attack on Bowles's conduct and moved a vote of censure ; Lord Folkestone, Mr. Benett, Crabbe, and ten or twelve other Whigs opposed it, but in vain ; the resolutions condemning the terms of the petition to the King were passed, and published in the newspapers a fortnight later.[2] They could do harm only to their authors.

---

[1] Cf. a letter to B., dated " TROWBRIDGE, 5th March, 1828 : I was wearied yesterday so much that I have not yet recovered : In the morning I was nearly five hours with my attention kept up, at the Woolpack's Inn, with a room full of noisy applicants for justice or for clemency. . . . [Then, in the evening] I was summoned to a meeting at the school-room where more than 100 persons assembled to consider the best method of watching the town by voluntary housekeepers " (riots were frequent at that time).

[2] The following are the documents relating to this incident in chronological order :

(1) A letter from Bowles to Crabbe : " BREMHILL, Jan. 13 [1828]. MY DEAR SIR,—I hear my petition will be taken up at Devizes by some magistrates, as if,

A patriarchal government, with each village taking care of its poor under the supervision of its clergyman—this seems to have been Crabbe's ideal. He had little knowledge of the great cities and their eager, unsettled population of workers. Trowbridge even was only a market-town. No doubt he had already noticed in it signs of antagonism between masters [1] and men [2]; he knew also what a pernicious influence the promiscuity of factory life has upon public morality.[3] But he had no inkling of the infinite complexity of the social questions which were arising in the large urban agglomerations. The England of his thoughts was that of his youth and middle age— the rural England prior to the "industrial revolution," and covered with farms rather than factories.

in doing my public duty, I had sought to reflect on them, and I hope as a friend to equity and humanity you will attend on Tuesday the 15th. . . . Your neighbour Waldron [cf. above, p. 383, n. 2] knew so little on the subject, by partial informers, that he considered I had taken my part headlong without consulting evidence or the prosecutor. . . ."

(2) A letter from Crabbe to B., dated Trowbridge, January 18th, 1828: "Mr. Waldron and I took a chaise to Devizes on the day of the sessions to meet the magistrates who assembled (the common business being over) to sit in judgment on my friend Bowles for his petition to the King respecting their severe sentence on a woman who had purloined from her master some cups and saucers, value 4s. 6d. [Here follow the facts relating to the sentence narrated above.] The magistrates assembled, thirty-two in number. . . . About twelve of us were for letting the matter drop, but the majority . . . drew up some resolves, viz. that the petition was not expressed with literal truth and exactness, and that the magistracy was reflected upon without cause, etc. Lord Folkestone, Mr. Benett, and about ten or twelve of us opposed all this, but we could not prevail, yet I think they will not be indiscreet enough to publish in the papers what they formed into resolutions, but let the matter die; if not and appeal be made to the public, they will in my opinion lose much more than they are aware of. The sentence was severe, and so the public will judge" (Broadley Collection).

(3) The number of *The Devizes and Wiltshire Gazette*, of January 31st, 1828, publishing the Resolutions.

(4) A letter from Bowles to B., from Bremhill, February 16th or 18th, 1828: "MY DEAR SIR,—I shall be delighted cum Zephyris et hirundine prima to come to Pucklechurch [where B. was curate] to meet my excellent friend your Father—who has acted like a *nobleman* towards me in my late wars with some of the merciless squires" (Broadley Collection).

[1] *Posthumous Tales*, ii. 120-5.

[2] Cf. the following passage in a letter to B., dated Trowbridge, December 14th, 1828: "Nothing particularly interesting has occurred in my absence: there is, however, a combination among workmen respecting wages to which every man is sworn to secrecy, which renders it unlawful, for the mere combination does not, nor ought it, for if masters may combine to fix what they will give, servants should be allowed to make agreements concerning what they will take, but the oaths and the secrecy are not to be justified." Here we are witnessing the birth of "trades unions" and "federations of employers."

[3] Letter to Mrs. Leadbeater, quoted by B. p. 72, col. 1.

IV

SOME time before his departure for Scotland in 1822
Crabbe had experienced the first attacks of a complaint
which troubled his closing years—facial neuralgia.
"It came," he writes to Mrs. Leadbeater,[1] "like
momentary shocks of a grievous tooth-ache: and
indeed, I was imprudent enough to have one tooth
extracted which appeared to be most affected; but
the loss of this guiltless and useful tooth had not
one beneficial consequence. For many months the
pain came, sometimes on a slight touch, as the application of a towel or a razor, and it sometimes came
without an apparent cause." On his return from
Edinburgh he stayed for two months at Beccles,
and on the advice of his doctors, William and
Henchman Crowfoot, his relations by marriage, he
was treated with "extract of hemlock," which had
recently been recommended as a success. "I am
certainly freed from the severity of my attacks," he
writes on October 23rd, "though I cannot boast
of my entire freedom. As the remedy has its
inconveniences and rather weakens me, I take bark
also, and between both am pretty well dosed."[2]
A London practitioner prescribed to him a remedy
which was well spoken of at that time[3]—carbonate of
iron, in the form of "blue pills," which he henceforth
took, though dreading them, for they affected his head
in a disagreeable way, and besides gave him only
temporary relief.[4] In December of the same year he
complains to the sculptor Chantrey[5] of "pain and
fever" which will prevent him from travelling to
London and to Belvoir Castle, where the Duke of
Rutland had invited him.[6] Eighteen months later, on
March 26th, 1824, he notes a slight improvement:
"Though I am not in a state of sound health, nor
of one free from pain," he writes to Mrs. Leadbeater,

---

[1] Letter of October 29th, 1824, quoted by B. p. 80, with a wrong date.
[2] Letter to George, dated Beccles.
[3] Cf. *Cases of Neuralgia Spasmodica, or Tic Douloureux,* by B. Hutchinson,
London, 1822. In modern medicine the tic is considered as "the transformation of a non-convulsive facial neuralgia" (Dieulafoy, *Manuel de pathologie
interne,* ed. 1896, vol. ii. p. 298, n. 1).
[4] Letter to B., dated Trowbridge, April 9th, 1829 (Broadley Collection).
[5] Letter quoted above, p. 4, note (British Museum).
[6] Cf. letter quoted by B. p. 79, col. 1.

" still I have not that which has been for the last two years my almost constant attendant, pain in a considerable degree, and with it (or rather in the intervals when it left me) lassitude and nervous weakness."[1] However, a crisis was gathering in which the neuralgia, reaching its acutest stage, changed into " tic douloureux."

At the end of September, 1825, Crabbe had left Trowbridge for London and Hampstead, where his excellent friends Mrs. and Miss Hoare awaited him.[2] "On the second day after my arrival," he writes,[3] " Miss Hoare and I went to the place of worship to which she is accustomed, where, just as the service of the day terminated, a sudden and overpowering attack of the disease was the commencement of an illness which was troublesome to my friends for about three weeks." He recovered sufficiently to stand the journey to Beccles and to enjoy the sea air at Aldborough, in November and December. " The pain has much abated," he said in February, 1826; but in the month of May of the following year he was seized once more, at Pucklechurch, in his son George's house, with the " electrical symptoms," the " spasms,"[4] which cause intense pain, all the more formidable that they may attack their victim at any moment. These crises, of an intermittent nature and always followed by great prostration, in the long run undermined his constitution.

With this exception, his closing years have no history. They were spent for the most part at Trow-

---

[1] *Leadbeater Papers*, vol. ii. p. 384.

[2] The widow and the daughter of Samuel Hoare, banker, of Hampstead Heath and Lombard Street, who died on July 13th, 1825, at the age of seventy-four, according to *The Gentleman's Magazine*. Cf. B. p. 80, col. 1.

[3] Letter to Mrs. Leadbeater, of February 3rd, 1826 (B. p. 82). In a letter to George, dated Beccles, November 6th, 1825, he says: " I am better in relation to pain, but I want strength, and certainly find the effects of the severe paroxysm which came upon me at Hampstead. . . . I trust, my dear George, that you will not feel anxiety respecting my health, but I too well know the alarm I gave, and to which Miss Hoare in her fright contributed " (Mackay Collection).

[4] Cf. a letter to B., dated Trowbridge, June 3rd, 1827 : " I ought to have written yesterday as you kindly desired me, but I had not then seen Mr. Cary [his Trowbridge doctor] of whom I meant to enquire what he thought of those spasms which teized me at your house and made me I am afraid teizing to you all . . . these electrical symptoms. . . . I went through the duties of yesterday (Sunday) with pain, but without the spasms, nor have they returned to-day, but the pain was very troublesome in the night, and I am taking steel again as my best defence against it."

bridge, in the bosom of his family. A young fellow-countryman of Mrs. Leadbeater,[1] who visited him at his parsonage in 1820 or 1821, gives us information about his habits : " He goes to bed at 12, rises at 9, and from breakfast till 4, his dinner-hour, he is alone in his study—from that hour till 12 he devotes to intercourse with his family." He himself confirms this account in a letter to Mrs. Leadbeater [2] : " I shall now bid you farewell, for my son and his Anna call me from my study to join them for the evening ; for so we live. I have my room, where I am monarch—sole sovereign, subject sole ! And when I please I enter their apartment—but this is not often, except on visits of friends, and at dinner. The evening brings us together. They are vastly good to me, and I put off the grave and querulous senior as well as I can, in gratitude for their attention to what cannot be put off." At night he would place a lamp and writing materials near his pillow, for, as he said to Lady Scott in 1822, " I should have lost many a good hit, had I not set down, at once, things that occurred to me in my dreams."[3]

His favourite amusement was no longer botany, but geology. With a hammer in his hand and a notebook in his pocket, he was perfectly happy exploring the quarries in the environs of Trowbridge. Sometimes he would make these expeditions in a gig driven by his son John. One day at the cliffs of the Avon, about four miles from Trowbridge, they had tied the horse to a rock, and, being free to move about, were beginning their investigations. Crabbe espied a stone which seemed to him of interest. He picked it up, but it slipped out of his hands and rolled down the slope with a noise which frightened the horse. The animal ran away with the carriage, which was smashed in a few moments, and the poet, looking philosophically at the wreck, said with a smile, " Well, it might have been worse."[4] A mischievous rather than malevolent destiny seems to have made Crabbe liable to accidents of this kind. In June, 1827, he was returning from

---

[1] John James Lecky (*Leadbeater Papers*, vol. i. pp. 421-4 ; cf. B. p. 76).
[2] Dated December, 1820 (cf. *Leadbeater Papers*, vol. ii. p. 371).
[3] Lockhart, letter to B. p. 79, col. 1.
[4] According to Taylor (cf. B. p. 73) : *Cullings from Crabbe, with Memoir*, Bath, 1832, a passage quoted in *The Athenæum* of April 21st, 1832, p. 256.

Westwood,[1] in a gig also driven by his son John, when, near the bridge over the Biss at Trowbridge, just at the spot where the road turns to the left in the direction of the church, a little monkey, wishing no doubt to show his prowess, darted in front of the horse. " He would probably have paid dearly for his honour," writes Crabbe good-humouredly, " had not John checked the speed of the horse, who instantly stumbled and fell, and I with him ; John likewise fell, but so deliberately that he immediately rose and came to me, whom the good people of the blunderbuss[2] had taken up, and it soon appeared that no material injury was done to either. I was a little bruised on the hip-joint, and felt no other pain."[3] The effects of this dangerous fall, however, did not disappear for some days.

Although constantly threatened by the tic douloureux, Crabbe undertook frequent journeys, either in the neighbourhood of Trowbridge or to London, and even into Suffolk. In August, 1824, he was invited to the Marquis of Bath's at Longleat, where he dined in a brilliant company consisting, among other personages, of Lord John Russell, of the elegant and cosmopolitan Genoese, Madame Durazzo, and of the poet Moore, to whom he related his visit to Edinburgh.[4] In the month of October, 1827, we find him at Bowood with his publisher, John Murray, and his brothers of the pen, Rogers and Moore, who repeatedly asked him for details of the character and conversation of Burke. But he could not summon any from the depths of his memory, except the " extreme kindness " shown him by the great orator.[5] On the other side of Trowbridge, Bath was often the goal of his excursions. It was there that, through Bowles,[6] he had made the acquaintance of the Hoares about the year 1818, and he liked to revisit the place, finding that the town, or rather the walks around it, agreed with him, although at the cost

---

[1] Four miles to the west of Trowbridge.

[2] With which the monkey performed his tricks (cf. Hogarth, *The Élection*, plate iv.).

[3] Letter to George, dated Trowbridge, June 30th, 1827 (Rivett-Carnac Collection).

[4] Moore's *Memoirs*, vol. iv. pp. 232 *seq.*, August 9th. Longleat is twenty miles to the south of Trowbridge.

[5] Moore's *Memoirs*, vol. iv. pp. 222-3 (October 26th).

[6] B. p. 76, col. 1 and n. 27.

of "no small inconvenience and discomfort."[1] He had also received some marks of public esteem there. On January 21st, 1825, the founders of the "Literary Institution" invited him to the opening ceremony and to the banquet presided over by Lord Lansdowne. Moore writes of this occasion : "Two Bishops present and about 108 persons altogether, Bowles and Crabbe of the number. On the healths of the three poets being given, though much called for, I did not rise, but motioned to Crabbe, who got up and said a few words."[2] We may admire the skilful deference of a man who keeps in the background in order to produce a greater effect. Crabbe, however, who was modest and almost timid, suddenly stopped, and, without any embarrassment, said simply that he had forgotten what he was about to add, and requested the indulgence of the meeting. "He was received with universal acclamation," says Bowles,[3] "and the simplicity and candour of his manner felt by every one in the room." In an old man of seventy-one a momentary loss of memory was only too natural, and in an author of repute the absence of all vanity and self-consciousness proved the amiable sincerity of his character. For these different reasons, therefore, he was fond of Bath. Besides, it was on the way from Trowbridge

---

[1] Letter of August 21st, 1831 (24, Brock Street).
[2] Moore's *Memoirs*, vol. iv. pp. 271-3.
[3] Letter from Bowles to B., dated Salisbury, January 31st, 1834. Bowles continues: "I sat next to him at table, and he remarked to me it was not surprising he should have hesitated in what he was about to say, for he was seventy. On my congratulating him, I remember, that there was no appearance of his being yet in that state of decadence which has been so truly and so poetically described—

. . . when old age began,
And time's strong pressure to subdue the man,
[*Tales of the Hall*, x. 462-3]

I asked him if he knew who wrote this powerful line. He instantly answered, ' Dryden.' ' No,' I replied, ' Crabbe !' He spoke, I have no doubt, with that truth and simplicity which were so characteristic of him through life " (Broadley Collection).

It is curious to note that a precisely similar story, and *about the same passage*, was related in 1833 by the brothers Smith (cf. *The Rejected Addresses*, ed. 1833, Preface, quoted by B. p. 81, n. 2). According to them, it was in William Spencer's house at Petersham that Crabbe was guilty of this more or less affected piece of forgetfulness. It seems to me much more probable that the Smiths heard this anecdote from Bowles, and afterwards dressed it up in their own fashion. Crabbe could not have gone to Spencer's house after 1820, one year after the publication of the *Tales of the Hall*, and he would not have forgotten so quickly a passage which all the reviews had picked out for commendation.

to Pucklechurch, a small village in Gloucestershire, where his eldest son [1] acted as curate, and where he himself often went. On returning from it for the last time, at the end of November, 1831, he had a disagreeable mishap. From Pucklechurch to Bath the road at first winds along the valley, and then mounts rather steeply to the plateau of Lansdowne, crosses the whole length of it up to " Beckford's tower," [2] and, descending again, forms the principal street of Bath. "At the first rising of the hill," writes Crabbe to the biographer, " I was requested to favour the horse, and, having no dislike to a walk, I proceeded in much comfort. After the first mile was past, I began to take a view backward, when no fly appeared : so, mile after mile, I moved on soberly, passing the Tower of Mr. Beckford and at last the turnpike at Bath, and, taking one look more as I was entering the Castle and Ball, I saw Lucas and his lame horse. . . . We dined, forgot our labours, and set forth again. Alas! our own beast was determin'd and we had to borrow again, and then, to end a dull story, we entered Trowbridge all in the dark, and, in a very short time, I neither felt nor thought of the troubles of the day." [3] In those times the shortest journey demanded some resolution.

Already for some years he had had many misgivings about returning to Suffolk. Two hundred and twenty miles by coach, even with a halt in London, was a formidable prospect. As early as September, 1825, he wrote : " I do not love the preparation for going away : the collecting of articles wanted, the brushing up portmanteaus, the saying good-bye to one's neighbours, and taking leave of the folk westwards. I do not love all this, and though Hampstead and Beccles have much to engage me, I need exertion, and am obliged to say to myself, ' It is a duty,' before I can be

---

[1] He had married, on April 3rd, 1817, Caroline Matilda, the youngest daughter of Mr. T. Timbrell, of Trowbridge, and had settled at Pucklechurch directly afterwards as curate-in-charge of that parish and its hamlet of Abson. He remained there till 1834, when the Chancellor Lyndhurst gave him the livings of Bredfield and Pettistree, near Woodbridge (cf. Edw. Fitzgerald, " Obituary Notice," *Gentleman's Magazine*, November, 1857).

[2] The author of *Vathek*, who, obliged to leave his residence of Fonthill, had built an observatory on this spot, from which he could descry the remains of his former grandeur. "Je ne conçois pas," said Durazzo on visiting Fonthill, " un homme doit avoir le diable au corps pour bâtir une maison comme ça " (Moore's *Memoirs*, iv. p. 234).

[3] Letter to B., dated Trowbridge, November 30th, 1831.

reconciled to the journey."[1] A warm welcome always awaited him in Beccles, at the house of his sisters-in-law and in the Crowfoot family. Up to the year 1824 he had preached in the church several times; but a new incumbent, Dr. Owen, and his curate, both ultra-Calvinists, now monopolised the pulpit. The sermon was transferred to the evening service and " called a lecture." It once happened that the young curate, a simple deacon, but " more vehement than becomes a dignitary of the church, and more cruel in his assertions than becomes any man," described Hell as "open for all who did not escape in the narrow way that he recommended "[2]; on another occasion Dr. Owen himself, hearing that a company of actors were giving performances in the town, informed his parishioners that the theatre was the " nursery of sin " and "the devil's hot-bed," so that the poor men played to half-empty benches. "Yet," writes Crabbe, "the manager and his family go to church, and are, as I understand, a grave and sober people." But Dr. Owen was not to be got over so easily. He thundered, and Crabbe condemned his intolerance. " I have been twice to the play," he declared, "and in truth have seen nothing offensive to good manners, but they who go not see this very clearly."[3] On December 12th he returned to Aldborough, where he had already stayed from October 23rd to the 30th. The health of his sister Mary was causing him anxiety; and, in fact, he saw her only once again, in 1826, the year of his last journey to Suffolk, on the occasion of the death of his brother-in-law Thomas Sparkes.[4]

---

[1] Letter to B., dated Trowbridge, September 17th, 1825 (Mackay Collection).

[2] Letter to B., dated Beccles, November 6th, 1825 (Mackay Collection).

[3] Letter to B., dated Beccles, December 9th, 1825.

[4] Cf. above, p. 371, n. 4 (end). The following, according to Fitzgerald's MS. notes, are the dates of his moves :

"1823: June 16, to London.—17, Hampstead.—Sept. 19, Fonthill.—29, Cromer.—Oct. 11 (or 17), Beccles.—31, Aldborough, Storms.—'More attached to Hampstead and less to London.'"

"1824: January 1 to 19, at Hampstead.—June 14, London.—Mr. Rogers, Haymarket.—July 16, Bath, balloon.—4 visits to London and Hampstead."

"1825: July 9, Nominated a magistrate.—Sept. 22, London, Hummums, Theatre—23, Hampstead [cf. letter, B. p. 82, col. 1].—Oct. 23, Aldbro'.— 30, Beccles.—Dec. 12, Aldbro'."

"1826 [Pocket-book, Broadley Collection] : At the end of May, London with Mr. Clarke.—June 7, London and Aldborough [cf. above, p. 455, n. 2].— 14, Aldb. and Beccles.—22, Aldb., London and Hampstead.—July 7, London morning, for Trowbridge in the evening. Mr. Rogers and Mr. Murray.—

From 1827 onwards he did not travel farther than Hampstead Heath, where Mrs. Hoare had a country house. He preferred the calm of this retreat to the agitation of the capital, to dining with Lord Holland and breakfasting with Rogers. In the neighbourhood lived Joanna Baillie, the "poetess of the passions," whose dramas have been forgotten by posterity, but whose intelligence and cordiality are attested by Miss Edgeworth [1] and by Crabbe himself.[2] It was also at Hampstead, in the year 1828, that he was able to have a long conversation with Wordsworth. The two poets had already met at Rogers's house; but Crabbe, as we are aware, did not shine in a large company, and Wordsworth had noticed the insignificance of his conversation. On Hampstead Heath, however, in the groves and by the pond, Crabbe, feeling more at his ease, interested his companion by the variety of his knowledge in "every branch of natural history."[3] But it was easy to excite Wordsworth's curiosity by conversing with him on such subjects. For several other reasons the journey of 1828 was particularly pleasant to Crabbe: he met Southey, no doubt at Rogers's house; he went up the Thames as far as Richmond in a steam-boat, which was a novelty in those days; he visited the Athenæum and the picture-galleries.[4] In other years he left Hampstead with

8 (Saturday), Returned from London.—9, Preached.—August, Wednesday 9, Bath to Portsmouth.—10–11, Portsmouth and Ryde.—Sept. 19, to Portsmouth and Salisbury.—20, Devizes and Trowbridge.—Oct. 18, Clifton.—Nov. 28–9, Bath and Pucklechurch.—Dec. 9, to Bath and Trowbridge."
This made an average of three months' holiday per year.
Of 1827 we know nothing. In 1828 he was at Hampstead on July 5th, and at Clifton on November 28th; in 1829, at Hampstead on June 27th; in 1830, at Hastings from September 26th to the beginning of November, at Hampstead up to December 8th; in 1831, at Clifton towards the end of October, and at Pucklechurch in November.

[1] Maria Edgeworth's *Letters*, ed. by Hare, vol. i. pp. 253-4.
[2] *Posthumous Tales*, xiii. 58-69. See also many passages in Lockhart's *Life of Scott* and a letter from Joanna to B. p. 85.
[3] Wordsworth's *Poetical Works*, ed. by Dowden, vol v. pp. 359-61, note dictated to I. Fenwick on the *Extempore Effusion upon the Death of James Hogg*, November, 1835 (*ibid.* p. 161), in which Crabbe's name is linked with the recollection of "Hampstead's breezy heath."
[4] I take this opportunity of showing by one instance the Biographer's inaccuracy when he quotes extracts from the correspondence. A letter (B. p. 81, col. 2) dated "Hampstead, June, 1825," is in reality composed of two fragments, one of them ("My time passes—I am too much indulged") perhaps written on the date mentioned, the other forming part of a letter sent from "Hampstead Heath" on July 5th, 1828, of which the following is the true text, without the corrections of the Biographer, or rather of Lockhart:

Mrs. and Miss Hoare for some place on the south coast—Ryde in August and September, 1826, Hastings in 1830. In this last place he nearly fell a victim to another carriage accident. On September 26th, as the coach entered Hastings, he had alighted from it in order to allow some travellers who had reached their destination to get out, and was about to resume his place when the shaft of a gig driven at full speed knocked him down. "The wheel went over one foot and one arm. Twenty people were ready to assist a stranger, who in a few minutes was sensible that the alarm was all the injury."[1] A month at the sea-side set him up again : he was able to "climb the cliffs and walk a mile or two after that exploit."[2] " It was on a cold November morning," writes Miss Hoare, " that he took his last look at his favourite element, in full glory, the waves foaming and dashing against the shore."[3] On December 8th he returned to Bath and afterwards to Trowbridge. He was not to see the ocean again.

In 1831, dreading the fatigue of a journey to London, he went to Clifton with Mrs. and Miss Hoare. " I

"... Except a return of my pain and that not severe, not as it has been, I have good health, and if my walks are not long, they are more frequent. I have seen many things and many people, have met Mr. Southey and Mr. Wordsworth, have been some days with Mr. Rogers and at last have been at the Athenæum, but not at the Royal Institution which however I purpose to visit. I have my home with my friends here and exchange it with reluctance for any other. If I add that I have gone up the Thames in a steam-boat to Richmond and seen the picture-galleries and some other exhibitions, I have related all my gratifications of this kind. Not only is my chief pleasure here, but in other places I am not satisfied, and especially I pass'd one day with discontent, doing no duty myself nor listening to another and I hope it was not merely breaking a habit that gave me uneasiness. I scarcely need inform you that this day was Sunday which was pass'd by a long lingering breakfast at Kensington and a late dinner about the same distance from Town, a dinner social and pleasant enough if the hours before had been rightly spent, but I would not willingly spend any more such nor, I think, I may add was I willing then, but compliance, I doubt, is nearly akin to will. . . . The time for my leaving Hampstead is not yet fixed : I dine at Lord Holland's on Wednesday next, the 9th inst. . . . Thank God I am well, as people say, considering, but the pain yet troubles me, though it does not torture . . . " (Broadley Collection).

[1] Miss Hoare informed John of the accident that day : " He is quite unhurt and, though a little stiff, is able to walk, and has been on his feet for an hour or so " (Broadley Collection). Cf. a letter from Crabbe himself, on the second day after it (B. p. 84). His address at Hastings was 34, Wellington Square.

[2] Letter to B. from Hastings, October 27th, 1830, and letter from Trowbridge of February 22nd, 1831.

[3] Quoted by B. p. 84, col. 2.

have to thank my friends," he writes on October 24th,[1] "for one of the most beautiful as well as comfortable rooms you could desire. I look from my window upon the Avon and its wooded and rocky bounds—the trees yet green. A vessel is sailing down, and here comes a steamer (Irish, I suppose). I have in view the end of the Cliff to the right, and on my left a wide and varied prospect over Bristol, as far as the eye can reach, and at present the novelty makes it very interesting. Clifton was always a favourite place with me. I have more strength and more spirits since my arrival at this place, and do not despair of giving a good account of my excursion on my return."[2] But the silence of the picturesque gorge, watered by the yellow stream of the sluggish Avon, was speedily disturbed by the echoes of the grave events which happened at Bristol. On seeing this town fall a prey to riot and incendiarism, Crabbe must have thought of London in 1780.[3] At the end of October there was a feeling of deep resentment throughout England against the House of Lords, which had rejected the second Reform Bill a fortnight previously. One of the bitterest opponents of this measure,[4] Sir Charles Wetherell, formerly Attorney-General in Wellington's ministry, and more conservative than his leader, was about to make a formal entry into Bristol as Recorder of the city, on Saturday, October 29th. A significant manifestation was got up against him by the more enthusiastic reformers. The Corporation, being alarmed, and feeling itself helpless, applied to the Home Secretary, Lord Melbourne, for an imposing military force. Ninety-three dragoons were sent under a commanding officer who was resolved not to fire, whatever happened. As early as the 26th Crabbe exhibits some uneasiness: "I have been with Mrs. Hoare at Bristol," he writes to his son, "where all appears still: should anything arise to alarm, you may rely upon our care to avoid danger. Sir Charles Wetherell, to be sure, is not popular, nor

---

[1] B. p. 87, col 2.

[2] He was at 4, Prince's Buildings (MS. letter of October 28th). In 1826 he lodged at 2, York Crescent.

[3] See above, pp. 101-4.

[4] For his comic attitude when Lord John Russell made his first speech, cf. *The Greville Memoirs*, ed. 1897, vol. ii. p. 125.

is the Bishop,[1] but I trust that both will be safe from violence, abuse they will not mind."[2] This was too optimistic a forecast. When Wetherell entered the city on Saturday at half-past ten, he was received with groans by a crowd which followed him to the Guildhall; stones were even thrown at his carriage. Taking advantage of this uproar and of the impotence of the authorities, the mob spread into the streets, besieged the Mayor's house, which it finally carried by storm on Sunday morning, got drunk in its well-stocked cellars, burned three prisons in the course of the afternoon, the Bishop's palace in the evening, and during the night the houses on the north and west sides of Queen's Square, then the central open space of Bristol.[3] From his window Crabbe could descry the glare of the conflagrations in the distance. On Monday morning he would have liked to go into Bristol, but Mrs. Hoare dissuaded him, being afraid that his clerical garb might mark him out for attack. Yet he had exact information as to the state of the city. "Queen's Square," he writes, "is but half standing; half is a smoking ruin. The Mayor's house has been destroyed, the Bishop's palace plundered, but whether burnt or not I do not know. This morning[4] a party of soldiers attacked the crowd in the Square; some lives were lost, and the mob dispersed, whether to meet again is doubtful. The military are now in considerable force, and many men are sworn in as constables: many volunteers are met in Clifton churchyard, with white round one arm to distinguish them; some with guns, and the rest with bludgeons." On Monday, in fact, the cavalry of the nearest garrisons, sent for by the Mayor, poured into Bristol and suppressed the disorders, which were due to Wetherell's obstinacy and Melbourne's want of energy.

After staying a month at Pucklechurch, Crabbe returned to Trowbridge on November 30th.[5] He

---

[1] Robert Gray. Like the Bishop of Bath and Wells, he had voted against the Reform Bill on October 8th.

[2] B. p. 88.

[3] Cf. *The Bristol Riots, their Causes, Progress, and Consequences,* by a Citizen, Bristol, 1832. The comments of this anonymous author, a Tory of the Tories, are very questionable, but the facts are accurate. Cf. also Sir Spencer Walpole, *History of England,* ed. 1890, vol. iii. pp. 226-30.

[4] The letter quoted by B. p. 88 is thus dated. It was on Monday, the 31st, at five in the morning, that the repression began (*Bristol Riots,* p. 139).

[5] See above, p. 469.

seemed to be in fairly good health; perhaps even he ate with too keen an appetite. All of a sudden, on January 27th, 1832, after having suffered from a cold, he felt a violent pain in the head, which was followed by fever and extreme weakness. His doctor bled him. This treatment, which was unusual in his case, alarmed his son John, who at once sent word of it to George at Pucklechurch.[1] An apparent improvement, however, took place on the 28th; but on the next day the fever and weakness returned, and recovery was seen to be hopeless. Crabbe, whose constitution was not strong, and who had been enfeebled for ten years by the tic douloureux, was succumbing to old age. His agony lasted for four days more, fits of delirium alternating with outbursts of piety. At last, on Friday, February 3rd, at one o'clock in the morning, he became

---

[1] The following are the two letters from John: "TROWBRIDGE, *Jan.* 28, 1832. MY DEAR BROTHER,—. . . The [? Dad] not being quite well, I wanted to send you an account of him. We came home after our week's absence [at Pucklechurch] quite well and found him so too, but during this last week we all three took severe colds producing perpetual coughing and which Mr. Cary says are very prevalent. Anna and I soon got pretty well by common medicine, but the D^d not taking aperients soon enough had yesterday such a violent pain in the head that Mr. Cary thought it requisite to bleed him last night: this is so unusual a remedy for the D^d to require that we began to be rather alarmed: that however and more medicine have eased the pain and coughing very much and he is this morning much better.

"I shall keep this letter open till Mr. Cary calls. . . . As to my judgment— though absolutely frightened last night—I now hope and believe that the only thing required is judicious reducing, and that that system and nursing for a week or two will make him much better than he was before: for of late he has lived as a person might do who took strong exercise, which of course he has not taken. . . .

"Mr. Cary has just been here and gives a good account. Weakness is now almost all that remains to be dealt with, and Mr. Cary says that is so immaterial that he does not want the appetite at all to be urged: reducing was the thing wanted.

"Though this opinion of his is so satisfactory this morning, you will probably be more comfortable by coming and giving him a look; and if he still continues going on well, we shall enjoy it very much as a visit. . . . "
On the following day, the 29th, John wrote: "As I know you would wish for constant intelligence, I must send a line to say that I do not think the D^d quite so well to-day as yesterday, and if you can come and pay him a visit, I think you should. The original complaint, pain in the head, is much better, but the weakness and fever make him frequently appear so ill as quite to alarm us. . . . The D^d has just enquired whether I had written to you" (Broadley Collection).
As John is mentioned here, I may add that he left Trowbridge in December, 1832, that in November, 1833, he received from Mrs. Sophia North (widow of Dudley North) the livings of Little and Great Glemham, that in 1837 he had a serious attack of paralysis, and that he died at Beccles on September 2nd, 1840, at the age of fifty-three. He had more taste for drawing than for literature.

unconscious, and at seven o'clock he passed away peacefully in the arms of his sons.

As soon as the sad news became known, Trowbridge went into mourning. The shutters of the shops in the town were half closed. On the day of his funeral the principal inhabitants, including all the Nonconformist ministers, met of their own accord in the schoolroom and followed him to the grave.[1] One and all felt the loss of the venerable old man, whom they knew to be illustrious and who had endeared himself to them by his goodness of heart.

[1] B. p. 90. A memorial tablet by the sculptor Baillie was put up in the chancel of the church in August, 1833, near the spot where Crabbe's remains are interred. It has no artistic value. It appears that during the restoration of the church in 1847 the poet's skull was stolen by a workman, and that in July, 1876, Mr. Mackay had it re-interred (cf. *The Skull of the Poet Crabbe*, by Clifford W. Holgate, *Wiltshire Archæological and Natural History Magazine*, vol. xxix. p. 3, December, 1896 ; *The Daily Telegraph* of July 19th, 1877 ; and *The Trowbridge Chronicle* of July 22nd).

CONCLUSION

CRABBE'S is a mind which can be explored without much difficulty. His life, his experience, his ideas, without being exactly narrow, move in a limited circle. Born in a large village of less than a thousand inhabitants, he passed from one hamlet to another, and died in a small country town. He sometimes stayed in London, and he visited Edinburgh. But he did not go farther afield. A confirmed John Bull, he was not one of those Englishmen who flocked to Paris after the Peace of Amiens; he did not accompany Moore and Rogers there in July, 1817. On the morning of their departure he went to say good-bye to them, but they had already started when he arrived.[1] Little curious about the unknown, Crabbe always confined himself to observing what came in his way, and never sought to refresh his mind by travelling. " The situation of a country clergyman is not necessarily favourable to the cultivation of the Muse," says Hazlitt; the isolation of a country parsonage, or, still more, the daily intercourse with the humbler parishioners, the calls on the squire, the composition of the weekly sermon, impart to this rather dull existence a monotony which, in Crabbe's poems, is revealed by their uniformity, so fatal to their permanence. Besides this, his poverty in youth and the crises successively experienced at Wickham Brook, at Aldborough, and in London, had, by throwing him back on himself, steeled his character and given him strength, but not breadth. His relations with the great, far from

---

[1] B. p. 70 (July 15th).

477

inclining him to expansiveness, had contributed to his isolation, in a sphere where humiliations were not spared him. It was only on the threshold of old age that he met with attentions, with the flattering civilities of persons conspicuous for their rank or their intelligence. He expanded under success, for his nature, which was amiable and sociable, had contracted and hardened only in order to make a firmer stand against adversity, against the mediocrity of his life. But this constraint had given it a bias which, in spite of all counteracting influences, never entirely disappeared. Again, his speculative and religious, his moral and political ideas, hampered by tenets which he was precluded from discussing, and by professional decorum, stopped halfway, smitten with apprehension: the daring of infidel revolutionaries such as Byron and Shelley frightened him. Prudence was his rule of conduct, the golden mean his ideal. As Wordsworth felt very clearly, "his motives for writing verse and his hopes and aims were not so high as is to be desired."[1] When he wrote, it was not inspiration which moved him, but rather the hope of gain. In short, he had no lofty aspirations.[2] He remained essentially *bourgeois*.

He became but was not born a poet. His sensibility, although lively and fairly keen, is not vibrant; his senses are far from having the subtle penetration of Shelley's. His austere temperament, in youth and middle age at least, lacks the softness, the richness, of those happy and slightly voluptuous minds from which poetry gushes forth without effort.[3] He does not fall into ecstasy over the "harmonies" of nature; the birds do not sing in his verses: we hear in them only the scream of the sea-gulls, the twitter of the swallows, the boom of the bittern, and often also the mutterings of the storm. He has no ear: if he takes an interest in music, it is simply out of curiosity.[4] The

---

[1] Wordsworth's *Poetical Works*, ed. Dowden, vol. v. p. 361.

[2] The expression is Jeffrey's, *Edinburgh Review*, vol. xxxii. July, 1819, p. 123.

[3] Cf. Shelley, *A Defence of Poetry:* "Poetry is the record of the best and happiest moments of the happiest and best minds."

[4] See as to this B. p. 8, col. 2: "Nature had given him a poor ear," and a piece of conflicting testimony, *ibid.* p. 80, col. 1. The point is decided by the following passage in the *Leadbeater Papers*, vol. i. p. 421, in which John James Lecky gives an account of his visit to Trowbridge: "He told me he never had any ear for music. In answer to my surprise at this, he laboured with

sense of taste and that of smell are very little developed in him : he never describes flowers by their perfume. He has the touch and the eye of a naturalist, not of an artist. He excels in observing and depicting the forms of things, but he sees colours only as patches, and never takes in their picturesque effects. The "bugloss" is "blue" and the "mallow" is "slimy," he tells us : is it a poet who writes thus, or a botanist copying out his notes?

Poetry, which is emotion expressing itself in rhythmical language, demands a bold intellect, an enthusiastic and passionate mind. Too uniformly reasonable and calm, Crabbe becomes animated only on rare occasions and emits only transient gleams. Besides, he is hampered by the prosaic nature of his favourite subjects.[1] He has none of the stuff of a lyric poet ; he does not carry within him the source of an inspiration always ready to be thrilled at the recollection of past joy or sorrow. What he wants to describe is the external world—the desolate landscape of his native shore, the characters and the manners of the small community around him, the misfortunes of the humble. Where is the spirit of poetry to come from, which alone can breathe life into this refractory material ? In a word, how is realism to be made poetical ? Wordsworth attempted it, finding his contemporary's treatment too crude, too "matter-of-fact."[2] In a few pieces of varying length, but of almost equal merit, he has described to us young "Lucy Gray," who goes to meet her mother in the town, and, caught in a snowstorm, slips off a rustic bridge and is drowned in the stream ; an old man who, bent double, wanders over the heath and picks up leeches in the ponds[3] ; an old beggar[4] who keeps on his

much earnestness to convince me that an ear for music and a taste for harmony of verses were quite distinct and did not of necessity go together." True, but a "musical ear" shows itself in a poet by qualities of harmony which Crabbe's versification possesses only in very rare passages.

[1] "A coarse and impracticable subject," says Byron (to Murray, September 15th, 1817—quoted by Moore in his *Life of Byron*).

[2] *Lucy Gray*, Prefatory Note, ed. Dowden, vol. i. pp. 368-9 : "The way in which the incident was treated, and the spiritualizing of the character might furnish hints for contrasting the imaginative influences which I have endeavoured to throw over common life, with Crabbe's matter-of-fact style of handling subjects of the same kind."

[3] *Resolution and Independence.*

[4] *The Old Cumberland Beggar.*

way in silence, or sometimes sits upon a stone to "eat his food in solitude." A little country-girl and two paupers, these are figures familiar to Crabbe's readers. But not content with photographing them, Wordsworth transfigures them by flinging the light of his imagination over them. Alike realistic and romantic, equally mindful of objective truth and subjective emotion, he communicates to all something of himself. Lucy Gray is compared to the mountain roe whose feet "with many a wanton stroke disperse the powdery snow"; the leech-gatherer is "motionless as a cloud," and his voice seems to his interlocutor to flow "like a stream." "With the aid of a few pleasing images,"[1] and of a poetic and moral commentary, Wordsworth idealises his humble heroes. He presents them to us, not only as they really are, but as he sees and conceives them; by a somewhat forced metamorphosis Lucy Gray is changed into a wandering fairy who—

> Sings a solitary song
> That whistles in the wind.

The solitary existence of the leech-gatherer becomes a lesson in calm stoicism and proud independence; that of the old beggar is a social blessing which "prompts the unlettered villagers to tender offices." By means of these reflections the poet takes a livelier interest in his personages; he loves them for what he imparts to them of himself; he envelops them in a deliberate sympathy. Nowhere is the union of realism and poetry more harmoniously effected than in the story of Margaret, the hapless heroine of the first book of *The Excursion*. What can be more commonplace, more devoid of interest, apparently, than the destiny of a poor woman deserted by her husband, whom poverty has driven from home, sinking from year to year, and finally dying of despair? And yet can anything be more touching than this narrative, in which the grave voice of the pedlar who relates it strives, as it were, against his own emotion? If realism is to reach the level of poetry, the writer must feel an intense sympathy for his personages: that is the sole and all-sufficing condition of this

[1] E. Legouis, *La Jeunesse de Wordsworth*, p. 456.

"sublimation." It is found sometimes in Crabbe: the death of the poor labourer in *The Village*, the portrait of Isaac Ashford, and the closing scene of *Ruth* are excellent examples of it. But one would like to have more of them. For Crabbe almost always, instead of making himself one with his heroes by force of sympathy, stands aside from them and loads them with reproaches, like a judge delivering a pitiless sentence.

This detachment with its tendency to irony has passed into the style, a faithful mirror of thought and feeling.[1] In form, as well as in inspiration, Crabbe is only a poet here and there. He seldom uses metaphor,[2] that figure of speech which makes language "a vision." Endowed with a penetrating psychological intuition, but unimaginative, he prefers comparison, "which is a syllogism." It serves as an adventitious ornament[3] to the uniform texture of his poetry. It is often scientific, suggested by his observation or his reading. The evening newspapers, for instance, are to him—

> Like bats, appearing, when the sun goes down,
> From holes obscure and corners of the town.

The innumerable daily journals are—

> Like insects waking to th' advancing spring,
> Which take their rise from grubs obscene that lie
> In shallow pools.[4]

Sir Richard Monday's greed attracts gold as—

> Steel, through opposing plates, the magnet draws,
> And steely atoms culls from dust and straws.[5]

---

[1] Cf. Guyau, *L'Art au point de vue sociologique*, pp. 290-3.

[2] Which is a condensed simile. It is very common in Shakspeare ("thy inky cloak") and in Shelley ("A light of laughing flowers along the grass is spread," *Adonais*), but rather rare in Crabbe (cf. however the description of Richard Monday as a child: "He was a footstool for the beggar's feet," *Parish Register*, i. 722; of the master of the workhouse: "And gauges stomachs with an anxious look," *ibid.* iii. 480; also *The Borough*, iii. 32, 63, 69, and *Tales*, iv. 264). It becomes possible only when the imagination is excited by inspiration.

[3] Jeffrey had already noted this in 1812, *Edinburgh Review*, vol. xx. p. 304 (cf. *Works*, p. 383, n. 3).

[4] *Newspaper*, 59-60 and 65-7.

[5] *Parish Register*, i. 747-8.

Gwyn, the free-thinker, wanting to express his horror of legal chicanery, says :

> Who would by law regain his plunder'd store,
> Would pick up fallen mercury from the floor ;
> If he pursue it, here and there it slides,
> He would collect it, but it more divides ;
> This part and this he stops, but still in vain,
> It slips aside, and breaks in parts again.[1]

These similes, much less concise than metaphors would be, have a tendency to become little scenes independent of the main narrative and to attain a disproportionate length. To quote one instance only, this is how Crabbe describes the humiliation of "Justice Bolt,"[2] isolated amidst a crowd of opponents, and then his triumph over Hammond, his discomfited antagonist :

> As a male turkey, straggling on the green,
> When by fierce harriers, terriers, mongrels seen,
> He feels the insult of the noisy train
> And skulks aside, though moved by much disdain ;
> But when that turkey, at his own barn-door,
> Sees one poor straying puppy and no more,
> (A foolish puppy who had left the pack,
> Thoughtless what foe was threat'ning at his back,)
> He moves about, as ship prepared to sail,
> He hoists his proud rotundity of tail,
> The half-seal'd eyes and changeful neck he shows,
> Where, in its quick'ning colours, vengeance glows ;
> From red to blue the pendent wattles turn,
> Blue mix'd with red, as matches when they burn ;
> And thus th' intruding snarler to oppose,
> Urged by enkindling wrath, he gobbling goes.[3]

Here we have quite a new description, a regular genre picture—excellent of its kind—inserted in the fabric of the narrative. We are a long way, assuredly, from the single, creative epithet, the lightning of thought which the mind flashes on an object to illumine its outline for a moment.

[1] *Tales*, iii. 113-20, and many other passages, among others *Borough*, iv. 160-7 ; *Tales*, xv. 97-9, xvii. 11-16, xviii. 9-10 ; *Tales of the Hall*, i. 9-10, 175, ii. 5 and 25 *seq.*, vii. 10 and 313 *seq.*, viii. 260 and 645, etc.
[2] See above, p. 453.
[3] *Tales*, i. 368-83. Cf. also *Village*, i. 79-84, ii. 119-26 ; *Borough*, iv. 48-55, vi. 71-80 ; *Tales*, xi. 123-33, xv. 275-88.

Unlike Wordsworth, who wants to revolutionise the style of poetry by clothing it in a rustic form of speech purged of all incorrectness,[1] Crabbe adheres to the classic model perfected by Dryden and Pope. The "poetic diction" of these great writers is, according to Johnson's definition, equally removed from "the grossness of domestic use and from the harshness of terms appropriated to particular arts."[2] It is recognisable by "its elegance" and its preference for the "flowers of speech." A young girl is called at least a "maid," and for choice a "nymph"; a peasant becomes a "swain"[3]; poets receive the appellation of "sons of verse"; fishes figure as "the finny tribe," and country-folk as "the rural tribe."[4] Not that Crabbe is afraid of using the proper term, or that Dryden and Pope were afraid of it, but the periphrasis seems to them an indispensable embellishment. It is one of the privileges which distinguish poets from mere prose writers, like the personification of abstract ideas[5] and inversion,[6] which is necessitated by the difficulties of rhyme. Still more characteristic of this style, created for satire, is the frequent occurrence of antitheses which oppose adjectives or substantives to one another in the two halves of the same line,[7] which

---

[1] Preface to the *Lyrical Ballads*, 3rd ed. 1802, and E. Legouis, *La Jeunesse de Wordsworth*, pp. 448 *seq.*

[2] *Life of Dryden* (Cassell, National Library, p. 104).

[3] In Crabbe's realistic *Village* as well as in Pope's *Pastorals*. The word was convenient for rhyming with "plain," "pain," etc.

[4] *Village*, i. 25, 27, 113.

[5] Cf., among many instances, *Village*, i. 111 ; *Borough*, ix. 287-90, and x. 230-7.

[6] The examples are so numerous that one will suffice. *Library*, 91 :

"Yet all are not these births of noble kind";

cf. *Borough*, xxi. 144, 220, etc., etc.

[7] Sometimes the word (adjective, substantive, verb) is simply repeated :

"And so obliging that he ne'er obliged"

(Pope, *Epistle to Dr. Arbuthnot*, l. 208);

cf. Crabbe :

"And sought awhile to find what he would seek"

(*Borough*, iii. 26);

or there is a symmetrical balancing of the adjective and the verb, or of the adjective and the noun, Cf. Pope (*ibid.* 203):

"Willing to wound, and yet afraid to strike"

and Crabbe :

"For no deep thought the trifling subjects ask"

(*Village*, i. 33),

etc., etc.

emphasise, if need be, this effect of contrast by means of alliteration,[1] and make a short poem a quiver full of

[1] This appears to me much more common in Crabbe than in Pope. Here is a perfect example of it :

> "They boast their peasant's pipes ; but peasants now "
> *(Village*, i. 23).

To this union of antithesis and alliteration are due Crabbe's verbal jingles, which are so pointless and ridiculous. They would form a curious collection. Here are some of them :

Parish Register, ii. 142 :
> "And Phœbe felt, and felt she gave, delight."

Ibid. 211 :
> "And now her path, but not her peace, she gains."

Ibid. 160 :
> "He serv'd the Squire, and brush'd the coat he made."

Borough, iii. (p. 184, l. 7) :
> "Oh had he [the poor curate] learn'd to make the wig he wears "

(criticised by Jeffrey and expunged in consequence).

Ibid. xix. 141 :
> "And prompted base desires and baseless schemes."

Ibid. xx. 286 :
> "He'd means of dress and dress'd beyond his means."

Ibid. xxi. 1-2 :
> "A quiet, simple man was Abel Keene,
> He meant no harm, nor did he often mean."

Ibid. xxii. 43 :
> "He [Grimes] fished by water, and he filched by land."

Tales of the Hall, vii. 258 :
> "The cows, though cowards, yet in numbers strong."

Ibid. xii. 819 :
> "And as I wept at large, and thought alone."

The well-known parody of Crabbe by James Smith, in the *Rejected Addresses* (ed. 1812, "The Theatre," by the Rev. George Crabbe, pp. 113-21), owed its success to the excellent imitation of these plays upon words. Drury Lane theatre is lighted up, and we see—

> ". . . short cotton wicks,
> Touch'd by the lamplighter's Promethean art,
> Start into light and make the lighter start."

On entering the theatre you pass the ticket office :

> "Hark ! the check-taker moody silence breaks,
> And bawling " Pit full," gives the check he takes."

One of the spectators is the young " Pat Jennings," whose calling is thus described :

> "Emanuel Jennings brought his youngest boy
> Up as a corn-cutter, a safe employ."

—(Cf. Crabbe, *Borough*, vi. 200-1 :

> "Swallow, a poor Attorney, brought his boy
> Up at his desk, and gave him his employ.")—

> "In Holywell Street, St. Pancras, he was bred,
> (At number twenty-seven, it is said,)
> Facing the Plough, and near the Granby's head."

Pat goes up into the gallery and drops his hat into the two-shilling seats. His obliging companions forthwith lend him their handkerchiefs, and, with the help of this " motley cable," he recovers his " beaver " :

> "Up soars the prize ; the youth, with joy unfeign'd,
> Regained the felt, and felt what he regain'd,"

like Phœbe Dawson.

pointed arrows. Thanks to these epigrammatic traits in which the intervention of the writer is manifested, the portrait of an insignificant or commonplace personage may acquire a relief which lifts it above the intolerable flatness of a prosaic realism. In form, as well as in conception,[1] Crabbe to a certain extent complies with the exigencies of art.

But our satirist is also a descriptive poet and a moralist. He tries to get as much reality,[2] as much truth into his works as possible. An object is not depicted to his taste unless all its details have been successively presented to us ; an argument, a piece of advice, should be considered, he thinks, in all their aspects. Hence a second characteristic of his " poetic diction," as important as the first and too often forgotten : the amplitude of the sentence in numerous passages where the couplets, instead of remaining isolated as in Pope, are linked together and form long periods, overburdened with dependent clauses or conjunctions,[3] and disfigured here and there by obscurities,[4] slovenliness,[5] and

---

[1] Cf. above, pp. 371-2 and 309-11.

[2] Contrary to Johnson's precept, his vocabulary, in other respects an ordinary one, contains a great number of technical terms, especially of entomology and botany.

[3] Cf. *Village*, i. 63-78 (where . . . from thence . . . there [three times]), *Newspaper*, 466-75 (then . . . meanwhile . . . and though), and *Posthumous Tales*, a very interesting passage, xiv. 150-69 (But when . . . when . . . 'tis then . . . and when [twice] . . . when . . . and while . . . ; then comes the main clause after fifteen lines of subordinate ones).

[4] Cf. among others, *Village*, i. 341-2 (the pauper's burial):
> " The bell tolls late, the moping owl flies round,
> Fear marks the flight, and magnifies the sound,"

where no doubt the meaning is, " the bell tolls towards evening," and not " later than the appointed time," and " the sound " probably refers to the sound of the bell and not to the cry of the owl (communicated by Mr. H. Bradley).
The following couplet (*Village*, i. 140-1)—
> " Or will you deem them amply paid in health,
> Labour's fair child, that languishes with wealth "—

wrongly interpreted by Mr. Kebbel (*Life of Crabbe*, p. 120), is clear if " Labour's fair child " is taken simply as an amplification of " health."

[5] As appears from the harshness of the following lines :
Parish Register, i. 742 :
> " He'd no small cunning, and had some small wit."

Jeffrey often blamed the poet for these too familiar abbreviations.
Cf. also *Borough*, x. 213 :
> " And gives old ill-told tales for new-born anecdotes."

Tales, v. 576 :
> " Which, cherish'd with such love, 'twas worse than death to lose. '

inaccuracies.[1] Between these two extremes, epigrammatic concision and wordy diffuseness, Crabbe's style fluctuates, being adapted, as is always the case, to the ideas and feelings expressed. From *The Village* to the *Tales of the Hall* he develops in the direction of liberty, or, to speak more accurately, of laxity. The same tendency is observable in the versification. A disciple of Pope at the beginning of his career, Crabbe in his early works closes each of his couplets regularly with the end of the second line. He never runs one couplet into another, and, to vary the cadence, he confines himself to alternate masculine and feminine cæsuras.[2] But later, from 1798 onwards, tired perhaps of this monotony and no doubt encouraged by the example of Wordsworth and Scott, he adopts for his minor poems the eight-syllable metre in irregular

Tales of the Hall, x. 247 :
"By whom that deed was very seldom done."

Ibid. xiii. 514 :
"With clean brown broadcloth and with white cut wig."

[1] Almost all of them in the rhyme, through the omission of the *s* of the third person singular of the present indicative. It appears that this fault is common in Suffolk.

In *The Village*, i. 49, 50 :
"No ; cast by Fortune on a frowning coast,
Which neither groves nor happy valleys *boast*,"
evidently "boasts" should be read, but in the first edition the line ran :
"Which can no groves nor happy valleys boast."
The inaccuracy dates from 1807.

Cf. also *Parish Register*, iii. 270 :
"E'en well-feigned passion for our sorrows *call*."

Borough, iii. 248 :
"Some tradesman's bill his wandering eyes *engage*."

Ibid. 312 :
"When our relief from such resources *rise*."

Cf. *Tales*, ii. 13 :
"Pain, mix'd with pity, in our bosoms *rise*,"
in which it seems that Crabbe yields to the attraction of the plural substantive which immediately precedes the rhyme.
Yet we find in *Tales*, ii. 461 :
"*Blaze* not with fairy light the phosphor-fly."

[2] For a detailed study of the prosody see the last part of Herr Pesta's thesis (*George Crabbe*, Wien, 1899). He points out that in *The Library* half of the lines have the masculine cæsura after the second foot, a quarter the feminine cæsura after the fifth syllable, and another quarter varied divisions, in which the masculine cæsura after the third foot and the feminine after the seventh syllable predominate.

strophes,[1] the Spenserian stanza,[2] for which he had always had a liking, and even the four-stress rhythm.[3] Sometimes he sketches a tale, intended for one of his regular collections, in octosyllabic metre, or in Spenserian stanzas.[4] Then, in the course of the four or five stages through which his first effort passed before it was sent to press, he reverts to couplets. Only he now handles them with greater ease, runs them into one another,[5] uses "triplets," groups of three lines united by the same rhyme,[6] and alexandrines, which Pope condemned ironically,[7] becomes more and

---

[1] In *Woman* (published in 1807), *The Hall of Justice* (cf. above, p. 461, n. 4), *Reflections* (published in 1807), *The World of Dreams* (cf. above, p. 401), and especially in *Sir Eustace Grey*, written in 1804-5, published in 1807, a remarkable work the hero of which, having killed his unfaithful wife, goes mad, fancies himself persecuted by two unrelenting demons who hunt him all over the world, finds peace if not reason in Methodism, and relates with animation his sad destiny.

[2] Cf. above, pp. 54-5, and *The Birth of Flattery* (1807), the two first stanzas. This poem is a frigid allegory in which "Flattery" is represented as the daughter of "Poverty" and "Cunning."—In a tale published by *The Monthly Review* (March, 1904, pp. 119-37), Crabbe uses, with some irregularities, Chaucer's favourite stanza, the "rhyme-royal" of seven lines.

[3] Cf. *Monthly Review* (article just quoted, p. 138). The manuscript of this poem was three years ago in the possession of Mr. Edwards, bookseller, of High Street, Marylebone, and Monsieur A. Feuillerat, of the University of Rennes, had informed me of its existence (see Appendix VII). It now belongs to the Cambridge University Press. It may be noted also that in a youthful poem entitled *Midnight*, the original of which belongs to Mr. Dowden, Crabbe has used blank verse. This imitation of Young, an incorrect and tedious production, has been published in its entirety for the first time by Dr. Ward, in his edition of *Poems by George Crabbe*, Cambridge University Press, 1905.

[4] In one of his rough drafts, for instance, I find *The Amours of George* (*Tales of the Hall*, vii.) written in eight-syllable verse. The following is the encounter with the cows :

> " As instinct prompted forth I ran,
> Resolved to show myself a man,
> And plucking forth an oaken bough,
> Ran like Guy to fight the Cow,
> And like a valiant champion fixed
> Myself the Maids and Cows betwixt ;
> And tho' I had not breath to say,
> Run, Ladies, for the stile away,
> Yet doubtless with a warlike grace
> My hand was pointed to the place," etc.

Cf. *Tales of the Hall*, vii. 243-51.

[5] "Barely half a dozen," says Herr Pesta (p. 65). There are many more than this, especially in the *Tales of the Hall*.

[6] Sometimes composed solely of pentameters, and more often of two pentameters and a final hexameter. They enable the poet to finish his sentence, and Crabbe uses them without any æsthetic intention. They increase steadily in number, as Herr Pesta has shown : cf. his table, p. 63.

[7] "A needless Alexandrine ends the song,
That, like a wounded snake, drags its slow length along"
                                        (*Essay on Criticism*, 357-8).

more flexible in his cæsuras, so that in the *Tales of the Hall* the rigid mould of the classical couplet is almost broken up, under the pressure of narrative and dialogue. Not that Crabbe is a great artist. With him, form remains a secondary consideration, and substance is the main point. The natives of Suffolk are deficient in the sense of beauty, say the writers who know them,[1] and Crabbe is no exception to the rule. His gifts are those of a man of science, and in no way those of a poet—observation, force, above all, a love of truth. And it is by them that he has achieved his fame and earned our sympathy. He came in an age when English poetry, which had long been imprisoned in the didactic and satirical groove, wanted to recover touch with the reality, to return to the study of nature. Taught by the experience of his sad youth, he perceived that, of all poetic schools, the pastoral was perhaps the most artificial. He attacked it with a generous intrepidity, with an infectious ardour, and the success of *The Village* was at once his own personal victory and the triumph of truth over convention. Even before Cowper he helped, more than any one, to " bring poetry back to Nature." He prepared the way for a poet like Wordsworth, who, endowed with a keener sensibility, added lyrism to realism. A writer of transition, classical by origin, realistic by temperament, and romantic on very rare occasions,[2] he failed to harmonise the contradictions which encountered one another in himself and in his poetry : taking his subjects from common life, he imposed on them the stiff, jerky movement of the heroic couplet ; by nature a satirist and a man of science, be became a poet and a clergyman. His character and his works lack the elevation and the harmony which are the stamp of true greatness. He remained isolated, without imitators and without disciples.[3] But he had wielded a decisive influence at

[1] Cobbett (*Rural Rides*, ed. 1893, vol. ii. p. 298), Mitford, Fitzgerald. We may note that along with Crabbe this county has given to English literature writers like Skelton, Nash, Robert Bloomfield, and Mrs. Inchbald, all of them prosaic.

[2] Cf. *Sir Eustace Grey* and, in the *Tales of the Hall*, the character of Richard, in the person of whom Crabbe introduces himself.

[3] This is Fitzgerald's opinion (MS. notes) : " And remarkably enough he has not up to this time, 1864, had any imitator. ' Crabbe has a world of his own,' said Alfred Tennyson to me in 1854." The two only possible exceptions would be Ebenezer Elliott, the sentimental and unreadable Corn Law Rhymer—who appears to me to draw his inspiration far more from Goldsmith

the right moment. Better still, he had been one of those men, rare in every age, who are bold enough to look reality in the face, if only in one particular, and who relate what they have seen, regardless of prejudices. Compared with this, how unimportant are the timidities of his philosophical and religious speculation, the defects of his style? His own method enables us to correct them. And his intellectual probity, his robust plain-spokenness, so conspicuous in *The Village*, remain a great example for us.

than from Crabbe—and Alexander Balfour (1767—1829), who contributed to Constable's *Edinburgh Magazine* a series of *Characters omitted in Crabbe's Parish Register*, collected in a volume in 1825. They are hopelessly dull. According to Mr. Clement Shorter (*The Sphere*, October 24th, 1903), Thomas Hardy, the poet-novelist of Wessex, said that "his earliest influence in the direction of realism was obtained from Crabbe's works." In that case Crabbe would seem to have lost nothing by waiting.

APPENDICES

APPENDIX I

THE following letter, often quoted in the first part of this book, is to be found in *The Correspondence of Sir Th. Hanmer . . . and Other Relicks of a Gentleman's Family*, edited by Sir Henry Bunbury, a now somewhat rare work, published by Moxon in 1838. This all-important document[1] had remained forgotten there. It occupies pp. 384-95, and we read in a note: "This letter was sent by Mr. Burke to Sir Charles Bunbury who took a warm interest in Mr. Crabbe's welfare." Here is the text of this third letter to Burke, or "Bunbury Letter," as I have called it in my references:

"SIR,

"It is my wish that this letter may reach you at a time when you are disengaged, but if otherwise, I intreat that it may not be immediately read, as it is sufficient to try your patience without the additional circumstance of asking your attention at an improper time. I think it right to lay before you, Sir, a farther account of myself, and lest my present or future conduct should appear in a light that they ought not, I venture to inform you more particularly of the past: nor is this my sole motive; it is painful to me to be conscious that I have given you only partial information, though the part I gave was strictly true. Nor can I, with propriety, beg your advice in my present difficult situation, without relating the steps which led to it; on the other hand, I consider how much I have troubled you, and that you probably know as much of me as you desire; I am apprehensive too that I shall not rise in your opinion by what I write, and it is my constant fear that, kind and benevolent as you are, these repeated attacks upon your patience may compel you to withdraw your assistance and leave me to lament the importunity of my applications. These reasons however do not balance their opposite ones; they oblige me to fear, but not to relinquish my purpose, and this long account is the result of a painful deliberation on the propriety of writing it.

"I do not recollect the particulars of my first letter, but I believe, Sir, it informed you that my Father has a place in the Custom hᵒ at Aldborough, that he had a large family, a little

_____
[1] The original now belongs to Mr. Broadley.

493

income, and no œconomy: he kept me two years at a country boarding-school, and then plac'd me with an apothecary, who was poor and had little business, but the premium he demanded was small. I continued two years with this man, I read romances and learned to bleed; my master was also a Farmer, and I became useful to him in this his principal occupation; there was indeed no other distinction between the boy at the farm and myself, but that he was happy in being an annual servant, and I was bound by indentures. I do not mean Sir to trifle with you, but it is by no means a small matter with me how I stand in your opinion, and now when I speak of my mingled follies and misfortunes, I wish to say all I can consistently with truth in vindication of the former. I rebelled in my servitude, for it became grievous. My Father was informed of his Son's idleness and disobedience; he came, and was severe in his correction of them: I knew myself then injur'd and became obstinate, and a second visit of my Father's put an end to my slavery; he took me home with him, and with me two thirds of the money he had advanced. He then placed me on very easy terms with a man of large business in a more reputable line; but I was never considered as a regular apprentice, and was principally employed in putting up prescriptions and compounding medicines. I was, notwithstanding, well treated in every respect but the principal one, for no pains were taken to give me an idea of the profession I was to live by. I read novels and poetry, and began to contribute to Magazines and Diaries. My Master occasionally prophesy'd my ruin, and my Father advised me to quit such follies; but the former would sometimes laugh at the things he condemned, and my Father was a rhymer himself. I therefore paid little attention to these instructions, but was happy to find my signature in the Lady's Magazine was known to all the Ladies round the place I liv'd in. After four years I left my master according to our agreement: he is a man much esteemed in his profession and I believe he knows something of it, but I had not the good fortune to find it communicated to me. My Father at this time was much distressed and could not send me to London for the usual improvements. I meant to serve in a shop, but an unlucky opportunity offered itself at Aldbro', the Apothecary there was become infamous by his bad conduct, and his enemies invited me to fix there immediately. My Father urged it, and my pride assented: I was credited for the shattered furniture of an Apothecary's shop, and the drugs that stocked it. I began to assume my late master's manner, and having some conscientious scruples I began to study also: I read much, collected extracts, and translated Latin books of Physic with a view of double improvement: I studied the Materia Medica and made some progress in Botany. I dissected dogs and fancied myself an anatomist, quitting entirely poetry, novels and books of entertainment. After one year, I left my little business to the care of a neighbouring surgeon, and came to London, where I attended the lectures of Messrs. Orme and Lowder on Midwifery, and occasionally stole round the hospitals to observe those remarkable cases, which might indeed, but which probably never would, occur to me again. On my return I found my substitute had contracted a close intimacy with my rival. He cheated me and lost my business. The second woman who committed herself to my care, died before the month after her delivery was expired ; and the more I became qualified for my profession, the less occasion I found for these qualifications. My business was the most trifling and lay amongst the poor. I had a sister who starved with me ; and on her account it now pains me to say we often wanted bread ; we were unwilling to add to my Father's distress by letting him see ours, and we fasted with much fortitude. Every one knew me to be poor ; I was dunned for the most trifling sums, and compelled to pay the rent of my hut weekly, for my landlord was Justice of the Corporation and a man of authority. My druggist, a good-natured Quaker, gave me some friendly hints. My friends and advisers who had been zealous for my fixing in this place, entirely deserted me for this reason only, that I had not been successful by following their advice. After three years spent in the misery of successless struggle, I found it necessary for me to depart, and I came to London.

" That part of my conduct which I am about to relate, I am afraid will be greatly disapproved, and I shall be happy to find, Sir, you think it not more than foolish and inconsiderate. I knew the wages of a journeyman apothecary were trifling, and that nothing could be saved from them towards discharging the obligations I lay under. It became me to look for something more ; I was visionary, and looked to him from whom no help cometh.

" My Father, some years since, attended at the House of Commons on some election business, and he was also with the minister ; I recollected to have heard him speak with some pleasure of Lord North's condescension and affability ; and renouncing physic, I resolved to apply for employment in any department that I should be thought qualified for ; I drew up a long and laboured account of my motives for this application, and to prove my ignorance in the proper method of managing such applications, I accompanied my petition with a volume of verses, which I begged leave to submit to his Lordship's perusal. I was admitted to Lord North on my second calling, and treated with more attention than I now should expect, though with none of that affability I had been led to hope for ; what I still wonder at, is the civil part of his Lordship's behavior ; my request was idle and unreasonable, he might, with the greatest propriety have dismissed me instantly, but whether through want of thought, or with an inclination to punish me, he gave me hope, was sorry for my circumstances, enquired who could recommend me, and was satisfied with those I named : he ordered me to apply again and fixed a day. I am even now astonished at this unnecessary and cruel civility, it has greatly added to the inconveniences I now labour under, besides the anxiety of a long attendance growing daily more hopeless ; for not only on the day fixed, but on all other days, I went regularly to Downing Street, but from my first to my last interview with his Lordship were three months. I had only a variation in the mode of answer as the porter was more or less inclined to be civil, the purport of all was the same : I wrote and entreated his Lordship to accept or refuse me : I related my extreme poverty and my want of employment, but without effect. I again begged him to give some message to his servant, by which I might be certain that I had nothing further to hope for : this also was ineffectual. At last I had courage to offer so small a sum as half a crown, and the difficulty vanished : His Lordship's porter was now civil, and His Lordship surly ; he dismissed me instantly and with some severity.

"I had now recourse to my rhymes, and sent a hasty production to Mr. Dodsley, who returned it, observing that he could give no consideration for it, not because it wanted merit, but the town wanted attention ; he was very obliging in his reply, for I am now convinced it does want merit. Mr. Becket returned me a similar answer to an application of the same kind. I yet indulged a boyish opinion of my productions, and determined to publish ; fortunately however I had hitherto concealed my name, and I continued to do so. Nichols, who had printed some remains of Dryden, and other poets, was for this reason fixed upon to usher my piece on the world ; he printed 250 copies of *An Epistle to the Authors of 'The Monthly Review'* which I believe are now in the warehouse of Mr. Payne the bookseller, as I never heard of any sale they had. My patrons spoke of my poem rather favourably ; but Mes.rs the Critical Reviewers trimmed me handsomely, and though I imputed this in a great measure to envy, I was very glad that I had not exposed my name on the occasion.

"I now began to think more humbly of my talents : disappointment diminished my pride and increased my prudence. I solicited a subscription. Mr. Nassau, the late Member for Malden, was well known to me, and this led me to apply to his brother for a permission to prefix his name to a dedication. Lord Rochford assented, but bade me hope more from the merit of my productions than that permission. I conveyed my proposals to my friends and obtained about 150 names, chiefly at Beccles, which are since increased, and are something more than

200. I have acquainted these people with the alteration in my intention, but I am desired to send my poem in whatever manner it comes out, and this is that certainty I spoke of to Mr. Dodsley. During a long interval betwixt my disappointment at Downing Street and that necessity which compelled me to write to you, Sir, it would be painful to me, and tedious to you, to relate the distress I felt and the progress of my despair; I knew that my subscribers would not more than pay for the printing their volumes. I was contracting new debts, and unable to satisfy old demands. I lived in terror, was imposed upon, and submitted to insults and at length so threatened, that I was willing to make use of any expedient that would not involve me in guilt as well as vexation. I could accuse myself but of folly and imprudence and these lessen'd by inexperience, and I thought that if my circumstances were known, there would be found some to relieve me. I looked as well as I could into every character that offered itself to my view, and resolved to apply where I found the most shining abilities, for I had learned to distrust the humanity of weak people in all stations. You, Sir, are well acquainted with the result of my deliberation, and I have in one instance at least reason to applaud my own judgment.

" It will perhaps be asked how I could live near twelve months a stranger in London and coming without money : it is not to be supposed I was immediately credited—it is not—my support arose from another source. In the very early part of my life, I contracted some acquaintance, which afterwards became a serious connexion, with the niece of a Suffolk gentleman of large fortune. Her mother lives with her three daughters at Beccles ; her income is but the interest of £1,500, which at her decease is to be divided betwixt her children. The brother makes her annual income about £100 : he is a rigid œconomist, and though I have the pleasure of his approbation, I have not the good fortune to obtain more, nor from a prudent man could I perhaps expect so much. But from the family at Beccles, I have every mark of their attention, and every proof of their disinterested regard. They have from time to time supplied me with such sums as they could possibly spare, and that they have not done more arose from my concealing the severity of my situation, for I would not involve in my errors or misfortunes a very generous and very happy family by which I am received with unaffected sincerity, and where I am treated as a son by a mother who can have no prudential reason to rejoice that her daughter has formed such a connexion. It is this family I lately visited, and by which I am pressed to return, for they know the necessity there is for me to live with the utmost frugality, and hopeless of my succeeding in town they invite me to partake of their little fortune, and as I cannot mend my prospects, to avoid making them worse. This, Sir, is my situation : I have added, I have suppressed nothing ;

I am totally at a loss how to act, and what to undertake. I cannot think of living with my friends without a view of some employment or design, and I can form none, and I cannot continue in town without such, where the expense is (to me) much greater; my present undertaking can be of no material service I find, and the unlucky circumstance of printing so much of my miscellany renders it less so. I finish this tedious account by intreating your consideration on my present state and my future prospects. I cease to flatter myself, Sir; I only wish to live and to be as little a burden as possible to my friends, but my indiscretion and my ill-fortune have so far carried me away that it requires a better judgment than my own to determine what is right for me to do; I do not wish, Sir, to obtrude my affairs too much upon you, but you have assisted and advised me, and even exclusive of the advantage I reap from your directions, I judged it right to give you this account: for all that is past I most sincerely thank you; you have comforted, you have relieved, you have honoured me; what is to come is in a situation like mine particularly mysterious; but whatever comes I will be grateful; and with a remembrance of the benefits I have received I will ever cherish the highest respect for the name and virtues of my generous benefactor.

"I will wait upon you, Sir, as soon as possible with a fresh copy of my poem, correct as I have power to make it. In this I shall yet presume to ask your opinion; on any other subject it will now become me to be silent; thus far I feel a satisfaction from what I have written that it is entirely unreserved, and that it goes to one who knows how to allow for indiscretion and to pity misfortune.

"I am, Sir,

"Most respectfully,

"Your much obliged and obed^t servant,

"GEO. CRABBE.

"BISHOPSGATE STREET, *June* 26th."

APPENDIX II

I GIVE here a description of the first (anonymous) edition of *The Library* (1781) compared with that of 1807.[1]

Lines 1-50 are identical, except that in l. 22 "prevail" should be read instead of "avail," and in l. 28 "with her old flattering art."

> 51 Come then, and entering view this spacious scene,
> 52 This sacred dome, this noble magazine
> 53-60 Where mental wealth . . . their sober influence shed.
> [It will be noted that two lines, 53-4 of 1807, have been added.]

Description of *The Library*:

> 61 In this selection, which the human mind
> With care has made, for glory has design'd,
> All should be perfect ; or at least appear
> From falsehood, vanity and passion clear :
> 65 But man's best efforts taste of man, and show
> The poor and troubled source from whence they flow ;
> [ll. 95-6 of 1807.]
> His very triumphs his defeats must speak,
> And e'en his wisdom serves to prove him weak.
> 69-72 Fashion, though folly's child . . . o'er her mother's foes
> [are ll. 167-70 of 1807].
> 73-80 Yon folios . . . and the sons deride
> [have been reproduced by B. p. 104, n. 15].
> 81-102 Our patient fathers . . . your rivals too.
> [Cf. 1807, ll. 179-200, except that l. 85 (183 of 1807) is, "Till, every note and every comment known," that in l. 89 (187 of 1807) "prov'd" should be read instead of "show'd," and that instead of 198-200 in 1807 we have 100-2 :
> Hard is your task who hope by manly arts to please
> (2nd ed. 1783: "Hard is your task by manly arts to please.")
> For all your secret faults are brought in view
> And half your judges are your rivals too.]

[1] Since this Appendix was written the comparison has been made by Dr. A. W. Ward (*Poems by George Crabbe*, vol. i. 1905, pp. 527-9). His study has not rendered mine superfluous.

103-9 But ne'er, discourag'd, fair attempts lay by,
For Reason views them with approving eye,
And Candour yields what cavillers deny.
She sees the struggles of the soul to steer
Through clouds and darkness, which surround us here,
And, though the long research has ne'er prevail'd,
Applauds the trial, and forgets it fail'd.

110-47 With awe . . . lie disdain'd below
[are ll. 105-42 of 1807 with these differences:
l. 113 (108 of 1807):
These are the tombs of those who cannot die.
ll. 146-7 (141-2 of 1807):
Wits, Bards and Idlers fill a tatter'd row;
And the vile vulgar lie disdain'd below].

148-51 Amid these works . . . our early offering pay,
[are ll. 201-4 of 1807].

152-96 Reproduced by B. p. 106, n. 26.

Description of books of Science, Moral Philosophy, Medicine, and Law:

197-304 Man crowns the scene . . . or while power defies
[are ll. 323-430 of 1807, with a few insignificant variations].

305-6 (431-2 of 1807):
"Ah, happy age!" the youthful poet cries,
"Ere laws arose, ere tyrants bade them rise"
[which in 1807 appeared to Crabbe too revolutionary,
even in the mouth of a young dreamer. This slight
correction is highly significant].

307-52 When all were blest . . . the savage state is gone
[correspond to ll. 433-78 of 1807, with a few differences:
ll. 315-6 (441-2 of 1807):
Bound by no tyes but those by nature made,
Virtue was law, and gifts prevented trade.
And l. 328 (454 of 1807):
Taught by some conquering friends, who came as foes].

Then this passage on theology:

353 Now turn from these, to view yon ampler space,
There rests a sacred, grave and solemn race;
There the devout an awful station keep,
Vigils advise, and yet dispose to sleep;
There might they long in lasting peace abide,
But controversial authors lie beside,
Who friend from friend and sire from son divide;
Endless disputes around the world they cause,
Creating now and now controuling laws;

362-79 Dull though impatient . . . by the foes she fought
[are the ll. 219-36 of 1807].

380-3 Reprinted by B. p. 105, n. 22.

384 (245 of 1807):
  Great authors whom the church's glory fir'd.
385-7 as 246-8 of 1807.
388 (257 of 1807):
  And let them lie—for lo! yon gaudy frames
389-97 All closely fill'd . . . though various in their way
  [are ll. 258-66 of 1807].
Finally, ll. 398-611 are very nearly an exact reproduction of
  479-692 of 1807, containing the description of books
  of history and the drama, of romances, of works of
  criticism and imagination.

From this comparison it appears: firstly, that Crabbe, in 1807,
touched up the first half of his poem much more than the second,
the style of which rightly appeared to him more finished; secondly,
that certain interesting passages were added in 1807, among
others, ll. 63-105, 143-79, 205-19, 249-56; thirdly, that the importance which he gave to philosophy in 1781 for "guiding mortals
through their mental night" was attributed in 1807 to theology,
without changing a single word (l. 206, ed. 1807). The plan of
his poem was modified in consequence: a clergyman was bound
to give theology precedence over philosophy and science.

APPENDIX III

"NATHAN KIRK" AND HIS SERVANT

THIS story is in *The Parish Register*, ii. 19-83.

Lines 19-34 have undergone no change, except in l. 19: "tried" instead of "tied."

But ll. 34-68 were completely recast in the second edition (1808), in consequence of the following remarks of Jeffrey (*Edinburgh Review*, vol. xii. p. 144: "The first pair here is an old snug bachelor who, in the first days of dotage, had married his maidservant. The Rev. Mr. Crabbe is very facetious on this match, and not very scrupulously delicate. We can only venture to insert a line or two of his animated address to this rustic Benedict"). This was enough to tempt readers of the first edition. Here is the original text (ll. 34 *seq.*) :

> Fie, Nathan ! fie ! to let a sprightly jade
> Leer on thy bed, then ask thee how 'twas made,
> And lingering walk around at head and feet,
> To see thy nightly comforts all complete ;
> Then waiting seek—not what she said she sought,
> And bid a penny for her master's thought ;—
> (A thought she knew, and thou couldst not send hence,
> Well as thou lov'dst them, for ten thousand pence ;)
> And thus with some bold hint she would retire,
> That wak'd the idle wish and stirr'd the slumbering fire ;
> Didst thou believe thy passion all so laid,
> That thou might'st trifle with thy wanton maid,
> And feel amus'd and yet not feel afraid ?
> The dryest faggot, Nathan, once was green,
> And laid on embers, still some sap is seen ;
> Oaks, bald like thee above, that cease to grow,
> Feel yet the warmth of spring, and bud below ;
> More senseless thou than faggot on the fire,
> For thou couldst feel and yet wouldst not retire ;
> Less provident than dying trees,—for they
> Some vital strength, some living fire display,
> But none that tend to wear the life itself away.
> Ev'n now I see thee to the altar come ;
> Downcast thou wert, and conscious of thy doom :

I see thee glancing on that shape aside,
With blended looks of jealousy and pride ;
But growing fear has long the pride supprest,
And but one tyrant rankles in thy breast ;
Now of her love a second pledge appears,
And doubts on doubts arise, and fears on fears ;
Yet fear defy, and be of courage stout,
Another pledge will banish every doubt ;
Thine age advancing, as thy powers retire,
Will make thee sure—What more wouldst thou require ?

The rest as from l. 61 of the later editions.

APPENDIX IV

REVERTING to the division already adopted for the study of the *Tales in Verse*, we shall have the following classification of the *Tales of the Hall*.

I. PATHOS

FIRST of all, in tale iii., *Boys at School*, come two narratives related to the brother by "Jacques," the Rector of Binning.

The story of Charles, in part that of James Elmy (cf. above, p. 47, n. 4), was one of Hazlitt's favourites (*Spirit of the Age*, ed. 1886, p. 315). The son of a widow, sent to school at the expense of a noble patron, Charles had a prepossessing countenance, gentle, polite and reserved manners, accompanied by a certain pride which he could not always subdue. Mediocre and conscientious, he worked hard, but never rose above the average. After five years at school he had to choose a profession : in spite of the nobleman's wishes, he refused to enter the navy, and so lost his protector's influence. He wanted to be a painter, and fancied himself a genius. Walking, as he thought, in Correggio's footsteps, he worked to earn a living and pay for his drawing lessons. No one could be more industrious and zealous, but he aspired to fame without having talent enough to obtain it. He soon grew soured, lost his mother, to whom he was devoted, and left the district.

Many years afterwards "Jacques" met him in a London alley, in some Grub Street inhabited by broken-down artists. Charles, still proud, slunk away. The workhouse was his last refuge : there Jacques found him again, lying on the "naked boards" of his bed, dying of hunger to avoid debt, reduced to this extremity by inability to pay his rent. The reader will remember the distress which Crabbe himself went through in 1780-1. Charles, less fortunate, passed away peacefully in the arms of his faithful friend Jacques. This tale is only a variant of *The Patron* (*Tales in Verse*, v., above, pp. 327-32).

Of a proud disposition, "Harry Bland" also had a painful disenchantment in store for him. His mother having died young, his father took a mistress. He was scandalised at this. Sometimes he would ask one of his playfellows if "all wicked people go to hell." Grown up, he left his father's house and, from a horror of vice, married "a lovely maid, approved of every heart as worthy to be loved." Well, this dragon of virtue has himself broken the seventh commandment! He has seduced the wife of his miller, whose connivance he purchases. Held back by remorse, driven forward by his appetites, he indulges his passion and despises himself.

The characters of the two sisters in tale viii., *The Sisters*, form a contrast. In their youth, one was tall, "with free commanding air," the other "mild, and delicate and fair." Jane's smile had archness, Lucy's cheerfulness. The latter inspired affection, Jane, more imperious, was alternately scolded and caressed. Jane's favourite reading consisted of satires, of romances like Mrs. Radcliffe's and *The Pilgrim's Progress*. Lucy preferred the Bible and love-stories. Both patriots, Jane waxed enthusiastic over glorious victories, Lucy deplored the death of so many brave men. The one had gentleness and simplicity, the other ambition. But they were attached to each other, in spite of the difference in their tastes. And both were courted, for they had a handsome fortune. Their lovers resembled them, in appearance at least. Lucy's, by name Barlow, was imperturbably calm and placid; Jane's, called Bloomer, was an elegant youth, with a certain boldness of language and ideas, and a somewhat dubious past.

Unfortunately for them, a dangerous adventurer started a bank in a neighbouring town. His promises won the confidence of his fellow-citizens, and a sumptuous abode testified to his success. Wishing to earn the good opinion of the two sisters, he approached them through his wife, who loaded them with small attentions; he paid them the hurried visit of a man absorbed in business, and placed his elegant carriage, his grapes, his library, and his roses at their disposal. Jane and Lucy eventually entrusted their money to him. Shortly afterwards the bank broke.

Barlow, Lucy's accepted suitor, heard of the catastrophe on his return from a journey to London. He had approved of her investment, but now blamed it, to himself. However, he resolved to display his generosity. He offered his hand to Lucy, counting on the effect which such noble conduct ought to produce, as he thought. He miscalculated: Lucy had determined to be brave, and he obtained none of the distress and gratitude which he had anticipated. In his disappointment he could speak only of money matters, so that Lucy, out of pride, thanked him and begged him to think no more of her. Bloomer behaved still more badly: his visits and his attentions to Jane redoubled; he assumed a caressing air, took more liberties, remained later of an evening, tried to be alone with her. As soon as he thought his sapping operations were sufficiently advanced, he delivered his attack and was ignominiously repulsed.

Jane has never got over this blow. Lucy, calmer and more valiant, has started a small school which gives her a living and enables her to take care of her sister. The latter, like Mira, has fits of silence, followed by intervals of exaggerated loquacity and gaiety. Sometimes she feels that she is going mad ; she sings in a low, melancholy voice, or takes up gardening to escape companionship. Disappointed in her affections, she avoids the male sex and takes refuge among her flowers.

The story of Sir Owen Dale (xii.) is a double one, containing his own and that of his farmer Ellis.

A rich widower at the age of forty-five, Sir Owen, feeling his passions revive, wished to marry again. He had fixed his choice on Camilla, a young beauty of about five-and-twenty, as intelligent as she was handsome, but unfortunately rather a flirt. Seeing that he expected some signs of love before declaring himself, she resolved to amuse herself at his expense. She flattered him and paid him many attentions, taking his arm and never refusing to play or sing when he asked her, with the result that Sir Owen at last plucked up courage and proposed. He was rejected, Camilla alleging the difference in their ages. The lover, therefore, humiliated and wounded in his pride, vowed revenge.

A very singular idea occurred to him. His nephew, "Captain Morden," a young and brave officer, owed everything to him. "Be my avenger," says the uncle, "swear to me—

> That by all means approved and used by man
> You win this dangerous woman, if you can ;
> That, being won, you my commands obey,
> Leave her lamenting, and pursue your way ;
> Take now an oath—within the volume look—
> There is the Gospel—swear, and kiss the book."

Out of devotion to his uncle Morden complies, but with reluctance. Of course he and Camilla fall in love at first sight, and Sir Owen, when asked to relent, threatens the nephew with his displeasure if he does not keep his word.

Sir Owen, however, remembers that he has a tenant, named Ellis, whose wife has been unfaithful. Wishing to justify his inflexibility to himself by the example of another, he calls on this farmer, who relates his misfortune to him. Ellis had married the too amiable Alicia, the niece of a clergyman, and, somewhat neglecting his young wife, was in the habit of spending his evenings in the inn of a neighbouring town. By way of distraction, Alicia encouraged the visits of a certain Henry Cecil, the natural son of a nobleman, who was living with a farmer of the district to learn agriculture. This acquaintanceship led to an irreparable fault. The guilty pair fled, and when Ellis discovered them months afterwards, they had sunk into the deepest destitution. Cecil speedily succumbed to his privations. Alicia was rescued by her husband, who supports her in a separate cottage, but "will never see her more on earth."

This half-pity is enough to soften Sir Owen, who on his return says to his nephew, "Take her : bring me the dear coquette," and let us forgive each other.

It will be noticed that Ellis's story presents some analogy to Th. Heywood's famous play *A Woman killed with Kindness* (1603), the heroine of which is called Mrs. Frankford. I do not know whether Crabbe had read this domestic drama.

The subject of tale xiii., *Delay has Danger*, has been sketched above (p. 263).

Gretna Green (xv.) is one of the least interesting of these tales. A young man named Belwood, a pupil of a "Doctor Sidmere," falls in love with Clara, his tutor's daughter. Having borrowed some money from a Jew, Belwood proposes to Clara to fly to Scotland, where the "blacksmith of Gretna Green" will marry them without waiting for the consent of their parents or guardians. Now, the doctor and his wife had discovered the intrigue, but had shut their eyes to it, hoping to benefit by Belwood's fortune. They are bitterly disappointed : the young man and his better half lead a cat-and-dog life after a few weeks of their marriage, and Clara's sole thought is to obtain her liberty from her husband, with an adequate allowance. But Belwood refuses, out of avarice.

Lady Barbara (xvi.) is based on a more romantic idea. A brother and a sister, brought up in Deism and deeply attached, have promised to communicate to each other the mysteries of the tomb. The one who dies first will endeavour to reappear in the form of a ghost and dispel the doubts of the survivor. A year after her marriage, her husband being absent, Lady Barbara is awakened by a strange noise, and sees her brother at her bedside. He declares to her that her doubts about religion should come to an end, that "the word revealed" is true, that she will soon be a widow and ought not to marry again, otherwise she will "wed despair." A week afterwards, in fact, she hears of the death of this brother, whose ghost had appeared to her. And the prophecies come true one after another : Lady Barbara becomes a widow, and takes up her abode with an old clergyman, whose young son George she brings up. The latter gradually falls in love with her and asks her hand, which she grants, in spite of the aversion and the warnings of the ghost. George, in fact, makes her very unhappy. As Canon Ainger has remarked (*Life of Crabbe*, p. 171), the character of the young man, at one time an excellent poet, at another a mean coward, is very incoherent.—Crabbe did not invent this story : he owed it, I believe, to Miss or Mrs. Hoare of Bath ("I owe [it] to the kindness of a fair friend," *Works*, p. 377, col. 2, Preface to *Tales of the Hall*), who perhaps had it from Lady Betty Cobbe "in Ireland or Marlborough Buildings, Bath."[1] The original is known as "the Tyrone ghost story," and the details, similar in every point to those of Crabbe's tale, will be found in *The Diaries of a Lady of Quality*, ed. by A. Hayward (Longmans, 1864), pp. 43-54. Cf. *Notes and Queries*, 7th series, vol. vi. p. 506, December 29th, 1888, where Dr. William Aldis Wright was the first to point out this source. Cf. also *ibid*. 8th series, vol. xii. p. 377, November 6th, 1897, where Mr. Arthur Mayall refers to an interesting article in *The Genealogical Magazine*, October, 1897, pp. 329-38 : " *The Beresford Ghost*, by the late Rt. Hon. Wm. Beresford, P.C., M.P." The following is the principal passage : " The account was written by Lady Betty Cobbe, the youngest daughter of Marcus, Earl of Tyrone, and granddaughter of Nicola Sophie, Lady Beresford (the Lady Barbara of the poet). She (*i.e.* Lady B. Cobbe) lived to a good old age, in full use of all her faculties, both of body and mind. I can myself remember her, for when a boy I passed through Bath on a journey with my mother, and we went to her house there and had luncheon. . . . It has never been doubted in the family that she received the full particulars in early life from her own father, Lord Tyrone, who died in 1763, and from her aunt, Lady Riverstone, who died in 1763 also. . . . These two were both with their mother, Lady Beresford, on the day of her decease, and they, without assistance or witness, took off from their parent's wrist the black bandage which she had always worn " (to hide the marks left by the ghost's fingers, pp. 331-2).

Tale xviii. has a very distant resemblance to the plot of *La Nouvelle Héloïse*. The heroine, "Ellen," was an only daughter and very anxious to learn. Like another Julie, she falls in love with Cecil, her brothers' tutor and her own. The affection is soon returned, although Cecil is not very young nor very handsome. With more control of his passions than Saint-Preux, he resolves to depart rather than incur the contempt of his pupils and of their father. He travels abroad. When he returns to England some years afterwards, he is informed that Ellen, who is now her own mistress, still lives in her native village. He calls upon her, and sends up his name. But she, by an inexplicable caprice, replies that the name is unknown to her. Without flinching, Cecil puts his affairs in order and sails for Greece, where he dies, after having bequeathed his property to the wretched Ellen, who was anxiously awaiting the return of her lover, so inconsiderately dismissed.[2]

---

[1] Cf. for Lady Betty Cobbe at Bath, J. F. Meehan's *Famous Houses of Bath*, 1901, pp. 161 *seq*.

[2] This tale, one of the feeblest, was suggested to Crabbe by Rogers. In his preface (*Works*, p. 337, col. 2) Crabbe, without quoting his friend's name, made him sufficiently known by an allusion to *The Pleasures of Memory*, and

The tale entitled *Smugglers and Poachers* [1] (xxi.) is one of the most tragic of the two collections. James and Robert Shelley, both foundlings, are of opposite natures : the first sedate and grave, the second bold, impulsive, and often generous. James enters the service of the squire, and becomes his gamekeeper ; Robert, a foe to all restraint and a lover of danger, joins a gang of smugglers. Another cause of discord is their common love for the young and gentle Rachel, employed, like James, at the hall. Their growing animosity eventually bursts forth. James, informed by his spies, captures some poachers, among whom is his brother. As blood has been shed in this encounter, the prisoners are liable to the penalty of death. But the gamekeeper, who is all-powerful with the magistrate, his master, promises Robert his life if he will agree to forego his claims on Rachel, who loves him. It is she who brings to him in prison this proposal from his brother ; she declares herself ready to die with him or to marry James, according as the love of Rachel or the fear of death will triumph in his heart (cf. Shakspeare, *Measure for Measure*, iii. 1). He renounces the hand of his beloved, who keeps her promise and accepts James as husband. At that very moment the prisoner's comrades succeed in breaking open the doors of the gaol. Once more free, Robert vows revenge. The poachers meet, and organise a battue in the squire's woods : the two brothers have an encounter in the darkness and kill each other without knowing it. Since that fatal night Rachel has sunk into a languid melancholy.

II. HUMOUR

IN the third tale will be found the ironical portrait of Sir Hector Blane, a school bully (cf. above, pp. 30-1), then a naval hero, and finally a petty village tyrant, a reproduction of Sir Denys Brand, minus the pride that apes humility.

The Preceptor Husband, Charles Finch (ix.), is a singular person who worries himself to no purpose. A pedant from his youth up, he declared that he must have " wealth, learning, and beauty " in a wife. He had to abate his demands a good deal, and ended by putting up with a semblance of learning. Augusta Dallas, a clever coquette of good family, won his affection. The amorous Finch attributed every perfection to her. When the honeymoon was over, the reality, alas ! fell short of his fancy. They both became bored when alone together. They tried reading. Finch gave his fair lady a first history lesson : she

---

' Rogers thanked him for it by a note dated July 1st, 1819 : " What can I say to you for the mention you have made of me ? If I was a vain man before, I must be a proud man now " (Broadley Collection).

[1] For the origin of the tale, see above, p. 459, n. 3.

mixed up the Reformation and the Revolution. They went into the garden, and Finch delivered a botanical lecture to Augusta, pointing out the different parts of the plant. She proved unable to repeat the learned names. She frankly admitted her preference for romances, and Finch, in despair, gave up his plans of conjugal instruction. It appears, according to Crabbe, that this disappointment made him morose—why, it is not easy to see.

The dialogue entitled *The Natural Death of Love* (xiv.), at once ironical and sentimental, is as witty and pointed as that of *The Frank Courtship*. A married couple, Henry and Emma, after a year of marriage, ask each other why the charm of courtship is a thing of the past. "It is your fault," asserts Emma, in substance; "you are growing irritable and exacting." "Yours rather, or that of nature, of passion, which threw a glamour over everything connected with you," replies Henry. "Since it has gone, never to return, let us resign ourselves to the commonplaceness of our life, and, abandoning recrimination, try to improve our lot. Let us be, if not lovers, at least unfailing friends to each other. Let us help each other along the rough paths of life : if we determine to be happy, we shall doubtless be so, and perhaps ever and anon we shall catch a transient gleam of that purple light which illumined our past."

Tale xvii., *The Widow*, tells us the history of Harriet, the widow of three husbands. The first, a wealthy merchant, was ruined by her extravagance. The second, his clerk, offered to Harriet to put her affairs in order if she would accept his hand : he succeeded, by dint of economy and authority, without any complaint from Harriet of this energetic management. The third, thinking to please the "Widow," made her travel, and plunged her into all sorts of burdensome pleasures. His death came in time to prevent a fresh insolvency. Harriet, having collected the remnants of her fortune, has retired to the country, gives herself youthful airs, and tries to attract admirers. She has been compared to the Wife of Bath in *The Canterbury Tales*, but how tame and colourless she appears by the side of that lively dame!

The Cathedral Walk (xx.) is a sort of parody of fantastic tales. The niece of a Dean, an orphan who has lost her lover, has been given a home by her uncle. He is a widower, and has made this young girl his housekeeper. Mystically inclined, she would like to see the ghost of her beloved. Of an evening she walks in the cathedral, hoping that her long expectation will not be in vain. At last she believes that her prayers are granted! A slight movement is heard in the sacred edifice : without a doubt it is the dear departed, who is coming to carry her off to Paradise. She falls into an ecstasy of joy. But, to her consternation, the supposed ghost is transformed into a living being, a grave-robber, half malefactor, half idiot. Terrified, she escapes with all speed.

III. RESIGNATION AND IDYLLIC LIFE

BOOKS i., ii., iv., vi., vii., and xxii., analysed above (pp. 407-21), fall within this class. *The Old Bachelor* (x.) is an aspirant to marriage, who has been four times disappointed. The son of a Whig, he had become attached in his youth to the gentle and kind-hearted Maria, the daughter of a Tory, and had asked her hand, his affection being returned. Unfortunately, Maria's mother, a haughty and implacable woman, had treated the young man's proposal with the utmost contempt. An illness, however, which brought her to death's door, extorted a tardy consent from her. But Maria in her turn fell ill and died. Some time afterwards the "Old Bachelor," at the suggestion of his own mother, courted a "grave and civil" lady, who soon discarded him for an old admirer, a cousin, who was jealous of this new rival. The third time, the unfortunate man discovered in a secret cupboard the liquors which had produced the glowing colour in the cheeks of his "tall and thin" dulcinea. He was then forty-six, and the humorous description of the first symptoms of his decay (ll. 458-86) has been often quoted. At about sixty years of age he fancied himself loved by a young girl, whose father, a clergyman, was one of his old friends. The mischievous child was amusing herself: she asked him one day to use his influence with her father on behalf of her favourite, young Henry Gale. And the "Old Bachelor," without further ado, has resigned himself to his fate, and preserves his good humour.

The eleventh tale, *The Maid's Story*, is the counterpart of the tenth. It is a highly complicated story of "Martha," an old maid in spite of herself. Her mother had soon taken a second husband, a Scotch physician, and had sent Martha to her grandmother, with whom she "kept perpetual Lent." However, she had fallen in love with a young man named Frederick, unaware that this requited affection had bitter disappointments in store for her. Irresolute and wavering, Frederick becomes successively a Methodist preacher, an infidel soldier, and a fifth-rate actor. Martha, in the meanwhile, has lost her stepfather, then her mother, whose property she has inherited. She has taken to live with her, as an equal and companion, an intimate friend named Priscilla, whose lover had sailed for India many years previously. He has prospered there, and returns unexpectedly to claim Priscilla's hand, who grants it him. Alone once more, Martha prudently refuses to listen to the advances of Rupert, a young enthusiast. She also is resigned to her lot.

Book xix., *William Bailey*, reminds us, in spite of important differences, of the sixteenth "tale in verse." William, a laborious and gentlemanly rustic, and Fanny, the daughter of a small farmer, have plighted their troth, but put off their marriage for fear of poverty. In the meanwhile Fanny is sent for by her aunt, who is housekeeper in a large country mansion. There she is seduced by Lord Robert, the son of the owner. Hence arise indignation in the father's breast, blank despair in that of William, who thereupon begins a wandering life and leads it for nine years. But one day, having alighted at an inn much frequented by Methodists, he is struck by a resemblance between the manner and the features of the landlady and those of Fanny. An explanation ensues, which leads to a reconciliation and a marriage, for neither William nor Fanny have ever ceased to love each other.

With the *Tales of the Hall* may be linked a dialogue called *Flirtation* (written in May, 1816, published in 1834) between two schoolfellows, Delia and Celia, the former of whom, reviewing all the infidelities of the latter, instructs her how to be ready with satisfactory replies to the questions of her old lover Charles, who has been absent for five years, and is on the point of returning. Celia defends herself with much skill. But at the last moment there appears a servant of Charles, or of his father, with a letter which makes her turn pale : " the fickle wretch " has married at Guernsey. The dialogue is not without psychological insight, but remains dull because deficient in point.

APPENDIX V

As a curiosity, I print this little poem, "Old Crabbe's Vision,"
as Blackwood calls it (vol. xii. pp. 349-50).

Of old, when a monarch of England appear'd
    In Scotland, he came as a foe ;
There was war in the land, and around it were heard
    Lamentation, and mourning, and woe.

In the bordering land, which the Muses love best,
    Was one whom they favour'd of old ;
With a view of the future his mind they impress'd,
    And gave him the power to unfold.

"Come, strike me the harp, and my spirit sustain,
    That these visions of glory annoy,
While I to the chieftains of Scotland explain
    What their sons shall hereafter enjoy.

" I see, but from far—I behold, but not near,
    When war on the border shall cease ;
New cities will rise, and the triumphs appear
    Of Riches, and Science and Peace.

" O ! give me to breathe, while this scene I describe,
    A Monarch in Scotland I see ;
When she pours from her Highlands and Lowlands each tribe,
    Who are loyal, and happy and free.

" The Islands at rest in their Sovereign rejoice,
    Lo ! the power and the wealth they display !
And there comes from the lands and the waters a voice,
    From the Shannon, the Thames and the Tay :

" ' All hail to our King ! ' is the shout of the crowd,
    I see them, a shadowy throng ;
They are loyally free, are respectfully proud,
    And joy to their King is their song.

" Yet bear up, my soul, 'tis a theme of delight,
That thousands hereafter shall sing,
How Scotland, and England, and Ireland unite
In their Glory, their Might and their King.

" Aloud strike the harp, for my bosom is cold,
And the sound has a charm on my fears—
A City new-clothed, as a Bride I behold,
And her King as her Bridegroom appears.

" 'Tis he whom they love, and who loves them again,
Who partakes of the joy he imparts,
Who over three nations shall happily reign,
And establish his throne in their hearts."

EDINBURGH, *August 15th*, 1822.

This piece is to be found at pp. 6 and 7 of the following
collection : *Broadsides, Newspaper Cuttings . . . on the Visit of
George IV. to Edinburgh* (1822) (British Museum, 1876, e).

APPENDIX VI

" THE DESERTED WIFE "

MR. EDWARD DOWDEN, to whose great courtesy I owe the communication of the manuscript, has already published a summary of this tale in *The Illustrated London News*, June 20th, 1891, p. 818. It was "begun at Hampstead (at Mr. Hoare's) on the 16th June, 1822."

A foreigner—is he a Frenchman?—named Frederick, is shipwrecked on the English coast. He is taken in by the squire of the place, Richard Vernon, and by the latter's sister, Matilda. In the course of a long illness, from which he eventually recovers, thanks to Matilda's nursing, he falls in love with the young girl and marries her, for his love is returned. A few years after his marriage, having been converted from scepticism to the Christian religion, he is seized with terrible qualms of conscience which disturb his sleep and even threaten his reason. Suddenly, he abandons Matilda and his young children, and disappears, leaving the following explanation of his flight :

Bear witness Heaven and all the Powers above,
Ye who in boundless, endless glory dwell,
It is with breaking heart I speak of love,
For I must bid to love and hope farewell.

I came to thee when thou wert all content,
Loving and loved, a creature half divine,
I came a robber for thy misery sent
Whilst thou wert anxious in removing mine.

On a sick bed, attended, soothed, caressed,
Healed of my wounds, but smitten in my heart,
" And must we part ? "—were words my Love expressed,
Some listening demon echoed : " Must you part ? "

" Art thou not dead to all the world beside,
Save these the kind preservers of thy life ?
Canst thou not ask that angel for thy bride,
And quit the woman who is now thy wife ? . . ."

515

Wretch that I am to wear a vile disguise,
With Virtue, Truth and Piety in view,
My words, my thoughts, my very looks were lies,
My vow alone and my fond love were true. . . .

Cheerful and gay my years of unbelief—
They fled, and now a sad reverse I see :
Like Judas I, or like the dying thief,
But not the one who said " Remember me."

I go, Matilda, for my peace is gone,
Nor would thy heart a lawless love allow.
I dare not die, but must a wretch live on,
And life, once bless'd, must be my torment now.

O ! when convinced that Jesus died for man,
For sinners suffered on the accursed tree,
A dreadful choice to shake my soul began :
Loss of the soul's best hope, or loss of thee.

A vain weak boy, I took the offered hand
Of one who with it her poor pittance gave,
Then fled to sea, and wrecked upon your land,
There, lived their bane who snatched me from the grave.

And yet to leave thee ! leave that rosy boy,
A life of toil and penury to share,
To quit all worldly good, all earthly joy,
It is too hard—and more than I can bear !

For none beside thee will I ever live,
For thee I must not, though so fond and true ;
But must to Heaven's high will my being give,
And pray for strength to bid the world adieu.

He becomes a missionary, while Matilda, plunged in grief,
gradually pines away. Many years pass. A doctor advises the
" widow " to go to the south of France to recruit. There she
meets her husband, a lawful one now that the other woman
is dead. But the climate of the Equator has undermined his
health. And the husband and wife, under the care of Richard
Vernon, spend together the brief space which separates them
from the tomb. The passage quoted by Mr. Dowden contains
the tender description of their decline. Such was the situation
which Crabbe considered new, and the tale, which only wants
a little finish to be really poetical.

APPENDIX VII

ON FRIENDSHIP

THE following piece, written in the four-stress rhythm, was composed about 1822, at the end of the five or six years of unclouded happiness which Crabbe experienced at Trowbridge, from 1816 onwards:

O give me the hour that I love to spend,
When the heart is quite warm and the words are all free;
When I sit at my ease and converse with the friend
Who sits at his ease and converses with me;

When both yield attention that neither need crave,
When restraint is unfelt and reserve is away,
When our freedom is kind and our pleasure is grave,
And we feel we are glad nor desire to be gay;

When our words are unstudied and come from the heart,
And our converse is truly the flow of the soul,
When we need not the spirit that wine can impart,
Nor ask to assist us the flow of the bowl;

When the world for our subject we wander about,
With a smile for its folly, a sigh for its sin,
When all that imbitters our life is barr'd out,
And all that enlivens and graces, shut in.

APPENDIX VIII

BIBLIOGRAPHY

As the bibliography of this book is to be found in the notes, it seemed superfluous to give in this place a list of the works consulted. I confine myself to enumerating, in chronological order, the successive editions of Crabbe's works and the principal magazine articles relating to them. I make no pretension to completeness.[1]

I. Editions

1772	Wheble's Magazine (known to B. but now not to be found): Hope, To Mira, The Atheist Reclaimed, The Bee, an allegorical fable. Signed G. C., Woodbridge, Suffolk (cf. B. p. 7, n. 5).
1775	Inebriety; a poem in three parts. Ipswich. Printed and sold by C. Punchard, Bookseller in the Butter Market. Small 4to, price 1s. 6d. Reprinted in full by Dr. Ward (Poems by George Crabbe, 1905).
1780	The Candidate: a Poetical Epistle to the Authors of the Monthly Review. H. Payne, Pall Mall. 4to, 2s. (B. p. 15).
1781	The Library: a poem. London, printed for J. Dodsley in Pall Mall. 4to, 2s.
1783 2nd ed.	Ditto, by the Rev. Geo. Crabbe, Chaplain to His Grace the Duke of Rutland, etc.

---

[1] The registers of the firm of Hatchard not having been preserved, it is almost impossible to enumerate all the editions of the various works. I mention those that I have seen or of which I have discovered the trace. A bibliography of Crabbe has already been written by J. P. Anderson (as an Appendix to Kebbel's *Life of Crabbe*, 1888), from the Catalogue of the British Museum. As regards the reviews, Poole's *Index of Periodical Literature* gives the main points. W. I. Fletcher (*American Library Association, Index to General Literature*, 2nd ed. 1901) furnishes some supplementary references, of no value whatever. Lowndes (*Bibliographer's Manual*, 4 vols. Bell) wrongly ascribes B.'s *System of Natural Theology* to his father, and is very incomplete.

1783		The Village : a poem in two books, by the Rev. Geo. Crabbe, Chaplain, etc London, Dodsley. 4to, 2s. 6d.
1879		Ditto. Reprinted in Blackie's School Classics. 16mo.
1783		Annual Register, vol xxvi. pp. 35-40. Character of Lord Robert Manners (cf. Works, pp. 121-3).[1]
1785		The Newspaper : a poem, by the Rev. Geo. Crabbe, Chaplain, etc. London, Dodsley. 4to, 2s.
1856		Ditto. Translated into German by Dr. Carl Abel : Die Zeitung. Ein Lehrgedicht von Georg Crabbe. Berlin, J. C. Huber.
1788		A Discourse on 2 Corinthians i. 9, read in the Chapel at Belvoir Castle after the funeral of the Duke of Rutland. London, Dodsley. 4to, 1s.
1795		The Natural History of the Vale of Belvoir, in The History and Antiquities of the County of Leicester, by J. Nichols, London, vol. i. part i. pp. cxci-cciii. Fol.
1807		Poems, by the Rev. Geo. Crabbe. London, Hatchard. 8vo, 8s. 6d.
1808	2nd ed.	Ditto.
„	3rd ed.	Ditto.
?	4th ed.	Ditto, in 2 vols., according to Davy (British Museum MSS. Athenæ Suffolcienses).
1811	5th ed.	Ditto.
1812	6th ed.	Ditto, in 2 vols.
„	7th ed.	Ditto (Davy).
1816	8th ed.	Ditto, 12mo.
1837		Ditto, with an essay on his genius and writings. G. Daly, London. 16mo.
1858		The Parish Register translated into Dutch : De Kerk-registers naar het Engelsch. . . . door K. Sijbrandi, Amsterdam.

[1] Some reviews of the time, and even *The European Magazine and London Review* of September, 1819, p. 200, attribute to Crabbe, for the year 1783, an absurd poem entitled *The Skull*, a short analysis of which may be read in *The Monthly Review*, vol. lxix. p. 598, *Supplement to the Monthly Catalogue for December,* 1783, art. 25 : *The Skull, a true but melancholy Tale, inscribed to the prettiest woman in England.* Bowen, 1783. 4to, 2s.

	1863	The Parish Register and other poems, and The Sabbath, by J. Grahame, London. 16mo.
	1886	Ditto, Poems in Cassell's National Library
1810		The Borough : a poem in twenty-four letters, by the Rev. Geo. Crabbe. London, Hatchard. 8vo, 10s. 6d.
	1810 2nd ed.	Ditto (Davy).
	1811 3rd ed.	Ditto. 2 vols. (Davy).
	1812 4th ed.	Ditto.
	1816 6th ed.	Ditto. 12mo.
	1903	Ditto, in Dent's Temple Classics.
1812		Tales in Verse, by the Rev. Geo. Crabbe. London, Hatchard. 8vo, 12s.
	1812 2nd ed.	Ditto. 2 vols.
	1814 5th ed.	Ditto. 1 vol.
	1891	Ditto, with introduction by H. Morley (Companion Poets, No. 8).
1816		Entire Works, 4 vols , 12mo (cf. European Magazine and London Review, vol. lxxvi., Sept. 1819, p. 200).
		Ditto. 4 vols., roy. 8vo, £4 12s. (Davy).
1817		The Variation of Public Opinion and Feelings considered as it respects Religion : a sermon preached before the Rt. Rev. the Lord Bishop of Sarum on his Visitation held at Devizes on Friday the 15th of August by the Rev. Geo. Crabbe, LL.B. London, Hatchard.
1819		Tales of the Hall, by the Rev. Geo. Crabbe, LL.B. London, John Murray. 2 vols. 8vo, £1 4s.
1821		A Series of Twelve Illustrations for Crabbe's Poems from designs by Corbould. 8vo (Lowndes).
1822-3		31 Plates to illustrate the Poems of Crabbe. Engraved by Heath from the drawings of Westall. Proofs, 4to, £44 ; 8vo, £3 ; fcp. 8vo, £2 2s. (Lowndes and Davy).
1822		Poetical Works. John Murray. 7 vols. 8vo (Davy).
	1823	Ditto. 5 vols. 8vo (Davy).
	1823	Ditto. 8 vols. 12mo (Davy).
1829		The Poetical Works of Geo. Crabbe. Paris, Galignani.

1833	Prospectus of the first complete and uniform edition of the Poetical Works of the Rev. Geo. Crabbe, with his letters and journals. London, Murray. P. 8, 8vo.
1834 (Feb.-Sept.)	The Works of the Rev. Geo. Crabbe, with Life by his Son (contains the Posthumous Tales). London, Murray. 8 vols. 8vo, £2.
1847	Ditto. Complete in one vol., 15s. John Murray.[1]
1854	Ditto.
1867	Ditto. 7s.
1901	Ditto. 6s.
1850	Posthumous Sermons, edited by J. Hastings, Rector of Trowbridge. London, Hatchard. 10s. 6d.
1905	Poems, by George Crabbe, edited by Adolphus William Ward, Cambridge University Press. Vols. i. and ii., 4s. 6d. net. each. The edition will be complete in 3 vols.

Incomplete Editions

1854	Universal Library, Poetry, vol. iii. (Borough, Tales).
1855	Works, with Life (does not contain the Tales of the Hall nor the Posthumous Tales). Gall and Inglis, Edinburgh. 8vo.
1881	Ditto, reprinted in The Landscape Series of Poets.
1858	Works, with Life (does not contain the Tales in Verse, nor the Tales of the Hall, nor the Posthumous Tales). Routledge's British Poets. 8vo.

[1] Cf. the following passage in a letter from J. Murray, the son, to B.: "ALBEMARLE ST., *May* 8 [1846]. MY DEAR SIR,—I have for some time past been contemplating the printing of Crabbe's Life and Works in one volume . . . if I can obtain your concurrence to this proceeding.

"The present edition of 8 vols. has come to a dead stand and there is no demand for it and although nearly 400 gs. were advanced to you in anticipation of profits, not only has no profit been realised, but there is still a debt of nearly £200.

"In the event of an edition in one vol. . . . if you make over to me the copyright of the Life and of the Poems forming the 8th vol. of the present edition, I will give you £300 by notes at 12, 18, and 24 months from the day of publication."—Conditions accepted. (Broadley Collection.)

1873   Works, illustrated in two parts (does not contain the Tales of the Hall nor the Posthumous Tales). London, J. Blackwood.

Extracts and Selections

1781, 1783, 1784-5, 1808, 1810, 1812, 1819. Annual Register : Various Extracts.

1789   Elegant Extracts in Verse, by Vicesimus Knox (book ii. pp. 522-3, of the 1801 ed.); Extracts from The Village (book i. ll. 218-317; book ii. ll. 87-106).

1827   The Living Poets of England. Paris, Baudry & Galignani. Crabbe, vol. i. pp. 175-278.

1827-8   The British Poets of the Nineteenth Century. Including the Select Works of Crabbe, Wilson, Coleridge, etc., being a Supplementary Volume to the Poetical Works of Byron, Scott, and Moore. Frankfurt (Kayser).

1832   Cullings from Crabbe, with a Memoir of his Life and Notices of his Writings (by Taylor, cf. B. p. 73, n. 25). Bath.

1832   Beauties of Crabbe, with Biographical Sketch. Effingham Wilson, London.

1882   Readings in Crabbe (Tales of the Hall), with an Introduction (anonymous, but by Edward Fitzgerald). Quaritch. 8vo (privately printed, 1879).

1883-4   The English Poets, by T. H. Ward. Crabbe, ed. by Courthope, vol. iii. pp. 581-95.

1888   Crabbe's Poetical Works, selected, ed. by Lamplough (Canterbury Poets).

1891   The Poets and the Poetry of the Century, ed. by Miles, vol. i. Crabbe to Coleridge. 8vo.

1899   The Poems of George Crabbe. A selection arranged and edited by B. Holland. London. 8vo.

1902   English Tales in Verse, with an Introduction by C. H. Herford (contains Edward Shore, Phœbe Dawson, The Wager). Blackie.

1903   Selections from the Poems of George Crabbe, ed. by Deane (Little Library). Methuen.

II. MAGAZINE ARTICLES

1780	Sept.	Monthly Review, vol. 63, pp. 226-7.	The Candidate.
,,	,,	Critical Review, vol. 50, pp. 233-5.	Ditto.
,,	Oct.	Gentleman's Magazine, vol. 50, p. 475.	Ditto.
1781	Aug.	Critical Review, vol. 52, pp. 148-50.	The Library.
,,	Oct.	Gentleman's Magazine, vol. 51, p. 474.	Ditto.
,,	Dec.	Monthly Review, vol. 65, pp. 423-5.	Ditto.
1783	July	Critical Review, vol. 56, pp. 60-1.	The Village.
,,	Nov.	Monthly Review, vol. 69, pp. 418-21.	Ditto.
,,	Dec.	Gentleman's Magazine, vol. 53, p. 104.	Ditto.
1785	April	Critical Review, vol. 59, pp. 345-8.	The Newspaper.
,,	Nov.	Monthly Review, vol. 73, pp. 374-6.	Ditto.
1808		Monthly Review, vol. 56, pp. 170-80.	Poems.
,,	April	Edinburgh Review, vol. 12, pp. 131-51.	Ditto (Jeffrey).
,,	June	British Critic, vol. 31, pp. 590-3.	Ditto.
1809	Jan.	Eclectic Review, vol. 5, pp. 40-9.	Ditto.
1810		Monthly Review, vol. 61, pp. 396-409.	Borough.
,,		Critical Review, 3rd series, vol. 20, pp. 291-305.	Ditto.
,,	April	Edinburgh Review, vol. 16, pp. 30-55.	Ditto (Jeffrey).
,,	June	Eclectic Review, vol. 6, pp. 546-61.	Ditto.
,,	Nov.	Quarterly Review, vol. 4, pp. 281-312.	Ditto (Gifford).

1811		Christian Observer, vol. 10, pp. 502-11.	Borough.
„	Mar.	British Critic, vol. 37, pp. 236-47.	Ditto.
1812		Monthly Review, vol. 69, pp. 352-64.	Tales in Verse.
„		Critical Review, vol. 2, pp. 561-79.	Ditto.
„	Nov.	Edinburgh Review, vol. 20, pp. 277, *seq.*	Ditto (Jeffrey).
„	Dec.	Eclectic Review, vol. 8, pp. 1240-53.	Ditto.
1813	April	British Critic, pp. 380-6.	Ditto.
1815	May	The Pamphleteer, vol. 5, pp. 437-43.	A Sketch of the History of Poetry (Sir T. N. Talfourd) : Crabbe.
1816	Jan.	New Monthly Magazine, vol. 4, pp. 511-17.	Memoirs of Eminent Persons : the Rev. Geo. Crabbe (by himself).
1819	Mar.	North American Review, vol. 8, pp. 276-322.	Hazlitt's English Poets (R. H. Dana).
„	July	Edinburgh Review, vol. 32, pp. 118-48.	Tales of the Hall (Jeffrey).
„	„	Blackwood's Edinburgh Magazine, vol. 5, pp. 469 *seq.*	Ditto (Wilson).
„	Sept.	British Critic, 2nd series, vol. 12, pp. 285-301.	Ditto.
„	Oct.	Christian Observer, vol. 18, pp. 650-68.	Ditto.
„	Nov.	Monthly Review, vol. 90, pp. 225-38.	Ditto.
1820	Feb.	Eclectic Review, new series, vol. 13, pp. 114-33.	Ditto.
1821	May	London Magazine, vol. 3, pp. 484-90.	Crabbe (Hazlitt), reproduced with numerous variations in The Spirit of the Age (1825).
1827	Nov.	Blackwood's Edinburgh Magazine, vol. 22, pp. 537-40 (Crabbe).	The Chronicles of the Canongate.
1832	Feb. 18	Athenæum, pp. 112-14.	Crabbe.
„	April 21	*Ibid.*	Taylor's Cullings from Crabbe.
„	Dec.	Fraser's Magazine, vol. 6, pp. 751-2	The Departed of the Year.

1834		Monthly Review, vol. 3, pp. 101-15.	Burns's and Crabbe's Poetry.
„	Jan.	Quarterly Review, vol. 50, pp. 468-508.	Life and Poems (Lockhart).
„	Mar.	Gentleman's Magazine, new series, vol. 1, pp. 253-64.	Life of Crabbe (Mitford).
„	April	Eclectic Review, 3rd series, vol. 11, pp. 253-78.	Ditto.
„	„	Tait's Edinburgh Magazine, new series, vol. 1, pp. 161-8.	Ditto.
„	July	British Critic, etc., vol. 16, pp. 56-70.	Ditto.
„	„	North American Review, vol. 39, pp. 135-66	Crabbe's Poetry (O. W. B. Peabody).
„	Aug.	Quarterly Review, vol. 52, pp. 184-203.	Posthumous Tales (Lockhart).
„	Aug. 30	Athenæum, p. 636.	Ditto.
„	Oct.	Eclectic Review, vol. 12, pp. 305-14.	Ditto.
„	Dec.	Gentleman's Magazine, new series, vol. 2, pp. 563-75.	Poetical Works (Posthumous Tales).
1835	Jan.	Edinburgh Review, vol. 60, pp. 255-95.	Life and Poems.
„	Mar.	New England Magazine, (Boston), vol. 8, pp. 215-20.	Life of Crabbe.
„	July	London and Westminster Review, vol. 30, pp. 316-41.	Life and Works.
1836	Jan.	North American Review, vol. 42, pp. 63-9.	British Poetry at the Close of the Last Century: Crabbe.
1837	Mar.	New York Review, vol. 1, pp. 96-109.	
1841	Oct.	Methodist Quarterly, vol. 23, pp. 514-34.	
1847	Mar.	Tait's Edinburgh Magazine, pp. 141-7.	G. Crabbe (Gilfillan), reprinted in A Second Gallery of Literary Portraits (1850).
1851		Sharpe's London Journal, vol. 12, pp. 21-8.	Life and Poems (F. Lawrence).
1854, etc.		Notes and Queries, 1st series, vol. 9, p. 35.	

1854, etc.		Notes and Queries, 2nd series, vol. 10, pp. 123, 178, 198.	
„		*Ibid.*, 3rd series, vol. 4, p. 375.	
„		*Ibid.*, 4th series, vol. 12, pp. 67, 96, 178.	
„		*Ibid.*, 5th series, vol. 6, p. 440.	
„		*Ibid.*, 7th series, vol. 3, pp. 306, 460.	
„		*Ibid.*, 7th series, vol. 6, p. 506.	
„		*Ibid.*, 7th series, vol. 7, pp. 114, 214, 373, 511.	
„		*Ibid.*, 7th series, vol. 8, pp. 116, 298.	
„		*Ibid.*, 7th series, vol. 9, p. 71.	
„		*Ibid.*, 8th series, vol. 12, pp. 308, 377.	
1859	Jan.	National Review, pp. 1-32.	Crabbe (W. C. Roscoe).
1864	Sept. 24	Saturday Review, pp. 394-6.	Tales of the Hall.
1869	Feb.	St. James's Magazine, new series, vol. 2, pp. 677-88.	
1872	July	North American Review, vol. 115, pp. 48-65.	Crabbe (F. Sheldon).
1874		Cornhill Magazine, vol. 30, pp. 454-73.	Crabbe (L. Stephen) reprinted in Hours in a Library, new ed. 1892, vol. 2, pp. 33 *seq.*
1880	May	Atlantic Monthly, vol. 45, pp. 624-9.	A Neglected Poet (G. E. Woodberry), reprinted in Studies in Letters and Life, 1890, pp. 29-46.
1887	July	Temple Bar, vol. 80, pp. 327-40.	
1888	Oct. 13	Saturday Review, pp. 438-9.	Kebbel's Life of Crabbe.
„	„	Athenæum, p. 478.	Ditto.
1890	Oct.	Temple Bar, vol. 90, pp. 270-9.	
1891	June 20	Illustrated London News.	Unpublished Extracts (Dowden).

BIBLIOGRAPHY 527

1897	Nov.	Temple Bar, vol. 112, pp. 350-61.	Crabbe (A. C. Hillier).
1899	April	Gentleman's Magazine, vol. 286, pp. 356-67.	Ditto (Maude Prower).
1901	Jan.	Quarterly Review, vol. 193, pp. 21-43.	Ditto (Heathcote Statham).
„	June	Cornhill Magazine, vol. 83, p. 750.	Some Memories of Crabbe (W. H. Hutton), reprinted in the Burford Papers, 1906, pp. 282-302.
„	Sept. 28	Literature, pp. 295-8.	Crabbe's Aldeburgh (F. Gribble).
„	Dec.	Atlantic Monthly, pp. 850-7.	A Plea for Crabbe (P. Elmer More).
1903	July	Edinburgh Review, pp. 30 seq.	Crabbe.
„	Oct. 31	Athenæum.	Ainger's Life of Crabbe.
1904	Mar.	Monthly Review, vol. 14, pp. 117-39.	Two Unpublished Poems of Crabbe.
1905		Proceedings of the Suffolk Institute of Archæology and Natural History, vol. 12, part 2.	Crabbe as a Botanist (J. Groves, F.L.S.).
1906	May	The Book Monthly, pp. 544-8.	A Treasure Trove (M. Jourdain).

In France

1827	May	Revue Britannique, pp. 61-70.	From New Monthly Magazine (1816).
1831	May 22	Revue de Paris, t. xxvi. pp. 197 seq.	Pierre Grimes, conte traduit de l'anglais de George Crabbe.[1]
1834	May	Revue Britannique, pp. 55-69.	Les débuts d'un poète (Crabbe).
1835	Feb.	Revue Britannique, pp. 252-84.	Poésie domestique de la Grande - Bretagne (Crabbe, pp. 273-9), translated from The Repository of Knowledge.
1845	Oct. 15	Revue des Deux Mondes, t. xii. pp. 333, 335, 337, 338.	La Poésie chartiste (Philarète Chasles). Crabbe.

[1] By P. Chasles, and reprinted in *Caractères et Paysages*, 1833 (cf. Michaud's *Biographie universelle*, art. " Crabbe ").

1854	Sept. 27, 28, 29.	Moniteur Universel.	George Crabbe (Cucheval-Clarigny).[1]
1856	Sept. 15	Revue des Deux Mondes, 2nd series, t. v. pp. 371-4.	Les Poètes des pauvres (Étienne), Crabbe.
1903	Nov.	Revue de l'Enseignement des Langues vivantes, pp. 357-60.	On Ainger's Life of Crabbe.

III. ESSAYS

1848 H. Tuckerman, Thoughts on the Poets, New York, 3rd ed. (Crabbe, pp. 122-36).

1850 H. Giles, Lectures and Essays, Boston (Crabbe, vol. 1, pp. 45-92).

1852 Earl of Belfast, Poets and Poetry of the Nineteenth Century, London (Crabbe, pp. 258-68).

1862 S. F. Williams, Essays, London (Crabbe, pp. 161-90).

1873 J. Devey, A Comparative Estimate of Modern English Poets, London (Crabbe, pp. 368-75).

1882 Mrs. Oliphant, The Literary History of England (Crabbe, vol. 1, pp. 184-216).

1895 G. Saintsbury, Essays in English Literature, 1780-1860 (Crabbe, pp. 1-30).

In France

1825 Am. Pichot, Voyage historique et littéraire en Angleterre et en Ecosse, Paris, 3 vols. (Crabbe, vol. 2, letter 63, pp. 330-62).

IV. ALLUSIONS BY CELEBRATED AUTHORS

1783 John Scott, of Amwell: An Account of the Life and Writings of James Beattie, by Sir William Forbes, 3 vols., 1807 (on Crabbe's Village, cf. vol. 2, letter 163, pp. 301-6, August 29th, quoted by B. p. 120, n. 8).

1808, etc. Wordsworth, Letter to Samuel Rogers, from Grasmere, September 29th, 1808 (quoted by Clayden, Rogers and his Contemporaries, vol. 1, p. 49).

Ditto. Letter to B., February, 1834 (quoted by B. p. 117, n. 19).

Ditto. Extempore Effusion upon the Death of James Hogg, November, 1835 : Wordsworth's Poetical Works, ed. Dowden, vol. 5, p. 161, ll. 29-36.

---

[1] Cf. Hoefer's *Nouvelle Biographie générale*, art. " Crabbe."

1808, etc. Wordsworth, I. Fenwick, Notes (1843) on Lucy Gray, Dowden, vol. 1, pp. 368-9. Notes (1843) on Extempore Effusion, *ibid.* vol. 5, pp. 359-61.

Ditto. Life of, by Wm. A. Knight, ed. 1889, vol. 3, pp. 305 and 376.

1808 Southey, Selections from the Letters of Rob. Southey, ed. by J. W. Warter, 4 vols., 1856, vol. 2, pp. 90-1, to Mr. J. N. White, from Keswick, September 30th, 1808.

1808 Ditto. The Life and Correspondence of Rob. Southey, ed. by his Son, 6 vols., 1850, vol. 4, pp. 355-6, to C. W. W. Wynn, from Keswick, July 22nd, 1819 (on the Tales of the Hall).

1809, etc. Byron, English Bards and Scotch Reviewers (towards the end).

Ditto. Moore's Life of Byron (1830), cf. at the dates of March 13th, 1809, of October 12th, 1813, and of September 15th, 1817.

1810 F. Horner, Memoirs and Correspondence of (1843), vol. 2, p. 53, letter to Jeffrey of July 16th, 1810 (on The Borough).

1810 Sir Sam. Romilly, Life of Romilly, vol. 2, p. 163, n. letter to M. Dumont of October 13th, 1810 (on The Borough).

1812 Sir J. Mackintosh Life of, vol. 2, ed. 1835, p. 218 (on The Borough), and p. 347.

1814 Leigh Hunt, The Feast of the Poets, 2nd ed. 1815, p. 6, and notes pp. 19-50.

1816 Carlyle, Letters of T. Carlyle, ed. by Ch. E. Norton, 1886, from Annan, July 15th, 1816, vol. 1, p. 73.

1819 Croker, The Croker Papers, vol. 1, p. 146, letter to Murray from Ryde, July 18th, 1819 (on the Tales of the Hall).

1834 Coleridge, Table Talk, ed. Bohn's Libraries, p. 276, March 5th, 1834.

About 1840 Landor, Imaginary Conversations : Southey and Porson.

1852 J. H. Newman, The Idea of a University (1st ed. 1852), 3rd ed. 1873, pp. 150 and 326.

1855 D. G. Rossetti, Letters to Wm. Allingham, 1854-70, ed. by G. B. Hill, 1897, p. 102, and note p. 107.

1856 Macaulay, Life of, by Sir G. O. Trevelyan, ed. 1878, vol. 1, p. 61 ; vol. 2, p. 426.

Ditto. Essay on Robert Montgomery, ed. Routledge, 1892, p. 139.

1856 A. Clough, Prose Remains, ed. Macmillan, 1888, p. 237, to Professor F. J. Child.

Tennyson, Life of, by his Son, ed. 1899, p. 659.

1884   Swinburne, art. on Byron in the Nineteenth Century, April, 1884, pp. 598-9.

1889   Cov. Patmore, Principle in Art, London, 1889, pp. 134-40 : Crabbe and Shelley.

For Edward Fitzgerald and Scott. cf. above, p. 421, n. 1, pp. 433-4.

V. Biographies

1857   A. Druzhinin, George Crabbe and his Works (in Russian). St. Petersburg.[1]

1875   F. Stehlich, G. Crabbe, Ein englischer Dichter, Dissertation, Halle.

1888   T. E. Kebbel, Life of G. Crabbe. London, W. Scott, (Great Writers).

1899   H. Pesta, G. Crabbe, Eine Würdigung seiner Werke. Wien and Leipzig.

1903   A. Ainger, Crabbe. Macmillan, London (English Men of Letters).

---

[1] For the influence of Crabbe in Russia, cf. also *English Poets* in biographies and specimens, compiled (in Russian) by Nicolas V. Gerbel (Crabbe ⁓ɔ. 178-95), and W. R. Morfill, *A History of Russia*, 1902, pp. 451-2 (information communicated by Professor Morfill, University of Oxford).

INDEX

531